Multiple Voices

DATE DUE

Multiple Voices

Multiple Voices

An Introduction to Bilingualism

Carol Myers-Scotton

Blackwell
Publishing

575496886   9-23-10

© 2006 by Carol Myers-Scotton

BLACKWELL PUBLISHING
350 Main Street, Malden, MA 02148-5020, USA
9600 Garsington Road, Oxford OX4 2DQ, UK
550 Swanston Street, Carlton, Victoria 3053, Australia

The right of Carol Myers-Scotton to be identified as the Author of this Work has
been asserted in accordance with the UK Copyright, Designs, and Patents Act 1988.

First published 2006 by Blackwell Publishing Ltd

4   2008

Library of Congress Cataloging-in-Publication Data

Myers-Scotton, Carol.
  Multiple voices : an introduction to bilingualism / Carol Myers-Scotton.
    p. cm.
  Includes bibliographical references and index.
  ISBN 978–0–631–21936–1 (hardcover : alk. paper)
  ISBN 978–0–631–21937–8 (pbk. : alk. paper)
  1. Bilingualism.   I. Title.

  P115.M494 2006
  306.44′6—dc22

                              2005001282

A catalogue record for this title is available from the British Library.

Set in 10/13pt Palatino
by Graphicraft Limited, Hong Kong
Printed and bound in Singapore
by Markono Print Media Pte Ltd

The publisher's policy is to use permanent paper from mills that operate
a sustainable forestry policy, and which has been manufactured from pulp
processed using acid-free and elementary chlorine-free practices. Furthermore,
the publisher ensures that the text paper and cover board used have met
acceptable environmental accreditation standards.

For further information on
Blackwell Publishing, visit our website:
www.blackwellpublishing.com

Contents

Preface

This is a book that tries to cover all of the important aspects of bilingualism that university students should know about. This means that the book deals with both what it means to an individual to be bilingual and what it means to a community to include bilinguals. The goal is to write the chapters at a level to make the book appropriate for upper-level undergraduates (in their last two years) or beginning-level Master's degree students.

Most generally, the book is intended as a textbook for courses that are particularly concerned with bilingualism as a socio-political phenomenon in the world. As such, it emphasizes overviews on why people become bilingual; why they maintain their first language or why they shift to a dominant language in the community as their main language; how they use the language varieties in their repertoire in interpersonal interactions; and how language policies in nation states and globalization as a phenomenon affect choices people make to learn certain languages.

However, the book also includes chapters on the more grammatical and cognitive aspects of bilingualism. That is, it deals with outcomes of grammatical combinations of two languages (e.g. codeswitching and convergence), as well as with how bilingualism is a factor promoting the borrowing of words across languages. In addition, there is a chapter on what psycholinguistic studies tell us about how bilingualism seems to be organized in the brain, as well as a chapter largely considering how child bilingualism differs from bilingualism acquired at a later age.

Other topics considered include how cultures differ in their views of appropriate language use. Also, there is a chapter on the ideologies that groups have about the linguistic situation in their community and attitudes that individuals develop about others based on the languages they speak. In addition, there is discussion of memory in bilinguals and aphasia (language loss) in bilinguals and how recovery differs across individuals. Still other topics considered are types of bilingual education programs and attitudes toward them, as well as explanations that researchers offer for outcomes in second language learning after a young age. Current theories about second language acquisition also are covered.

Instructors may choose to skip the more grammatically and cognitively oriented chapters, depending on the interests and needs of their students. Even without these chapters, the book offers students a very comprehensive view of various aspects of the communities that include bilinguals and the lives of the bilingual individuals themselves.

As the author, my assumption is that students using this book in their course work *need have no background at all in linguistics as a discipline*. But this isn't "bilingualism for dummies", either. Most of the chapters do cover complex issues – because the nature of bilingualism itself and bilingual communities is complex. But anything students need to know about any technical aspects is explained in the book. Further, all technical terms are defined in the text as they are used; there is no need to flip to notes or a glossary to understanding the meaning of what is being conveyed. Also, the many examples help, too.

I have tried to write an overview, but this book is different from many overviews because I have almost always put a good deal of "meat" into the examples so that regularly, an example will go on for an entire paragraph or more. The hope is that this extra detail brings alive to students what life is like for bilinguals and their communities.

So that students get a sense of the lives that bilinguals lead, each chapter opens with a verbal snapshot of a bilingual person. The bilinguals portrayed are not real persons, but they all are based on real persons in the community where they are situated.

Ideally, this book is the main course textbook that should be selected for a course titled "Introduction to Bilingualism". As such, it could serve as the sole text in a semester-long course; for a year-long course, other texts could be added to it to give more detail. It can also be used as a second text or as a supplementary reading for courses that are only partly concerned with such topics as how bilingualism arises, when and where it is maintained or not, who bilinguals are (in terms of their social backgrounds and cognitive makeup), when and why they use their two or more languages, and how bilinguals are treated in official decisions, including those for education.

Thus, this book could be a textbook for a variety of courses in departments of English, any foreign languages, linguistics, communication, and possibly psychology or sociology. Certainly, it would be appropriate for faculties of education because of the bilingual nature of the student bodies everywhere today that their graduates will teach.

Acknowledgments

This is a big book and it was a long time in the writing. But the journey was made easier by the help of many different individuals, some at my home university (University of South Carolina, *the* USC), but even more from other places around the world. At least five colleagues at other universities read drafts of entire chapters (Jan Bernsten, Judy Kroll, Judy Olinick, Terese Thonus). Many others responded to my requests for help, based on their expertise in various areas, so that I would get right certain details on everything from possible changes in the brains of aphasics, to bilingualism along the German-Danish border, to types of bilingual education programs in Arizona. These individuals include Ad Backus, Dominique Caubet, Michael Clyne, Elin Fredsted, Annick De Houwer, Joan Argenter Giralt, David Green, Jan Jake, Elizabeth Lanza, Joe Lo Bianco, Hyeson Park, Christina Bratt Paulston, Bethyl Pearson, Hal Schiffman, and the late Larry Trask. The following colleagues helped me breathe life into the verbal sketches that head each chapter: Ad Backus, Agnes Bolonyai, Dominique Caubet, Michael Clyne, Giuli Dussias, Sue Jenkins, Elizabeth Lanza, Yaron Matras, Alicia Myhrer, and Zhu Wanjin.

Several reference librarians helped me with one or more difficult references (Gary Geer and Sharon Verba at USC and David Nelson at the University of Pennsylvania). Harold Schiffman's Language Policy List (at the University of Pennsylvania) was an excellent source of current information on many relevant topics; many of the examples throughout the book appear only because I found them on this list. Linguist List provided information, too. Over several years, a number of graduate assistants looked up available materials on various topics and references to go with citations or read chapters; they include Eva Moore, Bevin and Helen Roue, Cherlon Ussery, Zhu Fan, and especially Laurie Sanders. Mila Tasseva at USC continues with good humor to provide answers to my computer-related queries. At Blackwell, first Steve Smith, then Tami Kaplan, and lastly Sarah Coleman have always been encouraging and helpful. Finally, I thank Glynis Baguley for her careful and intelligent copyediting that has made this a better book. I am sure I left out some names, but to everyone who helped me, I am ever so grateful. Of course any errors or infelicities that remain are my own.

1

Introduction

Multiple voices: The word from China

Zhao Min speaks two dialects of Chinese as well as English. He's a commodity trader for a joint venture of the government of the People's Republic of China and an international conglomerate. He comes from Nanjin, China, but divides his time between Beijing and Hong Kong in China, with extended stays in Europe. He studied English as part of his secondary schooling and university education. Today his job demands a good deal of English; he writes emails and has long-distance phone conversations – always in English – with his customers, for whom English is usually a second language, too (e.g. Serbs in former Yugoslavia, now Serbia). When he visits his family in Nanjin, he speaks his home dialect but when he deals with Chinese colleagues, he speaks the standard dialect of the People's Republic of China (formerly called Mandarin, a name some still use, but called Putonghua in the PRC). This is the variety he speaks with his wife, who was raised in Beijing. Zhao Min has little spare time from his job, but when he does, he often watches films and has a huge collection of English-language movies on DVDs.

1.1 Introduction

Bilingualism is the subject of this book. This is a study of the people who speak more than one language and the social motivations for bilingualism – why people learn a second language and the net result in their lives. It also considers how the fact that speakers are bilingual influences the structure of the languages themselves. In addition, the volume considers how the age at which a speaker learns a second language makes a difference in success as a fluent speaker of that language. Both bilingualism as a feature of individual speakers and bilingualism as a feature of communities or entire nation states are discussed.

Speaking only one language, typically the language you acquired as a first language or mother tongue (generally the language of your home), is called **monolingualism**. **Bilingualism** is the term for speaking one or more languages. Usually the speakers' mother tongue or first language is one of the two languages that make them bilinguals. Bilingualism is used as a cover term for multilingualism, too – speaking more than two languages. Some researchers use the term plurilingualism for speaking more than two languages.

It may come as a surprise to some readers, but more people in the world are bilingual than monolingual – a clear reason why bilingualism is worth studying. When the American comedian, Billy Crystal, introduced the Film Academy Awards ceremony in Hollywood, California in early 2004, he joked, "This ceremony is being broadcast in 57 languages – and that's only in Los Angeles." Yes, there are many bilinguals wherever we look; thus, it makes sense to study the various aspects of bilingualism that this book covers.

Who are the bilinguals? The sketch at the top of this chapter gives you an idea about such persons. You will find similar sketches at the top of all the other chapters, too. These mini-portraits are based on real people although the names are fictitious.

Throughout this book, we will refer to "first languages" and "second languages", assuming that most bilinguals started their speaking years as monolinguals. Of course for persons who acquired two languages simultaneously as young children, "first" and "second" won't work. You will read about some of these early "polyglots" in chapter 11.

Monolingual = a person speaking only one language
Bilingual = a person speaking *at least* two languages
Polyglot = sometimes used for a bilingual, especially one speaking many
    languages
L1 = first language (what's acquired first as a child)
L2 = any second language (what's acquired later, either as a child or adult)
Linguistic repertoire = the languages a person speaks

1.2 Bilinguals and their languages

"Being bilingual" doesn't imply complete mastery of two languages. Further, speakers are **rarely equally fluent** in two languages. All humans of normal intelligence speak at least one language. As will become clear in this book, as humans, we are innately programmed to acquire a language quite effortlessly as young children when exposed to it. We say that speakers are bilingual when they have also acquired or learned to speak or understand – as a minimum – some phrases that show internal structural relations in a second language. We'll give you more details later on about what this means. The problem is that there is no accepted formula for exactly what's necessary for a person to claim to be a bilingual. Usually, being bilingual is associated with being able to *speak* two or more languages, not just being able to read an L2 with a dictionary by your side. But how much "speaking" of an L2 counts as being bilingual? Just being able to produce some formulaic phrases (e.g. greetings and the equivalent of "please" and "thank you") isn't enough to label you a bilingual in our view.

One thing we do know: With some exceptions, few bilinguals are as proficient in any second language as they are in their first language. And, if they do speak several second languages, they generally don't speak all of them equally well. There are two socially based main reasons: (1) Few bilinguals have been equally exposed to all languages in their repertoire and (2) They don't use them with the same frequency or in the same situations. In chapters 10 and 11, we'll discuss some findings and views on differences in bilingual proficiency that may have to do with how language is organized in the brain. But for now, rest assured you can take most such claims as "she speaks five languages fluently" with a grain of salt.

1.3 Views about bilinguals

As a reader of this book, your perception of bilingualism will depend a great deal on your nationality or where you are living. Those North Americans who are monolingual in English have a hard time comprehending what another language consists of or how people can manage two languages. (For example, I once had an American student whose mother came from Brazil and who spoke Portuguese in addition to English, even though English was the only language she used with her own children. But when the mother spoke to her own brother, she spoke Portuguese. The student called using Portuguese "speaking another language". That is, the student never referred to Portuguese *as Portuguese*, but only as "another language", taking a "one size fits all" approach to bilingualism. Apparently, she had never heard anyone speak a second language *other than Portuguese*.

For many in the United States, **bilingualism used to be exotic**, because the stereotypical bilingual had either a romantic or a threadbare background, or both. That is, typical Americans envisioned the bilinguals they met in this way: Either the bilingual spoke more than one language because he or she was the child of European nobility (read: from Transylvania or some such mysterious locale), or because he or she was the child of refugees (read: from Argentina, Chile, or Russia). More recently, of course, for US residents, bilingualism is associated with migrant or unskilled workers (read: some Spanish speakers) or small businessmen (read: Korean grocer or South Asian motel manager/owner).

Most Canadians used to think of being bilingual as **coming from Québec** and "speaking French" in addition to English. Today, Canada has surpassed the US as the melting pot of North America and being bilingual there today just as likely means being a new arrival on Canadian shores and speaking anything from Haitian Creole to Hmong to Urdu as a first language.

1.4 Learning a second language

Typical Europeans in nations with a firmly established single national language used to think of becoming bilingual as not the by-product of everyday life, but rather a part of formal education (at places such as Oxford, Cambridge, Heidelberg, etc.). That is, for the English to study French or German and for continental Europeans to study at least one other language was **part of academic training**, whether in secondary school or at the university. At the same time, these Europeans did not expect to hear anything but their own national language spoken on their home turf. Today they overhear conversations in many other languages; for example, Britain has large numbers of immigrants from India, Pakistan, the Caribbean, and Africa, among other outposts. Even *la belle France* ('the beautiful France') is a multilingual nation today, with French the sole official language, to be sure, but with large numbers of North Africans who speak Arabic, as well as speakers of Turkish and various African languages, among others. The Germans encouraged *Gastarbeiter* **"guest workers"** from places like Turkey, who were meant eventually to go home. Just under nine percent of those living in Germany today were born outside Germany, according to the Organization for Economic Cooperation and Development. Some details about the current state of bilingualism and patterns of language use in North America and Europe will be explored further in a number of the later chapters.

While educated people in Western Europe and North America often study a second language in school, the rationale has been primarily to learn something about another (generally Western) culture and only secondarily to converse in that language far beyond having the words to order dinner when on vacation in another (Western) nation. True, Europeans have generally taken learning a second language more seriously than North Americans. Of course a major motivation was that the opportunities to use a second language were nearer at hand for Europeans. But only recently, especially with the establishment of the European Union (formerly the Common Market), have these people had regular opportunities – or the need – to speak a second language.

Certainly, **the rise of English** as the world's major lingua franca since the end of World War II (especially after the 1950s) has affected in two opposite ways the degree to which people become new bilinguals. Non-native speakers of English, from Capetown, South Africa, to Beijing, China, see the benefits and the need to learn English. In contrast, realizing that the world is learning their language, many native speakers of English are less willing to put effort into learning a second language. There are exceptions, of course; for example, anyone studying for an International MBA (Master of Business Administration) in the United States probably undergoes at least one intensive course in another major international language such as Spanish or Japanese and may also serve an internship using the language. The world status of English will be discussed further in chapter 3 and chapter 12.

A lingua franca = Any language that is used between two people who don't share the same first language. For example, English can be a lingua franca between a native speaker of English and a speaker of any other language. Or, it can be a lingua franca between speakers of any two other languages. Or, any other language can be a lingua franca between speakers of two other languages (e.g. Swahili is often a lingua franca in East Africa in multi-ethnic areas, or Italian may be a lingua franca in the area around the Adriatic Sea).

1.5 Where did bilingualism come from?

Why is bilingualism such a part of the human condition? Many of you know the **story of Babel**. Babel was a city named in the Bible (now thought to be Babylon in Shinar, an ancient country on the lower parts of the Tigris and Euphrates rivers) where the leaders were building a tower intended to reach heaven. The Bible tells us that such a goal smacked too much of pride and so God punished the builders by destroying their unity, giving them different languages. Building stopped when the builders couldn't work together because they couldn't understand each other's languages. Whether this picturesque explanation of the origin of diversity in languages is true doesn't matter because what we do know for certain is that in recorded history, the world has never been without hundreds of languages. The general view is that there are at least 2,000 different languages, maybe many more. And whether Babel was the cause of this linguistic diversity or not, the diversity didn't make people into bilinguals. What did in ancient times and continues to stimulate bilingualism is **contact between persons who don't share an L1**. Contacts arose in the past through such large-scale forces as colonialism. Today immigration, business travel, and education are major forces bringing peoples together. In order for these would-be conversationalists to converse, **someone has to learn another language**. Bilingualism on someone's part is the result.

1.6 Linguists: What they know and don't know

When new acquaintances find out someone is a linguist, the first question they always ask is, "How many languages do you speak?" The answer always disappoints them; most linguists only speak a few languages fluently – but they do know a great deal about the structures of many languages. You see, linguists spend most of their time studying *about* the structure of language rather than working very hard to learn to speak many languages. So we may be able to produce a smattering of many languages, but we don't really claim to speak those languages. Instead, most of us specialize in studying one language or group of languages, and we may well speak one or more of those. Just for your information, the second language your author (Carol Myers-Scotton) speaks best is Swahili and she has additional knowledge of several other eastern and southern Bantu languages. You will see some examples from those languages. Why don't I speak more languages? I'm no different from other people: If there were a need in my life to be able to carry on long conversations in another language, then I would make the effort to learn enough to be able to do that. But for example, right now, my abilities to speak German end with my being able to get myself to the train station, check in at a hotel, and order simple meals. I stop at that – something I can do as long as (1) I don't visit Germany often or (2) the Germans I interact with have more abilities in English than I do in German (as they generally do). Make no mistake about it: **Learning a second language is time-consuming work**, requiring a lot of memorization, at least for adults. You'll read more about this in a later chapter.

The second question linguists are always asked is one you, too, may be asking: **"How did languages originate?"** All we can offer by way of an answer is another disappointment. We have very little evidence about the origin of language. We don't know if the humans who developed the first languages all spoke one language or not, or if languages developed in only one place or several. We also don't know what the first languages were like, even though there is a good deal of speculation. The ancient inscriptions that we do have indicate that languages as far back as we have records certainly had complex structures. This is clear from the inscriptions in Greek and in Egyptian hieroglyphics on the Rosetta Stone. There also are inscriptions in demotic scripts (simplified apparently local forms) there as well. The Rosetta Stone, which dates from around 200 BC, was discovered in 1799 in Egypt and is now in the British Museum. Even older are artifacts with Sumerian cuneiform in Mesopotamia (now Iraq); there also are other Egyptian hieroglyphics in old kingdom sites, such as Abydos (about 250 miles south of Cairo). Predating even these are inscriptions at an archeological site in Pakistan (the Harappa site) that are about 5,500 years old. In 2003, archeologists found language-like symbols carved into 86,000-year-old tortoise shells in China. They were at a site that has been radiocarbon-dated to between 66,000 and 62,000 BC; this puts the symbols in the late Stone Age or Neolithic Age. As such, they predate the earliest recorded writings from Mesopotamia by more than 2,000 years.

What evidence we do have has been used by linguists to group together presently spoken languages (along with some extinct languages for which we have sufficient records) that share critical features into **"language families" and sub-families**. Even so, these groupings indicate a tremendous potential for the need or desire to learn another language, because most linguists would say that conservatively that there are **at least 12 major language families in the world** (not languages, but groupings of languages). The best-studied family is the Indo-European family. It includes languages spoken across northern India to the British Isles. And seven of the ten languages with the most native speakers are Indo-European (although the single language with by far the most speakers, counting all its various dialects, is Chinese). Within the Germanic branch of the Indo-European family, English and German have the most speakers. In the Romance branch, Spanish and Portuguese have the most speakers (remember that Portuguese is the main language of Brazil); the branch also includes French and Italian. What the grouping of languages in families means to you, if you are thinking of studying a second language, is that languages in the same sub-grouping as your own language will be easiest for you to learn because they should share some structural features and also some vocabulary.

1.7 Why so many languages?

Your next question might be this: We can imagine that there may have been many different languages when humans began developing languages, but why did so many different languages result?

The answer is this: **If groups are separated**, whether geographically or socially, for a long enough time, the differences in their speech become greater. Changes happen to language varieties for two reasons. (1) They happen because the speakers introduce some internally motivated organization of structures. For example, American English, at least, is losing the distinction between *fewer* and *less*. The old "standard" is *There are fewer people here than yesterday* (because *people* is a noun you can count), but the incoming standard is *There are less people here than yesterday*. (*Less* previously was used only with mass nouns, such as *water* or *flour*.) (2) Changes also happen because the speakers take in new features from contacts with speakers of other languages. For example, probably under the influence of English, Swahili speakers are changing the way they indicate something is "for someone". The "old standard" is something like example (1) if the speaker wants to say 'I cooked food for Mwangi'. The verb meaning simply 'cook' is -*pika*, but in this sentence a special form of the verb (with -*i*- added to make -*pikia*) is used to mean 'something is being done for someone'.

> (1) Nilimpikia Mwangi chakula.
>   literally: 'I cooked for Mwangi food.'

Instead, today's speaker, at least in upcountry Kenya, may produce a sentence such as that in example (2). So we see that a prepositional phrase (*kwa Mwangi* 'for Mwangi') is used instead of a special verb form. The result is that the sentence structure in (2) looks more like English structure because English also would convey the notion of 'for someone' with a prepositional phrase and a change in the word order.

> (2) Nilimpika chakula kwa Mwangi.
>   'I cooked food for Mwangi.'

That is, the net result is this: Even if two groups of speakers start life as one group, speaking more or less the same linguistic variety, if the two groups don't keep up frequent contacts (e.g. if one moves away) and if the now separated groups don't have exactly the same contacts with other groups, differences in the speech of the original unified group are bound to arise. American English has expressions that aren't found in British English and vice versa. The differences aren't so great that two separate languages have developed. But, given enough time, this is how new language varieties arise. The Roman Empire spread Latin in the parts of Europe where French, Spanish, Portuguese (and related languages) are now spoken. It's not too far-fetched to say that French is Latin as it is spoken in what is now modern France. And so on. French isn't the same as Spanish because speakers in the two different places didn't get together to iron out differences between their "versions" of Latin. This is **how different languages and different dialects come about from a single beginning**.

1.8 The rationale for many languages today

You now may be saying to yourself, "Okay, diversity happens, but wouldn't life be simpler for everyone if we eliminated languages with only a few thousand speakers so that everyone would speak either the same language or one of several major languages?" Communication might be simpler with fewer languages, but most groups are not willing to give up their languages. The reason is that **each language does "social work"** for its speakers. This notion is developed further in later chapters. Here, suffice it to say that languages often are the single most important symbol of group identity. And this is not just a pre-modern view that's lost when a group modernizes. Evidence that people consider their languages as essential symbols is that there are more official languages (serving as national symbols) in Europe today than existed in the nineteenth century.

Although the spread of international commerce and communication via long-distance phones, faxes, email, and the web may have shrunk the importance of geographical distances as an impediment to communication, **linguistic diversity is here to stay**. We can distill the reasons from the discussion about groups, their penchant for distinctiveness and their use of borders. **As long as groups wish to distinguish themselves** from other groups, many different languages will continue to be spoken. This is especially true for any language that is the official language of a nation – simply because nations have the funds to nurture a chosen official language at home. And sometimes nations go so far as to use funds to promote their L1s elsewhere as second languages; this is the case with the major European languages, especially English and French. They seek to develop or strengthen cultural and economic ties through a common language.

What is the attraction for a group of having its own language? It serves as a **positive badge of identification**. When groups are in contact, they both value their own language, but typically the less powerful group learns the other group's language, not vice versa. Or, sometimes near-peers communicate in a neutral language, giving no deference to either group's badge of identification. Either way, language's function as a badge promotes bilingualism because it promotes maintaining L1s and learning at least a neutral L2.

One of the main themes of this book is that **bilingualism is a natural outcome of the socio-political forces that create groups and their boundaries**. There are two reasons why bilingualism grows in the soil in which culturally distinct groups and their languages flourish.

First, this distinctiveness means that **some groups command more social or economic prestige** than others; when persons wish to join an attractive group, the entry fee is becoming bilingual in the language of the attractive group. Think what happens to immigrants all over the world; they almost always must learn the dominant language of their new home if they are to survive in this new setting. If a group is so attractive that others wish to cross into its territory – whether permanently or temporarily – then the group reminds those others whose territory it is that is hosting them. In most cases, this reminder comes in the form of the expectation – or the requirement, for long-term visitors – that the **newcomers will learn the host's language**.

Second, some groups are more powerful than others, meaning they **control desirable resources**. Previously, the source of such power was often military or colonial might; today, the source is more often technological expertise or economic clout. To interact with today's powerful groups, others often have to learn the languages of those groups. To take some relatively recent examples, think about such **results of colonialism** as the spread of Spanish and Portuguese in South America from the fifteenth century onwards, or Italian in the early twentieth century in the Horn of Africa (Eritrea, Ethiopia, and Somalia). Today, think about the need to learn English to **conduct business via computers** in much of the world, or the need to **read critical textbooks**, or the need to **interact with fellow workers** if your company has an international scope.

Some people learn a second language just because they like to learn languages or are attracted to a certain culture, but most L2 learners expect to benefit by improving their lives in a material way. Still, learning a language that facilitates self-improvement does not have to mean that speakers quickly lose their L1. If the immigrant group is large enough and speakers have strong networks composed of fellow immigrants who speak their language, then an L1 can be maintained for years for in-group talk with family and friends. Also, if people who have become bilingual because their jobs demand it live in nations or regions where their L1 is the main local language, many opportunities remain to speak their L1. All the activities outside of work hours can be in their L1. And even in the offices of foreign-owned conglomerates around the world, the chatter in the cafeteria is in the local language. However, depending on the circumstances, becoming bilingual can be the first step in loss of one's L1, as we will see in later chapters.

1.9 Attitudes about language

Although bilingualism has long been recognized, it has been little studied. Why is this? For much of the general public in nations with a long-standing single national or official language, bilingualism is considered something "to get over". At the same time, European nations such as France and Britain in the past limited their teaching of foreign languages in the schools, believing that this helped eliminate the barriers between territories. That is, persons in power have considered **bilingualism as a condition best changed**. If people want to participate in mainstream society, then fluency in the nation's dominant language is expected, but they should forget those other languages. Yet, today the languages heard on the street in many nations have become more, not less, diverse, thanks to never-ending conflicts and other events stimulating waves of migration. This does not mean the typical person interviewed on that street thinks this linguistic diversity is music to the ears. A few years ago, the noted linguist David Crystal asked passers-by in London what they thought about having only a single language in the world, and why. Most people plainly hadn't thought about it. But most who answered thought diversity was a bad thing, either citing the biblical notion that what happened at Babel was a curse, or saying that having only one language might promote world peace.

Until recently, Western European nations and the United States and many provinces in Canada and much of New Zealand and Australia either were largely monolingual or perceived themselves as such. The adage "facts are facts but perceptions are reality" applies here. This notion that monolingualism prevails – or that it should prevail – will be explored in chapter 12. Of course, the Western-oriented movers and shakers with this attitude know that in many parts of the world, actually using more than one language as a regular necessity has been commonplace for as long as people remember. But these observers also think of bilingualism as a characteristic of the less developed nations. The prime examples of multilingual nations are in Africa, parts of South Asia, such as India or the Malaysian archipelago, in New Guinea, and in some places in Central Europe and the former Soviet Union.

Even today, most of the bilinguals in the more developed nations are new arrivals from the less developed nations, such as the migrant workers from Turkey in Germany, the Netherlands, and Switzerland, or the North Africans in France, or the immigrants from the Caribbean who seek permanent resid-ence in Britain and Canada, or the South Asians in Australia. Thus, such topics as "Who are the bilinguals?", "What does bilingualism involve?" – that is, what bilingualism entails – have been placed low on the list of "things to study", either because **it was considered a transitory state in the West**, or because **it was only a fact of everyday life in distant, often agrarian, places**. The world's economic giants simply had other interests. But the world has changed under their feet. For example, all over, there are now large, estab-lished communities of immigrants and descendants of immigrants who all come from the same background where you would hardly expect them. Does it surprise you to know that there are many Nigerians in Hamburg, Germany or that Hmongs from Cambodia are prominent sellers of produce and flowers in street markets in downtown Minneapolis and St. Paul in the US Upper Midwest?

1.10 Linguistics and bilingualism

You would think that linguists, who refer to linguistics as the study of the structure of language (with a big L), would be very interested in bilingualism. However, they generally stick with one language at a time in their investiga-tions, even though they claim to be looking for universally present principles. This is especially the case with those linguists who study either the sound systems or the syntactic systems (how sentences are structured) of language; they almost always analyze structures in only a particular language. While these same linguists sometimes may test the same hypothesis about some structure by testing it first against one language and then against related structures in another language, few make comparing structures across languages their main enterprise. And even fewer have been concerned with studying the influence of the structure of one language on another when the two languages are spoken by the same bilingual speakers. There are two extreme positions that linguist take in regard to bilingual language. The first position is that bilingualism obscures their view of language (with a big L). That is, in order to study the structure of a language, or a particular type of structure across languages, issues about how languages are actually used are better set aside in order to focus on the main subject. A second position – and this is our own view in this book – is that **bilingualism offers a unique opportunity to understand the structures of a particular language** when we see how they pattern when in contact with structures of another language. That is, can speakers use certain types of words (e.g. verbs) from one language in the same clause as patterns from another language? What happens when the structures of two languages are in contact – because their speakers are in contact, or speak both languages – will be the topic of chapter 9 in this book.

Now, some linguists, who are called sociolinguists, *do* study the social side of language. They study either language use patterns in bilingual communities or the socio-psychological motivations for using one language rather than another in conversations with fellow bilinguals. We will survey such studies in this book. But most linguists who call themselves sociolinguists study dialectal variation in a single language, not any of the many aspects of bilingualism that we will survey in this book.

1.11 Why bilingualism matters to you

Now that we've told you about all the people who either have seeming misconceptions about bilingualism or aren't interested in bilinguals and bilingualism, you may wonder why we're asking you to read this book and study bilingualism as a subject.

First, there are two **intrinsic values in studying bilingualism**; they are intrinsic in the sense that they can't be easily observed or measured in any empirical sense.

The first value: We argue that simply because the competence to speak two or more languages is a part of the human blueprint, all aspects of language, including the potential to be bilingual, are worth studying. Studying **bilingualism tells us something about the genetic potential of humans**. For example, we know that monolingual speakers produce sentences in accordance with the rules of their language. When bilinguals produce sentences with elements from more than one language, are there rules that they seem to follow, and what are they? This information tells linguists more about how language is processed in the brain than they can find out from studying only monolinguals. Also, studying the steps children go through who acquire two languages at once gives us important insights into how humans acquire language in general. In summary, studying bilinguals expands our understanding of the human language faculty.

The second value: Simply **living in a community where two or more languages are spoken is a part of the human experience**. Part of the liberal education of all humans, including monolinguals, is developing an awareness of the many aspects of how humans live and interact. Knowing something about the place of language in the lives of bilinguals is part of this education.

1.12 Bilingualism: Practical considerations

Second, there are a number of practical values to be derived from reading this book; we hope to convince you that **bilingualism is relevant to your life**. No matter where you live, even if you are among those whose nation has only one official or nationally recognized language, you can't avoid having bilingualism impinge on your life. How is this? In your future or present life, some of your fellow workers may speak another language as their first language (their "best" language) even though they can communicate with you in your language. Consider the following: Your **fellow workers' backgrounds**, how they became bilingual, why they maintain bilingualism, how their first language affects the way they speak your language – these are some of the ways that bilingualism makes a difference in your life. Or, your children may be in classrooms with children who speak a different first language. Just as likely is that **your children** will be asked to study a foreign language starting in elementary school. Knowing something about how psycholinguists think language comprehension and production are organized and the relationship of two languages in the brain of a bilingual may help you understand how classes are organized and what is in the curriculum. Also, you may find that you yourself need to learn a second language – at least to some degree – because your job requires you to travel internationally or because of where you live. Furthermore, because of the **movement of populations all over the world** and in particular the flood of immigrants to Western nations, it is foolhardy to ignore bilingualism as a phenomenon that surrounds you even if you yourself are basically a monolingual. For example, the results of the 2000 census in the United States show that nearly one-fifth of school-age children there speak a language other than English at home. Of these children, seven in ten speak Spanish. However, in that group two-thirds rated themselves as speaking English very well.

1.13 How the book is organized

The goal of this book, then, is to **introduce you to bilingualism** in all of its main aspects. The discussions do not presuppose a background in linguistics;

they assume only that you, the reader, are willing to study a new subject. The chapters fall into five areas.

General introduction – chapters 1–3. This chapter and the next two introduce you to some general facts about bilingualism. Chapter 2 also discusses how linguistic varieties (languages, dialects, and styles/registers) are defined and perceived and the types of features that are involved when one language influences another. Chapter 3 considers the types of peoples who become bilingual and the conditions that have promoted bilingualism in the world.

Bilingualism and society – chapters 4–7. Once someone becomes bilingual, what are the motivations to maintain the first language (L1)? Under what conditions do peoples simply shift to a more dominant second language and leave their first language behind? Chapter 4 discusses the types of conditions that lead speakers to maintain their first language or to shift to another language. When speakers remain bilingual, another issue is how they allocate their different languages to different situations. Chapter 5 discusses ideologies (mindsets) that people have about their language in relation to their community. It also considers the types of attitudes that speakers have about different languages. Chapter 6 considers how speakers and listeners interpret choices in language use as a tool to negotiate interpersonal relations. Their choices also can serve to present a "verbal picture" of how they see themselves. Chapter 7 looks at cross-cultural differences in what is considered appropriate language behavior in different societies.

Structural aspects of languages in contact – chapters 8–9. When words are borrowed, what kinds of words are involved and how are these words integrated into the language on the receiving end? This is the subject of chapter 8. Chapter 9 broadly looks at what happens to the grammatical structures in a bilingual's languages when both languages are used frequently. This means the chapter looks at several examples of what are called language contact phenomena. Most attention is given to codeswitching (using two languages in the same conversation). Another topic is this: Under what conditions are creole languages created (such as those spoken in the Caribbean and the South Pacific)? What is their "mix"?

Bilingualism and the mind – chapters 10–11. Chapter 10 considers psycholinguistic research that gives us some evidence about how a bilingual's languages are organized in the brain. It also considers how memories are stored (in which language?). Finally, it deals with what happens to a bilingual's language when he or she has brain damage. How does it happen that young children seem easily to acquire more than one language, but most adults do not? Chapter 11 looks at becoming bilingual as a small child compared with as an adult. The chapter also surveys the current models in use to study and predict success in learning a second language in the classroom.

Globalization and language policies – chapter 12. What factors are considered when a nation sets language policies? This is the overall topic of the last chapter. Against the backdrop of the global nature of communication today, the chapter considers the provisions that multilingual nation states make for their citizens. It considers issues of bilingual education. In addition, the chapter looks at the position of English in the world and problems in international bodies, such as the European Union, in settling on a single working language.

Summing up – chapter 13. Some general themes to remember from the book as a whole.

1.14 Words and phrases to remember

monolingual
bilingual
first language
second language
linguistic repertoire

2

What's a Language? What's a Dialect? What "Social Work" do they do?

Multiple voices: The word from Italy

Monica Flori is a businesswoman who lives in a small town in northern Italy in the region near Modena, a city that is famous because the opera star, Pavarotti, was born there and also because the Ferrari car is made there. Monica owns a small clothing store that caters to adults for sports and casual wear. She studied finance at the University of Pisa. She lives in an area where there are lots of tourists, especially for skiing in the winter; in fact, the Italian Olympic ski team trains in the mountains nearby. Monica needs to speak English and French because many of her customers are tourists. With French tourists she speaks French, but English is the language she uses with German tourists or other non-Italians. She studied these languages at school. She speaks standard Italian to Italian customers, but speaks the dialect spoken in the Modena region to local people. Monica's husband's name is Giuseppe Capitani, but most people know him as Beppe; he also comes from the region and speaks the local dialect as well as standard Italian. He speaks English, too, but not as well as Monica and he doesn't use it as often.

2.1 Introduction

In this chapter, we try to make sense out of what the various terms mean that we'll be using in the rest of the book. That is, to give you the necessary background to understand future chapters, this chapter gives you an overview of what we mean by the basic terms **language**, **dialect**, and **style** or **register** that we use to refer to ways of speaking. Let's begin by making it clear that we can use the neutral terms **linguistic variety** or **code** for any way of speaking. That is, they are cover terms that are not judgmental in any of the ways that *language* and *dialect* are, as you will see. Sometimes we will use the term *language* itself as a cover term not referring specifically to what we'll define below as **a language**.

2.2 What counts as a language?

Here's a conundrum or puzzle for you: **Why can't we give you a firm answer** on how many languages are spoken in the area around the Baltic Sea in Eastern Europe or how many languages are spoken within the national boundaries of Cameroon in West Africa? The answer has to be: It depends. Depends on what? The answer depends on who you are listening to as your expert because there are two main ways of defining languages. (1) We may distinguish language A from language B on the basis of **structural (linguistic) criteria**. (2) Or, we may distinguish the two languages according to **socio-political criteria**, or because they've been differentiated historically. Sorry to make things complicated, but that's the way they are.

2.2.1 Distinguishing languages on the basis of structure

If we use structural criteria, then we usually separate one linguistic variety from another when the differences in their various linguistic systems are so great that speakers of one language can't understand speakers of the other variety. (By **linguistic systems** we mean **phonology** (pronunciation), **morphology** and **syntax** (word formation and sentence structure), and **lexicon** (vocabulary). Of course, when we say that these three are systems it means that speakers have to follow the rules of each system that make an utterance well-formed in the specific language that is under discussion; otherwise, they aren't speaking that language.

The term **grammar** can be vague in reference to a linguistic variety. Sometimes you'll see it used for morphology and syntax, but it also can be used to refer to everything about the structural requirements of a language that make it well-formed. This would mean it includes phonology, too, but also could include information on how words are related to each other in the lexicon and other matters having to do with semantics. We will try to avoid using the term "grammar" on its own, just because it is not always clear elsewhere what it covers in each instance of its use.

THE THREE MAIN SYSTEMS OF ANY LANGUAGE

Phonology: The sounds a language has and how they are organized into units, with one unit (a phoneme) being perceived as different from another by that language's speakers; i.e., /b/ and /p/ are two different phonemes in English, but what is one phoneme in English, such as /b/, may be divided into two phonemes in another language (e.g. various Indian languages). Not all languages have the same sounds and not all organize their sounds in the same way.

Morphology and syntax: The way that meaningful units of sound are organized into words (morphology) and then organized again on another level into clauses and sentences (syntax).

Lexicon: The vocabulary or store of words that a language has, with their meanings (semantics) and their connotations, including how they are interpreted in certain contexts (pragmatics).

Although there are many similarities across the systems in languages, especially in closely related languages, you can understand that if these systems are quite different, an addressee can't work out what the speaker means. And if languages are being **defined by structural criteria**, then if any one system of variety X has very different rules than those in a similar system of variety Y, the two are called two different languages. For example, consider some simple differences in the sounds that are put together. In Swahili, a word may begin with a sound that never occurs at the beginning of a word in English. This is the sound that is written as *ng* in English, as in *running*, but it occurs at the beginning of some Swahili words and is written *ng'*, as in the word for 'cow' (*ng'ombe*). Also, in Swahili the marker for 'past tense' (and other tense/aspect markers, too) comes before the verb so that the prefix [li] in *ni-li-pika chakula* 'I cooked food' corresponds to the sounds that are written as *ed* for 'past tense' and that occur after the verb stem in English. Or, even if one of the words a speaker uses sounds familiar to you as an English speaker (*mal* sounds like "malady"), how would you understand that *j'ai mal à la tête* is the French way to say 'I have a headache'? (Note that *ai* is the form of the French verb *avoir*, meaning 'have', that is used for a first-person subject in the present tense.) As these examples show, such differences in any one of the three main systems of language can make a huge difference in your ability to understand the other person.

When understandability fails, it usually means the speaker is literally "speaking a different language" – at least if we're defining languages by considering structure. From a structural point of view, we use mutual intelligibility to group together linguistic varieties and label them as a single language. **Mutual intelligibility** means that two speakers can understand each other; it

equals understandability. This isn't a perfect criterion, because remember that we are dealing with three main systems, not just one, when we are looking for similarities that permit understanding. When there are two varieties showing enough structural overlap so that mutual intelligibility is possible, we say we have two dialects of one language. What is **structural overlap**? This is when two varieties show a number of the same features in the three systems of language (phonology, morphology–syntax, and lexicon). These systems represent the "structure", and "overlap" means showing many of the same features. Dialects are discussed further later in this chapter.

Even though closely related languages do not have the same systems, their systems do show a good deal of structural overlap because the evidence (or claim) is that they come from a common ancestor. In fact, **the basis for saying two languages are closely related** is their structural overlap. So, it is no surprise that speakers of such closely related languages as Italian and French can "almost" understand each other, pointing up the fact that mutual intelligibility or "understandability" is not an all-or-nothing thing.

2.2.2 Paying attention to social factors in defining languages

This brings us to our second set of criteria for differentiating one language from another. Not only does the criterion of mutual intelligibility not always work, but people don't always pay attention to understandability, anyway, when they are saying what is a separate language and what isn't. Instead, they **use various socio-political criteria**.

2.2.2.1 National borders

First, linguistic varieties are often called separate languages just because they are **spoken in different nations**. The best example of how national boundaries figure in where the line between languages is drawn is the case of three Scandinavian languages, Swedish, Norwegian, and Danish. Even though these three varieties are clearly closely related and speakers of any one of these languages can more or less understand speakers of the two other languages, for historical reasons and because of present political boundaries, they are called three different languages.

When Scandinavians who are speakers of these languages meet, each participant speaks his or her own language in many conversations. This form of limited bilingualism is called **receptive bilingualism**; that is, the addressee only develops a receptive ability in the other speaker's language (meaning he or she can understand, but not speak the language).

Sometimes, Scandinavian speakers try to make communication easier by accommodating to the other speaker's language. They can do this by trying to speak the neighbor's language, but sometimes they produce various forms that are neither one language nor the other. For example, a Danish political scientist, being interviewed by a Swedish radio broadcaster, produced the form *stött* (with a final [t]) for 'support'. But this corresponded to neither the Danish *støtte* [sdøde] nor Swedish *stöd* [stø:d], both of which have a final [d] sound (Braunmüller, 2001). The problem is two-fold: He used a different "o" vowel from the vowel that both Danish and Swedish have for this word, and then he used a final [t], not a final [d]. His efforts at accommodation may have muddied the already murky waters of intelligibility!

In recent modern history, Norway was under the control of the Danish, but not today. Swedish is the Scandinavian language with the most speakers and it is spoken in Sweden as the majority language, but also as a minority language in Finland, where Finnish is the main language but Swedish also has official status. (Finnish is not related to the other three Scandinavian languages at all; it's in a separate language family.)

Another good example to show how mutual intelligibility doesn't count for much at national borders is the case of the **German-Dutch dialect continuum**. (A continuum is a linear representation without clear divisions between the elements on the line; that is, the elements just blend into their neighboring elements.) There is a well-known continuum of mutually intelligible varieties stretching from southeastern parts of the Netherlands across much of Germany. This is called a **dialect continuum** because there are overlaps in the structural systems of varieties as you move along the continuum. At both ends, speakers probably do not understand each other, but at points along the continuum, neighboring varieties are mutually understandable. What happens to a dialect continuum when you come to the national border? Speakers at this point in the continuum end up saying they speak different languages – even though, from a structural point of view, they speak mutually intelligible dialects! On one side the dialect at the border is called German and on the other side it's called Dutch.

An interesting sidelight is that this particular dialect continuum is losing out to the powers of national standard dialects. That is, young people on either side of the border now acquire the standard dialect of their nation's official language (they learn it in school and hear it on the electronic mass media). So it's only older people who understand with any ease the local dialect of their neighbors across the border. You'll read more about what a standard dialect is later in this chapter.

In other parts of the world, national borders divide up dialect continua into languages as well. Mansour (1993) argues that the multilingual nature of West Africa is exaggerated because of the **national borders that were artificially drawn** to suit colonial powers in the late nineteenth and early twentieth centuries. What she means is that a single ethnic group and its linguistic variety are or have been classified as two different groups and two different languages, just because a national border intervenes. She cites the case of the cluster of Mandingo dialects, which are spoken in a number of different West African countries and go by many different names (as if they are separate languages).

2.2.2.2 *Cultural borders*

Second, when speakers see themselves as **culturally different**, they often refer to their varieties as separate languages. That is, again mutual intelligibility is ignored. Since the 1990s, we have seen that the number of languages has grown in the southern Slavic group in former Yugoslavia. (Russian, of course, is the best-known Slavic language, but it's in the northern group.) Where there used to be three languages (Slovenian, Serbo-Croatian, and Bulgarian) there now are at least five. Slovenian has remained Slovenian, but Serbo-Croatian has split along ethnic and religious lines into Serbian, Croatian, and Bosnian. (Serbians are members of the Eastern Orthodox church, but Croatians are Roman Catholics.) The two languages are written in different scripts, too. Serbian is written in the Cyrillic script (like Russian), but Croatian is written in the Roman or Latin script that is used in most European countries. (This book is in Roman script or orthography.) Bulgarian has largely remained Bulgarian. A variety called Macedonian by its speakers is spoken in Bulgaria within Western Bulgaria, but it is just a dialect of Bulgarian, according to speakers of Bulgarian in Bulgaria. Why should the Bulgarians care? Because they want to unify all areas of Bulgaria under one language; they might also want to use language as a reason to extend Bulgarian borders. Macedonian is written in the Cyrillic script and so is Bulgarian.

But there are Macedonians elsewhere, giving Macedonian speakers in Bulgaria a rationale to claim they speak a language separate from Bulgarian that is called Macedonian. There is an area called Macedonia that is part of the former Yugoslavia; its administrative center is Skopje. In addition, there are Macedonians in Greece thanks to the Greek incorporation of Aegean Macedonia after the Second Balkan War of 1913, although many Macedonians migrated to other nations from this area, especially to Bulgaria.

A similar situation of "language creation", but of longer standing, exists in northern Uganda in East Africa between the Acholi and Lango peoples. Their languages, Acholi and Lango, are referred to as separate languages (within the West Nilotic language group). In fact, the two varieties are mutually intelligible. Yet, because the Acholi and Lango wish to differentiate themselves culturally, they refer to these as separate languages, not dialects of the same language. Around the world, there are many examples like this where the **salience of ethnicity** takes precedence over mutual intelligibility.

2.2.2.3 *Religious borders*

South Asia provides an example of how languages can be created along **religious lines**. When India and Pakistan were divided in 1947, a language formerly called Hindustani became two. Hindi is the version that is spoken in India by Hindus and other religious groups while the variety spoken in Pakistan by Moslems is called Urdu. The two languages are also written in different scripts.

Urdu is written in the Arabic script and Hindi is written in the Devanagari script of its ancient predecessor, Sanskrit. **Language engineering** of sorts has helped the two languages become more different than they were originally; Urdu has taken in many Persian and Arabic-based forms, true to its Moslem profile, while Hindi has made a number of existing words more closely resemble Sanskrit. But the two varieties are mutually intelligible. This suggests that if it hadn't been for the partition of India and Pakistan, there might not be the view that Hindi and Urdu are two different languages. We discuss this case again in chapter 12.

2.2.2.4 *Uniting linguistic varieties into one language*

In contrast, other groups may wish to see themselves as **members of one culture** and in that case, they say they speak the same language even if the dialects making up that language are not necessarily mutually intelligible. The most commonly cited example is the Chinese language. True, there is only a single writing system for all of the dialects of China. And there is only one spoken variety that is recognized as the standard dialect. Based on the dialect of the capital area, Beijing, this spoken dialect is still called Mandarin by many, but is called Putonghua in Chinese. But by no means are all the Chinese dialects mutually intelligible with each other or with Putonghua. That is, if we are using structural criteria, many of them should be called separate languages. This is especially true for the southern varieties, such as Cantonese (spoken in Guangzhou, formerly called Canton).

That there should be linguistic differences in such a wide expanse as China is understandable; so why do the Chinese want to ignore the differences? They do recognize a number of minority groups that speak their own separate languages (e.g. there are a number of Mongolian languages in the northeast). But by referring to all the varieties spoken by persons from the Han ethnic group as "Chinese", the Chinese government instills **the notion of national identity across diverse communities**.

Across the world, the Chagga peoples, who live in the area of Mount Kilimanjaro in Tanzania (in East Africa), see themselves as a single ethnic group and refer to their linguistic varieties as one language. Still, from a structural point of view, the dialects making up Chagga are different, especially regarding the sounds in their systems and therefore how certain words are pronounced.

2.3 Problems with mutual intelligibility

Let's return to mutual intelligibility for a minute. While it's a reasonable criterion (when it is followed), there are two problems with it that should be recognized. First, mutual intelligibility is not clearly something that is there or isn't. That is, it is a continuum, or call it a **gradient concept**. It is not a concept offering sharp divisions, because it's based on whether or not two linguistic varieties have systems that overlap. And within any of the three main systems of a language, we can see that there could be varying degrees of overlap. This would mean that the basis for mutual intelligibility is not an all-or-none sort of thing. Second, whether two different speakers even *want* to understand each other can affect the claim of mutual intelligibility. Speakers of the more powerful group seem less willing to make the effort to understand speakers of the less powerful group. For example, speakers of the three related Scandinavian languages sometimes say they have difficulties understanding each other; but the difficulties often have less of a linguistic basis and more of a psychological one, given their histories and differences in numbers of speakers. There are real structural differences between Danish and Swedish, but there are also subjective barriers that may be traced back to a history of negative experiences – first wars and, more recently, an unbalanced economic relationship between small Denmark and much larger Sweden (Braunmüller, 2001).

Not just in this case, but often the world over, **people "decide" to understand** other speakers – or not. For example, a study in the South-Central African country of Zambia showed that, of four fairly closely related languages, Nyanja was the one that native speakers of the other three languages found easiest to understand. Even though the author of this study is cautious in drawing conclusions, the fact that Nyanja must have had the most prestige as the main language of the capital (Lusaka) is hard to overlook (Kashoki, 1978).

2.4 Dialects as groupings under a language

Now, what about dialects? While our focus in this book is on speakers of more than one language, we can also discuss speaking several dialects as a form of bilingualism. In general, we use the term **dialect** to refer to linguistic varieties whose speakers can understand each other. The basis of this mutual intelligibility is the same structural overlap between the three linguistic systems outlined above in our discussion of languages. Let's consider explicitly the connection between the linguistic varieties called languages and those called dialects. What we call a language doesn't really "exist" as a single entity; rather, it exists in its dialects. That is, **a language is made up of dialects, and dialects, not languages, are what people actually speak**. While two closely related languages, such as French and Italian or German and Dutch, may show quite a bit of structural overlap in their systems, they still are not mutually intelligible. However, if the degree of overlap increases to the extent that mutual intelligibility exists, then we have two dialects of the same language.

But, again, we have to contend with the speakers themselves, not just the linguistic varieties, in labeling them as separate languages or dialects of the same language. In 1990, the district council of Anklam in Germany (in the federal state of Mecklenburg-Vorpommern) declared that the local variety, Plattdeutsch (Low German) would be its *second* official language (after standard German as its first official language). Commenting on this decision, Coulmas (1997: 37) observes, "Almost every district in every German federal state could pass a similar resolution, but not everyone insists as stubbornly as the Mecklenburgers on their own local, dialectal identity."

True, sometimes mutual intelligibility is strained across dialects. For example, many of our South Carolinian students pronounce "where" and "were" in the same way. They pronounce them both the way that I – not a native Carolinian – pronounce "were". That is, when they say *Where did you go?*, *where* sounds like *were* (not like *wear*, as in *to wear shoes*). Still, we northerners (the Carolinians would call me a "Yankee", largely because of the way I speak) can understand which word they mean (because of how the word is used). This is a good example to show that mutual intelligibility (speakers can understand each other) is not a perfect criterion for grouping together dialects as a single language, but it's the best we have.

Sometimes, it is true, what are called dialects of the same language are different enough that they are not mutually intelligible. This is the case for many languages, even languages with long written traditions. Consider English. Some of the dialects spoken in England itself, such as the northern dialects, are hard to understand for other English speakers, especially if you're a speaker of an overseas English dialect such as American English or Australian English (e.g. taxi drivers in Newcastle-upon-Tyne are famous for being hard to understand by outsiders and the drivers seem to enjoy this status).

2.5 The written language and dialects

At this point, you may be thinking, if a language doesn't actually exist, then what's in the book on my shelf that is titled, for example, *The English Language* (or *The X Language*, etc.)? The answer is that books that claim to contain the basics of any language generally contain only the basics of *one* dialect. This is called the standard dialect of any relevant language. By saying that it's the **standard dialect**, we are saying, in effect, that it is a version of the language that has been **selected to represent the language**. But it is not the entire language! Some writers refer to the standard dialect as the standard language, but we prefer the term standard dialect, because this dialect is only one of a number of dialects that make up the entire language. A grammar book of the entire language would have to include information about what are considered to be well-formed ways of speaking in all the dialects of that language. These other dialects simply are called **non-standard dialects**.

True, some people think of non-standard dialects as "less correct" than the standard dialect; they are often making this judgment on the basis of who is speaking, not on the dialect itself. We say this because **all the dialects are**

structurally equal in the sense that each one has its own structural principles for how to speak it. One difference is that **non-standard dialects are often only spoken varieties**; that is, only the standard dialect is written down. Sometimes the term **vernacular** is used for a non-standard dialect, or even for a language that is not written down. It may surprise you, but not all languages in the world have a written version.

2.6 Identifying the standard dialect

The standard dialect differs from other dialects in a number of ways. Sometimes the standard dialect represents **a leveling of several or more dialects**, meaning that the standard dialect may be something of a compromise. When this happens, the standard dialect often is largely based on **the way that educated people spoke** in the nation's capital when the standard dialect was being developed and recognized as the standard. This seems to be the case in France, for example. But speech in the capital isn't always the basis of the standard dialect; an obvious exception is Standard American English, since speech in Washington, DC is not the source of the standard dialect.

How is the standard dialect identified? Who selects it? In some nations, there is an actual official organization that formally rules on the features of the standard dialect. Many nations have such organizations, such as France and Spain. In other nations, the standard dialect has no more than an informal basis; this is the case with all the standard dialects of English – in the United Kingdom, the United States, Canada, Australia, and everywhere else. Yes, languages of wider communication, such as English, may have different standard dialects in the different nations where the relevant language is spoken as a native language or is the main official language. This means that what is standard in England isn't the same as the Australian view of a standard dialect, for example. It also means that nations, such as Nigeria, where English is an official language, have their own ideas about a standard dialect of English. Even in such countries as Malaysia, where English is no longer an official language, a variety called Malaysian English is used in corporate business and industry (Nair-Venugopal, 2001). Bahasa Malaysia/Melalyu, the official standard variety of Malay, is the official language in Malaysia.

French is an exception to the claim that different nations where a language is spoken may have different versions of the standard dialect. The same variety of French (based on Parisian, metropolitan French) is recognized as the standard in many places other than France, such as in the sub-Saharan African nations that have French as their main official language. However, it is no surprise that in French-speaking Canada, the norm of reference is local (Québec) standard French. This is reflected in Canadian dictionaries that feature Québec French and where usages that are typical of formal and informal European French are flagged as *francismes* (Mougeon, 2002, personal communication).

Here's **a set of overlapping criteria for identifying the standard dialect** of any language. Note that none of these criteria alone identifies the standard dialect perfectly because there are exceptions to each of them.

- Used in written works of a serious nature (but not necessarily in all fiction or poetry).
- Spoken by most "people of power and/or prestige", with "power" and "prestige" defined by community norms. (Not all such people speak the standard dialect; many politicians are notable exceptions.)
- Spoken by broadcasters on national radio or television network news programs.
- Taught as a subject to native speakers in the public schools (although this criterion assumes the teacher recognizes the standard dialect and uses it).
- Taught to students who study the language as a second language.

2.7 Who speaks a dialect?

Many people are not used to thinking of themselves as speaking dialects. In fact, the typical person, when asked, ordinarily says "I speak language X" *not* "I speak dialect X." The closest we may come to using the term "dialect" is to refer to our home dialect as if it were *the* language. In fact, a repairman at my house asked me if it was true that "American" was the hardest language to learn. He didn't seem to recognize that the accepted cover term for our way of speaking is English, that there are many others in the world who speak varieties similar to ours, that they are all called English. In some ways, though, he was correct, because – in a broad sense – American could be considered a dialect of English, but I don't think that's what he had in mind.

In its most neutral usage, speakers may employ "dialect" for **an out-group** – for example, to refer to how "people over there speak". Often, dialect is a somewhat pejorative term. People may say, for example, "I speak Spanish, but I sometimes hear people on the bus who just speak dialect." Or, some people may refer to languages spoken in the Third World as dialects, e.g. we've heard the question, "How many dialects are spoken in West Africa?" All of this shows that if many people use the term dialect at all, it is not something that they apply to themselves very often, but to others.

The same goes for **accent**. Most people do not think of themselves as speaking with an accent; it's *other* people who may "speak with an accent". This may be the reason that some people take offense at being told that they speak with "a heavy accent"; "heavy" isn't good because it is interpreted to mean "more" of an accent, with the implication that it is not the accent associated with the standard dialect of the country in question. In fact, of course, **we all speak with an accent**. All it means to say this is that we all have a phonological system, a way of organizing the sounds that come out when we speak.

2.7.1 Dialectal differences in identifying group memberships

We pay a lot of attention to differences in accents (pronunciation) and the reason is that they generally are the **most distinguishing features of dialects**. In fact, a pronunciation example that distinguishes dialects is famous (famous among linguists, at least!). It comes from the Bible and is the basis for our use of the word *shibboleth*. Today the word means "a custom or practice that portrays one as an insider or an outsider", but its original meaning was specifically "a pronunciation that identified one's ethnic group". The biblical story of how this worked is told in Judges 12: 4–6. The Ephraimites had lost a battle with the men of Gilead and were trying to escape across the Jordan river, but the Gileadites controlled crucial passages. In order to gain passage, when asked if they were Ephraimites, the Ephraimites said "no". But the Gileadites asked those who were fleeing to say the word *shibboleth*. They knew that only true men of Gilead pronounced the [sh] sound in this word while the Ephraimites would say instead [s]. Unfortunately, the unlucky Ephraimites revealed themselves by their pronunciation, and they were killed.

However, in judging whether someone sounds "educated", we generally pay more attention to morphological or syntactic differences. These are what we think about when we refer to the standard dialect. Why? A reason for this is that one dialect often shades into another in terms of pronunciations, so it's hard to draw a line based on pronunciation alone – even though the biblical Gileadites did. Take, for example, the variation between pronouncing the *-ing* in such words as *running* or *going* as either *-ing* (with the "ng" pronounced as what linguists call a "voiced velar nasal") or *-in*. In some social dialects – especially those associated with persons of the working class – this ending is usually pronounced as *n*. But then in other classes, including professional ones, some speakers *also* pronounce this ending as *n* when they are speaking casually. The result is that you can't say that *n* pronunciation really distinguishes an "educated" or standard dialect from others; you can say that the percentage of *n* does, but listeners don't necessarily make this calculation (Wolfram and Schilling-Estes, 1998).

In contrast, **grammatical differences tend to be more of an "either/or" thing**: Either a dialect has a certain grammatical feature or it doesn't. For example, most middle- or upper-class English speakers speak a dialect in which when a third person singular (a noun or *he, she,* and *it*) is the subject of a verb, and the verb is in the present tense, then speakers attach an *-s* to the verb (e.g. the contrast between *he like-s ice cream* and *they like ice cream*). Many lower-class speakers don't follow this rule, but have a rule for a "zero ending" no matter what the subject is (they say not only *they like ice cream* but also *he like ice cream*). It is the way that middle- and upper-class speakers speak that is considered the standard dialect.

2.7.2 How many dialects?

Every language has at least two dialects and many languages have many dialects. But just as it's hard to draw the line between languages according to structural criteria, it's hard to separate one dialect from another in all ways. As just indicated, differences in phonology (how the same written word is pronounced across dialects) represent the biggest difference between dialects. We often think of grammatical differences as definitively separating dialects; such differences may generally separate the standard dialect from non-standard dialects. But they don't necessarily separate one non-standard dialect from another.

Several non-standard dialects may have the same non-standard grammatical feature, yet we often think of them as separate dialects. For example, those African-Americans who are speakers of African American Vernacular English frequently use double negatives in a sentence (and be careful: Don't assume all African-Americans are speakers of this dialect just because they're African-American – it's a socially based dialect, not an ethnically based dialect, and many African-Americans are speakers of the standard dialect). These negatives especially occur on the verb and any following indefinite elements that can be negated (e.g. *They don't know nothing*). But speakers of *other* non-standard dialects also use double negatives! For example, they are especially prevalent in the speech of other Americans from a wide range of social classes, particularly when they're speaking in a casual way. That is, even someone who normally uses standard dialect features may use a non-standard form at times – just for a special effect. For example, using a double negative obviously adds emphasis of the negative meaning being expressed.

Some of us may be bi-dialectal; that is, we know and use two different dialects. But a problem is that it's not easy to say what constitutes "enough" to distinguish one dialect from another – because of the structural overlap between dialects as discussed above. **Some dialects do have rather distinctive features**, though, and if speakers use a cluster of such features part of the time and not at other times, they may be said to be bi-dialectal. Even so, the line is hard to draw.

2.7.3 Personal dialect continua

Rather than commanding more than one dialect, most of us have access to a **range of styles** in our dialect. Some writers prefer **register** as a cover term for linguistic varieties below the level of dialect, but we prefer to reserve register for the specialized lexicon that is used by persons in a certain profession or aficionados or fans of a certain sport or activity.

Styles/registers are sub-categories under dialect. That is, just as our language is, our dialect is also something of an abstraction that is realized by the styles we use. Just as languages and dialects are characterized by having the three systems of phonology, morphosyntax, and lexicon, so are styles/registers. You know that related dialects show a good deal of overlap; well, as you would expect, so do styles/registers. And, not surprisingly, they show even more overlap, so that often the difference between one style and another depends on only a few structural differences.

Earlier, we talked about dialect continua across national boundaries. We can also use the term **stylistic continuum** to refer to the stylistic scale along which each person moves, depending on situational factors and the persona she or he wishes to project. As we move along the continuum, we are calling into use the styles (or registers) that make up the configuration that is our dialect, our version of "the language". For example, consider the differences between the form of two directives, *Kindly finish that memorandum by Tuesday, please* and *Hey buddy, get that stuff to me by Tuesday, okay?* Also, the difference between pronouncing the sentence *Do you want to go?* as [dja wannego] and [du yu wan tu go] is a matter of casual versus a more formal style.

What determines where we place ourselves on our continuum? First, we have to consider who we are, in the sense that not everyone is able to speak the same way. That is, not everyone is going to have the same styles in her or his linguistic repertoire. This depends on who we are, our social identity features (age, gender, education, ethnic group, etc.), and our life experiences.

Whether someone is highly educated or not, everyone has her or his own dialect continuum in having at least both a formal and informal style. But not everyone who speaks a dialect of a given language has the same variety as her or his formal variety. And not everyone has the same informal variety, either. You slide along a continuum from further from to closer to the version of the standard dialect that's associated with serious writing – and generally you are further from it since written language is almost always more formal than speech.

You may have been taught somewhere along the line to think that you should speak something toward the formal (written) end of the standard dialect continuum all the time if you want to speak correctly. Well, that's not true. If you speak even your own formal variety to your garage mechanic you won't win any medals from him and he may not give you good service because he thinks you are a stuffed shirt. If you spoke that way with your fishing buddies, you would be laughed off the boat.

We hope you can see by now that choices of style depend on the situation and your goals, and, as a communicatively competent speaker, you have internalized notions about what is unmarked or appropriate for a range of interactions. (We'll give a fuller discussion of "unmarked" versus "marked" in chapter 6.) **Communicative competence** has come to be used for an ability to recognize what your community views as the unmarked (appropriate) way(s) of speaking in a given type of interaction. Bell (1984) refers to our sense of **audience design**; the basic idea is that we vary our way of speaking depending on who we are talking to, or who our audience is (actually present or via radio or TV).

Just as important is that we vary our speech depending on our own individual goals and desires. That is, we are concerned about our self-presentation and how others view us, as we are with meeting the expectations of others in terms of what's appropriate for the situation. The French sociologist Pierre Bourdieu (1982, 1991) popularized the notion of thinking of the linguistic varieties we command as **symbolic capital**. This idea applies not just to dialects, but also to the different languages in a bilingual's repertoire. Bourdieu's idea is that even fields that are not economic in the narrow sense are still economic in a broader sense in that the way we speak is oriented towards "profit" of some kind. That is, there is a link between interests and actions, and speaking is such an action. Bourdieu's ideas come up again in chapter 4. A **rational choice** model (cf. Elster, 1989) also makes such a link, and Myers-Scotton and Bolonyai (2001) have shown how such a model can be applied to linguistic choices. The basic idea is that speakers are selecting their choices rationally if they make choices based on weighing costs and rewards of competing choices. However, to say that choices are "rationally based" does not mean that choices are the best in any objective sense, but rather that speakers are making cognitive calculations about their choices and making choices that subjectively they judge to be the best for them. The notion of rational choices comes up in chapter 6 when the Markedness Model is discussed.

2.7.4 The bilingual's dialectal and stylistic repertoire

Of special relevance to this book are the dialects and range of styles a bilingual controls. Certainly, if we are referring to a bilingual's repertoire within a second language, that person probably does not speak a dialect that is exactly like any of the dialects of native speakers. It is true that some bilinguals speaking second languages do come very close to native speaker dialects. But many bilinguals **fossilize** in producing pronunciations or grammatical structures that are not like native forms in the language they are trying to speak. For example, native speakers of a language that doesn't have articles used before nouns as English does, or doesn't have the same usage patterns for articles as English does, may well not use articles in an English-like fashion much of the time. A Chinese speaker whom we know comes very close to speaking the standard dialect of American English, but he regularly leaves out articles in such sentences as *I'm going to (the) library now*. That is, his understanding of how to use articles in English has fossilized in a non-native form regarding this particular use of English *the*.

Or, you may know bilinguals whose grammatical production of your language is very native-like, but whose pronunciation is decidedly non-native, especially of certain words. For a variety of reasons, including the age at which they acquired your language, these bilinguals haven't mastered the range of sounds in your language or how they are organized in those words.

Also, while most bilinguals certainly have more than one style in their repertoire of a second language they know well, it's unlikely that they have the same wide range of styles in their repertoire as native speakers of that language. This is an important consideration for both the bilingual and the person who speaks her or his language as a native speaker to keep in mind. **Most bilinguals can't match exactly the native speaker's repertoire** or, just as important, the native speaker's notions about what style is appropriate for a given situation.

2.7.5 Regional and social dialects

Sociolinguists often write confidently of two different types of dialects, regional and social dialects. As you would expect, **regional dialects** are those that are identified with a particular geographic region. **Social dialects** are identified with a social group, with "social group" defined very broadly. Thus, we talk about the dialect of different socio-economic classes, but we also can talk about the social dialects of ethnic groups, of women versus men, and of speakers according to their age groups or educational level, as in the case of the young, more educated speakers at the German-Dutch border compared with their less educated elders. But while it's easy enough to think that we are differentiating regional from social dialects and then making distinctions among types of social dialects, think about it more carefully. Isn't the problem that we all live somewhere, so how can we avoid to some extent speaking like people from our region? But then, does this mean that we only speak a regional dialect and not a social one? And then, aren't we all simultaneously members of different social groups? For example, can't you be a male aged 35 of Jamaican descent, but have been raised in London, England since age ten, and also now be a dental surgeon? So when it comes to classifying the dialect you speak, what do we say? The question isn't easily answered, is it?

For this reason, we don't say that everyone in the same region speaks the same dialect. They may; that is, **geographical boundaries** can make a difference (e.g. rivers or mountains). But dialect boundaries are just as often **social boundaries**. Still, if asked, the average person probably would identify the way someone speaks more in terms of region than social group. But the social basis of dialectal differences (and ultimately, language differences) is more profound and **ultimately affects our evaluations of others** more. Again, we evaluate how good or bad a linguistic variety is according to who speaks it, and, in any one region, everyone doesn't have the same social identities.

At the same time, it is hard to disentangle region and social group in the identification and valuing of dialects. What happens when subjects in a study are asked to identify the region where the "best" speech is spoken? At least in the United States, Hartley and Preston (1999) found that "best" can apply along two different dimensions. The **dimension of "most correct"** is related to how closely the relevant regional dialect matches the criteria we've outlined for the standard dialect. Judging a dialect "most correct" is a socially based judgment that has become tied to region in the minds of speakers. People who live in the areas where the speech is perceived to be more standard-like (the Midwest and Upper Midwest) ranked their areas highest in terms of "correct". At the same time, others (e.g. Southerners) also identified these as the areas of most "correct" speech. But what is interesting is that on another dimension, Southerners are very positive about their own dialect area, identifying the speech there as **most "pleasant"**. Hartley and Preston refer to this feature of "pleasantness" as homestyle. Not just "correct" but also "pleasant" emerges as a measure of the prestige accorded to group membership and, in this case, positively identifying the local community.

2.7.6 Dialects and geographical barriers

Once you get to larger groups – ethnic groups, geographical regions, and nations – you find even bigger differences in the way different groups speak. Two sets of factors have promoted linguistic divisions. First, natural geographic features, such as the Appalachian Mountains in the southeast US that have helped preserve distinctive features in the dialects spoken there, have served as boundaries separating mountaineers both physically and symbolically (through the dialects) from other groups. And in Valle d'Aosta, an area in the mountainous region of Italy near France, a local variety that is neither French nor Italian has been preserved alongside French and Italian. (This variety is called a **patois** by the locals, a term often used in French for non-standard, regional dialects.)

2.7.7 Dialects and language as social barriers

Second, humans have made their own boundaries. The most obvious human-made boundaries are national borders; we've seen how they "create" languages. But just as potent are boundary-makers that one socio-economically based group or ethnic group has erected to separate itself from other groups. Those who do not speak the dialect of those who control desirable socio-economic opportunities face a virtual barricade.

2.7.7.1 Types of bilingualism and social barriers

Gatekeepers in the world of socio-economic power and prestige have always recognized the desirability of bilingualism in certain languages. (And, of course, not only the relevant language, but also the "right" dialect, matters.) For example, in eighteenth- and nineteenth-century Europe, it was mainly the upper classes which were bilingual, and they used their bilingualism to separate themselves from the common people. In many nations, members of the upper class spoke French among their peers and only spoke their national language to lower class citizens. Being bilingual in whatever language is associated with education and/or high socio-economic status has always been **the mark of a privileged few**. Latin was such a language in Europe in the Middle Ages; it was only when such writers as Chaucer in England and Dante in Italy began writing in local languages that such indigenous languages became considered as even possible vehicles of serious ideas.

Today, the prestigious languages in any community are still the main targets for becoming bilingual. In some cases, speakers becoming bilingual are still striving to separate themselves from the masses. We have in mind learners of English or other world languages that are passports to better jobs in businesses with an international base or involving technological expertise. But more often than not, people are becoming bilingual simply to join the mainstream in any nation. Now we have in mind immigrants. In contrast, with other bilinguals, these persons are often lower class workers. They must overcome the barrier of not speaking the national language in order to be active participants in the national economic life. Almost ironically, such bilingualism promotes a measure of egalitarianism. This does not mean bilingualism is reciprocal; there are few in the host country who want to learn the immigrant's language. Thus, in Paris, it is the North African factory worker who learns French, not the French who decide to learn Arabic. In San Antonio, Texas, no matter how many Mexican immigrants there are, it is the Mexican immigrant who learns English, and not often the Texan Anglo who learns Spanish. And in Zurich, located in the Swiss German-speaking area of Switzerland, it is the Italian immigrant who learns Swiss German more often than local residents learn Italian. Egalitarianism comes in this way: These new bilinguals may have entered the host society in lower class jobs, but by becoming bilingual in the national language they acquire one means to break through socio-economic barriers to mainstream membership. Future chapters will discuss further the role of bilingualism in the speaker's life.

2.8 Summing up

The theme of this chapter has been two-fold. First, we have defined as best we can the labels used for ways of speaking. Second, we opened discussion of how speakers use their linguistic varieties to "do social work", especially to distinguish themselves from other social groups.

- **Language**, **dialect**, and **style** are used in labeling the different ways we have of speaking.

- **Linguistic variety** and **code** are neutral labels for any way of speaking. The reason we need these neutral terms is that how we define what people X speak as a different language from one people Y speak, rather than calling what they both speak dialects of the same language, varies a lot, depending on many factors.
- What counts as a language on its own depends on what criteria are used.
- **Mutual intelligibility**, a criterion that considers whether speakers can understand each other.
- **Socio-political factors**, criteria that consider similarities or differences in histories and cultures, status as separate nation states or not.
- In general, a **dialect** is a sub-group under a language and a language consists of at least two dialects, usually more. Dialects generally show **structural overlap**, making them mutually intelligible.
- A **style** or **register** is a sub-group under a dialect; this time, there is even more structural overlap among styles than among dialects.
- Linguistic varieties are **social identity markers**. What we speak depends on our life experiences.

2.9 Words and phrases to remember

three main systems in all linguistic varieties
dialect continuum
receptive bilingualism
standard dialect
non-standard dialects
personal dialect continuum
communicative competence
symbolic capital
social dialects
regional dialects

3

Who is a Bilingual? What Factors Promote Bilingualism?

Multiple voices: The word from Ecuador

Alberto Gallegos is a civil engineer in Ecuador who speaks Spanish as his first language, but who also speaks English. In addition, he studied Quichua in the university but has very few opportunities to hear it or speak it because of the type of life he leads in Quito, the capital. Spanish, of course, is the main language in Ecuador, alongside Quichua, the first language of many of the indigenous people in the highlands. Alberto began to study English in Ecuador, but became fluent in English when he spent a year as an exchange student in high school in Pennsylvania in the United States. Alberto returned to Ecuador to study civil engineering at a university there. He now builds industrial plants in Ecuador, but his work takes him to the United States often to visit plants such as poultry- and milk-processing plants. He speaks English when he is in contact with Americans on the job and he also has several American friends in Quito and likes to watch baseball and American football on cable TV. He wants his four children to go to the United States as exchange students when they are teenagers. In contrast with Alberto, Pedro Lema, who also lives in Quito, does speak a good deal of Quichua there. He is a weaver from the province of Imbabura and his first language is Quichua. He sells garments and tablecloths, which his family weaves during the week, at an open market. He speaks Quichua with other vendors and with his family and friends, but speaks Spanish with most of his clients and in such transactions as going to the bank. If he spots a client who speaks English, Pedro will attempt a rudimentary conversation with him. He is eager to continue learning English and takes night classes.

3.1 Introduction

There have been many attempts to define bilingualism from many different perspectives, but none of them works in general or really characterizes the phenomenon very well. For example, defining bilingualism as "speaking two or more languages with native-like ability" would rule out most bilingual speakers.

3.1.1 Introducing bilingual children

There are extremely few people who really speak more than one language "like a native". Generally, these are people who were raised as bilinguals from infancy onwards. (Remember that we are using **bilingual** for two *or more* languages.) In chapter 11, we'll discuss some studies of child bilingualism and we'll see that, even as very young children, speakers develop dominance in one language (partly because it's the main language of the social milieu where they are raised). They also divide up their language use, with one language used more with certain persons (and therefore certain situations). Furthermore, even if they left childhood (almost) equally fluent in both languages, most bilinguals still gradually end up with more facility in one language for certain types of situations and facility in the other language for other situations – just because of their usage patterns. What we mean by dominance will become somewhat clearer later on.

There is a good deal of research on what's called the **critical age hypothesis** and this will be discussed in chapter 11. This hypothesis presents the notion that all children easily acquire any language to which they are exposed up until about the age of puberty; after that, acquiring a language becomes more arduous and more of a conscious procedure. Debate on this hypothesis continues.

Even so, there is plenty of good evidence that very young children do acquire more than one language as long as they are exposed to speakers of the languages. It's also very clear that **their ease of acquisition is generally different** from that of their parents in the same situation. For example, internationals from Asia or Africa who are graduate students at European or North American universities and have families with them are often chagrined when their young children whiz through learning the local language while the adults – after years of classroom study of the language in their home country – still speak haltingly and with a non-native pronunciation, even when they are now immersed in the milieu of their target language.

3.1.2 Good language learners beyond childhood

True, there are some persons well past puberty who – for reasons not entirely clear – seem to have an innate ability to pick up second languages very easily to the extent that they speak two or more languages with real facility. We all know people who claim they learned to speak French fluently by going to French movies – and some of them are telling the truth. We don't entirely understand how some adults do learn languages easily; one view is that there may be a specialized ability encoded in the brain for language learning, just as there may be such an ability for music. Generally, though, there is also clearly a social component to these **polyglots** (one word for people who speak many languages). That is, they are typically people who lived – or now live – in societies where it is necessary to speak more than one language on a daily basis. Thus, while these people may have special linguistic abilities, the fact that their lives place a good deal of **social pressure** on them to speak more than one language in order to participate fully in their communities may make the crucial difference. For example, these good language learners **often are members of minority groups** who must speak the dominant language in their society for any sort of socio-economic advancement, if not just to conduct their everyday lives. Thus, in Parus or Bolivia, a Quechua-speaking Indian from a rural village would have a hard time existing in urban areas without speaking Spanish, too. Our prototypical Quichua speaker in Quito sketched above exemplifies such a person. (Quechua is a cover term for the related varieties that make up the Quechua language, but in Ecuador and Argentina, Quichua is the name used for the local variety.) And in eastern Belgium, the German-speaking minority, who are in villages surrounded by French-speaking villages, almost necessarily must speak French as well as their native language. (French and Belgian Dutch (Flemish) are the two main (official) languages of Belgium, although German is also official.) Further, the Berbers are a minority group in most of the areas of North Africa where they live. It's a fact of life that they must learn the local variety of Arabic, the native language of most other people all through North Africa, unless the Berbers are isolated nomads. But many Berbers also have learned the main foreign language of the area, French, as well as one or more other European languages.

Clearly, for various possible reasons, there are many people in the world who do speak two or even three or more languages quite well. How many speak these second language (L2s) with **real fluency is another issue**. As you will see, the experiments reported in chapter 11 indicate that most late learners of an L2 do not have near-native abilities in an L2. We use "late" to refer to learning a language after about age 12 and possibly even a bit earlier.

3.1.3 Individual and community repertoires

Hearing about people who speak several languages, we can surmise **two important sociolinguistic facts** about all people and their linguistic repertoires. First, as we've indicated in chapter 2, people typically speak more than one language because an extra language does important **"social work"** for them.

When speakers add another language to their repertoires, they almost always do so for one reason – because **that language will be useful to them** in their community, or in another community that they want to join. That is, not many people acquire another language to any real extent just because it's "fun" to do so.

Second, although we can refer to the linguistic repertoire of a given community as a composite of all the varieties spoken there, not all people in that community speak the same varieties; that is, individuals have **individualized linguistic repertoires**. What makes the difference across individuals are their needs and desires to learn different languages, but perhaps even more so, their opportunities to learn them. This **unevenness in repertoires** and how it affects people's lives will be relevant in various ways in many of the following chapters.

Still, most people who are bilinguals do not regularly use two or more languages or speak them all fluently. So, when you meet people who tell you they speak four or five languages, give them a smile to show you're impressed, but don't take this claim very seriously. We're not doubting that they are bilinguals, but the question is, do they carry on all of their everyday interactions in *all* these languages? Keep in mind the following statement that's going to have relevance throughout this book: Bilinguals rarely have equal control of both languages, simply because **people rarely use two languages in exactly the same situations** with the same persons. So your "I speak five languages" friends may be able to ask directions to the train station or order four-course meals in several of the languages they "speak", but can they give a presentation or carry on a long conversation in a group of native speakers of these languages? Don't ask this question, though; just smile.

Our point is that there are very few **balanced bilinguals**, people who are equally at home in their several languages, simply because **everyone's life favors two outcomes**: (1) acquiring one language more fully than two, (2) using one language more frequently than others that may be known to varying degrees. That is, even most children who acquire two languages as their first language (if they are exposed to both at a very young age), and seem to speak them equally well as small children, do not maintain their equality in the two languages. Depending on how they live their lives, they use one language more; they definitely develop a wider vocabulary and possibly more complex sentence structures in that language.

3.2 Who is a bilingual?

Should we emphasize *knowing* more than one language in our definition of a bilingual, or should we emphasize *using* more than two languages regularly? The proverbial person-in-the-street probably thinks of being a bilingual as a matter of knowing two or more languages, being able to speak them, but doesn't think much about – or know much about – how the bilingual uses these languages. In the next section, we'll discuss what knowing two or more languages may mean and then move on in the following section to discussing how bilinguals use their languages.

3.2.1 Assessing proficiency

A first issue, and one that we cannot resolve, is **who decides that someone is a bilingual**. Speakers can identify themselves as bilinguals, or other persons may make the assessment. In either case, the assessment can be absolute ("She speaks Moroccan Arabic like a native") or gradient ("I can get around Jakarta in Indonesian, but don't ask me to carry on a conversation with the locals").

A second issue that also resists resolution is **how professionals assess language proficiency**. The simple truth is that even they do not have a good measure of proficiency. The reasons are complex, but they include the fact that linguistic varieties consist of three main systems (phonology, morphology and syntax, and the lexicon). All **L1 speakers** (native speakers of a language) of at least average intelligence have almost equal competence in the phonology and morphology and syntax of their L1, even if the size of their vocabulary may vary. But a speaker of a second language (**L2 speaker**) may have decidedly more ability in one or two of these systems than the others. And across speakers, this unevenness **especially applies to pronunciation skills**. Very few persons who learn a second language after early childhood master the sound system of their L2, but they may speak very fluently and have extensive vocabularies. So, how can you say a speaker is proficient or not if her or his abilities aren't the same across these systems?

Interestingly enough, while most L2 speakers try very hard to master the morphology (how words are constructed of bits and pieces) and syntax (how phrases and clauses are constructed) of their L2, some L2 speakers actually prefer *not* to speak their second language with **a native-like pronunciation**. There are several possible reasons. First, **not being mistaken for a native speaker** means that your fellow speakers don't have native-like expectations for you in other areas, such as knowing all the local customs. Second, speaking your L2 "with a foreign accent" (from chapter 2, remember we all speak with accents) may give you **a certain desirable dimension**. For example, it's been said that Henry Kissinger, the elder statesman and advisor to American presidents, speaks English with an accent reminiscent of his native German, so that he would sound like a European professor and therefore gain whatever connotations that identity brings with it. Some native speakers of French may have similar views because French accents in an L2 are considered "charming" in those cultures that admire the French cultural tradition.

Within the areas of **morphology and syntax**, a bilingual may have very good control of specific grammatical categories, but not of others. For example, some languages have a number of ways of referring to when an action happened and its present state (different references to tense and aspect) that are little used, even by native speakers, and bilinguals may not have much fluency in using them. This is the case with some tenses in French or references to remote past in some Bantu languages. And although English supposedly does not "have a lot of grammar", it does have enough grammatical pitfalls for the L2 speaker. For example, many L2 speakers of English use the progressive form when they really want to indicate a habitual activity (they say *Every day I exercise; I am running five miles* instead of *I run five miles*). Or, certain aspects of English word order may be difficult for them to master. Some have difficulty with question formation involving inversion of subject and verb (for example, L2 speakers may say *When you are going?* instead of *When are you going?*).

The area in which we seem to expect the least proficiency from a bilingual and still be willing to label her or him a bilingual is in **mastery of the lexicon (vocabulary) of the L2**. We expect the bilingual to know enough words to express everyday ideas, but bilinguals rarely have the same store of words as an L1 speaker of the relevant language. This is especially true in dealing with specialized topics. However, ironically, if the bilingual is a specialist in a certain topic, she or he may be able to discuss it with more facility than most L1 speakers, certainly more than non-specialists in the topic. Think of South Asian immigrants who are specialists in designing hardware or software in the computer industry.

3.2.2 Two kinds of linguistic competence

Another problem in assessing proficiency is that any evaluation ought to consider both **grammatical competence** and **communicative competence**. Grammatical competence is what the ordinary person thinks of when we talk about "knowing a language". It's what this ordinary person calls "speaking properly". More technically, grammatical competence refers to speakers' ability to recognize and produce what are considered well-formed utterances in the language in question. That is, when given a pair of sentences, grammatical competence enables you to say, "Yes, that's how we say it in our language" or, "No, that doesn't sound right". Such **grammaticality judgments** are often used in testing grammatical competence in a language.

Communicative competence refers to the ability to *use* those utterances in ways that are considered **unmarked or appropriate** in one situation as opposed to another in the relevant society. What is unmarked depends on who the participants are, the topic, and the setting, as well as other factors. Our communicative competence also enables us to recognize **marked usages** and what the speaker intends by such utterances. What someone says is marked if it is *not* what most people in your society would say in a given situation; instead, a marked choice of words or the entire conversational contribution is appropriate in some other situation altogether. For example, knowing when you can say *Hey, dude* to someone rather than *Good morning, sir* reflects our communicative competence. Speakers don't make many marked choices, but when they do, such a choice is a comment on how that speaker views the situation and may want others to view it. You'll see more on markedness in chapter 6 when interpersonal language use is discussed at length.

Communicative competence is sometimes referred to as **pragmatic or socio-linguistic competence**, especially when the emphasis is on how to interpret the speaker's intended social meaning in a particular utterance, a meaning that is not the same as the utterance's literal meaning. Thus, when someone stops you on the street and says, "Do you know where the main library is?", chances are good that he or she does not expect you to answer "yes" or "no", but to take this utterance as a request for directions to the library.

Note that the native speakers of a language (or someone who learns the language as a young child) does not need to be "taught" either grammatical competence or communicative competence. They acquire both types of competence with no obvious effort. This acquisition requires some exposure to the language in use in the speaker's community, and it is based on some innate mechanism or innate learning principles that all humans have. This topic is discussed more fully in chapter 11.

When L2s are taught in a formal setting, the emphasis generally is on teaching – as much as it can be taught – what native speakers know as their grammatical competence. That is, most programs that teach a language in an explicit way concentrate on teaching grammatical constructions. However, more and more second language programs are recognizing the need to pay attention to communicative competence. But because of the belief that "grammar" *is* "the language", most L2 speakers have paid more attention to studying grammar in their language learning.

For this reason, many L2 speakers have more control of the L2 grammar than of its appropriate use. For example, an international student from a culture that is stereotypically considered to be very "polite" once came into my office to find out the results of a quiz that I had given the previous day. But what he said was, "I want my quiz back." I said to myself, "Why is he being so rude?" Any American student would never have said that! Instead, an American might have phrased her or his directive as a pseudo-question ("Have you graded the quizzes yet?" or "Could I find out my grade on the quiz?"). Because I'm a sociolinguist, I could answer my own question: He had learned how to ask for something in English, but didn't realize that although there are various ways to make requests, only certain ways are appropriate in an American student–professor exchange.

This international student spoke very grammatically correct English, but because he was lacking in communicative competence, can we say he was a "full" bilingual? Certainly, he would face a rocky road in an English-speaking society. Chapter 7 deals with some differences in what is considered appropriate behavior cross-culturally.

3.2.3 Different uses for a language and proficiency

Not only is structural proficiency (that is, morphology and syntax) generally not an all or none phenomenon for bilinguals; the same applies to proficiency in *how* the L2 is used. Languages are used in a number of different ways and in different situations. First, consider the ways that languages are used; basically, we can talk about **speaking**, **listening**, **reading**, and **writing** skills. And, of course, not all speakers have the same degree of proficiency in any of these skills, nor is there an absolute way to say what counts as proficiency in any one skill. Second, consider the relevant situations of language use.

Fishman (1972) and others make an initial classification into **domains**; the basic domains include home, work, neighborhood, church and the more general public domain (both formal and informal activities). But under any of these domains, there are many different types of activities to consider. For example, conversation at home between two teenage siblings is quite different from conversation at home at a holiday family dinner with elderly relatives present. And assigning one language to one domain in a given community doesn't allow for the possibility of something some bilinguals do very often: codeswitching, using two languages in the same conversation. Domains are discussed more thoroughly in chapter 4.

3.2.4 Circumstances of acquiring a language make a difference

How it happens that a speaker knows the L2 is a major factor in determining how fluent she or he is in any of these skills. As background information, let's consider the distinction some linguists make between language acquisition and language learning. When a child speaks a language as a first language in the home, we refer to language **acquisition**. And a child can acquire either one language or two languages as a first language, or even more. For example, Lanza (1997) reports on a Norwegian child who acquired Norwegian from the father and English from the mother; this study is discussed in chapter 11. When speakers learn a second language later in life, we refer to language **learning**. We'll discuss the rationale behind this distinction in a later chapter, as well as the difficulty in applying it in any absolute sense. One potential source of confusion is that linguists often refer to the study of L2 learning as a subject (not the study of a specific L2) as "second language acquisition" (SLA).

If a child acquires two languages in the home, with each, really, as a first language, how well the child acquires either language depends on a number of factors; however, those linguists who put a lot of stock in an innate program that is called **universal grammar** argue that little exposure is necessary for very young children to acquire fluency in speaking and understanding speech in any language to which they are exposed. As you might imagine, acquiring ability in reading and writing requires more than simple exposure. Bilingual children and their language acquisition are main topics of chapter 11.

If a second language is learned in the school context, how proficient the child becomes also depends on a number of factors. First, of course, is **the matter of age**, with young children having the advantage, as indicated above. But also of obvious importance is **the type of language instruction** (immersion in the L2 or only scheduled L2 classes), how frequently the classes meet, which skills are emphasized, why the L2 is being studied and when and how it will be used, etc. There are also various psychological considerations, such as personal motivation.

In addition, we shouldn't forget that many bilinguals learn their L2s informally. The extent of **informal language learning** varies with both the individual and the community. In some parts of the world, this is how almost all L2s are learned; for example, in the hinterlands of Papua New Guinea it is certainly how Tok Pisin is learned. In Western societies, immigrants working in factories or outdoor construction or farming work often learn the national language almost entirely through informal contacts on the job.

In some multilingual communities, the norm is for certain languages to be learned informally, with others almost always learned only through formal schooling. For example, this is how the learning of Swahili differs from that of English in Nairobi, Kenya. Urban children become fluent in Swahili in two ways; in multi-ethnic neighborhoods they may acquire Swahili alongside their ethnic group language as a dual first language, or they may acquire Swahili from playmates at a slightly older age. Certainly, Swahili is the language of play among inter-ethnic groups of children in urban areas in Kenya. Later, they may also study Swahili in school as a subject. In-migrant adults (from other areas of Kenya) who do not already know Swahili from either earlier informal contacts or from schooling (less likely) may learn Swahili on the job in Nairobi. However, everyone generally learns English only as a school subject, although children may also learn at least some phrases from playmates and the electronic media. In Tanzania, Kenya's neighbor to the south, Swahili is much more widespread and often is learned informally (although it is generally also the medium of instruction at least in primary schools); it has replaced other languages as the L1 of some ethnic groups. But if English is learned at all, it is learned in the schools there, too.

3.2.5 Bilingualism and a fluency continuum

All of these factors result in bilinguals having what can be called a **fluency continuum** in each of the skills of speaking, listening, reading, and writing. While we expect all those that we call bilinguals to speak and understand their L2 to some extent, **their fluency typically varies in different situations**. Some of the main factors affecting performance are who the participants are, what the topic is, and what the goal of the interaction is. As you can imagine, simply how often a bilingual uses her or his L2 also makes a difference; if you speak or read your L2 every day you probably are more fluent in it than if you only use it on occasional trips to the home area of that language.

Given the fact that a primary use of language is to communicate with others, you would expect that speaking and listening skills would always be the greatest. This isn't always the case, though. In some communities, more emphasis is placed on learning to read and write an L2 than speak it. For example, until recently, this was the main feature of English-language instruction in Korea and Japan.

We don't want to leave out the possibility that bilinguals may show either **"active" or "passive" bilingualism**. That is, someone may be able to understand a certain L2, but not speak it, making him or her a passive bilingual. And in some societies, many conversations are carried on with one speaker speaking one language and the other speaking another language, with both speakers as passive bilinguals.

3.3 Defining bilingualism

So, who is a bilingual? If we can't use proficiency in speaking another language as our criterion, what can we use? Most books and articles on bilingualism spend several sentences, if not several paragraphs, looking at one definition and then another. Surely knowing just a few words or phrases isn't enough to qualify a speaker as a bilingual. But how many phrases *is* enough? It depends on who is doing the defining. You can imagine that any definition that calls for being able to use two languages "perfectly" or even "habitually" won't work for us – given our discussion above. Even definitions that refer to "minimal proficiency" in a second language run into problems; for example, how is "minimal" to be defined?

For our purposes, we are satisfied with a very broad definition based on being able to demonstrate minimal use of two or more languages. We have indicated that bilingualism may be based on reading or writing as well as speaking. But in this book we will consider speaking most essential in our definition. We'll say that **bilingualism is the ability to use two or more languages sufficiently to carry on a limited casual conversation**, but we won't set specific limits on proficiency or how much the speaker in question is speaking or demonstrating comprehension of another speaker. This definition does not limit bilingualism to speaking any one specific dialect of the L2 in question; it can be the standard dialect or any of the non-standard dialects (as discussed in chapter 2).

This definition does rule out some people who can use a second language in specialized ways. It rules out simply being able to read a menu and place an order in a restaurant. And, just because you studied Spanish for two years in secondary school or at a college or university and you can read some Spanish, you're not a bilingual by our definition unless you can use Spanish in a short conversation.

Our definition also means that persons who use some words from another language (lexical borrowings) in their own L1 are not necessarily bilinguals. In fact, one of the defining features of these borrowings is that they are words from another language that have become established in language X to the extent that at least some monolingual speakers of language X can and do use them. Discussing loan words (borrowings) has a place in a volume on bilingualism because their presence in a language depends on some bilingual speakers who brought in the borrowed words in the first place. Chapter 8 provides an overview of borrowing as a process and borrowed words.

3.4 Factors promoting bilingualism

To this point in the chapter, we've characterized bilinguals themselves in terms of what we can say about their proficiency in their L2s and how they use them. In the remainder of this chapter, the discussion centers on the factors that promote bilingualism and on characteristics of bilingualism itself. In chapter 4 the main topics are maintenance of an L1 in the face of bilingualism and shift from the L1 to an L2 as speakers' main language. Chapters 5 through 7 deal once again more specifically with the bilingual as a person and how bilingualism figures in her or his life. Chapters 8 through 11 look more closely at what we know about bilingualism and its mental organization, what happens to the bilingual's languages when they are frequently spoken together, and language acquisition.

Of course bilingualism is the **result of contact between speakers** speaking different languages, especially different L1s. If we look at bilingualism when it is a group phenomenon, bilingualism often results under two main sets of conditions. (1) **Close proximity**. That is, the ordinary conditions of life in their ethnic group regularly put speakers in close proximity to speakers of another language. Further, if learning the other group's language is not a reciprocal matter, then **the group of less power and prestige makes the effort** to learn the other group's language. (2) **Displacement**. Conditions of displacement promote the need or desire to learn another language. Displacement can mean either physical movement or a change in psychological outlook.

3.4.1 Close proximity = bilingualism for many

The conditions of close proximity with other groups that promote bilingualism include:

- Living in a bilingual nation, especially as a minority group member.
- Living in border areas between ethnic groups or nations.
- Living in a multi-ethnic urban area.
- Engaging in an occupation that involves many contacts with out-group members.
- Marrying outside one's ethnic group.
- Having a parent or grandparent outside one's ethnic group.

3.4.1.1 *Living in a multilingual nation*

Recall that we're using "bilingual" to cover speaking more than one language, so it may refer to more than one other language. In this section, we'll refer to *nations* with more than one language as "multilingual", just because the rule almost always is more than two languages. Almost every nation in the world is multi-lingual by this criterion; in fact, it is very hard to find a monolingual nation in the world. Iceland may still qualify and also Korea. Even Japan includes speakers of Ainu on its northern island, and it has many Korean immigrants as well as some Chinese. Before World War II, some other nations, especially in Western Europe, were close to being monolingual. But this isn't the case today, thanks to the large numbers of immigrants who now call these nations home.

Of course, there are monolingual areas in almost all nations, especially if the speakers there speak a dialect of the official language of the nation. But except in nations of broad expanses, such as the United States, Canada, Australia, or China, it is harder and harder to find monolingual enclaves. And remember that individuals may be either monolingual or bilingual, even if the nation in which they live shows what is sometimes called **societal bilingualism**; i.e., bilingualism at the level of a group.

3.4.1.2 *Minority groups*

Many nations include groups who speak a mother tongue that is not the official language of the nation state. Such groups are called **minority groups** and they can exist in either rural or urban settings. They typically are ethnic-ally based groups; that is, everyone claims membership in the same ethnic group. The name "minority" is used for groups in a nation state that do not have large numbers of mother tongue speakers when compared with the group whose L1 is the official language. But the real reason to call them minority groups is not just numbers. These groups **typically lack political power** within the nation state and/or socio-economic prestige. This is the most important sense in which they are minority groups. Their status by these criteria is re-flected in the fact that these groups lack the same level of official standing as the main official language. This language may be the language of the majority, but it may also be selected for other reasons.

We can think of only **two major exceptions** (we are sure there are others, too) to this characterization of minority groups as lacking both political power and high socio-economic status. First, there is the **prominent case of Catalonia** where a minority group has high socio-economic prestige, but little political power. This is the region of Catalonia in Spain, with Barcelona as the main urban area. The language of Catalonia, Catalan, is a Romance language closely related to Castilian, the standard dialect of Spanish, although it is possibly more closely related to the linguistic varieties of southern France, such as Occitan (now disappearing rapidly). Catalan is an official language in Catalonia, although of course Castilian is also an official language, because it is the official language all over Spain.

Catalonia (often called Catalunya) is a major industrial center. Related to this fact are statistics showing that Catalan speakers (especially native born individuals) have a higher standard of living and are better educated than L1 Castilian speakers there (Atkinson, 2000). The medium of schooling in Catalonia is now Catalan. Catalan L1 speakers are the numerical majority in Catalonia; in 2004 the issue of whether to give special status to Catalan within the European Union was under consideration.

The second case is found in Miami, Florida where there are many Spanish-speaking immigrants. Many of them, mostly immigrants from Cuba, are major forces in the economic community. In spite of this, Spanish has no official status there. But here, as in Catalonia, the minority group enjoys high prestige with out-groups and is considered a political force to be reckoned with on both the local and state, if not national, level. The connection between high socio-economic status and prestige in the larger community, as well as in-group **ethnolinguistic vitality** seems obvious. (Ethnolinguistic vitality is discussed further in chapter 4.)

3.4.1.3 What minority status means

Because almost all minority groups lack political and economic power, minority groups often become bilingual in the dominant national language for **both instrumental and psychological reasons**. Further, from the standpoint of the dominant group, the presence of minority groups can be an obstacle to communication and, more importantly, to national integration. It may sound cynical, but history supports the comment of Laponce (1987: 198) that **dominant groups tolerate minorities** "only on condition that they accept at least partial linguistic assimilation [learn the dominant language] and keep their numbers small."

At the same time, one can argue – just as cynically – that politicians in control of the central government can use the existence of minority groups who don't speak the official language to their advantage. They can **reduce the participation of such groups in decision making** at the national level and therefore in control of the state. Given that large segments of the populations in most sub-Saharan African states do not speak the official language, their inability to be heard in the political arena is a major problem if true nation building is a goal. In former anglophone Africa, all the nations have English as their main official language except Tanzania (where Swahili is the main official language). In former francophone Africa, all the nations have French as their official language. Cameroon is a special case and is discussed in chapter 12. In the former Portuguese colony of Mozambique, Portuguese is official, as it is in Angola and other formerly Portuguese areas. In these nations, it can be argued that the former colonial language is a neutral choice in nations with many competing ethnic groups, each with its own language – or it can be considered the best of bad choices.

> Anglophone describes English-speaking peoples or a nation where English is an official language and/or a former English colony.
> Francophone describes French-speaking peoples or a nation where French is an official. language and/or a former French colony.
> Allophone describes native speakers of languages other than English or French in Canada.
> Lusophone describes Portuguese-speaking peoples or a nation where Portugal is an official language and/or a former Portuguese colony.

Eastern and Central Europe may not have as many ethnic groups as Africa, but their minority groups are often more vocal in demanding linguistic rights. Hungary is something of an exception. Even though there are a number of minority ethnic groups, Hungarian is the first language of 98.5% of the population. The Roma or Gypsy peoples make up most of the remaining numbers (Fenyvesi, 1998a). But there are many Hungarians, as minority group members, in nearby nation states.

Other nation states, such as Bulgaria, have sizeable groups who self-identify as ethnic groups other than Bulgarian. In a 1992 official survey 85.5% declared themselves to be Bulgarian, but almost 10% said they were Turks, with Turkish as their mother tongue, although the younger generation speaks fluent Bulgarian (Boneva, 1998). In contrast, in the Caucasus across the Black Sea from Eastern Europe and in an area slightly smaller than France, there are 30 million people speaking at least 50 languages, plus at least 12 more spoken by recent immigrant groups. For example, in Armenia, except for Russians and Yezdi Kurds, all groups need to be bilingual to communicate outside of their rural settlements (Arutiunov, 1998).

3.4.1.4 Border areas

In many parts of the world, wherever there is a border between nations or between ethnic groups, at least parts of the neighboring populations show some bilingualism. Often, the **bilingualism is not reciprocal**, though; that is, speakers of the less dominant language are more likely to learn the language of the more dominant group than vice versa. For example, this is the case in western Kenya at the border between the Luo ethnic group and the less politically powerful Bantu groups of the area, the Luyia to the North and the Kisii to the east of the Luos.

Where there are borders between nations, speakers also often learn the language spoken across the national frontier. Again, though, bilingualism is not necessarily reciprocal. Interestingly enough, there may be more bilingualism today where closely related varieties are spoken on either side than there was years ago. In the past, there was less motivation to learn the variety across the border in order to communicate with inhabitants there. Why? Because if the varieties are closely related, a person on one side could speak his or her variety and a person on the other side could speak his or her variety and they could understand each other well enough to communicate. This used to be the situation at the German-Dutch border that was mentioned in chapter 2.

German and Dutch, of course, are closely related languages. But after World War II, two things happened. First, with more formal education at the secondary level becoming the rule, more people learned the standard dialect of their national language and spoke the local dialect less. Second, more education also meant that speakers unconsciously moved their local dialects closer to the national standard dialect and therefore the national language (Dutch or German); that is, local dialects became less like the dialect across the national border. So today, probably 80-year-olds from different sides of the border can talk to each other with more ease in their local dialects than teenagers. The teenagers would probably choose to speak Standard German to each other, if the Dutch person knows it (Backus, personal communication).

Farther north, there is bilingualism at the Danish-German border with minority groups on both sides. A German-speaking community is recognized as a national minority in the southernmost Danish county of Sønderjylland, and a Danish community is similarly recognized as a national minority in the northernmost German federal state of Schleswig-Holstein. The Danish minority includes some 50,000 persons, with concentrations around the city of Flensburg. The German minority in Denmark is smaller (12,000 to 20,000 persons). In both cases, the minorities have their own cultural and educational facilities, funded by both Denmark and Germany. Wars in the region from 1864 to World War II and subsequent border and population shifts resulted in the present state of affairs (Fredsted, personal communication).

In section 3.5.3 other changes in European borders that have motivated speakers to become bilingual are discussed.

3.4.1.5 *Urban multilingualism*

Today's **cities all over the world are generally very multilingual**. Consider Brussels, the capital of Belgium. Brussels is unusual as an urban area because it is an autonomous region within what is now the federal state of Belgium. This status largely came about because it has two official languages, French and Dutch. But not just one variety of either language is spoken there; various studies have distinguished four varieties of French and four of Dutch. This diversity exists partly because both French and Dutch have ties to neighboring countries. French is the sole official language in France and one of three in Luxembourg. And Dutch is the official language in the Netherlands. To make matters more complicated, two of the Dutch varieties are called Standard Dutch. One is Standard Netherlands Dutch, which is one of the national official languages, and the other is a variety called Standard Belgian Dutch, but which includes some Belgian regional forms as well as other differences (Treffers-Daller, 2002). In addition to French and Dutch, other European languages are spoken by personnel at the European Union (EU), which is centered in Brussels. But that is not all. There are also many immigrants (largely unskilled workers) from all over, including most prominently the former Belgian territories in central Africa (Congo, Burundi, and Rwanda). Once you get outside of Brussels, what has been called the **territorial principle of bilingualism** applies. French, Dutch, and German are now all official languages, but each only in its own areas.

In some nations that we call multilingual, there are large numbers of speakers of different languages who are mingled together, but largely only in the urban areas. For example, all the major cities in Africa are multilingual in this sense, but all rural areas are not. At least in West Africa, the nature of urban multilingualism differs from the smaller capitals of the rural inland countries to the urban centers on the coast. Upcountry capitals, such as Bamako in Mali have a more traditional pattern of households, with **a separate quarter for each major ethnic group**, with the quarter often associated with distinct activities, such as tailoring or metal work. This doesn't mean everyone comes from the same ethnic group in a quarter; just that most of the people do. The coastal urban cities arose as centers of trade with Europeans and later as centers of colonial administration. "As such, they have been multilingual from the beginning", Mansour (1993: 61) points out. We will see in chapter 4 how this difference has affected patterns of language maintenance and shift in these cities, such as Dakar in Senegal. The need to become bilingual in cities is obvious, even those with ethnic enclaves; that is, it is unlikely any person can hold a job outside her or his neighborhood in a city and speak only the mother tongue. In other places, even the rural areas are very multilingual, such as on the mainland of Papua New Guinea where there are many small ethnic groups, each speaking its own language, but with frequent contacts with other groups and their languages.

3.4.1.6 How one's occupation can matter

Speakers whose occupations involve many contacts outside their own ethnic group may well have reasons to learn a second language. This is especially so if our model speaker is a trader or anyone whose job involves selling something. Thus, it is no surprise to find that market stallholders, wherever in the world they are, often can carry on at least limited conversations (revolving around what they are selling) in whatever the dominant languages of potential buyers are.

Examples of how **trade has always promoted bilingualism** are everywhere. For example, in the late Middle Ages, trading communication in the Baltic area was largely controlled by the Hansa or Hanseatic League, a group of merchants and towns located mainly in Northern Germany. Middle Low German became a prestigious language around the Baltic Sea and in western and southern Norway because of the dominant position of the Hanseatic League (Braunmüller, 2000). Because business was conducted face to face and because the Scandinavian languages of non-German traders were closely related to Middle Low German, it was relatively easy for non-native speakers to understand Middle Low German or learn to use it.

In addition, in today's global economy, many people who **work for multinational corporations** find learning a second language almost an absolute requirement. Often, business meetings involve employees from branches of the corporation in different nations, bringing together speakers of different L1s. Or, employees are transferred from one branch of such corporations to branches in other countries. Such people often find it useful, or even necessary, to learn **whatever second language has the widest range of usefulness** in the corporation. That language often is English. As we've pointed out already, English is frequently the lingua franca of the international business world. Recall that a **lingua franca** is any language that is used between two persons who don't share the same first language, so a lingua franca need not be English. It could be one of the dominant languages in India if the conversation taking place is between Indians; or, it could be the Putonghua dialect of Chinese (standard Chinese) or another Chinese dialect, Cantonese, in parts of Southeastern Asia. But more often than not, it is English. English achieved this status partly because many recent innovations in technology happened in the US and so English is the default language for manuals and directions for new devices, from home computers to air traffic control devices. Also, the position of American businesses was influential in establishing **English as an international corporate language**. American corporations have branches everywhere or are in partnership with local enterprises.

Further, once English is established as a useful medium between many pairs of two business people who don't share the same first language, its momentum builds and it is becomes even more useful as a lingua franca in yet more international business contacts. And just because it is useful, not to mention because of the role of the US in scientific advancements, English is widely studied as a subject everywhere (at least in high schools), and often is the main language in which academic scholarship across many fields is published.

Speaking a second language may also be a necessary qualification in many other types of occupations, too. Obviously, people in the travel business find it useful to speak the L1 of the main groups of tourists that their countries attract. This may mean speaking some German in Spain, for example, or speaking English in Bavarian villages or speaking French or German at Disneyland in Florida. Teachers at all levels who have many students speaking an L1 other than the medium of instruction may find their jobs easier if they have some fluency in the language of the main group of such students.

3.4.1.7 Marrying outside one's ethnic group

With the recent huge movements of populations (migrants and refugees), inter-ethnic romances and subsequent marriages are on the increase. Marrying outside your group is called **exogamy**. In such cases, children may learn the language of either the mother or the father or even sometimes both, but which language dominates depends on which language has the most prestige where they live. The mother is usually the partner who encourages learning either the mother's or the father's language if it is not the language of local prestige.

3.4.1.8 Having a parent or grandparent outside one's ethnic group

Obviously, this factor may be related to exogamy on the part of one's parents, or of their parents. Again, when there are inter-ethnic differences in the L1s of key people in your family, whether you will learn the language of the "odd" person depends on a number of factors. For example, if you were raised by a grandmother who has a different L1 than any of the other members of your family circle, then it's possible you will acquire her language as well as the dominant family language. That you would acquire it *and* retain it would be especially likely if her language had high prestige for some reason in the larger community than the L1 of other family members.

To make more concrete the notion of having several languages in your immediate family, consider these two scenarios. Your immediate family lives in **Basel, Switzerland**, which is in a German-speaking area, but one bordering on France. Everyone in your family except your grandmother is a native speaker of Swiss German. She was raised in France and is a native speaker of French. Because your grandmother is your primary caretaker, you acquire French from her. But you also acquire Swiss German from the rest of your family and your playmates. At school, you learn the standard dialect of German. Because French has official status in some of the other cantons in Switzerland and because of its international standing, you maintain your French and study it as a subject in school, making you **a trilingual**.

Or, let's say you live in London and are the child of a Jamaican woman who speaks **Jamaican creole** as her L1 and of an Englishman who speaks only a London dialect of English. You almost certainly will acquire a London dialect of English, either that of your father or, more likely, something closer to the way your peers speak English. But you also may learn Jamaican Creole from your mother and her relatives who also live in London. If your mother takes you on a visit to Jamaica, it's even more likely that you will learn Jamaican Creole. Whether you will use it frequently in London with others in addition to your mother remains to be seen, but there are many speakers of this language in London.

3.5 Conditions of displacement

Speakers are likely to become bilingual under certain conditions of displacement. This **displacement can be physical or it can be psychological**:

- Speakers move, whether voluntarily or involuntarily (migration).
- The ruling class changes (wars and colonialism).
- Borders change (peace settlements).
- Circumstances encourage speakers to learn the territorially dominant language (incorporation for national integration).
- Speakers admire/espouse the characteristics of an attractive group (acculturation).
- Education in an L2 is a prerequisite for socio-economic mobility.

3.5.1 Migration

Throughout history, groups of people have been on the move voluntarily. Although there are certainly cases of a single person leaving the home village to seek his or her fortune elsewhere, generally such individuals are part of a group of members of their same ethnic group who move to seek a better life. The motivation for most migration has been to find better jobs, but it can also have other causes, such as to seek political or religious refuge. In every case, an outcome of migration has been bilingualism in the mother tongue and the dominant language of the nation receiving the immigrants. Not all first-generation immigrants become bilingual, but it is almost always a feature of the second generation, with a likely reversion to monolingualism (but in the dominant language, not their parents' mother tongue) by the third generation. Language shift such as this is discussed in chapter 4.

3.5.1.1 Migration for jobs

Labor migration has a number of common characteristics (Grillo, 1989). First, at any point in history, migrants looking for jobs often have a common destination in mind: Quite naturally, it is the nation or the core of nations that is at the current center of economic development. Second, the source of such immigrants changes with political and economic developments, too; countries with current economic problems or political upheaval are the current major donor nations (those supplying immigrants). Third, such immigrants typically are not distributed equally across the recipient nations. They **tend to cluster around urban areas and industrial centers**. Even within an urban area, proportions vary from one neighborhood to the next. For example, Grillo points out that although in the 1980s, 12% of the population of Lyon, France were classified as foreigners in the French census, the proportion varied from 6% in the middle-class western suburbs to 18% in working-class suburbs to the east. Fourth, within an industry employing many immigrants, their number will vary considerably depending on the department. There may be very few immigrants in white-collar and technical positions, but many on the factory floor. Fifth, labor immigrants are typically men, often young men. At a later stage, families come, depending on the policy of the recipient nation.

3.5.1.2 Immigration and the face of a nation

Of all places, immigration has most dramatically shaped the social profile of Australia and North America. Elsewhere (e.g. Europe), there are many immigrants, too, but there also is a large, relatively homogenous, group of long-term peoples. In both Australia and North America, the point to stress is that the vast majority of their citizens are the descendants of immigrants (who may be called "founding peoples" but they are still immigrants). The second half of the nineteenth century and the first decades of the twentieth century were times of mass migration of various European nationalities to these places, especially to the United States. In the twentieth century, there were many such migrations going on in other parts of the world, too. For example, both Malaysia and Singapore were destinations for many Chinese from southern China (e.g. Cantonese speakers) as well as Indians (e.g. Tamils) from the southern states in India.

3.5.1.3 Migration today

Since the Byzantine Empire, there has been a tradition of inviting various ethnic groups for economic purposes (Paulston, 1998), but the scale has changed. In Europe there are many immigrants, who were initially called "guest workers". They are generally unskilled, as are the many immigrants in the United States from Mexico and Central America. But there and elsewhere, many immigrants with specialized skills are especially welcomed. For example, in the 1990s and into the twenty-first century, the computer and biotech industries in the United States have recruited many trained engineers and scientists from other countries. To give one example, in mid-2002, the largest group of recent immigrants in the San Francisco area was from South Asia, mainly India, most headed for the computer-oriented industries. Today some of those Indians are returning home to join the growing computer-based industries in India.

Other migrants have moved from one country to the next because they are simply looking for a better life. Some of them are political refugees, such as the Cubans who were business people in Cuba, but who migrated to Miami, Florida where they now are very important in the local economy. But most people become migrants in the hopes of finding better jobs than they had at home. The middle of the twentieth century, continuing through today, saw new waves of migration to nations that had been largely peopled by immigrants (Australia and North America), but the new waves brought new faces.

3.5.1.3.1 New immigrants to the immigrant nations

After World War II, many continental Europeans joined the earlier Anglo-Celtic immigrants from the British Isles in Australia. In Australia, as late as 1947, 99% of the population was white and 90% were of British origin. That situation changed drastically in the years after World War II (Romaine, 1991), with Europeans from **new sources and many Asian immigrants**. Australian language policy is discussed at length in chapter 12.

By the end of the twentieth century, **Latino migrants** to the United States were the most visible immigrant group, although they are not a homogeneous group by any means. There are many Puerto Ricans, especially in New York City and northern New Jersey, while there are many Mexicans in the South-west and California, but also in Chicago and the southeastern states of Virginia, and North and South Carolina. As noted, in Florida, Hispanics come from Cuba, but also from many places in Central and South America. At the same time, the flow of Asian immigrants has increased, especially on the West Coast.

Findings from the 2000 census confirm that the US has a fast-growing population that speaks English at home less frequently, with California leading the way. The 2000 census showed that 13.3 million immigrants arrived in the US in the previous decade, well above the 8.7 million who arrived in the 1980s. The result is a tremendous change in the face of the US. For example, John Singler reports that the New York City press has commented on the **increase in the African presence** (up 127% from the 1990 census), with Nigeria, Senegal, and Liberia as the primary source countries. Such a dramatic influx has a variety of effects; one of them is an advertising billboard in downtown Brooklyn (Singler, personal communication). The ad was for Western Union, and it enjoined people to call Africa, featuring a smiling woman and a caption in Nigerian Pidgin English: "The call na 10 minutes and e go sweet your family dem well well".

3.5.1.3.2 Changes in Europe

What was especially noticeable by the end of the twentieth century was a change in the outward appearance of Europe, thanks to population movements. Europeans had been used to thinking of their nations as fairly homogeneous, at least in terms of the native language of most of the citizens. But that has changed for every single Western European nation. All of them have had an influx of **political and economic refugees from Eastern Europe**. In addition, the continental European nations have taken in many immigrants as persons whom they thought of initially as temporary "guest workers". For example, most noticeable in France are immigrants from areas in the former sphere of French colonial influence (North Africa and West and Central Africa); they fill unskilled positions in France. (Those who came before Algeria became independent in 1962 were French citizens, not technically immigrants.) All over Europe, from Switzerland to Norway, there are many Turkish immigrants. A walk down not just a London street, but also a city street almost anywhere in Britain, gives you an idea of this transformation. You will see the many **immigrants from areas with ties to the former British Empire** (Pakistan, the Caribbean, and Africa) seeking economic opportunities. Also, many Chinese, especially from Hong Kong and Southern China, have settled in Britain.

Other nations, ones that outsiders might think of as having more stable populations, also show a very cosmopolitan character today because of immigration. Canada has become the melting-pot that the United States was at the start of the twentieth century, with many immigrants from various parts of Europe, but especially Eastern Europe. In addition, it especially has welcomed many immigrants from the Caribbean and East Asia. For example, the far western Canadian city of Vancouver is **a veritable "new Hong Kong"**. Brazil also is showing the results of an immigrant flow from diverse sources. Today the **city of São Paulo** has more people of Japanese descent than any city outside of Japan, more people of Syrian-Lebanese descent than any city outside the Middle East, and more people of Italian descent than any city outside of Italy.

3.5.1.4 Forced migration

Forced population movements have also been important in group bilingualism as an outcome. We have in mind especially the **involuntary migration of Africans** during the slave trade era to the Caribbean and the southern states of the US until the early nineteenth century. In addition, there also was an ongoing slave trade in the Middle East. Other forced movements include the USSR's policy of sending dissidents to Siberia. Also, one could argue that the tradition of indentured laborers in various parts of the world, such as in the South Pacific and to the Queensland area of Australia in the nineteenth century, is a case of involuntary migration. In some cases, the workers remained. The linguistic result of the slave trade and the importation of large numbers of indentured workers was the development of pidgin and creole languages; that is, a special kind of bilingualism resulted, with speakers bilingual in their own L1 and the newly created language.

The structural features of pidgins and creoles, as well as their social motivations, are discussed in chapter 10.

3.5.2 Wars and subsequent colonialism

Examples of colonialism, sometimes preceded by war, and some imposition of the language of the conquerors on the local population, are easy to find. This is how what we today know as the Romance languages came into being. **The Roman legions** conquered parts of Europe, spreading Latin as the language of governance. At least in continental Western Europe where today Romance languages are spoken, the local populations were L1 speakers of Celtic languages as well as many other languages; many must have gone through a stage of bilingualism in their L1s and Latin before eventually shifting to the varieties of Latin that developed into the modern-day Romance languages. The original L1s were generally lost. Because local conditions varied (e.g. different varieties of local languages and variation in contact with Latin), people living in these parts of Europe today do not speak the same modern version of Latin. Even though they speak closely related varieties, their languages are different enough so that they are not truly mutually intelligible. In Western Europe, the main Romance languages spoken today are French, Spanish, Portuguese, and Italian, with Romanian in Eastern Europe.

In more recent times, **colonialism** in Africa, South America, and Asia resulted in bilingualism that still exists today. Although not all members of the indigenous populations learned the language of the colonials, many did add it to their linguistic repertoire and continue to do so today. The main reason is that generally, the colonial language is associated with upward socio-economic mobility, not to mention modernity.

3.5.2.1 Colonialism in India

If we count numbers of speakers, probably India is the nation where colonialism resulted in the most bilingualism that includes an international language. India was **"the jewel in the crown"** of the British Empire; it became a British colony in 1858 and achieved independence in 1947. But the history of the English language in India goes back further than the nineteenth century; from 1763 at least, the British East India Company and its agents were a dominant force in India. (Of course, bilingualism in two or more indigenous Indian languages probably existed in some areas before the British arrived.) During this long period when English-speaking civil servants and military personnel ruled in India, the English language was also being spread there, at least among the educated elite. After independence, English remained as what was to be a temporary official language, but has become a de facto official language. Indian language policy is discussed in chapter 12.

Hindi is certainly the **most widespread language spoken in India** and many people speak Hindi as a second language; it is the main language in six states, including all of north India (Dua, 1992). But for political reasons, notably resistance from speakers of the Dravidian languages that are concentrated in South India, English remains a neutral choice for the entire nation. This status naturally leads to **increased bilingualism in English**. (The Dravidian languages are in an entirely different language family from the Indo-European family, which includes Hindi. This means that basic resemblances between

Dravidian languages and Hindi are few; some do exist as the result of borrowings due to long contact between the two language families.)

3.5.2.2 Colonialism in Southeast Asia

In Southeast Asia, colonialism also promoted bilingualism, although the colonial languages have largely been replaced as official languages. In Indonesia, a former Dutch colony, Bahasa Indonesia (Indonesian) is the official language; its status is discussed in section 3.5.4. In former French territories, French is still spoken by some educated persons in Cambodia and Vietnam. Language policy in Cambodia is discussed further in chapter 12. East Timor surprised many by naming Dutch as its official language when it became independent in mid-2002; true, East Timor had been a Dutch colony before it was embroiled in a long conflict over statehood with Indonesia, another former Dutch colony. But making Dutch official was a surprise because relatively few people speak Dutch there.

3.5.2.3 Colonialism in Africa

Africa was divided up by the European powers in the late nineteenth century, with the result today that the European language of the colonial power still plays a prominent role in most sub-Saharan African nations even though most of these nations achieved independence in the 1960s. In most nations, this European language is either the sole official language or a co-official language alongside one or more indigenous languages. The only sub-Saharan nations with indigenous languages as their sole official languages are Tanzania, with Swahili; Somalia, with Somali; and Ethiopia, with Amharic.

A major reason the colonial language has survived in this role is that in any competition between indigenous languages, the colonial language is relatively neutral; that is, its use does not favor any one ethnic group over another. Partly because of its official status, but also because of its status elsewhere in the world, English is the language of education and status-raising positions in anglophone countries such as Nigeria and Kenya; French occupies this position in francophone countries such as Senegal and Ivory Coast; and Portuguese is this language in Angola and Mozambique and other former Portuguese possessions. Language policies are discussed further in chapter 11. No matter what their official status, indigenous languages are very robust in these nations as symbols of ethnic groups. The result is that speakers maintain their home language, but some also learn the official language as well as other local languages.

3.5.2.4 Colonialism in Central and South America

Spain, but also Portugal, were the main colonizers in Central and South America. Today, Portuguese is the main language of Brazil, spoken by both Portuguese settlers, Africans who came as slaves, and some of the indigenous peoples. The Spanish invaded these areas in the fifteenth century and Spanish dominates everywhere but Brazil, with some bilingualism where native American languages are maintained. For example, Quichua (also written Quechua), a native Indian language, is still widely spoken in Ecuador, Peru, and Bolivia, and there are many other smaller groups speaking Indian languages, too. In both Ecuador and Peru, about a quarter of the population speaks Quichua (either as monolinguals or bilinguals); the percentage is a little less in Bolivia. Quichua's legal status is highest in Peru, because it is a co-official language alongside Spanish in certain situations. But Ecuador has the most unified popular indigenous movement; the current constitution guarantees primary education in the language of the ethnic community (von Gleich, 1992).

In central Mexico, Nahuatl is spoken alongside Spanish. Nearly all speakers are bilingual. Nahuatl, which is called Mexicano by the people who speak it, was the language of the ancient Toltecs and was spoken as well by many other peoples of Mexico and Central America (Hill and Hill, 1986). In Paraguay, an indigenous language, Guarani, is widely maintained and has a special status as a national symbol, but many speakers of Guarani also speak Spanish. However, the widely held belief that nearly all of Paraguay is bilingual is not supported (Gynan, 1998). But Spanish certainly is the main language in urban areas all over the former Spanish colonies.

3.5.2.5 *Canada*

Another bilingual situation partially resulting from war and colonialism not often so considered is that of Canada. Eastern Canada was **initially colonized by the French**, but it was conquered by the British in 1759. The population in Québec remained largely francophone (i.e. French-speaking). Meanwhile, Canada's anglophone population grew with immigration largely from the British Isles as Canada spread westward. Today, some Québec pressure groups want "territorial unilingualism" at least for Québec, while still preserving minority rights. For them, bilingualism represents a threat to the future of French in Canada. How ideological differences affect Canadian discourse about language is discussed in chapter 5 and separatism in Québec is discussed in chapter 12.

3.5.3 Change of borders

As part of the settlements in various conflicts, national borders have changed, sometimes putting a group of people under a different official language than they previously had known. We discuss only several cases in Europe. For example, the **Hungarian-speaking people** of the village of Oberwart and the surrounding farm areas found themselves in Austria after World War I (Gal, 1979). Oberwart is located near the border of Hungary and Austria. For several hundred years, these Hungarian speakers have been surrounded by German speakers, and when Oberwart became part of Austria, German became the official language. Today, Hungarian speakers are a minority and all of them are bilingual in German.

At another border, this time between Germany and France, the term "Alsatian" covers the various Germanic varieties spoken alongside French in present-day Alsace, a part of France. That is, the political boundary between France and Germany, which follows the Rhine River, is not a linguistic boundary as such. The varieties spoken in Baden on the German side are very similar to those spoken at the same latitude in Alsace in France. Ever since at least the mid-fifteenth century, **Alsace has been passed back and forth between Germany and France**, following various wars. Following World War I (1918) Alsace was ceded to France. But it was annexed by Germany during World War II and only returned to France in 1945. Today active bilingualism between Alsatian and French, especially in the younger generation, is on the wane. In the last forty years, Alsace has gone "from being a predominately dialect-speaking [Alsatian] area in which French was used in certain clear-cut domains (administration, school-teaching) to being now a French-speaking area in which some sections of the population use the dialect [Alsatian] in some areas of their life", Gardner-Choloros (1991: 26) notes.

3.5.4 Bilingualism for national integration

Probably the best example under this heading of increased bilingualism involves the spread of what is called a dialect, not a language. In China, the standard dialect, called Putonghua, is spoken more and more widely as a second dialect. However, as we've pointed out in chapter 2, many of the so-called dialects in China are different enough to be called separate languages. The promotion of Putonghua, of course, leads to a greater and greater sense of national unity.

In other parts of Asia, **nation-building through bilingualism** also is occurring. The most notable case is Indonesia, a nation that was part of the Dutch East Indies colonial empire. Even though Indonesia has had some setbacks in its progress toward political and economic development, it has been very successful in building a sense of national integration through the Indonesian language. Indonesia is a nation of hundreds of indigenous languages, and the precursor to the language Indonesian was just one of several dialects of Malay and the native language of only a few million out of the more than 200 million people in Indonesia. Through language "engineering" (that would fall under corpus planning, as discussed in chapter 12), a non-ethnically based language, but linguistically based on Malay and now called Indonesian, has been developed. A large part of the success in getting people to learn and speak Indonesian is its "un-nativeness". That is, Indonesians see it as an "outgroup language without an outgroup" (Errington, 1998b: 3). This means that speaking Indonesian does not mean the speaker is favoring any particular "other" group – except the nation as a whole.

As **a Malay-based language**, Indonesian is related to other varieties of Malay in the region that have significant political bases. First, a variety called Bahasa Malay became the official language of nearby Malaysia following independence in 1957. Although English was, and remains, an important language in Malaysia, the decision to make Malay the official language was an act to promote national integration. Malay was already the language of some everyday interactions for many; further, some variety of Malay is the native language of the largest group of speakers (almost 47%) according to Jacobson (1992), followed by Chinese (34%), and various Indian languages (9%). Obviously, making Malay the official language has increased the necessity for many to learn Malay as a second language, notably those seeking government jobs.

Second, Malay is the language of one of the three main ethnic groups in Singapore, where it is referred to as Bazaar Malay. With this name, not surprisingly, it is widely used in everyday interactions, especially in the marketplace. Bilingualism is crucial to the national image Singapore politicians want to foster of a multiracial nation. "Virtually every student in the Singapore school system takes a specific language combination: English and Mandarin [Chinese], English and Malay, or English and Tamil", according to PuruShotam (1998: 75). The language situation in Singapore is discussed extensively in chapter 4.

3.5.5 How socio-economic mobility promotes bilingualism

In many parts of the world, speakers are adding a language to their repertoire because of the instrumental rewards and psychological values that are associated with that language. Everywhere, learning the language that enables speakers either to get a job or retain the one they have, or to get a better job, is a major motivation to become bilingual. In fact, as we've already pointed out, few people learn an L2 just because it's "fun". We refer to the motivation for learning a language for economic advancement as the main example of **instrumental motivation**. But we should keep in mind that people also show instrumental motivations when immigrants learn a language to meet citizenship requirements or for other reasons.

3.5.5.1 English as a world language and bilingualism

The best example we have today of learning an L2 for instrumental motivations is the learning of English for job-related activities all over the world. The most obvious reason is to do business with the many American and British multinational corporations. But another reason is that English is becoming the lingua franca of business in many places where native speakers of English are not necessarily involved. This is especially true in today's Europe. (Remember our **definition of a lingua franca**; it is a language that is used between two people who do not share the same L1. This means that a lingua franca may be the L1 of one of the speakers or it may be an L2 for both of them. For example, an article in *The New York Times* (May 19, 2002) outlines how an attorney found, much to his surprise, that he needed to know English when he joined a Paris law firm. He said, "I want to be a business lawyer, and I realized you just cannot avoid speaking English." Many European banks cross national borders in their operations and have made English the official corporate language.

Further, many European companies have made English their corporate language. This doesn't mean that everyone employed there speaks English; the average workers still speak the local language to each other. But the boardroom language is English. At an Italian appliance maker which has recently acquired both a Russian and a British appliance maker, English is the language of management, partly because many of the executives are now not Italian.

A second major instrumental reason that English is being learned around the globe is that the English-speaking US is the source of many recent technological advancements. This is especially evident in the computer industry. True, many manuals for new devices from computers to air conditioners are multilingual, but the controls often are just in English. The role of English as a world lingua franca is discussed further in chapter 12.

3.5.5.2 Is English too much of a good thing?

In some places, a local sense of "verbal nationalism" has resulted in a backlash against English's spread which goes far beyond business dealings. Predictably, this has been the reaction of some in France where English has burrowed its way into music and sports with such catchy phrases as *le hit parade*. French attempts to make up equivalents to English words used in the new technologies sometimes succeed, but also fail. For example, the French equivalent for *internet* as *inforoute* never caught on. Often, English phrases are less elaborate; for example, compare English *prime time* with French *heures de grande écoute*.

Across the ocean in Brazil, there also are critics of too much English in daily life. A *New York Times* article (May 15, 2001) details criticism of English words and phrases used in business and especially when they appear in advertisements. Portuguese, of course, is the official language in this nation of 170 million people. Brazil has the largest computer and internet industry in Latin America, complete with English verbs integrated into Portuguese in such forms as *attacher* or *deletear*, as well as nouns such as *mouse* and *site*.

Behind such cries of "too much English" is the recognition of another motivation for learning a language: A language carries with it associations with the culture where it is a native language. A point that we'll make over and over in this book is that the language one speaks is a paramount expression of identity. So it is no surprise that critics of the spread of English fear that their own language, and accordingly their own culture, will be abandoned if more and more of a nation's citizens prefer English, even if only as their public language.

This concern is certainly behind the pressure in Québec to give preference to French in public signs and advertisements. The spread of English figures again in chapter 12 when globalization is discussed.

3.5.5.3 *Speaking English isn't anyone's total identity*

At the same time, as many others have pointed out, every person perceives him- or herself as having more than one identity and is not always seen by others in the same identity. When a speaker of the Lwidakho variety of Luyia is at home in western Kenya, he identifies himself to a foreign visitor as a Mudakho, even if he speaks in English. If the conversation takes place in Nairobi, he identifies himself as a Luyia. If he goes to the United States, he becomes a Kenyan or an African.

Our point here is that **different identities also are conveyed by speaking different languages**. This idea is developed further in chapter 6 where linguistic choices are viewed as both indices of identities and tools to negotiate interpersonal interactions.

Here's an example of how bilinguals "change identities" depending on what they are speaking. Native speakers of Danish consider themselves (and are considered by others) as "just Danish" in Copenhagen. But in Paris, they may become someone who speaks French with a "Scandinavian accent", and in Chicago they may speak English, and be seen as "European" (with no special nationality recognized). Is conveying different identities by speaking different languages a threat to the mother tongue? We can't deny that sometimes it is. But bilingualism isn't an automatic threat to the home language and ethnic values. Obviously, it can be a unifying force across ethnicities. Also, it can give individuals a heightened awareness of what there is about their own language that they value.

3.5.6 How the psychological attractiveness of the "other" promotes bilingualism

We turn now to another reason why people learn an L2; this reason is psychological rather than instrumental. That is, when people become aware of other cultures, they may experience a **psychological displacement** in the sense that their L1 is no longer sufficient as the sole medium to express how they see themselves. For example, they may think of themselves as no longer just citizens of one nation, but as "world citizens". Or, they may wish to "join", if only symbolically through language, another culture. For these reasons, some people learn a second language because of its exotic associations. For an American student we know, this is the reason he has learned some Hindi and even how to write in the Devanagari script in which Hindi is usually written. Others learn a second language because of its cultural associations. Some learners of French are not professional chefs, but value that language for its standing in the culinary world; some learners of German feel there is something to be gained by reading the German philosophers in the original.

But at least today, the main psychological attraction of another language is its **associations with a modernity** that is not entirely definable. This is the cultural pull that today's youth feel from English. With them, English has prospered for exactly the same reasons that the English-based culture has prospered: They both symbolize openness to change and even a preference for innovations. It's partly for this reason that one sees so many advertisements in the world in English, whether the majority of the local population can understand English or not. Posters in Berlin advertise Volkswagen's "New Beetle" (not "Der neue Käfer").

Still, it's not just English that has this pull. Kulick (1992) details how a village in Papua New Guinea is becoming bilingual in Tok Pisin, the official language of the nation. Tok Pisin was introduced in the village by missionaries in the early 1950s, at a time when every young single male in Gapun spent at least a year working as a contracted laborer outside the village. When they returned, they brought back Tok Pisin. **The attraction of Tok Pisin** is that villagers view it as expressing an aspect of self that is not conveyed in speaking their own language, Taiap. Tok Pisin became associated with the dimension of self that is sociable and cooperative, a trait associated with people who are capable of participating in the modernization process. "In using Tok Pisin, villagers are thus expressing an important and highly valued aspect of self; they are displaying their knowledge and social awareness" (p. 21).

Conversely, one could argue that pervasive bilingualism is sometimes resisted for the very reasons that others value it. That is, a nation, or specific ethnic groups, may see that their national or ethnic identity is at stake when their citizens or members embrace a second language very enthusiastically. That is, the second language is a symbol of a way of life that is different from the recipient culture, a way of life not welcomed by everyone. This is largely what is at issue when groups resist the spread of English. On a more local scale, it is an issue wherever there is a minority group with its own L1 in a nation where another language has official status and is more the vehicle of political power and socio-economic prestige. It is also an issue when a population finds the second language so attractive that they gradually make that language their dominant language. This is an issue in Canada for the French-speaking population, which is losing numbers to the anglophone majority. In such situations, bilingualism is seen as **subtractive bilingualism**, meaning that to become bilingual leads to the eventual loss of one's first language. These are topics for chapter 4 and also chapter 12 when we discuss language policy.

3.5.7 The quest for education and bilingualism

Finally, speakers may well add a language through education. Which languages they add and how well they learn them depends on relevant arrangements at the local level. Whatever language is the official medium of instruction in the schools almost necessarily will be a language in which students attain some ability. Sometimes this is not the language of the home or the home dialect is very different from the standard dialect used in the schools. For example, Swiss German, a group of home dialects, differs considerably from the High German (Hochdeutsch) or Schriftdeutsch (written German) that are used in the schools. Also, in multilingual Switzerland, whatever language is the official language of the local canton (i.e. state) is the medium of instruction in schools; this is generally German or French, but it could be Italian or even Romansch. Children also are free to study other languages.

In most parts of the world, students are required to study a foreign language and sometimes certain ones. Above, we saw that in Singapore all students study two of the three main languages spoken there (English, Mandarin (Chinese), and Malay). In other places, children may choose the foreign language they study. English is the most widely studied foreign language in German schools, where most children start learning it from age 11. *The Times of India* (June 7, 2002) reported that a proposal to teach Punjabi or Swahili as a compulsory language, rather than French or German, in some British schools was made at the annual meeting of the National Association of Head Teachers in England, although no action was taken. Obviously, the proposal was an attempt to make language learning more relevant to the many Asian and African immigrant children in British schools. At present, the national curriculum calls for students to study at least one modern European language.

3.6 Summing up

This chapter has considered **two aspects of bilingualism**, what it means to be called a bilingual and factors that promote bilingualism.

- A characterization of a bilingual: **A bilingual is a person who can carry on at least casual conversations on everyday topics in a second language.**
- **Few bilinguals are equally proficient in both languages** that they speak.
- The reasons are that the conditions under which they acquire or learn the languages often differ, and where and the extent to which they currently use both languages often differ.
- Two major headings under factors promoting bilingualism: proximity and displacement (physical or psychological).
- **Proximity**: where people live, what kind of work they do, and whether there are speakers of second languages in their family circle.
- **Physical displacement** includes migration as a prime reason for a person to become bilingual. Wars and subsequent colonialism and changes in government also are major factors promoting bilingualism because of displacement.

- **Psychological displacement** is difficult to define precisely, but it includes those circumstances that encourage speakers to view their lives in a new way:
  - contacts with other ethnic groups or individuals who have different values and goals, or just awareness of how they live their lives differently.
  - changes associated with how the world works, especially **globalization of the economy**.

3.7 Words and phrases to remember

critical age hypothesis
balanced bilinguals
grammatical competence
communicative competence
factors promoting bilingualism
types of displacement
minority group
socio-economic mobility

4

Language Maintenance
and Shift

Multiple voices: The word from Algerians in France

Fadela Belarouci is a 12-year-old schoolgirl who lives in a suburb of
Paris, France along with many families that have moved to France from
Algeria. Fadela is the youngest of a family of six children. Before 1962
(the year Algeria became independent from France), Moslems in Algeria
were considered French citizens of a special class. Algerians living in
France who were born before 1962 became eligible to become French
citizens after a long process. Fadela's parents became French citizens.
Yet, Fadela's mother speaks very little French; she doesn't work outside
the home and only finds a need to use French in some shops. She speaks
Algerian Arabic with her women neighbors, even if they come from
Morocco or Tunisia and speak somewhat different varieties of Arabic
(they try to adjust their speech to each other). But Fadela's story and that
of her brothers and sisters is very different. They speak Algerian Arabic
to varying degrees, and are more fluent in French. In fact, the older
brothers have forgotten much of the Arabic they acquired as small
children. Even though the parents speak Algerian Arabic together, the
children often respond in French. Because she has lived in France since
birth and because all her schooling has been in French-medium schools,
Fadela speaks mainly French. Furthermore, she considers herself to be
French even though she is a Moslem. She watches the same French reality TV programs and likes the same French teenage singers as other
French girls of her age.

4.1 Introduction

This chapter considers the possible outcomes of becoming bilingual. We pay special attention to what happens to the first language of speakers when they become bilingual. That is, will this language be maintained? Or, will speakers shift to the new L2 as their main (or only) language? Thus, we introduce these two terms, **language maintenance** and **language shift** to refer to possible outcomes when speakers become bilingual. Actually, there are three main possible outcomes when speakers are exposed to a second language:

1   speakers simply retain their own L1 and do not learn the L2;
2   speakers learn the L2 as an additional language and retain both their L1 and the L2;
3   speakers learn the L2 as an additional language, but it replaces their L1 as the main (and generally only) language. In some cases, this third option happens within the lifetime of one person.

But in most cases, it takes an entirely different generation for the shift to the L2 to go to any sort of completion. In fact, shift to an L2 generally doesn't happen until the third generation, with the second generation bilingual in both languages.

There are other possible outcomes that happen less frequently; for example, speakers can learn a different L2 and that can replace the first L2 they learned. What happens even less frequently is that speakers can relearn at least some of their L1 in later life when they decide to "reclaim" it for its psychological value. Here we are most concerned with outcomes 2 and 3: bilinguals maintain their L1 alongside their L2, or bilinguals shift to their L2 as their main language. Although we may deal more with cases of shift, there are many, many examples of long-lasting bilingualism, too (outcome 2 above). We'll discuss a few of them in this chapter as well as cases of shift.

> First generation: Speak only their L1
> Second generation: Speak both their L1 and an L2
> Third generation: Speak only the L2

Some factors of human social organization favor monolingualism and some favor bilingualism; these factors are not necessarily the opposite of each other. For example, an individual can live in a city and still speak only his or her L1 while many others live in the same city and find it necessary to speak two languages in their everyday lives. The difference depends on not just one factor, but a set of factors and – this is especially important – **how factors are prioritized**.

But, as we've demonstrated in chapter 3, in today's world it's almost impossible to avoid the combinations of factors that favor bilingualism. True, **in some situations, bilingualism isn't favored at all**. People living in small, isolated, and homogeneous communities are often monolingual. So are those who are separated by natural barriers, such as mountains, from neighbors who speak a different language. So are many who have an occupation, such as farming, that requires little interaction with others. The same applies to people who hold low-level jobs within their own ethnic group and have little opportunity to get better jobs elsewhere. Such features are more or less the same as those promoting maintenance of an L1 in the face of a powerful L2 in the larger community. But, as we'll see, given the conditions of the modern world, becoming bilingual and then even shifting to that L2 is hard to resist.

4.1.1 Maintenance or shift? Many studies, few firm answers

There have been many published studies and analyses of the conditions that promote maintenance and its counterpart, shift. We will draw on a number of these sources in this chapter. Most consider the same sets of features, including ethnic and L1 loyalty, the rural–urban division, differences across generations and social classes, gender differences, and the degree of institutional support (e.g. the L1 in schools as either a medium of instruction or as a subject). But what we'll find is that **there is no "magic set"** that predicts what will happen in a given community. The reason seems to be that while the same features count everywhere, *how much* each one counts can vary from community to community.

In many places, many people become bilingual in a language with more official support and/or more international prestige, but still maintain their L1, usually as their main language. When speakers live in their home country, they are more likely to maintain their L1, even if they learn another language, than if they are immigrants in another country.

For example, it's unlikely those educated Shona ethnic group members in Zimbabwe who are fluent in English will make it their main language, even though English is one of the official languages of Zimbabwe (alongside Shona and Ndebele). True, they'll speak English frequently, but they'll still maintain Shona. And although some educated Brazilians speak Spanish or English, if they do business with either Spanish-speaking South America or English-speaking North America, their shift to either English or Spanish as their main language is unlikely. That is, Portuguese is firmly in place as the sole official language of Brazil and for all aspects of everyday life.

But there are other places where shift can happen for an indigenous group, even if it speaks an L1 with international status. A look at the **English-speaking community in Argentina** shows this is possible. (Spanish, of course, is the official language of Argentina.) The British have been in Buenos Aires since the nineteenth century as a major force in the economic sector. But a generational shift seems to be in progress in this Anglo community. At least, a self-report survey showed that almost 66% of those Anglos between the ages of ten and eighteen (N=99) responded "Spanish" to the question of which language they speak most of the time. Compare this to only 3% of those aged 66 and above from the same Anglo community who mentioned Spanish as their main language; that is, this older group uses mainly English. In the younger group, 59% said they speak Spanish better than English, although 49% said they speak both languages well (Cortés-Conde, 1996). These respondents were students in bilingual schools that were founded by the British for the community.

Although English retains its instrumental value for the workplace at the managerial level for doing international business, it is losing ground as the home language. But how can even a partial shift be happening here? After all, English is a language of international prestige and the Anglo-Argentinians studied come from an educated middle and upper class. Further, Argentinians of other backgrounds pay lots to give their children a bilingual education (in English as well as Spanish). So why is a shift to Spanish underway in the current Anglo generation?

Cortés-Conde points out that although the schools and parents are all for promoting bilingualism in English, school-age peers discourage its use. The children say that speaking English in a basically Spanish community is snobbish. "Some of them said that if one spoke English when school authorities were not present he or she was ridiculed," she reports (p. 121). Will they change their attitudes when they become adults? It is hard to say.

4.1.2 We can predict, but we can't promise

What this Argentinian example especially shows is that we can discuss general factors that figure in L1 maintenance and shift to an L2, and we can give persuasive case studies detailing what happened and what factors seemed to count, but we can't predict the future with absolute certainty. Still, as we'll see, some generalizations typically hold and do encourage predictions.

4.2 Three useful models of community organization

We'll see that these generalizations are encapsulated in three models of community organization. These models are theoretical "umbrellas" in the sense that they stand above specific factors, offering generally applicable "covers" that are useful in explaining whether group members are susceptible to shift away from an L1 or not.

- The first model divides communities according to the type of pattern that multilingualism takes in the larger society. Under this model, communities show either **horizontal multilingualism** or **vertical multilingualism**.
- The second model is used in the social sciences in general and has been applied within language studies to explain how dialects or other language-use patterns vary across individuals in the same area. It is called **social network analysis**; this is the study of types of connections that individuals have in a community.
- The third model cites the patterns of language use of a group and their beliefs as important in explaining whether group members maintain their L1 or switch to an L2 as their main language. This model is called **ethnolinguistic vitality**. This model is different from the others in that it aims to integrate group attitudes with sociological variables in explaining language behavior. The model aims to predict how the group will behave on the basis of how it sees itself in relation to other groups.

Keep these three models in mind as we look at the specific cases or predictions about language maintenance or loss and the factors that are present.

4.2.1 Horizontal or vertical multilingualism

The model of **horizontal or vertical multilingualism** proposes that there are two types of multilingualism if speakers are viewed in terms of how they are organized in space. Mansour (1993) employed this model to explain patterns of multilingualism in West Africa, but the division applies elsewhere, too. Speakers who live under **horizontal multilingualism** live in their own geographic spaces and are often monolingual. The idea is that multilingualism may be present at a higher level of society, but separate groups are not particularly integrated into this larger society. Each does its living in its own space. Mansour describes horizontal multilingualism as a patchwork quilt (with many monolingual squares).

Another spatial arrangement, under which people are in direct contact with others because of how they live and their daily activities, is called **vertical multilingualism**. When this type of spacing prevails, people work, live, go to school, and shop in communities with speakers of other languages. Obviously, vertical multilingualism is more associated with urban centers where people with different mother tongues interact frequently.

But, as Mansour points out, "These two types of multilingualism differ in more than their spatial arrangements . . . they differ – most importantly – *in the potentials inherent in each social situation*" (p. 19). With this claim in mind, we extend the notion of geographic spatial organization to cognitive spatial organization. Our idea is that we all have "cognitive space" in our minds. What notions of ourselves and our group in a larger community "take up the space" in our minds can make a difference in our patterns of language use. That is, there is a relation between how and where we live and **our mental outlook on life**. Mansour refers to horizontal multilingualism as "the road to socio-economic stagnation, cultural introspection, and marginalisation of the languages spoken by them [monolingual societies]." In contrast, she states that "vertical multilingualism is usually associated with social change, language shift among the speakers of minority languages and an expansion of one or several dynamic lingua francas" (p. 19). This means that speakers under vertical multilingualism don't perceive their individual spaces (whether they are real physical spaces or cognitive space) in the same sense as speakers living in a society with horizontal multilingualism.

If we look at L1 maintenance and shift to L2 in terms of these two types of multilingualism, we can predict what we will find, on the basis of the type of spatial organization and mindset that different groups have. Groups likely to retain their L1 and even resist bilingualism will be found under horizontal multilingualism. They will live in relatively isolated villages or they may live and work in towns or cities, but in only certain parts of the urban area. They identify with their ethnic groups, not the larger community. In contrast, groups more vulnerable to shifting from their L1 to an L2, or at least becoming very proficient in the L2 that is an urban lingua franca, will be found under vertical multilingualism. They are in-migrants to multi-ethnic cities or organizations where they spend most of their waking hours working with speakers of diverse languages, making the use of a lingua franca a necessity.

For example, even if we are considering only persons at a lower socio-economic level in the same city, consider the probable differences in language use and susceptibility to shift between cousins working together in a garage owned by a relative compared with military personnel who typically come from many different ethnic backgrounds.

4.2.2 Network models of social organization

The second model, **social network analysis**, tries to explain social behavior by examining who is connected to whom in a community along a social relation, such as friendship or a shared workplace (Wasserman and Faust, 1994). True social network analysis measures patterns of **relationships among a *group* of speakers**. Thus, a key contribution of this approach is to consider the connections among those people *to whom a speaker is connected*.

Also, under social network analysis, each relationship is treated differently so that all are not thought of as just one general relationship. And we will see how different relations affect outcomes in L1 maintenance; that is, "speaks L1 at home" is different from "speaks L1 at work".

Under the name "network theory", some sociolinguists look at the extent to which an individual speaker is involved in his or her community, but this approach measures attributes of individual speakers or their attitudes (e.g. Milroy, 1980). Researchers who practice social network analysis also can look at the networks of an individual (connections among the individual's connections), but we're more interested here in the networks that characterize an entire group of speakers.

Networks are measured along a number of dimensions, but the dimensions most important to us are **density** and **strength of ties**. A measure of density tells us what proportion of a network's members are connected through some relationship. For example, John Jones may interact with Alice Smith, but he also interacts with Roger Brown, who is also in contact with Alice. When we say that such and such a community is "tightly knit"or "everyone knows everyone else", we mean that its networks show a lot of **density**.

The **strength of a tie** is based on such things as frequency of interaction, but also the intimacy and intensity of interactions. So you have **strong ties** with a close friend whom you see every day and with whom you unload your personal problems, but weak ties with an acquaintance whom you meet only occasionally. You could have strong ties with someone who is far away, such as a distant mother, but the connection is strong because you see your relationship to her as one of high intimacy. A network of close friends would also be dense because it figures that your close friends know each other, not just you.

Strong ties are what you would expect within a home network in which members interact with each other in different settings because such interactions add up to much frequency. But if all members have strong ties within their home network, any multilingualism within the larger society would be horizontal multilingualism – just because members in each language group would be busy with people in their own group networks.

And you can imagine that an ethnic group where in-group networks show both density and strong in-group ties may well hold on to its L1 with a good deal of tenacity – more than a group whose members are parts of networks including out-group persons. For example, consider the German-speaking enclaves in Upper Silesia in Poland or the ethnically homogeneous villages elsewhere in Poland where Belorussian is the L1. You can imagine that their networks largely consist of in-group members only.

Now let's consider **weak ties** and why they are important. Again, frequency counts: If you and a former classmate don't see each other very often and just exchange impersonal news when you do, your social relation is one of weak ties. You can have strong and weak ties within the same network; for example, you can have both close friends (strong ties) and acquaintances (weak ties) in your "workplace network".

Weak ties are important for our discussion here because they are the way that **innovations** of any kind are transmitted from one group to another. We can see that "learning a new language" counts as an innovation. Such learning can take place because weak ties can connect a speaker with speakers of another language. The notion that weak ties can form a **bridge between two groups** and bring in innovations comes from Granovetter (1973). His contribution is the claim that not all weak ties are bridges, but **all bridges are weak ties**.

We can imagine that group members who have a lot of weak ties must be fairly marginal members of the home network (after all, there are only 24 hours in a day and an individual can't have both lots of strong ties at home and weak ties outside). We can also imagine that the "messengers" who bring in a new language (through a weak tie) aren't instrumental in whether or not the group as a whole adopts the new language. Their outside activities help make them marginal group members.

For innovations to be adopted, individuals who are central in the group have to become involved; for example, they have to decide there is good reason for group members to adopt the new language. **Centrality** is calculated according to the number of ties and the position a person has in the network. For example, consider a regionally based business in Asia or Europe with employees who speak different L1s. Company salesmen with contacts elsewhere may be the ones who have noticed (through these outside weak ties) that in other places it's useful to have a company lingua franca (i.e. a language everyone knows, but not necessarily anyone's L1). But the managers have to be the ones who decide to try to use one language as a lingua franca in some company meetings. They occupy positions of centrality.

Milroy and Milroy (1985) introduced students of language variation and change to Granovetter's ideas, especially those about weak ties. They also brought the notions of density and of plexity into discussions of networks within sociolinguistics. Density was discussed above. When speakers have **multiplex** ties with others, it means they interact in several different ways – maybe they work together, but also go to sports events together, and to the same cafés, pubs, or bars.

4.2.3 Ethnolinguistic vitality

A model of **ethnolinguistic vitality** was proposed initially by Giles, Bourhis and Taylor (1977), but since then others have contributed to its development (e.g., Allard and Landry, 1992). In the original formulation, the basis for considering a group's vitality included sociological variables, such as status of the group, numbers of speakers, and any official institutional support of the group's language. The idea is that the more positive a group is in regard to such features, the more likely its language will survive. Later, others contributed the notion of **subjective ethnolinguistic vitality**. For example, Allard and Landry (1992: 172) say, "a group's subjective assessment of its relative position on the variables affecting EV [ethnolinguistic vitality] may be as important in determining its inter-ethnic behaviours as its more objective position on these [sociological] variables." That is, what the group *thinks* about itself in relation to other groups may be as important as the more objective factors such as official status.

Thus, **this model has two components**. First, **at the sociological level**, the ethnolinguistic vitality of a group determines its members' opportunities for speech events in the group's language. (This level includes numbers of speakers, official provisions for using the language, and socio-economic status of the group and status of its culture.) These factors influence how well group members acquire their L1 or learn other languages. Second, **at the psychological level**, beliefs reflecting subjective ethnolinguistic vitality influence what languages group members use, and where and when. In turn, these patterns of language use contribute to maintenance or loss of an L1 (or other languages) (Allard and Landry, 1992). Landry and Allard edited a special issue of the *International Journal of the Sociology of Language* (1994) on ethnolinguistic vitality.

To give you an idea of what's involved in assessing ethnolinguistic vitality, here are examples of the types of factors considered. First, **objective measures are taken into account**. For example, how many speakers are there of language X? Are speakers of language X indigenous to the nation or are they immigrants? If immigrants, are they recent arrivals or not? What types of jobs do speakers of language X hold? Second, **more subjective measures are made**. For example, members of minority groups are asked such questions as these: On a scale of one to nine, how would you rate your feelings of belonging to your ethnic group versus belonging to the more dominant group in the community? Or, how legitimate do you think the present divisions are in terms of official support for your group's language versus support for the national official language?

Often, results on the two types of measures complement each other. In French-speaking communities in eastern Québec, a study showed a strong relationship between high ratings in terms of objective measures and high ratings in terms of more subjective measures. Based on this study, Allard and Landry drew some conclusions that link ethnolinguistic vitality to social networks. They state, "Ethnolinguistic vitality beliefs are formed in the individual's network of linguistic contacts. But an individual's beliefs can also lead to choices concerning the composition of one's ethnolinguistic networks, and to choices concerning language use in one's linguistic networks. There is a form of reciprocal determinism at work here" (p. 192). Ethnolinguistic vitality in French Canada is relevant when Canada is discussed again in chapter 5 and chapter 12.

However, Hogg and Rigoli (1996), studying ethnolinguistic vitality in another setting, present data indicating that having a network of personal contacts among speakers of one's ethnic group language did not predict ethnolinguistic vitality (i.e. identification with one's ethnic group) as well as factors having to do with how much societal-level support there is for the ethnic group language. These researchers studied second-generation Italians in Australia (N=75) who were born in Australia, but whose parents were born in Italy and came from rural backgrounds there. Hogg and Rigoli found that a better predictor of "Italian identification" was the amount of contact respondents had with Italian through Italian movies, television or radio programs, magazines, books, and newspapers. In general respondents in this study identified themselves more strongly as Italian than as Australian or as from a particular region of Italy. The authors do say that the fact that their respondents were well-educated schoolteachers may have caused them to place importance on Italian via the media as well as on support of Italian in the schools.

4.3 Allocation of varieties

Bilinguals don't necessarily use both (or more) of their languages in the same situation. This is a basic fact we pointed out earlier, but it bears repeating and even a fuller discussion here because of the topic of this chapter. How speakers **allocate** the languages in their repertoire tells us a lot about how stable their bilingualism is; that is, it tells us whether they are likely to maintain their L1 in the face of an L2 that is more dominant in their community.

But no matter what happens, whether **stable bilingualism** or **language shift** is the order of the day, **bilinguals are always very "economical"** about their languages. First, they don't learn or retain languages that they don't use frequently. Second, they don't use both languages equally in the same situation. Note that we can't say they *absolutely* do not use both languages together, although it is true that this generalization does hold for many types of interactions. What we can say is that either only one language is used, or one language predominates. This means we can roughly divide situations into three types according to the language used. (1) Only one language is regularly used. (2) Factors such as who is involved in the conversation, what the topic is, and so forth bias the choice toward one language or the other. (3) Speakers engage in codeswitching, meaning that they are using both languages in the same conversation and even in the same phrase or sentence. But no matter which type prevails, one language generally is still the main choice in a given situation.

4.4 Diglossia and domains

We owe the overt recognition that speakers make such allocations to two major sociolinguists, Charles Ferguson and Joshua Fishman. It may seem obvious to us now, but up until their writings, few linguists or ordinary people paid any systematic attention to where and when bilinguals used the languages they spoke. The implication was that there wasn't anything systematic about bilingual language use. We now know that's not so.

In a now classic article published in 1959, Ferguson introduced the notion of **diglossia** to English-language readers. He used this term to characterize a community with two genetically related varieties of the same language, but with their use rather strictly allocated to different situations. This means that in such communities, it would be unthinkable to use the same variety for all types of interactions.

Writing at about the same time, Fishman (1965; 1972) showed how one can discuss any bilingual community systematically in terms of **domains**; that is, speakers divide up when they use their languages in terms of the "major activity centers" in their lives. Also, Fishman (1967; 1970) introduced the notion that diglossia could be extended to societies with two genetically un-related languages.

Diglossia and domain analysis are introduced here because they bring in the notion of **allocation**. The allocation that speakers make for their two or more languages in different domains is an important clue as to whether an L1 will be maintained or not. Still, note that neither diglossia nor domain analysis is a theoretical model. They both offer descriptions of where, when, by whom, to whom, and for what purpose one language variety rather than another is used. But they differ from the three models discussed in the previous sections as explanations of susceptibility to shift. We referred to those models as theoretical because they offer explanations. Descriptions are necessary because they help us arrive at proposed explanations, but on their own they are not explanations.

4.4.1 Domains

Part of our communicative competence is recognizing (probably unconsciously) that most members of our community do not speak the same way in all of their daily interactions. Fishman uses the term **domain** in order to generalize bey-ond just referring to individual social situations and how language use varies from one situation to the next. Thus, he popularized the term domain to cover **a *like set* of social situations**. But domains are more than simply situations; as Fishman notes, they represent clusters of certain values, too.

Particular language use often identifies a domain. Fishman points out, "The very fact that a baseball conversation 'belongs' to one speech variety and an electrical engineering lecture 'belongs' to another speech variety is a major key to an even more generalized description of sociolinguistic variation" (1972: 43). What our sense that these two speech events require a different way of speak-ing tells us, according to Fishman, is that we view speech events as falling under different domains. The major domains that Fishman identified are **fam-ily**, **friendship**, **religion**, **education**, and **employment**.

In a given domain, the idea is not that every interaction is identical, but rather that the *majority* of interactions in domain X are the same at some level. They are the same in the sense that there is a usual (or unmarked, a term we'll use again in chapter 6) combination of elements in interactions in each domain. Each domain has its own constellation of expected factors, such as location, topic, and participants. So, for example, under the domain of "education", an expected interaction would include a teacher and students as participants, school as the location, and how to write a composition or solve a mathematics problem as the topic.

4.4.1.1 *Evidence of domain-specific codes*

The reason all of this is relevant to our study of bilingualism is, as Fishman goes on to explain, that each domain in a bilingual community is "commonly associated with a particular variety of language" (1972: 44). Fishman and his associates demonstrated this in a study of in-migrants from Puerto Rico (Spanish speakers) in the New York City community (Fishman, Cooper, and Ma, 1971). The authors conducted several experiments and surveys that showed that speaking Spanish was primarily associated with the domain of family and secondarily the domains of friendship and religion. Spanish was associated least with the domains of education and employment. The reverse was true for the domains associated with English. When choices didn't match these domains, the differences had more to do with participant differences than with topic or place (p. 251).

We will see more support for the concept of domains later in this chapter when we look at the language use in the home or at work as evidence of the extent to which an L1 is being maintained. Here, we cite some evidence that language use in bilingual communities does vary according to domain. The domain easiest to characterize is often the home domain where we can predict that the L1 of the speakers typically will dominate. But where multilingualism prevails, we can also predict that other languages may be used, too.

For example, a study of **language choice in multilingual Lusaka**, the capital of Zambia, showed that most people speak their L1 with family members at home, but not exclusively. In about half of the 352 households studied, speakers also use the two main lingua francas of Lusaka, Nyanja and English. The researcher (Siachitema, 1991: 480) described language use in Lusaka in this way: "It is normal for people to hold a conversation in the mother tongue on one topic and change to English or Nyanja on another", with the use of English or not depending largely on level of education.

A survey of language use in Luxembourg, one of the most multilingual countries in Europe, gives us a look at another domain, the workplace (Fehlen, 2002). Luxembourg is a small country, but it is unusual in having three official languages. One is Letzeburgesch, a Germanic variety that is the mother tongue of 85% of the respondents in a large survey (N=2002). The other official languages are French and German.

Of the three, French dominates in the domain of work. According to Fehlen's survey, it also is looked upon as the language of prestige. French is the language that most respondents said they could speak, and the language they said they used most frequently at work. Over 70% of the sample think it's necessary to be able to speak French in Luxembourg and 81% even think it's necessary to write it. Once a language is established for a particular domain, it tends to retain momentum there. So it's no surprise that French is the main language of communication between Luxembourgers and foreigners at work, too. This is the case even though many foreigners say they can speak

Letzeburgesch (69% of the Germans and even 57% of the Italians say this). There are many foreign workers in Luxembourg, some as immigrants, but many as daily commuters who come across the borders from Germany and France.

4.4.1.2 Self-reports and validity

Most studies about language use in different situations, such as the ones just mentioned, are based on self-reports; that is, speakers tell researchers what they speak. But speakers themselves are notoriously bad at paying attention to their own language use. And, for various other reasons, such as wishing to please the researcher or to appear more educated, speakers sometimes give answers that aren't accurate. But we don't want to castigate the researchers who do such surveys because there isn't a real alternative to self-report surveys if the goal is to get comparable answers across large groups of speakers (to the same questions about language use). Still, keep in mind that the results may not be entirely valid.

4.4.1.3 Other factors can override domain as a predictor

Of course, other factors can override the domain itself in influencing choice of a language. The most obvious factor is who the participants are, including what language varieties they are able to speak well. We've already noted that most subjects in a study of Lusaka, Zambia reported speaking their mother tongue at home. But we see a difference if socio-economic status is taken into account. Speakers living in the highest-cost area of Lusaka reported a considerable use of English in spouse to spouse conversations at home when the topic was the work domain (39% (24/62) said they spoke English on this topic). In comparison, speakers in the lowest-cost area reported no English at all when talking about their work (0/105) (Siachitema, 1991).

4.4.1.3.1 Topic

The effect of topic also seems to interact with that of socio-economic status in the Lusaka study. When subjects in the highest-cost area of Lusaka were asked what they spoke with a spouse when talking about the "strange behaviour of neighbours", 45% said they used their mother tongue and only 18% used English. Subjects in the lowest-cost area, who probably had fewer choices in their repertoire, reported they used their mother tongue between 61% and 63% of the time, no matter what the topic.

4.4.1.3.2 Negotiating interactional positions

Who the addressee is also can tip the scales toward one language or the other. Consider results from Elena, a child who is being raised as a English-German bilingual and who was studied between the ages of two and three (Bouchereau Bauer, Hall and Kruth, 2002). Even at this young age, in play activities Elena spoke the language of her adult playmate (English or German) most of the time. Other studies of young bilingual children show that they, too, select their language according to the language of their play partner. Interestingly, Elena did switch to English at times when playing with a German partner. Elena was being raised in the United States and she was already aware that English, not German, was the language of the dominant society there and therefore carried more authority in the local community. Thus, the authors explain this switch, not as an inability to keep speaking German, but as "a conscious, strategic use of language to maintain her authority as leader" (p. 69). This interpretation fits in with our general view that choices have social motivations much of the time. You'll see more on this view in chapter 6.

4.4.1.3.3 Times change, a domain's language changes

Of course, no bilingual situation is entirely stable and when a shift is in progress, it's hard to find entirely uniform language use in any given domain. In their study conducted in the 1970s (mentioned above), Fishman and his associates found that Spanish was clearly the main language spoken in the home domain by their New York City subjects. About twenty years later, Zentella (1997) studied one block (with a number of high rise apartment buildings) in what's known as *El Barrio* in the Bronx (New York City) and found diverse patterns of language use, even in the home. Everyone except for one Anglo male was Puerto Rican, but no single pattern of language use dominated. Zentella found six different patterns of bilingual usage in the 20 homes she studied. In every case, the children spoke both English and Spanish to each other and some-times to their caregivers, but whether the caregivers spoke Spanish to them or not varied (some spoke English or both English and Spanish).

4.4.2 Diglossia

In its original formulation and that used by Ferguson, the term "diglossia" applies only to closely related varieties used in the same society. Two features define this type of diglossia that we will call **classic diglossia**. First, everyone has the same L1 and acquires it in a home environment. But not everyone knows the second variety also in existence there; if they learn it at all, they learn it in school. Second, the two varieties are not used in the same situations. Allocation looks like this: If variety X is used in situation (or domain) A, then variety Y will not be used there. As we've already seen in earlier discussions, such generalizations are too strong in their absolute form. But this "if one, not the other" allocation generally does hold, at least in some domains, even in the small set of communities that Ferguson listed (discussed below).

Ferguson's major contribution was his insight that we can make gener-alizations about such communities and language use in terms of clusters of very different interactions – if they have a common feature. For Ferguson, the common feature was the **degree of formality** that the community attached to a type of interaction. Since Ferguson's study, clusters of interactions in any community are often referred to as either High (H) or low (L). These terms imply levels of formality, but also the related concept of out-group or in-group activity. The idea is that interactions that have society-wide prestige fall under the H rubric and those associated with in-group solidarity fall under the L rubric.

The examples that Ferguson gives in his original study show such an allocation. The H variety is the one that is used for more formal purposes, such as writing respected literary works, religious texts, and prepared public speeches. The L variety is used mainly for everyday conversation, especially within the family. The best example of classic diglossia is the allocation of varieties in the Arabic-speaking world. Classical Arabic is the H variety and the various regional varieties of Arabic are the L varieties. (However, today Modern Standard Arabic is also recognized as a modern version of Classical Arabic for use outside of religious purposes, and therefore it also can be called an H variety. More on this below.)

Here is where the notions of **domain and diglossia intersect**: In a given domain, most interactions are expected to display a specific set of values. Behavior in such interactions, including language choices, reflects these values. And diglossia is about dividing up language choices in terms of values. As already indicated, the idea of diglossia is primarily important, not so much for itself, but for this insight. That is, this notion has prompted later writers about bilingualism to see how **the notion of complementary allocation** (i.e. each variety is allocated to its own domains, but this is based on how it is valued) holds in communities in general.

4.4.2.1 Another view of diglossia

Soon Fishman (1972) extended the notion of diglossia so that it can apply to *any* bilingual community. We will call this extension **extended diglossia**. An obvious difference between classic and extended diglossia has to do with the relationship of the language varieties in question. Under classic diglossia, two varieties of the same language are involved. They can be called dialects because they are at least somewhat mutually intelligible, but they are definitely different from each other. Under extended diglossia, the H and the L varieties are recognized as different languages (they are **not mutually intelligible**).

Extending the notion of diglossia made clearer that the situations in which the H variety (in either version of diglossia) is used are not just ones calling for more formality, but are those where status and prestige are salient. In fact, we will call them **status-raising situations**. This aspect of diglossia is discussed further below. Thus, higher education, public speeches, most business meetings, serious written texts, news broadcasts and the like are carried out in the H variety. The L variety is what is often spoken in situations where status in the out-group world is not salient. Thus, it is used in casual conversations with the family and close friends, as well as for service encounters, such as shopping.

4.4.2.2 Diglossia as a continuum

Many observers have pointed out that diglossia is often a continuum, meaning that you can't draw firm lines around situations and say that variety X is the only one used there. Also, observers have said that strictness of allocation varies a great deal from society to society.

In many societies that show extended diglossia, we would have to speak of triglossia or something like that; that is, there isn't a true bipartite division. Either a third language can figure in the allocation, or else different dialects or styles (formal to informal) of the same language can be part of the equation along with another language. For example, in various parts of East Africa, there is a three-way division between a language clearly identified with one ethnic group (the L variety) and English as a lingua franca in status-raising interactions (the H variety), and then Swahili as a general lingua franca and therefore something in between L and H. Or, in French Canada, there is a division between standard Canadian French and an urban dialect of French called Joual, with English for contacts with anglophone Canada and many international purposes.

Or, codeswitching between the H and L varieties can occur in any domain (cf. Myers-Scotton, 1986). Even though university lectures in the Middle East are in the H variety (Modern Standard Arabic, not Classical Arabic), lecturers may codeswitch to the local dialect (the L variety) to clarify what they just said in the H variety. This same type of codeswitching occurs in many classrooms around the world when the medium of instruction is an international language (the H variety). The instructor switches to the L1 of the students (the L variety) to make sure they understand a point.

How flexible people are about the notion of a continuum depends somewhat on what Schiffman (1993) calls the "**linguistic culture**" of the society in question. He refers to the linguistic culture as "a shorthand for referring to the set of behaviors, beliefs, attitudes, and historical circumstances associated with a particular language" (p. 120). Schiffman's insight is that this "linguistic culture" makes a difference in how people actually value their varieties and divide up their use. When diglossia is viewed in terms of the linguistic culture, it becomes very clear that diglossia's existence and strictness is really a feature of the society in question, not the languages involved. For example, in those Arabic-speaking societies where the use of Classical Arabic is absolutely required for certain religious purposes, such a requirement is part of the linguistic culture, not a feature of Arabic itself. Similarly, it is part of the linguistic culture in the German-speaking cantons in Switzerland to expect all persons born in those cantons to be able to speak Swiss German (the L variety).

4.4.2.3 *Classic diglossia*

Ferguson identifies only four speech communities and their languages that he considered as diglossic: classical and colloquial Arabic, standard German and Swiss German (in Switzerland), French and Haitian Creole (in Haiti), and two varieties of modern Greek (in Greece). Others have pointed out other diglossic communities, notably the communities of Tamil speakers in India and in other places such as Sri Lanka (Schiffman, 1993).

Researchers agree that a classic diglossic situation still exists in two of the four examples Ferguson cited. The concept no longer applies in Greece, where the Demotic variety (the former L variety) is now in general use and a 1976 language reform established it as the language of publication administration, law, and education. In Haiti, Haitian researchers question whether diglossia ever existed there and state that it does not now (Dejean, 1993). We discuss briefly here the cases of Swiss German and Haitian Creole, as well as of Arabic.

4.4.2.3.1 Germanic varieties in Switzerland

In the German-speaking cantons of Switzerland, native German-speaking individuals speak closely related Germanic varieties as their L1 and they are used in a wide number of domains. The cover term for them is Swiss German (Schwyzertüütsch). Still, in school, all these German-speaking Swiss study standard German (Hochdeutsch), which is spoken as an H variety in the rest of the German-speaking world, too. Interestingly, the domains in which Swiss German is used are expanding, and certainly no one would be welcomed if they spoke standard German in everyday conversations. In fact, English might be a safer choice for tourists, even L1 speakers of German from outside of Switzerland.

4.4.2.3.2 French and Creole in Haiti

In Haiti, Haitian Creole is the L1 of almost everyone, but it is used everywhere, not just in L situations, Dejean (1993) reports. But it cannot be considered a variety of French and therefore, even in theory, Haiti doesn't belong under the heading of classic diglossia. True, Haitian Creole has many French lexical elements, but it has a grammatical base largely coming from the West African languages of the slaves who were imported to Haiti, and it is not mutually intelligible with French. French is spoken only by those with extended schooling, but the small minority who are bilingual in Creole and French do not compartmentalize their two languages, but use either one of them in both formal and informal settings. Further, Dejean states that for this bilingual minority, "Not to speak Creole in public is increasingly viewed as an overt expression of disdain and hostility toward the people" (p. 80).

4.4.2.3.3 Varieties of Arabic

In most Middle Eastern and North African countries at least three varieties of Arabic exist, Classical Arabic, and two other varieties called Modern Standard Arabic and Colloquial Arabic. (Arabic is also spoken as a minority group language in the northern parts of West Africa, such as in the city of Maiduguri in northeastern Nigeria (Owens, 2001).) Today, among educated Arabs, what Kaye (2001: 118) calls "a modern version of Classical Arabic" is replacing Classical Arabic in some domains; he is referring to what is generally called Modern Standard Arabic (MSA). Classical Arabic, the language of the Qu'ran, is only known by those with extensive education and/or students of religion. While being able to read Classical Arabic is useful, it is not spoken at all in ordinary conversation and is heard only at very formal occasions and at religious ceremonies. Modern Standard Arabic is studied in high schools, and is regularly used in literature and the media. This doesn't mean MSA is widely spoken, partly because only a limited group goes to school long enough to learn MSA well. Kaye (2001) points out that not even every university graduate could carry on a conversation in MSA without codeswitching with his or her regional dialect.

A main difference between Classical Arabic and MSA is that MSA does not have all the inflectional endings that the classical variety has. Also, MSA often uses a subject-verb-object word order that is in addition to the verb-subject-object order more often found in the classical variety. This may be under the influence of French and English (Ennaji, 2002). Of course the addition of MSA results in triglossia, not just diglossia.

Local dialects of Arabic exist everywhere Arabic is spoken, varying from one nation to another. They are what everyone normally speaks. In contrast with both Classical Arabic and MSA, there is no standardized version of any of these local dialects. Individually and as a group, these local dialects are referred to as **colloquial dialects**. (Linguists generally don't use the term "colloquial" in any scientific sense. However, "colloquial" is in general use, even outside the Arabic-speaking world, as a term for whatever variety is used in informal situations. This is usually a variety that is not written down.) In the Arabic-speaking world, these colloquial dialects are the L variety in the H versus L equation of classic diglossia.

The local colloquial dialect is used for **all in-group conversations** with family and friends, but also for a number of out-group situations that Ferguson noted, such as talking to clerks and workmen. These dialects are also used in the media for soap operas and in captions on political cartoons.

Kaye sees Arabic colloquial dialects moving into new areas. In the Arab world in general, he notes a continuous mixture of MSA and the colloquial dialect. Further, at least Egyptian Colloquial Arabic is even becoming more acceptable in the written form (some advertisements) and in some political speeches. Kaye comments, "Egypt is the most populous Arabic country, and one that has the greatest tendency to use its [colloquial] dialect for cultural identification and nationalistic purposes in situations bordering on the unthinkable or nearly unthinkable in other Arabic states" (pp. 121–2). But he agrees with Ferguson's distinctions by saying that a colloquial dialect would always be used on its own in some situations, even in Egypt, such as speaking to a maid or bargaining in a market.

4.4.3 Extended diglossia

Examples of extended diglossia abound in the bilingual world. It contrasts with classic diglossia because any case where two or more language varieties that are not closely related and are spoken in the same community and are perceived in terms of the H and L division will qualify. For example, in Ecuador, Spanish is the H variety and Quichua, the language of the indigenous Indians, is the L variety. In many countries, one would have to talk about triglossia or polyglossia; that is, a number of languages are spoken and some are more aptly called H or L than others, and some fall in the middle. Singapore, which is discussed later in this chapter, is a case in point.

This does not mean that all nations with bilingual populations are diglossic. In some nations, such as Belgium, different language groups have their own territories, so there is not an H and L functional distribution by languages within each territory, although, as is the case for dialects of the same language everywhere, one dialect may have more prestige than another. (Brussels, the capital, is officially bilingual in French and Dutch (also called Flemish) and does show some diglossic features, with French more of an H variety than Dutch, but this is because of French's international status. Major bodies of the European Union (EU) are located in Brussels.)

But this still leaves a wide variety of bilingual communities to analyze in terms of extended diglossia (cf. Fasold, 1984; Hudson, 1991; 2002; Schiffman, 1993). One also can argue that extended diglossia is the best way to characterize the relationship between the standard dialect (as the H variety) and the non-standard dialects (as the L variety) of a single language.

4.4.3.1 Is extended diglossia still diglossia?

Even though many analysts do use the term diglossia to refer to cases of languages in the same community, but not closely related, it's important to recognize that not all analysts, including Ferguson himself, favor extending the meaning of diglossia in this way. Instead, they want to use the term diglossia only for communities in which two closely related varieties are used, but in different situations. Writing in 1991, Ferguson made it clear that he saw diglossia as pertaining only to "a range of variation associated with different occasions of use" (1991, reprinted in 1996, p. 89). In this later paper, Ferguson is quite willing to include more language situations under the diglossia rubric, such as some language communities in South Asia. But he called these diglossic because two varieties of the same language are used in different situations in these communities.

Other researchers also argue against using the term diglossia for cases of unrelated languages. For one, Hudson (2002: 2) calls such situations "**societal bilingualism**", not diglossia. He states that to qualify as (classic) diglossia, a community has to show "stratification in situational context without much, or indeed any, sensitivity to differences in social class" (p. 3). Our view is that yes, these communities to which Fishman extended the concept of diglossia (that we are calling extended diglossic communities) aren't quite the same as those showing classic diglossia. But they are not different in the consequences for a society in viewing one or more varieties as H and one or more as L. In general, these communities do use the two different varieties for "different occasions of use" (repeated from Ferguson, 1991, as quoted above). Further, we find the substitution of the term "societal bilingualism" in this context more opaque than transparent.

Under extended diglossia, it is true that speakers come from **different social groups**, often different ethnic groups. That is, one social group (and this group may come mainly from one ethnic group because of the advantages that group has had) is more likely to command the H variety in the community than other groups. But what about under classic diglossia? Even though everyone speaks the same L1 under classic diglossia, this doesn't mean they are all from the same social class. Recall that the H variety has to be learned in school and not everyone comes from the social classes whose children receive advanced schooling. Therefore, it seems clear that differences in social background separate speakers and their participation in formal situations *under both types of diglossia*.

Following this train of thought, many other analysts continue to apply the term "diglossia" to any community where one can identify H and L varieties on the basis of **either the types of situations** in which they are used **or the social backgrounds** of the speakers. Keep this in mind whenever you read an article or book that mentions bilingualism and diglossia. We return to this topic below.

4.4.3.2 *Diglossia and predicting language shift*

Schiffman (1993), among others, states that the L1 variety under extended diglossia (i.e. societal bilingualism) is more in danger of shift than in the cases of classic diglossia. Everyone would agree that stable diglossia under extended diglossia is difficult to maintain – if there are many speakers who speak the H variety as a second language. In order for diglossia to be stable, these speakers have to maintain their **own L1 as the L variety alongside the L2** that they also know and to value mainly the H variety for status-raising.

Note that later in this chapter, we do discuss cases where bilingualism and extended diglossia both seem relatively stable for certain ethnic groups, if not the entire community (the Nupes in Ibadan, Nigeria, the Malays in Singapore), even though clearly the L1 is the L variety in the diglossic opposition. Also, in an email message on a language policy email list when the subject was types of diglossia and maintenance, Fishman gave 12 examples of language pairs showing maintenance in their communities for at least three generations, "each still going strong in at least part of their own speech communities." In terms of our discussion in this chapter, most of them would fall under extended diglossia, not classic diglossia. The examples include Yiddish-Hebrew, Basque-Spanish, and Mandarin-Cantonese (email of April 15, 2003 on Language Policy-List).

4.4.3.3 Diglossia and domination

As we've said more than once already, the initial insight of diglossia is worth attention (i.e. the recognition that community language use is so organized that in some interactions only one language variety is considered appropriate). But we can now see beyond that insight as it becomes obvious that diglossia is not simply a matter of dividing up situations or domains according to language varieties. **Power is also divided up in diglossic communities**. Those persons who know the H variety have access to the social and political power that is not available to those who don't know it. In order to participate in interactions where the H variety is used, you have to be able to use that variety, or not participate. (Under classic diglossia, participation means being able to read and write and understand the H variety, but it is not spoken except in formal speeches and the like; but under extended diglossia, it also means being able to speak the H variety.)

However, when we consider the socio-political ramifications of allocation, we see they are similar under the two types of diglossia, but for different reasons. Under **classic diglossia**, at least everyone in the community speaks the same L variety as a home language. That is, the L variety is everyone's L1. The H variety is always a variety that is learned through special study; it is not simply acquired as part of a natural process in the home. So sufficient schooling is the gateway to potential power. Under **extended diglossia**, everyone in the community speaks his or her L1, of course, and it is acquired in the home. But here's the catch: **For some people the L1 is *also* the H variety**, but for others, their L1 is only an L variety. Thus, by the accident of family, some people have more access to participating in status-raising interactions. Thus, under either type of diglossia, the same options of participation do not end up being available to everyone.

Thus, for example, if we look at France (or any other Western nation state in which one language dominates – or is the only choice – in out-group relations) as an example of extended diglossia, we can see how extended diglossia is as limiting as classic diglossia. In France, French is the H variety and it is the mother tongue of many people. It is also used in status-raising situations, giving L1 speakers of French an advantage. The various regional varieties, such as Breton and Alsatian, are L varieties. So are the L1s of the more numerous immigrants, including Algerians since Algeria became independent in 1962. The use of all these other languages is largely restricted to informal in-group interactions. Of course, if these other speakers learn French, they also can participate in status-raising interactions. The degree of this participation depends on many things outside of language, but certainly fluency in French is a necessary beginning.

Let's take another case of extended diglossia, a case where not many residents at all speak the H variety as their L1. Does this create more equality in access to power? In most of sub-Saharan Africa, the H variety is almost always an alien language for everyone; that is, it is not the L1 of more than a handful of local people (there are exceptions, such as South Africa where English is the L1 of about 5% of the population).

The languages of the indigenous peoples in sub-Saharan Africa are all L varieties. True, in some nations, some local languages have a middle status (e.g. Wolof in Senegal where French is the H variety; Yoruba, Igbo, and Hausa as co-official languages in Nigeria along with English as the H variety). Those who speak the H variety as an L2 are few (estimates across Africa are around 20%); but obviously these few are in a position to control political power and often they are clustered in only a few of the many ethnic groups.

Thus, the point is that in Africa, even though extended diglossia does not advantage one indigenous ethnic group as much as it does in almost all Western countries (not just France), it still makes it easy for those whose ethnic groups are well represented among those who speak the H variety to control political power.

In sum, we have seen that both types of diglossia are similar in that under both, only those speakers who command the H variety can participate in status-raising situations. What this means, of course, is that those who do not know the H variety have little or no access to power in the societies in which they live. Under either type of diglossia, the H variety is only available through schooling. This means advanced education takes on special importance, not just for the subject matter, but for learning the H variety.

If the results of diglossia were only a conservation of resources (two varieties aren't used in the same domain), this outcome would be no more than an interesting sociolinguistic fact. But remember what H and L stand for (High and Low), even though the terms are just supposed to be a convenience, and this distinction has serious socio-political implications of inequality.

One can observe that not everyone has the same socio-political power in *all* communities, anyway. But the difference that both types of diglossia make is that if only the H variety can be used for communication in status-raising situations, then not everyone can *even participate* in the power struggle. If you don't know the H variety, you have the right to remain silent, but with no or little potential power. Because this feature characterizes societies with both classic and extended diglossia, it makes sense to group them together.

4.4.4 Diglossia and the linguistic marketplace

Can you see a relation between the nature of diglossia and how language varieties are valued in the linguistic marketplace? In chapter 5 we discuss the writings of Bourdieu and the notions he has popularized of **linguistic capital** and **symbolic domination**. It's easy to see that under diglossia the L variety doesn't have the same value in the marketplace because its linguistic capital in status-raising situations is very low. Accordingly, speakers of the H variety may use that variety as a form of symbolic domination of non-speakers of the H variety. The discussion in chapter 5 of **elite closure** is in this vein; the idea is that speakers of the H variety can limit the access to socio-economic opportunities available to others.

4.5 Maintenance or shift?

In this section, we discuss some specific factors that seem to influence maintenance and shift in some case studies. A look at various studies makes obvious two generalizations: (1) there is always a combination of factors at work, and (2) maintenance and shift within a bilingual community fall on a continuum with those individuals who use only the L1 at one end to those who use only the L2 at the other end. The language use of individuals also generally falls on a continuum: What happens with any one individual is almost never black and white; even speakers who are in the process of shifting don't show the same degree of shift all at once in all of the purposes or situations for which they use any language. We have in mind such situations and uses as speaking (from family talks to more public conversations), listening comprehension (from household topics to technical subjects), writing, and reading.

There are many different ways that researchers have grouped the features. For example, Baker (2001) sets up three categories: political, social and demographic factors; cultural factors; and linguistic factors. Just as we've done, he makes it clear that ranking the importance of these factors "is simplistic because the factors interact and intermingle in a complicated equation" (p. 60). Another possible grouping that would cut across Baker's categories is one that we suggest below: the influence of societal-level factors; the influence of in-group factors; and the influence of individual views and aspirations.

4.5.1 Factors encouraging maintenance on anyone's list

No matter how the cake is sliced, there are certain factors that are on anyone's list. We list the main ones that encourage maintenance of an L1. In every case, their opposites would promote shift. Some factors are important no matter whether we are considering what happens to the L1 of an indigenous minority group or the L1 of immigrants in a new land. Other factors are only relevant under one scenario or more relevant under that scenario.

- Societal-level demographic factors encouraging maintenance
  - Horizontal rather than vertical multilingualism in the larger community
  - Large numbers of speakers living together, preferably in a homeland community
  - Physical separation from other groups (homogeneous village or own urban area)
  - If immigrants, recently arrived with proximity to home community or ability to visit it easily
  - International status of L1
- Societal-level occupational factors encouraging maintenance
  - Jobs with fellow speakers of the L1
  - Low level of education restricting socio-economic mobility
  - Stable source of salaried occupations in community
- Societal-level educational factors encouraging maintenance
  - Best: official provision for L1 as a medium of instruction, at least in lower primary levels
  - Or, provision to teach L1 as a subject
  - Literature available in L1
  - Provisions for radio and TV broadcasts in L1
- In-group factors encouraging maintenance
  - Overall sense of subjective ethnolinguistic vitality
  - Types of social networks (density and strong ties with in-group memberships)
  - A group culture with unique features
  - Group attitudes about L1 as ethnic symbol
  - Ties between group's religion and its L1
  - Beliefs that a separate nation for the group is possible
  - Emphasis on cohesion of the group
  - Standardized dialect of L1 and many group members know it
  - A literary tradition
  - L1 community institutions (language schools, other organizations)
- Individual views and aspirations as factors encouraging maintenance
  - Networks: both strong and weak ties with in-group memberships
  - Position in in-group networks (centrality)
  - Psychological attachment to L1 for self-identity
  - Importance placed on group identity versus identity in larger society
  - Personal emphasis on family ties
  - Low level of education
  - Low emphasis on education in dominant language
  - Low potential for occupational change
  - Religious fervor and group's religion (if different from that in the larger society)

4.6 Representative case studies

We will look at cases in which three main factors, **group size**, **institutional support**, and **generational differences** as well as related factors, seem to count in maintenance and shift.

4.6.1 Where numbers and related factors may make a difference

Are we referring to large groups of speakers or only a handful? Are we speaking of an indigenous group or immigrant peoples? Does it matter if the group lives closely together? How important are these factors in the hierarchy of all important factors?

4.6.1.1 *Hungarians as a minority group in Slovakia*

Size of group seems to mean more for an indigenous minority group in a nation with a different official language than it means for an immigrant group in a nation new to them. For example, consider the minority group of Hungarians living in Slovakia where Slovak is the official language. For these Hungarians, a combination of group size and a linguistic culture that equates language with ethnicity and even with nation are perhaps the two most important factors that figure in the maintenance-or-shift equation.

At least according to the 1991 census, more than 10% of the population in Slovakia listed Hungarian as their mother tongue. Furthermore, the Hungarian population is grouped in a compact area on the Slovak-Hungarian border. This is a rural area of small villages; in more than 400 villages, the Hungarian population is more than 50% and in more than 200 it is 80% (Lanstyák and Szabómihály, 1995).

Schooling in Hungarian and access to standard Hungarian via the mass media are both available. Still, in 1995 the Slovak majority tried to implement a program to increase the teaching of Slovak in minority schools. This move was rejected by the Hungarian minority and the issue has not been resolved. They see their ethnolinguistic vitality tied to full functionality in their language, and this includes education in the language (Langman, 2002). Given all these facts, but especially the size and distribution of the Hungarian community in Slovakia, as well as the proximity and psychological support of Hungary, it seems very likely that Hungarians in Slovakia will retain their L1 – even while they are bilingual in Slovak.

4.6.1.2 *Hungarians as a minority group in Austria*

These Hungarians in Slovakia contrast in their L1 maintenance with those around the town of Oberwart in Austria (Gal, 1979). There, the Hungarian minority also is near a border with Hungary, but it is surrounded by German-speaking villages and the number of Hungarian speakers is declining. The small size of the community may make the difference here, as well as the norm to speak German in the town when German monolinguals are present. All the Hungarians are bilingual in German, the only official language in Austria. Further, German is the language associated with socio-economic mobility and jobs in the town. At least at the time of Gal's study, a change for these individuals from Hungarian as their main language to German was in progress.

4.6.1.3 *Vietnamese as an immigrant language*

Evidence that a large number of speakers is not enough to guarantee that an L1 be maintained comes from the Vietnamese community in California. In the California schools, Vietnamese is the second-largest language group (not counting English), following Spanish (Young and Tran, 1999). But the fact that the Vietnamese are an immigrant community in the United States, where monolingualism in English is the pattern for many, seems to be an impetus pushing immigrants in general to shift to English.

A survey of 106 Vietnamese parents showed that although they claim Vietnamese is the sole language in almost 85% of the homes, children speak a good deal of English. A third of the children said they speak both Vietnamese and English among themselves, but almost 22% said they speak only English with peers and siblings. Clearly, the children are on their way to shifting to English.

In addition to the large numbers in this immigrant group, there are other factors that would make you think the L1 would be maintained better than it is. They live closely together; they celebrate Vietnamese cultural events; there are churches, temples and even a Vietnamese Parent–Teacher Association to reinforce Vietnamese. But the shift to English seems very rapid. The only factor that correlated with more Vietnamese use was a short length of stay. The longer the length of stay, the more shift to English, even though – ironically – the longer the stay, the more the parent encouraged the child to speak Vietnamese.

4.6.2 Shift or not in long-term immigrant groups

Another study, this time of a long-term immigrant group in Jordan, the Armenians, shows a shift that is not surprising, given the length of stay, although other factors might have predicted more maintenance than exists. The Armenian refugee community (forced to flee from their homeland in Turkish Armenia) has been in Jordan since the 1910s. Most of them are well integrated into Jordanian society; however, they do not frequently intermarry with other Jordanians and they are Christians in an Islamic society. For the 110 subjects studied, Arabic is their main language and is used in a wide range of domains (Al-Khatib, 2001). Even at home with parents, only 22% reported they used only Armenian while 49% said they used only Arabic.

The Armenians contrast with a Chechen immigrant community in Jordan. First, the Armenians are much fewer (about 4,000 compared with about 8,000 Chechens). Second, the Chechens live in tightly knit communities. The Chechens also have more institutional support, with their own cultural associations and magazines, dating back to the Caucasian Club, established in 1932 (Dweik, 2000). They also hold better jobs than the Armenians, jobs that involve more contact with other Jordanians. When asked, "Which language is more useful to you?" just over half of both male and female Armenians said Arabic and about 28% said both Arabic and Armenian. In contrast, in response to the same question, 30% of Chechens said Arabic was more useful and 58% said both Arabic and Chechen. High percentages of both groups of subjects said it was important to them to speak Arabic. But while half of the Armenian men said "yes" to the question "Is Armenian dying in your home?", only 5% of the Chechens answered "yes" to this same question about their language.

Most of the Armenians studied still identify as Armenians and believe as long as their names remain Armenian their culture will survive. But this attitude is weaker in the third and fourth generation and a few of them have Arabic given names. Even while Armenians say Armenian is "better", they clearly have an instrumental attachment to Arabic. That is, they see it as a valuable means of communication and more useful than Armenian. How do the Chechens differ? Clearly, they also find Arabic very useful at the societal level. But perhaps because they are more numerous and they live together and because their networks must show strong ties (for example, through their cultural associations), they also find Chechen useful at the group level.

4.6.3 In-migrants to the city: transitory or not

Finally, consider a case that is halfway between that of an indigenous minority and an immigrant group, the Nupe people who live in the large Nigerian city of Ibadan. Strictly speaking, the Nupes are not immigrants because they are an indigenous people to the north of Ibadan. But they are immigrants from the perspective that Ibadan was originally a city peopled by the large and power-ful Yoruba ethnic group. Even though today Ibadan is multi-ethnic, the Yoruba predominate and the Yoruba language is the main lingua franca. Details re-ported here come from field work conducted in 1986 (Oyetade, 1995). At that time, there were about 1,000 Nupe in Ibadan, but the numbers varied because of the movement of individuals back and forth to the Nupe home area. Oyetade studied a sample of 45 who were all bilingual in Nupe and Yoruba, with 84% reporting they learned Yoruba after coming to Ibadan.

4.6.3.1 Learning other languages, but maintaining the L1

The Nupe case is a good example of the effects of vertical multilingualism. That is, even though they tend to live in one urban area (with the Hausa, fellow northerners), which has its own market where products from the north are sold, the degree of ethnic mixing in Ibadan is great. Oyetade lists eight major ethnic groups (including Nupe) in the city in addition to the Yoruba. Many of the adult Nupes are traders or hold unskilled jobs in factories or the various institutions in the city; some of the women are market sellers. Almost half of the subjects (44%) were school-age children attending school; not surprisingly they were very proficient in Yoruba because it is the medium of instruction.

The result is that nearly every Nupe person who has contacts outside the home is bi- or trilingual. In a spatial organization and psychological outlook such as one finds in a city like Ibadan, the only way one can avoid becoming bilingual in the urban lingua franca is to stay home. And, in fact, many of the women do just that (the Nupe are Moslems) and so show much less proficiency in Yoruba than the men. (Only 12% of the women were considered very proficient in Yoruba compared with 53% of the men.)

4.6.3.2 Saliency of ethnicity counts

However, under vertical multilingualism, the interesting point is that the mother tongue is not necessarily threatened. Rather, what you find is an allocation of the L1 to some in-group functions and the L2 to some out-group functions, and both languages to those functions that are in between (neighbors and friends). Two pictures emerge: (1) Nupe is the definite choice in some situations. All the men said they used only Nupe in the home, except for one man with a Yoruba wife who used both Nupe and Yoruba with her. Also, in a sub-sample of adolescents and young adults (N=25 in the 8 to 21 age range), self-reports indicated that they used Nupe almost exclusively with parents and even with other children. The self-reports of parents corroborated these findings. (2) But when it comes to talk outside the home, then Yoruba takes on prominence. Adults use mainly Yoruba in their work. Children speak mainly Yoruba at school, and also some English, but no Nupe at all, not even when talking during class breaks. (The choice at breaks is Yoruba for 95%.)

When talking to neighbors, 55% of parents (N=20) reported using both Yoruba and Nupe, but 25% reported using only Yoruba. With friends, parents reported no Yoruba alone, but 65% said they used both languages. The adolescents and young adults reported more Yoruba with both neighbors and friends, with 40% reporting Yoruba on its own. A higher percentage reported both Yoruba and Nupe (48% with neighbors and 44% with friends).

At least on the basis of this study, it looks like the Nupe will continue to use Yoruba, the main local lingua franca, extensively outside of the home. Given the fact that English is the main official language in Nigeria (along with Yoruba, Igbo, and Hausa), it is also likely that the more educated young Nupes may also use a fair amount of English and probably also Nigerian Pidgin English.

But the point is that it also looks likely that they will continue to speak Nupe in the family.

How representative is this picture? Elsewhere, if the main place the L1 is used extensively is the family domain, that is not enough to mean maintenance for the L1 in succeeding generations. But it is possible that African attachments to the mother tongue are stronger than they are elsewhere, at least if we are talking about an indigenous group's mother tongue (not a true immigrant population).

There are three reasons why ethnicity may be more salient in African cities than it is among either the Vietnamese in California or the Armenians in Jordan. By extension, the same reasons can apply elsewhere. First, one practical reason: Even though they may live in a large city, indigenous in-migrants from other areas in an African context are typically not far from their ethnic homeland, so there is a good deal of traffic back and forth. Second, one very instrumental reason: Africans (and possibly others elsewhere) rely on fellow ethnic group members in helping them locate jobs. True, members of one's own ethnic group may be helpful, but possibly nowhere is speaking your group's language the ethnic password that it is in Africa. Third, a psychological reason: Speaking several languages is something most Africans have always done, even in the rural areas.

One might say it is part of the ideology of Nupes in Ibadan to be multilingual. And in cities, this expectation of becoming bilingual is simply magnified by the presence of many ethnic groups in close quarters. Learning a lingua franca makes communication across groups easy. Further, in the city, one ethnic group can see that their neighbors are all doing the same thing: Each group maintains its L1 while learning at least the main urban lingua franca, if not even more other languages.

4.6.4 French in Canada beyond Québec

Once French Canadians move beyond Québec (obviously the main stronghold of French in Canada), maintenance of French becomes problematic. This is even the case when francophones don't move far. Raymond Mougeon and Edouard Beniak (1989) document French maintenance and shift to English in Welland, a city close to the Niagara Falls and in Ontario Province, which has the largest francophone minority outside of Québec. In the 1996 census, 23% of the Canadian population said their L1 was French and 17% of the entire population said they were bilingual in French and English.

But in Welland, neither the Catholic Church nor the school system, traditionally crucial institutions in language maintenance, have been able to stem the move to English among French-Canadian families. Even when Mougeon and Beniak gathered their data in the 1980s, they reported that the current French Catholic parish priest had to take on a bilingual assistant to handle the various requests for religious ceremonies in English or in both languages (funerals, baptisms, weddings, masses, etc.). Already at that time, young French people could receive their entire education in French, but Mougeon and Beniak report that "the students overwhelmingly use English for peer-group communication on the school premises . . . They will even try to use English with school personnel if they can get away with it" (pp. 290–1).

The strongest evidence of a shift to English is that the Mougeon and Beniak study shows that 54% of francophone adults who are of the prime child-rearing age (25–44) use English as their home language. It is no surprise, then, that "significant proportions" of the groups aged 24 and less do not speak French at home. True, there is much bilingualism and 75% of the older bilinguals (55+) say they are French-dominant. But 52% of the younger adults (20–34) are English-dominant bilinguals. Therefore, they are more likely to give up using French, their weaker language, at home.

Finally, another factor promoting shift in the Welland area is the rising incidence of linguistically mixed marriages. By the period 1973–5, the rate of such marriages was already over 50%. In these marriages, English typically becomes the home language for two reasons. First, English has more instrumental value in the area (on the job, memos are written in English, foremen typically give instructions in English, etc.). Second, Mougeon and Beniak state that Welland anglophones are "massively unilingual" (i.e. they speak only English). An earlier survey by Mougeon in the 1970s showed that almost half of linguistically mixed couples chose to send their children to French-language schools. This finding and other studies imply the conclusion that for the children of these parents, any French they learn is learned at school and used mostly in that setting.

Whether French will survive in Welland is hard to judge; certainly, it is not a robust language there compared with English. At the very least, bilingualism will dominate among the francophones. Even at the time of the Mougeon and Beniak study, 90% of the age group 5–14 was bilingual. Other students of language maintenance and shift claim that bilingualism does not necessarily entail shift, and we have cited studies that show this. But becoming bilingual mainly (or exclusively) by learning and using the minority language in the school system means that children will be unlikely to have complete mastery of the grammar of that language. And what school learners often miss learning are the styles more associated with informal situations. Given these considerations, francophones in Welland are unlikely to pass French on to their children.

Mougeon and Beniak point out that the home language on any survey is often too gross to be a reliable measure of shift. If the survey has only a single question about language use in the home, it does not differentiate between language use among parents and between parent and child; nor do census questions generally take account of the type of situation, such as whether conversation is one-on-one with a child or when the child is also talking to siblings. With a finer-grained questionnaire, Mougeon and Beniak suggest that the reported rate of shift to English might be even higher than indicated.

4.6.5 Where institutional support matters: Singapore

At the same time as L1 maintenance without any official support works in Africa (as long as the speakers are bilingual), it does not work everywhere. In general, institutional support can make a big difference in whether speakers will retain their L1. An excellent example is what is happening in Singapore. What has been a multilingual nation is gradually becoming a three-language nation.

When the British Sir Stamford Raffles landed in 1819 at Singapore, a small island at the tip of the Malayan peninsula, it was a fishing village with only a little over 100 Malays and a handful of Chinese living there. It became a British colony, and today the island republic is one of the major economies in Southeast Asia, with a population of more than three and a half million. The sharpest increase has been in the number of Chinese. But there also have been many in-migrants from the other places in Southeast Asia and from India. Many people think of Singapore today in terms of these three groups, Chinese, Malay, and Indian, but there are many different sub-groups, each originally with its own L1. The Chinese immigrants came from different areas and spoke varieties of southern Chinese dialects that are largely very different from each other. Hokkien and Cantonese are examples. The majority of the Malays spoke Malay, but some spoke other languages, such as Javanese from Indonesia. Some Indians spoke languages from the north of India, such as Punjabi and Hindustani, but more spoke South Indian languages in the Dravidian family, especially Tamil.

One factor that has kept ethnic differences or ethnic "consolidation" very salient is the education system. In the early days, the British supported education in English and Malay. The reason behind Malay as a choice was that they thought of the Malays as the indigenous people. English was offered in order to supply workers in the local administration. The local communities of the various Chinese dialects and of the Indian languages supported their own schools. Only the English-medium schools were multi-ethnic, but enrolled especially Indian children.

Kwan-Terry (2000) refers to this situation as having created "socio-economic islands". The English-educated Chinese and Tamils had more advantages than others. And because the Chinese were – and remain – so numerous (they make up 57% of the population), the division between "Chinese-educated" and "English-educated" was a sore point.

Socio-economic considerations propelled a change to English for everyone. Everyone could see that English-educated persons had higher incomes and that enrollments in non-English-medium schools had declined. Two steps were taken. First, around the time of separation from Malaysia to become independent (in the 1960s), Singapore established a bilingual education policy, with English given priority. Second, by 1980, *all* the schools became English-medium schools.

At the same time, three language shifts were taking place for English, Chinese, and the Indian languages. In contrast to all other languages, the Malay language showed very little shift; one reason is that it retains its ethnic and religious associations.

(1) Overall English use in the home increased from 11.6% in 1980 to 20.2% in 1990 (Kwan-Terry, 2000: 98). In Chinese homes, 23% of primary one children reported that they spoke English at home (up from 9% in 1980).

(2) Along with a clear increase in English in Chinese homes, there was an increase in using Mandarin; this represents a shift from other Chinese dialects. A drastic change happened. In 1980, 64% of children in primary one said that they spoke a Chinese regional dialect at home, but by 1989 the percentage dropped to 7% and Mandarin usage increased greatly (to 69% in 1989).

(3) Today Indian languages other than Tamil are being replaced by either English or Malay. Tamil itself is not threatened in family domains, but its use among schoolchildren is declining as English use is increasing.

4.6.5.1 *The shift to Mandarin among Chinese*

Although the use of English in the schools and the shift to English in other domains is obviously motivated by socio-economic considerations, the shift in Chinese homes to Mandarin is quite remarkable. Mandarin shows the greatest gain as the principal household language as it replaces regional Chinese dialects. In 1980, only 13% reported Mandarin as their household language, but by 1990, it was 30%. The motivations for this shift are two-fold. First, the large Chinese population retains its strong sense of Chinese ethnicity, so it did not view a total shift to English favorably. Second, the government came up with a way to satisfy such feelings while not displacing the role of English: They launched a "speak Mandarin" campaign in 1979. The idea was to encourage all Chinese to speak Mandarin in the home *in place of* other Chinese dialects. These other dialects were also banned on radio and televison. Mandarin was "localized"; it is called Huayu "Chinese language" in Singapore. In mainland China (the People's Republic of China), Mandarin is Putonghua.

Four factors are making the shift successful: The extensive, ongoing government campaign, the low status of other Chinese dialects, the belief that speaking Mandarin best defines one's ethnicity as Chinese, and the increased commerce with the Chinese-speaking outside world. Wariness over the omnipresence of Westernization in the region also was a factor. Kwan-Terry (2000: 103) reports, "The result is that Mandarin Chinese is now widely used among the younger generation [of ethnic Chinese] across different educational levels, from schools to polytechnics and universities, even though the medium of instruction is English."

4.6.5.2 *Family multilingualism in Singapore*

A feature of multi-ethnic cities (and multi-ethnic nations such as Singapore) is that individuals shift languages, or how much they use a language, as their life experiences change. Gupta and Yeok (1995) details the linguistic developments in two Chinese families in Singapore. English was dominant for the children at all stages. The families' L1 was Cantonese, but speakers of other Chinese dialects were caregivers when the children were young and so the older children grew up speaking the caregivers' dialects, either Hokkien or Teochew. Changes in caregivers for another child meant that child spoke only Cantonese and English and yet another child, whose family had a Philippine maid when the child was young, spoke only English. At some point, the children acquired Mandarin. How much Cantonese was used varied. In one family, Cantonese was used a great deal, partly because of a friendship with a family from Hong Kong, a Cantonese stronghold. In one of the families, English was less used in the face of Mandarin, both within the home and with friends. Mandarin, rather than Cantonese, was even used with the grandmother.

4.6.5.3 *Summing up Singapore*

In summary, the Singapore case shows how much difference government policies, especially regarding schooling, can make. At the same time, though, there are other factors than government intervention at work here. First, a reason English-medium schools were acceptable was that everyone recognized the role of English in socio-economic mobility. Second, retaining a means of ethnic identity is obviously very important to the Malays and the Chinese. The Malays have the distinction of having their language as the national language. Further, because other Malay varieties dominate in the region (and even are the sole official languages in Indonesia and Malay), Malay's future preservation can hardly be in doubt. Third, because most speakers of the Chinese dialects perceive all varieties of Chinese as one and the same language (even though they are not all mutually intelligible), it was relatively easy to promote Mandarin for everyone as a unifying ethnic symbol, no matter how diverse the community is. Also, the rise in world-level economic stature of the People's Republic of China was nothing but serendipitous. To "speak Mandarin" became a very attractive alternative to home dialects, given that it is more or less the same as the standard dialect of the People's Republic of China. Third, because the Indian population was also divided by language, English-medium schools were an appealing unifying development. Tamil-medium schools had existed only at the primary level and were not well considered. Tamil itself was associated with plantation workers.

All Indians, even Tamils, welcomed the alternative of an education in English and its socio-economic benefits. By 1990, 34% of Indian households used English as their main household language.

Keep in mind that for any of the three groups, Chinese, Indians, or Malay, conversations are not necessarily carried on in only one language. One feature of today's Singapore is that many conversations show extensive codeswitching to English, meaning that they include words and phrases and whole sentences from English along with one or more other languages. Codeswitching, liberally peppered with slang from different languages, is informally called Singlish in Singapore. Given the extent to which language use in Singapore has been institutionalized, it comes as no surprise that Singlish is seen as "bad English" and that the government has begun a campaign to promote "good English". In launching this new campaign, Prime Minister Goh Chok Tong said, "Poor English reflects badly on us and makes us seem less intelligent or competent" (Asian edition of *Time* magazine, July 29, 2002).

4.7 The younger generation and bilingualism

In case after case, when a younger generation is exposed to a more dominant language in the nation than the L1 (through schooling and school peers), it is hard to stop a shift to that second language by the next generation. That is, as we've indicated earlier, especially in immigrant communities, shift by the third generation is almost a foregone conclusion.

4.7.1 Shift among the youth

One community where shift seems to be underway is the Chinese community in Tyneside in the northeast of England. A shift from Chinese-dominant to English-dominant usage within three generations is evident (Raschka, Li, and Lee, 2002). In these Cantonese-speaking households, the children acquire more complex networks as they get older and move from parent-oriented networks to peer-oriented ones. Peer groups favor the use of English or English-Cantonese codeswitching. The authors comment, ". . . while the children's Chinese ability may be related to the 'classic' sociolinguistic factors such as gender, educational level, and parents' proficiency, this only gives half of the picture that emerges from our data. A more complex, more plausible, explanation related to the peer networks of the children themselves" (pp. 22–3).

A second example of even more rapid language shift, and one that is initiated by the parents, comes from the study of some Xhosa-speaking families in Grahamstown in the Eastern Cape province of South Africa (De Klerk, 2000a). The crucial fact in ongoing shift is that some parents in the indigenous Xhosa community are sending their children to English-medium schools, not Xhosa-medium schools. Most of the children in these schools are whites whose L1 is

English. Part of the reason for choosing English schools was dissatisfaction with conditions in the Xhosa schools. But the major reason was that parents believe English will prepare the child for more job opportunities. Even though 17 of the 26 parents studied said they thought it was important to support and maintain the L1, their responses to other questions indicated they "were making every effort to increase their child's exposure to English, not Xhosa" (p. 101). Many wanted to use only Xhosa for conversations within the family, such as with grandparents. But a number of the parents reported having decided to use English in the home or both English and Xhosa. Among the children in these families, English was on the increase, with only six families reporting only Xhosa by the children.

De Klerk comments that it is highly problematic in the local Grahamstown context that the social networks of either the parents or the children will help foster English. The children have few friends whose L1 is English and the parents' friends are predominately Xhosa-speaking; they have English acquaintances only at work. But De Klerk states, "Yet this does not seem to matter too much . . . mind prevails over matter, a determination to master English and a will to succeed seems to be sufficient. More to the point, the commitment to maintain the MT [mother tongue] is notably absent in most cases" (pp. 106–7).

4.7.2 The youth as language brokers

In many communities where a language shift is underway, the L1 is still maintained in the home, of course. But children, not their elders, can be primary in deciding on the home language in immigrant families. A study in the Seattle, Washington area shows that the choice the children make for family talk is not the L1, but English, the language of wider communication. Tuominen (1999) studied language use in 25 bilingual or multilingual families who spoke a variety of languages from Russian to Tagalog. All parents had positive attitudes toward their L1 and most reported speaking their L1 to each other. But for conversations with children, English use or codeswitching with English was very common.

"It is true that children in all families 'test' their parents, but my findings suggest that children in multilingual families not only 'test' their parents but often 'run the show'" (p. 71). A major reason for this is that the US-born or American-raised children are often the experts in the family on how things are done in America, such as how to understand job applications, notes from school, and American holidays. Tuominen also gives the example of a junior high school daughter helping her Russian-speaking father understand words in an English-language novel he was reading. Ironically, those parents who know more English are more able to set family rules (and encourage the L1 if that is their choice), just because they also are more familiar with American culture thanks to their education and economic status and do not need to rely so much on their children.

4.8 Separating language maintenance from cultural maintenance

Another factor to consider is this: Many people think that if an ethnic group desires to maintain its culture, it follows naturally that it will place importance on maintaining its language. "Ethnic identity is allegiance to a group . . . with which one has ancestral links" (Edwards, 1994: 128). Maintaining shared group features is one way to retain ethnic identity, and we've already said in an earlier chapter that, certainly, language is the most "visible" symbol of an ethnic group. And there are many examples all over the world where language seems inextricably linked to ethnic identity (e.g. Arabic in the Middle East). But when group members are second-generation immigrants, maintaining one's L1 as a necessary ethnic symbol may not hold much attraction.

4.8.1 Latinos in the United States

For example, consider the case of young Latinos in the New York City area. A lengthy feature story in the *New York Times* (June 8, 2003) has this headline: "Redefining 'Latino' this time in English, language divides Hispanic culture in U.S.". Latinos make up 27% of New York's population. The 2000 census shows that there are 38.8 million Latinos in the US, with "Latino" used to identify anyone from a Spanish-speaking country. The author of the *Times* article, Mireya Navarro, points out that the census data for states such as New York and New Jersey show slightly more native-born Latinos than immigrants and that the "great majority of all Latinos speak both English and Spanish".

   To show the contrast between immigrants and US-born Latinos, the author compares the language-use patterns in New York of a first-generation immigrant and a second-generation person. The first person, a 33-year-old woman, came to New York 19 years ago from Colombia and lives in the city borough of Queens. She speaks English only to the children she teaches at a church agency and says she has no American friends. She shops only at stores where owners speak Spanish. Her husband speaks English only when he talks to customers at the parking garage in Lower Manhattan where he works. The two of them watch Spanish newscasts and soap operas.

   In contrast, the second-generation 26-year-old says, "I'm definitely Latino but Americanized." He is the son of immigrants from Puerto Rico. Even though he lives in a Latino neighborhood in New Jersey, he grew up speaking English. He codeswitches between Spanish and English with his grandparents but watches English-medium MTV and other English TV programs geared to the general American young audience. He's employed as a promotions manager for a magazine geared to second-generation Latinos.

   The story goes on to point out evidence of the divide between Hispanic immigrants and those born in the US in their language use and their attitudes, as well as attitudes toward them. A recently formed consortium of advertisers in New York and Florida aimed at Latinos says it favors focusing more on Latinos who are bilingual, or for whom English is the dominant language. A national cable channel is among media outlets beginning to offer talk, music, and news magazine programs mainly in English, but directed toward young Latinos. The Pew Hispanic Center/Kaiser Family Foundation 2002 National Survey of Latinos is cited, showing that "on question of attitude and social issues, native and immigrant Latinos differed sharply, reflecting the prevalent sensibilities of either the United States or Latin America." For example, 59% of Latinos for whom Spanish was their dominant language agreed with the concept of fatalism (the sense that a person does not have control over the future), not a notion embraced by non-Latino North Americans. In contrast, only 24% of Latinos who speak English most of the time shared a fatalistic view.

The *Washington Post* reported data from the same survey showing that most second-generation Latinos are either bilingual (47%) or English-dominant (46%). Only 7% consider themselves Spanish-dominant. English gains even more ground in the third generation; 22% say they are bilingual and the remaining 78% are English-dominant (June 16–22, 2003).

At the same time, there is evidence that Latinos retain elements of their culture, even while speaking English. For example, even though they speak English or are bilingual, the survey mentioned above showed that Latinos share certain views that set them apart from non-Hispanic whites and African-Americans (e.g. they are more likely than the other groups to say that they are willing to pay higher taxes for more government services). Also, another *New York Times* article (July 2, 2003) indicates that Pentecostal churches in the New York area that were founded in the 1950s to cater to Puerto Rican immigrants now conduct some services in English to attract young people who do not have the mindset of planning to go back to Puerto Rico. One minister said, "during the English service, people feel they are fulfilling their destinies here in New York. Their culture tends to be Latino, especially in food, but they prefer to worship and sing in English."

4.9 Summary on language maintenance and shift

Our discussion makes clear that minority languages, whether of indigenous or immigrant populations, rarely can survive in all the domains where the dominant language in the relevant nation rules. Yet, it is possible for two languages to survive if each language has its own domains. As Laponce (1993: 25) concludes, "they [two languages] can coexist harmoniously within the same population and maintain a *relatively* stable balance within the same geographic niche." But Laponce goes on to say, "However, *relatively* is a key qualifier." The reason is that few social domains remain the sole property of the minority language for long, especially if there is any prestige attached to them. The result is, as Laponce says, the more prestigious populations "will pressure, restrict, and eventually eliminate the lesser language, that associated with less prestigious individuals and roles" (p. 25).

4.9.1 Where the L1 is maintained

But what about cases where the L1 is maintained? For example, consider the Nupe in Ibadan, Nigeria, where the main indigenous language is Yoruba and Yoruba is also the main urban lingua franca. So far the Nupe seem to be holding their own, in the home domain almost entirely but also to an extent with friends and neighbors. The same seems to hold for other multi-ethnic cities, such as Dakar, Senegal, where educated Wolofs retain Wolof but learn French, the official language. Wolof is associated with ethnicity, but French with modernity.

Specifically referring to Indian urban centers where L1s seem to be retained by in-migrants from other Indian areas, Laitin (1993) offers "uncertainty" as an explanation that may apply to all of these cases. This is uncertainty about the linguistic needs of one's children. These multi-ethnic cities in the developing world, at least, are all cases where there is uncertainty about future language policy. Speakers know what the medium of the schools is today and what languages are needed for socio-economic mobility, but what about future policies? In India, for example, will English retain its preeminence? Will Hindi's role be expanded? Will Indian state languages retain their official, privileged position as the medium of instruction through primary school? The same sorts of questions apply elsewhere, such as in the Nupe case. Another point that Laitin also mentions applies as well: Migrants to the cities are in a tenuous position in regard to their relationship with the indigenous population. Attempts to throw out real or perceived non-locals have been made in many places in the world. Of relevance to the Nupe case is that this has happened very recently in northern Nigeria. Thus, in-migrants to cities in their own nation have two reasons to retain their L1, both connected with uncertainty about the future.

4.9.2 Learning an L2 as an investment of time and energy

The overall point to keep in mind is that learning a second language requires an investment of time and energy; true, it's a major psychological commitment, but it also is just plain effort for anyone past early childhood. (L2 learning past early childhood is discussed at length in chapter 11.) Compare the Indian situation with that in places where the major outlines of language allocation, at least in the official sector, are unlikely to change substantially. On the basis of this comparison, one can see why Vietnamese immigrants in California are quickly shifting to English in many of their domains of activity.

There is no reason to be "uncertain" about the future of English in schools and government there. The same thinking applies to North African immigrants in France; that is, French is not going to lose its preeminence in any major occupational or institutional roles. Thus, while all immigrants everywhere may value their L1, the extent to which they give up its use in everyday life to a dominant language will vary.

Where speakers of different L1s coexist with territorial separation (under horizontal multilingualism), it is another story. Individual persons who have the need or desire to speak two languages will be bilingual, but communities can be largely monolingual. Then coexistence of two or more languages in the same nation is possible, as is the case in Switzerland where coexistence depends on territorial separation. There are four national languages (German, French, Italian, and Rhaeto-Romansch) each with territorial status, although only German, French, and Italian have official status. Romansch (a language related to French and Italian), with only about 50,000 speakers, is protected with special provisions. Still, Switzerland is unusual. One would have to look hard to find another nation with such a "strong emphasis on local particularism" and its rejection of "the notion that minority status is a temporary phenomenon" (Schmid, 2001: 142). Further, even in such nations, groups recognize that, outside their home area, middle-class jobs for themselves and their children will go first to those who speak and read the languages with national or international prestige.

Finally, uncertainty about future trends in favored languages and official policies can matter to indigenous minority group members living on their own turf. How much they have to be concerned depends on their home nation. It is not only in the developing world that language policies may change; future policies in Eastern Europe, especially the former Soviet Union, are uncertain.

4.10 Summing up

In conclusion, the **general pattern for minority groups and immigrants** that we introduced at the beginning of this chapter remains in place.

- The same factors generally are in place when a group shifts away from its L1, but **no one factor or set of factors always predicts language maintenance or shift**; it depends on the specific hierarchy among factors in a specific community.
- The importance and possibility of **socio-economic mobility** promotes shift away from the L1.
- **Bilingualism by the second generation** with the dominant and/or official language in the nation state is a typical pattern.
- **Shift is slower** or may not happen at all if the subordinate group lives in its ancestral home (some minority groups in China).

- **Shift is also slower** if bilingualism comes because the group was colonized or its land annexed. Consider groups in the so-called developing world whose nations became independent in the 1950s and 1960s (e.g. in Africa and Asia or various island nations). Also consider parts of Europe including the former USSR.
- **Numbers of minority group speakers or immigrants** may matter, but do not always. Younger speakers may shift their dominant language, but maintain their L1 as well (e.g. many Latinos in the US).
- **Members of an elite** are slow to change. If circumstances give a minority group or immigrants political or economic power, they are slow to become bilingual (e.g. wealthy Chinese merchants in urban Chinatowns in various parts of the world).

4.11 Words and phrases to remember

horizontal multilingualism
vertical multilingualism
social network analysis
ethnolinguistic vitality
allocation of varieties
classic and extended diglossia
factors encouraging language maintenance
factors encouraging language shift

5

Ideologies and Attitudes

Multiple voices: The word from Papua New Guinea

Pukuntap lives on Kapataarund Island off the coast of Kavieng, Papua New Guinea. He is a member of the Tigak ethnic group and speaks Tigak as his first language; it is one of more than 800 indigenous languages spoken in Papua New Guinea. Since Pukuntap lives and works in his own language area, he uses Tigak every day with family and other Tigak speakers. He is an engineer working for the New Ireland Provincial Government in Kavieng. There, he uses English in the office and when working with foreigners or Papua New Guineans from other parts of the country. In town, but outside the office, he speaks Tok Pisin, the preferred language of social interaction in any ethnically mixed groups. English and Tok Pisin are two of the three official languages of Papua New Guinea. More people speak Tok Pisin than English and many are self-conscious about their English because they only used it in school (at least in most of the country). Even when speaking with English-speaking expatriates, if they show a willingness to speak Tok Pisin, most Papua New Guineans gladly switch to Tok Pisin. For every-day conversation, English is still the language used with expatriates by only a very small educated elite. (The third official language is Hiri Motu, but it is spoken by less than 10% of the population and only around the capital district.)

5.1 Introduction

In this chapter, we venture into the realm of how personal and group beliefs, mindsets, and psychological or cognitive orientations affect the decisions that speakers and even nation states make about becoming or remaining bilingual. All of this can be subsumed under the term **ethos**. We use ethos to mean "Characteristic spirit, prevalent tone of sentiment of a people or community" (following the Oxford English Dictionary (OED)). Ethos comes from the Greek ēthos, which means 'character'. We use ethos as a useful umbrella to cover both **attitudes** toward languages and **language ideologies**. Even though it is not derived from the same word as ethos, we have come to think of ethnicity as somehow related.

It's true that we see the term ethnicity more often than ethos. Any anthropology textbook or journal article about culture will refer to "ethnicity" and newspaper articles daily refer to "ethnic groups". So how is ethnicity the same and how is it different? *Ethnic* has a different source from *ethos*. *Ethnic* comes from the Greek word *ethnos* 'people'. When the Greek form was borrowed into Middle English via Latin (*ethnicus*), it meant "foreigner". (The OED's first citation is from 1375.) Today, the OED gives this as one of its definitions for *ethnic*: "pertaining to race or nation, pertaining to having common racial, cultural, or linguistic characteristics . . . hence, foreign, exotic." In this way, ethnic has part of the same sense as ethos because the concept of ethnicity implies a "group mind"; that is, members of an ethnic group are often considered to have a "collective consciousness".

As part of this discussion on attitudes and ideologies, it is instructive to realize that today, of course, *ethnic group* is often used in popular parlance for *any* group outside the mainstream, not just for foreign citizens within the relevant nation state. For example, it's used for any hyphenated group in the United States, from African-Americans to Italian-Americans. In Australia, it's used interchangeably with "migrant groups" except that "ethnic group" includes later generations, too – but not, interestingly enough, the "so-called mainstream" English, Irish, and Scots, Michael Clyne tells us (personal communication). But it's not used for indigenous Australian peoples, who tend to object to being covered by the label. And in Canada, John Edwards tells us, francophones in Québec are "ethnics" in the eyes of anglophones outside of Québec. For academics, the term "ethnic group" is strictly neutral, although it may retain a sense of "the other" or "outsider" in the general public. Some academics differentiate ethnic groups and minority groups. But others do not, and we don't see much gain for our purposes in doing so.

Ethnicity itself consists of what one writer calls "social facts . . . or ideas experienced by the group mind and expressed or 'reincarnated' in the minds and behaviors of the individual members of the social group" (Williams, 1999: 170). Also, as we've just indicated, the designation of certain people as an ethnic group exists in the minds of others, too. We, of course, are interested in ethnicity in this chapter because many groups so labeled see their language as an intrinsic part of the group's identity. Some see ethnicity (and therefore ethnic groups) as primordial, meaning that the designated group *always* existed. But others, such as the anthropologist Frederick Barth (1969), argue that the existence of at least some ethnic groups depends on where boundaries are drawn. And boundaries, whether psychological or political, are not primordial and therefore can be redrawn. What's important for us – as we have argued before in this book – is that who speaks what language is often a sign of a boundary. This is the reason why we take pains at least to bring up ethnicity in a book about languages. Further, the notion of symbolic boundaries comes up often in writings about language attitudes and ideologies. Within the same nation state, the term **"we" as opposed to "the other" or "they"** is often cited as part of an ideology and the basis for language policies that favor the "we". Especially writers about language ideology emphasize that they wish to shift the attention from discussing languages as properties of communities to discussing languages as boundaries of communities (Gal and Irvine, 2000: 77).

For an example of how boundaries separating the "we" and the "other" are symbolized in language, consider the case of the Welsh. It is more than an interesting fact to note that the English word *Welsh* (for speakers of Welsh) was *wælisc* in Old English where it meant "foreign". Of course the Welsh are a people who were among the Celtic peoples who inhabited the British Isles *before* the Anglo-Saxons arrived. The Welsh in the west of Great Britain spoke then – and some still do today – a language very different from English, although all are bilingual in English today. But, obviously, their language was one reason for the early conquerors to label them as foreigners, even if the Welsh were there first.

Very soon, we'll give you a fuller discussion of attitudes and ideologies. For the moment, think of **attitudes** about languages as **assessments that speakers make** about the relative values of a particular language. Attitudes are largely unconscious, but this doesn't mean that people can't make judgments or act on the basis of their attitudes. As for **language ideologies**, think of them for now as perceptions of languages and their uses that are constructed **in the interest of a specific group**. Again, speakers typically are not consciously aware that they even hold such ideologies, nor are they necessarily aware of the potential effects of such ideologies. But it seems that because ideologies refer especially to group interests, leaders are likely to make them the basis for mobilizing a group to action of any sort. So, in this sense, ideologies rise more easily to the level of consciousness.

5.2 Language attitudes vs. language ideologies

What unites studies of attitudes and ideologies is that they are both concerned with bringing to light evidence that not all linguistic varieties in any community are equally valued. Both types of studies recognize that the value of a variety depends on the value that mainstream society assigns to the main speakers of that variety. We will see that it's generally social psychologists and linguists who conduct studies of language attitudes while linguistic anthropologists are the main writers about language ideologies.

Attitudes and ideologies overlap in that they both consist of evaluations, but we will see below that what speakers conclude from these evaluations differ under the two categories. How they use these evaluations in the broader political arena also differs. And it may help to keep in mind **"attitudes as more unconscious assessments"** and **"ideologies as more constructed assessments"**. At the same time, we think you will see that whether particular events involving bilinguals are discussed under the rubric of language attitudes or ideologies depends a great deal on the particular theoretical stance of the author.

5.2.1 Attitudes

Students of attitudes are interested in how a person's language variety is socially meaningful to others. They focus on what makes a variety **socially diagnostic**. It is socially diagnostic if its use leads others to associate the speaker with a particular social group or set of activities. That is, *who* uses the variety and *where* it is used makes the difference. For example, studies look at a variety's value to its own speakers (e.g. is it used beyond the family?) and its value in the larger, dominant community in status-raising situations (e.g. is it used in official interactions with out-group members?). For example, if mainly relatively uneducated immigrants are the speakers of a language and it is not used in official interactions, such as Turkish in much of Western Europe, then someone who speaks Turkish there is assumed to be an uneducated immigrant (even though this speaker may be well educated and hold a professional job). Further, attitudinal research often shows how the valuations of the language of a group affect judgments of individuals in seeming unrelated ways (e.g. judgments of intelligence or trustworthiness).

5.2.2 Ideologies

Students of language ideologies focus more on competing ideologies in the same community and see them as "various representations of reality which are pitted against each other" (Blommaert, 1999a: 9). That is, the interest is still on the values that both in-group and out-group members place on a language variety, but more emphasis is placed on how real or fabricated differences in languages (their histories or who is most associated with speaking one as opposed to another) are exploited in the political arena. For example, part of the ideology in German-speaking Switzerland is that the local dialects of

German (*Schwyzertüütsch*), which are quite different from most other varieties of German, are "more down-to-earth, more honest, . . . more direct, and in general, more Swiss than standard German" (Watts, 1999: 74–5). Part of this ideology is to consider Standard German as the "first foreign language".

5.2.3 Language as identity

Both sets of writers, whether they are in the tradition of referring to "attitudes" or see themselves in the arena of "language ideologies", use the term **identity**. That is, exploring the nature of group identity and the role that language plays in symbolizing a positive or negative identity for a group is behind all these studies. And, of course, as a reader of this volume, you can understand how "language as identity" can be the most obvious outward sign of a group's **ethos**, the cover term for a group's disposition or character that we introduced at the beginning of this chapter.

5.2.4 Attitudes and ideologies: links with nationalism

We begin our discussion at the macro-level of groups and nation states where both attitudes and ideologies are tied up with notions of **nationalism**. Safran (1999: 78) defines nationalism as a politically mobilizing and state-seeking ideology. That is, a group that invokes the slogan of nationalism is looking for independent status (i.e. as a separate nation state).

The term "collective consciousness" that we used in reference to ethnicity is relevant here, too. And there is no doubt that language is an important part of the collective consciousness of any group. But there is no natural hierarchy that places language above religion, race, or territory as a marker of collective identity. Nor is it "natural" that a group will seek independent status on the basis of language or any other group-defining feature. But when it is seen as a defining symbol of a group, it often becomes a rallying symbol if the group mobilizes to promote various changes in its favor. That is, when a group mobilizes, politically generated collective consciousness can make the importance of "language rights" appear to be natural. (Such rights refer to granting various forms of official recognition to the group's language, such as its use in public schools and in interactions between group members and government officials.)

Of course, part of what makes this possible is that **language may be the most "visible" symbol of a group**. After all, it "appears" every time anyone speaks or writes. In addition, the instrumental importance of your language is also evident every day. That is, where your group's language is considered appropriate becomes an open or closed gate for your chances for socio-economic mobility. Language attitudes and ideologies may have an emotional basis, but even then, they almost always have **an instrumental basis** as well – just because you can't avoid speaking and the varieties you can use are admission tickets to membership in various groups.

Thus, because "language" is so "visible" and because it has this instrumental value, groups and even nation states can be easily persuaded to mobilize to protect or advance their language. Consider some current examples of how nations and groups react.

- France protects the use of French in many ways. In a later chapter we will refer to France's influence regarding the medium of communication used in the European Community, the multi-nation body that preceded the European Union (EU). But protective measures surface in everyday ways, even in the labeling of foodstuffs. French law requires that the labels of foodstuffs imported into France be written in French only. This is in opposition to the European Commission that forbids national regulations to impose a specific language for labeling foodstuffs without allowing the use of another language that could be easily understood by the consumer (Treaty and Directive 2000/13/EC). France has said it will revise its law (to include another language, one assumes) but the proposed amendment to the law still was not adopted as of late 2002).
- Minority groups within a nation state agitate for various types of official status for their languages. In response to such pressure, the Swedish parliament passed legislation affecting a number of northern municipalities. From 2002 onwards, Finnish, Meänkiele, and Saami became official for possible use in local administration and certain functions, such as care of the elderly and children in these areas. (Finnish, of course, is a well-known language as the main language of Finland and the L1 of a sizeable number of Finnish immigrants to Sweden. The other two languages are less well known: Meänkiele is the language of Tornedalians, a group of Finns who remained on the Swedish side when the Swedish-Russian border was drawn in 1809; and Saami is the language of the peoples who were formerly called Lapps.)
- Consider a final example. In Moldova, formerly part of the USSR, the education minister was removed in 2002 because he planned to require schoolchildren to learn Russian. The plan brought unruly street protests from thousands of people. The protesters said that such a plan would erode cultural ties with neighboring Romania and tug Moldova back into Moscow's orbit.

Nevertheless, it is problematic whether a group will assert "language rights" and what they will mean in regard to official actions. The point we are trying to make is that **"rights" to a nation state based on language** are "imagined" rights in a way similar to the notion that nation states are "imagined communities" (Anderson, 1983, cited in Billig, 1995). (Anderson's use of this term referred to the notion that communities are claimed to "exist", even though there is no community in the sense that all supposed members have met, or even seen, the other members.) The notion that nation states can be "imagined" means that we can't predict where state boundaries will be drawn and when, or why. And when they are drawn, they are not "natural" in any primordial sense.

In addition, we can't predict when language will be a major ingredient in the call for a new nation state or what the end result will be. If "language rights" were the sufficient reason to create new nation states, there would be several thousand of them, rather than the existing approximately 200. Safran (1999) cites examples of different outcomes. Croatian nationalism, based on a combination of socio-economic resentments and religious differences, led Croatians to put renewed stress on language differences. They proclaimed Croatia a nation state in 1991 (separate from Serbia), leading to its recognition by the European Union in 1992.

But certainly not all speakers of one language are in the same nation state. The Middle East presents a different picture regarding language. Arabic is the classic vehicle in which Islam, a major ingredient in Arab nationalism, is expressed. But speaking a common language does not translate into a common nation in the Middle East. If it did, there would not be separate Arabic-speaking nations in the Middle East.

Safran also points out other nation states in which having a common language is not a major concern; what holds them together is something else. He argues that "[I]t is money that holds multilingual states such as Switzerland and Singapore together; it is economic interest, as well as tradition, that holds the United Kingdom and Spain together; and it is religion and common historical experiences that hold Jews together. The nationalisms of Pakistan, Israel, and (in part) Ireland, Sri Lanka, and Poland are based not (or not only) on language but on religion" (p. 81).

Some writers about nationalism see a reciprocal relation between nation states and having a single, dominant language. This is so to an extent. Certainly, a pre-existing dominant language facilitates the creation of a state. And its presence also can promote national integration. But, as a whole, the language itself benefits more than the state when it is the main language. Generally, **the state bestows legitimacy on a language** and also aids in its development. In fact, the state can help transform a dialect into a language. (That is, a variety can start out as one of a number of related varieties, and therefore be a dialect of a language, but if the state uses that dialect in spoken and written official business and proclaims it to be the official language, then the dialect becomes a language in the eyes of that state and usually the rest of the world, too.)

This is what happened with Slovak in Slovakia recently, with Bahasa Indonesia in Indonesia, and with Malay in Malaysia, and it's what has happened many times over around the world. What is important to note is that as one particular language receives official status (i.e. receives the mantle of legitimacy), almost always becoming the sole language of public administration and instruction, the role of *other* languages is arrested. And of course their status is diminished. In a later chapter, we'll discuss language policies further, but here we hope you can see already how language attitudes and ideologies both are forces (causes) in setting official policies and also are the effect of such policies.

5.3 Power and the economy of language

On both a societal and an interpersonal level, the languages that a person is able to speak are an index of that person's position in society. A number of researchers, most prominently Pierre Bourdieu (1982; 1991), have written about a person's linguistic repertoire as a source of **symbolic power**. A key concept for Bourdieu is that of *habitus*. The term is very old, but Bourdieu uses it for a set of "dispositions". These dispositions generate practices and attitudes that are very much like norms, because without being consciously coordinated, they incline individuals to act and react in similar ways in daily life in line with the social conditions in which they were raised.

As applied to the concept of the **linguistic marketplace**, the idea of dispositions refers to the relationships that speakers establish – generally unconsciously – between the "value" of a linguistic variety and other "products" (other linguistic varieties) offered in the same market at the same time. Don't think of the linguistic market so much as a place; it is rather a metaphor for the figurative location in which speakers interact. It may represent a place, too, but its existence doesn't depend on a set location any more than the "financial market" does. (There is a financial market whether or not there is a specific (single) stock exchange building.)

The key to understanding the linguistic market is to understand that it is "where" power relations are expressed. Those controlling the linguistic varieties that are most valued have more power or more **symbolic capital** in this market than others controlling varieties of lesser value in the market. So the market shapes the **symbolic value** of different ways of speaking; therefore, speakers of different language varieties possess different quantities of **linguistic or symbolic capital**. The value of a language variety as an "asset" is related to other forms of capital associated with the specific variety in question (economic capital, cultural capital). Altogether, these forms of capital define the place of an individual in social "space" (i.e., the person who speaks that specific variety).

For those speakers with power and prestige (because of other features of their lives) and for those others who have the ability to speak more than one variety, the choices that speakers make reflect what languages are most valued in the linguistic market. How do we know this is so? Because speakers are looking for **symbolic profit**, and they choose the variety they speak with this in mind. Just as important, current choices help to create *future* value for a language variety (depending on who chooses to use the variety, people of power and prestige in the community or not).

We will see that especially writers about language ideologies make use of Bourdieu's framework and his vocabulary. But the basic ideas apply to the discussion of attitudes as well. The difference is a matter of where emphasis is placed and the conclusions that are drawn. All writers on both attitudes and ideologies would agree with Bourdieu's main position and this is that language is not only the medium for expressing ideas, but also the medium for expressing evaluations across groups and therefore for expressing power.

5.4 How languages identify groups

We begin the discussion not with studies that explicitly refer to either attitudes or ideologies, but with studies that straddle the line. These are studies in which the authors typically refer to the attitudes about **group identity** that are behind various actions, but group ideologies about expected language choices clearly underlie the attitudes and actions.

Recently, and specifically in regard to language policy, whether there are two ways of viewing ideologies about identity has become a topic. John Myhill raises the issue, arguing that one ideology is what he calls *language-and-identity* and the other is an ideology of *language-and-territory* (Myhill, 1999). He argues that the ideology based on identity is more an emotional connection with language, while an ideology based on territory means that its proponents argue that in each territory, only one particular language "should be the one used in public circumstances and intergroup communication" (p. 34). Further, the implicit view under the territorial argument is often that "whoever got there first" (or, who among immigrants got there first) has inherent rights in any competition between languages. However, David Atkinson responds to Myhill citing the case of Catalonia (in Spain). He argues that *both* types of ideologies about identity can be salient at the same time, as they are among Catalonians, who value their L1 (Catalan) in both ways (Atkinson, 2000). This side of ideologies and identity is not developed here, but keep it in mind when we consider language policies in chapter 12.

5.4.1 An example of identity decisions in projecting a persona

In Tunisia, learning languages, or the "right variety"of a language, is at stake for anglophone wives **(women whose L1 is English) who have married Tunisian nationals**. Walters (1996) discusses the dilemmas of this particular group of immigrant wives in Tunisian society. Although there are features about social identity, power, and language in Tunisia that may be specific only to Arabic-based societies, many of the issues this study raises about identity decisions exist for "outsiders" in any nation. Your gender makes a big difference in the struggle for power in Tunisia's male-dominated society. Colonial history (Tunisia was a French colony) also affects current practices and perceptions to an extent because it gives the colonial language (French) a special status. But such issues as gender inequality and history are at issue in the many other nations, too.

The personal goals anglophone wives have to consider in Tunisia make it clear that different languages can have equally positive connotations; even in Bourdieu's linguistic marketplace it is not always a matter of one language outweighing the other. So these wives operate in a double bind: (1) They possess a good deal of "linguistic capital" because they command English and often also French, both recognized and valued as international languages. Just being able to speak English or French earns clear value in the Tunisian marketplace for these wives. (2) But the entrée into their husbands' families and most facets of Tunisian society is being able to speak Tunisian Arabic (TA), the national variety of spoken Arabic. But this isn't so easy to do. For a myriad of reasons, from the fact that Arabic grammar is very different from that of European languages to a lack of willing teachers, it is difficult for anglophone wives to learn TA. For example, husbands seem ambivalent about helping their wives learn TA. Or, they may not seem able to do so: Even if they may teach or have taught at the university level, they are not trained language teachers.

Further, in general, the behavior of the highly educated Tunisians with whom these wives interact is often a mixture of politeness and expediency. In the name of politeness, they don't correct errors that these wives make in TA. But the effect of this is that the wives don't become better speakers of TA and just keep making the same errors. So otherwise intelligent wives who may reflect badly on their husbands with their "kitchen Arabic" are discouraged from trying to speak TA. In the name of expediency, husbands and other educated Tunisians prefer to switch to English or French to converse with these wives, because these are languages that both speakers know well.

The situation in Tunisia is similar to that in other cultures for persons from outside the culture. Not speaking the local language means a person is perceived by others in a certain way; speaking the local language changes perceptions. But either choice has both potentially positive and negative outcomes. One anglophone wife commented that knowledge of TA by an anglophone wife might be a threat to some Tunisians because it would give her access to interactions that would otherwise be closed to her. Walters comments, "For the couple it would mean renegotiating relationships in the marriage, in the nuclear and extended family, and in the society at large" (p. 543).

Walters's conclusion has general applications: As the choices of these women illustrate, speakers have choices; but their choices "can never be neutral, because they occur within the context of pre-existing social structures. Likewise, power comes in many forms, and relative or apparent powerlessness in some situations may translate into great power in others" (p. 549).

5.4.2 How advertisements construct identity

Piller (2001) looks at the role the media play in identity construction. Her subject is **multilingual advertisements in Germany**, where she reports that from 60% to 70% of all advertisements on various television networks and in two national newspapers in a two-week period in 1999 were multilingual. In the corpus of 658 TV commercials, German, understandably, was most frequently used. But in 70% of the ads English was included, followed by French (8%), Italian (6%), and a number of other languages.

The content of the ads points to the conclusion that multilingualism is part of a prestige identity that German advertising projects. Piller comments that the implied reader of bilingual advertisements is often someone who wants to shape the future, with ads often making overt references to the future. For example, TV commercials may have such messages in English as "The Future in Metal" (Corus) or "In Touch with Tomorrow" (Toshiba). Other parts of the implied identity of consumers of multilingual advertisements is that they take a world, not a local, perspective. In addition, they are sophisticated and also oriented to having fun.

The body of most commercials was in German, but the commercial might end with slogans partly in another language, with that part printed on the screen while it is spoken by the voice-over. An example of a typical ending is this one: "Deutsche Börse. We provide access".

Even though most bilingual advertisements imply a male reader, the implied relationship between bilingualism and maleness is not the right conclusion. There are fashion ads that feature women, but a particular kind of woman, those who "dress for professional success". Thus, the relationship with bilingualism depends on the other characteristics of the implied reader beyond strictly maleness, although it is more often men than women who meet the image of "a business executive who identifies with an international environment".

At the same time, Piller also points out that some non-profit organizations produce ads that are implicitly or explicitly critical of the lifestyle that the use of English implies. For example, in one ad the headline says *rush hour = Rasche aua*, with the equal sign formed by two strips of bandage. *Rasche aua* means 'quick ouch'. The organization sponsoring this ad promotes bicycle use as an environmentally friendly alternative to cars; the implication of the ad is that there are too many cars at rush hour and this is an unwelcome feature of the modern (bilingual) world.

In conclusion Piller notes that in bilingual advertisements, German does the work of providing factual information, while the L2 (often English) does the symbolic work of providing stereotypical associations that Germans have with the cultures where the L2 is spoken. In urging readers to perceive their lives in a particular way, or aspire to such a life, these bilingual ads in Germany are an example of how bilingualism itself has a role in identity formation.

In many other countries, foreign words, especially English words, occur in advertisements, sometimes in monolingual ads, but sometimes in patterns of codeswitching (Martin, 2002a). As you might expect, the use of English seems to symbolize modernity and technology, but it also symbolizes the universalism of what it advertises, "giving the targeted audience **the impression that the product is being used worldwide** and that consumers in every country on the planet consider it to be essential to their everyday existence" (cf. Martin, 2002b: 19).

Writing about English in advertisements in the French-speaking part of Switzerland, Cheshire and Moser (1994) take the argument about universalism even further. They argue that in Switzerland, English is not seen as external to the country. They see English used "in **advertisements to present an image of the Swiss to the Swiss** . . . that symbolises the favourable image held by foreigners" (p. 468). For example, they counted almost an equal number of ads for Swiss watches in English (21) as those not using English (24).

5.4.3 Constructing a national identity

Lebanon occupies an unusual position in the Middle East, geographically, politically, and culturally. Most notably, it is the only Middle East nation with a large Christian population. Since its creation in the 1920s, Lebanese leaders and intellectuals have argued over **Lebanon's identity: Is it "Arab" or "Lebanese"?** Even the Lebanese constitution, written in 1943, does not take a firm stand; it states *lubanaan duu wajh 'arabii* translated as "Lebanon [is a country that] has an Arabic face/character" (Al Batal, 2002: 94). Most Moslem Lebanese and some Christian Lebanese see Lebanon as an Arabic country, but others, mainly Maronite Christians, view the country as something else. Those who stress Lebanon's Arab ties symbolize this identity by favoring a variety of Arabic (*"fusha"*) used elsewhere in the Arabic world largely only for formal topics and situations. But on the other side, some claim that the distinctly Lebanese colloquial variety (LC) is what reflects a Lebanese identity. In addition, those asserting a distinctly Lebanese identity also use a great deal of French, especially the Maronite Christians but also some of the Moslem elite. They view the emphasis on LC and French as evidence of Lebanon's close ties with Western culture and thought. (Both French and English were introduced by Christian missionaries in the second half of the nineteenth century and Lebanon was under a French mandate from 1925 to 1943.)

News broadcasts on the largest TV station in Lebanon reflect the conflict between the two national identities of Lebanon. Broadcasts begin with the headline news and local (Lebanese) news briefs in the formal variety of Arabic that is used elsewhere in the Arabic world for TV news. But then when on-location reports begin, the language shifts from a pure formal variety to a composite of the formal and the colloquial (LC) variety. This mix is used only during Lebanese national news, not for Arab or international news.

This station obviously straddles the identity question in various ways. First, it recently added "international" to its name (Lebanese Broadcasting Corporation International or LBCI). Also, as if reflecting this name change, it has a number of programs using French and English in order to appeal to some upper-class Lebanese. However, all this is done while "emphasizing all things Lebanese, including the Lebanese dialect, which now has a strong presence in almost every program at LBCI" (Al Batal, 2002: 93).

The LBCI language variety is not the same as what has been called by some Educated Spoken Arabic or Modern Standard Arabic. That variety draws more on a regional colloquial variety as its grammatical base (i.e. it varies from country to country in the Middle East), with insertions of more formal words from formal (Classical) Arabic. That is, in broadcasts elsewhere, the local colloquial variety is the source of the grammatical frame, but with many pan-Arabic words inserted (from Educated Spoken Arabic). In contrast, the LBCI variety has a strong *fusha* (formal Arabic) base, with Lebanese Colloquial (LC) features and words inserted into it.

Thus, the grammatical frame into which words are inserted is fairly different because it comes from LC. This makes the LBCI variety sound "more Lebanese" because of all the Lebanese words in it. Also, while Educated Spoken Arabic is just that (it is only spoken), the LBCI variety has a "scripted" nature because reporters often write it and then read from their notes in the broadcast. In this way, the LBCI variety manages to have both the formal nature expected of TV broadcasts across the Middle East, and also a spontaneous (Lebanese) quality.

Al Batal concludes that the choice of this LBCI language variety is a compromise, making it *daat wajh lubnaanii* **"[a language that] has a Lebanese face"** (p. 112). In this way, linguistic tensions are "managed" in order to meet competing needs. It would be unthinkable in the Arabic world, even in Lebanon, not to have formal Arabic in a news broadcast. But using this LBCI variety for local news gives the broadcasts the desired Lebanese flavor. However, this variety serves an economic purpose, too. With a grammar from the formal base that is known by educated persons everywhere in the Middle East, such broadcasts are possibly more comprehensible to audiences in the rest of the Arabic world than broadcasts in other countries (because they have a local grammatical base). The station's broadcasters have used this compromise variety for the last fifteen years, but recently, via the new LBCI Satellite Channel, these broadcasts are going beyond Lebanon's borders.

5.4.4 Ideologies and African-American English in the US

Winford (2003b) discusses ways of looking at the language variety that many African-Americans speak as an indication of the ideology that other (white) Americans have in regard to African-American people. Linguists call this variety

African American Vernacular English (AAVE) and most consider it one of the dialects of American English, but a variety that has a number of distinctive grammatical features.

The **ideologies about African-Americans themselves** are reflected in views about this language variety. Some scholarly attempts to study the history of AAVE contribute to a negative bias toward the variety by arguing that AAVE largely shows continuities from various British English dialects. This view, and the attitude of the average American, deny a distinctive history for African-Americans and a legitimacy for their culture. Many African-Americans are well aware of the social advantages of Standard American English in any linguistic marketplace, but at the same time, AAVE is "an expression of community membership and solidarity across class lines" (p. 30).

5.5 Language attitudes

We turn now to discuss the types of study that consider language attitudes more specifically as attitudes. Attitudes can be defined as **subjective evaluations** of both language varieties and their speakers, whether the attitudes are held by individuals or by groups. This may be another way that they contrast with ideologies. You know that an evaluation is a judgment that fixes the value or weight of something. If that evaluation is subjective, this means that it is an opinion and therefore the value it fixes does not have an objective basis. In contrast, ideologies are more often closely related to a factual base, such as that language X is the sole official language used in the schools. This doesn't mean facts aren't involved in attitudes, but does mean that the evaluation itself isn't directly based on facts.

For example, facts may show that speakers of a certain language (or dialect) are primarily persons of high socio-economic status. But to judge their language as superior (e.g. "clearer", "more logical") to other languages spoken in the same community has no direct factual basis. Yet, many times community members place a high value on the linguistic varieties spoken by persons of high socio-economic status and a low value on those varieties spoken by persons of lower status. You can say that such attitudes are unfair, but in every community speakers come up with such judgments. Almost always, these subjective evaluations are based on the characteristics of the speakers of the linguistic varieties.

But the important point for us to notice in this chapter is that such evaluations are attached to the varieties, too, not just to the persons who habitually speak them. And evaluations make a difference in whether people will make an effort to learn certain languages, as well as in their attitudes. For example, people who don't speak certain languages as their L1 typically make an effort to learn to speak certain languages, but they ignore others. For example, in San Antonio, Texas, not as many English-speakers make an effort to learn Spanish as the Spanish-speaking immigrants from Central and South America make an effort to learn English.

5.5.1 How attitudes arise

Social psychologists tell us that a major motivation for holding attitudes is that people strive for positive self-esteem and this esteem is established at least in part through comparisons with others and their groups. Clearly, holding attitudes involves categorization of individuals, both self-categorizations and categorization of others. One way of improving self-esteem is to compare yourself to other individuals. But everyone also makes classifications based on his or her in-group in comparison with relevant out-groups. Social psychologists talk about the need for both distinctiveness (i.e. differentiation) of the self, and inclusion of the self into larger groups (Hogg and Abrams, 1993). These needs are the source of attitudes (i.e. evaluations) toward others and, ultimately, of ideologies that may be used to mobilize one's group in opposition to the "other". As we have argued in earlier chapters, because language is such an omnipresent group marker, making comparisons of the status of your group's language with that of other groups' languages is a readily available way to give our group cohesion and distinguish it from other groups.

Just as we make comparisons with other groups, we should recognize that in the eyes of others, the identity that they attach to our group is the identity they attach to us. As John Edwards (1999: 103) notes, "people are evaluated in terms of characteristics that, in a broad-brush sort of way, reflect perceptions of the group to which they seem to belong. The implication is obvious: *individuals* – **with all their personal strengths and weaknesses – are viewed in stereotypical *group* terms**."

5.5.2 How do attitudes evolve and how do they matter?

Political and socio-economic forces can change community attitudes toward language varieties and motivate learning a second language that has gained prestige among the powerful persons in the larger nation state. As you can imagine, studies have shown that individuals prefer to speak language varieties that are associated with the members of high-status groups. So, if speaking a particular language variety seems to be one qualification for joining a high-status group (and the individuals in question have other qualifications, such as education, and can see that mobility is an option in the society where they live), people will learn and use that variety. The quest for mobility is typically reflected linguistically in this way.

This is what has happened in the case of both **the standard dialect of Chinese, Putonghua, and Cantonese in southern China**. Both are gaining speakers among migrants to Guangzhou, the capital of Guang Dong Province (Miao,

2001). Putonghua has been the national standard variety of Chinese since the 1950s, but it wasn't widely used until recently. And remember that many of the so-called dialects of Chinese are different enough from each other to be called different languages. For this reason, it isn't as easy for all Chinese citizens to learn to speak Putonghua as it may be to learn or at least understand the standard dialect in your country. This is especially the case in the south of China because Putonghua is based on a northern dialect of Chinese.

Cantonese, one of the main southern Chinese varieties, is the L1 of many people in Guang Dong province, as well as in neighboring Hong Kong. Cantonese is very different from Putonghua. In fact, Yuling Pan (2000: 22) states, "In terms of phonological, lexical, and syntactic features, Putonghua and Cantonese are as different as two languages like Italian and English." Certainly, for a Cantonese speaker to learn Putonghua amounts to having to become bilingual.

Thus, one reason why Putonghua wasn't widespread in Guangzhou is that it is not easy to learn. This is so not only for the natives of Guangzhou, but also for migrants from the neighboring areas who speak a native dialect closer to Cantonese than Putonghua. In addition, the rural migrants often share more than their language variety with Guangzhou residents; as fellow southern Chinese, they share more cultural values with Guangzhou than with the north (and Putonghua speakers there).

But there is another reason why Putonghua wasn't widespread until recently and remains in competition with Cantonese. First, consider the socio-economic prestige of Guangzhou City (formerly called Canton). Guangzhou has an exceptionally strong economy compared with most other areas in China and a good deal of local pride for this reason. The only other Chinese city where a local dialect rivals the prestige and use of Putonghua is Shanghai, also an industrial center (and also in the south). In both places the local dialects are common even in official settings. Guangzhou's industrial success has attracted short-term rural migrants who have been more loyal to their local capital than to the nation as a whole because economic advantages have come largely through local connections.

But, in addition, Guangzhou has also attracted more urban-based migrants who come to Guangzhou after graduation. (This generally "urban to urban" movement is allowed under a government provision for migration to "seek employment after graduation".) These more educated migrants are more likely to know Putonghua than Cantonese. At the same time, the central government is strongly encouraging the spread of Putonghua in general. The kind of jobs these better-educated migrants hold down require a good deal of inter-group communication, much more so than the factory jobs of the rural short-term migrants where not so much interaction is necessary.

Thus, these new migrants and the growing use of Putonghua across the nation and in other places result in more use of Putonghua in at least some of the more powerful circles in Guangzhou. (The proximity of Hong Kong, which was transferred from British control to China in 1997 and where Putonghua is now encouraged as a replacement for English in many areas, also is important in raising the use of Putonghua in neighboring Guangzhou.)

5.5.3 If you can't change national boundaries, change attitudes

If the boundaries of groups are rigid and therefore it is difficult for non-dominant group members to take advantage of possibilities for socio-economic mobility that the dominant group enjoys, then a less dominant group may do one or both of two things: (1) either engage in inter-group competition regarding the relative recognized statuses of the groups or (2) engage in creative strategies to enhance the low-status group's image.

Various forms of inter-group competition initiated by the French have marked English–French relations in Canada since the 1960s, especially where the French in Québec Province are involved. Everywhere, conflicts over official use of languages in the schools and in other official venues are examples of inter-group competition. For example, recently in Britain there have been at least occasional calls to add the languages of such immigrant groups (e.g. Punjabi or a West African language) to official choices for study of a second language.

More often than may be realized, groups use **various creative strategies to enhance the value of their languages**. One strategy a group may use is to draw attention to its literary or other universally valued tradition (or even invent such a tradition). Nations have been known to invent noble pasts, complete with invented royalty. Such strategies figured when Denmark, Norway, and Sweden sought to distinguish their nations and the three mutually intelligible Scandinavian varieties they speak as three separate languages (Norwegian, Swedish, and Danish).

A strategy employed in Uganda in the 1990s was **to "invent" a language** (Bernsten, 1998). This language, Runyankitara, is emerging through a realignment of four western Bantu varieties. In the colonial period, these varieties became considered as separate languages in large part through the efforts of competing missionaries. Each missionary group established a separate orthography for the one of the four mutually intelligible varieties in its area. The four, from north to south, are Runyoro, Rutooro, Runyankore, and Rukiga. In the 1990s movements to amalgamate them began, and Runyankitara was born. Some of its advocates are instructors at Uganda's Makerere University, who are speakers of these varieties, and they managed to get courses in Runyankitara added as an option in the university's offerings.

In many ways, the creation of this new language is a reflection of the Western Bantu speakers' resistance to the role of Luganda in government policies. Like Runyankitara, Luganda is a Bantu language. Luganda has had a privileged place as the most prestigious indigenous language in Uganda since colonial days under the British. The rise of Runyankitara (as a combination of what previously were four separate languages) challenges Luganda's position as the

Ugandan Bantu language with the most speakers. Of course any challenge to the place of Luganda also is directed against the economic and political power of Luganda's speakers, the Baganda.

5.6 Theoretical models and the expressions of attitudes

In this section, we begin a discussion of how individuals negotiate their way through everyday interactions by selecting among the linguistic varieties they know. They do this against the backdrop of the different values that different languages have in the linguistic marketplace and the unconscious recognition that different linguistic practices are marks of social identity. In this chapter, we only discuss those models and studies that most directly have to do with expressions of attitudes directed more toward groups than toward negotiating interactions with individuals. These are models most associated with social psychologists. In the next chapter, we devote much more attention to choices in interpersonal interactions, choices, admittedly, that can hardly not involve attitudes or ideologies.

We look at language attitudes across groups through three models developed by social psychologists. When we wrote about language maintenance and shift in chapter 4, we introduced the first model, **ethnolinguistic vitality**. The basic idea behind this model is that researchers can predict whether a group will maintain its language on the basis of measurements of a group's attitudes about itself. A second model is implied in the **matched guise test**. This is a test conducted under experimental conditions (in a laboratory, not in everyday situations) that claims to measure the attitudes that test subjects hold about speakers of the languages used by speakers in the experiment. The idea is that the attitudes that subjects express in the experiment reflect attitudes that are held by people in general in the community. Finally, we consider a third model, **Communication Accommodation Theory**, as it applies to groups. This theory used to be called Speech Accommodation Theory. And for convenience, we'll just call it **Accommodation Theory**.

5.6.1 Ethnolinguistic vitality

Ethnolinguistic vitality was introduced more than 25 years ago as an umbrella to explain why groups maintain or shift from their languages (Giles, Bourhis, and Taylor, 1977). They formalized their ideas as **ethnolinguistic identity theory**. Up until today, ethnolinguistic vitality is the construct most often used in discussions of the attitudes of groups toward how their own language is holding up in competition with other languages in the community. The basic notion is that ethnolinguistic vitality has a cognitive basis. That is, ethnolinguistic vitality refers to the mental image that a group has of itself, and the assumption is that groups with little ethnolinguistic vitality are likely to disappear as entities, while those with high ethnolinguistic vitality are likely to survive, and even thrive, as groups.

Two notions of this vitality developed, one based on objective measures (things that can be counted) and the other on more subjective measures (attitudes). But under both types of vitality, status depends on comparisons that a group makes between itself and other groups.

5.6.1.1 Objective ethnolinguistic vitality

Researchers "operationalized" ethnolinguistic vitality by arguing that the extent to which a group has a positive ethnolinguistic identity can be measured with various objective factors. These factors include such measures as the size of the group in a given territory, institutional support (e.g. support in the schools, official interactions), and the number and type of domains in which the group's language is used.

Obvious examples of languages showing low vitality are those that have small numbers of speakers and little or no community support system or much, if any, official support. These include many indigenous languages in parts of Central and South America, especially those with small numbers of speakers and little or no official support. (Official support includes such practices as using a language as a medium of instruction in schools, giving it status in the courts, etc.)

In contrast, consider two examples showing strong vitality. First we look at Korean as spoken by Korean immigrants in the United States as a case showing a specialized vitality and then look at Welsh in Wales as a case showing a widespread vitality.

5.6.1.1.1 Korean vitality in the United States

Even though there are many Korean immigrants living in the United States, the Korean language has little "presence" in the lives of the average American. Few Americans even hear it spoken and wouldn't recognize it (as Korean) if they did hear it. Further, Korean has little official standing; that is, it isn't used in government offices, street signs aren't in Korean, etc. Certainly, it is not used in public interactions, nor do Koreans expect non-Koreans to show an interest in learning it.

But at least in the larger urban areas where there are large Korean communities, **Korean definitely has vitality in the lives of Koreans**. In these areas, speakers have a number of support groups (e.g. Saturday school to teach Korean to the community's children, Korean churches with large memberships). Further, in these same urban areas (e.g. New York, Chicago, and parts of California), Korean is a subject in some high schools and in some elementary schools. In 1988, Korean was studied by 2,000 students. Korean is even one of the languages that can be chosen on the second part of the Scholastic Assessment Test (SAT II). A number of foreign languages fall in one of the five general subject areas on SAT II. In 2001, over 3,000 students applied to take the Korean test. Factors such as these increase the vitality of any language.

Why all this vitality? Doesn't the normal "third-generation rule" apply to Korean immigrants? As you'll remember, by the third generation, children in many immigrant families no longer speak the L1 of their parents. How does it happen that third-generation Korean-Americans speak Korean, and why? First, if they don't learn it at home as small children, at least some Korean-Americans are choosing to study Korean in high schools in at least nine states. Where will they use it? There are a number of Korean businesses with offices in New York (or other American cities) and in Korea itself that want to hire graduates who are bilingual in Korean and English. Such graduates would live, at least for a time, in either the US or Korea. Korea is basically a monolingual nation, but it has a formidable place in the world's economic markets. Thus, we see that a language that we would expect to die out in the US really has quite a bit of vitality, but a specialized vitality.

5.6.1.1.2 Welsh vitality in the United Kingdom

While Welsh in Wales (in the west of Great Britain) does not have a totally secure future, it now has **an established support system** that is the sort that leads to strong positive ethnolinguistic vitality and a "presence" in the British Isles that cannot be denied. Welsh was spoken in Wales before the Anglo-Saxons arrived in the British Isles. Gradually it was used less and less, but there was a revival in the mid-nineteenth century when the Welsh national anthem was written. In the aftermath of World War I and the Great Depression (mainly the 1930s) in the twentieth century, Welsh almost died out. But a Welsh Language Society was formed in these years, agitating in various ways for recognition of Welsh as a legitimate language in Wales. Finally, the Welsh Office was established as a separate government department in the United Kingdom in 1964 and in 1970 responsibility for primary and secondary education was transferred to the Welsh Office.

Since then, involvement of the schools and the media has sparked a true revival. The Welsh schools movement is especially vigorous in the primarily Welsh-speaking non-industrial areas. Today there should be enough bilingual primary schools (Welsh and English) available to allow parents the choice of a main language with the other language also used. In secondary schools, Welsh is taught as a second language where English is the main medium of instruction. Overall, local control prevails and each county fine-tunes its policy to fit its needs. Also, the Welsh Language Act of 1967 gave Welsh "equal validity" with English in legal proceedings in Wales. Wales receives national radio and television broadcasts in Welsh. The rise in popularity of Celtic (Welsh is a Celtic language) music affected youth sentiment, too. Today, while Korean in the US is somewhat invisible to non-Koreans, Welsh is very visible in Britain and beyond.

5.6.1.2 *Subjective ethnolinguistic vitality*

When subjective ethnolinguistic vitality is studied, the emphasis is on a group's perceived status and this status may differ from the status that would be based on actual conditions. Various researchers have developed Subjective Vitality Questionnaires. These seek to measure group member perceptions about the status of their group in relation to other groups. Some of the questions have to do with objective measures (such as institutional support), but the questions ask what measures the speakers *think* exist; they don't actually consider what the measures *are*.

Bourhis and Sachdev (1984) discuss group attitudes in terms of such ethnolinguistic vitality. Allard and Landry (e.g. Allard and Landry, 1992) have their own measures that include ways to assess beliefs about what a group thinks that its legitimate vitality should be as well as what it thinks about its future vitality. Many of the first studies dealt with French-English relations in Canada, but today everything about vitality among groups – whether they are indigenous or immigrants – all over the globe are studied.

5.6.2 Matched guise tests

When Wallace Lambert developed **the matched guise test** in the 1960s, his object was to study inter-ethnic attitudes in Montreal (where he taught). His research question was, how do French and English Canadians (francophones and anglophones) view each other? He believed that public statements and replies to questionnaires about this issue did not get at the views that people really held. The premise of the studies he and his associates did (and the premise behind the many later studies done employing this test) is that hearing a person speaking language X will trigger an expression of the attitudes a judge has about speakers of language X. The attitudes studied refer to both abilities (e.g. competent), attributes (e.g. educated) and personality traits (e.g. friendly, loyal, ambitious).

The "trick" in these studies is that the judge hears the same person speaking the two different languages under study (i.e. the person has a "guise" or "false appearance" as only a speaker of language X when, in fact, he or she also is heard speaking language Y). The recordings of the same person in the two guises are interspersed with other recordings so that the judges will not realize they are hearing the same person twice. In the initial experiments, judges thought they were hearing an anglophone Canadian speaking English and a francophone Canadian speaking French.

After hearing the speakers, the judges rate the speakers along a number of dimensions, as mentioned above. That is, the study is supposed to test the judges' privately held attitudes about speakers of two different language varieties spoken in the same community. In Lambert's initial study the anglophone Canadians rated the same speaker in the anglophone version more favorably on half of the traits, including abilities and attributes such as "intelligent" and "educated". This study was done at a time when French Canadians were just beginning to assert the value of their group and eventually demand special rights, especially in Québec. For this reason, it's not surprising that the francophone judges not only went along with the anglophone judges in rating the anglophone version very favorably on a number of traits, but they actually favored the anglophone on ten out of the 14 traits.

A major theoretical value of the matched guise technique is that the initial study, but also most further studies around the world, show that judgments cluster around two sets of traits: **(high) status** and **solidarity**. In some cases, judges rate the voice that is associated with their own group favorably regarding the solidarity traits, but in all studies the judges consistently rate more favorably on the ability and attribute traits the voice associated with the language variety spoken by people with power and prestige in the society. That is, there is a split between the types of attitudes judges hold about speakers from different groups. In-group speakers may be rated as "honest" or "friendly", but out-group speakers (if they are from the group dominating in high-status positions) are rated as "educated" and"competent".

5.6.2.1 *Matched guise tests and inter-group attitudes*

More of the studies that followed Lambert's initial work looked more at differences in judgments about dialects of the same language than at different ratings for different languages. One study using the matched guise technique that does deal with different languages is that by Woolard and Gahng (1990) of **changing cross-group attitudes in Barcelona**, the capital of the Catalonian autonomous region of Spain. Recall from our earlier references to Barcelona that Catalan, a language closely related to Castilian (the standard dialect of Spanish), is the local language. Under the regime of Franco (1939–75), Catalan was repressed. Further, the Spanish Constitution of 1978 obliges all citizens to know Castilian. But later, the Catalan language became co-official with Castilian in Catalonia under a Statute of Autonomy, and in 1983, the Catalan Parliament passed a law establishing full co-official use of Catalan in a wide number of public uses. For example, Catalan is now the medium of instruction in at least some subjects in many schools and teachers are officially required to know both Castilian and Catalan.

Woolard and Gahng repeated their 1980 study in 1987 to see if all these changes in official policy (and therefore presumably the increase in knowledge and use of Catalan) affected attitudes toward a Catalan speaker. They used the "matched guise" format with the same stimulus tape recording in both studies. Four young women, two Catalan-dominant and two Castilian-dominant, each read a text of about one minute, once in Catalan and once in Castilian. Respondents evaluated the speakers, but were unaware they were hearing the same speaker in both languages.

The listeners were secondary school students (N=276 in 1987 and slightly fewer in 1980). They included both male and female and reflected a range of social classes; most were natives of Catalonia, but their parents were not necessarily born there. According to the language they used at home, listeners were classed as either Catalan or Castilian speakers or as bilinguals.

Listeners rated the speakers on 14 personal traits that the authors classified in terms of two factors, Solidarity and Status. Ratings under Solidarity included "likeable" and "generous", and those under Status included "intelligent" and "leader-like".

In a comparison of the data of 1987 and 1980, the most interesting findings are those on the Solidarity dimension because the language used had little effect on the Status dimension. Both times, the Catalan version rated higher in regard to Status. This is not a surprise because Catalonia is a major industrial center and has a higher standard of living than most other parts of Spain. In contrast to Catalan speakers, Castilian speakers in Catalonia are typically immigrants who hold skilled and semiskilled jobs.

In regard to the Solidarity dimension, patterns did change. True, listeners still gave the highest scores on the Solidarity factor to speakers using their own common in-group language, especially the girls. But, as Woolard and Gahng note, "there has been a loosening of the bond between the Catalan language and native Catalan ethnolinguistic identity. It no longer matters so much to Catalans *who* speaks Catalan, but rather simply that it is spoken" (1990: 326). Also, the responses from Castilian-dominant listeners indicated that speaking Catalan in Barcelona was not just for Catalan natives anymore. When Castilian listeners heard someone who was clearly Castilian-dominant (obvious from the pronunciation), but speaking Catalan, they did not penalize the speaker with lower ratings on Solidarity. This indicates that by 1987, **Catalan had lost its label as an ethnic language reserved for Catalan natives**. As the authors put it, "in 1987, being addressed in Catalan had become a part (even if only a small part) of most school-aged Castilian speakers' day" (1990: 327).

5.6.2.2 *Where evaluations come from*

What was important about these studies was that they demonstrated that listeners make evaluations of people based on the language they speak. It didn't matter whether their judgments coincided with any objective measurements or not. True, to some extent they did reflect community norms because at the time of Lambert's studies in Canada, English had considerably more prestige than French in Canada, especially as a language spoken by persons with the higher-status jobs. But, for example, the more favorable rating for the English guise in terms of "good looks" could hardly be anything but a subjective judgment.

Where do these evaluations come from? Many of them are based on experience with other speakers. That is, if the listener knows that people "who speak language X" are often people who have Y set of attributes, he or she uses previous experience when encountering a speaker using language X. That is, previous associations with language X are a basis for judging the speaker or what the speaker "means" by using language X in this particular context.

5.6.2.3 *Attitudes and validity and reliability of evidence*

Attitude tests have been criticized on a number of grounds. Listeners/consultants may say something on one day when asked about their views toward a language choice, but can we assume that their set of attitudes is constant and unidimensional? One problem with studies involving attitudes toward languages is that the meanings attached to hearing different languages have a number of potential associations. For example, are speakers who seem to be "making an effort" rated more favorably (for whatever reason, but often to speak what is a second language for them when the addressee is a native speaker of that language)? Also, several important questions arise in many attitude studies about listeners: Are they even trying to tell "the truth" or do they give answers that they think the researcher would like, or answers that make them "look good"?

There are some methodological problems with matched guise tests, too. For one thing, such tests imply that listeners hold a constant set of evaluations about a speaker of a given language. In fact, it's more likely that the social meanings attached to a given language vary with the context in which it's used.

But these tests did demonstrate what we care about: **Listeners can and do evaluate an individual in regard to a number of personal attributes**, just from hearing that individual speak language X. And we can go on to say that it's not just listeners who "know" about these evaluations; so do the speakers themselves.

Studies based on self-reports from speakers have a special problem (as discussed in chapter 3). Whether we researchers like it or not, there is evidence that self-reports about what speakers do are often misleading or downright wrong. For example, Bourhis used self-reports in a survey in Québec in Canada in the early 1980s to test ethnolinguistic vitality. One result was that English Canadians reported being more likely to converge to French (with French speakers) than they had in the past. And French Canadians said the opposite – that they were less likely to converge to English with English speakers. But a follow up study designed to test **whether self-reports matched actual behavior** (Bourhis and Sachdev, 1984) found little support for the self-reports, especially for the English Canadians. In real life, French Canadians were more likely than English Canadians to converge and speak the other person's language in inter-group encounters.

5.6.3 Accommodation Theory

Like the theory of ethnolinguistic vitality, Accommodation Theory was developed by the social psychologist Howard Giles and his associates. Giles's Accommodation Theory grew out of matched guise tests conducted in the early 1970s to study evaluations of speakers of various British dialects. For example, Giles found that listeners rated a male speaker as having a higher socio-economic status when they heard the more "posh-accented" guise than when they heard the same speaker in his non-standard regional dialect guise. (In England and in the former British Empire, "posh" is associated with so-called RP pronunciation (and grammar), with RP standing for "received pronunciation".) Giles's associates and others went on to study differences in language with versions of the matched guise test. In many contexts, these studies show that standard-dialect speakers are rated higher on factors having to do with education and authority, while they are downgraded on traits relating to solidarity and integrity, in comparison with non-standard speakers.

With the knowledge in hand from these dialect studies that speakers are judged by the way they speak, Giles and his associates went on to study **under what circumstances speakers change the way they speak** in a conversation. In the process, they developed Speech Accommodation theory and showed how it can explain choices speakers make.

The implicit assumption of this theory is that speakers are motivated to make changes in order to be evaluated more favorably by listeners. Such notions gave rise to viewing such changes as **accommodation** or **divergence** (disaccommodation). And the kernel meaning of Accommodation Theory became this: **Speakers tend to accommodate their speech to persons whom they like or whom they wish to be liked by**, and they tend to diverge from those persons whom they don't like. In the next chapter, we will discuss accommodation again in interpersonal relations, but accommodation has become seen as a general phenomenon, applying in group relations as well. And everything from making one's pronunciation more like the dialect of a listener to switching to the language that is the mother tongue of a listener can be considered accommodation. Also, convergence and divergence can be either "up" (to a more statusful dialect or language) or "down" (to a less statusful one). More recently, Giles and his associates have expanded their focus to study non-verbal and other aspects of communication and that is why they now refer to their theory as Communication Accommodation Theory.

5.6.3.1 *Bilingualism and accommodation or not*

Some studies by Giles and his associates have looked at evaluations in bilingual groups where there is tension regarding the use or value of the languages involved. The idea being tested was that when speakers of one of the languages were presented with statements threatening the value of their language, they would respond by showing some sort of divergence in their answers. An experiment in Wales conducted in English, but with Welsh-speaking subjects, showed that when subjects were asked questions that challenged the value of Welsh by a very English-sounding voice (via tapes in a language laboratory), they broadened their Welsh accents and some subjects even produced Welsh words and phrases in their answers (Bourhis and Giles, 1977).

A follow-up study in Belgium conducted in English with Dutch-speaking (Flemish-speaking) students as subjects (who spoke Dutch, French, and English) also investigated language divergence. When the experimenter said something negative about Belgian Dutch, 50% of the Dutch-speaking subjects shifted to Dutch for their response (the questions and answers had been in English). In a repeat of the experiment, when the experimenter himself switched from English to French for his negative remark about the Dutch-speakers, then nearly 100% of the Dutch-speaking students switched to Dutch (Flemish).

5.6.3.2 *Accommodation and divergence across groups*

We've been discussing Accommodation Theory as it applies to individual speakers and their listeners in experimental situations, but it also applies in real-life situations to both individuals and groups.

First, one way of looking at any **attempts at learning the dominant group's language** in any society is to recognize the very attempt as one of the best examples of accommodation. When individuals or entire groups go beyond learning the dominant group's language and actually switch over to that language as the main (or only) language they use, we can say that they are going beyond accommodation to practice **assimilation** in the sense that they are attempting to become part of the dominant group. Especially many immigrants, or the children of immigrants, go through this process. This is why the language of immigrants is often lost by the third generation. Some reasons for assimilation are psychological and some are more instrumental. A psychological reason is simply to "fit in" and "have a sense of belonging"; an instrumental reason is to improve their chances for **social or economic mobility**.

As you can imagine, there are various degrees of assimilation – from simply learning the dominant language and using it when necessary with dominant-group members to making that language one's primary language, even at home. As we will see in the next chapter, codeswitching (using the dominant language along with your L1 in the same conversation) can sometimes function as a "middle station" along the road to completing switching to the dominant language for all interactions.

Second, **divergence** can be practiced in group relations, either simply to make a language "more distinctive" or to separate its speakers from others. A dominant group may make its language more different from other varieties (more divergent) in various ways for a variety of purposes and results. It may do this to ensure that its language is distinctive. This may make its language more difficult for others to learn, sometimes a desired effect and sometimes not.

Such divergence can be done consciously or unconsciously. If it's done consciously, there may be some sort of official or semi-official body that tries to introduce new words into the language, often from archaic sources. Or, at various times in history and in various places, governments have tried to get rid of foreign words that have been borrowed into the official language. In their place, the government suggests new words from its own language or some other indigenous source.

For example, when India was partitioned after Independence in 1947 into India and Pakistan (with two closely related varieties as official languages in the two nations, Urdu in Pakistan and Hindi in India), Hindi scholars sought ways to raise the status of Hindi in India by making Hindi more distinctive. One way was to introduce words from Sanskrit into Hindi. (Sanskrit is the ancient precursor of some Indic languages and the classic literary language of Hinduism; it is not a spoken language today.) While making Hindi more different from Urdu by making Hindi more associated with Sanskrit, giving Hindi speakers added social prestige, it also made Hindi more difficult for non-Hindi speakers in India to learn. So, in some ways this was a bad move because it didn't win supporters for Hindi as the "real" official language in India, and up until today English serves in many official roles. This example is mentioned again in chapter 12.

And in France today, it is no accident that the French distinguish themselves by having their own word (*ordinateur*) for what is called a 'computer' in much of the rest of the world.

5.6.3.3 Divergence as a symbolic protest

When a group is marginalized by the dominant group and either does not want or does not see the possibility to assimilate to the dominant group, it may respond with its own creativity. That is, minority groups can also – and do – practice their own brand of divergence. One of the best examples of minority-group divergence today is hip-hop music, with lyrics that aren't understandable to everyone.

Speech divergence also is practiced by various local populations in geographic locations that have become trendy because it distinguishes the locals from the often more wealthy newcomers. In the 1960s, William Labov showed how natives of Martha's Vineyard separated themselves from tourists by how they pronounced certain vowels. Martha's Vineyard is an island off the coast of the US state of Massachusetts; the main local occupation used to be fishing, but today the island has become a favorite place for the wealthy to buy summer homes. When locals practiced what can be called **social comparison**, they could see they didn't have the same material possessions as the new arrivals, and they reacted by **placing value on their "authenticity"** as natives. They advertised this by their speech (cf. Labov, 1972). Walt Wolfram and Natalie Schilling-Estes (1998) report similar findings among the long-term residents of Ocracoke Island, off the coast of the US state of North Carolina. The Ocracoke economy is being transformed from a marine-based economy to one based on tourism, too. Men who used to have high status based on their fishing abilities and earning power are losing such sources of status. Today women have more of the steady jobs on the island (in restaurants and hotels). This difference is reflected in the speech on the island; the men maintain the local dialect more than the women. The women converge more and more toward the standard dialect, but the men are the ones who say "hoi toide" (for "high tide"), among other features. In doing so, they are diverging from mainstream speech. This divergence earns them some symbolic capital (status as being "true islanders").

5.6.3.4 *Elite closure as a form of divergence*

Your author uses the term **elite closure** for a form of symbolic domination that is based on the type of speech divergence that is practiced perhaps universally, not by minorities, but by the elite. Taking examples especially from educated Africans, Myers-Scotton (1990; 1993c) shows how members of the elite reinforce their position in a society through their distinctive patterns of knowledge of both particular languages and how they are used.

That is, members of a high-status group do two things with their linguistic varieties (languages, dialects or styles). First, **the elite are very fluent in the official language**, which is English, French, or Portuguese in much of sub-Saharan Africa (which one depends on the colonial history). Second, because they are very much at home in this official language, **their use patterns mark "who they are"**. That is, they don't reserve it just for formal occasions, but use it frequently, either on its own or in codeswitching patterns (with a local language). Average people can't duplicate these use patterns because they don't have the same facility in the official language. In most African countries, far less than 50% of the general population speak this language at all, let alone with ease in a variety of situations. Thus, the elite shut out from elite status those groups who cannot manipulate the same linguistic varieties in the same patterns as the high-status group.

Even though the articles cited deal specifically with elite closure in Africa, people of power and prestige everywhere use the languages they speak as a way to distinguish themselves. Closure in a single language is often done through pronunciation and word choices that set a high-status group apart. For example, some years ago a British writer wrote an article setting out which words were "non-U" and "U" in England ("U" stood for "upper class"). Saying *toilet* rather than *lavatory* was given as an example of "non-U" speech.

Not only are there obvious relations between elite closure and accommodation theory; there is also a relation between elite closure as a concept and Bourdieu's notion that to enter the realm of the elite, one must know how to act as the elite do. Whether they are conscious or not (and they are not necessarily so), for the elite to set up patterns that diverge from the common folk is a major way to keep the common folk "down".

Such patterns of language use, of course, reflect a role for linguistic choices already discussed in this book: The languages one knows and uses often can serve as boundary markers, setting off one social group from another. And speaking a language not known to the masses is not new. After the fall of the Roman Empire, Latin was such a language among the educated for another millennium or more. Two other great imperial languages of this era for clerics and governmental administration were Chinese in Southeast Asia and Sanskrit in South Asia. Arabic as the language of the Koran also fulfilled a similar function where Islam prevailed.

A good deal later, French replaced Latin as the language of diplomacy and learning in Europe. If you read Tolstoy's *War and Peace*, you will find enough snippets of French to work out that French is what the upper-class Russians spoke to each other.

In some parts of the world today, speaking English serves to distinguish the elite. Alternatively, the ability to engage in codeswitching back and forth between English and a local language is a mark of the educated elite. We have an example of such codeswitching in the next chapter; a clever, non-elite, but successful businessman codeswitches in the manner of the elite, and fools some strangers about his non-elite background.

5.7 Language ideology

The main notion that differentiates studies of language ideology from studies of either language attitudes or identity is that academics who write about language ideology almost always focus on the legitimacy of the present status relations between competing groups. Further, often these academics "take sides", usually against the legitimacy of domination by one group in a nation state and the ideology on which it is based.

Here is a general definition of ideologies that can be applied to languages: **Ideologies** are patterns of belief and practice, which make some existing arrangements appear natural and others not. To a dominant majority, existing arrangements almost always seem "natural", because they (or their forebears) are the ones who put these arrangements in place. For example, most of those in political power in the US support having English as the main, or even *the only*, medium of instruction in public schools, no matter what the home language of students is, even at the beginning levels. To these supporters, giving other languages this status is "not natural". However, to minorities in many countries (e.g. Hungarians in Slovakia discussed in chapter 4), giving their languages status in the schools (in areas where they are numerous) is also viewed as natural.

Students of ideologies are especially interested in how the ideology of the dominant group in a society brings about **political and social consequences for everyone** in that society.

On the one hand, they focus on the roots of specific ideologies, such as "who uses language X" and "where it's used". But on the other hand, they emphasize ideologies as evolving forces and so also highlight the effect of how ideologies are played out in the life of a group in a nation state (what people do under the influence of their ideologies). Thus, a focus for ideologists is most often on **official language policies and their negative effects on the less dominant groups** in a nation state. A view uniting ideologists is that not just policies, but also the social role of language, can be changed. They use the term **agency** for the possibility of change.

5.7.1 Globalization, nation building, and language ideologies

In many ways, the current interest in competing language ideologies falls out of the globalization that the world economy is experiencing. Deliberations surrounding ongoing regional political consolidations, such as the European Union (EU), also bring competing ideologies to the surface. Most language ideologists see problems, or at least potential problems, surrounding such economic and political consolidations. They point out that globalization promotes an ideology of uniformity in production and marketing.

You can imagine that promoters of the various forms of economic globalization view uniformity in language as beneficial, too, because it makes for efficiency. This is not the view of language ideologists because of what uniformity means to non-dominant groups. And it does seem clear that **globalization promotes the increasing power of various languages that are already established as the languages of wider communication**, whether in a single country or in the world. English, of course, is a prime example of such a language.

Because of this, not only language ideologists but also nation states fear what globalization means for their national language. Thus, for example, France rejects the lesser role for French that globalization brings to it in other nations, and even in France itself. French used to be the preferred language of international diplomacy, but now English is more common. In the last 30 years, France has responded to threats to its role in certain parts of the world with **"francophonie"**, a term covering **France's efforts to strengthen both economic and cultural ties** with nations where French traditionally was – and often still is – the most important non-native language. And, indeed, francophonie has connections in nearly 50 countries and regions in all parts of the world, from other European nations outside of France to Southeast Asia, the Pacific, the Indian Ocean, the Caribbean, and of course Canada. Instilling an ideology that promotes French as the "natural" language for educated people to speak and use in any international dealings is a major goal of francophonie. For example, in former French West Africa, France encourages nations such as Senegal and Ivory Coast to retain French as the main official language and the medium of the schools. And the islands of Mauritius and the Seychelles in the Indian Ocean have two official languages, French and English.

5.7.2 When local languages get left behind

The ideology that international languages are the route to modernization percolates down from the global to the national level. Views about not only national integration, but also economic efficiency, make having only one language in government and business a goal. Thus, whether on a global or a national scale, minority languages lose out. The goal of many of the writings on language ideology is to point out such results. We cite two examples where the choice of a main official language is part of the engineering of a national identity in newly independent nations and therefore an ideology about the nature of the nation. In one case (Mozambique) the ideology is one that, in effect, legitimizes a nation of two separate groups, the elite, who know Portuguese, and the "others", who do not. In the other case (Indonesia), the language policy promotes homogeneity across ethnic boundaries, at least suggesting equality.

5.7.2.1 *Mozambique: Keeping the former colonial language*

When Mozambique, a Southeastern African nation, became independent, a natural issue was formulating a national language policy. Yet, even after centuries of Portuguese colonial subjugation, those in power were still willing to embrace the Portuguese language and it emerged as the sole official language. Again, **this is a case of elite closure** because the elite, of course, spoke Portuguese as a second language. A long civil war followed independence, with the FRELIMO party winning control not only over the territory, but also over the government and therefore over language policy. Stroud (1999) details how FRELIMO promoted an ideology "normalizing" Portuguese as the language of unity.

There were other possible choices among languages of wider communication, Swahili or English. Mozambique is surrounded by anglophone countries; Swahili is already spoken in parts of northern Mozambique as an inter-ethnic language and is the main official language in Tanzania (just north of Mozambique) and is widely spoken throughout East Africa. Also, Swahili is a Bantu language and all of the 20 indigenous languages spoken in Mozambique are Bantu languages, some relatively closely related to Swahili.

What is most interesting is how Stroud shows that the colonial language of **Portuguese** was not only embraced by the ruling party, but was also **reworked as a "national treasure"**. Portuguese became considered a symbol of cultural authenticity and tradition, rivaling and even trumping the local languages. For a time, whether Portuguese would be "localized" (e.g. with borrowings from local languages) was an issue, but a more conservative Portuguese won out. Use of Portuguese in government circles became associated with these very institutions. Most Mozambique citizens, of course, did not speak anything like this variety, if they had the opportunity to learn Portuguese at all. "Most importantly, the performance of good Portuguese demonstrated the excellence and legitimacy of the authority's right to talk and to govern" (p. 367).

Writing in the parlance of many language ideologists, Stroud concludes, "In a sense, Mozambican national unity and disunity can . . . be understood as rhetorically imagined, interpreted and commented upon, and also partly constituted (or toppled) through discourse on language" (p. 371).

5.7.2.2 Indonesia: Working toward egalitarianism

In contrast to Mozambique and many other African nations, the powers that be in Indonesia promoted a language that is "conspicuously unattached to any politically salient ethnic native-speaking community" (Errington, 1998a: 272). Thus, Indonesia became **a linguistic success story** in the eyes of students both of ideologies and of language planning. Formerly part of the Dutch East Indies colonial empire, Indonesia became independent at the end of World War II. At that time, what is now called Bahasa Indonesia was only an artificial dialect of Malay used by the Dutch administration and later in the nationalist cause. (Various varieties of Malay are spoken in the region; another variety of Malay is now the official language of Malaysia and it is one of the three official languages of Singapore.) As Errington tells us, "Now [Bahasa Indonesia] is the fully viable and universally acknowledged language of the Indonesian nation and citizenship, over and against the native languages of about 190 million members of four hundred or so ethnolinguistic groups" (p. 272).

What is remarkable is that leaders managed to make **Bahasa Indonesia the vehicle of the "state-idea" of development**, as Errington puts it. Various speeches by state employees speak of Bahasa Indonesia as a necessity to promote unity and facilitate modernizing the economy. Over thirty years of discourse on development, Indonesian leaders move from metaphors of the rise of Bahasa Indonesia as a natural process to metaphors that imply craftsmanship or engineering. This is one of the ways of making the **language engineering** that was needed to "develop" Bahasa Indonesia a logical part of the overall ideology of development in Indonesia. (Language engineering refers to making overt changes in a language. Such engineering can involve making up new words from existing ones or borrowing words from other languages so that a language has the vocabulary necessary to talk about the affairs of a nation state. Engineering also involves agreeing on what counts as acceptable spelling in written works and even preferred grammatical constructions for certain formal purposes.)

5.7.3 Symbolic domination

Students of language ideologies often refer to "discourses or debates" on language; their interest in these discourses or debates often is to show how a group in power imposes its values. This is referred to as **symbolic domination**. A dominant group can place constraints on everything from what type of language use is to be valued to how what is said is to be interpreted. Such issues are especially relevant to inter-cultural communication when different groups are at odds about how what is said is to be interpreted. Chapter 7 includes some examples of cross-cultural communication problems in interpersonal interactions. But here, we give an example of symbolic domination in relation to public policy.

5.7.3.1 Canada: Symbolic domination and competition

Heller uses the term **symbolic domination** in writing about the struggle for power among Canada's different ethnolinguistic groups. She often focuses on the relations of power between majority anglophones and minority francophones in Canada, but also on the role of the French language in education outside of Québec (Heller, 1995). In the 1980s, francophones won a number of concessions in Ontario, especially in education at the primary and secondary levels. Also, in Canada as a whole, persons holding government jobs had to pass examinations in both English and French.

Still, **anglophones retain a great deal of political and economic power**. And the powerlessness of speakers of other languages (native Canadians, francophones, and immigrants) is tied up with their position in respect to the anglophones. Even if these other groups learn English, this does not mean automatic access to power. Citing Bourdieu, Heller says that members of the English-speaking mercantile class are able to define what forms of "knowledge" and behavior are acceptable – or even required – for participation in mainstream Anglo-dominated interactions.

Also, under the newfound approval for bilingualism, another problem for francophones is competition from anglophone bilinguals. Heller notes that many francophones feel **threatened by bilingual anglophones**, having felt that bilingualism was their terrain and a way to gain a measure of power.

Another language-related issue in Canada, but this time within the francophone and immigrant community, is the type of French taught in French-medium schools in Ontario. Heller brings this up in relation to the legitimacy of Canadian French vernacular and to the languages immigrants speak who go to these schools. She refers to Canadian French vernacular as "the authentic voice of working-class francophones" in comparison with other varieties of French (1995: 376).

Not surprisingly, the francophone establishment in Ontario considers having **French-medium schools** there an important accomplishment. But ironically, these schools do not serve the needs of all students who attend them. Students are required to study specific kinds of French in these schools, and this is fine for some who represent the educated middle class. But for others, the world in which they live may require some other language, such as a casual style of French (vernacular French) for children from the working classes. Among immigrants, their out-of-school lives require such home languages as Somali, Haitian Creole, or Farsi. Their world also requires English in order to function in an English-dominant world outside of school. Thus, Heller argues that the type of "school French" taught "has had the effect of **privileging the interests of the upwardly mobile** [francophone] bilinguals (who can utilize this type of French in their jobs) over those of vernacular speakers or immigrants whose French does not correspond to the standard as defined by the school" (p. 402). Thus, the type of education offered, even though it is in French, is a form of symbolic domination that is practiced against large numbers of students by those French who are among the upwardly mobile bilinguals.

5.7.4 Ideology as an instrument of language maintenance

A group's sense of itself as expressed through its ideology about its language can be an important force in the maintenance of that language, even in the face of a dominant culture. A case in point is that of the **Arizona Tewa Indians**. Almost three hundred years ago their ancestors moved west to Arizona at the invitation of the Hopi Indians. Although they have accommodated in various ways to both the Hopi and Euro-Americans, they live as a distinct cultural group and still speak Tewa (Kroskrity, 2000).

Their language ideologies are a main resource in this maintenance. First, they have a "ceremonial ideology" that emphasizes fixed prayer and song texts with no innovations. Repetition of past performances is the goal. Second, the Tewa compartmentalize what is called "Tewa talk" for ceremonies only. Third, they have a "purist ideology" regarding input from other languages into Tewa. While fluency in Hopi and English is not criticized, any form of language mixing is frowned upon, whether it is the borrowing of words or mixing two languages in a conversation. Switching within the same conversation does happen, but usually Tewa claim to do this to signal something about the culture of speakers of the other language. For example, a switch to Hopi may show disapproval of the Hopi conservatism or indecision on a certain matter (Kroskrity, 2000: 341).

5.8 Summing up

In this chapter we've given an overview of studies of language attitudes and language ideologies when the speakers or communities studied are bilingual.

Try to associate the following points with the examples of actual situations of language use discussed in this chapter.

- **Attitudes** about language varieties are subjective evaluations (assessments) that are made about the value of both the varieties themselves and their speakers.
- **Attitudes regarding a speaker** often take the form of a set of attributes (e.g. intelligence, trustworthiness, etc.) that may be little or nothing to do with the variety.
- Three models have been employed to identify or explain language attitudes. **Matched guise tests** identify attitudes. The model of **ethnolinguistic vitality** seeks to explain the attitudes that a group has about its own language variety. **Communication accommodation theory** seeks to explain how speakers communicate attitudes toward others, especially in interpersonal conversation.
- **Ideologies** are perceptions about how language varieties are used **in the interest of a specific group**.
- **Studies of ideologies** explicate a particular group's ideology and the consequences of holding that ideology. Some say that an ideology is **a system of beliefs**.
- **How a group in power imposes its values** is a topic many studies of ideology address. **Linguistic choices** can be a sign of the identity of a person or a group.
- **Boundaries** separating the "we" and the "other" are symbolized by languages.
- Because different varieties are valued differently in **the linguistic marketplace**, a person's linguistic repertoire can be a source of **symbolic power**.

5.9 Words and phrases to remember

attitudes toward language varieties and speakers
ideologies as sources of beliefs and practices
language varieties as boundaries
language varieties as sources of identity
matched guise tests
power and solidarity as theoretical constructs
accommodation and divergence
measures of ethnolinguistic vitality
globalization and ideologies
elite closure as an ideology
egalitarianism as an ideology
linguistic marketplace

6

The Social Motivations for Language Use in Interpersonal Interactions

Multiple voices: The word from Turks in the Netherlands

Bahar Solmaz is a young woman in her late twenties living in the Netherlands who is of Turkish ancestry. She works as a reporter for a Turkish ethnic magazine, having studied for several years at a Turkish university. Her father came to the Netherlands in the early seventies as a migrant worker. He was looking for a better standard of living than he had in Turkey, but returned to Turkey to visit often. Bahar, her mother, and her older brother didn't follow him to the Netherlands until 2000. Throughout her day, Bahar associates with numerous people and her conversations necessarily involve different linguistic choices. For example, she always speaks Turkish with her parents and her older brother, but then speaks Turkish and Dutch alternately with her peers and her three younger siblings. With her Dutch friends, she speaks Dutch. Bahar says it makes a difference where she is: When she is visited by her younger sister in her own home, she alternates between languages much more than when the two of them run into each other in their parents' house, where she automatically will use more Turkish. Similarly, in the highly ethnic environment of her job, she uses Turkish exclusively with a colleague, but when she goes out at night with that same colleague, they will speak both Turkish and Dutch. Because of the number of Turks where she lives (the city of Tilburg) and the visits she regularly makes to Turkey, it is unlikely she will stop using Turkish extensively.

6.1 Introduction

In previous chapters, we've argued that the reason speakers become bilingual is that the second language will be of some use to them. Specifically, we have emphasized that people learn an L2 because of its instrumental value, meaning that it opens up socio-economic opportunities for them. But that's not the only value that second languages have for bilinguals. In this chapter, we explore another reason for learning a second language (or maintaining a first language). We consider how linguistic varieties in general serve as social identity markers. A second language identifies speakers as belonging to additional groups outside of that of the L1. This chapter looks at how bilinguals use both their L1 and L2 to say something about their group memberships in relation to how they view themselves and in relation to others. Thus, a second language is an addition to the speaker's store of ways to indicate who they are and to relate to others. The topic now becomes the **interpersonally based motivations to choose** to use one language rather than another – or to choose both – in a given interaction.

What is behind this choice? Our basic premise is that a major reason for selecting a particular language to speak in a particular interaction is to call up the socio-psychological values that are associated with that language. The basic notion is this: In any community, the linguistic varieties (languages, dialects, styles) in that community's repertoire each take on distinctive social meanings. Speakers "know" these meanings as part of their communicative competence (a concept introduced in chapter 3).

The basic claim we will support is this: When speakers use a particular variety, they are **indicating both their view of themselves and their relationships** with other participants in the conversation. Of course this claim does not rule out other reasons for speaking one language in one situation and another language in another situation or for switching languages in the same conversation. Speakers may feel better able to speak about a certain topic in one language. Or, they may switch languages because they think an expression in one language conveys what they want to say better than one in another language; that is, an expression or word from one language fills a **pragmatic gap** in the other language. (There's more below on what "pragmatics" means.) Or, a word in one language may refer to a concept or object that doesn't exist in the home community of the other language; that is, a word from one language may fill a **lexical gap** in the other language.

But while there are many reasons for selecting one language over another, our research shows that the major reason is the **symbolic value** of speaking that language, not to fill gaps. So, a major concern in this chapter is to show how a bilingual's choice of one linguistic variety rather than another symbolizes or stands for something beyond itself. We will show how choosing a variety is both **a tool and an index of interpersonal relationships**.

6.1.1 The basis for associated meanings: Speakers and communities, not varieties

Keep in mind that varieties don't take on symbolic values from thin air. The social meanings that they take on largely depend on the group of speakers in the community who are most associated with that variety. What we think about a given variety is what we think about the merits and shortcomings of its usual speakers.

Let's go back to our discussion of dialects in chapter 2. The standard dialect of any language is *not* primarily valued because it sounds nicer or is easier to understand than other dialects of the same language, no matter what many people will tell you. No. The standard dialect is valued because of its association with the type of people who speak it most of the time. Those are the people with prestigious jobs or at least people on a track of socio-economic mobility (such as college and university students, we hope). We make similar associations between non-standard dialects and the qualities of their speakers. The same idea applies to languages in the bilingual community. For example, if language X is spoken by people with lots of schooling, including higher degrees, then when someone speaks that language, listeners form a **psychological picture of speakers of language X** as someone who is highly educated, someone who may hold a professional job or live in the nicer sections of town. Depending on the situation, listeners may form other pictures of that person, too. For example, if our model educated speakers uses this same language X in those situations calling for informality, they may come across as snobbish and too full of themselves and even out of place. This could happen just as easily at either a market stall in the developing countries or at a flea market or garage sale or a pub or sidewalk café in the industrialized countries.

6.1.2 Socio-psychological baggage

Thus, there are two important points to keep in mind in this chapter: First, all linguistic varieties carry with them **socio-psychological baggage**. Each variety gets this baggage largely from the speakers most associated with using that variety and from the situations in which the variety is used as the most appropriate choice. Second, **the baggage is almost never uni-dimensional**. That is, there are many social messages packed into the baggage and which ones come to the listener's mind often depend on community norms that have developed through experience and over time about expected or usual language use in different types of interactions. (As a cover term for varieties and their choices sometimes we'll use the term **code choice** instead of specifically referring to choosing one language, dialect or style/register over another.)

6.2 Linguistic varieties as social indices

We referred to the choice of one linguistic variety rather than another as having symbolic value in the sense that such choices have a social meaning. More specifically, we can refer to linguistic choices as **indexical signs**. When a verbal or non-verbal sign is functioning as an indexical sign, we mean that it "points to" something else. For an example of an indexical sign that is not linguistic, consider smoke coming out a window; smoke is indexical of a fire within. An indexical linguistic "sign" can be a word, a phrase, or an entire variety. We emphasize that the variety *itself* is not the message, but it "points to" the message, so it has a special type of meaning. More on this below.

(Just for your information, there are two other kinds of signs that are relevant to your life. You see examples of them on the two sets of public restrooms (toilets) in the English-speaking world. First, there is usually the word *men* on some restrooms and the word *women* on others. These are examples of **arbitrary signs**. When signs (words) are arbitrary, there is no natural connection between the actual written word (or the sequence of sounds when it's spoken) and what it stands for. So *women* in English stands for the same entity as *femmes* in French or *abakazi* in Luganda, a Ugandan language. Most words in any language are arbitrary. There's a second kind of sign that you see every day. Such signs are a "picture" of what they stand for; they are called **iconic signs**. For example, on many restrooms there are iconic signs that are stylized pictures of a man or a woman. Most road signs are also iconic signs because they "show" rather than "say".)

Think of the way that we speak as a form of social behavior not too different (but probably with more and larger consequences) from the way we dress, the kind of music we like, the way we decorate our dorm room or apartments or houses. These all "say something" about **who *we* think we "are"**. So, for a bilingual, choosing to speak one language in a given encounter rather than another says something about how that bilingual thinks of himself or herself. When a bilingual (or a monolingual) makes such a choice, it "says something" about how the speaker wishes to relate to others in the conversation, too. It is in this sense that making a code choice is **indexical** of the self. All linguistic varieties are indexical in this way.

Keep in mind that, as indexical signs, the choice of a way to speak itself is not the social message. Rather, the choice "points to" one of at least several interpretations that can be attached to the choice. **The interpretations are the social messages**. For example, when teenage children in an immigrant family in England refuse to speak the family's L1 with their parents, but prefer to speak only English, what is the social message? (For this example, we assume the parents know enough English to understand the conversation, but have indicated that they prefer to speak their own mother tongue in family interactions.) The teenagers could simply be showing off their ability to speak English, the language of the dominant community. Parents would view this as the social message in their speech. But teenagers also could be indexing a social message about their **persona**. A persona represents a role one assumes in public life, generally reflecting how an individual views him- or herself. So in this case, one possible message indexed by the choice of English is that these teenagers view themselves as disassociated from their ethnic group identity and associated instead with the mainstream culture and its values. In contrast, if the teenagers spoke the mother tongue, parents could interpret this as indexing at least a minimal respect for parental wishes or a valuing of ethnic identity.

6.3 More than meets the ear

Note that looking at linguistic choices in this way implies that there is more to what is communicated when we speak than simply a decoding of the meaning of the words and their combinations. For a long time, researchers studying language implicitly indicated that everything that is communicated is contained in the linguistic elements in the "bundle" that is sent via the airwaves. The idea was that unwrapping the dictionary meanings of the words and their combinations, as conveyed by the sounds and their combinations and any grammatical elements attached along with word order, gave us the entire message. And the expressions the general public still uses imply this view. Think about such expressions as "putting thoughts into words". But then think again – all of your thoughts when you say something are *not* contained in just the words you speak; the choice to say something in a particular way at a particular time and place is part of the message, isn't it?

6.3.1 Implicational messages

In fact, as many researchers are now pointing out, part of the intended message in any utterance is the interpretation the utterance calls up in the mind of the listener (and was in the mind of the speaker at some level of consciousness or, more likely, unconsciousness, too). The study of this aspect of messages is called **pragmatics**. (Some have referred to pragmatics as "language in use", but we think that definition is too vague and not to the point, either.) We see the basic premise of pragmatics as of two parts: (1) There is a gap between decoding words and sentence structures and what is actually meant to be communicated; and (2) the gap can be filled in by **inference**, a process driven by the certainty that the message can carry intentionality in addition to the dictionary meaning of words and their combinations. So **we define pragmatics** as the study of language choices and the intentions or inferences those choices carry in specific contexts. In contrast, **semantics** is the study of sentence meaning. Thus, "meaning" is a composite notion, involving both semantics and pragmatics.

6.3.2 Cooperation and relevance

Some linguistic philosophers have been instrumental in changing our notions about the full meaning of utterances by recognizing the pragmatic messages in them. A major figure is H. P. Grice (1975), who coined the term **implicature** to refer to such indirect messages, for the messages that accompany those "bundled in the words". **Conventional implicatures** do depend on what is coded in the linguistic system, but still are not the sum of words. For example, saying *How are you*? upon meeting someone almost always implicates the speaker's intention to give a greeting, not to ask a question about that person's health. **Conversational implicatures** are of more interest to us. They are inferred from the context, as well as from assumptions about the nature and purpose of conversation. Grice's basic notion about the nature of conversation was that speakers (and writers) operate under **the cooperative principle**. This principle enjoins speakers to be cooperative in various ways. Here's the principle:

> Make your conversational contribution such as is required, at the stage at which it occurs, by the accepted purpose or direction of the talk exchange in which you are engaged.

By following this principle, listeners (and readers) can interpret what is said (or written) with the assumption that the speaker is following a set of maxims having to do with being informative, truthful, relevant, and not being obscure or ambiguous. Speakers sometimes violate the maxims. But whether they follow them or violate them, the listener recognizes that the way the utterance is phrased has its purpose. Thus, for example, if a speaker says on an extremely rainy day, "Wonderful weather we're having", the listener must assume that the speaker says this for a communicative purpose and not just to follow or violate the maxim to be truthful. If there's been a drought, the speaker may really be truthful and mean that rain is "wonderful" in this context. Or, the speaker could be violating the maxim about being truthful in an attempt to be amusing. But the point is that the listener can expect that the way something is said, in a given context, is part of the intended interpretation of the message.

Later, Dan Sperber and Deirdre Wilson (1986/1995) argued that interpretations depend on just **the principle of relevance** (with no extra maxims necessary). This principle states that whatever is said (or written) comes with a guarantee of relevance. Sperber and Wilson also pointed out that utterances can produce both strong and weak implicatures. Listeners are enjoined to assume relevance in any utterance, and therefore to interpret utterances by looking for the interpretation that requires the least effort. Strong implicatures about the interpretation are most obviously more relevant than weak ones, but a given utterance can convey both types at once. So if John says to Mary, "Let's go on a cruise to the Caribbean", and Mary replies, "I don't like ostentation", the strong implicature is that she thinks going on such cruises is ostentatious behavior. A weaker implicature might be that she wouldn't like to live on her own in a huge house with eight bedrooms and one bathroom for each.

Recently, Stephen Levinson (2000) has argued that not only are there implicatures in utterances, but there is a particular layer of what he calls **generalized conversational implicatures**. These are implicatures that are based on world knowledge or knowledge about the specific context that most people have in the community in question – that's why they are called "general". An example Levinson gives is this: The utterance *there's a taxi at the door* doesn't indicate that a taxi is literally right outside the door, but rather where anyone familiar with taxis would expect a taxi to be, such as at the curb (in the street). In Levinson's scheme, he refers to such implicatures as part of a "level of utterance-type meaning" that is different from a "level of sentence-meaning" (more or less semantics). It is also different from a "level of speaker-meaning" (speaker-intentions) that includes more speaker-specific conversational implicatures. You will see that this level (of speaker-specific conversational implicatures) is most important to our discussion of choice of languages.

Although Levinson's discussion is concentrated on generalized conversational implicatures, the important point is that he, as well as Grice, and Sperber and Wilson, clearly establish **the role of pragmatics in utterance interpretation**. So the main point you should get out of all of this discussion of implicatures is that there is more to be interpreted than word meaning in most utterances.

6.3.2.1 *Pragmatic implicatures about referential meanings*

However, while all of these linguistic philosophers (and others) are interested in conversational implicatures, they are still most directly concerned with how listeners are able to work out interpretations of the basic "referential meaning" of a conversational contribution. To take an example from Grice, when the speaker says "There's a station around the corner" to a man carrying a gas can who has just asked, "Do you know where I can get gas?", the meaning the speaker is conveying indirectly is that there is a station nearby, it is probably open, and one can generally get gas there. Thus, the interpretation in this example has to do with both utterance-type meaning (referential meaning or semantics) and how language is used. It's easy to see how the listener must use any or all of the three frameworks we've discussed in interpreting the speaker: The listener can assume what is the speaker says is "cooperative" under Grice's cooperative principle; it is "relevant" under Sperber and Wilson's relevance theory; and it fits under Levinson's generalized conversational implicatures about general expectations about how language is normally used. But the interpretation doesn't have to do with the speaker's presentation of self, nor is it a comment on the interpersonal relationship.

6.3.2.2 *Pragmatic implicatures about socio-psychological meanings*

So, while these pragmatic theories are useful in establishing that we make inferences way beyond form–meaning correspondences in understanding an utterance, we need to enhance these theories to explain **socio-psychological pragmatic meanings**. For the sake of brevity, we'll just call them **socio-pragmatic meanings**.

Let's return to indexical meaning. Under what we'll now call a theory of socio-pragmatics, we argue that many code choices carry indexical meaning of a social nature. When there is a choice of languages (as there is for bilinguals), selecting one language rather than another calls up interpretations (implicatures). Often such a choice is based on the social and psychological features or attributes that the community has come to associate with that language. That is, a language becomes an indexical sign of these attributes. The interpretation that is placed on such a sign is what we mean by **social meaning**.

6.4 Language varieties absorb meanings from situations

But where do the social meanings come from? The situations in which a particular language variety is regularly used are one source of their social meanings. We remind you of the discussions in earlier chapters and how the different varieties in a community's linguistic repertoire generally are allocated to different uses. Recall especially the constructs of "domain" and "diglossia" that we discussed in chapter 4. For a variety of reasons, different varieties take on different values so that their use is associated with different domains or types of situations. We referred to such **domains** as "home" versus "work" and the association of different varieties with each.

Recall **classic diglossia**, a construct used to describe the situation under which two varieties of the same language are in use in the same nation, but for different situations. One of these is the variety that all native-born people acquire in their home setting as their L1. Largely because of where it is acquired and subsequently frequently used, whether by children or adults, this variety becomes associated with the home domain. In addition, it is associated with other interactions that incorporate the informality, if not the intimacy, of the home domain. For example, it is used in shopping encounters. The other variety is only learned formally (i.e. through schooling). This variety is associated more with public speech of a serious nature and written work. Such classic diglossia exists in the Arabic-speaking world where at least two varieties of Arabic exist side by side in the same community.

Extended diglossia shares with classic diglossia how varieties are allocated, but the varieties themselves are different. The variety analysts call the H variety is the one also associated with education and formal occasions. The difference is that this variety may or may not be the L1 of some native-born citizens, and it almost never is the L1 of all local citizens. Further, it might have no (or few) native speakers in the nation in question, but be spoken as an L1 elsewhere (e.g. the status of certain international languages, such as French in a number of African nations, such as in Rwanda and Burundi). Under this type of diglossia, the L varieties almost always are L1s of the local peoples. Such extended diglossia exists in many multilingual nations, such as most African and Asian nations, and the extent to which it exists in the former Soviet Union is in flux.

Refer back to chapter 4 for more details about domains and diglossia. The reason to bring them up again here is to remind you that, depending on the society in question, **some varieties are valued for one set of situations and not for others**. Individual bilinguals are aware of these evaluations and they can influence choices people make to speak one variety rather than another. In the following sections, we introduce a number of theoretical approaches to explaining speaker motivations for the choices they make in interpersonal interactions. In various ways, these approaches all relate back to the basic notions of societally based differences in valuations placed on linguistic varieties.

6.5 Speakers have their own motivations for choices, too

But the situations in which language varieties are regularly used are not the only factors influencing the choices that speakers make. In fact, they may not be the main factors at all. Instead, speakers' motivations regarding how they wish to present themselves and how they view their interactions with others may be most important. So we turn now to speakers themselves. In a now classic paper, social psychologist Roger Brown, along with Albert Gilman (Brown and Gilman, 1960), used the two dimensions, "power" and "solidarity", to refer to the basic factors that influence interpersonal interactions and therefore language choices that speakers make.

Solidarity is an attribute of relationships that arises through **a shared membership** with another person. An obvious shared membership is coming from the same family, so solidarity characterizes relations between most family members. Working in the same office or on the same factory line is also a source of solidarity. The more shared memberships, the more potential for more solidarity between the two persons.

While speakers can share solidarity, power is more defined by **its asymmetrical nature**, meaning there is inequality present. **Power** is an attribute that exists in relationships through one participant having more control over outcomes and factors that affect the other participant than the other way around. For example, an office supervisor has some measure of power over the office staff. Participants may have equal power in a relationship, but more often they do not. Sometimes both power and solidarity exist in the same relationship. For example, parents generally have power over their children, even while they also have solidarity with them.

Social distance is an attribute of relationships that obviously is related to both power and solidarity. How much social distance there is between speakers is related to how much solidarity they share and how great the power gap is between them.

Specifically, Brown and Gilman used the concepts of power and solidarity to discuss changes in European languages of the use of the second-person pronouns. Many languages around the world have two second-person pronouns used similarly to those in French. That is, even though one is a "singular" in form and the other is a "plural", either one can be used as a "singular" (i.e. when "you" is just one person). For example, French has a second-person singular pronoun *tu* that is used most often in relationships where solidarity is strong, although it can also be used in a downward fashion in a relationship where there is a big power differential. French also has a second-person plural pronoun *vous* that is used when addressing two or more listeners. But *vous* also can be used to one person, either in an upward fashion (to a superior) or between strangers. In discussions of the use of second-person pronouns in those languages that have both singular and plural forms, no matter what the language, the pronouns have come to be called T and V (after the French forms, which, of course, came originally from Latin). Later in this chapter we'll discuss how these forms can be used in ways that are unexpected (in what we will call a marked way) so that their use can be considered especially friendly or the opposite, insulting.

For our purposes, the details of how these pronouns are used in Brown and Gilman's 1960 study aren't as important as their theoretical model. The heart of the model, of course, is to claim that the linguistic choices that a speaker makes can be neatly characterized in terms of the speaker's solidarity and power relations with an addressee.

6.5.1 The dynamic aspect of solidarity and power

But their model contains another important insight: Brown and Gilman suggested that the **saliency** of either solidarity or power could change over time, either for an entire society or for an individual speaker and his or her addressee. This means that solidarity and power are **dynamic concepts**. And when something "becomes salient", this means that it becomes "more prominent". For example, consider a relationship in which two speakers regularly use the V form to each other. In such a relationship, because of something that happens, or just over time, the speakers can begin to view the attributes of their relationship differently: Those that point toward solidarity become more salient than those pointing toward power as a basis for the relationship. When this happens, the speakers can switch to using T forms with each other. All this usually happens unconsciously, but it can result from a conscious decision, too. That is, a change in the salience of power and solidarity doesn't mean that either one "disappears"; it just means that either one becomes more or less important in the linguistic choices speakers make.

6.5.2 Using linguistic choices to change relationships

For example, let's consider a professor and a graduate student. Up until the time when the student gets his or her first real job, they may have had what we will call a **non-reciprocal relationship** because the student called the professor by the V form and the professor called the student by the T form. But now that the student is no longer a student, the two may begin to call each other by T forms. This indicates they now think of their relationship more in **reciprocal terms**. It may already have occurred to you that the use of **terms of address** is just like the use of the T and V pronouns. In our example, using their first names with each other is equivalent to using the T forms; it also signals a reciprocal relationship.

This example illustrates something important about language use that is applicable to bilingual communities and conversations that take place there. We can refer to whether one language or the other is used in a given interaction as an index of the power and solidarity relationships between speakers. Also, we can see that changes in the pattern of how languages are used can be seen as reflecting perceived (or hoped-for) changes in these relationships. We will see that much codeswitching (changes of language within the same conversation) can be viewed as indexing bids for changes in the salience of power or solidarity.

At the same time, we must keep in mind that how much the relative salience of power and solidarity is open to change varies a great deal at the societal level. Many of the readers of this book live in relatively open societies where change in possible. But in some traditionally oriented societies, power is highly salient and relationships based on the power differential are rigorously maintained. That is, non-reciprocity is a feature of language use in many interactions in such societies. For example, persons in positions of much power are called the equivalent of "your excellency", or they are not spoken to *at all* by common people. In many more societies, while children obviously have a lot of solidarity with their parents, the power dimension of parent–child relationships is more salient in language use. The result is that children may be expected to avoid speaking to their parents, especially fathers, or not to ask questions. And when they do speak, they are expected to use their mother tongue rather than a second language they might have heard on TV or learned from playmates or in school.

In summary of this section, keep in mind the following terms and their meanings: (1) power and solidarity and how they can affect social distance; (2) reciprocity vs. non-reciprocity in language use; and (3) how all of these are dynamic concepts and that, therefore, their salience can change over time, meaning their importance changes in the minds of an entire community or individuals.

6.6 Models to explain conversational choices

In the next sections, we move on to discussing models that emphasize the role of individuals in negotiating their way through everyday interactions by selecting among the linguistic varieties they know. They do this against the backdrop of the different values that different languages have in the linguistic marketplace, the extent to which they encode power or solidarity in general and in specific in the relationship at hand. Another part of the backdrop is that speakers operate with the unconscious recognition that different linguistic practices on their part, and on the part of others speaking to them, implicate social as well as referential meanings.

6.6.1 Matched guise studies and linguistic choices in bilingual communities

Many of the models to explain attitudes toward speakers and how they affect linguistic choices grew out of the research of Wallace Lambert in the late 1950s. This statement applies especially to accommodation theory (Speech Accommodation Theory and Communication Accommodation Theory), discussed below. Matched guise tests were introduced in chapter 5. Working in Canada, Lambert and his associates asked subjects to rate speakers on a number of attributes. As we indicated there, Lambert's original studies conducted in Canada generally showed that subjects rated the English guise more favorably than the French guise along a number of scales (e.g. intelligence, education) and the French guise more favorably in others (e.g. humor). Matched guise tests continue to be used, especially in bilingual communities; they aim to uncover various subconscious attitudes about people based on which of the community languages they speak. One recent study (data were collected in 1994–5) was conducted in Ukraine to assess evaluations of women vs. men, who spoke Ukrainian or Russian in the experiment (Bilaniuk, 2003). After the breakup of the Soviet Union, Ukrainian became the official state language of Ukraine in 1989. Still, the **diglossic relationship** that had been in effect under Soviet rule lingers. That is, Russian is still considered by many to be the "high" language and Ukrainian is considered more of a "low" or "peasant" language, although these attitudes vary depending on historical and other factors. In the matched guise tests, subjects, who were students, identified themselves as either "Russian" or " Ukrainian".

As in other matched guise tests, subjects in Ukraine heard recordings of the same person speaking first one language and then, later, the other language; subjects thought they were hearing two different persons. Subjects then rated each version of the speaker on a set of personal attributes, from "likeable" to "likes to joke" to "proud".

On all 12 traits studied, the interest was in comparing evaluations of men vs. women. Results showed a cross-over: The female readers were rated higher in their Russian guise and the male readers were rated higher in their Ukrainian guise. Because women previously have been seen in Ukraine as the guardians of traditional values, these results are somewhat surprising; speaking Ukrainian should be more associated with such values than speaking Russian. Less surprising was the split in the guise preferred for the ratings of "self-confidence" and "hard-workingness". For both women and men readers, their Russian guise was rated higher in "self-confidence", and for both, their Ukrainian guise was rated higher for "hard-workingness".

The researcher, Bilaniuk, suggests that a number of factors could be responsible for different evaluations by speaker gender. For example, differences in the reading style of the readers in one language not found in the other language may partly explain these evaluations. But she also suggests that evaluating women positively in their Russian guise may be related to the connotations of Russian as a prestigious, urban language for women. As such, Russian may be attractive to women because it gives them opportunities for socio-economic advancement in the cities. Perhaps this makes women speakers of Russian themselves more attractive – even though this runs counter to the view that women are (and should be) the preservers of Ukrainian traditions. Note the observation made above that Ukrainian is not yet a well-established language of prestige in comparison with Russian.

6.6.2 Interpretations of interpersonal language

We turn now to three models that help us understand the language choices that bilinguals make in interactions with each other. The first, **Communication Accommodation theory** (formerly called **Speech Accommodation Theory**) was developed by the social psychologist Howard Giles and his associates; it was introduced in chapter 5. We will call it simply **Accommodation Theory**, although it is also abbreviated as CAT. We will see how **Accommodation Theory** considers adjustments speakers make toward the speech of their listeners. The second, the **Markedness Model** (sometimes abbreviated as MM), views linguistic choices as "negotiations of identity" and comes from your author (Myers-Scotton). This model attempts to explain language choices as negotiations of self-identity and desired relationships with others. A third approach is called **conversational analysis**; its practitioners call it CA. Applications of this model to bilingual speech are most associated with Peter Auer, stemming from the work of John Gumperz (discussed in section 6.10). This model views social meanings as a product of the conversation itself as they are co-constructed by participants; language choice is part of this construction. (Under any of these approaches, much goes into the social message a speaker can convey: word choice, various aspects of pronunciation, and the sentence phrasing that a speaker prefers. But since our subject in this volume is bilingualism, we are most concerned about the models in relation to what the choice to use one language rather than another can convey.)

6.7 What accommodation means

In chapter 5, we introduced Accommodation Theory. Its original meaning revolves around the choice of **accommodation** or **divergence** in how speakers present themselves to others. The basic premise of the theory is this: Speakers tend to accommodate their speech to persons whom they like or whom they wish to be liked by, and they tend to diverge from those persons whom they don't like.

This model is especially relevant in this chapter because the model's premise is that what speakers say is not just a product of "who they are" (in terms of their group membership), but also a product of **what speakers wish to accomplish**. This is important in this chapter because the chapter's overall theme is that speakers don't talk just to convey information, but to imply their own views about who they are, as individuals, and about their relationships with their listeners, and the notion that these relationships are not set in stone, but can evolve.

Accommodation Theory is listener- or audience-centered. That is, speakers choose the way they talk with their audience foremost in mind. Accommodation is often referred to under this theory as **"the reduction of linguistic dissimilarities"** (Giles, Coupland, and Coupland, 1991). Wishing approval and therefore trying to build solidarity (or showing disapproval and no solidarity) is clearly a motive for changing one's speech. For example, Jeff Siegel points out that in Indian films, multiple mixing with different Hindi dialects, Punjabi, and other Indian languages happens very frequently in supposedly Hindi movies. In one film, the hero switches from the Hindi variety associated with Christians with his landlady to standard Hindi when he talks with his girl-friend. Siegel sees this as "an important marker of linguistic accommodation" (email September 6, 2000).

But the theory can also cover switches to promote efficient communication or to achieve instrumental goals. For example, salespeople in bilingual settings who speak language X will often switch to Language Y if it is the language of the customer. They are not necessarily doing this to be liked, but rather because the customer has the power advantage. So we can see how either the solidarity or the power dimension can be salient when a speaker accommodates in different interactions, or even at the same time. In more recent writings, Giles (2001) emphasizes that speakers are not unidimensional: They wish to **signal multiple identities and have multiple goals**.

6.7.1 In the tradition of Accommodation Theory

Other researchers, such as Allan Bell, have developed a theoretical framework related to Accommodation Theory that views variation in speech as **"audience design"** (Bell, 1984; 2001). Most of Bell's work deals with dialectal and stylistic variation, but he sees his overall point as relevant to languages in bilingual situations, too. His basic claim is that "[S]peakers design their style primarily for and in response to their audience" (2001: 143). The idea is that "audience" can be one person or a group and be physically present or not (as in a broadcast). Note that Bell emphasizes the speaker as responding to an audience just as Accommodation Theory does, although he recognizes that speakers can initiate choices to change a situation (always a major tenet of the Markedness Model discussed below).

Nikolas Coupland shares many of Giles's and Bell's views, but in his recent writings (2001: 201)) he speaks of **"style as self-identity"**. That is, he puts more emphasis on the speaker's presentation of self (again, as does the Markedness Model). He indicates that when most sociolinguists discuss style, they tie style to dialect differentiation, as if the style one uses is a function of dialectal group identity. Coupland recognizes social group factors as relevant in stylistic choices, but states that it is "equally likely that the designing of acts of linguistic display would be geared to the speaker's *self*-perceptions, projecting various versions of his or her social and personal identity" (2001: 200).

6.7.2 Bakhtin and multiple voices

Coupland quotes a writer often mentioned in discussions of stylistic choices, Nicolai Bakhtin. Bakhtin is cited for two main ideas. First, he refers to **the multiplicity of "voices"** in any utterance. Take "voices" to mean that any turn at talk gives rise to multiple implications about the intended pragmatic meanings, both because of the speaker's multiple intentions and our own previous multiple experiences. Second, Bakhtin emphasizes the need to pay attention to the "existence of previous utterances" in the current discourse or earlier interactions. These points are similar to ones that we've made before, that utterances have multiple implicatures (implications) and the idea that we partly build on previous turns at talk, previous experiences, to arrive at interpretations of what the speaker means in a current turn at talk.

6.7.3 Accommodation between bilinguals: valued or not

But there may be yet another dimension to the issue of why people accommodate or not in their speech and how they are evaluated for doing so. Life is often more complicated than operating on the premise that similarities attract or that people will like you better if you make your speech more like theirs. Evaluations may depend on other factors, such as how the individual listener relates to the speaker. For example, Burt (1994) found that listener reactions to conversations in an experimental condition between two students, one American and one German, varied considerably.

Although her sample is very small (5 American listeners and 7 German listeners), the results are instructive because they show that whether and how speakers make themselves more like their addressees is not necessarily what evaluators pay most attention to. Burt's study compared evaluations for two types of accommodation; she compared evaluations for what she called convergence (using the other person's native language) with evaluations for compliance (using the language the other person had just used).

Listeners heard conversations between two bilingual students, one German and one American. Burt's hypothesis was that listeners would give higher evaluations to speakers in the conversation in which each speaker complies (switches languages to match the language to which the other speaker has just switched). All evaluators spoke both English and German to some degree. They heard two sets of audio tapes with a number of switches in language, but one tape showed convergence and the other showed compliance.

A few turns from the conversation showing compliance are given below. Note that even though the conversation begins in German, Kay (the American) switches to English in her second turn. And then Maria also switches to English. The conversation goes on with switches back and forth, following the other person's switches.

> Maria (German): Und wo kommst du her? ('Where do you come from?')
> Kay (American): Aus Urbana. Urbana. ('From Urbana. Urbana.')
> Maria: Die Stadt kenne ich nicht. ('I don't know that city.')
> Kay: Urbana liegt südlich von Chicago. <u>Right in the middle of the cornfields</u>.
>   ('Urbana is south of Chicago.')
> Maria: <u>Is it in Illinois or another state</u>?
> Kay: In Illinois, in the middle of Illinois. Und du? Wo kommst du her?
>   ('And you? Where are you from?')
>
> > (Burt, 1994: 542)

In another conversation showing convergence (speaking the other speaker's own language), the American listeners rated both the American and German speakers more positively than they did when they heard the compliance conversation (following the other speaker's lead as to which language to speak). But the German listeners had mixed reactions, showing no clear preference for either convergence or compliance, and giving both speakers some negative ratings in both conditions.

Even more interesting is that while both sets of listeners had some positive and some negative reactions to the speakers, the comments they added to their ratings did not always focus on whether the speakers accommodated to each other or not. For example, in the compliance conversation, the American was often perceived as showing lack of self-confidence when she didn't speak German, and was downgraded for that. One German listener said, "Her reverting to English very early on in the conversation makes me feel that she wasn't trying very hard." Another said, "She should have been able to express everything said in this conversation in German." And an American listener said, "I felt that she was a bit rude because she didn't ask if Maria could speak English." Another American listener thought that the German speaker switched back to English (which she did, but her American partner switched to English first) because she wanted to "assert her superiority."

Burt suggests that although wanting to be similar is a motive for accommodation, accommodation strategies are **socio-pragmatically ambiguous**. She concludes, "we must temper the obvious truth of similarity attraction with another obvious truth – the idea that we also will like people who do what we want them to" (1994: 557). That is, we often don't know exactly what a speaker means to convey, but we like people who seem to project whatever are the messages that we think should be conveyed.

6.7.4 Accommodation and divergence

Both accommodation and divergence are probably more unconscious acts than conscious ones. As we'll argue in the next section, speakers come equipped with a faculty that gets filled in through experience that enables them to make what are ostensibly unconscious judgments, to evaluate the social outcome of speaking one way rather than another, using one language rather than another.

Divergence may be more conscious sometimes than accommodation, simply because speakers may be more aware of going against the flow rather than going with it. For example, the Tariana are a very small ethnic group in the Brazilian jungle who avoid assimilation to the more numerous Tucano group, even though the Tucano language and the East Tucanoan people are reported to be increasingly dominant over the Tariana (Aikhenvald, 2003). Because Tucanos are viewed as invaders, a Tariana person who inserts Tucano words into his or her speech can be ridiculed for divergence from Tariana group norms and for succumbing to pressure from the Tucano.

6.8 Markedness Model: Another model of social motivations

Another model, covering some of the same ground as Communication Accommodation Theory, is the Markedness Model. You can see how the accommodation model is primarily concerned with converging or diverging from the listener or a larger audience. In contrast, the Markedness Model is more centered on the notion that speakers make choices because of their own goals. Of course, they can't ignore some consideration for listeners. After all, without listeners, there is no conversation. Your author introduced this model into discussions of language choice in 1983, focusing initially on social motivations for codeswitching. (Remember that "code" is just one of the cover terms for ways of speaking, so it can refer to separate languages, dialects, or styles.) Many others have discussed the social motivations for switches, especially those between languages, some using this model and some not.

What does "markedness" mean? The Markedness Model tries to establish a principled procedure that both speakers and listeners use to judge any linguistic choice that they might make or hear as more or less **marked**, given the interaction in which it occurs. The procedure that is used is this: As part of our communicative competence, and based on experience in our communities, we develop a sense that there is a continuum of choices for a particular interaction type that are considered **unmarked**. Recall that our communicative competence involves structures that are innate, but also includes what is stored and assembled in the course of language use.

6.8.1 Unmarked choices

Unmarked choices are those that are more or less expected, given the ingredients of the interaction (participants, topic, setting, etc.). Myers-Scotton (e.g. 1993a) refers to a Rights and Obligations set (RO set) as part of the normative expectations for each interaction type. These expectations refer to an unmarked way to behave. In regard to language, **the unmarked choice is the linguistic reflection of any specific RO set**, but only in a specific interaction type. For example, for bilinguals in France, the unmarked choice to use in a government office is French, not any other languages that they speak. Or, for most Spanish-English bilinguals in the United States (especially if they are recent arrivals), the unmarked choice to use to elderly relatives at family gatherings is Spanish. To use the term we introduced earlier, the linguistic choice is **indexical** of the RO set. Thus, when a speaker makes **the unmarked choice**, he or she is causing no social ripples because participants expect such a choice, based on experience.

Who decides what is unmarked? There is no exact answer except community norms (based on cultural values). But whose values? Certainly, with family and friends, in-group values prevail. But in out-group, status-raising situations it is **the more dominant members who can influence the unmarked choice** (remember the power dimension). It's like this: If the boss wears a suit to the office and says wearing a suit shows an attitude that the job is serious business, then junior partners (at least those who aspire to occupational mobility) will wear suits, too. And remember what we said in chapter 5 about **symbolic domination**; those in power can influence everyone's language choices.

6.8.2 Marked choices

However, one of the main features of the Markedness Model is not what it has to say about unmarked choices, but what it says about **marked choices**. Marked choices are those that are not predicted, given the RO set that is in effect. So why do speakers make marked choices? The model's keystone is a **negotiation principle**. It states:

> Choose the *form* of your conversation contribution such that it indexes the set of rights and obligations which you wish to be in force between speaker and addressee for the current exchange. (Myers-Scotton, 1993a: 114)

Under this principle (and the model as a whole), making a marked choice is **a negotiation for an RO set other than the one that is unmarked** for the current exchange. In other words, the speaker making a marked choice is calling for a new situation, for a new RO set to be in effect. Thus, a choice that is marked in interaction X would be unmarked in interaction Y, the one that the speaker wishes to be in effect. Generally speaking, a marked choice is a negotiation about the speaker's persona (who the speaker is) and the speaker's relation to other participants. Thus, making a marked choice is a negotiation about either the solidarity or the power dimension (or both).

We'll look at a number of examples of switching between languages, but begin now with an example of different choices that involves styles within one language. A young man meets his girlfriend's father for the first time. This is an important occasion; after all, the father is an older person with status as the parent of an important person (the girlfriend). Also, the father is a potentially very important person in the young man's life (i.e. a potential father-in-law). In most societies, the unmarked choice would be relatively formal, something along the lines of "It's a pleasure to meet you, sir". What if instead the young man's greeting is only "Hi there" or some equivalent and no more? This is a marked choice. By saying this, the young man is not making the choice that the expected Rights and Obligations set would call for (special respect for age and parenthood). By making a marked choice, the young man would be signaling that he does not see this meeting as anything different from a first encounter with any stranger. He's implying that the father is not someone he cares to recognize as having a higher status. (He's also implying that he has in mind making the relationship with this girlfriend very short!)

Now, an example between bilinguals. A young man from the rural areas comes to Nairobi, the national capital of Kenya, to visit his brother at his brother's office. The brother has an important white-collar position at the national utility. The unmarked choice would be for the brother to greet the young man in their shared ethnic group language. Instead, the city brother greets the rural brother in English, an official language in Kenya and the language that is common in higher-level business offices. What is the city brother doing by this choice? He is basically treating the rural brother as if he were like *any* friend or acquaintance who comes into the office. Given that the visitor is his brother, not to greet him in their shared language is a marked choice. His choice of English downplays the ethnic connection he has with the rural brother. Why would he do this? If we recognize the expectations of many rural people about their city relatives – relatives who have salaried positions – a likely explanation is this: The city brother suspects the rural brother is there is ask for a loan or some other favor, and the city brother is letting him know that ethnicity won't get the rural brother anything special. But, at the same time, the city brother risks alienating his rural brother, as well as the folks at home who will hear about this encounter.

6.8.3 Making "Rational Choices"

An important premise of the Markedness Model is that speakers not only make choices with a sense of which choices are more unmarked and which are more marked. Just as important, they make choices with a sense about which choices will bring them the best outcome. To do this, they use their minds to make assessments. What do they assess? In regard to language choice, **they weigh the relative costs and rewards** of speaking one language rather than another. This premise that speakers make mental assessments brings the Markedness Model into the tradition of **Rational Choice models**. But note this: To say that a choice is rational doesn't mean that it is the best choice! Under such models, what makes choices "rational" is the premise that the speaker makes **cognitive calculations** that take account of how the speaker views available evidence that indicates likely outcomes of choices, but the speaker also considers his or her own values and beliefs. So rational choices are subjective, with the **emphasis on mental calculations** about getting the best outcome.

6.8.4 Marked choices in codeswitching

Much of my field work was done in Kenya, especially in Nairobi, where my research assistants audio-recorded many examples of codeswitching. Code-switching is the use of two language varieties in the same conversation. It can occur between speakers, or between sentences in the same speaker's turn, or within a sentence.

6.8.4.1 On the bus in Nairobi

Here is one example from Nairobi that shows codeswitching as a marked choice. The speaker may have had too much to drink or he's just being funny, but he speaks to the conductor in his own L1 (a Luyia variety, part of the Luyia dialect cluster (a Bantu language) which is spoken as an L1 in western Kenya and of course by in-migrants to the city from that region). Swahili is one of the official languages of Kenya alongside English, but it is better known as a widely used lingua franca between people who don't share the same L1; it is used especially in casual conversations. As such, Swahili is the unmarked choice for any transaction with a bus conductor in Nairobi. This means that the speaker's use of **his own L1 is clearly a marked choice**. In this context, it represents a bid to establish a shared group membership (solidarity) with the bus conductor. His choice implies that he hopes the conductor won't charge him the full fare. Perhaps the speaker does think that the conductor looks like a member of his ethnic group (i.e. looks like a Luyia person); or else he is just taking a chance. The Luyia man speaks loudly and in a joking voice – almost as if he knows he is making a marked choice.

> *Luyia man (in a Luyia variety): (Holding out his hand with some money in it)*
>   *Mwana weru, vugula khasimoni khonyene.*
>   *('Take only fifty cents, dear brother.')*
> *(Other passengers laugh)*
> *Conductor: (Also just laughs)*
> *Luyia man (still in Luyia): Shuli mwana weru mbaa? ('Aren't you a brother?')*
> *Conductor (Swahili): Apana. Mimi si ndugu wako. Kama ungekuwa ndugu*
>   *wangu ningekujua, ningekujua kwa jina. Lakini sasa sikujui wala sikufahamu.*
>   *('No. I'm not your brother. If you were my brother, I would know you. I would*
>   *know you by name. But now I don't know you nor do I understand you.')*
> *Luyia man (now in Swahili): Nisaidie, tu, Bwana. Maisha ya Nairobi imenishinda*
>   *kwa sababu bei ya kila kitu imeongezwa. Mimi ninaketi Kariobang'i, pahali*
>   *ninapolipa pesa nyingi sana kwa nauli ya basi.*
>   *('Just help me, mister. The life of Nairobi has defeated me because the price of*
>   *everything has gone up. I live in Kariobang'i, a place to which I pay much*
>   *money for the bus fare.')*
> *Conductor (Swahili): (Taking some money out of the Luyia man's outstretched*
>   *hand)*
>   *Nimechukua peni nane pekee yake.*
>   *('I have taken 80 cents alone.')*
> *Luyia man (English first, then Swahili): <u>Thank you very much</u>. Nimeshkuru*
> *sana kwa huruma ya ndugu wangu.*
>   *('Thank you very much for the pity of this one, my brother.')*
>   *(Myers-Scotton, unpublished Nairobi corpus, 1988)*

6.8.4.2 Switching to lower oneself

Codeswitching often occurs not just in consecutive turns, but within a turn. Another example from Kenya, this time from the provincial capital of Kakamega in western Kenya, shows this type of switching. The following represents half of a telephone conversation. The speaker is a local accountant and he is talking to a client. Both are well educated. Both are trilingual; they speak different Kenyan languages as their L1s, and they also speak both English and Swahili fluently. Because they come from different ethnic groups and are educated men talking about a business matter, English is the unmarked choice in this interaction. Remember that you are reading only one side of the conversation. (Dots indicate the other man is talking.) Swahili parts of the conversation are underlined.

> Accountant: Hello, Bwana Muchanga. Good Morning! . . . Well, I've told you good morning, but it is not a good morning. <u>Hee . . . namna gani, bwana?</u> ('What's happening, mister?')
>
> For so many days and so long that you have disappeared? . . . No, even if you come around, you will see my mother is here . . . I don't know if she will die or whether she will survive. . . . No, in my house in Kakamega. I took her to hospital, Bwana. We have got a poor hospital. I am telling you. I took her to the hospital at night . . . There was no treatment . . . These people claiming no medicine – nothing in the store . . .
>
> I think this is what I shall do – because I am (interrupted) . . . Where is the time, bwana? Time is the problem with me . . . <u>Wewe, unajua mimi niko mwandikwa, bwana</u> ('You know I am an accountant, mister'). I have always to squeeze myself. <u>Niko taabu, bwana</u> ('I have worries, mister'). . . . <u>Na sasa watu ya kusaidia taabu yangu ni watu kama wewe, tu</u> ('And now the people who can help [me] are only people such as you'). No, what do I do, bwana? I will come, but – <u>huyu mzee yangu, nahitaji unisaidie, bwana na mzee yangu</u> ('My dear old mother, I need your help, mister with my dear old mother'). . . . <u>una</u> EXPERIENCE <u>nyingi</u> . . . <u>Umezoea mambo haya [na wewe] unaweza kusaidia mimi na mzee yangu</u>. ('You have lots of experience, you're used to these matters, and you can help me with my mother').
>
> (Myers-Scotton, unpublished Kenya corpus, 1977)

Note that in this conversation, except for the greeting, the accountant does not speak Swahili until he begins to ask the other man for help (and help implies "money" in this context). Thus, in switching to Swahili, the accountant uses the language that they have in common that indexes informality. Swahili, as an African language (and an indigenous language to Kenya) is the best index these two men from different ethnic groups have for in-group membership.

Given its placement in this conversation and the Kenyan context, the pattern of switches to Swahili represents a bid for shared group membership or solidarity, but not just with the addressee. Given who the speaker is (educated and probably fairly prosperous, at least in the past) and that he is making a request for "help", the use of Swahili also indexes the accountant's desire to present himself as having solidarity with the masses as an "ordinary" person who is in need of help just like anyone else might be. Note that it is important to recognize that this speaker (and others) can have multiple goals, and they may well be ambiguous. This analysis only suggests the main ones that his language choices imply.

6.8.4.3 *Turning a non-prestige variety on its head*

Another example from another part of Africa, South Africa, also shows a marked codeswitch as a bid for solidarity, but with a switch to a language that is an unmarked choice in a very different type of interaction than where it is used here. The language that is used is Fanakalo (Fanagalo) and it was used in colonial South Africa in asymmetrical master–servant relationships. Fanakalo is a pidgin/creole language that has been used in South Africa at least since the arrival of the British in the mid-nineteenth century. It has elements from English, Zulu, and also some Afrikaans. (Afrikaans is the language derived from the L1 of the white Dutch settlers in South Africa.) Fanakalo was – and still is to some extent – used in the mining industry in particular. The less powerful person in the interaction was always a black worker, especially in conversation with a white supervisor.

Because of this history, Fanakalo remains an unmarked choice between unequals and may be avoided because of its racist associations. However, as the example will show, when Fanakalo is used between peers, especially outside of the work setting, it can be a marked choice and it can index shared group membership. What makes this example especially interesting is that a white speaker uses Fanakalo to other whites in a tennis match at a private club outside the South African city of Durban.

Four middle-class white males are playing tennis doubles at a private club. Three of the players immigrated to South Africa earlier from Europe, and the fourth, a younger man, was born and brought up in South Africa. These are men whose unmarked language in this interaction would probably be English. One of the older residents (of British origin) checks on the score by asking:

Ini lo telling?
'What's the score?' (Adendorff, 1993)

In saying this, the speaker combines Fanakalo (*ini lo* 'what's the') with Afrikaans (*telling* 'score'). In doing this, he is using the two "indigenous" South African languages that all the participants would be likely to know, at least in part. But note that he himself would be a native speaker of English. Adendorff (1993) comments that the speaker is indexing an assumed common South African identity among a group of status-equal white South Africans. Adendorff continues, "The speaker is confident that the other players will recognize that he is providing them with a linguistic display and that they will appreciate the display." He goes on to say, "this is further evidence that F [Fanakalo] is a strategic interaction resource – one connoting power and domination when it is an unmarked choice, and solidarity, when it is a marked choice" (1993: 21–2). A related interpretation is that the speaking is "showing off" how much of a South African he has become (by speaking uniquely South African languages).

6.8.5 Codeswitching to claim a multi-dimensional persona

Of course marked choices in codeswitching are often used to assert attributes on the power dimension, too. Persons engaged in commerce all over the world, but especially open-air market sellers, may switch their languages either to claim solidarity with a potential customer or to assert their modernity. Trying to speak the customer's language is a way to associate oneself with the customer (a bid for solidarity), but it also shows how multidimensional the seller is – and therefore how powerful he or she is. Also, another ploy that sellers use is to speak another language that has some international status; this could show the customer that the seller is a worldly person.

6.8.6 Codeswitching as a neutral choice

In Jaffna, Sri Lanka, among members of the Tamil ethnic group, Canagarajah (1995: 209) describes what he calls an "Englishized Tamil" that is becoming a separate code in its own right. Following independence, there is a strong social pressure among Tamils in Sri Lanka against excessive use of English. But speaking Tamil on its own can be considered excessively formal. So what happens is that "Englishized Tamil is becoming the unmarked everyday code".

Sri Lanka (formerly Ceylon) became independent in 1948, but has been racked by three decades of conflict between the Sinhala state in the south (in control of the national government) and Tamils in the north. The Tamils see the Sinhalese language (the L1 of the majority) as something being imposed on them, one of the reasons for the conflict. Jaffna, as a Tamil center, has become a highly politicized and ethnolinguistically conscious community. Thus, the speaking of only Tamil has many supporters. Also, for a variety of reasons, including the civil strife, there has been a decline in English proficiency in the community.

But while proficiency has declined and Tamil has taken over some domains previously belonging to English, English is more used than ever before because of codeswitching. As Canagarajah states, "code alternation activity enables English to continue in a more widely distributed and pervasive form than ever before, with both 'monolinguals' [in Tamil] and bilinguals [in Tamil and English] using English in conventional and unconventional contexts" (p. 209).

The following example shows how codeswitching can be used to level inequalities between speakers and is a neutral choice in this sense. In this example, a bilingual senior professor is interviewing a candidate for a junior lecturer's post. By opening the interview in English, the professor is making an unmarked choice for a typical academic encounter in university. However, note that the candidate replies first in a codeswitching pattern of both English and Tamil. He can expect that the professor is a native speaker of Tamil just as he himself is. In effect, he is negotiating a relationship with the professor of less social distance than had he replied in English only. But note that the professor responds only in English. Still, the candidate persists with English and Tamil codeswitching. Finally, the professor switches to such codeswitching. Canagarajah (1995), who is the source of this example, explains that it is entirely possible that the candidate lacks the confidence to produce complete utterances in English. But, at the same time, to speak the formal variety of Tamil that would be expected in this situation, but show no facility in English, would only accentuate the status difference. Engaging in codeswitching allows the candidate to show some academic expertise, but also frame his responses in acceptable, educated Tamil. Either the Accommodation Model or the Markedness Model can explain what has happened when the interviewer switches to codeswitching himself. Clearly, the professor has accommodated to the candidate; one implication (implicature) of this accommodation is that the professor is narrowing the social distance between them. One can even argue that such accommodation indicates that the professor looks favorably on the candidate and that he will get the job. Under the Markedness Model, the argument would be that the candidate has successfully negotiated a change in the Rights and Obligations set that is structuring the social side of the interview. In this example, you can see how Accommodation Theory offers a more addressee-centered explanation and the Markedness Model makes a more speaker-centered explanation. But explanations under both models have to take account of both participants and their choices and reactions.

INTERVIEW IN A SRI LANKA UNIVERSITY

> *Interviewer: So you have done a master's in sociology? What is your area of research?*
>
> *Candidate: naan sociology of religion-ilai taan interested enTai thesis topic vantu "the rise of local deities in the Jaffna Peninsula".*
>
> 'It is in sociology of religion that I am interested. My thesis topic was "The rise of local deities in the Jaffna Peninsula".'
>
> *Interviewer: Did this involve a field work?*
>
> *Candidate: Ooom, oru ethnographic study-aai tann itai ceitanaan. KiTTattaTTa four years-aai field work ceitanaan.*
>
> 'Yes, I did this as an ethnogragraphic study. I did field work for roughly four years.'
>
> *Interviewer: Appa kooTa qualitative research taan ceiyiraniir?*
>
> 'So you do mostly qualitative research?'

The example comes from Sri Lanka, but the same type of interaction could happen anywhere in the bilingual world. Myers-Scotton (1976) gives evidence from Lagos, Nigeria, and Kampala, Uganda, that codeswitching functions as a strategy of neutrality in white-collar office interactions by defusing the stuffiness associated with speaking only the official language to one's officemates.

6.8.7 Codeswitching and an unmarked group identity

In some communities, codeswitching itself is the unmarked choice. One can argue that individual switches within a conversation with switches have their own social messages; but we argue that an overall pattern of constant switching has its own meaning, too. In effect, such codeswitching conveys the message of **dual identities** or memberships in both of the cultures that the languages index.

The following example of a conversation between several Nairobi teenagers from different ethnic groups shows this. Their Swahili is not the standard dialect, but shows some features from their own ethnic languages (for example the suffix -nga in the first line is from the speaker's L1 (it's not present in standard Swahili) and conveys the idea of continuous action).

> *Taita ethnic group member: Ukisha ikanyaganganga hivi <u>pedals</u>, unasikia <u>air</u>*
> *umeshakishwa. Sasa unashangaa kama ni <u>bike</u> au ni ma-<u>ghosts</u>.*
> *'When you step on the pedals you hear the air coming out. Now you wonder whether it's the bike or the ghosts [that do that].'*
> *Luyia speaker: Wewe pia una-<u>believe</u> habari ya ma-<u>ghosts</u> kumbe?*
> *'You also believe about ghosts?'*
> *Taita ethnic group member: Ah, <u>ghost</u>, lazima una-<u>believe</u>, usiku unaona <u>something</u> kama <u>bones</u> na inatembea <u>on the road</u>.*
> *'Ah, ghost, you have to believe [when] at night you see something like bones and it's walking on the road.'*
> *Luyia speaker: (the topic shifts and he is talking about a party)*
> *Kulikuwa na <u>table long</u> namna hii, mazee, imejaa tu chakula ya kila aina . . .*
> *Nilikwenda pale nikaangalia, nikapata chakula nyingine iko <u>grey</u>, nika-i-<u>taste</u>*
> *nikaona ina <u>taste lousy</u> sana.*
> *'There was a long table like this, my friend, full of food of every kind . . . I went there and looked and I got another kind of food [that was] grey, and I tasted it and I thought it had a very lousy taste.'*
>
> (Myers-Scotton, unpublished Nairobi corpus, 1988)

Across the world, highly educated immigrants in the high-tech and scientific communities of the United States and Britain also make such a pattern of codeswitching their unmarked choice for in-group conversations. Many of these immigrants come from the Indian subcontinent. In their jobs, they probably speak English almost exclusively. But at home and with friends from their own ethnic group, they often speak their L1 (for example, Hindi) and English in a codeswitching pattern. The same generalization applies to educated Arabic-speakers in the United States. Again, codeswitching becomes their unmarked choice for in-group interactions. At the same time that it indexes their dual identities, it helps them retain their ethnic distinctiveness while also fitting into the culture where they live now.

6.8.8 Combining codes to mark a unique identity

Other groups that do not have high status may just as easily mark "who they are" by what linguistic varieties they use and how they use them. For example, if using lines from hip-hop songs in a codeswitching pattern with phrases from African American Vernacular English is the unmarked choice of some African-American youths, this identifies them as distinctive from ordinary users of AAVE. Similarly, Rampton (1995) has written about "crossing" as a style of speaking used by some urban adolescents in England. They use words and phrases from the languages of other urban groups. For example, white and black adolescents can use Punjabi and Creole along with their variety of British English in the same conversational turn. Punjabi is the L1 of some Pakistani or Indian immigrants in the community and Creole is the name used in this context for an Afro-Caribbean variety. (There are many immigrants in Britain from both the Caribbean and the Indian subcontinent.) Rampton refers to this code alternation as involving some violation of co-occurrence expectations, although he does not discuss "crossing" in terms of markedness. Under the Markedness Model, crossing, even though its exact pattern is not predictable, would be an example of the unmarked choice for a particular group that is identified by network and neighborhood ties, not by racial or family/ancestral ties. Crossing is a cultural convention for these adolescents and its use distinguishes its speakers from "others" and therefore is a form of closure, too.

6.8.9 Exploiting codeswitching to claim an identity

An example from Nigeria shows how speakers can circumvent elite closure by using what is an unmarked choice for a high-status group to claim membership in that group. In this case, codeswitching between Ibibio and English is the unmarked choice in informal conversation among an elite who have a shared background, with a Western education. However, in the Akwa Iborn State in the Cross River area where they live there is a class of successful and rich businessmen who have little education, but who know some English. "For such people, code-mixing is a wonderful opportunity to camouflage their illiteracy and join the 'we-type solidarity' of the educated class," Essien (1995: 281) suggests. He goes on to relate what happened when he and some university colleagues met a very rich businessman at the Governor's Office in Uyo. He knew the businessman, but the others did not. After introductions, the group began to speak to each other, unconsciously, but predictably, switching between English and Ibibio. Essien reports that when he and his colleagues left, one asked "which university the rich businessman attended". Essien responded, "His mansion in his village."

6.8.10 One person's unmarked choice, another's marked choice

In many interactions in a multi-ethnic community, someone gets "left out" when two speakers of the same language decide to speak their language exclusively. Incidents such as the one reported in Beijing (below) happen the world over. Sometimes the speakers from the same group are purposely leaving the other person out and may even be saying something negative about the odd man out. Thus, some think that ethnic group co-members use their own language in order to engage in "back-biting". Or, they may do this with no ill feelings toward the person who is left out, but an expression of solidarity to one person can be an expression of increased social distance to another. A student of mine when I taught in Beijing, China reported this incident:

"One student (the host in this story), who doesn't come from Beijing, is having a friendly conversation in Putongua (standard Chinese) with another student from another part of the country. There is a knock at the door and a visitor comes in. It's an old friend of the host. Greetings and introductions follow, still all in Putongua. But the host suddenly switches to the regional dialect that he shares with the visitor. The two of them talk in this dialect. Finally, the first visitor leaves because he can't participate in their conversation. The two from the same region may think that they should show familiarity to each other by speaking their regional dialect. But they ignore another aspect. They don't know that they establish separateness with the third student while they are shortening the social distance between themselves."

In conversations between bilingual parents and their children, each "side" may have its own unmarked choice. In immigrant families, typically the parents prefer their L1 as the unmarked choice of family conversations and the children typically prefer the language of the dominant community. In the following example from the southwest United States, the conversation begins with English on both sides (mother and 14-year-old son). But then the mother switches to Spanish to express her annoyance with her son's gum chewing. As Valdés (1981: 101) notes, "By this switch, the mother alters the relationship maintained in the conversation up to that point. While previously she had acted as a trusted confidante, she now steps back into her role as parent."

Mother: An' then what?
Son: Well, we dint really say nothing . . . Poncho got on his bike an' went off.
Mother: Umm.
Son: Yeah . . . and . . .
Mother: Listen, your gum is driving me up a tree.
Son: He . . . took off . . . And . . . [Son continues to chew his gum noisily.]
Mother: <u>Tir el chicle y luego me dices</u>
  'Throw your gum away and then tell me.'

6.9 Code choices within a Conversation Analysis approach

Peter Auer and others who study codeswitching within a Conversation Analysis (CA) framework come up with some distinct differences from the Markedness Model and other approaches that emphasize the role of norms about the social meanings that are associated with using one language variety rather than another. Auer makes four main points about the choices bilinguals make in a bilingual conversation: (1) CA analysts try to avoid using what Auer calls "pre-established external categories" in interpreting the social meaning in interactions involving bilingual codeswitching (1998: 2). That is, they downplay the role of societal norms regarding language use and emphasize instead that social meanings can be "locally produced". (2) Thus, they argue that there is a level of conversational structure which is "sufficiently autonomous" from larger societal factors (1998: 3). (3) CA analysts emphasize paying attention to the overall organization of the discourse, especially sequences of how codes are alternated. Auer (1995: 123) states, "The situated meaning of code-alternation . . . cannot be stated unless a sequential analysis is carried out. The same cue may receive a different interpretation on different occasions." (4) CA analysts in general emphasize that a fine-grained transcription of any speech event is necessary to capture potential nuances in how social meaning is produced.

6.9.1 An example in a Conversation Analysis transcript

The following example gives us an idea of what a CA transcript looks like and how its social meaning is interpreted.

Setting: An informal conversation among a group of young Spanish-German bilingual speakers of South American origin in Hamburg: J and U are hosts, C is a guest. Spanish is in italics.

1	J	*qué estás buscando?*
		'What are you looking for?'
2	C	*cigarros*
		'Cigarettes'
3	J	*ay por qué?*
		'Oh why?'
4	(1.0) (one-second silence)	
5	C	*por qué?*
		'Why?'
6	J	*por qué por qué quierres ir al* <u>flur</u>?
		'Why why do you want to go out in the corridor?'
7	C	*para fumar*
		'In order to smoke'
8	J	*aha*

9	L	*a(h)!* <u>*fl(h)ur*</u>	[*a(h)! a(h)!l*	[*a(h)l*
		'To the corridor to the to the		to the'
10	J		[*y dónde*	[*al* <u>*flur*</u>? *h h*
			'And where	in the corridor?'
11	A	*he he he* [*he*		
12	U		[*fuerte*	
			'Cool'	
13		(2.0) (two-second silence)		
14	L	*ahí donde está la bicicleta* [*está*		
		'there where the bike is . . . it is'		
15	J			[*aquí no hay aquí no hay* <u>*nichtraucher*</u>=
				'Here we don't have "no-smoking"'
16	L	=*donde está la bicicle- he he*		
		'Where the bike is'		

(Peter Giese, unpublished data 1992/93, cited in Auer, 1998: 4)

In analyzing this interaction, Auer notes that in a basically Spanish conversation, the German word *flur* 'corridor' is used three times and the German *Nichtraucher* 'no smoking' is used once. He recognizes that without knowledge about recurring patterns of use in this group, it is difficult to tell whether *flur* is a borrowing into these speakers' Spanish, but its uses in lines 9 and 10 are followed by laughter. But it's also difficult to tell whether the laughing is just at the idea of smoking in the corridor and not in the living room.

Auer attaches more importance to the use of *Nichtraucher* 'no smoking' in the turn that is otherwise in Spanish and which translates as "Here we don't have no smoking". Auer states that the choice of German for 'no smoking' gives the decisive clue: It is a certain segment of German culture which is contrasted with these South American participants' way of living in terms of how it deals with smokers. He couples this clue with background information (not in the conversation itself) that smoking in German society has been a topic for these speakers. He claims that "[I]t is only on the basis of an analysis of the sequential position of this insertion *together with* this background knowledge . . . that a full understanding of code alternation can be reached" (p. 7).

6.9.2 Contrasting Conversation Analysis and the Markedness Model

Clearly, Auer doubts that one can refer to a particular language as a marked choice in a given interaction type unless the discourse structure of a specific interaction itself gives evidence as to the markedness of that choice. The implication is that CA analysts would not agree that speakers, through experience and the workings of a markedness evaluator, arrive at markedness readings for how different languages will be normatively perceived in a specific interaction type. That is, CA contrasts sharply with the Markedness Model on this point.

Let us look at the example cited above. Most non-CA analysts would agree that speaking German would call up different associations for young South American men, even though they live in Germany, than speaking Spanish. The Markedness Model goes a step further. Even without knowledge of the specific persons involved, that model would predict that German generally would be a marked choice for informal conversations among young South American men living in Germany. In this particular conversation, the markedness of *Nichtraucher* seems even more likely. Given the way the interaction has progressed in Spanish, the strong implicature of "no smoking" said in German is that the speaker wishes to call up not just restrictions on smoking, but the German mindset about such restrictions. For these speakers (who already know speaker C wants to smoke and have questioned why he is going out in the corridor), shifting to a marked choice (German) is a way to make fun of the restriction and the would-be smoker, and their laughter reinforces this interpretation.

The difference between a CA analysis of bilingual conversation and that under other approaches discussed here seems to be a matter of degree, not absolutes. Most other analysts would agree that large-scale societal factors cannot tell the whole story of why two languages are used in the same conversation. But they do pay much attention to previous associations of the languages in the community (i.e. the situations in which they are regularly used, by whom, and for what purposes). The difference is that most CA analysts instead emphasize the "local" construction of meaning. By this they mean that they do not so much emphasize the choice that a speaker makes, as attach special meaning to where in the interactional episode the switch occurs.

Finally, CA analysts claim that their focus on discourse structure provides an interpretation more true to the role of language in the interaction because it limits external evidence. For an argument that the type of detailed transcription that CA analysts use necessarily results in a more interaction-internal explanation, see Li (2002: 174–7). Other analysts respond that they also take account of the sequence in which the two languages are used in interactions and the use of other cues, such as the use of silence. The difference is that these other analysts also argue that the participants bring with them to the interaction knowledge of the symbolic value of the languages in the community, as well as their own statuses and values of persons of like statuses.

6.10 Summary on explaining bilingual conversations

In some sense, all three approaches to explaining bilingual conversations discussed here have the same theoretical forerunner, John Gumperz, and his notion of **contextualization cues**. Beginning at least with his 1982 volume, *Discourse Strategies*, Gumperz has emphasized that listeners find social meanings in conversations by paying attention to various "pointers" that are embedded in the discourse. They are called contextualization cues because the idea is that the cues give listeners the context (or connections) that help in interpreting the speakers' meanings. However, even though all three approaches base their analyses on language choices as one of the most important of those cues, the different approaches use the cues in different ways.

In addition, all three approaches assume that speakers send social messages by switching from one dialect or one language to another, sometimes within the same conversation. All speakers select their speech code on the basis of calculations that they make, even though most of these are unconscious.

The three approaches also differ in these ways:

- Both Accommodation Theory (and related approaches) and the Markedness Model are deductive in the sense that they argue from a set of premises about the basis for what is communicated in interactions; they then seek to argue how empirical evidence supports these premises. That is, their claim is that these premises explain what goes on in interactions. In contrast, CA analysts operate inductively, arguing that conclusions arise in describing details. So theirs is more of a methodology than a theory, and the premise is that the methodology leads to discovering social meanings. As Li (2002: 162) puts it, "extracts are repeatedly scanned for evidence of procedures whereby the participants accomplish an interactional task, such as disagreeing or changing a topic."

- Accommodation Theory and the Markedness Model both are based on premises about the speaker's motives that both speakers and addressees bring to the conversation. Under Accommodation Theory, choices are interpreted as attempts to stress the speaker's similarity to (or dissimilarity from) the addressee. Instead, the premise of the Markedness Model is more that speakers make choices to promote their own self-identities. CA analysts reject the premise that speakers necessarily bring any intentions to the interaction; instead, they argue that what goes on in the interaction itself will constitute whatever social meaning the interaction has (the idea of locally arriving at the meaning of language alternation).

- To put the difference another way, all three approaches are interested in arriving at the same goal, working out what the interaction "means". But how can this be done? CA analysts seem to see the social meaning of bilingual choices as available from an examination of the linguistic structures. A large part of this examination involves close attention to the surface structures of the interaction and their classification.

- Instead, the other two approaches would argue that linguistic decoding (classifying surface structures) is only one type of input to arriving at social meanings that are communicated. They would say that a more important input comes from the participants' inferential system. This system derives pragmatic inferences not just from the current linguistic input, but also from conceptual resources (memory, etc.) based on prior experiences.

Pragmatic inferences are notions about other people's thoughts and intentions in the interaction. This means that these approaches necessarily assume that humans have inferential mechanisms as part of their cognitive structures. CA analysts reject reliance on "external categories"; it is not clear how they view cognitive resources.

6.11 Summing up

Overall, this chapter has dealt with the notion that language varieties have different socio-psychological values associated with their use and that bilinguals take advantage of this notion when they speak one variety rather than another.

- Most analysts see these values as coming from two general sources: These are (1) the **settings or situations** in which a particular variety is habitually used in the community; and (2) how different persons use the varieties so that their use comes to reflect relationships of **power or solidarity**.
- In regard to reflecting relationships, language variety choices reflect the degree of **social distance** between participants; as a construct, social distance is derived from degree of solidarity and asymmetries in relationships.
- **Pragmatics** is based on the notion that a speaker's meaning depends on inferring meaning from utterances, not just linguistic decoding.
- Three approaches that have been employed for analyzing changes in code choice within the same interaction were considered: **Communication Accommodation Theory, the Markedness Model, and Conversation Analysis**.

6.12 Words and phrases to remember

language choices as indexical
language choices as generating implicatures
power and solidarity as dimensions of interactions
relationships as reciprocal (symmetrical)
relationships as non-reciprocal (asymmetrical)
convergence
divergence
unmarked choices
marked choices
contextualization cues

7

Inter-cultural
Communication

Multiple voices: The word from Indians in England

Kirit Patel owns a chain of laundries in Manchester, England. He came to England as a refugee from East Africa in the 1970s. Even though he is of Indian descent, he was born in Uganda where he was a prosperous owner of a large grocery store. He left because the Ugandan government at the time was expelling persons of Indian origin and he felt he would have more political freedom in England. He and his wife have four children, now grown with their own families. At home, he and his wife try to speak only their first language, Gujarati, and encourage the children to speak it, too. But the children prefer to speak English and engage in codeswitching (using both Gujarati and English in the same conversation) when speaking to their parents. Kirit's grandchildren speak only English. Kirit himself speaks English a good part of the day since most of his customers and business associates are native Britons, or immigrants themselves. But hardly any of them know Gujarati. This means that English is the main language he uses because it an obvious choice as a lingua franca between immigrants from different groups and with native Britons.

7.1 Introduction

With its benefits and its problems, globalization is the order of the day. In particular, three changes are important: changes in transportation technology have made it easier to travel to faraway places; changes in communication technology have made it possible to have instant interactions via telephones and email around the world; and changes in immigration patterns have meant we see new faces and hear new languages where they were unknown even a few years ago. A major consequence is that peoples from very different societies are now in contact and have reasons to speak to each other.

When conversations take place in a language that's not the L1 of both speakers, we refer to such interactions as **inter-cultural communication**. These conversations also go under the name **cross-cultural communication**. In particular, many conversations that bilinguals have take place in the L1 of one speaker, but not the other (that is, when two people speak language X, it may be an L2 for one of them). What is one's "culture"? Perhaps most important, culture is learned; it's not something you are born with. Second, it's always a group phenomenon in the sense that it's at least partly shared with others who live in the same society. While there are many definitions of culture, a useful one for this discussion is that of Hofstede (1991: 5). He refers to culture as "the collective programming of the mind which distinguishes the members of one group or category of people from another". Also, we must keep in mind that within any so-called national culture, there are important subcultures; the ones that probably influence our patterns of language use the most are those based on gender, ethnic group, social class, region, and religion. Because we come from different cultures, either cultural differences or different understandings of what something means in our mythical language X can result in anything from humorous misunderstandings to serious problems.

Much of the study of inter-cultural communication has focused on the problems that can arise when people from different societies interact. But there is no inherent reason that problems must arise, and they don't always. When they do arise, they do so because **we attribute intentions to utterances** that go beyond the surface utterance itself. Recall that in chapter 6 we pointed out that most utterances have both referential meanings and meanings of intentionality (also called implicatures). In attributing intentions, we typically draw on our past experiences that have developed in our own societies, and that bears repeating: experiences that have developed in our own societies.

Samovar and Porter (1991: 12) put it this way, "The degree of influence culture has on inter-cultural communication is a function of the dissimilarity between the cultures." When speakers from different societies don't use their language resources as speakers do in our societies, it affects our assessments of them.

Be aware that cross-cultural communication can be more broadly defined than the way that we consider it in this chapter. Whenever a message is produced by someone from one society and has to be processed by someone from another society – that's cross-cultural communication in the broadest sense. The term "message" can mean non-verbal communication (including body movements that sometimes go under the name "body language"). And any behavior that is just observed by someone can be considered a "message" if it elicits a response from that observer. (For example, singing at 2 a.m. in the street or a physical action, such as dropping trash or smoking in a non-smoking restaurant, all could provoke responses and therefore be messages.) Further, different studies of inter-cultural communication may focus on very different aspects of the subject. For example, Clyne (1994) is a book-length treatment of discourse strategies in workplace environments in Australia, with the speakers coming from diverse language backgrounds but using English as a lingua franca.

Any individual's conception of culture is not everything he or she knows and thinks or feels about the world. Rather it is what almost always provides his or her interpretation of not only his or her own world, but of the world in general. In this sense, **culture is an individual's explanation** (i.e. his or her theory) of the code that people are following in interacting. It is our theory of the "game being played", as Keesing (1974: 89) aptly puts it. At some level, we are aware that there is a "game", but we are not necessarily consciously aware of the rules that we follow, nor could we explain them, if called upon. We know that not everyone in our own society has exactly the same view of how the game is to be played, but we expect that most members of our group do share our views. We can easily imagine that other societies see the rules of the game of life differently from us, but when they are very different, this is often a surprise and a puzzle to us. This is because everyone views his or her ways as normal; that is, we are all ethnocentric to some extent. **Ethnocentrism** is the view that one's own group is the center of everything, and other groups are rated in reference to how they stack up in relation to one's group.

Sharwood-Smith (1999) makes a practical suggestion relevant to student readers of this volume. He advises students to be aware of what might be called "an international youth culture". What he means is that there is a culture among young people that transcends some features of national cultures. So if students travel to other countries and just interact with students of their own age, they may not think there really are cross-cultural differences. Furthermore, the students they meet tend to be like-minded and the interactions in which they meet are almost always very casual. The visiting students are not observing the local students in all of their activities in their own culture and they are not interacting frequently with non-students. Looking at cross-cultural communication is important, Sharwood-Smith advises, "precisely because it is possible to go to another country and fail to notice differences, to behave inappropriately and never get corrected" (pp. 61–2).

7.2 Languages are different and so are cultures

We know that languages are different; we found that out when we studied a foreign language in school. But we often don't realize that **views of appropriate**

ways to use language in conversation also differ across different languages. That is, not only social identities emerge when conversation is exchanged between persons, but different ideas about cultural values too. Unfortunately, even when we learn an L2, we often assume that our own views about appropriate language use are universal. But they are not. Each culture has at least some different views as to **the "proper" way** to greet people, to offer them hospitality, or to carry on any conversation in general. Consider this example from a meeting of a Polish organization in Australia at which a distinguished Australian is introduced. One of the Polish hosts greets her cordially and offers her a seat of honor with these words: *Mrs. Vanessa! Please! Sit! Sit!* Wierzbicka (1991b: 27) points out that in Polish, the equivalent of *Mrs.* can be combined with first names (Vanessa in this case), but "what is more interesting . . . is the use of the short imperative *Sit!*, which makes the utterance sound like a command, and in fact like a command addressed to dog." And Victor (1992: 33–4) points out how the Swedish manufacturer of Electrolux vacuum cleaners used the slogan: "Nothing sucks like an Electrolux" in Britain without any problems, but how this slogan was unusable in the United States because as a slang word, *sucks* means something has a terrible quality, and the word also has an obscene overtone.

And here's an example showing how different cultural norms can cause serious misunderstandings. In the 1970s, a Vietnamese refugee physician, initially working as a lab technician at an American medical laboratory, thought he had made a punishable mistake at work. His crime? He responded in a casual way to a phone call, not realizing the call was from his boss (Erickson and Rittenberg, 1977). Here's the conversation:

> *Phone rings. The technologist who is expected to answer the phone isn't there;*
>   *Ky is, and he answers.*
> Ky (the Vietnamese): "Lab, Ky speaking."
> Dr. Smith (boss): "How's everything going?"
> Ky: (not recognizing voice) "Oh, pretty good."
> Dr. Smith: "This is Dr. Smith."
> Ky: "Sir! Yes, sir!"
> Dr. Smith (gives Ky his phone number and asks to have Jim, the medical technologist, call him when he gets back to the lab).
> *Conversation ends.*

Because of this conversation Ky thought he might lose his job! Dr. Smith did seem to notice that Ky had not recognized him at first, but Dr. Smith never said anything about Ky's having offended him. Even so, Ky was still anxious two days later about his "error" of giving a casual response to a superior. Clearly, Ky was operating with Vietnamese cultural norms, and apparently in the Vietnamese system speaking casually to a superior would be regarded as definitely insubordinate and maybe punishable.

7.2.1 What's marked in one culture is unmarked elsewhere

In an earlier chapter, the notion of communicative competence was introduced alongside grammatical competence. Developing abilities regarding these competencies involves both some interaction between our cognitive faculties and exposure to our language in use. Evidence of our grammatical competence is our ability to produce and recognize well-formed sentences in our own language. Our **communicative competence** shows up in our ability to recognize what would be called unmarked and marked choices under the Markedness Model (discussed in chapter 6). That is, for each of you, unmarked choices would be considered not only expected, but also appropriate, for certain interaction types in your community and marked choices would be unexpected, given the interaction type. Each carries a different type of social message (see chapter 6 for details). But the overall point of this chapter is to show how different cultures have different ideas about unmarked and marked choices. One can refer to knowing what's marked or not as **conversational etiquette**.

7.2.2 Major themes in discussing inter-cultural communication

Analysts who study inter-cultural communication come up with a variety of ways of discussing why different societies have different views about appropriate conversational etiquette. But most analysts start from the assumption that Lim (2002: 76) expresses. He states, "Forms of language not only reflect people's social position and the circumstance, but also express their **view of the way society is organized**, and of their own position within the social network . . . The forms of language encode a socially constructed representation of the world." With this in mind, we discuss three classifications of cultures that some analysts have followed. These are:

1   Do cultures favor individualism or collectivism?
2   Do they expect messages to be indirect or direct?
3   Do they expect relationships to be based on hierarchy or equality?

7.3 Dividing up societies as individualistic or collectivistic

First, many analysts view cultures by making a simple but useful two-part division based on attitudes toward group membership. Under such a scheme, cultures can be classified as **collective cultures or individualistic cultures**. The emphasis in individualistic cultures is on individuals and their striving for self-realization and achievements. In contrast, the emphasis in collectivistic cultures is on belonging to groups, and cooperation in shared activities within the group (Hofstede, 1991; Gudykunst and Kim, 1997).

Even within this division, most societies fall along a continuum, as more or less one type of culture or the other. Further, they can be collectivistic in some ways and individualistic in other ways. We mention here only some general characteristics attributed to these two types of cultures; you can see how the extended examples discussed later fit into either of these types.

In **collective cultures**, emphasis falls on **showing you belong to and respect your own group**. In such cultures, individuals don't often express their own opinions if they are different from those of the group in general; or, if they express them, they do it very indirectly. Speaking indirectly obviously means not coming right out and stating your views and desires because you must **worry about offending group members** who might not agree. "Putting oneself forward" in a variety of other ways is also frowned on, such as taking credit for anything as an individual (instead as of a group member). It's been claimed that about 70% of the population of the world lives in collectivistic cultures (Ting-Toomey and Chung, 1996).

In contrast, in **individualistic cultures**, it's considered appropriate for individuals to express themselves in various ways (i.e. they can "**speak their minds**"). The listener pays most attention to the ideas a speaker presents, not his or her group membership.

7.3.1 Equality and personal freedom

How much equality and personal freedom between group members is valued can vary in either collectivistic or individualistic cultures (Triandis, 1995). That is, relations among people can be **more horizontal or more vertical**. Thus, the fact that collectivistic cultures emphasize the group as the source of values does not mean that everyone in the group is perceived as equal. For example, even though traditional society in the Central African nation of Burundi is collectivistic, it is also vertical in the sense that there are recognized divisions in the society so that not everyone is considered equal. Also in India, another largely collectivistic society, some people see themselves as different from others. In contrast, Japan is often cited as an example of a collectivistic culture in which relations between individuals are more horizontal; that is, high value is placed on equality, or at least in not standing out from your fellow group members. You can guess that the United States is an example of a vertical, individualistic culture, but it's not the only one (Germany and France are also mentioned by Triandis). People are admired who act as individuals and stand out in these cultures. Sweden and Norway represent more horizontal, individualistic cultures.

It's important to understand that ways of speaking and attitudes pointing toward both individualism and collectivism exist in every culture, but one type tends to predominate in most nations. Examples of nations showing more individualism are Australia, Great Britain, Belgium, Canada, Denmark, France,

Germany, Ireland, Italy, New Zealand, Sweden, and the United States, according to Gudykunst (1994). And he states that most Arab, African, Asian, and Latin cultures are collectivistic. For example, he includes Brazil, China, Egypt, Ethiopia, India, Japan, Korea, Nigeria, and Saudi Arabia.

You will see how some of the extended examples given below come from collective cultures, but here's an example now, illustrating a collectivistic culture's reaction to your author, a representative of an individualistic culture. When I was in Malaŵi in East Central Africa doing field work in order to write a learner's grammar of Chicheŵa, the main language of the country, it was understandable (to me, at least!) that I had to ask Malawians a lot of questions about the language. These questions often required pinning someone down (e.g. "Is this the way you say it, or is that way better?"). To my face, I was "the professor". But since the Malawians found me to be so direct, they thought I wouldn't mind being told that behind my back I was referred to (in Chicheŵa) as *wovuta* 'the troublesome one'. I was amused, but in fact, I minded a little, since it's mainly only a child who is referred to as *wovuta*.

7.3.2 The importance of in-groups

Many analysts argue that how much value a society places on in-groups is one of the major factors differentiating individualistic and collectivistic cultures. **In-groups** are groups to which individuals have ties that are especially important to them. They almost always include family, but can include members of the same religion, members of the same organization or social group, fellow workers, etc.

Although what counts as an in-group doesn't necessarily differ between individualistic and collectivistic culture, the **in-group's influence does differ**. In collectivistic cultures, an important in-group affects behavior in many aspects of a person's life, and its effects may last for the individual's entire life. For example, in an individualistic culture, the university a person attends generally is a major influence on that person's behavior only when he or she is a student at the university (although support of the university's athletic teams may last for some graduates). In contrast, in collectivistic cultures, such as Japan and Korea, the university individuals attend influences who they choose to associate with and how they act and think throughout their adult lives (Gudykunst and Kim, 1997).

You may remember from an earlier chapter that we discussed people's social networks; you can see how in-groups are related to the networks to which people belong. In individualistic cultures, individuals may have **strong ties within an in-group**, but they also often have ties outside their group, even if these are weak ties. Such ties provide them with information about "how the other half lives" and are the route that innovations may travel into the individual's home group.

In collectivistic cultures, the views of the in-group assume more importance than any differing views the individual might have. **Emphasis is on coopera-tion** with fellow in-group members, not on the individual's own goals. Which primary in-group is more important varies across collectivist cultures; the family is the primary in-group in many Latino cultures, but in Japan, the company one works for is often considered the main in-group. Further, the individual is often viewed first and foremost as not just a member of an in-group, but a member of a sub-group within that group, so there are circles within circles. An important sub-group may be persons of the same age. Or, people from the same village constitute a sub-group.

7.3.3 Judging what others say/don't say

Viewing cultures as either collective or individualistic can offer an explanation for inter-cultural communication differences between Westerners and Asians. Many Westerners often consider Asians to be timid, or at least reserved in expressing opinions or ideas. After a conversation, a Westerner may say about an Asian participant, "It's hard to know what he's thinking." And in turn, some Asians consider many Westerners to be pushy and egotistical because do they exactly that (i.e. make clear what their views are). Communication patterns receive more attention in the next section where differences on how much speakers rely on indirectness in speech and the context to convey their meanings are discussed.

7.4 High- and low-context messages

Edward Hall (1959/1976) differentiates cultures in a related, but somewhat different way, that is more relevant to how bilinguals carry on conversations. He focuses on the types of messages that people send to each other, as either **high- or low-context messages**. In turn, cultures themselves are called **high- or low-context cultures**. A **high-context message** is one in which most of the information being conveyed rests in the context of the interaction. This means that the setting, the topic, and other situational factors are interpreted as carry-ing a large part of the message, as are the different statuses of the participants. Body language is part of the context, too (e.g. smiles, the speaker's posture, etc.). Hall says that in such a message, "very little is in the coded, explicit, transmitted part of the message" (p. 70). What he means is that the linguistic utterance itself (i.e. "what is said") carries little information about what the speaker intends to communicate. In order fully to understand what is said, the listener has to rely heavily on **working out what the speaker's intentions are**.

In contrast, in a **low-context message**, the words and phrases that the speaker produces contain the main message. If the listener can understand these words and phrases in combination, he or she can arrive at the main part of what the speaker intends to communicate. Notice we don't say that arriving at intentions is ever entirely a matter of simply decoding the linguistic utterance. There is almost always (maybe always) part of understanding an utterance that requires the listener's powers of interpretation in order to arrive at the speaker's intentions. So mutual assumptions provided by the context always matter to some extent. (Recall the discussion in chapter 6 of pragmatic intentionality and implicatures.)

Misunderstandings when high- and low-context individuals interact should come as no surprise, given the above descriptions. Listeners from high-context cultures tend to interpret what others say as **an expression of the context**; that is, they find meaning in factors external to the speaker. Listeners from low-context cultures not only **pay attention to the literal message** in the words and phrases the speaker uses, but go on to base any interpretations of the speaker's "real" meaning on his or her personality.

You can see the relationship between high- and low-context communication and individualistic and collectivistic cultures. High-context cultures **make a greater distinction between insiders and outsiders** than low-context cultures do and don't perceive people as individuals as much as they are seen as group members. Although no culture exists at either end of the high- and low-context continuum, most individualistic cultures prefer low-context messages and most collectivistic cultures prefer high-context ones. The United States is one of the cultures most favoring low-context messages. Most Asian cultures are at the high-context end of the continuum.

7.4.1 Deconstructing low- and high-context societies

Within the context of viewing cultures as **low-context and high-context societies**, Samovar and Porter (1991) argue that the interpretations of messages that we develop are based on three sets of constructs. These are (1) our belief/value/attitude systems, (2) our world view, and (3) our social organization. They go on to break down these constructs in this way.

- **Beliefs, values, attitude systems**. Our beliefs are what we accept as sources of knowledge (for example, it could be the Bible, the Qu'ran, even animal entrails or tea leaves, etc.). Our values are the qualities we think are important; normative values make up a set of rules that a culture has implicitly adopted for making choices and reducing conflicts in a given society.
- **World view**. For Porter and Samovar, a world view refers to a culture's morals or the truths it lives by, such as God, humanity, and the world of nature.
- **Social organization**. Social organization refers to how a culture organizes itself and the institutions it establishes or values. This also has to do with such issues as the use of space, the concept of time and what these mean to a particular group, etc.

Whether a culture is high- or low-context depends on how all of these constructs are interpreted in a given culture, but social organization is particularly important. Samovar and Porter make the following distinction. **In a high-context society**, most of the information about **societal priorities is "invisible"** because what is important is not said directly or may never be said at all. Further, people in high-context societies expect that others will understand their unarticulated meanings. **In a low-context society**, most of the information about what is considered important is "**right out in the open**".

Thus, the biggest difference between these two types of societies is that high-context conversations do not reveal much information about what people really consider when they organize their lives. In individualistic cultures, there is typically ongoing public discussion all the time about the pros and cons of existing social organization. That is, there is **a lot of talk**.

Just as we could immediately imagine that many Asian societies would be classified as collectivistic, not individualistic, in the first dichotomy discussed above, we also can see that in this second division, these same **Asian societies would count as high-context societies**. Reischauer (1977), who served as the US ambassador to Japan, made this comment: "The Japanese have a genuine mistrust of verbal skills, thinking that these tend to show superficiality in contrast to inner, less articulate feelings that are communicated by innuendo or by nonverbal means" (p. 136). This points to a final feature of the low-context/high-context division that we've made; that is, people in high-context societies think of people in low-context societies as less attractive and less credible. **Their lack of talk** must be a reason for this judgment.

Given the emphasis on non-verbal signals, it's not surprising that the Korean language contains the word *nuwn-chi*, literally 'eye-sense'. It is a very common expression meaning to have a sixth sense that enables you to size up the situation, just through using your eyes. A Korean colleague gave me this example:

"I visit a colleague's office when she is busy with her class preparation. She expects my visit to be brief, but I keep talking about my classes, my life, etc. without noticing that I am not welcomed there. In this situation, my colleague will think I don't have any *nuwn-chi*."

7.4.2 Confucianism and communication patterns in East Asia

A look at the writings of Confucius, who lived in about the fifth century BC, reveals an additional dimension to the concepts of collectivism and high-context messages beyond what most Westerners can imagine. (For Confucius, collectivism seems to have little to do with twentieth-century organized collectives under Communism.) In writing about the impact of Confucianism on East Asian cultural values, June Ock Yum (1991: 78) argues that ethics in Confucianism are based on **good relationships and harmonious interactions** rather than some absolute good. She states, "In East Asia, the emphasis is on proper social relationships and their maintenance rather than any abstract concern for a general collective body. In a sense, it is a collectivism only among those bound by social networks." In line with this emphasis on relationships, but not necessarily an abstract "group" in these societies, actual role terms are used rather than "you" to get someone's attention and as terms of address. Examples of occupational terms as terms of address are easily found across a variety of collectivistic cultures. For example, in Yoruba in Nigeria, a blacksmith is addressed as *alágbède* 'blacksmith' and in Chinese, a factory supervisor whose surname is Wang is addressed as *Wáng jīng lǐ*), with the Chinese term of address for 'supervisor'. Such role terms clarify and accentuate the relationship between the two speakers better than "you", according to Yum and others.

In Thailand, occupational titles are also used as second-person reference terms, and sometimes as first-person terms, too. Most denote a social superior. So university students may call their instructor *zaacaan* 'professor' and the instructor in return uses *zaacaan* to refer to him- or herself. This usage shows both social distance and closeness, because a *zaacaan* is someone of high rank who is supposed to take care of them in the context of the school (Iwasaki and Horie, 2000).

In order to develop relationships in East Asia that will meet the dictates of Confucianism, one must have frequent contacts that, if possible, create some common experiences and therefore establish a personal relationship. Thus, there is not the distinction between personal and business relationships that typically exists in Western societies. Yum states that under Confucianism, warm feelings of *jen* are generated according to one's relationship with another person. So even though Westerners may perceive East Asians as shy and retiring, they may find Asians are more willing to communicate personal information than Westerners – if their goal is to develop a social relationship. For example, I was surprised to hear (from one of her students) that a young East Asian faculty member teaching in the United States told her undergraduate class about her tendency to just leave without a certain wanted item in a supermarket if she couldn't find it on her own rather than have to speak and ask for it (thereby labeling herself as a foreigner). That's not the sort of personal information we would reveal to a class.

What Yum refers to as **"anticipatory communication"** is common in Japan; that is, the listener guesses at the speaker's point or needs. Thus, when East Asian students visiting the US are invited to American homes, they are puzzled when they are asked what they "would like". "The host is supposed to know what is needed and serve accordingly." Americans emphasize freedom of choice, but in East Asia, it is important to indicate you can anticipate what someone would like.

When you are speaking to someone whose L1 is different from yours, and your type of culture differs from theirs along the high-context/low-context continuum, you might want to consider how the way you normally carry on a conversation with just speakers of your own language would be viewed in their culture. Bear in mind that whether you are speaking in that person's L1 or yours or a neutral third language, all participants will view the exchange through the lens of their own culture.

7.5 Five areas of potential differences

We've selected five interactional elements that speakers must consider how to handle: if and when silence is valued, how what's appropriate in common conversational exchanges varies, what counts as politeness, how to make requests, and how power differentials are verbalized. Then, how these elements function in different societies is illustrated. These elements were selected for two reasons. First, they are all obvious components of interpersonal talk in any culture. For example, requesting that someone do something for you is something you have to do often. Second, they are strategies about which different cultures can have very different ideas about what's an appropriate version of the strategy and what is not. Politeness is discussed on its own, but you'll see how it affects almost all ingredients of conversation as well.

7.6 Is silence golden?

When should you remain silent and when not? Remaining silent unless called upon to speak is favored in many collectivistic cultures, especially if you are the less powerful person in a relationship. In some American Indian cultures, for example, the Navajo, long periods of silence are normal parts of any conversational exchange. By Western standards, people from many Asian cultures are considered very silent – too silent. "So and so doesn't hold up his end of the conversation," some Westerners may think. But in some Western cultures, such as among some Scandinavians, **silence is favored** unless the person has something pressing to say. Finns, especially, have a reputation for saying little. At a dinner party in Sweden recently, fellow linguist Elin Fredsted found herself seated between two male Finns. She recalled, "They did perhaps speak four or five sentences each the whole evening. And I think that they thought they were being very entertaining!" In contrast, in other Western cultures, such as among North Americans, silence in a conversation is uncomfortable. People will even end up bringing up inane topics ("Just look at how hard it's raining!") just to **fill up silences**. For most North Americans, silences maintained very long are a sign of some kind of failure of rapport between the potential speakers.

The value placed on silence in American Indian interactions often has been recognized. Scollon and Wang-Scollon (1990) offer this explanation of why silence is the choice in some conversations among the Athabaskan Indians in northern Canada whom they have studied. They write, "there is a real difference between Athabaskans and English speakers in how much they choose to speak . . . Athabaskans have a high degree of respect for the individuality of others, and a careful guarding of one's own individuality. As a result, any conversation can be threatening because of the possibility of a negotiated change of point of view. Athabaskans avoid conversation except when the point of view of all participants is well known" (1990: 263). Scollon and Wang-Scollon say the difference between how Athabaskans and English-speakers view conversation has to do with the negotiation of what they call intersubjective reality. This term refers to a frequent conversational goal (especially found in Western societies) for each person to check out his or her sense of reality (i.e. point of view) against the reality of each other person in conversation. Part of this checking out may result in encouraging others to change their point of view; Athabaskans may view this as disrespect for individual rights.

Wieder and Pratt (1990) provide some personal examples that illustrate how silence has worked in interactions among another group of Indians (although the Indian group is not identified). Based on their research among Indian consultants, the authors conclude that "the real Indian . . . must know that neither he nor the others has an obligation to speak – that silence on the part of all conversants is permissible" (p. 59). For Indians, **silence is a way of being with others**.

The consultants of Wieder and Pratt related a number of narratives showing how silence is considered in their group. One said this: "I passed this Indian girl on the way to class for two months, and we never spoke – she knew who I was, and I knew her name." The reason for such behavior comes clear after the authors discuss rights and obligations in this group's conversations. Once acquaintance is established, then participants must engage in further interaction whenever the two cross paths. The consultant's narrative goes on, "After we started talking, I had to stop and talk each time I saw her. We both usually wound up being late for class, but if I hadn't stopped to talk, she would have thought I was 'acting-some-kind-of-way'" (p. 53). Another consultant had this to say about a conference he attended: "When I was at this conference, this other Indian girl and I never did talk to each other until the last night. There was one girl who was there and did come up and talk to me who said she was Indian, but I could tell she wasn't because if she was, she probably wouldn't have come up and talked to me." That is, "a real Indian would not initiate an interaction so casually, abruptly, and idly" (p. 52).

Another consultant related what happened when his professor organized a group of Indians and gave them a topic to discuss. "Most did not participate and those who did participate knew the least," the narrator says. Those who knew the most said such things as "I don't know, what do you think?" and "I guess so. That sounds all right to me" (p. 57).

Long pauses of silence represent one end of a continuum of how much speech is appropriate. At the other extreme, in Antigua, the West Indies, loud talk is frequent and **talk can become a competition** of who can dominate the conversational floor. Reisman (1974: 111) describes such conversations in this way: "there are a variety of ways of speaking that Antiguans sometimes call 'making noise' . . . 'To make noise' may refer to **the assertion of oneself** by the sound of one's voice." For example, taking turns in conversations hardly exists because while taking what would count as a turn, the speaker may break the turn to greet someone, make a remark to someone else, and then take his turn back on the original conversation. Also, there are no norms against interrupting others, and not even any norms governing the need to stop if one is not heard. Reisman says that one can go right on, with only one listener or even no listeners. Also, loud boasting as one walks by the house of the intended addressee is a show of strength as a response to a tease or challenge. It is also a form of defense against any attacks or criticism.

7.7 Ideas about "good" conversational routines differ

Can we find similarities in all routine exchanges of words? It seems that certain everyday conversational routines can be very different.

7.7.1 Greeting routines

An investigation of the best way to communicate in initial face-to-face interactions (i.e. the greeting routine) showed significant differences across four different Spanish-speaking groups and United States Anglos. Two findings were of special interest: (1) The US Latinos had much more in common with US Anglos than they did with the other three Spanish-speaking groups. (2) The findings didn't allow for many generalizations across all the Spanish-speaking groups, even if the US Latinos are excluded. The study by Johnson, Lindsey, and Zakahi (2001) relied on self-reports via a questionnaire that was given to 458 persons, with relatively equal numbers of both sexes and respondents from these groups: US Anglos, US Latinos, Mexicans, Chileans, and Spaniards. Subjects were asked to rate more than 20 possible characteristics of a greeting routine as to what would be considered a good part of communication in an initial encounter in their culture. These characteristics included: pay close attention, make eye contact, and exhibit appropriate posture.

Although these results are based on what respondents judge is appropriate, not what they actually do, the results still indicate trends and show that not all Spanish L1 speakers have the same ideas and that living in the same nation (Anglos and Latinos in America) seems to lead people to express similar views.

As some readers might expect, Mexicans, Chileans, and Spaniards differ from American Latinos and Anglos in their expectation that **appropriate initial interaction** includes kissing, but they also differ regarding the degree of appropriate head nodding, and appropriate posture, among other characteristics. The Mexicans, Chileans, and both American groups all place importance on eye contact. Among the non-US groups, Mexicans and Spaniards differ from Chileans in the rated importance of attentiveness and maintaining eye contact during a social interaction.

7.7.2 At a loss for words

It may come as a surprise to some readers, but the concepts encoded by the English words *thanks* and *apology* don't really fit all cultures. Consider how expressing thanks is handled in Japanese. It's been said that societies can be divided into two types: those preoccupied with rights and those preoccupied with obligations. If that's correct, Japan clearly falls in the camp focusing on obligations (Wierzbicka, 1991a).

To most Westerners, **an appreciation routine** including *thanks* is the unmarked ("normal") expression to show that one feels good toward someone about something that person has done. But, for example, in Japanese culture, with its stress on obligatory repayment of all favors or acts of kindness, saying *thanks* is not so normal (Coulmas, 1981). Rather, a more normal response is to say something, such as *sumimasen* (literally, 'it never ends', but meaning "I recognize my unending indebtedness to you" (that is, this is used in situations when Westerners would use *thanks* or its equivalent in their languages). But Japanese use the same expression in situations calling for an apology. To make sense of this, you must realize that the emphasis in the Japanese culture is on **recognizing an obligation**, not on conveying a good feeling toward someone who does something for you. So you incur a debt either for what someone does for you or for a mistake or omission you make. And because whatever the Japanese say in circumstances calling for gratitude expresses a feeling of "**unrepayable debt**", we can imagine that the net result is a link between "a feeling of quasi-gratitude with something like a feeling of guilt" Wierzbicka (1991b: 158). Not a happy ending!

Further, the stress in Japanese culture on hierarchical relationships means it's unlikely that one word to express thanks could even be appropriate in all the different circumstances in which you thank someone. Thus, it is not so surprising Japanese doesn't have a verb corresponding to the English verb *to thank*. There is a verb borrowed from Chinese *kansha suru*, but this is largely used only in the written language.

Wierzbicka also points out that in the Australian language Walmatjari, spoken in Western Australia, there is a speech act related both to English *to ask (for)* and English *to order*, but not the same as either. Walmatjari has a special word, *japirlyung*, for requests based on kinship rights that cannot be refused. But, of course, such speech acts are not really requests. In effect, such a speech act means "I want something and everyone has to do good things for others because of the way we are related; therefore, I think you will do this". So the speaker expects the addressee will do what is asked, not because of a hierarchical relationship, but because of a system that involves everyone in reciprocity.

7.7.3 Differing views about a conventional service encounter

Differing views between Korean owners and African-American customers in Los Angeles about what constitutes showing respect is the subject of Bailey (1997). Bailey videotaped and analyzed 25 interactions in a Korean-owned liquor store in Los Angeles. One problem is that the two groups have different concepts of the **relationship between customer and storekeeper** and different ideas about appropriate talk in a service encounter. But a bigger problem is that culture-specific frameworks, as stereotypes about other cultures, influence perceptions. Bailey states that his observations and videotape do not reveal the stereotype of the "inscrutably silent, non-greeting, gaze-avoiding, and non-smiling Korean storekeepers which were cited by African-Americans in media accounts and in interviews with me" (p. 339).

But videotaped records do reveal "subtle but consistent differences" between the two groups in their forms of talk. African-American customers consistently offer sociable comments. When Korean store keepers respond, "Many responses display an understanding of referential content of utterances – but no alignment with the emotional stance of the customer's talk, e.g. humor or indignation" (338). That is, Koreans do respond, but tend to respond with what Bailey calls **"restraint politeness"** rather than **"involvement politeness"**. What is lacking in the responses of many Korean storekeepers is what African-American customers (and probably many other Americans) would interpret as a show of interest in the other speaker or a willingness to "take a joke" by responding in a joking way to what's intended as a joke.

7.7.4 Culturally distinctive strategies

Many other cultures have types of conversational routines that are distinctive, if not unique. Daniel and Smitherman (1990) describe and analyze the significance of call–response routines in traditional African-American churches in the United States. These routines function to emphasize group cohesiveness and cooperation. A **call–response routine** beginning with the well-known gospel song "How I got over" illustrates this strategy between the church leader and the church congregation:

Leader (call): How –
Background (response): How I got over
Leader (repeat with emphatic feeling): I said how –
Background: How I got over
Leader: My soul –
Background: My soul look back and wonder –
Leader: How
Background: How I got over

(p. 35)

The **ritual insults** of African-American adolescents in the United States are well known. Such speech acts are also called "playing the dozens". This way of talking is a way to show one's wit and daring in breaking the rules of mainstream society. In many societies there are culture-specific speech acts that men engage in involving apparent insults that are a form of "shared fun", and ritual insults are most associated with boys. Of course, in many ways, the current hip-hop industry in popular music simply follows in the footsteps of these speech styles in African-American adolescents. But African-American girls can and do produce ritual insults, too. Marjorie Harness Goodwin (1990) gives some choice examples said by a girl. Here's one of them between a girl and a boy.

The interaction begins when Malcolm makes a negative comment about Ruby's shoes (he says, *Shoes all messed up.*) The confrontation progresses until a point when Ruby implies Malcolm's house is full of roaches:

Ruby: One day (0.2)
  *H(my)**brother** was spendin' the night with **you***
  hAnd// the next mornin' he got up,
Malcolm: I don't wann hear about it.
  *Your brother// ain't never been in **my** house.*
Ruby: THE NEXT TIME HE GOT UP,
  heh He was gonna brush his teeth
  so the roach tri(h)ed ta(h) bru(h)sh hi(h)s!

(pp. 291–2)

H, h = a breathy addition that is not part of a completed word
// = a slight pause

Writing about Israel, Katriel (1986) provides an analysis of a speech event called "a *dugri* talk". To "speak *dugri*" means '**to talk straight**', but also to say something the speaker thinks the addressee needs to hear, whether it's welcome or not. Katriel refers to speaking *dugri* as a ritual act of confrontation at the expense of harmony, but resulting in a moment of true contact. The sentence "he is *dugri*" means "that the speaker tends to be direct and straightforward in expressing his non-complimentary thoughts or opinions" (p. 15). The idea is that such talk symbolizes the cultural values of frankness and hardness associated with native-born Israelis.

7.7.5 Communicating personal information

In general, members of individualistic cultures tend to use a direct style of speech and members of collectivistic cultures use a more indirect style. This difference is apparent not just in their requesting behavior, but in all of their language use. For example, speakers from individualistic cultures **feel free to ask questions**. Still, in many individualistic cultures many personal questions are considered as "nosey" except among close friends (about topics such as one's age, religion, or political affiliation). For example, some Americans we know say "my parents taught me never to talk about religion or politics in polite company". Some British persons consider it prying when Americans – who think they are just making small talk – ask "What do you do?" (i.e. "What is your occupation?") at a social event. This is something Americans routinely ask American strangers when they meet for the first time at a social event. But if they get more personal, it is often only to give compliments about one's appearance, even to strangers. Especially women do this.

But it may surprise any readers from individualistic cultures that persons from collectivistic cultures who supposedly value indirection can be very direct at asking what others consider personal questions. For example, when I was teaching in mainland China in the early 1980s and Western foreigners were still rare, frequently persons who spoke enough English to question me would stop me on the street. The first question they asked me was predictable ("Where do you come from?"). But the second question always surprised me ("How old are you?"). One reason for a question about age in any Asian society may be that it's very important to show the appropriate conversational **deference to match the age of the individual**. The older the person, the more deferential you're supposed to be. Jan Bernsten, who lived in Indonesia for several years, offered this explanation, "My Indonesian friends told me that they have a very hard time estimating a white person's age by looking at us (we Anglos all look the same). So, in order to decide on a style that would be considered polite, they ask our age."

What is interesting here is that people from individualistic societies value their own individuality, but aren't necessarily willing to engage in a lot of self-disclosure (i.e. revealing information about themselves as individuals). This may be a reason behind the description that Daun (1991) offered of typical Swedes as persons who readily participate in formalized social interactions (they join voluntary associations, take courses, etc.) but don't extend their circle of informal interactions far beyond their families and a few close friends. The reason may be that one can participate in such formalized social interactions without much self-disclosure, thereby maintaining personal independence. And it's possible that persons from collectivistic cultures may ask people from these individualistic cultures certain questions because they don't view them as private individuals, but want to find out something about them *as group members*.

7.8 The faces of politeness

Don't think of being polite as saying the equivalent in your language of "please" and "thank you". Rather, think of politeness as a technical term that means **attention paid to self-respect** of the addressee and ultimately of oneself. Brown and Levinson (1987) refer to politeness as **meeting a person's "face needs"** for self-respect. But not all cultures have the same idea about appropriate ways to meet face needs.

Everyone has two faces that need attention. A person's **positive face** is one's need to have self-worth recognized. The way to preserve someone's positive face is by paying positive attention to that person. In some cultures, positive attention can be such conversational moves as complimenting a person on his or her appearance or achievements. Another way is to use language that builds solidarity with that person (e.g. remembering the person's name, using "we" to include the person in your group). (But how much such solidarity is welcomed depends on the culture.)

A person's **negative face** is one's need not to be imposed on. But the problem is that any time you ask someone to do something, you are imposing on that person. The solution is that there are ways to cut down on the imposition, based on how you ask (saying "Give me that!" can be very imposing in comparison with "Would you please give that to me?" and "If it's not too much trouble, could you please hand that to me?" is even less imposing).

The problem cross-culturally is that cultures can differ a lot in terms of how much attention people like to have paid to their positive face and in what is considered imposing to a person's negative face. In fact, it can be argued that some cultures are basically positive politeness cultures and others are more negative politeness cultures.

What does this mean? This means for some cultures, paying a lot of attention to meeting positive face needs is expected (i.e., using a lot of **strategies that express approval**). In such cultures, giving compliments and offering many and varied expressions of gratitude is expected.

In other cultures, paying a lot of attention to avoiding impositions is important. Protecting a person's negative face through a good deal of indirection is expected, and this means there are many **mitigations** to weaken requests and many apologies for any impositions.

But there are **tensions between meeting the needs of an individual's positive and negative faces**. A problem is that paying positive attention can be seen as imposing, and attempts to avoid imposing can be viewed as ignoring a person's desire for clarity in messages (a form of positive attention). For example, even though giving compliments is a form of positive attention, they can be considered imposing in some cultures because they are viewed as unwelcome attention to self. And very indirect requests that may seem to the speaker as appropriate ways to avoid imposing can be viewed as annoying by the addressee from another culture because they "beat around the bush" too much.

Further, we must always keep in mind some of the limitations of our own views of politeness, as Rosaldo (1982) points out in her analysis of speech acts, especially directives, among the Ilongot peoples in the Philippines. She cautions that "concerns for 'politeness' themselves are dependent on local forms of social inequality and hierarchy, forms which differ considerably between such relatively 'egalitarian' peoples as the Ilongots and ourselves" (p. 230).

Three examples of specific studies that illustrate contrasting views of politeness follow.

7.8.1 Paying attention to positive face in Tlaxcala, Central Mexico

In the peasant culture of Tlaxcala, Mexico, bilingual speakers of Nahuatl and Spanish have ideas about meal time politeness that contrast with any views in other cultures that guests should be reserved. Hill (1980) characterized these Nahuatl-Spanish bilinguals as "paying **attention to mutual solidarity**, managed through constant attention to positive face" (p. 4). This view of politeness was especially evident at meals. First, upon arrival for a meal, Hill and her husband, who were doing linguistic field work in the area, were greeted with elaborate attention to their efforts at making the visit ("What a miracle! We thought you weren't going to come!"). As part of the "we" attention to positive face and "feel-good" politeness, the Hills would be figuratively included in the family.

But as guests, this meant they **could refuse neither food or nor drink**. Refusing food would be a threat to the host's positive face in this culture. There was no place for a Western refusal, even a refusal that could attend to both the host's positive face and the speaker's own negative face, such as, "Oh, it looks absolutely delicious, but I'm trying to lose some weight." Hill writes, "Solidarity is valued over freedom to negotiate . . . the negative-face option of not eating is simply unavailable in interactions with Tlaxcalan peasants." (p. 9). The following exchange (the original was in Nahuatl) illustrates Hill's point: when another guest urged Hill to drink more, Hill said, "I cannot drink any more, or I will vomit." Replied her friend, "You can vomit here! This is your house!" (p. 11).

7.8.2 "I will need to see you about the report." French and Australian office requests

Another example of differences across cultures concerning what is polite or not comes from interactions between French and Australian English-speakers in a study of interactions on the job in a large French company in Melbourne, Australia (Béal, 1998). All interactions were in English and the French-speakers had studied English at school and had been in Australia between six months and two years. When interviewed, the workers made comments that showed a **clashing concept of politeness in directives**. ("Directive" is a cover term for any request for action on the part of the addressee.) First, results of the interviews and the workers' actual behavior indicated that the French people differentiated "giving instructions" from "asking for a favor". This meant that the French expected requests in the office to be given in a relatively direct fashion. The French requests looked like this: "Start on that tomorrow" or "I want you to have a look at it before I send it", whereas the Australians expected all requests to be given with some indirectness (e.g. "If you don't mind, leave that there").

Altogether, the Australians and French co-workers differed considerably in requests that asked for information. The overall results showed mirror patterns for the two groups of speakers in their use of any softening device when they made requests. For the Australians, 60% had one or more softening device in their requests. (Softeners might be openers such as "Could you/would you", or minimizers such as "a little".) But only 40% of the French requests contained similar softeners, so 60% of them did not.

There were also a number of more subtle differences that surprised Australian workers. For example, French-speakers seemed to translate the standard French apology of *Excusez-moi de vous déranger* 'excuse me for disturbing you' into English, and then use the English equivalent at times when English speakers would not use it. The Australians thought this expression was often too elaborate for an office interchange. For example, a French-speaker telephoned a fellow worker [at work in the same business] and said, "Ann? Sorry for disturbing you. It's Béatrice. Could you check something for me?" One Australian (who knew no French) said, "It's the sort of thing you'd [only] say if you were waking someone up at three in the morning."

7.8.3 Entschuldigung. Ich habe eine Frage. "Excuse me. I have a question."

The preceding example shows how easy it is for speakers of language X to assume that speakers of language Y have a strange sense of politeness. We turn now to another case where things are not what they seem. Scandinavians are often considered taciturn, the kind of people who say only as much as is required. So it's assumed they don't pay much positive attention to their listeners' face needs because they just say "the facts". However, a study in a Danish tourist information office showed that yes, **Danes do say little**, but they communicate positive attention to their listeners in subtle ways, some of which are **non-verbal ways**. Fredsted (2005) compared politeness strategies in interactions in Danish and German tourist offices.

In the Danish office, Danish tourists showed a clear tendency to start off by explicitly saying what they wanted (the equivalent of "I have just arrived in town and I would like a couple of tips about what one ought to see when here"). They also ended with an similarly unvarnished conclusion (the equivalent of "Then we will take this flyer with us and study it"). Although 65% of the Danes (35/53) said *tak* (Danish for "thank you"), they were no more elaborate than that and some walked away without saying anything.

In contrast, the German tourists in a German tourist office typically showed more **attention to building solidarity** through their speech, thus showing positive attention. They typically began their interactions with a pre-request (the equivalent of "Excuse me. I have a question"). They ended with elaborate thanks. In fact, in general, the German tourists (and even the tourist official) used many **lexical upgrades**. That is, the Germans said things like "such a lovely old city" and "I like it very much". So, on the surface of talk, it seems as if the Germans give a good deal of positive attention to the official and express their approval of the local sights, but the Danes simply mention the necessary details.

However, Fredsted shows that, in fact, the Danes express some attention to the tourist office official's positive face (i.e. sense of self-value), too, but in less obvious ways. First, the Danish tourists use hesitation markers (saying "eh", "mm") or shaking their heads when they make the type of requests that they might expect won't be met (e.g. asking about a guide who gives tours). And there is much more eye contact by the Danes with the tourist officials than there is on the part of the German tourists in eight videotaped conversations that Fredsted analyzed (27% of the time by Danes compared with 18% by Germans).

7.9 How to ask for something in different cultures

Expectations about how people will ask for something vary a great deal across cultures. Still, at least in the cultures looked at here, speakers and listeners seem to implicitly "know" what counts as a reasonable way to make a request. As you will see, a survey of respondents from five different Western societies showed that in all societies, speakers are expected to make overt requests, but often they are also expected to mitigate them. They do this by making their requests indirect, but in ways that, by convention, make them recognizable as requests. In contrast, in the Igbo society requests can be very direct, and the addressee knows what is expected of him or her in the given context, and does the task. In contrast, in another non-Western society (in Malagasy), requests are very indirect.

7.9.1 Requests in Western societies

Blum-Kulka and House (1989) compared five national groups in five situations to see how they made requests. The groups were native speakers of Hebrew, Canadian French, Argentinian Spanish, Australian English, and German. They were provided with a set of 16 scenarios in their own languages and were asked to fill in the request form (directive) they would use in each scenario. In effect, this was a self-report survey. Each scenario had a specific addressee and dealt with a specific situation; these were the same for all languages. For example, in one scenario the speaker is to think of him- or herself as a policeman who asks a driver to move his or her car; in another scenario, a student asks his or her roommate to clean up the kitchen the other left in a mess.

Overall, what the authors call **conventionally indirect requests** outnumber all others. They classified requests into three general categories: direct, explicit requests (e.g. imperatives such as "Clean up the kitchen"); what they called **non-conventionalized indirect requests** (e.g. "The kitchen needs to be cleaned"), and conventionally indirect requests. When requests show conventional indirectness, they are indirect because they include **mitigations** to cut down on the force of the utterance. (Mitigations include words such as "possibly" and phrases such as "when you get a chance".) These requests are conventionalized because they follow a certain formula that makes them recognizable as directives in the relevant community. Such directives have a beginning with a modal verb plus "you" (e.g. "can you") that gives them the same syntactic form as some questions, even though they are interpreted as directives. The "could you/can you" beginning is found across all language groups. For example, in Australian English, "Could you please clean up?" or "Can you give me a lift home?" were favorite choices. Another common conventionally indirect form has to do with willingness ("Would you mind?"), but in this form it appeared only in Hebrew and Australian English. In both Spanish and French an express questioning of a hearer's willingness or wishes was more common (the equivalent of "Would it bother you" or "Would you like").

Blum-Kulka and House found that Australian English-speakers switch the form of their request the least, using requests that show conventional indirectness as a first preference for all situations. Over 82% of their directives fell into this category. Speakers of Hebrew and Argentinian Spanish varied their requests the most, depending on the situation, and they were generally more direct than the other speakers; they both had just 59% in the conventionally indirect category.

In general, the authors found that speakers from all the cultures shared the common feature of **varying the directness of their directives by situation**. But the groups disagreed on which situations received the most direct directives. An important overall finding was that there weren't sharp differences in the degree of directness in requests across the speakers of the different languages, only gradient ones. Still, the authors conclude that "these results do confirm the importance of directness levels as cultural indicators of interactional styles" (p. 150).

7.9.2 Requests among the Igbo

The Igbo ethnic group of southeast Nigeria follows many of the tenets of a collectivist culture but this does not mean that the directives that Igbos use with fellow Igbos are indirect. "The Igbo disposition to care more for the collective image of the group than for that of the individual accounts for why acts normally regarded as impositions in some other societies are not so regarded by the Igbo" (Nwoye, 1992: 316). It's expected that **inconveniences are simply suffered** in the interest of communal or societal cohesion, and in the belief in the reciprocity of hospitality. Thus, requests don't take the form of conventional indirectness that they often do in Western societies.

Nwoye relates an example from his own experience. When his car broke down on a lonely road, he went to a nearby house, extended customary greetings, and requested help from a man and his son there. He had never met them before. His request was very direct, but he reported that the man and his son followed him and helped him and then waved him on. Here is what was said (in Igbo):

> moto m nokatalu kwusi bia nyelu m aka kwaa ya aka.
> "My car has suddenly stopped, come and help me push it."

Nwoye argues that a conventionally indirect request (e.g. the Igbo equivalent of "Can you help me push this car?") would have been marked (unexpected) in this situation.

7.9.3 Requests in Malagasy

But in yet another collectivistic, non-Western society, the Malagasy community of Madagascar, extreme indirection is the valued form of requests (Keenan, 1974). Their requests must observe overall social norms that call for avoiding direct affronts and confrontations. For example, a person who insults another is ignored by those sympathetic to the insulted person; in one case, the insulting person was physically cut off from the village by blocking her footpath to the village.

Because requests, no matter how small, are necessarily a form of confrontation in any society, of course Malagasy people always use **indirection with their requests**. Keenan discusses requests as falling into two categories, requests for those things that the speaker knows the addressee is obligated to give, and those things for which no obligation exists. Both types call for indirection, but the degree varies. For example, a kinsman may enter a house and say as a greeting, *Iona no maska?* "What's cooking?" This is taken as a request for food, which the speaker has a right to, but even in this case, the request is not very direct. For many other things, the request must be made in a very indirect manner or even through an intermediary. Keenan gives these examples. Young boys suddenly speak of a journey to be made that night and how dark it is and the need for candles. (This is taken as a request for candles.) In Keenan's presence, women chatter about the poor quality of Malagasy soap as compared with European soap. (This is a way to ask Keenan for soap.)

Especially men operate very indirectly and, partly because of this, they are claimed to be more skillful speakers than women. It is the women who communicate sentiments that men share but dislike expressing. That is, women are expected to be direct when it's useful. For example, they are the ones who buy necessities and they sell village produce (men weigh produce and take the money). Men typically sell only those items having a fixed price.

7.10 Cross-cultural ideas about power differentials

In any society, no matter how small, there is inequality, no matter how much at least some cultures desire and promote equality. Some people always have more power and more recognized status than others. For our purposes, power is "the control someone has over the outcomes of others". And status in the context of this discussion is "the respect that someone enjoys because of physical or intellectual capacities or wealth".

Because what counts as a power differential exists outside of conversation in a sense that views about silence and politeness do not, we need to pay special attention to the ways in which different cultures deal with power differentials in their patterns of language use. Some of the different views on the necessity to recognize this control in conversations may surprise you – or not.

Hofstede came up with a construct to refer to the extent to which people accept power differentials. He uses the term **power distance** to define "the extent to which the less powerful members of institutions and organizations within a country expect and accept that power is distributed unequally" (1991: 28). Note that this construct explains attitudes toward power from the standpoint of the *less* powerful members. The idea is that authority only survives where it is matched by obedience. That's an excellent observation, but "power distance" itself strikes us as a rather opaque term. Instead, we will take Hofstede's basic idea, but refer to **inequity tolerance**. This term stresses the tolerance less powerful individuals in any interaction have for inequity and the degree of such tolerance high-status people expect. This leads to a third way to divide societies – along the dimension of **equality and hierarchy**. That is, some cultures value equality among individuals, but other cultures value, or at least expect, hierarchy in interpersonal relationships.

Because of our interest in language use in this volume, we are especially interested in what conversational strategies less powerful persons will put up with in conversational interactions. That is, what level of inequity will they tolerate in turns to speak, speaking time, and how they are spoken to by the more powerful persons?

At the societal level, we can roughly classify whole societies in terms of the degree of inequity tolerance high-status people expect and receive from low-status people. Inequities are visible in the existence of different social classes and different occupations or roles within the same job site. Inequities surface especially in terms of ethnic, age, and gender differences.

7.10.1 Equality and hierarchy in the family

Expectations about tolerating inequities are first shaped in the family. Consider how talk from children is viewed. In many traditional cultures, children do not speak unless spoken to. Obviously, such societies fall at the high end of the hierarchical end of the equality–hierarchy continuum. That is, power is not distributed equally and the **children accept the inequality of the situation**. For example, in the Gonja ethnic group in West Africa that Goody (1978) studied, men are traditional weavers. But sons may not ask their father questions. How then is a son to learn how to weave if he can't ask his father questions? He must ask his father's brother for help.

In general, children are expected to show a good deal of obedience toward their parents when tolerance for hierarchical relationships, based on familial role, is expected. In such societies, the pattern of obedience and dependence on seniors lasts throughout the children's lives. When they are young, children are looked after with much affection, but they are not encouraged to show independence. In contrast, in other societies which fall at the other extreme of the continuum (i.e. they have a low tolerance for inequities based on age or parental power), the goal is to raise children showing initiative and independence from an early age.

Mealtime conversations vary cross-culturally in regard to the degree of deference that is expected from children. In some Western cultures, children who ask questions of any family member at mealtime or volunteer news are admired and even praised for their initiative; being inquisitive is seen as a sign of intelligence and even maturity. But a comparative study of mealtime conversation across Swedish, Finnish and Estonian families found that Finns and Estonians spoke less than did Swedes, even those Finns and Estonians living in Sweden, and the difference was statistically significant (Tulviste, Mizera, de Geer, and Tryggvason, 2002). In Swedish L1 families, children were much more active than in the other families. The norm in Sweden is that everyone should enjoy the same kind of social arrangements (Daun, 1991).

The social class and education level of parents often play a decisive role. In some middle class families children seldom show formal respect and deference to their elders and when they grow up, they replace the child–parent relationship with one of equals or near equals. For example, parents and grown children can have animated discussions about current events, including politics. "Family relations in such societies often strike people from other societies as cold and distant," Hofstede remarks (1991: 33).

A recent *New York Times* article about Iraqi family bonds reinforces this point. Both young adult and elderly Iraqis express pity for American parents and children living thousands of miles from each other. "Families are supposed to be together," said an adult son. "It is cruel to keep children and parents apart" (September 28, 2003).

In some countries, there is a division in views toward authority in the family and in the workplace, too, that is along class lines. That is, studies have shown that lower-status employees, even in various Western countries, hold more "authoritarian" values at work than their higher-status compatriots. This carries over into their views about family interactions.

7.10.2 Decisions in a factory

Tolerance for expressions of inequities in the workplace varies from one culture to the next, with collectivistic cultures showing both more and less tolerance. This becomes more obvious if we look at how authority is expressed. Consider the following case study.

Maquiladora is the Spanish name given to twin factories on the border between the United States and Mexico. Most are American-owned, but some are owned by other nations, such as Japan. When US, Japanese, and Mexican workers are all located within a single organization, there is a potential for discord when different groups have **differing views about expressing and accepting power inequities**. We interpret these views in terms of degrees of worker-based tolerance for explicit expressions of power differences. McDaniel and Samovar (1997) describe cross-cultural differences in a Japanese-owned maquiladora. In both Japan and Mexico, relatively high differences in inequity are accepted, but for different reasons. And this acceptance is expressed in different ways. In Japan, workers advance by a system of seniority, but the way the system works is accepted, even though the bottom line is that not everyone is equal. Recall that the Japanese value harmony, so before implementing a new policy or changing procedures, a Japanese supervisor will try to establish consensual agreement. In Mexico, workers accept that those in charge have authority and seldom question authority; in turn, higher-status persons take an autocratic approach when making and implementing decisions. In contrast, in the United States, upward advancement is largely based on individual accomplishment and initiative; talented workers can be promoted ahead of others with more seniority.

When workers and management interact, US workers "have little difficulty in openly disagreeing with their superiors ... This world view, focusing on the individual and his or her personal achievements, can produce conflict when Americans interact with people enculturated with differing concepts of authority" (p. 292). When speaking to the managers, Mexican workers try to provide only positive information and the Japanese, who place emphasis on indirectness, avoid a direct "no".

7.10.3 Requests as expressions of power

You can imagine that societies also differ in views about the extent to which power distances are appropriately conveyed in language-use patterns in the workplace. Requests are one of the most frequent components of workplace conversation. Above, we discussed requests as politeness strategies. But they belong here, too. Power differentials often show up, not just in who makes requests, but in the **structure of a request** that one person gives another. Ervin-Tripp (1976) offers an extensive discussion of the structure of requests (also called **directives**) in the United States and the ingredients of situations where each type is expected. Above, we noted that conventionally indirect requests are common in the five Western societies studied, and Ervin-Tripp indicated that such directives are almost the all-purpose choice in the United States, too. Recall that these types of directives typically consist of a modal verb plus *you* (e.g. "can you" or "could you") preceding the actual request (e.g. "Can you help me with this?").

But studies of American office interactions do show variation in the preferred directives across the statuses of the speaker and addressee. People in positions of power give more direct requests than their subordinates (i.e., imperatives such as "Get that done as soon as you can", "Mail this today"). But this pattern isn't always found. One obvious reason is that the view in many American workplaces is that accepting and expressing a high power distance is frowned upon. In such cases, everyone in the same office uses the same directive type most of the time; of course there still is a power differential, but it's not salient in making a request.

Still, especially in "blue-collar" workplaces (employing many manual workers), power differentials are very salient and show up in bald imperatives from the supervisors in charge (cf. Bernsten, 1998). A student of mine studied requests in a warehouse where he worked part-time in the evening. He found that the supervisors there normally gave direct directives most of the time; they peppered them with obscenities, too, as the evening wore on and work piled up.

But in another student's study, the senior attorney in a law office used mainly conventionally indirect embedded imperatives to subordinates (e.g. "Could you please do x?"). Was it that he felt he was so powerful that he could afford to weaken his requests but still expect everyone to comply? In this same office, a young attorney (several steps down the pecking order) used more bald imperatives to secretaries and law student interns than the senior attorney did. One explanation is that the young attorney (a woman) was negotiating a position of power (i.e., as deserving recognition as powerful) through these choices.

7.10.4 Who speaks first or the most

In many cultures, the sign of power differentials is who speaks first and who speaks later or not at all. Consider who speaks or **the order of speaking** when everyone is an adult. Often, no one expresses an opinion before the most powerful person speaks. And then agreement with whatever that person says is the expected choice. This scenario is played out in the boardrooms of international corporations in individualistic cultures just as often as it occurs in a collectivistic Third-World village council. Also, consider who speaks the most. Even in the most individualistic societies, most participants in conversation expect the more powerful or statusful persons to take the most turns at talk and to talk the most.

Also in any conversational group, people in positions of power can nominate topics for discussion much more freely than persons of less power. For example, generally a boss may ask how the secretary's son is doing in his first year as a university student much more easily than the secretary can inquire about the boss's son.

7.10.5 Negotiating status

Still, even where power differentials are explicit (depending on age, sex, and caste as well as achieved prestige resulting from wealth or reputation for morality), there is often some room for negotiation. Irvine (1974) demonstrates this in her discussion of **status manipulation in greeting routines** among Wolof ethnic group members in Senegal, West Africa. The name of the game here is to lower one's status. Why should anyone want to do this? "Although high status implies prestige, respect, and political power, it also implies the obligation to contribute to the support of low-status persons. Thus high rank means a financial burden, while low rank has its financial compensations" (p. 175). Anyone may use this strategy, no matter what his or her previous standing is in terms of the categories of caste, age, and sex, etc.; purposes vary depending on what that previous standing is.

If two Wolof people meet on a road or elsewhere, because both physical activity and speech activity are duties which low-status persons perform for persons of higher status, the person who initiates the greeting can claim to be lower in status. But he must keep the initiative in the conversation, too. He does this by asking many questions about the other's welfare (a sign as well that the other is higher in status). The other person can ignore the questions and try to take over the role of initiator. In this way, greetings become an arena to battle over the issue of who gives favors and who should receive them.

In some cultures, how people speak is a reflection of their power or at least of their social standing. For example, in the Wolof greetings just mentioned, low-caste people, including griots (singers/story tellers) exhibit high, strident, rapid speech, and this contrasts with the low-pitched, quiet speaker style of high-standing people. Similarly in Burundi, low-status people are expected to speak haltingly in comparison with those who hold the power in their society.

7.10.6 How to behave like a manager in Germany and the US

Friday (1991) contrasts the expectations of German and American managers when they meet. He argues that Americans and Germans **contrast in their emphasis on hierarchy** (the Germans pay more attention to it) and the need to be liked and accepted (this is what Americans are looking for in a relationship). To this end, Americans use first names more quickly in a relationship than Germans and use a more casual speech style. Another difference has to do with establishing credibility. For Germans, credibility depends on acknowledging or adhering to known barriers (one's credentials including education and qualifications or position in the hierarchy are important). Americans, with their emphasis on the individual and equality and the possibility for social mobility, want to reduce barriers (and possibly hierarchies, too). Thus, for American managers, "acceptance of what one is doing in the present and plans to do in the future is a great part of one's identity" (p. 299).

7.11 Managing cross-cultural conflicts

When one bilingual clashes over cultural differences with another bilingual who is a native speaker of a language other than the first one's language, they should begin by following general suggestions on how to manage conflict that apply whether or not cultural differences exist. Experts recommend that the first step is simply to speak to the other person in order to clarify what the problem is. Once our two bilinguals at least are talking to each other, experts stress the need to be cooperative, not competitive. The goal is to arrive at a common definition of the problem. This means trying to understand the other person's position. Above all, both bilinguals have to make it clear that they are interested in finding a solution. A final general stance is to show the other person that he/she is valued; that is, pay attention to the other person's positive face needs. If possible, any agreement should spell out how both sides will try to act differently in the future; this means developing more awareness of the other person's views on preferred conversational strategies as well as developing more conscious self-awareness about preferred ways of speaking.

When different cultures are involved, bilinguals need to add a number of considerations if they wish to solve their mutual problems. Even if we assume that the problems arose because of cultural differences, in order to solve the problems both bilinguals need to recognize their similarities rather than just focusing on differences. Finding a solution to a problem requires building on similarities (Gudykunst, 1994).

Finally, bilinguals need to be as aware as they can how the culture of the bilingual with whom they are in conflict differs from theirs. Here are some points based on the suggestions from Ting-Toomey (1994) of how persons from individualistic cultures can handle conflicts with persons from collectivistic cultures and vice versa.

First, individualists need to remember that collectivists see their positive face (their sense of self-respect and self-worth) as an extension of their group's status. Collectivists see their actions as reflecting on their group, so they take their group's image into consideration in managing conflicts. So as far as their conversation goes, individualists need to tread lightly in how they refer to the collectivist's group; this means using indirect and tactful speech.

Second, Ting-Toomey recommends that individualists should try to deal with conflicts when they are small. Because collectivists view their conflict as placing their group's image on the line, they may see the conflict as more serious than an individualist would. This is a special reason why the sooner a conflict is resolved, the better. But individualists should be prepared to recognize that collectivists may want to use a third party to mediate the conflict.

Third, individualists need to help the collectivists maintain face. Again, remember that the public image of the group is important. This means avoiding saying or doing anything that might embarrass collectivists in public.

Fourth, individualists need to pay special attention to how collectivists use non-verbal communication and indirect messages. Possibly, individualists should try to be more indirect and tentative themselves. They should avoid statements that sound absolute, including saying "no".

Finally, individualists should remember that avoidance is a favorite strategy of collectivists. So if collectivists do not seem to want to deal with the problem, individualists may find that simply letting go of the conflict is the only reasonable course of action.

On their side, collectivists need to recognize that they may have to make adaptations in dealing with individualists if their misunderstandings or problems are to be solved.

First, collectivists need to recognize that individualists tend to separate the person with whom they are having a conflict from the problem. That is, they often can be less emotionally involved and not feel that their positive face is as much at stake as a collectivist might feel. Therefore, individualists can and do focus on the issue itself and expect others to do the same.

Second, collectivists need to try to alter their unmarked conversational strategies toward the strategies that individualists favor. This means they need to attempt to be more direct and more assertive than they usually are. They should state their opinions, if possible, and provide more verbal feedback to the opinions of individualists than they usually do. While they may value periods of silence in conversations, they should recognize that individualists do not.

7.12 Summing up

This chapter has included both general and individualized portraits of how cultures differ. The main general portrait depicts cultures as one of two types: either more collectivistic or more individualistic. Still, bear in mind that most cultures have features of both types.

- In **collectivistic cultures**, from childhood onwards, people are integrated into cohesive groups. The group is the main reference point in any individual's life.
- To maintain harmony within the group in collectivistic cultures, **indirectness in speech** is favored to deflect confrontations.
- East Asian societies are good examples of collectivistic cultures.
- In contrast, in **individualistic cultures**, the ties between individuals are loose, except often those within the immediate family. But even within the family, personal freedom is important.
- In individualistic cultures, **a direct style of speech** is favored; people tend to express their opinions.
- Whereas in collectivistic cultures, loyalty to the in-group provides people with their identities, in individualistic cultures, individuals are expected to try to realize their own goals and these are not necessarily tied to any group membership.
- Many Western societies have individualistic cultures.
- A related way of looking at cultural differences is to classify cultures as **high-context or low-context cultures**. This classification emphasizes the patterns of speech individuals use with each other.
- Like collectivistic cultures, **high-context cultures** favor an indirect speech style. But indirection goes further than this: Interpreting the words that are said means paying attention to the context in which the talk is situated.

- **Low-context cultures** share features with individualistic cultures. In low-context cultures, the sum total of the words and their organization is the message speakers mean to convey. Largely, "what you hear is what you get".
- Variation across a number of conversational strategies is discussed: the use of **silence**; common **conversational routines** varies; types of politeness; variation in appropriate **requests**, and the expression of **power differentials**.
- A third way to look at cultural differences situates cultures along an **equality–hierarchy continuum** (from those that favor equality across individuals to those favoring hierarchical relationships).
- A final word from Yong Yun Kim (2001: 5–6) to travelers and immigrants seems appropriate:

> Regardless of resettlement circumstances, all newcomers are compelled to make adjustments . . . Those who fail to do so may have to return home prematurely or find themselves staying on yet experiencing emotional and social isolation from the new environment. Most people, however, learn to detect similarities and differences between their new surroundings and their home cultures, and they become increasingly proficient in handling situations they encounter. Each adaptive challenge, in turn, offers them an opportunity to grow beyond the perimeters of the original culture.

7.13 Words and phrases to remember

ethnocentrism
communicative competence
collectivistic cultures
individualistic cultures
low- or high-context messages
Confucianism and harmonious interactions
"face" and self-respect
types of politeness
valuing equality or hierarchy

8

Lexical Borrowing

Multiple voices: The word from Kenya

Nifreda Mbira is a Kenyan who speaks two different varieties of the Luyia language cluster (Lumaragoli, her L1, and also Lwidakho, the L1 of her husband's family). Whether to call these varieties separate languages or dialects of a single language is an open question; they clearly are very similar to each other. In Luyia communities such as hers, it is customary for women to marry outside their own immediate sub-ethnic (language) group; she married a native speaker of Lwidakho and that is how she learned that language variety. Nifreda also speaks Swahili and English. She studied English long ago in a school run by missionaries, but just learned Swahili from informal contacts. There are many words borrowed from Swahili into the two Luyia varieties she speaks; some of these words were borrowed into Swahili from Arabic or English. In addition, she can carry on a limited conversation in Luo, a major neighboring language totally unrelated to her own language variety, because two of her sisters are married to Luo men and she sometimes visits them. Nifreda is a retired primary schoolteacher, now 60. She lives in Western Kenya on a small farm with an extended family (her husband, who was also a teacher, and one of their sons, the son's wife, and their three children). Although these days she doesn't go to towns often, when she does go to the main commercial center in the region, Kakamega, she speaks Swahili in some shops, depending on the shopkeeper. Many of the shopkeepers in Kakamega are first language speakers of Kikuyu, even though their home area is rather distant, around the Kenya capital of Nairobi; they speak Swahili with customers. Nifreda also may speak Swahili or one of her Luyia varieties in other places, such as the produce market. If anyone speaks to her in English, she responds in English. She reads English-language newspapers or magazines, but these are not often available in the rural area where she lives. If she writes letters to any relatives who live in Nairobi or other distant places, she writes in English. Swahili and English are both official languages in Kenya.

8.1 Introduction

When people speaking one language are in regular contact with other people speaking another language, two things are likely to happen in the early stages of this contact: (1) Some speakers on both sides will learn how to say at least some useful phrases in the other group's language. (2) One group will actually take into its language some words from the other group's language to refer to objects, activities, or concepts that the other group has, largely for those things that are new to the first group. This second happening is the subject of this chapter. Words from one language appearing in another are **lexical borrowings**.

The key to understanding this exchange of phrases and words that accompanies any exchange of goods or other relations between the two groups is this: **the exchange is never equal**. That is, one group always does more taking, and – almost ironically – the group that takes the most is the one with less prestige in some vital public area, such as socio-economic status or political control. (Later, the less prestigious group often shifts to the other group's language, but that's discussed in chapter 4.)

8.1.1 Why call it "borrowing"?

Three rather unfortunately chosen terms occur in the linguistics literature to refer to such incorporations. Two are inaccurate and the third has negative connotations. The first term is **borrowing** and the second is **loan word**. When one language takes in words from another language, the process is referred to as **borrowing**, but the elements taken in aren't truly borrowed (or loaned) – because the recipient language never gives them back! Just because these terms are very established, we will use them, too, and there's no harm done as long as you realize that what's taken isn't returned. However, we will use the term "borrowing" only to refer to **lexical elements**, not grammatical elements. When "lexical" is used, it means content words, such as nouns or verbs.

The third unfortunate term is **interference**, and its use is more objectionable because of its connotation. This word is often used as a cover term for whatever effects one language has on another. This includes the borrowing of words, but "interference" also refers to a number of other effects, such as adopting the way sentences are structured. In fact, all forms of language-contact phenomena (i.e. whatever happens to the structures of languages when their speakers are in contact) are often subsumed under "interference". What we don't like about using "interference" in reference to bilingualism is that when in daily life we say an act constitutes "interfering", we normally mean that it's purposeful meddling – and definitely not welcome. Well, this isn't the case with language contact. Most speakers of any language have no views at all about borrowings; in fact, they hardly consider such words as unusual (if they notice them at all), because lexical borrowing is such a natural process. In chapter 9, **convergence** is discussed, another natural process that can change word meanings or sentence structures.

8.1.2 Motivations for change

In general, we can say that speakers (generally unconsciously) make changes in their languages under the influence of another language for two reasons: (1) First, those speakers fall under the influence of another language because there is **something more "attractive"** about that language – the attraction largely being associated with the higher prestige of the speakers of that language or its wider use in the community where both languages are spoken. (2) Second, certain innately based **language universals push speakers in certain directions**; admittedly, this is a controversial notion, but it will be supported in future chapters. To take a quick example that applies to this chapter – across many language pairs, most of the words that are borrowed are nouns. Doesn't this suggest there may be a universal basis at work?

The upshot of this discussion is that while you will see both "borrowing" and "interference" used in many texts that discuss bilingualism, you won't see "interference" used in this book. We prefer to consider what happens to languages in contact as the result of universally present processes, based on the political-social relations of the speakers, their demographics, and their innate linguistic predispositions. Thus, we will use the neutral term of **contact phenomena** as our cover term for whatever happens to languages in contact, as you will see in chapter 9.

8.2 Lexical borrowing

Now, back to borrowing – that is, **lexical borrowing**. As we've already indicated, while it's true that one language can take in grammatical structures from another language, "borrowing" is best used only as the term for the borrowing of words – i.e. lexical borrowing. The reason is that we will argue in chapter 9 that taking in grammatical structures depends on different cognitive processes than does lexical borrowing. Here, we talk about lexical borrowing as incorporating words from one language (the **donor language**) in another (the **recipient language**).

8.2.1 Borrowing as a one-way street

We can make two generalizations about lexical borrowing. The first generalization is already obvious from the discussion above: Borrowing is almost entirely one-way, from the more prestigious language to the less prestigious one. What counts as prestige will vary from one era to another and from one pair of languages to another. Generally, however, the more prestigious language controls more of whatever resource is valued – whether it is political power or socio-economic status or even *cachet*, a French borrowing into English that we will define for our purposes as "being more with it" – whatever "it" is. For example, when the Norman French conquered England in 1066, they not only had the political power, but their mode of living was considered more civilized, more sophisticated (i.e. it had *cachet*). Thanks to this contact and to the prestige accorded to Latin and then to French throughout succeeding centuries, about half of the words in the English language today were borrowed from Latin or French. Appropriately, new words or expressions in English are called **neologisms**, a word borrowed from French.

Come today, the tables are turned. The French are embracing English words, so much so that the French establishment complains. This is not a new battle. More than 30 years ago, "in its first skirmish of a war against the invasion of French by foreign words", the French Academy barred from its dictionary the word *score* in French sports parlance, replacing it with *la marque* while reluctantly accepting *set* in tennis because it helps distinguish the set from the game (*New York Times*, February 27, 1967). Overall, it seems to be a losing battle. Recently, an American columnist considered the chances as slim of stopping French people from using English. The headline read, "Stop the spread of English, *'Bonne chance, mes amis'*!" ('Good luck, my friends').

Generally, languages that are widely spoken as second languages become the source of borrowed words for other languages. Both French and English are good examples, but so are other languages that have been, or now are, lingua francas in other parts of the world. An obvious example is Arabic in areas where there are many Moslems. Russian, especially during the USSR regime, also has been the source of many loan words not only in the Soviet republics, but also elsewhere in Eastern Europe. Other languages in Southeast Asia have taken in words from Chinese. During the period when Portugal was a great power on the oceans, many Portuguese words were incorporated into languages around the world, including many of the emerging pidgins and creoles.

8.2.2 The process of borrowing: English as an example of a donor language

Not just in France, but all over the world, languages are borrowing words from English for two main purposes. (1) The success of English speakers in making advancements in science and technology, especially from the United States, means that English becomes the source of words that persons everywhere use to discuss the fruits of these advancements, such as any computer-based activities and space-launchings. (2) This success feeds the view of English as the language of modernity, the language of *cachet*. Thus, English borrowings are entering languages everywhere, and in more domains than just science and technology. Not surprisingly, the reported reaction of a Paris disk jockey to the French Academy's latest pronouncements against English borrowings was to use an English borrowing to call the pronouncement *"Pas très cool"* ('not very cool').

While today English is the leading source of borrowings into many languages, other languages are also currently important as donor languages as well, if on a more limited level. All it takes are opportunities for two cultures to be in contact, with some lexical borrowing as almost an inevitable consequence. But the process requires both **innovators**, who are bilingual, and **adopters**, who are centrally placed in the society and are open to new developments. Sometimes even only a few well-placed innovators can introduce alien words to any language. If these are words for important new objects to the culture, then others will take them up. Adopters need not be bilingual themselves in order to pair up a new word with a new object. However, if a large part of the population becomes bilingual, then the extent of lexical borrowing increases, too. It stands to reason this will happen as the number of "models" to follow increases.

8.3 Cultural and core borrowings

Our second generalization about borrowing is that borrowings can be divided roughly into two categories: **cultural and core borrowings**

8.3.1 Cultural borrowings

Cultural borrowings are words that fill gaps in the recipient language's store of words because they stand for objects or concepts new to the language's culture. Perhaps the most common cultural borrowings around the world are versions of the English word *automobile* or *car* because most cultures did not have such motorized vehicles before contact with Western cultures. For example, in Swahili a car is *motakaa* and a locomotive train is *gari la moshi* (literally 'car of cloud/steam').

Any of the new vocabulary items that have to do with computers qualify as cultural borrowings. Many of these words are new even to English, because computers are new to native speakers of English. Consider *email* or even the word *computer* itself (why is it no surprise to you that the French powers-that-be made up their own word, *ordinateur*, rather than frenchify *computer*?). Often the words themselves in new technological or scientific areas, such as the computer industry, are not new, but their specialized meanings or combinations are new; for example, consider the combinations *software* or *website*, or the verb *crash* and *hard drive*, as in *my hard drive crashed*. Or consider the use of *map* in the phrase *mapping the human genome*.

Many times the names of articles of clothing or types of food new to a culture are borrowed with the item itself. German has borrowed *blue jeans* and English has borrowed *pizza* from Italian along with this favored food, as have many other languages.

8.3.1.1 The classical languages as a supply source

Many of the technical terms in the fields of science, medicine, and the law come from Latin or Greek. David Crystal (1987: 380) points out that "[S]cience is in fact **the main birthplace for new words** in a language: in a comprehensive English dictionary, the vast majority of the words would be scientific (or technological) terms." He lists some of the now well-known words and the years that they first appeared in the *Oxford English Dictionary*. For example, *vitamin* was first listed in 1912; its base comes from the Latin word *vita* 'life'. The word for the partial or total loss of the ability to speak, *aphasia*, was first listed in 1867. This word is based on the Greek word *aphatos*, which is a combination of the prefix *a-* 'not' and *phatos* 'spoken' or 'speakable'. Aphasia in bilinguals is discussed in chapter 10.

In the field of law, many Latin words are in use, such as *habeas corpus* 'a writ that may be issued to bring a party before a court or judge, serving to release the party from unlawful restraint'. It comes from the Latin for 'you may have the body'. Some legal terms have become part of everyday language, too, such as *alibi*. Its technical meaning is 'a form of defense whereby a defendant attempts to prove absence from the scene of the crime' but in its everyday usage it can just mean 'an excuse or explanation to avoid blame'. It comes from the Latin *alibi* 'in or at another place'. French is also a source of such legal terms as *tort* 'a damage or injury done willfully or negligently'. The original source is Latin, but the word came into English through French. In some English legal expressions, a French or Latin term is used with one of Anglo-Saxon origin, such as *breaking and entering* or *will and testament*. Crystal says the use of two words with about the same meaning "reflects the uncertainty of early draftsmen as to whether the two terms had the same meaning. In such cases, the safest course of action was to include both" (p. 386).

8.3.1.2 *New words that are home-grown*

Some languages are less inclined to borrow a new word along with a new object and **instead make up words from their own lexical stock** for the new object. German and Japanese do this much more than English, for example. So when the telephone was invented, Germans called it *Fernsprecher* ('far' + 'speaker'). But today, most Germans simply call a telephone *Telefon* although they still use *Ferngespräch* for a 'long-distance call'. Planners for some languages in the Third World that have recently become official languages, such as Swahili in Tanzania and Somali in Somalia, also are anxious to achieve a unique identity and so avoid too many foreign borrowings. For example, Swahili planners introduced *kamusi* for 'dictionary' in the 1960s in preference to using a borrowing based on the English word.

8.3.2 Cultural borrowing in reverse

An opposite process from borrowing is to **replace existing borrowings with native words**. That is, for a variety of reasons, but all having to do with promoting a group's unique identity, speakers have been known to rid their languages of borrowings. A famous case is Turkey. When Turkey became independent of the Ottoman dynasty in the 1920s and under reforms introduced by Atatürk, Arabic script was replaced by the Latin alphabet in 1928. Atatürk also created the Turkish Language Society for the Purification of the Language which replaced Arabic words with Turkish-based words. This example of language planning in Turkey is discussed further in chapter 12.

Also, **a more recent case of reverse-borrowing** is what is happening in southern India. The Tamil ethnic group in India has been cleansing the "High" version of its language of words that have a Sanskrit base. (Recall from chapter 5 that even though it was not one of the languages originally mentioned as showing classic diglossia, Tamil is one of the languages with both High and Low varieties in use.)

Why avoid words related to Sanskrit? Tamil is a member of the Dravidian language family. Although Sanskrit has prestige as the sacred language of Hinduism, it is also the ancestral language of Indian languages that are not Dravidian languages. Rather, they are in another grouping, the Indo-Aryan language family, with Hindi as the most prominent of them. Tamils see their language in competition with Hindi in regard to official policies about languages that can be used most widely for inter-group communication. For this reason, they want to keep their language as distinctive in its own right as possible; this provides a reason to oppose use of Hindi for inter-group communication in Tamil-speaking areas. (Since India became independent from British rule in 1947, English has remained the unofficial main public language. However, the constitution (in 1950) called for Hindi, the major Indo-European language in India, to replace English. Although it is now unlikely this will happen in the foreseeable future, Dravidian language speakers, especially the Tamils, resist any hint of Hindi domination.)

Thus, the motivation to replace words is two-fold: One is to preserve Tamil as a language with its own character and the other motivation is more socio-political, to maintain Tamil identity as an ethnic group in the face of pressure from the more numerous speakers of Indo-European languages in India, most notably Hindi.

For these reasons, Sanskrit words in Tamil are being replaced. Sanskritized poets, writing in the High variety of Tamil in the fifteenth century, used many Sanskrit words – as many as 35% or 40% of their words came from Sanskrit. Educated estimates are that in the last fifty years, the influence of Sanskrit has been reduced to about 20% of the entire vocabulary of High Tamil (Zvelebil, 1983).

Attempts to remain pure of any borrowings whatsoever mean that in High Tamil, loans from English are also avoided. But in more informal (Low) Tamil, there are many English loans, as well as some from Portuguese, Telugu, Arabic, and other languages, and no one tries to prevent any of these from coming in. Sometimes the results are funny when scholars replace English words in High Tamil. For example, English *fan* (< *fanatic*) was replaced in High Tamil by /viciri/ which was an existing term referring to the object used for fanning oneself or even an electric fan. Because High Tamil is used in written work, such as newspapers, this word for a 'hot weather fan' is the word used on the sports pages for a 'sports fan'. Whoever came up with the idea of using the High Tamil word didn't realize that the two words *fan* and /viciri/ didn't mean the same thing (Schiffman, personal communication).

8.4 Core borrowings

Core borrowings are words that duplicate elements that the recipient language already has in its word store. They are gratuitous – by definition, another layer on the cake, because the recipient language always has viable equivalents. Then, why are they borrowed? One answer is cultural pressure: When two languages are spoken in the same community, but one language prevails in most public discourse and certainly in all status-raising discourse, then **the other language loses some of its vitality** to that language, and it becomes the recipient language in borrowing and will even replace its own words with words from the dominant language.

For example, in Harare, the capital of Zimbabwe, where both English and Shona are official languages, native speakers of Shona sometimes use the English word *problem* instead of the Shona counterpart, *dambudziko*. In fact, Bernsten and Myers-Scotton (1993) found that *problem* was used in 10 out of 129 interviews, even though it was in response to a question asked in Shona by a native speaker of Shona. Also, there was a specific direction to use the Shona word for 'problem' as a prime (just to see if the interviewee would follow his lead or not). You can see that the English word *problem* is clearly *not* filling a gap in Shona; still, it is being used in variation with its Shona counterpart.

Probably the most common core borrowings are discourse markers. In Myers-Scotton and Okeju (1973), we reported on discourse markers borrowed from Swahili into Ateso as spoken in Uganda. Swahili, a Bantu language, is the major indigenous lingua franca in East Africa; Ateso is a Nilotic language totally unrelated to Swahili. Ateso speakers have incorporated *alakini* 'but' (< Swahili *lakini*), originally from Arabic.

Looking again at the Shona study just mentioned, we see another borrowing in progress in Harare. Two English discourse markers, *because* (in place of Shona *nokuti*) and *but* (in place of Shona *asi*) are showing up in discourse that was supposed to be all in Shona. For encoding the concept of 'because', English *because* appears in 7 percent of the cases (24/367). For the concept of 'but', English *but* appears in 8 percent of the cases (25/315). Obviously, the English discourse markers do not rival the Shona counterparts. Still, they are frequent enough so that we can refer to a borrowing in progress. It is true that educated bilinguals in Harare do a good deal of codeswitching back and forth between English and Shona, and interviewees in this study did engage in codeswitching, even though monolingual Shona was called for. But analysis showed that neither *but* nor *because* was dragged along by other English words in a codeswitching pattern. When *because* or *but* occurred, generally Shona material both preceded and followed the discourse marker. That is, one cannot claim that their occurrence is just "triggered" by English material either preceding or following these English discourse markers.

Mougeon and Beniak (1991) discuss the distribution of another discourse marker, English *so*, in the French spoken by a sample of French Canadians. It is a replacement for *alors* or the more informal variant, *ça fait que* (meaning approximately 'and then' or 'for that reason'). Interestingly enough, their study shows that the prevalence of *so* doesn't correlate as much with the degree of bilingualism of its users as it does with the extent to which speakers use both languages.

8.4.1 Motivations for borrowing core lexical items

We suggest two major motivations to borrow a word for which the recipient language already has a word. First, as Mougeon and Beniak (1991) point out, core borrowings occur in the speech of bilinguals who regularly use *both* of their languages. In their study, those French speakers with roughly equal use of English and French used *so* more than other groups – that is, even more than speakers who use English more than French.

Second, the sheer magnetism of the dominant culture of the donor language seems to motivate speakers to borrow core elements. And it doesn't even seem to matter if the donor language is widely spoken in the community in question. For example, in Malaŵi, a southern African country next to Zimbabwe, English is also an official language, this time alongside Chicheŵa, a Malaŵian language. Simango (2000) reports that English is not widely used by your ordinary person in the street. Yet, even such people have borrowed the English word *madam* to use it as a frequent replacement for the Chicheŵa word for 'wife'.

Also, Zentella (1997) reports that even those Spanish speakers living in New York City who are monolingual in Spanish are among the users of core borrowings from English. They use such words as *londri* ('laundry'), *lonchar* ('to lunch'), *biles* ('bills'), and *el bloque* ('the block'). According to Zentella, such words are so completely adapted to Spanish phonology and morphology that second-generation speakers think they belong to the Spanish lexicon and have no idea they come from English.

8.4.2 Reverse core borrowing

Sometimes core borrowing goes the other way for a few words. That is, speakers of the dominant language take up a word or two of a language that is less prestigious in their eyes. For example, this often happens when speakers of the dominant language are temporary residents in another culture. For example, English-speaking expatriates living in China may be able to utter only a few sentences in Chinese, but they may well sprinkle their English with a few Chinese expressions, such as *méi yǒu* 'not have/not be', as what is for them a novel way to say 'no'. Also, if they have lived in China, English speakers might use the Chinese word *guānxi* to each other when they are back home. *Guānxi* doesn't quite have an English equivalent, but translates roughly as 'personal connections', with the connotation of 'people who are important to your wellbeing'. (A friend recently used it to me when she was indicating she understood how I wanted to spend time with certain people at a conference I was attending in her city; we had both lived in China and knew the word.) Also, under British colonialism in Kenya, for expatriates living there a journey – in a sentence otherwise all English – became a *safari* (< Swahili *safari* < originally from Arabic for 'journey') and one's garden became a *shamba* (Swahili *shamba* 'a cultivated plot' < also borrowed from Arabic). Today, of course, *safari* is known by any visiting tourist, not just long-term residents.

We suggest two reasons for such borrowings. One reason for adding such words to one's conversation would be just to claim some understanding (no matter how limited!) of "the local culture". This showing that you know something others from your own culture do not know adds a dimension to your persona. By the same token, when I say *my bad* in front of either teenagers or university students, I am showing off my very marginal (and very temporary) membership in their cool culture. (*My bad* means '(I admit) my mistake'.)

A second reason is that words from a culture very different from one's own have always smacked of the exotic; that is, they have a magic quality about them. Consider how words from the jazz culture entered mainstream English and other languages from the 1920s onwards. Today words from hip-hop music are being adopted by teenagers for the same reason.

8.5 Less direct borrowings

In addition to direct borrowings as discussed above (i.e. a donor word becomes part of the recipient language's vocabulary with no alterations), there are three more indirect types of borrowing. Still, they all fall within the general framework already outlined; that is, they become either cultural or core borrowings.

Although single words that are borrowed directly are by far the most frequent, the first indirect type is more common than you may realize. This is the **calque** or **loan translation**. These loans differ from other borrowings in two ways. First, many calques consist of more than one word. Second, the actual word (i.e. phonological shape) from the donor language is not borrowed; instead, how that language conveys a particular notion is borrowed. What happens, then, is that the recipient language replaces the words that the donor language uses to convey the desired notion with its own. So what is "loaned" is a translation, not words. Some of the most commonly cited calques are compounds based on English *skyscraper*. German has *Wolkenkratzer* (literally 'cloud scratcher') and French has *gratte-ciel* (literally 'scratch-sky').

But there are many other calques. While *weekend* is an accepted borrowing in Italian and, somewhat grudgingly, in French, Germans know the word, but prefer their German equivalent, *Wochenende*, which is a calque on *weekend*. English modeled its expression *trial balloon* (as in *send up a trial balloon*) on the French expression *ballon d'essai* 'balloon of trial or attempt'. A recent calque used by Dutch young people is *er voor gaan* (literally 'it for to go') that is modeled on the English expression, *to go for it* (Backus, personal communication).

Over time, ideas as to what is "politically correct" may change the popularity of a loan translation. Schiffman (personal communication) reports that when he first visited India some years ago, a simple restaurant was referred to by English-based words adapted to Tamil: *miils-hoom* (<*meals* + *home*). But ideas changed and the latest incarnation is Tamil through and through: *uNavakam* (<Tamil *uNavu* 'nutrition' + *akam* 'home') (N stands for a retroflex consonant). Note that it is now a loan translation when before it was more of a direct borrowing. A more or less opposite process results in **loanshifts**, the second type of indirect borrowing. In this case, speakers borrow the phonological form of a word, but give it a different meaning from its original. In the last twenty years, both the French and the Spanish have borrowed English gerunds (verb forms ending in *-ing* that are used as nouns, as in the sentence, *brushing my hair is a lot of trouble*). But their meanings are shifted from what they are in English. Thus, in French, *le shampooing* is the product (a bottle of shampoo), not the process, and *le brushing* is a blow-dry at the hairdressers.

AN ADVERTISEMENT FROM A COIFFEUR'S WEB PAGE

200 francs pour 4 brushing dans le même mois – soit 50 frs le brushing!!!
('200 francs for four brushings in the same month – it is 50 francs per
brushing')
Shampooing Ordinaire: 25
Shampooing Spécifique 35
(Source: http://parallelecoiffure.free.fr/salon/salon_.htm)

Third, there also are less frequent borrowings called **loanblends** or **hybrids**.
As you might guess, they consist of two or more parts, with input from both
the donor and the recipient languages. English *grandfather* is a blend of English
father and French *grand* from the French word for 'grandfather' *grandpère*. And
back at the French hairdresser's, we have English *shampoo* + *in* + a French
derivational suffix (to make it into a process) becoming *shampoo-in-age* for 'the
process of shampooing'.

8.6 How borrowed words are integrated

A statement from a general linguistics textbook of the 1960s reads, "[when
words are borrowed] they are normally adopted to the structure of the borrowing language, in sound and in form" (Hall, 1964). Many linguists still
present this as an accurate statement about borrowings. The problem is that
such a statement oversimplifies the facts, especially regarding how borrowings are treated phonologically.

8.6.1 Phonological integration

Let's look first at **phonological integration**; this is the process of making
borrowed words fit the sound system of the recipient language. True, as the
1960s textbook states, many borrowed words are so modified that it's hard
to tell that they were not original words in the recipient language. But there
also are many words that show only partial integration and some that show
hardly any integration at all, if any. So, it's important to recognize that the
degree of phonological integration should be represented as a continuum
(i.e. a matter of sometimes more and sometimes less), but definitely not
always a done deal.

There are many aspects to phonological integration, and we won't discuss
them all. But here are some of the key areas for integration.

8.6.1.1 Phonotactics

Consider the **phonotactics** of the recipient language. A language's phonotactics are the combinations of sounds that are permissible in that language. If we know about a language's phonotactics, we can answer these questions: What types of syllables does the language in question allow? Does it have only open syllables (ones ending in a vowel) or does it allow closed syllables (ones ending in a consonant). Does the language allow two or more consonants together (called consonant clusters)? Many languages have a CVCV system, meaning that consonants and vowels alternate, but they allow no consonant clusters and the word must end in a vowel. There are more questions, too, such as what consonants are allowed in these clusters? Are there any requirements on the sounds that may begin or end a word?

For example, a moment's reflection tells you that the phonotactics of English allow many words to end in consonants and there are many consonant clusters (two or more consonants in a row). Consider a word such as *streets* [striyts] that both begins and ends with consonant clusters. But some languages, such as Polish, have even more and more complex consonant clusters.

As we just noted, many languages have a CVCV pattern, so when they borrow English words, they may break up consonant clusters or make other changes. For example, Japanese does not have consonant clusters (only CVCV sequences), so if English *drama* is borrowed, Japanese speakers would be likely to break up the /dr/ cluster or change the sounds in some other way. Italian does have some consonant clusters, but not the sequence /kstr/ in English 'extra', so Italian speakers might render 'extra' as *estra*.

There are variations on the CVCV system. For example, most Bantu languages allow consonants clusters of a nasal consonant + another type of consonant and such clusters often begin words, too (e.g. the Swahili word for 'goat' is *mbuzi*). But in loan words, many consonant clusters will be broken up (see below what happens to *mudguard*).

8.6.1.2 Inventory of distinctive sounds

Not all languages have the same **inventory** of distinctive sounds (phonemes) by any means. So consider the sounds in the recipient language compared to the donor language. For example, Spanish has a /x/ sound (a voiceless velar fricative) not found in English. Thus, when English speakers pronounce a Spanish loan word containing *x*, most substitute the [ks] sequence for [x], which is how the letter *x* is pronounced in English (e.g. in *exit*). Consider, for example, even the name of the closest southern neighbor to the US, *Mexico*.

8.6.1.3 Attitudes toward sounding 'native'

Different cultures and different individuals vary in how much importance they place on the importance of **approximating native sounds**, or attempting to "sound like" when they borrow a word. When Chinese borrows a word, Chinese speakers want to make it "as Chinese" as possible. Speakers try to find Chinese characters that stand for a similar reference to the borrowed word. But speakers also want the characters to "sound like" the borrowed word. They end up with some very imaginative ways of accommodating a borrowed word. For example, in recent years some Chinese citizens are giving up their bicycles for cars and some of the cars are expensive imports. For example, a Mercedes Benz is called by the characters *bēn chí*; they mean 'running quickly/speed'. And a BMW is called a *bǎo mǎ* 'treasured horse'. The word for *gene* is *jī yīn* 'basic reason' and the word for *vitamin* is *wéi tā mìng* 'keep his life' or a sequence that is more of a calque than a "sound alike", *wéi shēng sù* 'element that keeps life' (Zhao, personal communication).

8.6.1.4 Trying to stay true to the donor language or not

Do speakers want to sound like they speak the donor language? Consider chewing gum, which becomes [chuvingam] in Russian. Whether borrowed words are integrated may depend on any value that is attached to sounding like a speaker of the donor language. But another issue is this: Are speakers *able* to sound like they speak the donor language? The more the pool of users of borrowed words in the recipient language includes speakers who are not, in fact, also speakers of the donor language, the more phonological integration there seems to be. It's important to keep in mind that far from all users of borrowed words are actually bilingual in the donor language. Many of these users may have no idea how a word is pronounced by donor language speakers themselves, because the borrowers don't speak the donor language. So all the new users can do is fit the borrowing into their own sound system. For example, as noted earlier in this chapter, many French words were borrowed into English in the centuries after the Norman Conquest by the English-speaking population in Britain, but most of these people didn't actually speak French. Once a word was borrowed, it would have undergone the same phonological changes as native words, so that now it isn't even recognized as a borrowing. For example, English borrowed *nation* at this time, but most English speakers wouldn't recognize the word in French. (In modern French, *nation* is pronounced [nasyõ], but in English it is [neyšn].)

In recent times, some English native speakers (and others) may try to approximate a French pronunciation for what they know is a French word because they associate speaking French with exhibiting "culture" (whatever "culture" means in this context). But most speakers do not succeed entirely – unless they've studied French extensively and, preferably, as young children. The problems are two-fold. First, these speakers need to have the opportunity to hear the relevant word spoken by native speakers of French. Second, there may be big differences between the sounds of the speakers' language and those of French; certainly, there are big differences between the French set of sounds and those of English for some words. Consider *croissant* 'a French bread roll'. In French, this word has three non-English sound features: (1) The sequence *oi* is pronounced as [wa], (2) the vowel [a] is nasalized, (3) and the final [t] isn't pronounced at all. The result in French is [krwasã]. The English speaker who knows some French makes a stab at emulating the French pronunciation (although few succeed entirely!), but other English speakers may anglicize the word to [kresant] in blissful ignorance.

8.6.1.5 Bilinguals can do better

Conversely, when the pool of recipient language speakers includes many who are fairly fluent in the donor language, then you will hear very close approximations of how the borrowed word is pronounced in the donor language. For example, with the spread of English as an international language, there are more or more speakers who are aware of the English sound system. They often pronounce borrowed words in ways approximating how English speakers themselves would do it.

And it's not just educated speakers, either, who master at least some English sounds not found in their own languages. For example, languages in the Akan cluster in Ghana (e.g. including Ewe and Fante) don't have [l] as a distinctive sound that contrasts with [r] in all environments in a word. Ansre (1971: 159) points out that in Ewe, one would expect *raincoat* and *reader* to be pronounced with an initial [l] (because [l] instead of [r] appears before [i] or [e] in Ewe). Yet, instead, such words beginning with [l] in English are pronounced as they would be in English. And Forson (1979: 27) makes this comment about Akan speakers in general, whether bilingual or monolingual, when the word *lorry* is pronounced as a borrowing: "the pronunciation of *lorry* approximately coincides with Standard English pronunciation, with an [l]".

In a quantitative study of a sample of native speakers of Shona in Zimbabwe, Bernsten (1990) found that only 35 percent of all the types of English borrowed words were fully phonologically integrated into Shona by all speakers. (Shona words have a basically CVCV pattern.) She defined "fully integrated" as (1) breaking up English consonant clusters, (2) adding final vowels to English words ending in a consonant and (3) changing English [l] to Shona [r]. Such findings may not be so surprising for urban speakers who are bilingual in English; but even rural speakers who were basically monolingual speakers of Shona often reported certain words in an English fashion. So even a rural mother, when asked how many children she had, said *va-na* [siks] 'children six'. That is, she produced an English consonant cluster and ended 'six' in a consonant.

How the extent of phonological integration into Shona of just one word, *school*, changed over fifty years is an indication of the impact of first use of the donor language in the mass media (e.g. radio in rural Africa) and also – even more influential – bilingualism in the donor language. When *school* was first borrowed into Shona in the early part of the twentieth century, it was as phonologically integrated into Shona as it could be. Thus, *school* became *e-chi-koro*. Further, because the English cluster [sk] was broken up and [s] became [č], the word now began with the sound that marks Shona noun class seven (*-chi-*). Then, the pre-prefix of this class was added, resulting in *e-chi-koro*, and so 'school' was totally integrated into both the Shona phonological and morphological systems. However, by the 1980s when Bernsten's study was conducted, such phrases as *school fees* were being produced in Shona as [skul fiyz]. Notice that the consonant cluster that begins *school* is no longer broken up and both words end in consonants, as they would in English, but not in Shona.

8.6.1.6 *Staying close to the classics*

In all the languages of Europe (and probably in many other languages today), learned words – coming from Latin directly or a Latin form of a Greek word – are an important area of loan words. They are largely technical terms and, perhaps partly for that reason, they've undergone very little modification in their sounds. The result is that they are still very similar in form at least across most European languages. For example, *technology* takes these forms: French (*technologie*), Spanish (*technologia*), German (*Technologie*), and Russian (*texnologiä*). (Another reason that such learned loans remain very similar is that, relatively speaking, they have been borrowed quite recently and have therefore undergone little modification.)

Part of the reason probably is that the borrowed words stand for a very specific, if abstract, concept and speakers want to be sure the pronunciation is as true to the original as possible, just so that the concept being expressed can be identified. Another reason is that words from the so-called classical languages are associated with extensive formal education and so being able to pronounce them in a way approximating their original form gives the speaker a certain prestige.

8.6.1.7 *Summing up pronunciation*

In summary, yes, it's reasonable to recognize that borrowed words are frequently adapted to the sound system of the recipient language. But it is just as important to recognize that this is not how borrowings are always treated, either because the borrower wishes to associate him- or herself with the donor language's culture, or because the borrower speaks the donor language as an L2. In fact, bilingualism in the donor language seems to go against tendencies toward phonological integration of borrowed words from that language. After all, if bilinguals can speak the donor language, when they speak it, they would pronounce the words as close as possible to the way a native speaker of that language pronounces them – just to be understood. So, unless bilinguals wish to disguise their bilingualism, it is no surprise that this pronunciation carries over into the bilinguals' L1 when these words are introduced as borrowings.

8.7 Morphological integration

The second type of integration that can affect borrowings is **morphological integration**. Now, here we have something closer to a universal. That is, borrowed words are *almost always* adapted to the recipient language in morphology (adapted in form). In fact, as you will see in chapter 9, one of our basic theoretical claims is that there is a division between the roles of the participating languages in most contact phenomena. In regard to lexical borrowing, this division shows up most especially in the fact that the borrowed element fits into the frame of the recipient language.

There are a few exceptions that we'll point out shortly, but an examination of any language shows that nearly 100 percent of its words – both borrowings and indigenous ones – are treated the same by the morphosyntax. That is, both receive the same inflections and they follow the same requirements for word order. (Morphology is the study of word forms, including any affixes added to words, and syntax is the study of how words are put together into phrases and clauses. Each language has its own constraints on morphosyntax.) Thus, when a Spanish speaker, speaking Spanish, uses an English borrowed word, such as *weekend*, it receives a Spanish determiner (realized as a singular with masculine gender, the default gender for Spanish) and it is therefore *el weekend*. And when a Swahili speaker borrows a noun from English, it receives the noun class agreement prefixes of one of the Swahili noun classes. Thus, in example (1) the borrowed noun *sweta* 'sweater' receives the demonstrative form (*hii* 'this') that integrates it into the noun class that is called class nine by Swahili grammarians. Class nine is the default class for singular items that are borrowed into Swahili. Notice that *sweta* is phonologically integrated into Swahili by ending in a vowel (Swahili has a usual CVCV pattern, with words ending in a vowel).

> (1)   Hii sweta Mummy ndiyo alishona.
>   'This sweater, Mummy indeed sewed it.'
>   (Swahili-English, Myers-Scotton, unpublished
>   Nairobi corpus, 1988)

Example (2) shows how a borrowed word, Norwegian *matpakke* 'lunch bag' is integrated into a Turkish frame when used in a sentence by a Turkish immigrant to Norway who is very fluent in both languages. Note the Turkish particle (*de*) that modifies *matpakke* 'lunch bag/box' and the Turkish verb for 'spread' (*sür*). In fact, the speaker has borrowed not only the word for lunch bag/box, but the entire Norwegian expression as a loan translation in which the verb – with a Norwegian meaning – has been realized in Turkish (Norwegian *smøre matpakke* 'prepare a lunch box/bag' (which literally means 'butter [your] lunch bag'). In Standard Turkish the verb for 'prepare' would be *hazırla-*.

(2) Bi   de   **matpakke**   sür   de-di
     one particle lunch bag/box spread say-PAST3SING
     'He also said [to me], "prepare a lunch bag/box".'
                              (Turkish-Norwegian, Türker, 2000, p. 174)

8.7.1 Reanalysis as part of morphological integration

Furthermore, in the case of many borrowings, they are fitted so firmly into the morphosyntax of the recipient language that they are treated as members of a specific gender or noun class or case. (Recall that this is what happens with *echikoro* 'school' in Shona, as discussed above.) To take another example: in Swahili, some English words also are treated as members of the Swahili noun class system. The English word for a flap on a car to deflect mud (there's a long rainy season in East Africa!), *mudguard*, received this treatment when it was borrowed in the early part of the twentieth century before many Africans spoke English. First, it was phonologically integrated into Swahili, which means that it received a CVCV syllable order. So its consonant cluster was broken up and the word received a final vowel. It became *ma-di-ga-di*. Now, in this form, the Swahili speaker viewed the word as beginning with the prefix *ma-* that marks noun class six, a plural class. So, *ma-di-ga-di* was taken to mean 'mudguards'. In order to express the concept of 'one mudguard', the *ma-* was removed so that its form corresponds to a possible noun in the singular noun class five (that pairs up with the *ma-* class, class six). So 'one mudguard' became a *di-ga-di*.

8.7.2 Some examples of special treatment

True, some words, especially learned words borrowed from the classical languages of Latin and Greek via Latin, do not always receive full morphological integration into the recipient language, just like we noted above that they do not necessarily receive full phonological integration. Or, they are treated variably, depending on the speaker. Probably only highly educated speakers of English speak of *criteria*, but most of them treat it as a plural (with *criterion* (<Gk. *kritērion*) as its singular). In English, the Latin plural form *data* is treated as a singular by many people (e.g. *once the data is in . . .*) and these speakers do not use its singular at all (*datum* < Latin *datum* 'something given'). Those speakers who treat *data* as a plural do not give it the -*s* suffix that you would expect on integrated loans, but they do give it a plural verbal agreement (e.g. they say *His data leave something to be desired* not *his data leave-s . . .*).

But, at least in English, there is a good deal of variation in how such borrowings from Latin and Greek are treated; even university professors alternate between giving *syllabus* a plural as *syllabuses* or its Latin plural *syllabi*.

Finally, some languages have special derivational suffixes so that foreign words can be integrated into their morphological system. For example, German integrates alien verbs by *ieren* (for example *shop* > *shop-ieren*).

Overall, the point is that even if some borrowed words receive special treatment, most show morphological integration into the recipient language. That is, they are treated similarly to the recipient language's own words when it comes to inflections and word order – something that is by no means always the case regarding their sounds.

8.8 Nouns vs. other categories

From the standpoint of lexical categories (parts of speech), your guess about which category is most frequently borrowed is probably right on target: By far, singly occurring nouns are the lexical category most frequently borrowed.

This fact is very clear from studies of the speech of immigrants to the United States. For example, a study of English loan words in the speech of Finnish immigrants to the United States showed that out of 378 different vocabulary items, 78% are nouns and adjectives and 15% are verbs (Virtaranta, 1971, cited in Karttunen, 1977). There was one preposition and the remainder includes unanalyzed phrases such as *aitunnou* < 'I don't know' and *enuvei* < 'anyway'. The statistics for Norwegian immigrants studied by Haugen (1969b) were similar; he reported that 75.5% of the words in his corpus were nouns and only 18% were verbs.

Studies elsewhere show the same pattern. A study of borrowings from French into two Germanic varieties (Alsatian in Strasbourg, France and Brussels Dutch (Flemish) in Brussels, Belgium) showed nouns in first place. Treffers-Daller (1999) reported that of single word insertions of French into Brussels Dutch, 58.4% are nouns (2,329/3,988). Only 9% (353) were verbs. And in Strasbourg, 67% of single word insertions were nouns (297/452). Of the English loan words in *El diccionario del español chicano* (based on field work in Texas Spanish), nouns accounted for 74% while verbs account for 20% (Galván and Teschner, 1977, cited in Smead, 1998: 121). Farther afield, Heath (1981) reports on a case of unusually high borrowing across a number of aboriginal languages in Australia's Arnhem Land. Even though the direction of borrowing is open to speculation, borrowing is extensive in nouns of all types. In fact, in some domains (trees/shrubs, human age/sex terms) two languages share even over 50% of their nouns.

Why should this be so? We can only speculate, but a combination of hypotheses explains this skewing in favor of nouns.

(1) Consider the main motivation for borrowing. Speakers generally borrow words to fill lexical gaps in their language when the speaker wants to talk

about entities (things or notions) that in some sense are new to the recipient language. (Recall that these are most often cultural borrowings but they also can be core borrowings that don't add a meaning, but do add a dimension, to the speaker's speech.) The bottom line is that nouns are so often borrowed because they are the referents for most of these entities.

Let's approach this from a different angle. Talmy (2000), who has made extensive studies of how languages encode what speakers want to express, refers to **figure** and **ground** as the central entities that speakers map onto sentence structure. Thus, in the sentence *the bottle floated into the cave*, *bottle* is the figure and *cave* is the ground. Verbs are the grammatical elements that do the mapping of nouns. Semantically, they carry the meanings of what speakers wish to say about the figure and ground (e.g. Did the bottle *float*? Or, did it *sink* in the cave? Or, did someone *put* it in the cave?). Syntactically, verbs control what types of nouns can occur in a particular syntactic structure. These fall into patterns, but these patterns show variation across languages. For example, if we have an English verb expressing a state, we typically can't have a noun expressing an agent in the same sentence – i.e. *The door fell down* but not **The carpenter fell down the door*.

Now, back to why so many nouns are borrowed. We can imagine that in a sentence, figure and ground are the two components that will always be expressed and, once more, are open to insertions carrying a variety of semantic messages. This means there will be many possibilities for speakers of a recipient language to be exposed to many donor language nouns. For example, after the Norman conquest of England in 1066, the French naturally controlled the armed forces. The French word for 'military forces' was the figure in any discussion of armies. There was an existing Old English word for armed forces, *hera*. But after the Norman conquest, armed forces came to be called an *army* (<Fr. armée) – because *army* stood for a different type of army than *hera*. The French armed forces were organized on a different basis and with a hierarchical system that has survived until today. Here is another example showing how nouns present themselves for borrowing. Under the French, time was divided not only into *morning* and *evening* and *day* and *night*, but also into *hours* (<Fr. *heures*). The English latched on to this new way of dividing time and called it by the French word.

(2) Another hypothesis to explain the prevalence of nouns as borrowings is that most borrowed words are cultural borrowings. Most of these are for new "things", and "things", of course, are usually conveyed by nouns. Thus, we predict a quantitative study would support this hypothesis.

(3) A third hypothesis has to do with adding words to one's vocabulary in order to make new distinctions in what you want to convey. Some words are borrowed because they encode fine differences not made previously in the recipient language. Again, it is the nature of nouns, as filling the roles of figure and ground, to be able to make distinctions in larger categories that also

are referred to by nouns. For example, again under the Norman French, the various domestic animals retained their Old English names, but for the French the distinction between the animal and its meat was important. Thus, the flesh of animals became called by French names. The flesh of cattle was now *beef* (<Fr. *boeuf*) and sheep were still *sheep* but their flesh was called *mutton* (<Fr. *mouton*). Here is another, more modern distinction: Among Czech immigrants to Canada in the twentieth century, *kompeni* is used for 'company in Canada and the US' and the traditional Czech word, *společnost* is used for 'company elsewhere' (Rakusan, 1985). Also, before speakers of Igbo had any contact with English speakers, some Igbo speakers (women?) may have been the designated ones who cooked food. But it's unlikely Igbos had a word to distinguish persons who cooked from those who did it professionally. In Igbo of today the English word *cook* has been borrowed into Igbo as [kuk], but its meaning is 'a professional food preparer, usually a man' (Acholonu and Penfield, 1980).

(4) Next, we offer a hypothesis based on the grammatical nature of nouns vs. verbs. By their semantic nature, nouns largely encode entities (whether concrete or abstract). This nature is relatively fixed in some ways; for example, generally only animate nouns can be "agents", but many types of nouns can be "patients" (in the sense that they are acted upon). It follows that what is an "agent" or a "patient" in one language tends to be able to appear as an "agent" or "patient" in another language – just because you're speaking another language doesn't mean the nature of entities changes. (In this English sentence, *Alice* is the agent and *the tree* is the patient: *Alice cut down the tree.*) That is, nouns, by their intrinsic semantic nature, can either encode various thematic roles or not. For example, *Alice* and other humans can be patients, but *tree*s can't be agents in any strict sense – no matter what language you are speaking. Now, syntactic roles are something else. That is, the syntactic roles of nouns in a sentence may differ cross-linguistically. For example, a noun that has the thematic role of Experiencer cannot function as a subject in all languages (in English, Experiencers can be subjects as in *I feel hot* while in Hungarian the Experiencer cannot function in this way. Instead, 'hotness' would be the subject , as in *mert meleg-em vol-t akkor* (literally 'because hotness-mine was then'). Even so, an expression of the Experiencer can still appear in the Hungarian sentence; it is just that it cannot appear as the subject (Bolonyai, 1998).

(5) Finally, we note that functional elements that "go with" nouns are hardly borrowed at all – except when they are perceived as part of a noun. We specifically have in mind determiners and derivational affixes. Determiners add meaning to a noun by making the meaning more specific (more or less definite in many languages). Derivational affixes (they can be either prefixes or suffixes) change the meaning of nouns in some way. Consider how the prefix *in-* adds the meaning 'not', as in *inaudible* 'not audible'. Some derivational

affixes change the category of a word; for example, -*er*/*or* makes a verb into a noun, as with *actor*. These "go with/add on" elements are discussed under the 4-M model as early system morphemes in chapter 9. The basic idea is that nouns are the type of words whose underlying forms are accessed early in the language production process, and then determiners and derivational affixes are accessed along with them and therefore are "early".

So, the main point to grasp here is that in addition to their availability and their ability to accommodate new semantic distinctions, nouns are relatively transferable in their semantic sense across languages. Furthermore, they don't carry a lot of syntactic baggage with them in the sense that even if they control the form of some other words in the source language, they can be stripped of those properties when they are borrowed. For example, a Spanish noun is encoded for masculine or feminine gender in Spanish and its determiners and adjectives have to agree with it by also showing the appropriate gender; but when borrowed into English, the Spanish noun leaves behind its gender. Thus, *salsa* 'a sauce' can appear in an English sentence without any sign of gender – just like English nouns, and be treated with the same morphology that an English noun would receive. We can't assume all function words (e.g. determiners such as 'the') get left behind when a word is borrowed, though. Nouns borrowed from Arabic were sometimes borrowed with their determiners. A word such as *algebra* comes from the Arabic *al* + *jabr* 'the science of reuniting'. It came to English through medieval Latin.

In contrast, verbs do not transfer cross-linguistically so easily. The reason seems to be that verbs are syntactically more complex than nouns. As we've already mentioned, nouns are "mapped" onto syntactic structures, but verbs are the elements that do the "mapping". This means that verbs not only have their own semantic content, but they control the number and type of nouns that are present as "arguments" in a clause. For example, in English, some verbs take a double object construction, with one object standing for a Beneficiary and the other noun standing for a Patient (e.g. *Alice gave John a gift*.) In some other languages the Beneficiary could only be expressed in a prepositional phrase (English can do this, too: *Alice gave a gift to John*). We think you can see that it's pretty arbitrary how one language differs from another in how verbs express "arguments" (objects in this case). And because they control argument structure, it is their nature to carry with them a lot of baggage. But, because verbs differ cross-linguistically in what they carry (and how this baggage matches the requirements of the recipient language), they are not so easily transferable from one language to the next.

In summary, we offer the four hypotheses above to explain why nouns are so readily borrowed cross-linguistically and why verbs are not.

Similarly, discourse markers (particles) also are easy to borrow because they encode universally present discourse roles such as "contrast" or "consequence" or "addition", as noted above.

8.9 What borrowings can tell us

If we look at the stock of borrowed words in a language today, it will reveal to us the footsteps of time. That is, to put it less poetically, the non-native words that are there today didn't come on a meteor from outer space – rather, they are evidence of earlier cultural contacts. Often, of course, we don't need these words to tell us about past history because we have written documents or even oral histories to rely on. But this isn't always the case. We may know little about the history of certain parts of the world before modern times. For example, this is the situation for much of Africa. More than 40 years ago, a famous Africanist linguist wrote an article about loan words in Hausa, demonstrating that the course of history for Hausa speakers was different from what was the accepted view at that time. Hausa is the major lingua franca (language of wider communication) in many parts of West Africa; it is spoken as a first language in northern Nigeria. The usual view was that Islam was introduced to Hausa speakers in the fourteenth century from the kingdoms to the west of Hausa speakers. Well, Greenberg showed that Hausa has certain key borrowed words from Kanuri (another northern Nigerian language) to Hausa's east. Here's what he says: "Since Islam was established among the Kanuri in the eleventh century and the Kanem Empire [of the Kanuri] was an important political power during the next several centuries, it seems . . . likely that it would have exercised important cultural influence on the relatively weak and disunited Hausa states to the west" (1960, p. 206).

Here's the line of Greenberg's detecting. First, he must have figured that the basis of common vocabulary in Hausa and Kanuri couldn't be a common ancestor that would have passed the words on to both languages. The reason is that Hausa is in one language family (Afro-Asiatic) and Kanuri is in another (Central Saharan or Sudanic), so any words they had in common must have been borrowed. Second, Greenberg focused on words having to do with writing because he knew that before the coming of Islam, Hausa did not have any knowledge of writing. In fact, the Hausa words for "book", "pen", "ink", etc. are all clearly borrowed from Arabic into Hausa. But what interested Greenberg was that the word for "write" itself didn't come from Arabic, but from Kanuri. Further, even though the word for "read" clearly was ultimately from Arabic, its immediate source also was Kanuri.

Greenberg reached his conclusions by comparing the sound systems, semantics, and grammars of the two languages. For example, both Hausa and Kanuri have a word for "writing" that ends in a suffix composed of [tu] in Hausa and [te] in Kanuri. Since the [te] suffix is a regular way of forming verbal nouns from verbal roots in Kanuri and there is no such form in Hausa, the chances are good that Kanuri is the source of the forms in both languages. Greenberg also looked at the related languages of both the suspected recipient (Hausa) and donor language (Kanuri). If a form is found in languages related to one of the languages, but not in languages related to the other, then it must be older in the first language, and this first language must be the source of the form in both languages. We won't go into other details here, but on this basis, he could conclude that a number of cultural-historical terms in Hausa came from Kanuri. Examples are the words for "gun" and "saddle". Even though Arabic is the ultimate source, linguistic evidence indicates the words were borrowed directly from Kanuri. Greenberg could even make a case that the words for "father's sister" and "mother's brother" came into Hausa from Kanuri. If such words were borrowed, clearly this is evidence of strong influence upon the Hausa of their eastern Kanuri-speaking neighbors. From this vantage point, we can argue that Kanuri may well have brought Islam to Hausa several centuries earlier than previously thought.

8.10 Summing up

In this chapter, we've given you an extensive look at lexical borrowings. These are the main points to remember:

- The borrowing of words is **the most common type of structural change** that results when people speaking different languages are in contact and some of them become bilingual.
- The borrowing process is **generally a one-way street**; the recipient language generally has less prestige (however, how "prestige" is defined may vary with the cultures and the times) than the donor language.
- There are two main types of borrowed words, **cultural borrowings** and **core borrowings**. Cultural borrowings stand for objects or concepts that are new to the recipient culture and they are much more frequent than core borrowings. Core borrowings duplicate already existing words in the recipient culture's language and only seem to appear after long or intensive contact.
- Over time, which language(s) are the major source of borrowings can **change as socio-political factors change**.
- Because of English's present position as the main language of cross-cultural communication on the international scene, many languages include words borrowed from English today, especially cultural borrowings.
- Not all speakers of recipient languages are "happy borrowers". At least some influential people in some recipient cultures try to keep out alien words (e.g. the French Academy).
- **Nouns are borrowed more frequently** than another other lexical category.
- Function words and inflections (affixes) are rarely borrowed on their own, although they may come along as part of a borrowed content word.
- Generally, borrowed words **are integrated** into the recipient language. There is almost always morphological integration, but often less phonological integration.
- Borrowed words in a language are **evidence of past historical contacts**.

8.11 Words and phrases to remember

lexical borrowings
cultural borrowings (loan words)
core borrowings (loan words)
phonological integration
morphological integration

9

What Happens to Grammars in Bilingual Contacts

Multiple voices: The word from Palestinians in the US

Abdulla Shalabi is a Palestinian from the West Bank who speaks both Arabic and English fluently. He immigrated to the United States a number of years ago and today he is a professor in the pharmacy school at a large US university. He uses English in his job; that is, he teaches, meets with colleagues, gives papers at conferences, and writes academic articles, all in English. But at home and with Arabic-speaking friends, the main vehicle of communication is a combination of Arabic and English, an example of codeswitching. That is, he sometimes switches languages between sentences and often switches languages within a sentence (e.g. he says such things as *el pharmacy*, with the Arabic article for 'the'). His university-age daughter and her friends with parents from the Middle East speak Arabic fluently, although not as fluently as their parents. English has become her more dominant language and their Arabic shows some signs of converging to English grammatical features. She plans to study pharmacy, too.

9.1 Introduction

When speakers regularly use two (or more) languages in their daily interactions, there can be a number of different outcomes affecting the grammars of those languages. This chapter looks at some of those outcomes; they are usually called **language contact phenomena**. These phenomena come in many different forms, but they all have to do with either (1) how the elements of two language varieties are used together in some way or (2) how the grammar of one variety affects the grammar of another. We'll sometimes use the term **contact phenomena** but we also use the term **bilingual speech** for the subject matter of this chapter.

We define bilingual speech as any clause that includes elements from two or more languages. From here on, we will just refer to two languages, although, as throughout this book, we intend bilingual speech as a cover term for two or more than two languages. The elements that make a clause bilingual may be actual surface-level words from two languages. This is called **codeswitching**. But sometimes speech is bilingual even though it only has surface-level words from one language; that is, speech is also called bilingual if two languages are the source of the underlying structure of a clause. That is, the "elements" making the clause bilingual that come from one of the participating languages are abstract rules, not actual words. How such speech qualifies as bilingual becomes clearer below when we discuss such structures under the term **convergence**.

We can't cover all contact phenomena in one chapter, so we have to limit discussion to three phenomena, codeswitching, convergence, and pidgin and creole development. These will be defined and discussed below. Within that limit, we devote most of the space to codeswitching, largely because it currently generates a great deal of attention from linguists interested in contact phenomena. For more on language contact in general see three overviews (Thomason 2001; Myers-Scotton, 2002; Winford 2003a). Also see Muysken (2000) and Clyne (2003) who also offer overviews, but deal mainly with codeswitching and convergence.

Remember from earlier chapters that when we use the term "language", it is a cover term in the same sense that "linguistic variety" is a cover term. Either of them could refer to either a standard or a non-standard dialect of what is generally called a "language". The point of this comment is to ensure that you don't assume when a language "name" is used that any specific variety of that language is intended.

Further, especially in this chapter, it's important to remember that it is often hard, or even impossible, to point to distinct boundaries between one dialect of a language and another dialect. In addition, it is difficult to draw the lines between "separate" languages in some cases. A simple rule of thumb is that what are called different languages are not **mutually intelligible**. But mutual intelligibility is not an "either/or" matter (because we need to consider not just words, but pronunciations, and grammatical structures). Further, as we indicated in chapters 1 and 2, sometimes mutual intelligibility is not even the basis used for differentiating languages. Instead, political or socio-historical considerations count. For example, Dutch is structurally very close to German, but they are called two different languages partly because they are the official languages in two different nation states. And the variety spoken in Galicia in northwest Spain is closer to Portuguese than it is to the standard dialect of Spanish, but the Galician variety is generally subsumed under Spanish. Like it or not, there is a lot of fuzziness in separating one linguistic variety from another. And even the fuzzy boundaries can change because changes in use patterns and attitudes indirectly affect the language varieties themselves.

9.1.1 Guidelines to watch for

We begin with some general principles about the effects of language contact that seem to apply to all varieties, no matter how they are classified.

In language contact in general, we will find that there are two kinds of asymmetries that operate. There is **structural asymmetry** between the languages involved and also **asymmetry involving content words vs. grammatical elements**.

Recall that we found these differences between the participation of different languages in chapter 8 on lexical borrowings. In such borrowings, one language generally is the donor and the other language is the recipient; it's not a two-way street. And more content words, especially nouns, are borrowed than anything else. Very few, if any, function words are borrowed, except for discourse markers, and we'll comment below on how they can be considered as a special case of content words.

Notice throughout this chapter how the notion of asymmetry prevails in the forms of language contact discussed here. For example, when we discuss convergence we will see that there are very few true "mixed languages" (if we define mixed languages as varieties with certain types of grammatical elements from both languages). In general, we will see that there are distinct constraints or limits on what can happen to the grammatical outcomes when two languages are in contact. We will argue that these are based on asymmetries that have their roots in differences in how languages are stored in our abstract linguistic competence and accessed in actual language production.

9.1.1.1 Structural asymmetry

Both languages do not participate equally in resulting structures. That is, almost always, **one language supplies the main grammatical frame** for a clause containing words from two (or more) languages. This means that the instructions from only one language on what makes a clause well-formed are followed in many types of contact phenomena. We will call this the **Matrix Language**; another name that would fit is the "frame language". The contribution of the other language comes largely from supplying some content elements. We will call this the **Embedded Language**; some researchers have called it the "guest language".

9.1.1.2 *Asymmetry between content vs. grammatical elements*

Also, the restrictions on how elements from the participating languages can be combined apply differently to content words than to grammatical elements. Content words come from both languages in all types of contact phenomena; these include nouns most prominently, but also verbs and adjectives and some adverbs. The difference to watch for concerns grammatical elements. Certain types of grammatical elements can come only from the Matrix Language in at least one major type of language contact, codeswitching (using two languages in the same clause); such elements also pattern differently from other elements in other contact phenomena.

9.1.2 Some technical terms

We will be discussing language contact using a few technical terms that all readers may not know well. Our focus is on morphemes and syntax. We will not be dealing here with what happens to sounds in contact situations, simply for lack of space.

First, you need to know that a **morpheme** is the basic building block in words. Some introductory textbooks say that morphemes are "the minimal meaningful units in language", but this is misleading because the class of grammatical morphemes carries little, if any, meaning. Instead, they signal relationships among more meaningful elements (words or phrases).

Languages differ considerably in the relationship between what are considered words and in how many morphemes they contain. In some languages, whole words may be one morpheme. For example, English has a lot of words that consist of one morpheme only, such as *tree* or *often*, but it also has some of those morphemes that largely signal relationships, such as -s, as it occurs with a regular verb when the subject is he, she, or it in the present tense (e.g. *Rover chew-s bones*). Chinese and southeast Asian languages, as well as many West African languages, have even more words that are only one morpheme long, such as *táng* 'sugar' and *běi* 'north' in Standard Chinese. In other languages, such as Turkish or Japanese or American Indian languages, most words are composed of two or more morphemes so that what is expressed in an entire clause in some languages is expressed by one word (composed of a number of morphemes) in other languages. Also, in the group of Bantu languages including Swahili, clauses can be one word long. Thus, in Swahili, *ni-taka-po-ku-on-a* is considered one word and means 'when I will see you' (it's a dependent clause).

Note that the number of morphemes in a word doesn't correspond to the number of syllables, but rather to the number of units that either have some meaning or indicate structural relationships. So, in English, *tree-s* has only one syllable but two morphemes, with -s indicating plural.

It will help you to know that there are two main types of morphemes, **free and bound morphemes**. Free morphemes can occur by themselves (e.g. a noun such as *girl*), but bound ones cannot (e.g. English plural -s is a bound morpheme). **Affixes** are bound morphemes. There are three possible types of affixes. **Prefixes** occur before a content element (or another prefix in some languages). For example, *pre-* itself is a prefix. **Suffixes** occur after a content element (or another suffix). For example, *-ed* in *finished* is a suffix (note that in this verb, *-ed* is pronounced [-t]). **Infixes** can actually be inserted into a content element, but don't occur in many languages (they are found in some languages in the Pacific Ocean). Some affixes are called **derivational**; their presence changes the meaning of the word in some way. For example, in English *-er/-or* is a suffix that changes a verb into a noun (e.g. *act-actor*).

Other affixes are called **inflectional** (although in some books "inflectional" is used for any affix). These affixes do not change meanings as such, and they are something of a mixed bag. Generally, inflectional affixes signal relationships, not meanings as such. Thus, English third-person singular *-s* signals that the subject of the verb is a third-person singular element or actor (e.g. *Bora bark-s at strangers*).

Some researchers pay attention to other divisions between morphemes. Some (especially psycholinguists) make use of the division between open and closed classes of words or morphemes. Open classes can take in new members, so nouns represent an open class in most languages. Closed classes do not ordinarily take in new members, so most affixes are closed-class elements, as are some functional words, such as determiners. This is not an especially useful division to apply in accounting for what takes place in naturally occurring speech.

9.1.3 Syntax (phrase, clause, and sentence structures)

You also will need to know a few things about **syntax**. A language's syntax is its sentence structure; syntax is most obvious in word order, but there is more to syntax than word order, although we don't have the space to elaborate. It is true that across languages, the clearest difference in syntax is word order. In many languages, to meet the language's well-formedness requirements, most subjects come before verbs and most objects follow verbs (SVO order). But in some languages, the verb is at the end (SOV order) and in others the verb may come first. But the word order of the basic elements of subject, verb, and object is only the beginning. Order can also vary across languages within phrases; for example, we will see below that in some languages noun phrases have the form modifier + noun and in other languages modifiers follow nouns.

A more important issue regarding syntax is how phrases including these and other elements can be put together in order to qualify as utterances in the language in question. Thus, each language has its own **well-formedness**

constraints (or conditions); you can think of these as "grammatical rules" even though that oversimplifies what "grammatical" means. But this is as much as you must know now about syntax; in the examples, any differences across languages that you need to be aware of will be made clear to you.

9.1.4 The clause: Either an entire sentence or only part of a sentence

There is one more technical term for you to understand now, the **clause**. Clauses are the basic building blocks of sentences. There are two main types of clauses, an **independent clause**, which can stand alone and make up a sentence all on its own, and a **dependent clause**, which can only occur in a sentence with an independent clause. Most clauses have a verb that is marked to indicate tense (e.g. future) or aspect (e.g. progressive).

Complete sentences in most languages can have any of these structures: (1) a single independent clause, (2) an independent clause, along with a dependent clause that modifies the independent clause, or (3) two (or more) independent clauses joined together by coordinating conjunctions. Exact structural requirements depend on the language in question, but all languages have clauses. See the English examples below, with numbers corresponding to the types just discussed. Note how what is an independent clause in (a) becomes a dependent clause in (b1) when headed by a dependent (subordinating) conjunction. In (b2) a dependent clause with a relative pronoun (*who likes big dogs*) is inserted into a new independent clause (Alice . . . plans to buy a Great Dane).

(a)   *Alice likes big dogs.*
(b1)   *Because Alice likes big dogs, she plans to buy a Great Dane.*
(b2)   *Alice, who likes big dogs, plans to buy a Great Dane.*
(c)   *Alice is going to buy a Great Dane but her friend is buying a dachshund.*

One more point related to clauses: Models that seek to describe or explain language contact phenomena frequently use the term **constituent**. They often pay attention to setting up constraints on the possible combinations of content words and affixes (bound morphemes) from two or more languages in the same constituent. **Constituents** include everything from an element heading a larger constituent to the larger constituent itself, and that larger constituent is often a full clause.

The head of a constituent is often a noun or a verb, but single words, such as nouns or verbs, can be constituents on their own. Thus, in one example of a noun phrase, *the little dog*, *dog* is the head constituent. But the full noun phrase *the little dog* is also a constituent, and so is the verb phrase *ate the whole cake*. This particular verb phrase includes a verb and its direct object which serves the thematic role of Patient. (More on thematic roles later.) Some researchers refer to maximal projections. **A maximal projection** is a head *and* its expansion to the phrasal level. Thus, constituents differ from maximal projections in that a single noun can be a constituent (and a noun phrase).

The important thing to note here is how syntactic units are embedded in larger syntactic units. The constituents just discussed are part of a larger constituent, which is also a full independent clause, *the little boy ate the whole cake.* (And, course, this clause is also a sentence.)

9.1.5 Summary on technical terms

Except for something more on morpheme types in a later section, this is all the introduction that you absolutely need to technical terminology. So, if you have in mind (1) that morphemes are building blocks *within words*, (2) that syntax refers to structure in clauses *beyond the word*, and (3) that the clause is our *unit of analysis*, the material in this chapter is easily understandable.

9.2 Codeswitching

We begin our discussion of what happens to the grammatical structures when two languages are in contact by considering one of the most studied topics in contact phenomena today, codeswitching. There are many journal articles, dissertations, and even entire books specifically on codeswitching. We mention only a few of these to give you an indication of the scope of this research: Canut and Caubet (2001) on codeswitching including French and such languages as North African Arabic; Hlavac (2003) on second-generation Croatian-English switching in Australia; Türker (2000) on Turkish-Norwegian among immigrants in Norway; and McConvell (2001) on Australian indigenous varieties.

The most **general definition of codeswitching** is this: the use of two language varieties in the same conversation. Examples (1) and (2) show the range of structures that qualify as codeswitching. In (1) we see **inter-sentential switching**; that is, the example includes full sentences in both English and Swahili. Each of these sentences is a single clause (that is, *Have some vegetables* is a sentence in English and it is a single clause; *nipe kabeji hizi* 'give me these cabbages' is a sentence in Swahili and it is a single clause. Within each sentence there is no switching of languages, but there is switching between the sentences. In (2) we see **intra-sentential switching**, but a specific type of such switching, **intra-clause switching** (because inter-sentential switching could be between two clauses in the same sentence). Example (?) includes two clauses, each showing intra-clause switching (that is, *él le cambió los fans* 'he changed the fans' is an independent clause in this example showing codeswitching within the clause because it includes elements from both Spanish and English in the same clause). In all examples in this chapter, bold face will highlight a switched element.

(1)   Setting: A vegetable market in Nairobi, Kenya. Part of the conversation between the stallholder and a well-dressed customer from different ethnic groups and therefore with two different Lls. The stallholder is from the Kikuyu ethnic group and the customer is from the Luo ethnic group. They converse in Swahili, the main informal inter-ethnic group language in Nairobi, and English, an official language in Kenya alongside Swahili.

Stallholder: Habari, mheshimiwa. ('Hello, respected sir'.) **Have some vegetables.**
Customer: Mboga gani? Nipe kabeji hizi. (Which vegetables? Give me these cabbages.') **How much is that?**

(Myers-Scotton, 1993a: 40–1)

(2)   Setting: Spanish-English bilingual friends, originally from South America, who now live in the United States.
Porque son **two fans**, él le cambió los **fans**
because be two fans he it changed the fans
'Because there are two fans, he changed the fans.'

(Spanish-English, Jake, Myers-Scotton and Gross, 2002: 81)

We already met codeswitching in chapter 6 where we discussed social motivations for engaging in switching between languages. In this chapter, we concentrate on grammatical structure, not the social side of bilingualism. Further, we're not so much interested in conversations of one sentence in one language and the next sentence in another language (as in example 1), but rather in how two languages can be used together in the very same clause (as in example 2).

Specifically in regard to codeswitching, we'll be looking at their answers in this chapter for the following general questions: (1) What sort of "traffic control" is in place when two language varieties occur together in the same clause? Specifically, can both varieties participate equally in supplying content words, grammatical elements, and word order? (2) Are singly occurring words that are switched related to longer constituents (full phrases) that are switched? Or, are these words more closely related to established lexical borrowings? There are many other issues to address in codeswitching within the same clause, but space devoted to codeswitching must be limited.

9.2.1 The clause as the best unit of analyzing bilingual data

Although some researchers who study codeswitching try to work out constraints on switching by considering the sentence as their unit of analysis, we do not discuss such switching any further. We deal only with the clause, because it is only within the clause that the language varieties involved in codeswitching are in contact. Think about it: A sentence can qualify as bilingual, but it might be on the basis of having one clause from one language and the other clause from another language. You can say such a sentence shows codeswitching, but it doesn't show the two languages actually in contact, so the question about "traffic control" given above has no meaning. Other types of codeswitching may answer various other questions, but **intra-clausal switching** gives us answers to the most interesting questions about the grammar of codeswitching.

9.2.2 Defining codeswitching

When two languages are used within the same clause, theoretically both could control aspects of grammatical structure. For example, noun phrases (nouns and their modifiers) could meet the well-formedness conditions of one language, and verb phrases (verbs and their predicates) could be structured by the other language. However, that does not happen. Empirical evidence shows that the grammatical structure of one language prevails in what we will call **classic codeswitching**. Here's a definition of classic codeswitching:

> Classic codeswitching includes elements from two (or more) languages varieties in the same clause, but *only one of these varieties is the source of the morphosyntactic frame for the clause.*

Below, we refine the definition, discussing as bona fide codeswitching both singly occurring words and full phrases from one language within the frame set by another language. In the definition, **morphosyntactic frame** means all the abstract grammatical requirements that would make the frame well-formed in the language in question (concerning word order, morpheme order, and the necessary inflectional morphemes).

9.3 A model for classic codeswitching

We introduce classic codeswitching by presenting details from the Matrix Language Frame (MLF) model, our own model (Myers-Scotton 1993b [1997], 2002). The reason for situating the discussion within the terms of the MLF model is that it is one of the more comprehensive treatments of intra-clausal codeswitching, making it a good backdrop against which to discuss examples of codeswitching, as well as other approaches to codeswitching.

However, the MLF model is not intended to apply to all types of contact phenomena. Still, we will see that some of its provisions are relevant to other contact phenomena because the model highlights the importance of asymmetry in characterizing bilingual speech and differences between morpheme types. For other current approaches to codeswitching that go beyond classic codeswitching, see especially Clyne (2003) and Muysken (2000).

9.3.1 More on classic codeswitching

An important consideration behind the definition of classic codeswitching is that to engage in such codeswitching, speakers must be proficient enough in the language structuring the clause so that they can follow the well-formedness constraints of that language in providing the morphosyntactic frame for the bilingual clause. Speakers may also be very proficient in the other language involved; some proficiency is necessary, but a high degree of proficiency is not so critical. The assumption is that the two varieties participating in classic codeswitching are not mutually intelligible (they are called two different languages).

Composite codeswitching contrasts with classic codeswitching. This type of switching is less frequently described and its structure is less well explained just because its structure is less "neat" (the MLF model was not designed to explain it). Here's a definition of composite codeswitching:

> Composite codeswitching is bilingual speech in which even though most of the morphosyntactic structure comes from one of the participating languages, the other language contributes some of the abstract structure underlying surface forms in the clause.

Sometimes in composite codeswitching the "other language" contributes some of the surface grammatical elements themselves, but more frequently its influences are abstract and therefore "below the surface". As a phenomenon, this type of codeswitching is called a composite because it is a **combination of codeswitching and convergence**. Convergence is defined in section 9.9 and composite codeswitching is briefly illustrated there. Note that a speaker can be very proficient in the language that is the sole supplier of the morphosyntactic frame in classic codeswitching, but still select composite codeswitching as an option. That is, social or psychological considerations can influence how a speaker chooses to speak, even if this choice is at the unconscious level.

9.3.2 The Uniform Structure Principle

But before we present the explanations the MLF model does offer for classic codeswitching, we offer a "mega-backdrop" to the model itself. This is the Uniform Structure Principle. It is the ultimate backdrop because it applies universally, to monolingual language as well as to bilingual language. The reason something along its lines is not discussed often (in other linguistics studies of one language) is that we just take a version of the principle for granted in regard to monolingual language where, because we're only dealing with one language, there is obviously no competition as to which language is the language of grammatical structure. The principle only really assumes importance when it would be possible to have grammatical structure from two languages in the same clause. In effect, the principle makes the claim that such an outcome is unusual; it states that structure from only one source is the preferred option. Here's the principle (Myers-Scotton 2002):

> **The Uniform Structure Principle:** A given constituent type in any language has a uniform abstract structure and the requirements of well-formedness for this type must be observed whenever the constituent appears. In bilingual speech, the structures of the Matrix Language are always preferred, but some Embedded structures [i.e. Embedded Language islands as discussed below] are allowed if Matrix Language clause structure is observed.

9.3.3 Premises of the MLF model

The MLF model benefited from the insights of earlier researchers who recognized the unequal participation of languages in codeswitching. Joshi (1985) was one of the first to refer to the frame-building language as the **Matrix Language** and to the other participating language as the **Embedded Language**. The MLF model itself has three main premises.

The first premise is that the Matrix Language and the Embedded Language do not participate equally in constituent structure. Note how this premise follows from the Uniform Structure Principle just stated above.

The second premise is that not all morpheme types are equal in the sense that not all types can come equally from the Matrix and Embedded Languages. As you will see, these premises limit the Embedded Language to specific types of participation.

A third premise is that both languages are always "on" when a speaker engages in codeswitching, although the Matrix Language is always more activated. The MLF model doesn't support this premise with empirical evidence (as it can for the first two premises), but patterns in codeswitching do offer strong indirect support.

9.3.4 How to identify the Matrix Language

The heart of the MLF model consists of two principles that are specific versions of the general premise that languages do not participate equally in codeswitching. Only one of the participating languages supplies the morphosyntactic frame of the bilingual clause in codeswitching. The principles, in effect, identify this language as the language meeting their requirements. Of course, by default, the principles identify the other language as the Embedded Language, the language that does not meet their requirements.

These principles apply to what are called **mixed constituents** (constituents including morphemes from both languages). These constituents may consist of an entire clause, but smaller phrases within the larger clause are also mixed constituents.

It's important to recognize that both of these principles are **testable hypotheses** in the sense that they are open to falsifiability. This means that it is possible to see what sort of examples would be counter-examples to the principles. Falsifiability is an important feature of any hypotheses that claim some scientific value.

THE MORPHEME ORDER PRINCIPLE

In mixed constituents consisting of at least one Embedded Language word and any number of Matrix Language morphemes, surface word (and morpheme) order will be that of the Matrix Language.

THE SYSTEM MORPHEME PRINCIPLE

In Matrix Language + Embedded Language constituents, all system morphemes *which have grammatical relations external to their head constituents* [italics added] (i.e. which participate in the sentence's thematic role grid) will come from the Matrix Language.
(Original statements of the principles from Myers-Scotton 1993b: 83 [1997]; reprinted in Myers-Scotton 2002: 59.)
Note that under the 4-M model, a new model that refers only to morpheme types, the one type of system morpheme referred to under the System Morpheme Principle is named as an outsider late system morpheme. The 4-M model is discussed in section 9.8. You'll see there why this morpheme type is called "late".

9.3.5 Separating content and system morphemes

Now you may wonder what system morphemes are! Here's the last, real technical discussion for you: An important component of the MLF model is that it divides morphemes into content morpheme and system morphemes.

9.3.5.1 Content morphemes

Content morphemes are those that either assign or receive thematic roles. What are **thematic roles**? First, they are also called theta roles. Second, they are basically semantic roles, although they are often discussed by linguists as tied to syntax. But they are semantic in the sense that they refer to such relations within the sentence as whether a noun is the Agent or the Patient of the verb. Linguists say that verbs "subcategorize" for different thematic roles. For example, the verb *give* subcategorizes for (meaning "can take") three thematic roles, an Agent, a Patient (the element that is given) and a Beneficiary or Recipient (e.g. *Alice gave the dog a bone*). Because verbs most typically assign thematic roles and nouns most typically receive them, verbs and nouns are prototypical content morphemes.

We won't have space to discuss them in detail, but note that in this model **discourse markers** (e.g. *therefore, so, but*) are considered content morphemes *at the discourse level*. No, they do not assign thematic roles *within the clause*, but they limit the interpretation of what comes after them in the clause. In that sense, they assign discourse-level thematic roles. They frequently come from the Embedded Language in codeswitching (e.g. Torres, 2002 on English discourse markers in New York Puerto Rican Spanish). They often become established borrowings when social conditions promote borrowing words from another language.

9.3.5.2 *System morphemes*

In contrast with content morphemes, **system morphemes** do not assign or receive thematic roles. When the 4-M model is discussed in section 9.8, you will see how system morphemes are classified as falling into three types. System morphemes overlap with those elements that some linguists call functional elements, but the overlap is not complete at all. For example, free-standing independent pronouns in languages such as English are content morphemes (cf. Jake 1994 on pronouns), not system morphemes, although they are also called functional elements.

Prototypical system morphemes are **all affixes (bound morphemes) and some function words** that stand alone (e.g. determiners and clitics). Some languages (e.g. French and Spanish) have clitics in verb phrases; think of these as reduced pronouns; they are free forms, but they cannot occur by themselves, so they function more like affixes than content words.

Some lexical categories, such as adverbs and prepositions, straddle the division between content and system morphemes. Clearly, degree adverbs, such as *very*, are system morphemes. Even though they have more of their own content than affixes, they do not receive or assign thematic roles.

Some prepositions are more certainly content morphemes and some others are system morphemes. The ones with more content do receive thematic roles when they head prepositional phrases (e.g. *outside, inside, down, up*).

In contrast, two types of prepositions are system morphemes. First, those prepositions that are satellites to verbs are system morphemes. They result in what are sometimes called phrasal verbs (e.g. *up* in *look up the number*). But they mainly have content by adding content to the verb, not on their own. That is, they don't assign thematic roles on their own. Second, there are those prepositions that clearly have little or no content; they also are system morphemes. For example, *in* or *on* in the clauses *I live on Buchanan Street* (American English) /*I live in Buchanan Street* (British English) are system morphemes. Also, such morphemes as *of* in English, as in *book of Alice*, are system morphemes.

9.3.5.3 *Content and system morphemes across languages*

Even though all of these examples are from English, the basic definition holds across languages. That is, content words either assign thematic roles or receive them. True, not all linguists agree as to how many thematic roles there are or about their assignment. But that need not worry us here; in this overview, we're mainly concerned with separating the main content words (nouns and verbs) from those elements that are clearly system morphemes, such as inflections.

9.3.6 Examples showing how the principles of the MLF model are played out

Now, we'll give you some examples to illustrate some mixed constituents so you can see how the Morpheme Order and the System Morpheme Principles work.

Example (3) comes from an Italian-Spanish-English multilingual who has immigrated to Australia.

(3)   No porque quiero   dispressare a   mi **language italian**
      Not because seek-1SING undervalue INFINITIVE my language italian
      'Not that I want to undervalue my Italian language.'
                                          (Italian-English, Clyne 2003: 87)

What to pay attention to here: Note that the only material from English in this bilingual example is the noun and its adjective, *language italian*. But note that it follows Italian word order, not English order. This example supports the Morpheme Order Principle because this phrase and everything else in the clause follows Italian order, indicating that only one language supplies morpheme order. This identifies Italian as the Matrix Language. Also note that the subject–verb agreement element (the suffix on the verb *quiero* 'I seek' for first person singular) comes from Italian. This suffix is the type of system morpheme that must look outside the verb itself for information about its form; here, it looks to the larger discourse (i.e. the speaker). This supports the System Morpheme Principle that requires such morphemes to come from only one of the participating languages. This marks Italian as the Matrix Language in this clause, too.

In example (4), switching includes English and Ewe, a language spoken in Ghana in West Africa. Here, an English verb occurs with a suffix from Ewe (*weed-na*).

(4)   wo   tsɔ-na   wo fe   asi-wo   tsɔ-na
      they   take-HABITUAL   they POSSESSIVE hand-PL   take-HABITUAL
      weed-na   **garden**-a   me-ɛ
      weed-HABITUAL   garden-the   in-FOCUS
      'They take [use] their hands to weed in the garden.'
                (Ewe-English, Amuzu 1998: 56, cited in Myers-Scotton 2002: 89)

The verb (for 'they weed') is followed by what is called a postpositional phrase in which the postposition marker follows the noun in the phrase (*garden-a me-e* 'garden-the in'). A postpositional phrase corresponds to a prepositional phrase in English and other languages that have prepositions and in which the preposition comes first in the phrase. Ewe, not English, obviously controls word order in this phrase.

In this example, we actually have two clauses even though the best English translation includes only one clause. Literally, the example reads this way: 'they take their hands, they weed garden the in'. Because the word order in this example identifies only one language (Ewe) as the source of morpheme order, the example supports the Morpheme Order Principle. The example also supports the System Morpheme Principle because the outsider morphemes marking "habitual" on all the verbs in the example, including the English verb (*weed-na*) come from only one language, Ewe. The aspect 'habitual' is an outsider system morpheme because its form is not required by the verb with which it occurs, but rather by the overall proposition that the clause expresses. Thus, based on both the Morpheme Order Principle and the System Morpheme Principle, Ewe is identified as the Matrix Language and it is clear that only one language, Ewe, is supplying the morphosyntactic frame in this codeswitching example.

Example (5) comes from a French Canadian French-English bilingual.

(5)   A côté il y en a un autre gros **building high-rise**.
      at side there is an other big building high-rise
      'Next door there's another big high-rise building.'
                (French-English, Poplack 1988: 224)

French word order of *building* and *high-rise* is evidence that French is controlling word order, not English, in line with the Morpheme Order Principle. In addition, note that French provides the indefinite article (*un* 'an'). This is *not* the type of system morpheme that the System Morpheme Principle states must come from the Matrix Language; you will see later this is called an early system morpheme. But according to the Uniform Structure Principle, grammatical elements in general from the Matrix Language are preferred. As in the other examples above, only one language (French here) supplies the elements that structure the morphosyntactic frame. They all support the idea of asymmetry between the participating languages.

9.3.7 Other evidence of a single Matrix Language setting the frame

Example (6) shows a structural outcome that is not covered by the Morpheme Order Principle or the System Morpheme Principle. It shows how extensive is the influence of only one of the participating languages, the Matrix Language, on all the grammatical structures in a mixed constituent (with morphemes from both languages). In (6) Swahili is the Matrix Language. This is evident from the fact that it controls the verbal prefixes for subject–verb agreement and for tense on the verb. That is, again, these are the type of morpheme that has to look outside its head (the verb here) for information about its form. In this case, these morphemes look to the larger discourse to determine who the subject is (a third-person singular subject) and what the time frame is (past event). Because Swahili is the source of these morphemes, the example supports the System Morpheme Principle.

But we are citing this example to show that the Matrix Language also controls how attributive adjectives are handled in Swahili. Swahili itself has few attributive adjectives, but when they occur Swahili grammar utilizes the structure of "X with Y" (that is, the possessor *gari* 'car' precedes the adjective and an associative/possessive element (*ya* 'of') joins the noun for 'car' with the adjective for 'red'. (The prefix on this element (*i>y*) is the agreement marker for Swahili noun class 9, the class into which the borrowing *gari* is placed; this prefix is also the type of system morpheme that must come from the Matrix Language.) Note how the idea expressed in Swahili would be typically expressed in English, the Embedded Language. The speaker would have said *he bought a red car*, with the adjective 'red' preceding the object being described.

(6)   A-li-nunu-a gari   ya red
      3s-PAST-buy car   of red
      'He bought a red car.'
      (Swahili-English, Myers-Scotton, unpublished 1988 Nairobi corpus)

Here's another example that shows the same Swahili construction, but with English elements: *Hawa chicks hawakuwa* <u>*standard ya mine*</u> 'those chicks [girls] weren't of my standard'. Notice that in English the construction would have been *my standard*, with a possessive adjective (Myers-Scotton 1988: 61).

Example (7) is another indication of how the Matrix Language is in control.

(7) Ils pass-ont des petites   notes **back and forth** à **each other**
     they pass-PL   little   notes back and forth to each other
     'They pass little notes back and forth to each other.'
(French-English, King 2000: 100)

Note that in (7) the French preposition for 'to' (à) is used to join together the English parts of the fixed expression 'back and forth to each other'. This shift to French, the Matrix Language, in the middle of a fixed expression supports the Uniform Structure Principle, giving preference to Matrix Language grammatical elements.

Here is one more example to show the control that the Matrix Language exercises. In example (8) the English word *weather* receives a Finnish determiner *(se)* and the English infinitive *change* receives the Finnish suffix that marks infinitives in Finnish (-*ii*).

Note that in the English clause *the weather can change*, there would be no infinitive marker present; that is, *the weather can **to** change* would not occur. This is strong evidence that the well-formedness conditions of the Matrix Language are in control, not those of English. This example comes from a Finnish immigrant to Australia.

(8) Ikukaa   ei tii   millon, milloin se **weather** voi   **change-ii**
     anybody no know when, when   the weather may   change-INF
     Nobody knows   when, when   the weather can change.'
(Finnish-English, Kovács 2001: 145)

9.3.8 The principled basis of codeswitching

In effect, the extent to which the Morpheme Order Principle and the System Morpheme Principle are supported is an answer to the question, is there "traffic control" in bilingual clauses in codeswitching. That is, the answer is "yes". These principles are generally supported across various sets of codeswitching data reported in other studies, with only a few apparent exceptions. The few counter-examples do not change the general pattern of overall support. We stress the universality of support, no matter which languages are involved.

This support is evidence that codeswitching has a principled basis. It is not haphazard – speakers don't just mix words from two languages together freely. This finding goes against the popular view of many people, even many speakers who engage in codeswitching themselves. That is, many people think of codeswitching as "broken or bad language" just because it includes two languages. Alternatively, when some people hear codeswitching, they think it is amazing. But it is neither "broken" nor mysterious. The ability of bilinguals to engage in

principled codeswitching seems to be as much a part of the human competence for language as is acquiring and speaking any single language.

But if codeswitching is so systematic, why don't at least the codeswitching
speakers themselves realize this? The answer is that typically speakers don't
realize they are following well-formedness constraints for codeswitching any
more than they realize they are following them when they produce sentences
in their L1, or in any other language that they speak fluently. Abstract constraints on well-formedness are part of our implicit knowledge of language.
This means we have the constraints as part of our cognitive knowledge,
but can't report on its details. The difference between this type of knowledge
(called **procedural knowledge**) and **declarative knowledge** (what we overtly
learn and can report on) will be introduced in chapter 10 when types of memory
are considered; the difference is discussed in chapter 11 in relation to second-
language acquisition. Recall that in chapter 5, we discussed social and pragmatic motivations for codeswitching.

9.4 How other approaches to codeswitching differ from the MLF model

As we've indicated, codeswitching is a very popular topic for linguists interested in language contact. But exactly how it is studied varies a great deal. It is
something of an oversimplification, but these researchers fall generally into
two groups (under 9.4.1 and 9.4.2).

A major difference is that some researchers treat singly occurring Embedded Language words as a type of borrowing, even those with Matrix Language inflections. Others include these forms as codeswitching. Those who do
exclude single forms generally deal mainly or exclusively with the syntactic
organization of sentences or clauses that contain codeswitching. It is fair to say
that in not dealing with Embedded Language singly occurring forms, those
researchers leave out attempting to account for the structuring of one of the
most challenging aspects of codeswitching.

9.4.1 Paying attention to surface-level differences

One group of researchers is mainly interested in devising constraints on points
in a sentence where codeswitching can occur on the basis of **surface-level
linear differences** between the languages involved. That is, they see limits
on codeswitching in terms of differences in word order, either across clauses
(inter-sentential) or on phrases within clauses. This was the thinking of many
early researchers. For example, Poplack's Equivalence Constraint (1980) claims
that switching is not allowed when the syntax of two languages does not
match at a potential switch point.

Today, some researchers, including Poplack and her associates (e.g. Budzhak-Jones 1998) continue this line of thinking, as do others. For example, Muysken (2000: 118) states that "the evidence overwhelmingly supports more surface-oriented constraints". Yet, others point out that there are many counter-examples to such approaches. When the surface word order of two languages does not match, switching is still possible (as we've seen in examples cited above – recall example (4) in which Ewe is the Matrix Language and therefore supplies word order that includes a "postpositional" phrase from Ewe. English, of course, doesn't have postpositional phrases, but has prepositional phrases instead. Also, in example (6) *building high-rise* follows French, not English, word order. English places its modifiers before the noun, not after it.

Some researchers discount supposed counter-examples to the Equivalence Constraint by claiming that any "out of order" Embedded Language words are borrowings, not codeswitches. This is the line taken by Shin (2002) in regard to Korean-English codeswitching when she finds a number of English words in what would be accusative (objective) case position in Korean. Korean is a language with the verb in final position and a preceding direct object (that sometimes receives an overt accusative case marker and sometimes doesn't). She reports that the percentages of English- and Korean-origin nouns that occur with an overt accusative case marking suffix or with no suffix are similar. Because of this, she argues that the English nouns are borrowings into Korean and so their "wrong order" in Korean-English codeswitching doesn't count.

9.4.2 Extending current syntactic theories to codeswitching

Another group of the researchers also does not consider singly occurring Embedded Language words as codeswitches, but is looking for explanations at a more **abstract level than linear structure**. They do this by framing their explanations in terms of current versions of what are called generative theories of syntax. That is, they claim that the grammatical structure of codeswitching can be explained just in terms of the principles of current syntactic theories, even though these theories were only formulated to explain monolingual data. They do not recognize any theoretical (or useful) value in recognizing the asymmetry between a Matrix Language and an Embedded Language. In attempting to rework syntactic theories intended to explain monolingual utterance structure, these researchers are looking for explanations at an abstract level of grammatical structure.

Because they do not recognize single content words as part of codeswitching, these researchers can view them as borrowings, even though they generally receive inflections from the language the MLF model identifies as the Matrix Language. It can be argued they are borrowings since established borrowings also generally receive the inflections of the recipient language (corresponding to the Matrix Language). However, these researchers offer no theory to explain how the production and use of these forms differ from that of established borrowed words that are in the dictionary of the Matrix Language.

This group includes a number of researchers who try to explain codeswitching within the terms of the syntactic theory of Government and Binding (e.g. DiSciullo, Muysken, and Singh (1986), Belazi, Rubin and Toribio (1994), and Halmari (1997)). More recently, a later model, Chomsky's Minimalist Program (e.g. Chomsky, 1995), has been employed by Toribio and Rubin (1996), MacSwan (1999, 2000) and Bhatia and Ritchie (1996). Other researchers have cited serious counter-examples to Government constraints on switching. Also, Jake, Myers-Scotton and Gross (2002) argue that the Minimalist Program on its own (without the Matrix Language versus Embedded Language distinction) is not sufficient to explain what occurs in codeswitching.

9.4.3 Researchers who cast a wider net

In addition, there are a number of other researchers who fall into neither of the groups outlined above, but who can't be said to comprise a single group, either. They differ from the above two groups because they typically consider all Embedded Language material (both singly occurring forms and full phrases and sometimes full clauses or full sentences) in their analyses. They differ from the MLF model, which considers codeswitching (and other contact phenomena) as contact between languages only within the clause. Instead, many of these researchers are interested in citing bilingual examples at different levels of structure, some in phrases, some in clauses, and some in sentences. Clyne (2003) looks at various levels of structure and is more interested in what is here called composite codeswitching, but which he includes under the label transference.

If these researchers try to provide a theoretical basis for their analyses, they often do so by considering their data as tests of the MLF model (e.g. Park, 2000). Others operate within their own frameworks that may include features of the MLF model or a modified version of it (e.g. Backus, 1996; Boumans, 1998; Hlavac, 2003).

Yet other researchers are mainly concerned with describing the types of structures that occur in their data sets; that is, it is not their main purpose to explain the types of structures that can occur. Muysken (2000) provides a typology of bilingual structures across various data sets. Although many of these researchers do not offer theory-based analyses, some discuss their data in terms of a Matrix Language in relation to an Embedded Language (e.g. Kovács, 2001).

9.4.4 Reviewing the main features of the MLF model

Now, let's recap the main characteristics of the **MLF** model.

- First, the model is based on abstract premises regarding two basic asymmetries. These asymmetries are: (1) There is a division of labor between the languages participating in contact phenomena, with one language, labeled as the Matrix Language, supplying the morphosyntactic frame for the bilingual clause. (2) There is a division between types of morpheme that limits their occurrence in codeswitching. Specifically, content morphemes can come from either participating language, but a certain type of system morpheme (to be called outsiders under the 4-M model described in section 9.8) must come from the Matrix Language and other system morphemes generally come from the Matrix Language (following the Uniform Structure Principle).
- Second, only intra-clausal switching is considered (in contrast with inter-sentential switching).
- Third, only classic codeswitching is considered. This is bilingual speech within the same constituent but with the morphosyntactic frame coming from only one participating language.
- Fourth, the model's constraints apply only to language varieties that are not mutually intelligible.
- Fifth, the model emphasizes what happens on the abstract level of language production when bilingual constituents appear on the surface (cf. Myers-Scotton and Jake, 1995 and Myers-Scotton, 2002, 2005 for more on this). Both Muysken (2000: 274–7) and Clyne (2003) also raise the need to pay more attention to the cognitive aspects of language processing.
- Finally, most other discussions imply that only one language is active in production at a time. This seems especially to be the case when only alternation between clauses or phrases in different languages is considered. In contrast, the MLF model explicitly views both languages as always "on", even though the Matrix Language is more activated all the time. When we have examples such as *back and forth à each other* in example (7), with an English set phrase broken up with a French preposition, it is pretty hard not to argue that both languages are activated in the same phrase. (We will see in chapter 10 that there is good evidence from psycholinguistic experiments that both of a bilingual's languages are "on" to some extent, even when he or she is asked to recognize or speak a word in only one language.)

9.5 Singly occurring words as borrowings or codeswitches?

As we've indicated, a number of researchers do not consider singly occurring Embedded Language words as part of what needs explaining in codeswitching data. They say these single words are a type of borrowing. Still, they generally recognize that such words are different from established borrowings, and

Poplack (1980), one of the major early researchers, calls these words **"nonce"** **borrowings**. ("For the nonce", of course, means "for the moment".) Most of these words are nouns; as noted in chapter 8 on lexical borrowing, nouns are the most frequently borrowed element.

Because the status of these words is controversial, they deserve some attention. But because of limited space, we'll only present some examples of the words in question. We argue that one can conclude that they resemble Embedded Language phrases in codeswitching more than they resemble established borrowings. In fact, one could argue that there is a continuum of Embedded Language elements in bilingual clauses, with single words as one end point and full phrases as the other. Further, many singly occurring words that are codeswitches could (and do) become established borrowings if they are adopted by trend-setters.

9.5.1 Typical examples of singly occurring forms

Examples (9) through (11) give examples of the type of singly occurring words that some researchers call borrowings and that the MLF model views as codeswitched elements in mixed constituents. They are the most frequent type of Embedded Language elements across many and diverse codeswitching data sets.

In (9) the nouns *application* and *interview* occur in a conversation between a manager at a business in Nairobi, Kenya and a job applicant. The manager is speaking. True, either *application* or *interview* could be considered temporary borrowings into Swahili, but they clearly are not established borrowings. Further, the concepts could have been conveyed in Swahili just as easily (*haja* 'request for interview', an established borrowing from Arabic; *mkutano* (*wa watu wawili*) 'meeting of two people'). So there is every reason to consider the English words as instances of codeswitching on the same footing as long English phrases.

> (9)   Ulituma barua ya **application**?   Ikiwa ulituma barua, tutakuita
>   Did you send letter of application . . . if it be you sent letter, we will
>   call you
>   ufike kwa **interview**   siku itakapofika.
>   that you may arrive for interview   day it will when arrive
>   'Did you send a letter of application? If you sent a letter, we will call
>   you so that you may come for [an] interview when it [the letter] will
>   arrive.'
>   (Swahili-English, Myers-Scotton, unpublished Nairobi corpus 1988)

Example (10) comes from a conversation among Chinese graduate students studying in the United States who are bilingual in English.

(10) wo you   liang-fen   **paper** mingtian bixu jiashangqu
    I   have   two-CLASSIFIER paper tomorrow must turn in
    'I have two papers [which] I must turn in tomorrow.'
                                       (Chinese-English, Wei 2002: 699)

Note that in examples (9) and (10), the Embedded Language words are "bare" forms. That is, they do not receive any inflections that would make them well-formed in the language that supplies the morphosyntactic frame (the Matrix Language). For example, in (9), Swahili is the Matrix Language and nouns in Swahili normally receive noun class prefixes, so *application* and *interview* are both "bare". However, the missing prefixes are not the type that are required by the System Morpheme Principle. Many singly occurring Embedded Language words occur as bare forms; these are discussed again in section 9.5.2.

In contrast, example (11) shows examples of nouns that do receive Matrix Language inflections, so they aren't bare forms. But, again, these aren't the type that must come from the Matrix Language according to the System Morpheme Principle. Example (11) comes from a Zulu speaker in the urban township outside Pretoria in South Africa.

(11) **So** i-**language**   e-khuluny-w-a   a-ma-**gangs** . . .
    so CL.9 language COMP-speak-passive CL.6 PRE-PREFIX-PREFIX- gangs
    'So the language which is spoken by gangs . . .'
    (Zulu-English, Finlayson, Calteaux and Myers-Scotton, 1998: 408)

In this case, the English nouns receive noun class prefixes from Zulu. These prefixes are referred to by numbers by grammarians and this example includes one example with a class nine prefix (*i-language*) and one with a pre-prefix and a prefix from class six (*a-ma-gangs*).

9.5.2 Whose word order do singly occurring Embedded Language forms follow?

In all the examples considered so far of Embedded Language words in a Matrix Language frame, the two languages have the same word order as far as the singly occurring words are concerned. Now we consider some examples where there is *a conflict* in word order. When this happens, the Matrix Language order wins out. This is what the Morpheme Order Principle above predicts – that only the order of one of the participating languages prevails and that language is called the Matrix Language.

Consider example (12) from a second-generation Croatian living in Australia who is bilingual in Croatian and English. In English the typical word order is SVO (subject-verb-object). But in (12) the English verb *supervise* occurs in final position. In Croatian, the verb typically comes last in a clause. So this positioning of the English verb shows that Croatian, not English, is setting the frame of the clause and that, therefore, Croatian is the Matrix Language. Clyne (2003: 87) uses this example to point out that the verb of a clause does not always determine the word order. He notes that this example is an argument against Klavans (1983) and later researchers who argue that the verb of the sentence determines word order (and therefore the language of the verb is the Matrix Language or frame language).

> (12)   Ne on radi taj posao I   ja njega **supervise**
>   no, he does that job and   I him   supervise
>   'No, he does the job and I supervise him.'
>   (Croatian-English, Hlavac (2000: 353), cited in Clyne)

9.5.3 Aren't such examples very like established borrowings?

One might claim that example (12) shows that because singly occurring forms from an Embedded Language are integrated into the word order of a Matrix Language, this is evidence that they are borrowings of some sort and not codeswitches. Yes, it is true that established borrowings fit into the word order of the recipient language. But on another level of structure, words such as *supervise* aren't integrated as established borrowings are. The English verb *supervise* is pronounced as it is pronounced in English, not as it would be if it were phonologically integrated into Croatian. In fact, almost all singly occurring Embedded Language forms in codeswitching data sets *that occur only once in that set* are pronounced just as they would be in the Embedded Language. They do not conform to the pronunciation conventions of the Matrix Language. In a corpus of Swahili-English codeswitching, there are 91 English verb forms that receive Swahili inflections for person and tense or aspect and sometimes an object; still, the verb stem is pronounced as it would be in English (e.g. *ni-ka-i-rub* means 'and I rubbed it' cf. Myers-Scotton 1993a: 103; 1993b: 88). If *rub* were integrated into Swahili, it would have to be something like [raba] instead of [rəb] as it is in this example.

We also note that when Einar Haugen, one of the early "greats" in contact linguistics, gave a definition of codeswitching, he referred to singly occurring words and specifically mentioned their unassimilated status. Here's what he said would count as codeswitching: "the alternate use of two languages including everything from the introduction of a single, unassimilated word up to a complete sentence or more into the context of another language" (1973: 521).

Yet, most established lexical borrowings are pronounced *as words in the recipient language*; that is, they show complete or at least partial integration into the recipient language. Although speakers don't always succeed entirely, with most borrowings, they clearly are attempting to pronounce them as they would pronounce them in the recipient language. Thus, examples, such as *supervise*, are simply more evidence in support of the Morpheme Order principle in mixed constituents. Because examples such as *supervise* and *rub* retain the pronunciation of the Embedded Language, it is hard to argue that they are a type of borrowing. Instead, they are codeswitched forms that occur, perhaps only once, in a particular conversation.

9.5.4 Examples in the same syntactic slot, but longer switches

The problem with calling singly occurring forms from the Embedded Language any kind of borrowing becomes even clearer when we look at more examples of phrases (more than one word). They qualify as Embedded Language islands (defined below) because they retain their Embedded Language word order.

Still, what is important to note is that these new examples (with more than one word) pattern very much like singly occurring Embedded Language words *in their placement in the overall clause* framed by the Matrix Language, and they retain the pronunciation of the Embedded Language. For example, consider the noun phrase *school bus* in example (13). The example comes from the same set of conversations (among Chinese-English bilinguals in the United States) as example (10), and *school bus* occurs in the same place as a single noun (*paper*) can occur in Chinese-English codeswitching, as in (10) above.

> (13)   zhu zai zheli hen fangbian, meitian you **school bus**.
>   live LOCATIVE here   very convenient everyday have school bus
>   'It's very convenient to live here [since there is a] school bus every
>   day.'
>   (Chinese-English, Wei 2002: 699)

One more example illustrates Embedded Language word order in a two-word phrase. In example (14) two women, who came to the United States as immigrants from Palestine, consider moving to other houses in the city where they are now living. They produce an English noun phrase that is part of the larger noun phrase (*el new houses*) that includes the Arabic determiner (*el*) for 'the'.

> (14)   jibna majalli zan kul el **new houses** fi Columbia ...
>   we bring magazine about all the new houses in Columbia
>   'We brought [a] magazine about all the new houses in Columbia.'
>   (Palestinian Arabic-English, Myers-Scotton and Jake, 1996: 13)

9.6 Conclusions on singly occurring words in codeswitching

If we look at codeswitching data and compare established borrowed words with singly occurring Embedded Language words that are not established borrowings, we find there is little evidence for grouping them together. Here is what we find.

9.6.1 How established borrowings and single Embedded Language words are similar

There is one major resemblance between established borrowings and single Embedded Language words in codeswitching data sets. Both typically show morphological and syntactic integration into the Matrix Language (i.e. they both take Matrix Language inflections and function words and always follow Matrix Language word order). For example, the French borrowings into English, *omelette* and *sauté*, can occur with English affixes as in the sentence, *I sauté-ed mushrooms for two omelette-s yesterday*. In example (11), a codeswitched form, *gangs*, occurs with the plural marking from Zulu (*a-ma-gangs*). (Yes, it is accessed with an English plural marker, too. Double marking happens occasionally, but it does not happen with the type of morpheme covered by the System Morpheme Principle; those morphemes come only from the Matrix Language (cf. Myers-Scotton 2002: 91–3)).

9.6.2 Embedded Language words can be bare in codeswitching – rarely when they are established borrowings

But the resemblance between established borrowings and single Embedded Language words in codeswitching stops there. In codeswitching, there are many "bare forms" from the Embedded Language that do not receive Matrix Language inflections and function words, even though they follow Matrix Language word order.

What accounts for bare forms? In many data sets, they are very frequent. For example, Hlavac (2003: 202) notes that over half (236 out of 455) of English nouns or nouns plus modifiers that would require overt Croatian affixes do not have them in his study of Croatian-English codeswitching among second-generation Croatians living in Australia. Myers-Scotton and Jake (1995; 2001) have suggested that lack of congruence between languages regarding abstract grammatical features is behind the occurrence of bare forms from one language in the frame set by another language, but they do not go beyond this general suggestion. Obviously, more study is needed, but that is not a topic that we can pursue here.

In contrast, bare forms are very rare as established borrowings. Instead, most established borrowings receive the same system morphemes as native words in any language. The few exceptions seem to be learned words (in European languages, words borrowed from Greek or indirectly from Greek through Latin). Some of these do receive only their original number markings. For example, in standard dialects of English *phenomenon* is the singular form for which *phenomena* is the plural; that is, there is no *-s* plural such as *phenomenons*.

9.6.3 Only single forms in codeswitching retain their original pronunciation

As noted above, establish borrowings tend to be well integrated into the recipient language in regard to pronunciation (phonology). One can find such words in many codeswitching sets, too. That is, codeswitching and established borrowings can occur together, even in the same sentence. In her data set from Finnish immigrants in Australia, Kovács (2001) recorded about 100 English words that occurred at least three times in her corpus. On the basis of this frequency, she said that they may be considered borrowed forms. These English words that occur more than once all show some signs of being pronounced as they would be in Finnish, not as they would be in English. For example, English *nurse* becomes *noorss(i)*, *nodssa*, or *norssi* in a bilingual clause with Finnish as the Matrix Language.

These contrast with other single words in the same corpus that occur only once and that Kovács considers more akin to codeswitching such as *country* (p. 16) or *upstairs* (p. 116) in sentences or fragments that are otherwise all in Finnish, such as *kai upstairs* 'perhaps upstairs' (in response to where someone is).

9.6.4 Most Embedded Language words in codeswitching aren't predictable

Established borrowings occur with some level of predictability (although, admittedly, they may not reoccur in the conversation under study). Conversely, those Embedded Language singly occurring words that the MLF model sees as codeswitching elements have no "reoccurrence value" in codeswitching. They almost always occur only once in a single conversation and may not occur again – ever – in any further conversations.

9.6.5 Phrases are not often established borrowings

Lexical units, such as the phrases in examples (13) and (14), contrast with established borrowings in another way: Phrases are hardly ever borrowed. Instead of borrowing phrases, languages sometimes borrow the "sense" of a phrase and "translate" the phrase. These translations are called calques and were mentioned in chapter 8 (e.g. English *skyscraper* becomes *gratte-ciel* 'scratch-sky' in French).

9.6.6 Who are the speakers who use Embedded Language words in their speech?

Another reason not to call such words and phrases in codeswitching borrowings of any sort is that monolingual speakers (who therefore aren't codeswitchers because they don't know two languages) do not generally use singly occurring Embedded Language words that are pronounced in codeswitching as they would be in the Embedded Language. With this pronunciation, these words are generally found only in codeswitching (or in the Embedded Language on its own, of course).

Writing about English singly occurring words as they are used in Cantonese-English codeswitching in Hong Kong, Kang-Kwong Luke (1998: 147) comments that *"they are generally perceived, unlike full-fledged loan words, as English words* [italics added]: they are much less likely to be used by monolingual speakers of Chinese."

9.6.7 Conclusions about Embedded Language words

Let's be clear: we aren't arguing that *all* Embedded Language single words in codeswitching data sets are bona fide instances of codeswitching. Some singly occurring Embedded Language words could have become established borrowings. But, as we've shown above, there is good reason to treat *most* of these singly occurring words as codeswitched forms. Therefore, a model should provide an explanation that accounts for why these Embedded Language contact morphemes can occur in a Matrix Language frame, but Embedded Language system morphemes either cannot at all (outsiders) or generally only occur as doubling Matrix Language counterparts (what will be called early system morphemes under the 4-M model).

In effect, the MLF model and the Uniform Structure Principle do provide for these Embedded Language words. Specifically, the Morpheme Order Principle indicates how they must be placed (in accordance with Matrix Language morpheme order requirements). And the System Morpheme Principle indicates the type of Embedded Language elements that must *not* appear (those system morphemes that we now call outsider late system morphemes). And the Uniform Structure Principle gives preference to all Matrix Language system morphemes.

9.7 Characterizing larger Embedded Language phrases in Matrix Language frames

We have just offered arguments for considering Embedded Language singly occurring words in codeswitching as bona fide instances of codeswitching rather than some sort of borrowings. As we've noted, the ranks of researchers are split on whether they consider singly occurring forms as "real" codeswitching. In contrast, we can assume that everyone considers what are called Embedded Language islands as examples of codeswitching.

What is important to keep in mind is that these full phrases from the Embedded Language, which everyone accepts as codeswitched forms, pattern very much like singly occurring Embedded Language words. This is a motivation to accept the single words as codeswitched elements, as part of a continuum of Embedded Language material in bilingual constituents. We now discuss the full phrases as Embedded Language islands.

9.7.1 What are Embedded Language islands made of?

Embedded Language islands have three important features: (1) They are phrases within a bilingual clause, (2) their words show structural dependency relationships (discussed below) that make them well-formed in the Embedded Language, and (3) they are often collocations. As background, consider this: In a conversation including codeswitching, there can be three types of clause. There may be clauses with elements from both the Matrix and the Embedded Language – the type of clause that we have been discussing. Also, there may be whole clauses in either the Matrix Language or the Embedded Language. **Embedded Language islands** only occur in the first type of clause (bilingual clauses) and they are only phrases, not full clauses (and therefore, of course, not the same thing as monolingual Embedded Language clauses). Also, they occur in a bilingual clause that is framed by the Matrix Language.

What makes them different from the rest of the material in the bilingual clause is that within an Embedded Language island, all the content and system morphemes come from the Embedded Language and follow other well-formedness requirements of the Embedded Language (e.g. word order). This means that, within the island itself, the Morpheme Order and the System Morpheme Principles of the MLF model don't apply.

9.7.2 Hierarchical structure of Embedded Language islands

Also, Embedded Language islands must show Embedded Language **structural dependency relations** to qualify as islands. This means that words in an island show a hierarchical structure, with some words "higher" than others in the structure in which they occur. Just two Embedded Language words next to each other are not necessarily islands. Thus, in example (15) the Dutch phrase *een glas water of zo* 'a glass of water or something' is an Embedded Language island with *glas* 'glass' as its head, with the other elements modifying *glas*. Thus, the other elements "depend on" *glas*.

> (15) žib li-ya   **een glas water of zo**.
>   get-for me   a glass of water or so
>   'Get me a glass of water or something.'
>   (Moroccan Arabic-Dutch, Nortier, 1990: 131)

9.7.3 What types of word combinations are Embedded Language islands?

Finally, a third feature of any Embedded Language islands is that they generally are **collocations**. Collocations are phrases of words that usually occur together. Other Embedded Language islands are even more set than collocations; they are **formulaic** in their composition (the words they include hardly vary at all). Maybe the most formulaic phrases are idioms. An **idiom** is a phrase or clause whose meaning is not the meaning of the sum of its parts, but something else. Thus, in the sentence *Doing that will be a piece of cake*, the idiom is *piece of cake* and it means it will be "easy to do that", not that you will get a piece of cake doing whatever "it" is!

Example (16) shows a common formulaic phrase in English as an Embedded Island in a Finnish frame.

> (16)   Han luki sen   **from cover to cover**
>   He read it-ACCUSATIVE
>   'He read it from cover to cover.'
>   (Australian Finnish-English, Kovács 2001: 160)

Example (17) is a longer example than others we have cited. We cite a long example to show you how smoothly a speaker can switch languages, even when three languages and several different types of switches are involved. Here, this example is cited especially because of the Embedded Language islands it contains. Note that they can be considered collocations. The speaker is a first-language speaker of Luyia; she comes from western Kenya, but is working now in Nairobi, the capital. She is speaking about urban problems to a fellow L1 speaker of Luyia; they both also speak Swahili and English. To save space, we don't give a morpheme by morpheme gloss, but gloss by words. Luyia words are underlined and English is in bold.

> (17)   <u>Okhujia khu milimo</u>   <u>ndumisilanga</u>   **a company vehicle**.
>   To go   to work   I use   a company vehicle
>   Na yale matatizo   inayoikabili   ni   kile kitu
>   And those problems   which I encounter   are   that thing
>   tunaita **traffic jams**.
>   we call traffic jams.
>   **There are very many vehicles in Nairobi town as a whole**.
>
>   Na wengi wa **drivers** wakati mwingine   hugonganisha magari
>   and many of drivers time   some   they hit   cars
>   **causing traffic jams** ...   **And in general**   iko ile tabu
>   causing traffic jams ...   and in general there is that problem

iye tsiuymba   ha Nairobi hano.
of houses   in Nairobi here
'To go to work, I use a company vehicle. And those problems which
I encounter are that thing we call traffic jams. And many of [the]
drivers sometimes they hit cars causing traffic jams. . . . And in general there is that problem of houses in Nairobi here.'

(Swahili-Luyia-English, Myers-Scotton,
unpublished Nairobi data 1988)

In the first clause (a sentence), Luyia is the Matrix Language, followed by
the English island, *a company vehicle*. We can tell that Luyia is the Matrix
Language because the verb inflections are all from Luyia (in accordance
with the System Morpheme Principle). The next sentence is entirely in English,
so the issue of which language is the Matrix Language doesn't come up. In
the third sentence, there are several clauses, but Swahili is the Matrix
Language, with an English island, *traffic jams*. Here, Swahili word order
prevails (*wakati mwingine* 'time some') over English order and all the verbal
inflections come from Swahili. There is a singly occurring English noun
(*drivers*) and also an English island (*causing traffic jams*). The last clause (also
a sentence) begins with an English conjunction (*and*) and an island (*in general*). The rest of the clause is all in Luyia; the inflections indicate Luyia is the
Matrix Language.

9.7.4 Collocations: words that seem to go together

As should be obvious from the examples, many of the Embedded Language
islands can be considered **collocations**, combinations of words that often appear together as a single phrase. Note that many function just like Embedded
Language singly occurring content words.

Backus (2003) argues that most Embedded Language phrases, especially
collocations and idioms, should be considered as single **lexical units**. For Backus,
many elements of more than one morpheme are lexical units (or "chunks").
These units are accessed in language production as single units rather than
being "put together" on the spot every time they occur. He includes under
lexical units such Embedded Language examples as a noun plus its plural
marking (a relatively frequent Embedded Language form), or a noun and its
modifier, or even a verb and its object.

Backus frames his argument within the assumptions of those linguistic theories that fall under the general rubric of **cognitive linguistics**. He states that
"[T]he most important one of these assumptions is that lexical units can be of
any length and complexity" (2003: 84). Referring specifically to codeswitching,
he argues that phrases that cannot be considered as single units are rare. To
support his argument, he gives rather convincing quantitative evidence from

a corpus of Turkish-Dutch codeswitching recorded in the Netherlands. He states that "with very few exceptions, EL [Embedded Language] plurals, compound nouns, and verb-object collocations were fixed units in the Dutch lexicon" (2003: 122). That is, they already are single units in Dutch – they are collocations. However, note that he doesn't say that *all* Embedded Language material should be so considered. He warns that "[S]peakers can insert two separate EL morphemes; if they appear next to each other, that doesn't make them a lexical unit" (p. 122). Backus's idea is attractive; many Embedded Language multi-lexical units that occur in codeswitching do seem to be collocations. Look again at the examples of Embedded Language islands given above.

9.7.5 How do Embedded Language islands figure in overall clause structure?

We've given you three well-attested features of Embedded Language islands, but here is one more that often applies: Although the type and internal structures of Embedded Islands have not been studied extensively, Myers-Scotton (1993b) and Treffers-Daller (1994) both point out that (1) they are frequently adjuncts, meaning they are "add-ons" to the main structural/semantic elements of the clause and (2) many islands are time or place adverbial phrases. Example (17) above illustrates a locative Embedded Language island, and (18) illustrates two typical Embedded Language islands from English, the Embedded Language in a conversation for which Swahili is the Matrix Language. They are typical because (1) they are adjuncts (not part of the main elements in the clause) and (2) they are time adverbial phrases.

> (18) Huja-sikia, kutoka **next week** wafanya kazi wa serikali hawa-ta-ku-wa wa-ki-enda kazini **on Saturdays**.
> 'Haven't you heard yet, from next week government workers will not be going to work on Saturdays.'
> (Swahili-English, Myers-Scotton, 1993b: 137)

9.7.6 Placement within the overall bilingual clause

Consider Embedded Language islands from the point of view of the Matrix Language. Although Embedded Language islands must follow the principles of well-formedness of the Embedded Language regarding their internal organization (i.e. order within the phrase), they follow the *placement rules of the Matrix Language* within the clause. In this regard, they are just like singly occurring Embedded Language forms. Above, we indicated that this is an important reason to argue that singly occurring forms and phrases from the Embedded Language are part of the same codeswitching continuum.

Example (20) illustrates this because the instrumental phrase precedes the verb, as it would in Turkish, but not in Dutch. Recorded in the Netherlands, this example comes from a Turkish immigrant, who is a Turkish-Dutch bilingual, discussing how he washes a particular item. The Dutch equivalent of 'warm water' is inflected with -*nan*, the Turkish marker for "instrumental" case. Note also that Turkish is a verb-final language and this example conforms to Turkish well-formedness conditions in line with the fact that Turkish is the Matrix Language.

(20)   . . . ondan sonra **lauw water**'nan   yı kayınca
           then   after lukewarm water-INSTRUMENTAL   I wash it
       '. . . then I wash it with lukewarm water.'

                                   (Turkish-Dutch, Backus, 1992: 112–13)

9.7.7 Internal Embedded Language islands

Some Embedded Language islands are more firmly integrated into the Matrix Language than others. The type of Embedded Language island that we will call **Internal Embedded Language Islands** include a Matrix Language element to frame the Embedded Language phrase. That is, they are part of a larger phrase. Example (20) illustrates such an internal island because the Dutch phrase *lauw water* is framed by the Turkish case marker for instrumental, resulting in the meaning "with lukewarm water". The larger phrase is a postpositional phrase, with the head of the phrase coming in final position (the instrumental suffix -*nan*). There are many internal Embedded Language islands across data sets (cf. Myers-Scotton, 2002: 149–52). Example (21) comes from a French-English bilingual living in eastern Canada. In this case the Embedded Language island *real thing* is headed by a determiner from French.

(21)   J'étais   certain que c'était   pas   la **real thing**
       I be/PAST/1s certain that it be/PAST/3s NEGATIVE DET/FEM real thing
       'I was certain that it was not the real thing.'

                                     (French-English, King, 2000: 100)

9.7.8 Why do Embedded Language islands even occur?

Why do speakers shift from just using singly occurring words from the Embedded Language to using the full phrases that are Embedded Language islands?

9.7.8.1 Pragmatic considerations

First, it seems likely that *both* most single words from the Embedded Language and full phrases (i.e. islands) express "better" the speaker's intentions than the Matrix Language equivalent. That is, the typical switch of languages is *not* because speakers can't finish a phrase in the language in which they began. There may well be words or phrases with the same "referring meaning" in the Matrix Language, but speakers may switch because there is no Matrix Language equivalent that has the same **pragmatic force** (i.e. carries the preferred connotation) as the Embedded Language counterpart. For example, in a conversation in Uganda between two Acholi-English bilinguals (with Acholi as the Matrix Language), one woman uses the phrase *family planning* as an Embedded Language island. It's unlikely there is an exact equivalent to this phrase in Acholi because even though the speakers certainly could have produced a paraphrase in Acholi, it would not have had the same associated meanings (of government-sanctioned birth control).

Also, as we mention in chapter 6, we must consider the social or psychological associations that come with using words and phrases from the Embedded Language. It's no surprise that these will be different than those associated with the Matrix Language. For example, two English Embedded Language islands that occur in a Swahili-English data set are *old habits die hard* and *once in a blue moon*. They may convey the speaker's intentions better than a Swahili proverb or idiom with the same referential meaning, but, perhaps just as important, they also serve to index the speaker's facility in English, possibly a source of social status in this particular conversation.

But why full phrases rather than single words from the Embedded Language? We can imagine that there is more "**psycholinguistic stress**" in shifting to the Embedded Language for a full phrase. But it may be that a phrase just allows for more of a pragmatic impact than a single word. Both from the psycholinguistic and the sociolinguistic perspectives, this issue deserves more study.

9.7.8.2 Congruence and Embedded Language islands

We also need to recognize that **congruence problems** between the grammars of the two languages in codeswitching may be behind a speaker's saying something in an Embedded Language island. Differences in the grammars of the two languages, often at an abstract level, may block accessing an Embedded Language element in any other way than as a full phrase. That is, the speaker may have intentions that involve saying something in the Embedded Language (e.g. perhaps he or she wants to use a particular Embedded Language verb) and this activates "a chain of requirements" at an abstract level, resulting in an Embedded Language island. This idea deserves much more consideration; Myers-Scotton and Jake (2001) explain the many Embedded Language islands in a Palestinian Arabic-English corpus on the basis of congruence problems between how verbs are accessed in the two languages. Also see Myers-Scotton (2002: 146–7).

9.8 The 4-M model

Research on codeswitching under the MLF model made it clear that all morphemes were not equal in patterns of distribution in bilingual clauses. These findings led Myers-Scotton and Jake (2000; 2001) to develop a new model to explain this distribution in codeswitching. The model is called the **4-M model**.

The 4-M model doesn't change anything in the MLF model, but in refining the divisions between content and system morphemes, it offers a more precise explanation of some of the codeswitching data that the MLF model covers. Once more, it also offers explanations for findings in related phenomena, too – everything from second-language acquisition (Wei, 2000) to creole development (Myers-Scotton, 2001). The model divides system morphemes into three types.

Space doesn't allow a full discussion of the 4-M model's division or of its ramifications in explanations of what happens in language contact. All we can do is present the bare essentials of the model and some examples of how the model can be used (see Myers-Scotton and Jake, 2000 and Myers-Scotton, 2002 for more details).

The 4-M model begins by distinguishing four morpheme types in terms of the differences in their role in syntactic structures in general as well as empirical evidence about their distribution in codeswitching. Note that this model uses the term "morpheme" for both the abstract element in language production that underlies surface forms and the actual surface level forms.

9.8.1 The major premise of the 4-M model

Ultimately, the 4-M model is especially concerned with viewing morphemes in terms of how they are activated in a model of language production. Earlier, surface distributions in codeswitching had told various researchers that content morphemes pattern very differently from certain system morphemes in codeswitching. This difference is already reflected in the System Morpheme Principle of the MLF model; recall that it states that a certain type of system morpheme must come from the Matrix Language and never from the Embedded Language.

In devising the 4-M model, Myers-Scotton and Jake recognized this difference with more parsimony by splitting up system morphemes into three types. They went on to derive a new hypothesis about differences among morphemes at an abstract level, but based on the evidence about their differences at the surface level in codeswitching. This is the **Differential Access Hypothesis**.

The hypothesis explains these observable differences by postulating that the "where" (what level is involved) and the "how" (how are they activated) for late system morphemes differs from that of the other morpheme types. The hypothesis is this:

Relevant information in lemmas supporting surface-level morphemes does not all become salient at the same level of language production. Information supporting content morphemes and early system morphemes is salient in the mental lexicon, but information about late system morphemes does not become salient until the level of the formulator when larger constituents are assembled (cf. Myers-Scotton, 2002: 76–8 for more details).

The meanings of mental lexicon and formulator become clear below.

9.8.2 Conceptually activated morphemes: content morphemes and early system morphemes

Under this hypothesis, content morphemes remain as they were under the MLF model. The only difference is that they, along with the type of system morpheme called an **early system morpheme**, are specifically characterized as **conceptually activated**. What this means here is that a speaker's pre-linguistic intentions (before any specific language is indicated) activate them. This activation happens at the first level of the 4-M model's sketch of how language production works. This level is called the **mental lexicon** and the overall model is derived from that in Levelt (1989).

The mental lexicon consists of elements called lemmas that are tagged for specific languages; the speaker's intentions call up language-specific lemmas. **Lemma** is the name for the abstract elements that **underlie actual surface-level morphemes** (and therefore words). They contain the information necessary to produce surface-level forms. (The mental lexicon also contains language-specific generalized lexical knowledge (in addition to the knowledge in individual lemmas); this general knowledge is discussed in Myers-Scotton, 2002: 129–31.)

Lemmas in the mental lexicon that underlie content morphemes (e.g. nouns and verbs) are **directly activated** via the speaker's intention. In turn, these lemmas activate the lemmas underlying early system morphemes. These **early system morphemes flesh out the meaning** of the lemmas of the content morphemes that call them. They are called "early" because of the hypothesis (above) about their early activation in the language production process.

Examples of early system morphemes include plural markings, determiners (e.g. the definite article *the* and the indefinite articles *a, an* in English), and those prepositions (also called satellites) that change the meanings of phrasal verbs in certain contexts (e.g. *out* as in *Alice* <u>*looks out for*</u> *her little brother* or *through* in *the actor* <u>*ran through*</u> *his lines before the performance*).

9.8.3 Late system morphemes

The other two types of system morphemes are called "**late**" because the model claims they are not activated until a later production level, at a second abstract level that is called **the formulator**. These two types are bridge late system morphemes and outsider late system morphemes. The formulator is viewed as an abstract mechanism that receives directions from lemmas in the mental lexicon (those underlying content morphemes). Remember that content morphemes are the ones that assign and receive thematic roles, so they are the ones indicating the semantic outlines of the clause that is being constructed; they also contain information about syntactic structures.

Thus, directions from the lemmas underlying content morphemes tell the formulator how to assemble larger constituents. The formulator's most important function is to assemble combinations of noun phrases and verb phrases, resulting in a full clause. The late system morphemes are activated to indicate relationships within the clause; **they are the cement** that holds the clause together.

As the name implies, **bridge system morphemes** provide bridges; they **occur between phrases** that make up a larger constituent. The best example of a bridge is the associative or possessive element that occurs between a possessor noun and the element that is possessed in many languages. Thus, in English *of* is a bridge, as in *book of John*. The possessive *'s* in English is also a bridge morpheme (*John's book*). A bridge morpheme depends on the well-formedness conditions of a specific constituent in order for it to appear. That is, the constituent isn't well-formed without the bridge morpheme. For the particular construction in which they occur, nothing but the bridge morpheme will make the construction well-formed. So *of* must appear in a possessive construction if the possessed noun occurs first (*book* is the possessed element in *book of John*). And if the possessive construction begins with the possessor, then *'s* is the bridge morpheme (as in *John's book*).

The other type of late system morpheme is the **outsider system morpheme**. These late system morphemes also meet well-formedness conditions. But outsiders differ from bridges in that the presence and form of an outsider depends on information that is outside the element with which it occurs and therefore outside its immediate phrase, and usually outside its immediate constituent. That information comes from an element in another constituent or from the discourse as a whole.

The clearest example of an outsider morpheme in English is the element that shows subject-verb agreement on the verb in many languages. The form of the agreement marker depends on the subject. Can you see how this outsider looks outside of its placement for information about its form? Thus, in English, we say *the dog like-s chewing bones*, but *dogs like-Ø chewing bones*. The suffix -s only occurs when there is a third person singular content element in the present tense to call that suffix; otherwise, in English, there is no suffix (Ø here is a "zero" marker). Subject-verb in French is signaled by clitics (such as *je* for first person, as in *je suis de Paris* 'I am from Paris'). In French, these clitics contrast with what are sometimes called the "strong pronouns", including *moi* 'I/me'; these pronouns are content morphemes and occur in other syntactic contexts than the clitics.

Outsiders differ from bridges in that, with bridges, it is the particular syntactic construction that tells you that a bridge morpheme must be used, and which one. But with outsiders, it is information outside the construction in which it appears that matters, not the syntax of the construction itself. That is, different outsider morphemes may appear in a particular construction, and which one appears depends on the outside information that calls it.

To illustrate this last point, let's take another example, one that is a bit more complicated. In some languages, the relationship of a noun or a larger noun phrase to the rest of the clause is indicated by outsider system morphemes that are called **case markers**. These are often suffixes. But other languages have markers that function in a similar way and they may be prefixes, as they are in Bantu languages. These markers occur on nouns or other parts of the noun phrase (or sometimes as clitic-type elements in verb phrases).

What makes these elements outsiders is that their form depends on information outside the phrase in which they occur. For example, in German, information from verbs or prepositions indicates the case marking that should appear on parts in a noun phrase, notably determiners and adjectives. This makes the case markers outsiders – because they look outside the constituent in which they appear for information about their form. Thus, in German, when nouns or pronouns that are objects of the verb *lehren* 'to teach' appear, part of the abstract information underlying this particular verb is that its objects must be marked with accusative case (as in *sie lehrte mich Computerwissenschaft* 'she taught me computer science' with *mich* as the accusative form of 'me'). But the verb *stand. . . . bei* 'stand by' marks its objects with the dative case (as in *sie stand mir bei* 'she stood by me' with *mir* as the dative of 'me'. So we can see that in German both *mich* and *mir* mean 'me', but which one appears depends on the type of verb that requires them.

9.8.4 Why all this attention for late system morphemes?

We give all this attention to the 4-M model and the divisions it makes among morphemes because what can happen to different types of morpheme in language contact situations differs. In brief, content and early morphemes are much more open to various kinds of change than are late system morphemes.

Because of space limitations, we can only indicate evidence supporting this claim in three types of contact data, codeswitching, convergence/attrition, and creole development. But we hope readers of this volume will keep in mind the 4-M model if they ever consider other language contact phenomena. (You never know what you'll study . . .)

We have already discussed codeswitching, so we just remind you to look back at the System Morpheme Principle as it applies to classic codeswitching. In line with that principle, the **type of morpheme that we now call outsiders** must come only from the Matrix Language in mixed constituents. Look back at examples (3) and (4) and (6) and (7) to see how this works. You don't find any morphemes that can be called outsiders coming from the Embedded Language. And this principle is overwhelmingly supported across many data sets. In the following sections we illustrate how the 4-M model helps us understand convergence/attrition and creole development.

The 4-M model also helps explain why plural markers (early system morphemes) sometimes come along with their Embedded Language nouns when the nouns appear in bilingual constituents (cf. Myers-Scotton, 2002: 91–3).

9.9 Convergence and attrition

To put it simply, convergence and attrition occur when one language becomes more like another. **Convergence** is speech by bilinguals that has all the surface-level forms from one language, but with **part of the abstract lexical structure** that underlies the surface-level patterns **coming from another language** (or languages). **Attrition** involves the same outcome, but is generally thought of as language change within the speech of one individual. Both tend to happen to the Ll of bilinguals when they live in a community where the "invading" or other language is socially and politically dominant. One can refer to convergence or attrition in regard to either an Ll or an L2, but just for the purposes of this discussion, we deal with changes to an L1 only.

Codeswitching often precedes (or combines with) convergence or attrition, but either can occur without extensive codeswitching, too. Earlier in this chapter we used the term composite codeswitching. Clauses that show this type of switching include what's involved in convergence and attrition. That is, in composite codeswitching you find surface-level morphemes from both languages (as in classic codeswitching), but also abstract structure in the frame itself from both languages. If we want to describe the outcome by using the construct of the Matrix Language, we would say that the morphosyntactic frame of the clause has become a composite of two languages – even though one language remains the main source of the frame.

9.9.1 Some comparisons

Even though from a structural standpoint, convergence and attrition are very similar as outcomes, there are differences in how they are perceived and also there are some differences in the degree of change. Convergence is often thought of as something that **affects a community** and involves gradual change, even over several generations.

Further, the changes that affect the L1 due to convergence aren't necessarily huge. Even when the changes are many, convergence doesn't necessarily mean that the speakers involved will shift over to the "invading" language as their main language. In some circumstances, speakers simply incorporate into their

L1 features from the other language, but continue speaking their Ll as their main language even though they also use the other language. For example, French affected some structures in English after the Norman Conquest in 1066 and during French rule in England during the next century, but English was maintained as the Ll in England.

In contrast, attrition is more often seen as happening within the lifetime of one person and it is typically studied as it affects individuals. But the very term "attrition" implies the **first steps toward loss** of a language and replacement by another. Most typically, attrition of an Ll is studied, but of course there are many cases of speakers who no longer can speak a second language they have acquired as children or learned as adults. Also, there seems to be a surer link between attrition and shift to another language as the speaker's main language than there is with convergence. A language can converge to another one, but still be a separate language (e.g. for many Latinos in the US, their Spanish has taken on some English features through convergence).

Some researchers refer to the changes that are discussed under convergence or attrition as a "loss" of a distinction that is no longer made in the Ll. But **loss** does not consider the interplay between languages in the speech of bilinguals. We prefer to see these changes as **substitutions** because looking at them this way brings in the role of the "other" language in a way that loss does not.

9.9.2 Examples of convergence showing conceptual activation

When the structure of one language converges to structures of another language, the change affects content morphemes more than others and especially nouns or verbs. Here is an example showing how the distinction between the meanings of two verbs is neutralized (so that one verb form serves for both meanings) under the influence of a bilingual's more dominant language. In Hungarian, two verbs cover two different types of 'knowing'. If you know something, the verb is *tud*. If you are familiar with someone (or another animate), the verb is *ismer*. Bolonyai (1999) reports an example from a Hungarian-English bilingual child who is not making the distinction of 'knowing' found in Hungarian. Instead, she is following the English pattern of using only one verb for both senses of 'to know'. In Standard Hungarian, 'I know' (someone) would be *ismer-em*. This particular type of convergence (substituting one word for two in another language) happens frequently when the dominant language in the bilingual's community is the one that employs only one word for a meaning that is divided up between two words in another language. This child is growing up in the US.

(21) én   tud-om   ezt   a cicá-t
      1s   know-1s/PRES/OBJ   this   the kitty
      'I know this kitty.'
                        (Bolonyai, 1999: 100; cited in Myers-Scotton, 2002: 1999)

Clyne gives many examples from German immigrants to Australia whose speech shows convergence that involve content morphemes (although he uses the general term **transference**). Many of these immigrants retain German, but have become bilingual in English, which, of course, is the main language spoken in Australia.

Some of Clyne's examples also show how one word is replacing a distinction between two content words in the German of these immigrants. Many languages, including German, Dutch, Italian, and French have two different auxiliary verbs (one translated as 'have' and one translated as 'be' that is used with verbs marking movement or change of place or state). Clyne points out that some Australian speakers in the later generations (children of immigrants) are using one auxiliary form for all uses. That is, they have done away with the distinction between 'have' and 'be' as an auxiliary.

Clyne (2003: 78) also points out that sometimes immigrants converge to the new community's language in regard to "the way to say something". In example (22) the speaker is making a word-by-word translation into German of the English offer to 'have a cool drink'. (Such word-by-word translations are called calques and were introduced in chapter 8.) Because this example shows **both convergence and codeswitching** (the speaker uses the English word *drink*), this is an example of composite codeswitching.

> (22)   einen   kühlen **drink**   hab-en
>   a   cool   drink   have-INFINITIVE
>   'Have a cool drink.'
>   Homeland German: Etwas kühles trinken 'Something cool to drink'

Examples paralleling the types of change illustrated in (21) and (22) can be found in the speech of bilinguals in many communities. In line with the 4-M model that we have just discussed, it's of interest that many of the examples of convergence (and attrition) involve changes that can be considered conceptually activated. That is, they involve content morphemes, but not system morphemes and especially not outsider system morphemes.

9.9.3 Convergence in word order

Clyne also gives us examples of another very frequent form of convergence: Bilinguals substitute the word order of the language that is dominant in the community for word order in their L1. Example (23) comes from a German who migrated to Australia before World War II, but still speaks German along with English (Clyne, 2002: 117). Notice that all the words come from German, but this speaker places *jeden Tag* 'every day' in a place in the clause where it would be more likely to occur in English than in German. Clyne says that in homeland German this time phrase would come after the verb for 'start', not at the end of the sentence.

(23)   Mein Mann fangt   um drei Uhr an zum Arbeiten jeden Tag
       my husband starts/3s   at three o'clock to work every day
       'My husband starts work at three o'clock every day.'

9.9.4 Convergence and content system morphemes

We have cited only three examples of convergence in the speech of bilinguals. Note that these, and many other changes that can be considered convergence to another language, involve the type of morpheme that can be called either content morphemes or early system morphemes under the 4-M model.

At many places in the world, the evidence we can look at today indicates that convergence affected a number of languages (but not necessarily at the same time) so that today these languages have a number of structures in common. These areas are sometimes called "convergence areas" or *Sprachbunde* 'language leagues'. A well-known area is in the Balkan region in Eastern Europe (cf. Hock and Joseph 1996). It includes four sub-groups of the Indo-European family: at least four Slavic languages, Romanian in the Romance group, and also Albanian and Modern Greek.

The type of features that show convergence in such areas also are largely those involving content morphemes or early system morphemes, in other words, those involving the lexical-conceptual level of words and phrases. For example, the Balkan languages share a number of features, including placing the definite article before the noun, a marker for future tense based on each language's verb for 'want, wish', and a replacement of infinitive constructions with dependent or coordinate clauses. Many times, convergence areas show that the same derivational affixes (early system morphemes) are present in a number of different languages in the areas. Also, see Myers-Scotton (2002: 207–12) on early system morphemes and convergence and a suggestion that word order can be considered an early system morpheme at the abstract level.

Here is one more example of convergence that shows *the adding* of a content morpheme (one for a subject pronoun, *yo* 'I'). Spanish is what is called a pro-drop language, meaning that it does not have self-standing pronouns for subjects unless the subject is to be emphasized. The use of the subject pronoun here can be considered convergence to English.

Furthermore, here the subject pronoun is used to express the Experiencer (as in *I like . . .* in English). In contrast, in home varieties of Spanish, an Experiencer is not expressed as a subject, as it is in English, but only as a Beneficiary (as in *to me*). In this sentence, *me* does occur as the Beneficiary, so the presence of *yo* is very much out of place. Further, *yo* is not the subject of the verb, either. The verb (*gusta* 'please') agrees with *casa* 'house'.

This sentence comes from a nine-year-old boy from Peru, whose family are now migrant workers in Georgia in the US southeast. He is going to an English-medium school and his Spanish is heavily influenced by English because of his school contacts. This example (24) comes from a study of the Spanish of these migrant workers (Smith, 2003).

(24) Yo   me   gusta   esa   casa   mami
      1s/SUBJ   1s/DATIVE   please/3s/PRES   that/FEM   house/F   mommy
      I   to me   please   that   house   mommy
      'I like that house, mommy.'

9.9.5 Examples of convergence/attrition involving late system morphemes

The discussion of convergence so far has dealt with morphemes that are conceptually activated to express speakers' intentions. These morphemes are very full of content and are considered to be activated at the level of the mental lexicon. In contrast, **late system morphemes** seem to be **more resistant to change**. Recall that the Differential Access Hypothesis (section 9.8.1) suggests that these are only activated at the level of the formulator (after directions are sent from the content morphemes that are salient at the level of the mental lexicon). Differences in the level at which they become salient and the fact that they signal grammatical relations within a phrase or in the larger clause may be behind this difference.

9.9.5.1 Retention and substitution in Croatian

An example from Australia shows how **outsider late system morphemes** that are case markers in Croatian are **largely retained or show a substitution** in a convergence/attrition setting. The speakers studied are second generation speakers of Croatian (but whose dominant language is now English). Are they losing their L1 of Croatian? It is hard to say. Instead, one can argue that under the influence of English, their Croatian is changing. But the change is more a matter of substitution than loss.

Let's consider some statistics from Hlavac's study of 100 young adult Croatian-English bilinguals. Many of the expectations some writers have voiced about attrition as (1) very advanced by the second generation and (2) characterized by simplified or "lost" grammar simply don't match the results in this study.

First, overall, 91% of all Croatian noun phrases (8,444 out of 9,318) do receive the case assignment they would get in homeland Croatian. True, both masculine singular nominative case and masculine singular accusative inanimate nouns have no overt case marking (it is zero), so it is hard to argue with any certainty that their marking is not "lost" (since it was never overt in the first place) or influenced by English, which also has no overt case marking for these cases. Still, if these forms are not considered, then **75% of the nouns still show the same case markings** as they would in homeland Croatian. Second, what is even more interesting is that 92% of those forms that aren't as they would be in homeland Croatian include **substitutions of other Croatian case markers**. For example, Hlavac (2003: 314) points out that the accusative case marking replaces marking for other cases in 33% of the non-target-like forms (287 out of 874). That is, the picture shows substitution more than loss.

Example (25) from Hlavac (2003: 314) shows how minor case suffixes are beginning to be replaced by the more central case affixes. In this example, homeland Croatian would call for a locative case marker on both the preposition heading a prepositional phrase and the noun in that phrase (the phrase translates as 'in life'). Here, we see that the speaker marks the preposition (*u* 'in') as a locative, but substitutes an accusative marker on the noun (život 'life') for a locative marker. (Note that this is not so obvious because in Croatian, many of the inflections marking gender, number, and case are all represented by only one phonological form.)

> (25) ...što ću ja radit   u   **život**...
>   what will 1s do/INF in/LOCATIVE life/MASCULINE/S/ACCUSATIVE
>   '...what will I do in life...'

9.9.5.2 Case substitution in Russian

Examples from children who are now living in another community where their Ll is not widely spoken show similar results. Schmitt (2000) studied five Russian boys at two different ages (around nine and around eleven) who moved to the United States around the age of five, with their Russian fully developed. These boys retain their Russian because they use it with their grandparents and to an extent with their parents (also immigrants). Clearly, English is fast becoming their dominant language; it is the language they use with each other and the language that allows them to "fit in" outside the home at school and at play. Still, even after seven years in an English-speaking milieu, when they speak Russian, they retain most of the case markers that Russian calls for.

What attrition their speech shows largely can be termed **substitutions, not losses**. Example (26) shows a consistent pattern in Schmitt's data set. The boys **replace instrumental case with nominative case** (-a) in those contexts in which Standard Russian calls for an instrumental case marker (-ej) with past or future tenses.

> (26) Ona   budj-et uchitel'nits-<u>a</u>
>   3/S/NOM   be-3/FUTURE   teacher-NOMINATIVE/FEMININE/S
>   'She will be a teacher.'
>   (Schmitt, 2000: 208, cited in Myers-Scotton, 2002: 224)

9.9.5.3 An English pattern replacing a Hungarian pattern?

In her data set from Hungarian children who are being raised in the United States, Bolonyai (2003) pays special attention to what happens to Hungarian's accusative case marker. The children largely produce this marker when it is appropriate, but it also is often omitted. In this way, it contrasts with other cases markers (for types of spatial arrangements) that may show substitution, but not omission.

Bolonyai offers evidence showing that the accusative marker is **most likely to be absent in contexts when the clause structure is similar to that of English**. (In Hungarian, nouns functioning as objects are marked for accusative case.) For example, the most instances of accusative marker absence occur when word order matches English subject-verb-object order (Hungarian can also have SOV or OSV order). If the accusative marker is missing, one can argue that the children are substituting the English "rule" for marking a noun which is an object (accusative case). Of course in English there is no surface marking at all for object nouns (accusative case). Overall, Bolonyai argues that both substitution and omission by these Hungarian children show that their Hungarian is converging to English-like patterns.

9.9.6 General discussions on convergence/attrition

In summary, we can see that the asymmetries we have mentioned before in regard to codeswitching also apply in convergence and attrition. The elements with more content (content morphemes themselves and their "helpers", early system morphemes) pattern differently than the late system morphemes that do the work of signaling relationships between syntactic units (phrases within the clause); that is, content morphemes are more affected by convergence. Also, even though one language variety is a likely source of changes in another variety, an asymmetry remains here – because the affected variety still is largely the source of the structure behind any clause. Remember, too, that in both convergence and attrition, all the surface elements still come from one variety only.

True, there are such varieties as "mixed" languages that show important surface elements coming from both languages, but they are very few and far between. Even in these varieties, there is not an equal split between the two languages in supplying structure (cf. Matras and Bakker, 2003, as well as Myers-Scotton, 2002; 2003).

There are a number of recent discussions of the processes we are talking about, either in book form or in academic journals. We cite some examples in book form. For example, Clyne (2002) offers an entire volume on what we are calling convergence (he calls it transference) among immigrants to Australia. Winford (2003a) includes an extensive discussion under a section titled "structural diffusion" and some of the examples of what Muysken (2000) calls "congruent lexicalization" can be considered convergence, too. Also Myers-Scotton (2002) has a chapter that considers convergence and attrition together. Also, Thomason (2001) and earlier Thomason and Kaufman (1988) are devoted to discussing what they often call "contact-induced language change".

Also, there are many studies of what the authors call attrition. This was a frequent topic in journals and edited volumes in the last decades of the twentieth century (e.g. Seliger and Vago, 1991). More recently, a number of journal articles and volumes resulting from dissertations or conferences have appeared. We mention only a few of the more recent ones: Bolonyai (2002); Köpke (1999); Schmid (2002); Schmid, Köpke, Keijzer, and Weilemar (2004). Also, especially the *International Journal of Bilingualism* has devoted a good deal of space to articles on attrition in recent years.

9.10 Creation of pidgins and creoles

The few pages that can be devoted to pidgins and creoles can give you only a glimpse of what these languages are like and how they come about. First, though, let's make it clear that the terms "pidginized" and "creolized" are bandied about too much, and not just by non-specialists. Many use these terms as another way to say "simplified". They are wrong both to appropriate these terms to describe some other processes affecting languages, and also to assume that pidgins and creoles are simplified versions of some other language – or, for that matter, to assume that they are simple. Both **pidgins** and **creoles** are "real" languages in the sense that they have well-formedness conditions of their own that their speakers follow. Admittedly, not all of their structural constraints are as elaborate as those for other languages, and those for some pidgins are somewhat flexible. Here, we pay the most attention to creoles because their structures are more complex and we show how constraints on these structures can be related to the 4-M model and to principles we've already introduced in this chapter.

9.11 Pidgins

First, a few comments about pidgins. For a long time, creolists accepted the notion that creoles were versions of pidgins that had developed elaborated grammars over time and that had become the first language of a generation. However, at best, today most creolists see a continuum between *some* creoles and an ancestor-pidgin. Some other creolists argue that a creole does not necessarily have a pidgin in its ancestry (i.e. creoles can develop in other ways); they point out that pidgins do not necessarily develop in the same social circumstances as creoles.

The key notion to understand about pidgins is that they were (and are) developed for short-lived and very specific interaction types. Pidgins are created by adults for these restricted contacts, with speakers on both sides involved in the creation and with simple levels of communication as the goal and not much more.

Most researchers now accept the claim that the word *pidgin* comes from the English word *business*. Records indicate that a pidgin developed on the southern China coast in the early eighteenth century between traders and local businessmen. But pidgins go under various names, including "jargon" or "lingua franca". These terms have other uses, too, so don't assume every jargon or lingua franca is a pidgin. Further, some varieties that seem more like creoles (e.g. Nigerian Pidgin English) have names that label them as pidgins. Especially in regard to pidgins and creoles, you can't tell a book by its cover; you have to examine the structures to determine how any given variety is best classified.

9.11.1 Why pidgins develop

Most pidgins developed as a medium of communication between people speaking different languages, but wanting to do business with each other. Other pidgins developed in master–servant relationships, often involving colonial civil personnel and their indigenous subordinates or house servants. For this reason, most pidgins include only the type of vocabulary and morphosyntactic structures needed to do the business at hand. You can imagine that they would have a lot of simple, declarative sentences as well as commands. It should be no surprise that many pidgins share the same ways to form sentences and that these are a limited set. Still, as Winford (2003a: 269) points out, pidgins are "conventionalized means of communication", meaning that their speakers know what is a well-formed structure in their pidgin and what is not. This separates pidgins from the beginning efforts of second-language learners (now often called interlanguage, a topic in chapter 11).

Pidgin lexicons show a version of the asymmetry we saw in codeswitching (and that characterizes other contact phenomena): There is a split in the type of words they contain; their vocabularies consist mainly of the prototypical content morphemes (nouns and verbs) and include few or no system morphemes (functional elements). What this means is that relationships between and among content words are largely signaled by word order only.

Jahr (1996: 116) cites example (27) from Russenorsk, a pidgin that survived for 150 years until the 1920s in a northern area of Norway among Norwegians and Russians. It was spoken only during the summer when the Russians were bartering grain for Norwegian fish. One of the constraints of this variety is that the negative element always occurs in second position, a constraint not found in either Norwegian or Russian (even though *ikke* in this example is from Norwegian).

(27) pa den dag ikke   russetolk robotom
      on that day, not   russians work
      'On that day, Russians do not work.'

9.11.2 Pidgins fade away

Because they are used in specific types of interactions, not for all the day's activities, when the reason for those interactions no longer exists, most pidgins also no longer exist.

Probably the best-known pidgin was called the (Mediterranean) Lingua Franca or Sabir. Texts of this pidgin from the sixteenth century exist, but it was probably mainly spoken during the period of the Crusades from Europe to the Christian Holy Land in the Middle Ages. A pidgin sometimes called Chinook Jargon existed in the Pacific Northwest in the United States before European settlers arrived. It was used for trade between the local Indians who spoke different L1s. European traders in the early days of European settlement used it as well. With the expansion of European plantations and settlements in the South Pacific, various versions of Melanesian Pidgin developed (cf. Keesing, 1988; Siegel, 1999 *inter alia*). Tok Pisin, which is a creole if grammatical criteria are followed, seems to have developed from such a pidgin or a composite of a number of pidgins. (Tok Pisin is now one of the official languages of Papua New Guinea.) In the colonial settings of the British Empire, various pidgins came into being, such as a "Butler English" in India and Kisettla Kiswahili in East Africa. Today, various new pidgins may develop, serve a purpose, and then fade away, too.

9.12 Creoles

Before linguists began studying these languages, the term "creole" was already in use as the term for people who lived in European colonies, especially people of mixed descent. Then, the language varieties that developed in these colonies came to be called creoles. These languages were **created by speakers of non-European languages** who worked on European plantations, whether as slaves, indentured workers, or indigenous workers. The creoles developed through contacts with their fellow workers and with the overseers who were speakers of colonial varieties of a European language. They largely arose during the seventeenth through the early twentieth centuries.

Today, however, other varieties that developed among speakers who all were non-Europeans are also called creoles (e.g. Sango in the Central African Republic). And there may be new creoles developing today, just as there can be new pidgins, but the social conditions that promoted creoles would have to exist. Probably the Atlantic (Caribbean) creoles have been studied the most extensively, but so have the South Pacific pidgins and creoles (e.g. Tok Pisin on Papua New Guinea, as well as Hawai'i Creole English) and also the creole spoken on the island of Mauritius in the Indian Ocean.

Almost as a sign of the implicit bias many people originally had about creoles, they are typically referred to as **"X- or Y-based creoles"**, with the

European language that is part of the mix filling the "X or Y" blank. Thus, the creoles in the Caribbean on the islands that were under British control until they gained their independence are still referred to as English-based creoles by many. Such names imply that the European language is the main source language. A minority of creolists do make this argument (e.g. Chaudenson, 2001), but more would not. It is true that much of the lexicon **(vocabulary) of a creole** comes from the language that was spoken by most of the European overseers present when the creole was developing. Creolists call this language the **superstrate** or **lexifier** language. But it is also true that a speaker of one of the native dialects of English elsewhere would have a very hard time understanding one of these creoles.

9.12.1 How did creoles develop?

In fact, for a long time (e.g. since Alleyne, 1980) many have argued that the languages of the workers provide the basic **grammatical structure for creoles** and that they therefore are the foundation of any creole. Creolists call these languages **substrate languages**. Especially these creolists devote a lot of their efforts to trying to establish which ethnic groups were involved as slaves or other types of workers when and where a given creole was presumed to have developed. Not having many written records makes this quest difficult.

Then in 1981 Bickerton rocked the creolist world with his volume titled *The Roots of Language* in which he argues that neither the overseers nor the workers were very important in creole formation. Instead, he argues that children in the plantation communities are the major source of expanded creole grammars. How so? The argument is that children still have access to their innate **"bioprogram"** that enables them to acquire or develop a language in a sense that adults do not (this is the same innate component referred to as Universal Grammar (UG) in chapter 11). Since then, controversies regarding this proposal and counter-proposals are one reason why the numbers of creolists and publications about creoles have grown considerably in the last 25 years. For some recent views, see three edited volumes (Arends, Muysken and Smith, 1995; De Graff, 1999; and McWhorter, 2000).

9.12.2 Why the interest in the structure of creoles?

Why all this interest in creoles? A major impetus may be the two features that distinguish creoles as a linguistic category. First, they **arose in specific types of social situations** and not elsewhere. There are reasons for this: The main ones are (1) the plantation-like situations with slaves and workers with no common Ll and typically no dominant Ll and (2) the workers' limited access to overseers with their very different Ll, usually a European language. For these reasons, creoles represent a type of second-language learning, but they do not turn out as do second languages that are learned in other natural settings or in classrooms.

A second distinguishing feature of creoles is that, even though we don't have written records on the development of most creoles, the morphosyntactic structures visible in creoles all over the world show **a number of striking similarities**. Explaining why this is so makes their grammars challenging to study. For example, many creoles have what are called **serial verbs** (sequences of two verbs for a meaning for which one verb would serve in other languages, e.g. "walk go town"). In the case of some creoles, substrate languages with a clear tie to related languages, which are languages with a clearly defined family tree, have serial verbs, too. For instance, West African coastal languages have serial verbs (and so do many Caribbean creoles with ancestral ties to this area). But some other totally unrelated languages also have serial verbs. Perhaps more striking, many creoles have **similar ways of expressing tense-mood-aspect** with verbs; they do so with single morphemes for each such meaning and they are placed before the main verb. Again, some languages, which are known to be involved in creole formation and with a clearly defined family tree, also have such auxiliary verbs (e.g. English). But in some creoles, the languages of plantation overseers (e.g. French or Spanish) do not have these pre-verbal elements, even though the creoles that developed with such overseers have this feature. The list goes on; for more details on similarities, see general overviews in Holm (2000) and Winford (2003a), as well as articles in the *Journal of Pidgin and Creole Languages*. Also, though, bear in mind that some creolists stress that there are many differences, not just similarities, across creoles (e.g. Siegel, 2000).

9.12.3 Creole structures explained

How is it that creoles all around the world have similar features? Is there some universally present innate language component at work? To what extent might Bickerton be right about the role of children in creole development (even though much of the empirical evidence he cites is disputed)? Or, even when the persons forming a language are adults, are they working with universal principles that are part of their innate language faculty? Or are they using innate learning mechanisms that are not language-specific?

At least in those cases where a pidgin ancestor seems likely or is known, creolists agree that **structural expansion** or **restructuring** provided the more elaborate vocabularies and grammatical systems that distinguish creoles from pidgins. But this doesn't address the question: What is the basis of this restructuring, transfer from either the superstrate or the substrate languages, or language-specific innate mechanisms? See the 1986 volume edited by Muysken and Smith titled *Substrata Versus Universals in Creole Genesis* for some of the flavor of the controversy. Those creolists with chapters in De Graff (1999) are some of the major ones arguing for universal mechanisms.

9.12.3.1 The argument for substrate transfer

Still, probably most creolists argue that creoles have the structure they do because of transfer of features from the substrate languages, not because of innate universals. But most of these creolists make an argument that is largely based on comparing lists of words or structures that appear in a given creole with similar words in the substrate languages that may have been present when the creole was formed; that is, they don't offer a principled basis for why some matches occur and not others. Many creolists seek to reinforce the substrate argument by citing (or still seeking) what historical evidence there is about which groups were present at the time of creole formation.

Instead of citing lists, some of the creolists arguing for substrate languages' role in creole formation suggest that one of two processes that are at work in other forms of language contact were especially important in creole development. These are **transfer** or **relexification**. Among others, Siegel (1999, 2000) makes a transfer-from-substrate argument based on **similarities in grammatical features** between the creole and likely substrate languages. That is, he argues for the language-learning strategy, **transfer** of Ll (substrate) grammatical features onto L2 (superstrate) forms as the basis for a creole. Transfer is a strategy that beginning learners of an L2 do employ, but the overall importance of transfer in second-language learning is controversial. A recent contribution from Siegel is on Hawai'i Creole English or HCE (2000) in which he argues that this creole shows input from two pidgins (Chinese Pidgin English and Pacific Pidgin English), as well as immigrant languages, including Portuguese, which Siegel states was dominant among these workers when a stable tense-modal-aspect system was emerging in HCE. Even though HCE includes English grammatical morphemes, Siegel claims they show substrate influence. For example, he argues that the use of *stei* as a non-punctual (progressive or habitual) marker is similar to Portuguese *estar*, which is the form of the verb 'to be' used for non-punctual mood. Example (28) illustrates this.

(28)   Wail we **stei** paedl, Jaon **stei** put wata insai da kanu.
'While we were paddling, John was letting water into the canoe.'
(Siegel, 2000: 218, cited from Bickerton 1981: 29)

9.12.3.2 The argument for relexification

Another explanation, the **relexification hypothesis** of LeFebvre (1998) and Lumsden (1999) focuses on one language, Haitian Creole. This hypothesis suggests interaction between two specific languages that resulted in Haitian Creole. These are (1) the West African language Fongbe, thought to be one of the principal substrate languages spoken in the slave population (although the extent of a major presence for Fongbe speakers is disputed) and (2) the French variety spoken by plantation overseers.

The hypothesis is that Fongbe speakers were able to intuit the structure of their own language and replace grammatical elements in the relevant French variety with structures from Fongbe. For example, LeFebvre notes that in both Haitian Creole and Fongbe the plural marker may occur within the same noun phrase as a determiner, but it follows the determiner rather than occurring on the noun itself. This doesn't happen in French where plural is marked by a suffix on nouns. Lefebvre (1998: 85) gives example (29) to show this similarity. She also notes that at least several other creolists have suggested that the Haitian plural marker *yo* is a relexified version of the French third person pronoun *eux* 'them', which is a content morpheme in French and which has a similar pronunciation.

(29) krab la yo   (Haitian Creole)
      crab the PLURAL
      ason o le   (Fongbe)
      crab the PLURAL
      'The crabs'

9.12.3.3 *Comparing transfer and relexification*

The issue is: How do transfer and relexification differ? They both refer to the objective process of restructuring. Winford (2003a: 345) states that they just "reflect differences in perspective". Transfer emphasizes the effects of substrate (L1) influence; relexification focuses more on how lexifier elements are incorporated into the developing creole version projected by substrate influence. The result is the same under both arguments. That is, the creole ends up with superstrate forms functioning in grammatical roles derived from the substrate.

A problem with highlighting the role of transfer of substrate grammatical features onto superstrate forms is that this argument leaves unexplained why superstrate forms, *not substrate forms*, carry the key grammatical elements in most creoles. A problem with the relexification hypothesis is that it doesn't explain why – if the substrate abstract grammatical frame is so important – relexification from the superstrate *happens at all*. Also, if creole speakers are going to use superstrate elements at all, why don't they simply take in superstrate grammatical forms? That is, why do they import superstrate content elements *and then* reanalyze them as grammatical forms?

9.12.3.4 *Restructuring*

Another creolist, Mufwene (e.g. 2001) refers extensively to **restructuring** from a "feature pool" drawn from the various language varieties spoken in the period of creole formation. The evidence that there is restructuring is obvious; "the structures of the output and input varieties are not identical" (p. 4). In general, he gives few details or motivations as to why certain features from certain sources win out (although he mentions that the relative "markedness" of competing features may matter). For example, he states that "[T]here is no particular input–output ratio of number of varieties . . . What matters is that the structures of the output and input varieties are not identical" (p. 4).

9.12.3.5 *A two targets hypothesis for creole formation*

Your author (Myers-Scotton, 2001; 2002) offers another explanation for creole formation that also gives the substrates the major role in providing a morphosyntactic frame for the developing creole. Call this the **Two Targets Hypothesis**. What makes this approach different is that it specifies the *type* of superstrate participation and offers an explanation for it, particularly in regard to the supplying of grammatical elements. This participation is limited in a principled way derived from the 4-M model discussed above.

This approach begins by arguing that speakers had two different "targets" when they created creoles. Obviously, the speakers needed a common language to communicate among themselves. One substrate language would have been a good choice. But it appears from what is known of the social history of most creoles (there are exceptions) that no group of slaves or workers was large enough to push its language on the others. Another choice for the needed single variety was the language of the overseers. Certainly, it had more social prestige in the community, and whatever limited means for upward mobility existed involved this language.

Given these conditions, creole creators settled on two target languages. Their innate linguistic faculty pointed them toward a composite of grammatical features from their own languages (the substrates) for the frame of a new language; their recognition of social conditions led them to seek as much input from the overseers' language as possible. But creole developers had only limited access to this language; they largely saw only each other, not speakers of the overseers' language. So, they took in that part of this language that was most accessible to them.

Enter the 4-M model. Given the fact that content morphemes and early system morphemes have the most semantic content, they would be easiest for creole speakers to pick out of the stream of speech of those who spoke the superstrate language. Therefore, under this two targets hypothesis, many of these should appear in a developing creole. This is largely what happens; study after study supports the claim that most of the actual words in a creole come from the superstrate.

However, gaps in the developing frame for grammatical elements (late system morphemes) would be hard to fill with superstrate grammatical elements because they were less available than contentful elements. Why less available? Not only do these elements have less semantic content, but they are harder to acquire because of *how* they are acquired.

This argument follows from the Differential Access Hypothesis discussed above. Late system morphemes are only accessed late in language production (at the level of the formulator). Therefore, they have limited salience compared with content and early system morphemes (accessed earlier and more directly at the level of the mental lexicon). The net result is that late system morphemes are not so available for any type of language learning. Evidence from first-language acquisition and especially second-language acquisition shows that most late system morphemes are accessed late (e.g. Wei, 2000 on second-language learners).

Then, this question remains for creole formers, how are the gaps in the frame filled for those elements needed to indicate grammatical relationships among phrases and in the larger clause? The answer is that content morphemes from the superstrate can be reanalyzed to fill these gaps. Examples from a wide variety of creoles show this **reanalysis**. Under reanalysis, a content morpheme with a meaning that has something in common with what is needed from a grammatical element is reconfigured as a late system morpheme. For example, in the so-called English-based creoles of the Caribbean, in many cases the tense–aspect markers are reanalyzed content morphemes (for example, *de* marks a past time in many creoles; many creolists argue that it comes from the locative indicator *there*). In French-based creoles, a form of Frenc *après* 'after' has become a marker of future tense.

Here's another example. Creolists who study Tok Pisin (spoken in Papua New Guinea) have long recognized that the marker of future in that creole comes from *by and by*. Jenkins (2000: 138) shows how *bai 'n bai* has been reduced to *bai* (still to mark 'future tense') at least in one variety of Tok Pisin. In this variety, it occurs in the same position as the future marker in some of the likely substrate languages of Tok Pisin. One such language was studied by Jenkins; it is Tigak, spoken on the island of New Ireland in Papua New Guinea. Examples (30a) and (30b) compare Tok Pisin and Tigak in regard to this marker. Note that *sitor* is a borrowing for 'store' in both languages; also note that *long* in (30a) probably comes from *along*, but is similar to the locative marker (*lo*) in Tigak.

> (30a) **bai**   em   i   go   long sitor
>   FUTURE   3s   TRANSITIVE   go   to   store
>   'He will go to the store.'

> (30b) **yo**   gi   inang lo   sitor
>   FUTURE   3s   go   LOCATION   store
>   'He will go to the store.'

Thus, this example shows how the "two targets" operate together (the substrate language setting the frame and the superstrate language supplying the grammatical morpheme).

9.13 Summing up

We know that the length of this chapter has tested the reader's stamina. Even so, we've only discussed part of what there is to say about codeswitching and given only snapshots of convergence and attrition and then of pidgins and creoles. These three phenomena share characteristics (ones that are shared, too, with other contact phenomena)

- Two types of **asymmetry** characterize contact phenomena in general.
- Even though two languages come together in codeswitching, the basic grammar of neither language is necessarily changed because of this participation.
- In contrast, the essence of either convergence/attrition or pidgin/creole development is that structural changes happen.
- Two theoretical models are introduced:
- **The Matrix Language Frame (MLF) model** is intended to explain constraints on the structure of classic codeswitching, although some provisions of the model are useful in discussing other contact phenomena, too.
- A newer model, **the 4-M model**, turns out to be more ubiquitous; it refines divisions in codeswitching that the MLF model makes and it figures prominently in convergence and attrition as well as in creole development.
- **Substitution and reanalysis** are processes in convergence/attrition.
- **Restructuring** occurs in creole formation, whether it is viewed as **transfer, relexification, or reanalysis**.

9.14 Words and phrases to remember

language contact phenomena
asymmetry across languages
asymmetry in morpheme types
classic codeswitching
composite codeswitching
Matrix Language
Embedded Language
four types of morpheme
convergence
attrition
substitution
reanalysis
pidgin languages
creole languages

10

Psycholinguistics and Bilingualism

Multiple voices: The word from Hungary

Eva Polgar, a Hungarian, is an economist near retirement age who works for the national government in Budapest. In addition to speaking Hungarian, she studied Russian under the Soviet regime, but she never used it. She also studied German in school; then, in her late twenties, she began to study German again on her own and then with a tutor. She wanted to watch the Austrian TV channels (in German), which were available in the area where she used to live (at Lake Balaton). Also, there were lots of German-speaking tourists who visited that area in the summer. About four years ago, Eva began to take classes in English. She lives alone and travels a lot alone and doesn't like to depend on other people to interpret for her. Also, it's her personal belief that to be an educated person, one should speak at least one foreign language. Nevertheless, in the department where she works, she is the only one who speaks or reads English.

10.1 Introduction

When you are first faced with a chapter with psycholinguistics in the title, you also must figure that this is a going to be a pretty dry subject of little interest to anyone except psycholinguists. Surprise! Answers to sets of related questions about bilinguals and their minds interest just about everyone. Some of these are: First, there are questions about bilinguals and how their languages are organized in the brain. Are the language centers in the brains of bilinguals different than those in monolinguals? And if bilinguals speak more than two languages, do they have their different languages in different areas of the brain, each one in a different area? When bilinguals' brains are injured so that they suffer some language loss, are both languages affected in the same way? Second, there's a cluster of questions about the two (or more) languages and their activation, beginning with this one: How do bilinguals keep their two languages apart? That is, when they want to speak using only one of their languages, what about the other language? Is there a language switch that can be turned "off"? Or, is the other language always "on" in some sense, too? You'll find attempts to answer these questions, and more, in this chapter.

Readers probably know that cognitive psychologists in general are primarily interested in studying mental processes. The mental processes that interest psycholinguists are those that relate to **how language is produced and understood**. That is, psycholinguists are interested in assembling data to support theories of how language is organized in the brain. These theories underlie models that psycholinguists posit about the parts of the brain devoted to language processing.

Language processing is a cover term for **both the comprehension and production of language**. A moment's thought tells us that studying such processes generally has to be done indirectly by studying various aspects of actual behavior, although new imaging techniques that show brain activation during speech make some more direct study possible.

Recently, more and more psycholinguists have become interested in bilingualism. A major reason is that the ability to use two languages, and how they are used, can tell us something about what features or processes in the brain underlie language abilities in general that studying only one language may not reveal. That is, findings on various relationships between two languages (e.g. differences in proficiency, differences in age of acquisition) as they relate to performance in experiments and learning situations often can tell psycholinguists more than just making the same studies with monolinguals as the subjects.

Most studies by psycholinguists are **experimental studies**. That is, experimental researchers study human participants in a laboratory setting where the researchers can control exactly what information is presented to the subjects. Also, they can vary the information with similar or different participants in order to test specific hypotheses. Thus, these researchers who study bilinguals also mainly do it in laboratory settings, too. Some psycholinguists do study speech as it happens in the world (naturally occurring speech) and in chapters 8 and 9, you read about some other studies of bilinguals and their naturally occurring speech.

Some psycholinguistic studies are less directly concerned with the cognitive organization of language and are more interested in the developmental aspects of language. Especially as psycholinguists use the term, "developmental" means "how something changes or grows". So, for example, both psycholinguists and linguists may study children who are acquiring two languages at once or study the extent of success in second-language learning at a later age. The attention that is paid to late bilinguals should be of special interest to those readers of this volume whose main experience with attaining any degree of bilingualism was in high school or college and university classrooms. Studying how the results of second-language learning after childhood are different from first-language learning is one research topic. Another one is how skilled adult bilinguals process sentences in each of their two languages in contrast with less skilled learners of an L2. Some of these topics come up in this chapter and they are discussed more thoroughly in chapter 11.

It is fair to say that experimental psycholinguists in general have devoted more attention to studying comprehension (understanding language) than production, possibly partly because it is easier to study understanding. In fact, many people assume that studies labeled "language processing" must be about comprehension. In such studies, the researcher can select sentences and words to present to a subject. Getting participants to speak and produce the specific grammatical constructions or even specific words that interest the researcher is harder to control. Thus, much of the research on monolingual language has been on comprehension, involving often either **grammaticality judgments** (i.e. "Is this sentence possible in your language?") or **reaction time** (e.g. "How quickly can you report as many words as you can remember in a sentence with one syntactic structure vs. another structure but with the same meaning?").

Some of this research, especially studies of parsing (the hierarchical organization of a sentence) underlies efforts in **Artificial Intelligence**. This is the name given to studies concerned with modeling human mental functions.

The goal of some of the psycholinguists concerned with bilinguals also is to study comprehension, but many study production. The objects of study for both groups of researchers are single words and reaction times in processing them across the speaker's two languages. For example, some researchers are interested in such topics as how fast bilinguals who are shown a word on a computer screen can identify which of their languages the word comes from under various conditions (it might be the bilinguals have just been shown a word from their other language). This is **a comprehension study**. Or, with some sort of distraction present on the screen, bilinguals may be asked to produce the word in a specified language that names a picture. This is **a production study**. In addition, there have been a few studies of reactions to whole sentences in which two languages appear, to determine if the point of the switch to the other language makes any difference in response time (e.g. Dussias, 2001).

10.1.1 Where is "language" in the bilingual brain?

Whatever the differences in what psycholinguistic studies emphasize, whether **comprehension** or **production** is involved, we can answer one of the questions at the top of this chapter now: It's safe to say that bilinguals rely in general on the **same mechanisms** in acquiring, producing, and understanding language that monolinguals employ.

Further, at least to date, studies of electro-magnetic imaging of the brains of right-handed bilinguals show activation for language in the same areas of the brain as those activated in monolinguals. That is, language capacities in general are located in the **left hemisphere** of the brain for almost all humans.

This is not to say there are no differences in brain activity for language across individuals. For example, some differences in language areas in the brain (from right-handed persons) for left-handed persons and ambidextrous persons have been reported. More important to this volume, recent studies using imaging devices show some possible differences between **early and late bilinguals** regarding areas of the brain that seem to be activated. An early bilingual is defined as someone who acquires his or her two languages before the age of seven to nine (although the term can refer to an earlier age), and a late one is someone who acquires them at some later point. Such studies are discussed in chapter 11.

Still, studies continue to appear claiming that the right hemisphere of the brain is involved in bilingualism, especially in the case of any L2s learned after an early age. Among others, Michel Paradis, a prominent researcher in neurolinguistics, speaks out strongly against the validity of such findings. He recognizes that some reliable studies do show differences between monolinguals and bilinguals and within bilinguals as a group (e.g. differences in areas of brain activation, or qualitative differences in activation). But, if there are such differences, he suggests that the explanation may be that some bilinguals *add to* the systems that most speakers use. For example, bilinguals may be more tuned in to contextual cues or assessing the relevance of selecting one of alternative ways of presenting the same information. So in Paradis (2001: 83), he suggests that bilinguals may use "the same cerebral mechanisms available to unilinguals, but to different extents in order to compensate for the gap in their linguistic competence by relying more heavily on the other available systems."

Here's another piece of evidence. Fabbro (1999) points out that when the left hemisphere is damaged, over 95 percent of individuals show some language loss. This finding is solid evidence that certain **crucial mechanisms of language** are the same across individuals – in the left hemisphere.

10.1.2 A limited overview

We finish this introduction with a disclaimer: By no means does this chapter survey all of the important psycholinguistic research on bilinguals. For example, we hardly consider studies on language comprehension that involve sentence processing, concentrating instead on word recognition studies of either production and comprehension. We also ignore studies of eye movement during language comprehension or production. Even on some topics that we do cover, details are sometimes very sketchy (e.g. on memory and aphasia). There simply isn't space for everything in a volume devoted to bilingualism in a general sense. So we do wish to make clear that there is a large, fascinating literature, untouched here, out there in academic journals and books. Further, lots of questions will still remain at the end of this chapter, and there are many conflicting findings, making it difficult to reach firm conclusions even in areas where much research has been done.

10.2 Themes in psycholinguistics and bilingualism

There are five main themes in psycholinguistically oriented studies of bilingualism that are surveyed in this chapter. We present them in a group now, in terms of the questions they address. Then we discuss some of them together (if they are closely intertwined) and some separately. Again, we remind readers that in this volume a "bilingual" is a person who speaks two *or more* languages. Some studies test more than two languages.

1 The nature of **the bilingual lexicon** is a theme that is relevant to just about every other theme. Think of the bilingual lexicon as a sort of abstract dictionary in the mind. Some of the main questions about the bilingual lexicon are these: Is there a single lexicon for each language or one common lexicon? Are synonyms or close synonyms in both languages activated when a speaker wishes to say a word in only one language? If both languages are activated, is it equal activation? Although the discussion here is on experimental study of the nature of the lexicon by psycholinguists, its nature is also studied based on naturally occurring data by linguists interested in second-language learning or the grammatical structure of languages when they are spoken together in the same clause, as we saw in chapter 9 and will see in chapter 11.

The other four themes are all very much related to the nature of the bilingual lexicon and other abstract components involved in language comprehension and production. They all refer to questions generally studied only in a laboratory setting.

2 When bilinguals speak first one language and then the other in an experimental setting, is there a language switch that gets turned on and off for each language or are both languages "on" all the time? Investigating **the levels of activation** of the bilinguals' two languages is a major goal.

3   Some experiments are comprehension tasks (called **word recognition tasks**). These include **lexical decision tasks**. For example, a participant is asked whether a string of letters (shown on a computer screen) is a real word in the language under study. Experiments also include production tasks (**lexical access tasks**), such as translations or picture naming. They give indirect evidence about differing activation levels across languages. These experiments also provide indirect evidence for those psycholinguists interested in constructing models of language production or comprehension (e.g. Levelt et al., 1999).

4   The **study of memory** is another theme in experimental studies of bilingualism. Are words in a speaker's L2 seemingly as directly available as those in his or her L1 in **short-term memory**? What about types of memory in the speaker's **long-term memory bank**? Are memories in the bilingual's two or more languages equally accessible?

5   Studies of aphasic patients give indirect evidence about the areas of the brain involved in language processing. **Aphasia** is the name for the state of affairs when the production or comprehension of speech or written language is disturbed, either by disease (including strokes or dementia) or by accidents. Even if bilinguals have both of their languages in the same "language centers" in the brain that seem to function for monolinguals, what happens to the different languages of bilinguals when their apparent language areas are damaged?

Two themes not discussed here are closely related. These are related to the bilingual's acquisition of languages and they address the question of whether there is a critical age after which fluent language acquisition is difficult. The two themes are differences in early and late bilinguals and simultaneous acquisition of two languages as a very young child. These themes come up in chapter 11, which is concerned with those theoretical aspects of bilingualism that are more related to issues about age of acquisition and attempts to explain levels of success in second-language learning by adults.

10.3   Classifying bilinguals

As you may have noticed already in this volume, it is hard to know the current prevailing views about many different aspects of bilingualism, partly because research results in new findings and methodologies of research change quickly (we hope they become more precise). This is definitely the case concerning how bilinguals are classified in regard to either the supposed mental organization of their languages or their history as bilinguals.

For example, researchers from the 1960s up until recently discussed bilinguals as either **coordinate or compound bilinguals**. This division was loosely tied to how the languages were acquired, but it referred to how the bilingual's two languages were supposedly represented in the brain. If speakers acquired them in the same context, they were called **compound bilinguals**. The assumption was that the languages of compound bilinguals were interdependent in the sense that one abstract concept (supporting a meaning) was realized as two different words, one in each language, but there was only one concept involved. In contrast, a **coordinate bilingual** was learned his or her languages in different environments (e.g. one at home and one at school). For the coordinate bilingual, the claim was that words in different languages that stood for the same object or concept each had their own ties to the pre-linguistic conceptual level (in a model of language). But this supposed distinction on abstract differences between types of bilinguals, based on how they acquired their languages, didn't hold up. That is, dividing bilinguals in this way didn't result in any consistent predictions. Researchers couldn't produce consistent results in various tasks that might have indicated that how bilinguals performed was related to the claimed division between coordinate and compound bilingualism.

Two other divisions on which there is general agreement may or may not make a difference in how their languages are organized. First, bilingualism can be either **active** (the speaker actually speaks and understands both languages) or **passive** (the speaker understands his or her L2, but either can't or chooses not to speak it). Second, a bilingual may be a **simultaneous bilingual** (both languages acquired at the same time) or a **sequential bilingual** (one language acquired before the other). You can assume that participants in psycholinguistic studies discussed here are active bilinguals, unless indicated otherwise. But it seems that distinction between simultaneous and sequential bilinguals only receives attention in studies of bilingual child language acquisition.

A division that is part of many studies is that between **early and late bilinguals**. We'll see in chapter 11 how some results seem to be linked to differences in **age of acquisition** of another language. In assessing any studies of bilinguals, it's important for you to know that exactly what a given researcher means when he or she uses the terms "early" and "late" often is not entirely clear. Or, when and how the distinction is used may be inconsistent across researchers. Yet, there is general agreement that the age at which someone becomes a bilingual does matter, but how and why is not entirely clear.

10.4 Validity and experimental methodologies

Before we go into details about studies of how adult bilinguals seem to access their languages in various tasks, we remind readers that no matter what the theme, psycholinguists in general tend to study language experimentally (i.e. participants respond to prearranged stimuli in a laboratory setting). Also, at least in experiments on normal bilinguals (those without brain damage), the emphasis in studies of both comprehension and production has been on

single words, and often words for concrete objects or their attributes, such as color terms. That is, experiments largely consider how bilinguals handle single words that may be presented in a bilingual context, but not how they handle full clauses or sentences. True, as might be expected, studies of syntax (sentence structure) do consider full sentences. Most of these are studies of comprehension, not production. For example, an experimental task in this area might require participants to repeat sentences in one or the other of their languages. (As we've already indicated, this chapter hardly considers such studies, not just for lack of space, but also because researchers of bilinguals haven't concentrated on syntactic studies.)

We can imagine that studying speech as it's produced in naturally occurring situations seems preferable. And, as we've indicated in chapter 9, normal bilinguals in such situations often use single words or clauses from both of their languages in the same conversation. Studies of bilingual speech in full clauses as they are produced in naturally occurring speech are discussed in chapter 9 as **codeswitching**. Such studies offer a window on the nature of bilingual language production, with insights that sometimes complement experimental studies in the laboratory focusing on single words.

But there is a good reason to conduct experimental research. Testing some hypotheses isn't possible with natural speech because what is said across participants is not necessarily comparable. Further, the specific types of hypotheses tested in word recognition and lexical decision tasks require data produced under strict controls. And, even though such experiments do not deal with natural bilingual speech in all its parts, much has been learned by restricting research to single words and their production in one or both of the bilingual's languages. (Most studies of aphasia do collect more extensive natural data from patients; patients are often asked to tell stories. But this is partly because these patients often have short attention spans and don't respond well to other requirements of experimental conditions.)

A methodological problem that is hard to avoid concerns the issue of which of the bilingual's languages is **dominant**. That is, which of his or her languages is the one in which **judgments about grammatical well-formedness** of sentences are most native-like. Remember that bilinguals rarely have equal facility in both languages. The reasons are many, but largely have to do with the conditions under which each language was learned and how frequently and where the different languages currently are used.

For researchers, the problem is that assessing results in experiments may hinge on whether the language tested is the speaker's dominant language or not. Many times experimenters assume that the speaker's L1 is his or her dominant language. And it may be – but not under certain circumstances (for example, if the speaker no longer speaks that language as regularly as he or she speaks the L2). Or, experimenters may ask bilinguals to state which language they think is their more dominant one. In either case, is the judgment valid? Another problem centers around the issue of the participant's **level of**

proficiency in his or her less dominant language. In most studies to date, the researchers claim the participants are "proficient" in both languages. But at least up until recently, experimenters rarely have based this judgment on actual tests. Even if they use tests, the validity of tests claiming to test proficiency is open to question. So both "dominance" and "proficiency" remain thorns in the side of bilingual experiments, no matter what.

10.5 The mental lexicon

Humans may all think alike, but there is a difference between thought and language. Certainly, speakers think (in some sense) before speaking, and they can think without speaking. But when they do speak, they all formulate their speaking in terms of a specific language. And languages definitely differ in many ways, but especially in the forms that they use to refer to different objects and concepts.

10.5.1 The relationship between thought and a specific language

There is an age-old argument under what is called the **Whorfian hypothesis** (also called the Sapir–Whorf hypothesis) about the connection between the structure of a specific language and how its speakers conceptualize the world. The strong version of the hypothesis suggests that the way a person understands the world is controlled by his or her language. For example, a hypothetical language may require that a different noun form be used to refer to long, thin objects from the noun type used for round objects. When speakers of this language classify objects in the world, do they group them using the same criteria that the hypothetical language follows (e.g. in terms of shape, not in terms of color or purpose, etc.)? This hypothesis has some more current, generally weaker, versions, too. Consider Pavlenko (2000: 3), who argues that some differences exist in how different bilinguals conceptualize the world that are based partly (apparently) on input from their languages and cultures. She writes that "in the study of bilingualism, conceptual representations should be treated as related but not equivalent to word meanings . . . While some concepts may overlap partially or even completely between any two languages/cultures in question, any claim of correspondence requires evidence and cannot be implicitly assumed." Also see Gumperz and Levinson (1996) and Gentner and Goldin-Meadow (2003).

However, it's hard to see what would constitute a real test of the Whorfian hypothesis or its modern versions, as they've been formulated, although there have been, and continue to be, attempts. It seems reasonable to assume that all humans have access to a similar conceptual system, which allows them to have thoughts and intentions which they express in their own languages, if they choose to express them linguistically. Yes, the languages may shape how thoughts and intentions are expressed, but languages do not seem to shape the actual thoughts and intentions. But study of the extent of the relationship continues.

10.5.2 A common semantic system or not?

Once we reach the level of the production and comprehension of actual languages, we reach an issue that is certainly not settled. This is the issue of how the bilingual's languages are organized in the mind. Remember, of course, that we are dealing with hypotheses about abstract representations in the mind and that ideas about how language in general is represented are based on indirect evidence from experimental and other data.

An early proposal was that words from the bilingual's several languages were represented separately, but that they shared a **common semantic system**; that is, under this view, there would be a single memory store with semantic representations for both languages. This has been referred to as the **interdependence model**. Some researchers still support this view, basically arguing that there is a single memory store for both languages. But later studies of various aspects of bilingualism suggest otherwise. They support an **independence model**. That is, the more current view is that bilinguals have two distinct memories and semantic systems. However, as will become clear in later sections and in the next chapter, this view about separate entries (i.e. an abstract item in the mental lexicon) does not mean that both systems could not be activated at the same time. Further, it's agreed that of corresponding entries, one would be more activated. The claim of the comprehension model of Dijkstra and van Heuven (2002), which is discussed in a later section, is that activation of word forms is integrated across the bilingual's languages. But it is not entirely clear what "integrated" means. Also, they are dealing with actual surface-level word forms and their activation, not abstract entries in any mental lexicon.

Even though all languages can refer to the same objects and concepts, differences in how these objects and concepts are viewed and the contexts in which they are discussed would limit the notion of a common semantic system for two or more languages. For example, objects may be classified differently or viewed differently in relation to other objects across languages. For example, an object such as "rice" is not necessarily the same entity cross-linguistically. For some cultures (and their languages) "cooked rice" and even rice cooked in different ways are called by a number of different names than uncooked rice. Also, not all containers that may be called a "bottle" in some languages will be called by a counterpart to "bottle" in other languages; instead, a "bottle" may be called by the word for "container" or some other word. And how about a concept such as "loyalty" or "the family"? Are they understood the same in all languages and therefore categorized with the same like concepts in all languages? Also, some languages have words standing for concepts or states of affairs that aren't lexicalized in another language (e.g. there is no word in English that exactly corresponds to the time of day near sunset that the French word *crépuscule* refers to, nor is there one for German *Schadenfreude*, which roughly means gloating over someone's bad luck).

So in the end, most psycholinguists who study bilinguals agree that while there is a common system at the **pre-linguistic conceptual level**, bilinguals do not have a common semantic system at the linguistic level. Still, the idea of **a common mental lexicon** across languages is supported, as we'll see in the next section.

10.5.3 The mental lexicon and lemmas

Once beyond the level of concepts and at the level underlying actual language, research supports the idea of a **common mental lexicon**. But this abstract lexicon is not fused; it has different entries for the bilingual's two (or more) languages. These entries are generally called **lemmas** by psycholinguists (philosophers and lexicographers use the term differently, each somewhat differently from the other). Psycholinguists generally agree that lemmas are tagged in some way so that **all lemmas are language-specific**. The idea is that lemmas are not words, but underlie the actual words that are produced in speech (i.e. on the surface level as opposed to the abstract level); that is, lemmas only exist in an abstract sense.

Note that this level of the mental lexicon is linguistic in the sense that it is language-specific. But intentions at the conceptual level are pre-linguistic; therefore, they are not tied to a specific language at this level. Think about it – you can conceive of something or have intentions that are not expressed through actual language production. For example, pictures can stand for concepts. There may well be overlapping conceptualizations across languages at the conceptual level, but we expect lemmas to be at least somewhat different cross-linguistically, just because they are tagged for a specific language. When the term "surface level" is used, it refers to language that is actually produced, whether spoken or written.

Unfortunately, different researchers use the terms "**semantic**" and "**conceptual**" in sometimes confusing ways; some use them for constructs on the same level (either the conceptual level or the level of the mental lexicon). For example, Levelt et al. (1999: 3) refers to an apparent conceptual level as "conceptual preparation in terms of lexical concepts". But as used here, "conceptual" always refers to something that is on a pre-linguistic level and "semantic" refers to properties of an element in a language even if they are abstract properties. So both properties of entries at an abstract level and actual words on the surface level are semantic. This means that some concepts have more than a single word to express them, even in the same language, and, as noted above, some concepts don't have a word in all languages to express them.

Still, exactly what a lemma contains is controversial. Levelt and his associates (1999) narrowed the characterization of a lemma found in Levelt (1989) so that the 1999 version refers only to the lemma nodes representing syntax (constraints on what makes a surface phrase in a specific language well-formed). To accommodate semantics, Levelt et al. (1999: 66) posit what they call a "node" with apparently language-specific abstract entries containing word meaning (semantic) information (the node is called just "lexical selection" in the 1999 model). However, the earlier model of language production (Levelt, 1989) has a broader characterization of lemmas so that lemmas include semantic-pragmatic specifications, as well as all of the morphological and syntactic specifications that make the surface realization well-formed. (This is how lemmas are viewed in Myers-Scotton and Jake, 1995 and Myers-Scotton, 2005.) Where phonology comes in is another matter and is not considered here.

Do the lemmas of one language totally differ from those of another language? The answer is "no" if the languages are historically related. Many researchers agree that a lemma in language X may contain a meaning (or partial meanings) and even some grammatical directions that are similar to those in a lemma from language Y. (For example, a lemma from Spanish may have some similarities to a lemma from a closely related language, such as Portuguese, but it's unlikely to have any similarities to a lemma from Japanese.) De Groot (1992) demonstrated that fluent bilinguals translate concrete words more quickly than abstract words. This indicates **concrete words may have more overlap of conceptual features**, but also that "concept mediation" exists across languages, possibly because speakers have a mental image that corresponds to experience. Still, lemmas seem best seen as tagged for specific languages.

10.5.4 Bilinguals and their access to the mental lexicon

Even though earlier models of bilingualism (and still many today) depended on indirect evidence from speech errors by normal speakers or data from brain-damaged speakers (with aphasia), many psycholinguists today rely on **response time (RT)** in experiments for evidence to support their models. As we've already noted, experiments testing for response time generally require participants to name objects in pictures or say words on a screen or their translations. (Some researchers supplement support for their models with computer-generated simulations of language production.)

10.6 Levels of activation

The early view was that a bilingual's languages were not both activated at the same time. The idea of a language "switch" in the bilingual's mind (to turn one language off and the other on) has been replaced by general agreement that both languages are always "on" to some extent. For example, even though Grosjean (e.g. 2001) speaks of a continuum along which speakers can move in his **Language Mode model**, he says that if the bilingual has just been using both languages and he or she then shifts to speaking only one language, the speaker is still "in the bilingual mode". That is, activation varies. In Grosjean's model, a bilingual's motivation to move from a "monolingual mode" to a "bilingual mode" depends on a number of factors, including proficiency but also the task and the situation.

We can surmise that both languages are activated at some level *whenever* bilinguals speak – even when they speak in only one language. In fact, citing a large body of literature Kroll and Dijkstra (2002) can argue that there is strong evidence for **"nonselective access"** to words in both languages in an experiment when the participant is asked to select or produce a word in one language only. What this means is that when a word in one of the bilingual's languages is called for, there is some activation of the other language. But is this **parallel activation**? That is, is this activation identical? Is there activation at both some semantic level and a phonological (pronunciation) level? Many studies address this issue (cf. Kroll and Sunderman, 2003; Jared and Kroll, 2001 for overviews; Von Studnitz and Green, 2002a; 2002b).

Because many psycholinguists study activation (along with other issues) by looking at responses to words in experiments, these studies of bilinguals and word-related tasks are discussed in extra detail. Such studies give some indication of why psycholinguists reach the conclusions that they do about how the mental lexicon is organized and how levels of joint activation seem to vary across the dominant and less dominant language in the bilingual's repertoire. (Other methodologies are also possible; for example, eye tracking while reading a sentence in language X that contains a word from language Y may be studied for the level of fixation on the language Y word.)

10.6.1 Is the unintended language active?

Lexical decision tasks (used to study comprehension) and **lexical access** tasks (used to study production) are among the most frequently used ways to study language processing in either monolinguals or bilinguals. In lexical decision tasks for bilinguals, participants may be asked to decide as quickly and accurately as possible whether a string of letters that has been presented to them on a computer screen is a word in the language under discussion. Note that the object in such studies is to see the effects of **words related in form**. For example, if a string of letters (e.g. *glurk*) follows a permissible pattern for word forms in English, is reaction time for identifying it as a non-word slowed down? Or, if a string of letters that is a word in the bilingual's language that is not being tested is on the screen, does this slow down reaction time (e.g. *Wort* 'word' in German for a German-English bilingual when English is being tested)?

Or consider lexical access tasks. In one such study, participants can be asked to name pictures, using only one of the bilingual's two languages. At the same time various types of distractors can appear in the picture's background. Note that the object in lexical access studies is to see whether **words related in meaning** slow down reaction time. For example, if the participant is a Russian-English bilingual and is being tested in English and is shown a picture of a book, but with the Russian word for book (*knig*) in the background, does this speed up or slow down reaction time?

A variety of hypotheses can be tested, most having to do with levels of activation of the bilingual's two languages. Differences in reaction time under different conditions offer indirect support for such hypotheses. As you can imagine from the above examples, most studies look for answers to questions such as this: Even though the task to be performed involves only *one* pre-designated language, if reaction time is slower when words from *both* of the bilingual's languages are present in some form, is this evidence that both languages are "on" during the task?

10.7 Testing for selective access

Thus, the general question that lexical decision tasks seek to answer is, do speakers have **selective access** for just one language or **simultaneous access**? The answer seems to be "simultaneous access". That is, both languages seem to be active at some level, even when the speaker is speaking or identifying only one language in the experiment. The reason for this conclusion is how response time (RT) is affected by certain conditions in the experiment. That is, experiments show that it's possible to interfere with access and speed it up or slow it down, and both languages can be involved. For example, in monolingual English studies, if the word *dog* appears on the screen, followed by *cat* after a brief delay, response to *cat* as a possible word in English is faster than without the "semantic priming" of *dog*. Similar studies with bilinguals show that such semantic priming with a word from the speaker's *other* language also speeds up response. For example, a French-English bilingual may see the French word *chien* 'dog' on the screen and then immediately after this be asked if the word *cat* on the screen could be an English word. If the presence of the French word speeds up response time, this is evidence that a French word, as well as an English word, is accessed in the bilingual's mind. Many studies have shown this result, with more priming from the bilingual's more dominant language (the L1) to the L2 (Gollan and Kroll, 2001). In this overview, we will concentrate on such lexical decision studies as examples of the type of experiments that psycholinguists do with normal bilinguals.

10.7.1 Cognates speed up reaction time

In one version of such experiments, a non-target word may appear on the computer screen at the same time that the participant is being asked to speak or identify a target word. Isn't it possible that activation will be speeded up if the non-relevant word from the other language is a word that is **cognate** with the target word? The answer is "yes". (The target word is the word that the participant is supposed to speak or indicate in some other way.) Cognates are defined in the box on this page.

For example, consider an experiment in which the participant is supposed to name a target word in language X that appears on the computer screen. If a cognate word from the bilingual's other language (language Y) is presented as a stimulus word (a non-relevant word) before a target word comes on the screen, **response time is faster** than if the stimulus (cognate word) is not. On the basis of a number of experiments, Dijkstra and van Heuven (2002: 183) state, "Even when the orthographic and phonological overlap across languages is incomplete, cognates may be recognized faster than noncognates" (and speed up reaction time on a target word). But the claim is that nearly identical cognates (in terms of their sounds and letters) help more than cognates that differ even a little. For example, French *text* and Spanish *texto* are cognates, but differ in how the word ends. But in a study of French-Spanish bilinguals, while having such a cognate as the stimulus word (non-relevant word or prime) cuts down the response time, having identical cognates cuts down the time even more. Researchers think cross-linguistic relations in semantic processing are most evident with cognates.

Words are called cognates across languages if they come from the same source, because the languages in question come from a presumed common ancestor. Cognates share form and meaning. Thus, English *hound* is cognate with German *hund* "dog" and the two languages are related in their origins; both English and German are Germanic languages. Many languages have similar words because they are borrowed from a single source language; for example, *democracy* is borrowed from Greek. But such similar words do not count as cognates.

10.7.2 Distractors that slow down reaction time

Past research with monolingual participants (dealing with only their own language) has shown that having **distractors** present on the computer screen influences how long it takes the participant to respond. **Distractors are strings of letters that resemble the test word** in some way.

Sometimes **neighbors** are used as distractors; these are real words in either of the test languages. They are defined as **words differing by a single letter**, but with order and word length maintained. So, for example, the English word *word* has neighbors in English that include the word *work*. In both identifying and processing distractors and target words, spelling conventions as well as phonology (pronunciation) are involved.

Sometimes there are distractors that are called **enemies**. An enemy may resemble the target word in its spelling, but it **differs in how it's pronounced**. So in English, *word* and *wore* are enemies because their vowels are pronounced differently even though they are both written as "o".

A word from the other language that is **a translation generally speeds up reaction time**. But it is also possible that a word from the other language that is semantically related to the target word, but is not a translation, will slow down response time. For example, an English-Spanish bilingual may be told to judge whether words flashed on a screen can be words in English. The participant may say "yes" to the English word *man*, but if it is followed by the Spanish word *mujer* 'woman', it may take the participant longer to reject this as a possible English word. The reason, of course, is that the concept of "woman" is related to the concept of "man", even though *mujer* is not an English word.

10.7.3 Distractors from both languages

The interesting issue with bilingual participants is **to what extent neighbors matter**, and whether their effect varies if they are from the participants' L1 or their L2. One representative study involved Dutch participants who were bilingual in English. They were asked to judge whether a word on a computer screen was an English word. The study showed that response time was slowed down if there were neighbors from *either* language on the screen at the same time as the test word (Van Heuven et al., 1998). In a related test, the response times of monolingual English speakers weren't slowed down at all with Dutch neighbors, only English ones. The obvious conclusion is that monolingual English speakers do not access Dutch words, but English-Dutch bilinguals may well access them, even when told to pay attention only to English words.

But there was another interesting finding. In a second block of tests, the fluent Dutch **bilinguals got used to having English neighbors on the screen**. What happened is that having them present didn't slow down response time on Dutch as much as it did in the first block of tests. In commenting on this finding later, Dijkstra and van Heuven (2002: 179) said this response suggested that **very fluent bilinguals can filter out one of their languages** under certain conditions.

10.7.4 Distractors and level of proficiency

One study about distractors did compare bilinguals who had three different levels of proficiency. In this study of French-English bilinguals, more advanced bilinguals seemed to have a harder time avoiding paying attention to distractors than the less proficient ones (Bijeljac-Babic et al., 1997). The experiment took this form: A "prime word" (a non-relevant word) in either English or French preceded the actual test or target word, which was in English in one series of tests and French in another. The prime words were high-frequency words and could belong to either of the bilingual's two languages. The target words were low-frequency words or non-words that were pronounceable (their spelling conformed to the spelling rules of the language).

The key general result was this: **Very proficient bilinguals had slower response times** than less proficient ones. That is, very proficient bilinguals had slow response times when both the prime and the target words were from the same language, but had even slower response times when the prime and target words came from different languages.

Here are the details. First, when the prime word was in the *same* language as the target word and the two words were similar, response time in general was slower. It seemed that competition between processing the prime word and the target word canceled out any "same language help". For example, when English was the target language and *real* was the prime word and the target word was *heal*, response time was slower than when the prime word for *heal* was *roof*. Second, when the prime word and the target word came from *different* languages (e.g. a French prime word, such as *beau*, and an English target word, such as *beam*), this also slowed down response time. This second result is important because it indicates that both languages are "on" to some extent. Dijkstra and van Heuven (2002) cite these results to support their BIA+ model discussed below, as you will see.

10.7.5 Global effects as distractors

Another possible distractor in bilingual tests is what has been called **global lexical activation**. The idea is this: Does it matter if the subject has been using language X and then is asked to use language Y? Does the activation of language X carry over (i.e. become global)? Most studies seem to show there is some "**activation carryover**" from one language to the next. This includes not only carryover from what has been going on in the session, but also from what the participant is told at the beginning of the session about which language will be used. Again, a finding such as this indicates that both of the bilingual's languages are "on".

10.8 Summary on experiments

10.8.1 Lexical decision tasks

Here is a summary of the main issues that lexical decision tasks address. Recall that these are one type of word-recognition tasks involving comprehension. Lexical decision tasks can consist of presenting words from only one language or from more than one of the bilingual's languages. Words can be presented on a computer screen or in a picture (cf. Kroll and Dijkstra, 2002).

- **Speed**. Response time is a little slower in proficient bilinguals than it is in monolinguals. In one test, response time was about 500–50 milliseconds for English monolinguals and about 660 milliseconds for relatively proficient Dutch-English bilinguals. The time to name pictures is faster in L1 than in L2.
- **Proficiency and other factors affecting selection**. L2 proficiency matters a good deal, but the demands of the particular task and the expectations about language choice that instructions set up also matter.
- **Frequency effects**. As you might guess, common words are responded to more quickly than uncommon words. This result seems to hold even if words are matched for length. So we would expect the word for *table* to be responded to more quickly than that for *token*, whatever the language.
- **Context effects**. It should come as no surprise that words in the context in which they normally occur are responded to more quickly than words with no context or an unnatural context. So if a subject has been asked to respond to the English word *bacon* on the screen and then *eggs* is the next word, response time is faster than for *eggs* with no context, or in the context of terms for clothing.
- **Stimulus effects**. Sometimes participants are asked to respond to a picture of an object, not a string of letters; this can make some difference. Also, sometimes a letter string is hard to see because some pattern is superimposed over it. Generally, this does not slow down word recognition.
- **Neighbors and enemies**. If words that resemble the target word (and are in the same language as the target word) appear on the computer screen, having either neighbors or enemies can slow down response time in bilinguals. Recall that neighbors and enemies are defined in section 10.7.2.
- **Late activation.** When a distractor word in the non-target language is present, its effect is some slowing down of reaction time on the target word. But there is no evidence that these non-target words are actually pronounced.
- **Word/non-word effects**. When nonsense words (e.g. *tlurk*) are flashed on the screen, they are generally rejected pretty quickly. Nonsense words that conform to the phonotactics of the test language (phonotactics = permissible combinations of letters) are also rejected, but it takes the subject slightly longer to do this.

10.8.2 Lexical access tasks

Some of the generalizations just mentioned for lexical decision tasks (which are comprehension tasks) also apply to lexical access tasks, even though these are production tasks. Again, whether the speaker is a monolingual or a bilingual makes a difference; monolinguals respond faster than bilinguals. Also, frequency matters; that is, if a word is frequently used in ordinary speech, response time is shorter than with less frequently used words. And finally, if a context has been established, and the target word normally occurs in that context, response time is shorter. Here are some other generalizations about findings; see Kroll and de Groot (1997) for more details.

- **Proficiency**. Research centers on whether the nature of processing of the L2 is different from that of the L1 and on changes in processing with increased L2 proficiency.
- **Competition**. Evidence from a variety of experiments indicates that the bilingual's languages compete for selection, especially if there are no language-specific cues on which language to select (e.g. in naming pictures).
- **Conceptual effects**. Concrete words and cognates are translated faster than abstract words and non-cognates, but the effects of cognates are greater for less fluent L2 speakers.
- **Response time**. Producing a word (**lexical access**) takes longer than performing a comprehension task (**lexical decision**).
- **Language effect in translation**. Translation from an L2 to an L1 is slower than from an L1 to an L2. (The explanation offered is that restoring the L1 to its level before the L2 was activated requires more effort (time) than going from the L1 to the L2. This effect is discussed further under the Inhibitory Control model in section 10.9.1.)

10.9 Models of language production

In most models of language production, either monolingual or bilingual language, the model begins with the mental lexicon; that is, the pre-linguistic conceptual level is not discussed. The bilingual's intentions determine whether a lemma from language X or language Y is called to satisfy the intentions to be expressed. But considering what might affect the speaker's decision to use language X rather than language Y is another story. Obviously level of proficiency is a factor, but so are various social considerations. A full discussion is beyond the scope of this chapter, but see the speculative discussions in Myers-Scotton and Jake (1995); Myers-Scotton (2002).

10.9.1 When is the phonological form in place?

One big difference across models is in the answer this question: At what level is the phonological form of a word (its actual surface-level form) in place? This difference is related to the general issue of whether production involves **serial activation** (first one level of production is activated and then another, but with no feedback) or if there can be **interaction of levels** ("cascading" or spreading of activation from one level to the next).

Compare two models. The **Levelt et al. model** (1999) predicts serial activation. Thus, there is no activation of actual word form (phonology) until what is basically the surface level. The **Dell et al. model** (1997) allows for feedback and early interaction between words that are similar in form, such as *dog* and *frog*, or similar in meaning, *cat* and *dog*).

10.9.2 Other issues about timing in production

Another issue, of course, is the relationship between syntactic and phonological information; that is, is all syntactic information retrieved before or after word-form (phonological) information? Yet another issue is whether all directions to assemble units larger than a word (phrases and full clauses) are available in the same way or at the same time.

10.9.3 Adding bilinguals to language-production models

Models that are more strictly for bilingual production have more to consider; they must account for how the speakers control output so that they are performing whatever task is at hand in one language rather than the other. This can be thought of as **the selection problem**. Although many of the researchers refer to the problem as if selection involves a full language, their focus is on selecting words, possibly because most of their experiments have dealt only with words. That is, it is important to recognize that bilingual models are often models of the bilingual lexicon, *not of the entire system* (including grammar) that is involved in language production.

Three current models are discussed briefly, but there are many alternative candidates. Two of the models discussed are production models (the **Inhibitory Control model** and the **Revised Hierarchical model**. These are "top-down" models, with accounts beginning at a conceptual level and comparing languages in regard to how one language is more activated than the other or how meanings may be differently accessed in the two languages. The third model, the **BIA+** model, is a model of how both languages may be activated in word recognition or comprehension. It is a "bottom-up" model because it deals with word form, not word meaning.

10.9.3.1 The Inhibitory Control model

As its name suggests, the **Inhibitory Control (IC) model** of Green (1998) offers answers to the questions related to how bilinguals keep from producing both of their languages at the same time when this isn't their intention. This model assumes that there is a supervisory attentional system (SAS) that controls the activation of "task schemas". A task may be something such as naming a picture or translating a word, so the motivation to inhibit a language depends on non-linguistic contexts external to a language or its word.

The key to this model is that **the activation or inhibition of schemas is what regulates language selection**. Language-task schemas can send directions to access a word from "the lexico-semantic system" (i.e. the mental lexicon, composed of abstract entries underlying actual surface forms). But the SAS has to specify the required language to the task schemas (information the SAS gets from the conceptualizer in a top-down fashion). Green states, "A language task schema regulates the outputs from the lexico-semantic system by altering the activation levels of presentation within that system and by inhibiting outputs from the system" (p. 69). If a task is not maintained as a goal, other schemas can inhibit the original schema, possibly producing different results (a different language).

Motivation for the model is that research shows that when the participant is asked to switch in the context of an experiment, the switch has costs in terms of reaction time (Meuter and Allport, 1999). If the participant has been using L2, the L1 has to be suppressed for the speaker to activate L2. Now, if the participant is told to switch to L1, the reaction time is relatively long because the former suppression of the L1 has to be changed to suppression of the L2. Note that it doesn't matter that the L1 is the dominant language; what matters is the cost of switching to the L1 because the L1 had been suppressed before the switch.

Note that at least one other study, using the brain-imaging technique of Event Related Potentials, shows that for very fluent Spanish-English bilinguals, to read and recall the switching of one final word in an English clause to a semantically related Spanish word when the expected word would have been English is less costly (in response time) than processing an unexpected English synonym of the expected word (Moreno et al., 2002). The implication is that the intention to produce a certain meaning (even in another language) is more salient (in terms of reaction time) than maintaining the language in use. That is, the lexico-semantic system is more salient in language-task schemas than other systems at this point.

10.9.3.2 The Revised Hierarchical model

In a second model oriented to bilingual production, Kroll and Stewart (1994) hypothesize differences in how L1 and L2 words are accessed in order to explain at least part of selection in their **Revised Hierarchical model**. Like many others, they propose that words that are translation equivalents are connected. In this model, counterparts across languages are connected in two ways – both through a common concept that they stand for, but also by direct associative links that are at the word level. But the critical point is that **this model gives preference to the L1**. Its words are more strongly connected to concepts than are L2 words. L2 words have a stronger connection of another sort: they are assumed to be more strongly connected to their L1 counterpart words than L1 words are connected to the L2 counterparts.

Motivations for this model come from what is assumed to happen with late learners of an L2, such as students in a high school or college classroom. Obviously, they have strong connections between concepts and their L1 words. The model claims that the learners initially have strong connections for L2 words with L1 words, *not* with concepts themselves. As bilinguals become more proficient, they develop stronger and more direct associations with concepts (and do not mediate them through the L1). This model has been tested in a number of experiments involving translation tasks, but with mixed results.

However, one pattern consistently emerges: the performance (reaction rate in translating) of more proficient speakers of the L2 was more similar in both directions (from L1 to L2 and from L2 to L1). That is, for very proficient bilinguals **translation in both directions involves a connection to the concept**, not a connection to the word (L2 word to L1 word) as originally hypothesized.

10.9.3.3 *The Bilingual Interactive Activation + model*

Finally, consider a model that is oriented toward comprehension, the **Bilingual Interactive Activation** (BIA+) model of Dijkstra and van Heuven (2002). The BIA+ is the latest version of the BIA model of 1994. It's called an interactive model because feedback between levels in the system of language production is allowed. But it is also a bottom-up model. This means selection of a language, in effect, **starts with activating the phonological and orthographic features** (sound and letter features) of a word. Furthermore, the assumption is that lexical access to both languages occurs at the same time (counterpart words in both languages are activated together). That is, **this model rejects a powerful language-specific inhibition mechanism** that would be found in a top-down model (in which the initial selection is to inhibit one language and activate the other). There is inhibition within the BIA+ model, but it is more like the task schema inhibition of Green's model (i.e. task demands affect which language is more activated and which one is inhibited). Dijkstra and van Heuven recognize that it's possible that selection of the language of a word may be a global choice (for example, made at the clause level or larger discourse level). But they say a second option is more compatible with their model. This "option" (really a theoretical claim) is that "language nodes cannot activate or suppress word activation to any considerable extent" (p. 187).

As noted earlier, a bottom-up model seems to assume an integrated (bilingual) lexicon of sorts in the sense that one word form can activate a similar word form in another language. In contrast, a top-down model assumes the possibility of activating both languages at once, but, perhaps more importantly, the possibility of one language as more active than the other and therefore as able to suppress the other. This must mean maintaining separation between the languages at the lemma level. For more on speech production models, see Nicol (2001) as well as contributions to Kroll and De Groot (2005). See especially Kroll and Tokowicz in the Kroll and De Groot volume.

10.10 Memory

Many studies have attempted to understand what we call **memory**. That is, are there changes in the brain after animals (and humans are animals) learn a task or have an experience? And how long does that change stay in effect? Most researchers agree that there is some modification in some structures in the brain, including some structural modification of synapses (connections). Neurologists have identified areas of the brain associated with a storing process (Luria, 1976; Squire, 1987). These are the cortical areas that also support cognitive processes, including language. But what changes occur are largely unknown, even though a name has been given to what happens, **long-term potentiation**, with the implication that a potential exists to recall the task or experience.

10.10.1 The history of memory studies

We can point to two important advances in the history of memory studies. First, objective criteria have been established to study memory capacity, with the most important criterion known as **span**. Memory span for numbers and words corresponds to the number of elements in a sequence that a person can repeat correctly at least 50% of the time. We also learn pattern recognition, such as their pattern and how many numbers to expect in phone numbers. In general, the average human can remember (and repeat) seven digits "plus or minus two". (But an individual's span varies with the type of material that he or she is asked to repeat. For example, sound sequences not found in the individual's language or nonsense words are hard to repeat.)

Second, William James's distinction between primary and secondary memory (James, 1890) was refined to referring to **short- and long-term memory**, but then in the 1960s to **short- and long-term store**. Evidence from normal persons supported this distinction, but even stronger evidence came from comparing memory loss in patients with brain lesions, especially two patients.

One patient, called HM, has been observed for more than 30 years by the Canadian neuropsychologist Brenda Miller. In order to treat this patient's epilepsy, the connection between his temporal lobes was severed. After surgery he still showed his normal level of intelligence and linguistic competence. But his **capacity to store new memories** in his long-term memory had been affected. For example, he couldn't remember his psychologist's name or whether he had read a magazine or not. But he could remember what he had learned or events that had happened before the operation, such as his school or childhood friends. He also could learn certain tasks calling for motor control, such as drawing pictures, but then he couldn't remember having done it.

A few years later, English neuropsychologists observed a patient (called KF) who had the reverse problems; he had only **limited short-term memory**. KF had suffered a left hemisphere lesion, but he didn't have symptoms of language loss (aphasia). Instead he had a very limited short-term verbal memory span of only two to three numbers. He had a normal learning capacity and long-term memory.

Findings from these two patients substantiate the existence of two general memory systems, a short-term memory system and a long-term memory system (Fabbro, 1999). HM had lost his long-term memory capacity but kept his short-term memory and KF kept his long-term memory but had only limited short-term memory.

10.10.2 Dividing up long-term store

By the 1980s, research on memory in amnesic patients indicated that there were divisions within the long-term store. Some patient retained skills from the period before their injury/loss and acquired new skills after the loss. But "in no case did patients have any significant recollection of the events that gave rise to this learning" (Parkin, 2001). For example, a patient could be shown pictures in an experiment, but then not remember them an hour later. Such findings led researchers to divide up the long-term store into three parts: episodic, semantic, and procedural memory. **Episodic memory** refers to recollections of specific events as opposed to other types of consciously available memories (**semantic memory**). Some studies of this type of memory, as it applies to bilinguals, are discussed in the next section. Many researchers now group semantic and episodic memory together under the label "declarative", referring to any memory that is consciously accessible (Parkin, 2001). Declarative and procedural memory, and their relation to second-language learning, are discussed in chapter 11.

10.10.3 Bilinguals and their episodic memories

When bilinguals are recalling a past experience, what language do they use? Does it matter what language is being used in the current interaction? Does our memory system store a memory in the language in which the recalled experience actually occurred? Reports from bilinguals about their memories are intriguing. To take one example, an L1 English-speaking student of mine reports that he remembers *in English* conversations he had in German even though he speaks German very fluently. Experiments about bilinguals and their memories of events study such individuals. We will review just two experiments. A special issue of the *International Journal of Bilingualism* is devoted to articles on episodic memory (Pavlenko, Schrauf, and Dewaele, 2003).

10.10.3.1 *The reminiscence bump in memories*

One study of older bilinguals focused on what researchers call the "**reminiscence bump**". This term stands for the frequent finding that participants recall a greater number of memories for events between the age of 10 and 30 than would be expected by chance. The vividness of memories in this bump is generally explained because it is the period when a young person assumes an adult identity.

Schrauf and Rubin (1998) wanted to see if the **time of immigration** was a second "bump". They observed 12 Spanish-English bilinguals between the ages of 61 and 69 who had all immigrated permanently to the United States between the ages of 20 and 35. Although these bilinguals still used Spanish at the time of the experiment (especially with family), English was their dominant language in many situations, such as with workmates and neighbors. They indicated both languages were used in some situations, especially with their children and friends. Five of the 12 said they used only English with their spouses.

All participants took part in two sessions, one with English as the language of the interaction and one with Spanish as the interaction language. They were given priming words and asked to associate each word with a memory and then write a few words about it. The participants who had immigrated in their early 20s did have more memories from the 10 to 30 age range. But those who immigrated later (34–5) showed a marked decrease in memories from the 10 to 30 "bump" range; instead, the period around immigration seemed associated with the most memories. This finding supported the hypothesis that **immigration (a vivid event) has an effect** on the distribution of numbers of memories over the life span.

Finally, the researchers asked participants to comment on any sense they had of an "internal language" associated with specific memories. The participants said that about 20 percent of the total memories occurred internally in the language that didn't match the priming word or the written descriptions they produced. The self-reported match with other findings was mixed. Some participants said they "thought in Spanish" for certain memories even though the prime word and the written descriptions they produced were in English. But some said memories occurred in English as inner memories, even though the session was in Spanish.

What was interesting is that 82% of memories identified as Spanish in internal speech occurred before migration. So only 18% of internal memories from that period were in English. After migration, the percentage of internal memories in English is higher (65%), with only 35% of such memories in Spanish.

When a speaker learned English also mattered a great deal. Almost everything that happened to a participant before he or she learned English was remembered in Spanish. Of 110 memories recalled in English, only two are of events occurring before the participants' first formal contact with English, and these two came from the same person.

10.10.3.2 Does language choice follow the interaction language?

Memory studies of bilinguals frequently have centered around whether the language of a "priming" word makes a difference in the language the bilingual uses to tell his or her story. In a second experiment, the researchers tested the effect of such priming words. Results are mixed. Schrauf and Rubin, whose participants were in their sixties, found that Spanish words did not, on average, call up older memories than English words. But Marian and Neisser (2000), who studied younger bilinguals, found that the L1 did call up more memories overall, but the language of the interview also made a difference.

In addition to considering the effects of priming words, Marian and Neisser paid attention to what they called the "ambient language" (that is, the language that was being used by the experimenter and the participant in conversation in the particular test). Participants were told the experiment was a study of "storytelling in different languages" and they were told they could speak either of their languages, or use both in codeswitching. They were told a priming word would be heard just to bring to mind a story. They found that the **ambient language seemed to make more of a difference** than the language of the priming words.

In the first of two experiments, participants were 20 Russian-English bilingual university students who had immigrated to the United States at a mean age of 14. Their average age was 22 at the time of the test. The prediction was that participants would recall more stories in the language of the priming word than in their other language. (Half of the time the priming word was in English and half of the time in Russian.) This indeed is what happened, but **overall the bilinguals accessed more stories in Russian than in English** (160 Russian memories, 92 English memories, and 66 in both languages, i.e. codeswitching). When interviewed in Russian, they accessed more Russian memories (5.15 out of a possible 8) than when interviewed in English (2.85 memories out of a possible 8). When interviewed in English, they accessed more English memories. They accessed mixed Russian-English memories more or less equally when the interview language was either Russian or English. Also, results showed that stories were told in Russian when an event had occurred in Russian, in English for English events, and in Russian-English with bilingual Russians or sometimes mixed company of English and Russian speakers.

In a second experiment, 24 similar Russian-English bilingual university students took part. Half of the interactions had Russian as the medium of interaction and half had English. The difference was that four of the eight priming words were in a different language from the interaction language. This time both the language of the interaction and the priming word had significant effects, but the interaction language (the "ambient language") had stronger effects, and there was no interaction between the two effects. Participants recalled **more Russian memories when interviewed in the Russian than when interviewed in English**. They also recalled more memories to Russian word prompts than to English ones; but they also recalled more Russian memories overall to either prompt. Still, **when the interview language was English, they retrieved more English memories**. There were 248 memories of events in which Russian was spoken, 91 of events in which English was spoken, and 45 in which both languages were spoken. (In both experiments, more participants said they considered English their dominant language than those who said Russian was.)

These results imply that speakers do get into a particular mode, but this seems to be a little different from the "bilingual or monolingual modes" that Grosjean (1998a) proposes exist for bilinguals, since it is the mode or "mindset" for a particular language, not just the idea of speaking monolingually.

10.10.4 Declarative and procedural memory

Leaving aside the debate about dividing episodic and semantic memory or grouping them together under declarative memory, we will concentrate on the more semantic aspects of declarative memory as it relates to bilinguals. **Declarative memory** is also called **explicit memory**, and **procedural memory** is also called **implicit memory**. Think of these as two different stores for two different types of knowledge. Declarative memory refers to knowledge that is learned and the individual can express it at will (e.g. What is the capital of Russia? What is the word used in most of the world for what Americans call soccer?). There are two subtypes of declarative memory: **semantic memory** (encyclopedic knowledge of things learned about the world); and **episodic memory** (past experiences that we can recall consciously). Note that semantic memory includes the meaning of words that you've learned.

Procedural memory refers to learning (or acquisition) that may have depended on repeated execution of a task, but how much awareness was involved in the task varies. A defining feature of such knowledge is that "what it is" is not something you can articulate. And it's knowledge used without conscious control.

The best example of knowledge in procedural memory is the acquisition of certain aspects of your first language. Without your awareness, you acquired sensory-motor sequences for the production of sounds in that language, well-formedness conditions on how sentences are constructed in that language, etc. If asked to tell someone these things about your language, you will be hard pressed to do it unless you've studied your language formally when you were in school. And even then, you "know" much that you can't relate.

There is evidence that declarative and procedural memory are involved in the learning of different systems of a language. Clinical studies using neuroimaging techniques to study which areas of the brain are activated during specific tests show different areas for different linguistic tasks. Specifically, tasks involving grammatical elements show activation in different areas of the brain than when the task is to name content words (nouns, verbs). Also, a related proposal is that a bilingual's L1 is stored in a different memory than an L2 learned after early childhood. You'll read more on this in chapter 11.

10.10.5 Working memory

Researchers postulate that a system called **working memory** exists. It is assumed to contain and process information but to contain it only temporarily. The assumption is that working memory takes part in tasks such as reasoning, comprehension, and learning. It includes a phonological store (where verbal information is kept for two or fewer seconds). **Subvocal rehearsal (inner speech)** can refresh traces in the phonological store so that verbal stimuli are maintained for about ten seconds.

Working memory, especially the phonological store, may have something to do with acquiring the ability to speak both one's L1 and any L2s. When an individual is just learning an L2, his or her memory span in that language seems disrupted. At least, if participants in an experiment are performing the number span test and at the same time they are asked to pronounce irrelevant syllables, this causes a problem for the **subvocal rehearsal process** and partially inhibits memory span. Problems involving the individual's working memory may be at the root of some learning disorders, such as types of dyslexia.

If you speak a language in which numbers have more than one syllable, you may not perform as well on a span test as a speaker of another language. Digit span tests and various other mental calculations prove the effects of working memory because **storage "space"** is needed in order to perform such calculations. Studies have shown that bilingual Welsh children take longer to memorize Welsh numbers than English numbers and, if they use Welsh, don't perform as well as English children (using English) in a span test. But the reason seems to be that numbers in Welsh have more syllables than numbers in English. So the memory span for the same number of digits in languages with more syllables is shorter than in a language, such as English, with numbers that contain only one syllable. That is, Welsh takes up more "space".

Some researchers claim that phonological short-term memory plays a role in enabling individuals to learn both native and L2 vocabulary (Brown and Hulme, 1992). For example, a study found a relationship between how well four-year-old children could repeat non-words that they were taught and their vocabulary skills in a real language a year later. Another study showed that skill in repeating non-words predicts success in learning English as a foreign language.

A "verbal trace decay model" has received some support to explain span in short-term memory. That is, "memory span is equal to the amount of material that can be rehearsed [as subvocal inner speech] in a fixed time" (Brown and Hulme, 1992: 109). For example, as children grow older, their speech rate corresponds with an increase in memory span. But production in an L2 may depend on other factors. Still it is the case that memory span (of digits) seems to be shorter in an L2 than in the speaker's L1.

One hypothesis to explain this **reduced memory span in an L2** is that the speaker's long-term memory contribution to the short-term memory capacity is somehow reduced. The study by Brown and Hulme of memories of lexical items supports this hypothesis. They found that memory in English speakers who did not know Italian was less accurate when Italian words were simply presented in their pronunciation form than it was when the speakers learned the meanings of the Italian words along with their pronunciation. The assumption is some construction of long-term memory representations of these Italian words (based on learning their pronunciation *and* meaning) aided their short-term memory. The evidence that their short-term memory increased was that their speech rate in Italian and their ability to repeat the words improved. If this is so, then any process that increases the rate of pronunciation of L2 materials or improves long-term memory for their pronunciation will aid in L2 learning.

10.10.6 Separate memory systems for L2s?

A recurring research question for psycholinguists and neurolinguists has been whether the bilingual's languages are stored in separate memory systems. Instead, a better question seems to be: If a bilingual's languages are learned at different ages, does this make a difference to how the memory systems are differentially involved in their learning? Among others, M. Paradis (1994; 2001) has had much to say about this. Evidence points to this answer: An L1 is learned by means of implicit strategies (procedural memory results), or at least, critical aspects of the L1's grammatical apparatus depend on procedural memory. But an L2 may be learned more formally, involving memorizing words and grammatical structures, employing mainly or entirely declarative memory). Evidence comes from many sources, but especially from certain types of aphasia in which the bilingual's two languages are not both lost or both retained. Again, this difference between how procedural and declarative memory function in language acquisition is discussed further in chapter 11.

Two techniques for the study of neural structures provide new information about cognitive tasks and activation in brain areas. These are positron emission tomography (PET) and functional magnetic resonance imaging (fMRI). PET involves an injection of slightly radioactive substances. The prime structures activated during the execution of a cognitive task take up the injection more than others. The resulting images are called ERPs (event-related brain potentials). Many researchers, using electrophysiological techniques, have substantiated the hypothesis that syntactic and semantic processes are organized in separate areas of the brain (e.g. Neville and her associates, 1992; 1996; 1997).

Of most interest to readers of this volume is that studies show that there seems to be a difference in brain activation, depending on when an L2 is learned. For example, certain areas of the frontal lobe structures seem to organize certain grammatical components of language only if the language is learned at an early age. Some results from brain imaging studies of early versus late bilinguals are discussed in chapter 11.

10.11 Bilingualism, the brain, and aphasia

Aphasia is the formal term for the partial or total loss of the ability to speak and/or comprehend language; it is caused by injuries or disease, including stroke. And it is more common than many people realize. Worldwide, there are about 300,000 new cases of aphasia every year. Of these, 40,000 may be cases of bilingual aphasia (M. Paradis, 2001). There is more study of bilingual aphasia than ever, partly because most studies are conducted in the Western nations that have seen a good number of immigrants, either bringing bilingualism with them or developing it in their new homes.

Some of these patients recover their speech and some recover only partially. But the fact that the different languages in a bilingual aphasic's repertoire may be affected differently is evidence for the claim that languages are supported by different subsystems, not by a single common system (Fabbro, 2001). We speak of bilinguals in this overview, but many times the aphasic patient speaks more than one L2; speakers of more than one L2 are sometimes called **polyglots** (especially in the aphasic literature).

More than with any other topic in this chapter, those psycholinguists who study aphasia almost necessarily are expected to propose a theory of how language is organized in the brain. That said, in spite of much research since the late 1800s, researchers still do not have clear answers to many basic questions regarding language loss in bilingual aphasia. The general idea that Pitres proposed in 1895 still seems like the best starting point. He suggested that when a language is lost, whether temporarily or permanently, it is not destroyed, but inhibited. On this view, the popular reference to "language loss" seems misdirected; the ability to speak may be lost, but the language may still be represented in the brain.

But the big questions still remain. To date there is no reliable correlation between aphasia and sites in the brain affected, or for that matter correlation with the patient's history of bilingualism (which language was acquired when and its pattern of use at the time of the injury). Thus, M. Paradis, one of the main figures in aphasia study, ends his 2001 survey of aphasia in reference to bilinguals with these rather basic questions: (1) Why does any particular bilingual aphasic patient have the particular pattern of language loss that he or she shows? and (2) Why does this same bilingual aphasic show better language recovery in one of his or her languages than the other? (M. Paradis, 2001).

There are practical as well as theoretical benefits in answering these questions. As Green (2005) points out, we need to understand bilingual aphasic recovery patterns in order to challenge current accounts of how language is represented in the brain, but also we need to understand better the patterns that aphasics show in recovery in order to have principled rehabilitation programs. Keep in mind that, in general, bilinguals make use of the same neural mechanisms as monolinguals; the results of brain damage are just complicated in bilinguals by the number of languages involved.

10.11.1 Patterns of recovery

There are a number of generalizations about bilinguals who are afflicted with aphasia.

(1) Aphasic bilinguals do not necessarily recover both or all of their languages. If they do recover either language or both, it is not necessarily at the same rate or to the same extent.

(2) The variation on patterns of bilingual aphasia and their recovery is surprising. In 1997, Paradis surveyed the world literature on this issue, classifying results into six basic patterns of recovery. (Some other researchers use other names for types of bilingual aphasia.) Aphasia is especially complicated with bilinguals: One or two languages may follow the same path, but then a third isn't recovered at all or much later. So even these basic patterns don't cover the entire scope of bilingual aphasia. Once more, there are a number of disorders having to do with translating problems.

- Parallel recovery: The most common pattern is that both languages are impaired in the same ways and both are restored at the same rate.
- Differential recovery: Each language shows a different degree of impairment.
- Successive recovery: One language doesn't begin to recover until the other has been largely recovered.
- Antagonistic recovery: One language loses ground as the other one improves.
- Selective recovery: The patient doesn't regain any recovery of one of the languages.

- Blended recovery: The patient systematically, but inappropriately, mixes his or her languages at all or nearly all levels of language (pronunciation, word and sentence structure, vocabulary, and meanings).

(3) Even though we can point to one type as most common (parallel recovery), if the numbers of recent cases are considered, you can see how spread out they are. Further, parallel recovery only accounts overall for 40 percent of the cases, according to Paradis (1997). To show how hard it is to generalize, Paradis (2001) categorizes the 132 cases of bilingual aphasia reported since 1978. Of these, 81 showed parallel recovery, 24 differential recovery, 12 blended language, 9 selective recovery, and 6 successive recovery.

10.11.2 Paradoxical aphasia

Some cases are truly mysterious and go under the name paradoxical aphasia. In these cases, the patient doesn't recover his or her main language immediately, but begins recovery by speaking a language the patient had been exposed to through religious services or only long ago and had not used recently. For example, in one case the patient was a Catholic priest whose L1 was French, but who also knew Latin, classical Greek, and basic biblical Hebrew. After the stroke, he could speak French, but his sentences consisted largely of a subject noun and a verb and nothing more. However, he continued to serve Mass and one day the researcher attended a service and was surprised to hear the patient speaking quite fluent Latin which was free from errors (Fabbro, 1999: 128).

In another case, a 70-year-old woman who had always spoken the Veronese dialect of Italian suffered damage in her left brain hemisphere. She was in a hospital where the staff spoke mainly her home dialect. The patient was mute for two weeks, but then started speaking Italian, a language she had only studied in elementary school for three years and which she spoke only two or three times a year as an adult. After a month, she understood both her home dialect and Italian, but spoke Italian. Eventually she spoke her home dialect (Veronese), but her verbal production was better in Italian (Fabbro, 1999: 132).

10.11.3 Some other representative cases

The following is a case of what is called selective crossed aphasia. A polyglot patient (he spoke more than two languages) who at age 24 underwent a neurosurgical operation initially spoke his home language of Gujarati (a language in India). But he was born and had lived in Madagascar and so spoke Malagasy as well. At age six, he learned French, which he later used in his work as an accountant. Two weeks after the operation, he spoke French normally. He had trouble with Gujarati, but after four months he recovered Gujarati.

At the same time, he had more difficulty in using Malagasy. Two years after the operation, tests showed his Gujarati was normal, but he had reduced fluency and made syntactic errors in Malagasy. Finally, four years after the operation, no disorders were detected in any of his languages (Fabbro, 1999: 135–6).

Just to illustrate another case, consider EG, who had a stroke at age 55 which affected the left temporal lobe. His L1 was Slovene and Italian was his L2. He also spoke Friulian (a Romance variety spoken in northern Italy) and English. After the stroke, he had semantic and syntactic problems with all of his languages (he suffered from what is called Wernicke's aphasia). Furthermore, he mixed all of his languages. For example, in answer to the question (in English), "Did you live in Germany?" EG said, "just think the wife, for [switching to Friulian] *su e ju, su e ju*, because would the problem here in [switching to Italian] *Italia* . . ." (Fabbro, 1999: 154).

Here's an example of a case of parallel recovery. This case involved a Korean-Japanese patient (Sasanuma and Park, 1995, cited in M. Paradis, 2001). The patient was raised in a monolingual Korean environment until age six. However, Korean and Japanese both figured in his education. His first nine years of schooling were only in Japanese and then his high school and college education was in Korean. For the two years before his stroke at age 62, he worked for a Korean-Japanese trading company. Also, he had maintained Japanese through yearly visits to Japan and by reading Japanese books and journals. Following his stroke, he could understand, read, and write both languages; but in speaking, he had more severe word-finding problems in Japanese than in Korean.

10.11.4 Tentative explanations for aphasia

To date, two general explanations about the relation between aphasia and how language is organized in the brain receive support: problems with activation and evidence for different subsystems for different languages. First, results suggest that a basic problem that aphasics experience is a **problem with activation** and/or related problems with other aspects of the control system. Also, this focus on activation is compatible with Green's general model (1986) accounting for how bilinguals control their languages. That model includes the components of resource input (i.e. language), activation, and inhibition.

Modern imaging techniques such as positron emission tomography (PET) and functional magnetic resonance imaging (fMRI) can identify areas of the brain associated with one task compared with another. And other studies have been able to associate a lesion in the basal ganglia of the left hempishere with a number of the features of aphasia, whether in a monolingual or a bilingual. The most prominent feature of aphasia associated with this lesion is just a general reduction in spontaneous speech, as well as voice disorders and writing disorders. Lesions in other areas of the left hemisphere seem to be related to many difficulties in retrieving words, either spontaneously or in a test.

But as Green (2005) points out, knowing that a certain area is activated does not tell us about its necessity. So he makes the point that a minimum of three techniques are necessary: neuropsychological assessment (studying the patient), data on lesion site, and neuroimaging data. Also, instead of just considering the lesion site, Green suggests that certain patterns of recovery can be a function of problems in controlling the language systems, rather than of damage to them. "Damage to different components of the control system may yield different outcomes." Or, the same outcome may be the result of different problems of control.

Further, Green points out that a basic question is the extent to which an L2 is processed differently from the L1. Recall the statements at the beginning of this chapter indicating that the languages of bilinguals seem to be located in the same regions (left hemisphere) as the language of a monolingual.

Analyses by M. Paradis (e.g. 2001) also support the role of activation in language. Also, Fabbro (1999: 212) points out that "[A] cerebral lesion can lower the activation threshold of a language, which is thus not lost, but simply inaccessible through the usual activation threshold." Recall that focusing on activation is similar to what Pitres suggested in the 1890s.

In proposing a second general explanation for aphasia, M. Paradis (2001) argues that patterns of recovery by aphasics support a **subsystem hypothesis**. Under this hypothesis, within the same cognitive system, there are subsystems for each language the bilingual speaks. Both languages have neural connections to this cognitive system, namely, the language system. In support of this hypothesis and against other views of how language is organized in bilinguals, Paradis states: "only [the subsystem hypothesis] is compatible with all patterns of recovery as well as with the bilingual's ability to mix languages [codeswitch] at each level of linguistic structure" (2001: 81). The issue of problems with activation comes up in studies of brain-damaged bilinguals who no longer can speak both of their languages equally (or equally well).

On this view, when both languages are impaired, this would mean that the linguistic system as a whole is impaired. And when only one language is impaired, this would indicate damage to only the subsystem supporting that language.

Paradis also points out that differences in performance by aphasic patients indicates that there is no need to argue that comprehension and production are two different and separable systems. Paradis says that if comprehension and production were in different systems, there would be patients who could produce in a language, but not comprehend in that language. And so far no cases exist of a patient who can produce speech or written language that express propositions but who can't comprehend propositions, either spoken or written (Paradis, 2001). If both are not affected in the same way by aphasia, the explanation may be that they have different "thresholds of activation", an idea present in Green's model mentioned above.

10.12 Summing up

Even though psycholinguists studying the mental processing of bilinguals must do so largely indirectly, they have been able to propose a number of conclusions based on experimental findings, some of which are linked with recent brain-imaging techniques.

- **Language in the brain**: Both monolinguals and bilinguals generally have their language centers in the left hemisphere of the brain.
- **Languages are not fused**: The bilingual's languages are separate subsystems within one cognitive system.
- **Abstract mental lexicon**: It contains lemmas (abstract entries) tagged for both languages.
- Both of a bilingual's languages can be **"on" at the same time**.
- Language comprehension: One way to study this in bilinguals is via **word recognition tasks** in experiments.
- Language production: One way to study this in bilinguals is via **lexical access tasks** in experiments.
- Studies of lexical access imply that the **bilingual's L1 is more activated** than the L2.
- **Studies of memories of events** in bilinguals indicate that when events happened and which language was dominant for the bilingual at that time seem to influence memory recall. Still, explanations of the association between memories of events and the language in which they are recalled are largely incomplete.
- **The neural basis of aphasia**, loss of language due to an illness or accident, largely remains a mystery although advances are being made with modern imaging techniques.
- Studies of asphasic patients give **indirect evidence about the areas of the brain** involved in language processing (both comprehension and production).

10.13 Word and phrases to remember

role of cognates in word-based experiments
distractors and reaction time in experiments
short- and long-term memory
declarative and procedural memory
reminiscence bumps in memory recall
subsystem hypothesis
paradoxical recovery in aphasia
parallel recovery in aphasia
differential recovery in aphasia

11

Age of Acquisition and Success with a Second Language

Multiple voices: Croatian-Australians in Australia

Peter Hlavac is an Australian businessman of Croatian descent who lives in Sydney. He was born in Australia, but acquired both Croatian and English as a young child. He travels to Europe often because he works for a manufacturer of optic instruments that does a lot of business with a German optic firm. Because of this business contact, he has learned enough German to carry on simple conversations with his German counterparts, but they speak English better than he speaks German, even though he studied German in both primary and secondary school. And because he doesn't trust his German ability well enough to carry on business, final negotiations are in English. Peter also studied French in school, but he has few opportunities to use it except when reading menus in French restaurants in Sydney. He and his wife, who also comes from a Croatian-speaking background, are trying to raise their first child bilingually on the one person, one language approach; Peter's wife speaks only Croatian with their three-year-old son because her Croatian is better than Peter's and he speaks English only with their son.

11.1 Introduction

Are those two- and three-year-olds who speak two languages really budding geniuses? And why, after years of study, can't you speak your second language "like a native" no matter how hard you try? This chapter considers questions and answers that have to do with when a person becomes bilingual. First, we consider children who are raised as bilinguals, basically from infancy. Then we consider others who become bilingual at a later age and in generally a formal way – through classroom instruction in a second language. As we'll see, the two ways to become bilingual have very different results.

There are two general questions and their answers that we'll be considering. First, why is the degree of bilingualism of child bilinguals different from that of speakers who acquire a second language (L2) at a later age? That is, is there a cut-off point in language acquisition so that second-language learning is less successful after a certain age? Second, what are the factors that account for the difficulties and degree of success that later learners have in acquiring an L2?

Bilingual child language acquisition generally refers to acquiring two or more languages when exposed to them as a very young child. For such children "acquisition" means spontaneous learning with little or no obvious effort or instruction. However, researchers who study later bilingualism also use the term "acquisition", but they use it to cover both bilingualism as a later event with no formal instruction *and* learning as an event involving classroom teaching. In fact, the name given to the study of theories to explain degrees of successful bilingualism beyond early childhood is **second language acquisition** (SLA). One of the main figures in SLA defines SLA as "the way in which people learn a language other than their mother tongue, inside or outside of a classroom" (R. Ellis, 1997: 3). In this chapter, we will use "acquisition" and "learning" somewhat interchangeably when referring to this later bilingualism. Keep in mind, though, that generally more explicit learning than unconscious acquisition seems to be involved in late bilingualism. Without pinning down the exact age, we'll use the term **late bilingualism** for a second language added to one's repertoire after early childhood.

We end this introduction by beginning to answer two questions many people have about the relation between childhood language acquisition and later L2 acquisition. First, is it possible to acquire these linguistic systems in **two languages simultaneously** with **native-like competence** as a young child? The answer is "yes". Child bilinguals can acquire two (or even more) languages. They can do this as long as they are exposed to them, although they tend eventually to develop dominance in one of them because it's used more. Now another introductory question: Why does native-like acquisition of an L2 seem so difficult at a later age? Sorry, but there isn't a clear answer to this question. True, **near-native** acquisition at a later age can occur for a few learners. But note that we say only "near-native". Very, very few learners who start a language beyond early childhood achieve native-like competence. Whether there is a clear cut-off age for true native-like acquisition and what that age is still remain controversial; but evidence clearly shows there is a decline in the ability to achieve the same control of an L2 that L1 speakers of that language have. We all know bright and motivated teenagers or adults who have studied a second language conscientiously and who may speak the studied language well, but certainly not as native speakers do. In the following sections, we'll elaborate on the answers just given by presenting relevant research findings.

11.2 Introducing child bilingualism

There are many questions that most people have about what is involved when very young children speak two or more languages. (As we've noted in other chapters, our discussion will refer to two languages, while assuming that bilingualism can mean more than two languages.) These questions revolve around two themes: The first theme concerns **differentiating the two languages**. Is it possible for the child to speak both languages well, but keep them separate? When these child bilinguals speak, do they just speak whatever comes out first, or do they mix languages, or what? The second theme concerns the **age of acquisition**. Is there a cut-off point in language acquisition so that second-language learning is more difficult after a certain age? That is, what kind of support is there for a **critical age hypothesis**, the proposal that after a certain age, second-language learning cannot be done with the same ease as it can for very young children? Another question is, how do the abilities in a given language of early bilinguals seem to differ from those of later bilinguals? These questions are answered in the following sections.

11.2.1 Doing what is natural: acquiring language

Many readers who come from largely monolingual societies (e.g. the United States) or societies where second languages are usually learned only in school (e.g. many Western European countries) look upon very young children who speak two or more languages as linguistic marvels. We sometimes think such children must be super-intelligent to "master" speaking two languages before they can tie their shoes or ride a bicycle. But these little bilinguals are not linguistic wizards; they are simply doing what children of normal intelligence can do. That is, they acquire the language varieties to which they are exposed.

All normal children come with a genetic program that predisposes them to acquire human languages. Exactly what this program includes remains controversial; it's part of the general **"nature–nurture" debate** as to how much language development is dependent upon **cognitive pre-programming** specifically designed for building a language. Those who favor "nature" refer to the role of Universal Grammar (UG), which is more fully defined and discussed in 11.8.3 where second-language acquisition and UG is discussed. One of the most prominent researchers on UG in SLA, Lydia White, defines UG this way: "UG constitutes the child's initial state (S_0), the knowledge that the child is equipped with in advance of input" (2003b: 2).

The contrasting view (the "nurture view") is that language development is the product of **general learning mechanisms**. The idea is that humans, with exposure to a language in use, can use these general mechanisms to develop language through analogical thinking and other forms of associationism.

No matter which side one takes, evidence supports the assumption that **some sort of innate faculty** underlies language acquisition. This evidence is the finding that children all over the world go through similar stages when they acquire the grammatical systems of their specific languages. If we didn't have an innate faculty that figures in language acquisition, it would be hard to explain the similarities that are found around the world in these steps in acquiring different languages. Also, both children who end up as monolinguals and those who are early bilinguals go through **similar stages of acquisition**. De Houwer (2005) surveyed studies of 29 bilingual children between the ages of one and nearly six years old and established that the children's language-specific development differed little from that of a monolingual's development in only one of their languages. In addition, Genesee (2003) surveyed 14 published studies of young bilinguals who were compared with monolinguals of a similar age. With two exceptions, the rate of bilingual development was comparable to or within the same age range reported for monolingual children. A difference, of course, is that the bilinguals went through the developmental stages for two languages. Thus, **the natural outcome** for children is to speak whatever parents and other caregivers speak with them, whether it's one language or two or even more.

11.2.1.1 *Exposure to language is important*

Do small children need actual **exposure to a language in use** (by other humans) in order to develop a linguistic system (i.e. a language)? This question is not really open to the amassing of empirical evidence (after all, experiments that isolate babies aren't acceptable!), but we can confidently assume the answer is "yes". How important the *extent and quality of exposure* is remains a question, but clearly exposure is vital. We only know about a handful of children who were somehow isolated from exposure to a language. But they were found when they were no longer very young children. For example, there is the case of two girls in India in the 1920s who were possibly raised by animals in the wild and the case of Genie, a girl discovered in 1970 in California, who had been deprived of human contact. Such **feral children** did not ever fully acquire a language after they were found, but there were other factors to consider, such as their unknown level of intelligence and, of course, their age.

Evidence does show that whatever language(s) children are exposed to are acquired. Acquisition is largely complete by the ages of three or four; this depends somewhat on the complexity of grammatical elements in the language. Further, all children – monolinguals or bilinguals – acquire languages apparently effortlessly; that is, they do so **without overt instruction**, no matter how much parents or others think their "teaching" is involved in the success story. Understand that we are referring largely to pronunciation and grammar and a limited vocabulary as child language acquisition. To learn anything like an adult vocabulary takes longer and requires the experience that comes with age and possibly schooling. Also, learning certain syntactic structures found in formal styles almost certainly requires schooling.

Some readers may mistakenly think that children (or adults) who speak a non-standard dialect of a language have not acquired the language "properly". True, these people may not have acquired the standard dialect of that language, but that's not the point. Children **acquire whatever variety** of a language they are exposed to. That is, they are able to produce and understand sentences that their community considers well-formed (i.e. "grammatical" in that community's view). Some speakers never acquire the standard dialect, simply because they are not sufficiently exposed to it, or because they have no desire to do so for many possible reasons. Many learn the standard dialect in school, possibly replacing certain structures in their home dialect with these structures. All of us slide along something like our own dialect continuum, meaning that we unconsciously use certain pronunciations and grammatical forms in one situation, but use them less or not at all in other situations.

11.2.1.2 *Social motivations can matter*

Now, from the **socio-cultural standpoint**, the process of acquiring two languages may well be different from acquiring only one language. For one thing, although every child of normal intelligence will acquire one language, **children may resist acquiring some additional languages**. How much the family and community support acquiring certain languages does matter. This is especially true when we are talking about a minority group's L1 because the desire to acquire a second language is related to how much substantive and psychological support a language has from people around the child and the community. Do family members actively encourage acquisition of the language in question? The answer to this question matters for very young children. Children a little older may have acquired two languages, but one of them may then later fall into disuse unless there are domains in the community where the language can be used outside the home. Recall the discussions in chapters 3 and 4 about conditions favoring becoming and remaining bilingual. So just because children are around speakers of a second language does not always mean they will really acquire it – especially if they have begun to speak another language that is more in use around them and whose acquisition is more favored.

Still, one finding sticks out if we compare acquiring two languages as a small child with acquiring only one language: At least on the surface, **the process of language acquisition itself seems no different** except that child bilinguals speak two instead of one. However, in many ways, this does not mean that a bilingual is a monolingual times two. There are differences in how a bilingual uses his or her two languages and possibly in how being bilingual affects thinking abstractly. Also, even though the left hemisphere of the brain is the site of language for both monolinguals and bilinguals, how the bilingual's different languages are situated in that hemisphere seems to show variation across individual bilinguals. More on these subjects follows.

11.2.2 Terminology for early child bilinguals

We just mentioned the ages of three or four as major thresholds for child language acquisition. However, those researchers who specifically study bilingual children from infancy follow other age limits and have their own technical terms that may not be in place with all psycholinguists or other researchers dealing with children and their language.

First, consider the **terminology**. When children hear two languages from birth, Meisel (1989) has called this **bilingual first language acquisition**. De Houwer (2005) also uses this term, stating that she applies it to studies of children under the age of six who were exposed to two languages from birth and who continued to hear these languages fairly regularly up until the time of a reported study. Other researchers studying early bilingualism use the term **bilingual child language acquisition** for the object of their study (to distinguish it from acquisition of only one language, which is simply called child language acquisition). All these acquisition researchers try to avoid calling *either* language the L1 because, in effect, *both* languages are the child's first language.

Researchers use a different term for any child who is of pre-school age and who was exposed to language B more than one week after language A. Such a child shows **early second language acquisition**. It's important to note that a child who acquires a signed language along with an oral language also as a first language falls into one of these categories, too.

Second, many of the researchers set very stringent **time limits** on what should count as **bilingual acquisition**. De Houwer (1990) proposed that bilingual acquisition means the child is exposed to language B no later than a week after exposure to language A, and exposure is fairly regular on a daily basis. Whether all researchers follow this sharp division, most do refer to acquisition before age three as **simultaneous acquisition** to distinguish it from **successive acquisition**.

Bilingual child language has received increasing attention since 1990. There are many articles in diverse academic journals and there have even been three edited volumes devoted to child bilingualism in general just from 2000 onwards (Cenoz and Genesee, 2001; Deuchar and Quay, 2001; and Döpke, 2001). In recent years, there has been special interest in studying children acquiring more than two languages (e.g. a special issue of the *International Journal of Bilingualism* edited by Cenoz and Hoffman, 2003). In this volume, we offer a limited overview, singling out only a few studies of bilingual children.

11.2.3 Terminology problems

Before reading any further (here or elsewhere), we hope you realize from the discussion of terminology above that it's often not clear what the author means by the term "bilingual". For example, when the term "child bilingual" is used for a participant in a study, you can't be sure at what age he or she acquired language B – maybe from a week after exposure to language A, maybe not. When the term "bilingual" is used on its own, with no reference to age of acquisition, the possibility for different meanings multiplies. Also, many of the psycholinguistic studies of bilinguals deal with immigrants and use the terms **early or late arrivals**; these terms refer to their age when they arrived in the host country, but fine distinctions according to age are rarely made. And their age of arrival as immigrants says nothing about their age of acquisition of an L2, whether as a young child or not. Even if the study deals with speakers who became bilingual in their own home country, you can't be sure all the speakers being tested became bilingual in the same way and at the same ages. And of course one researcher's definition of a bilingual may not be the same as that of another. Just keep in mind that mysteries related to the terminologies researchers employ do exist.

11.2.4 Why study child bilingualism

Genesee (2001) offers a strong case for why child bilingualism is worth re-searchers' attention. First, there are, of course, obvious, **practical reasons**. The most obvious reason of all, as readers of this volume already know, is that the majority of the world's population is bilingual and many of them acquired two languages simultaneously as young children. Thus, not to study their linguistic profiles would be to ignore an important part of the lives of many people. There are also clinical, practical reasons to study these bilinguals; ensuring the normal development of their languages and treating any patho-logical problems both deserve attention.

Second, there are **theoretical reasons** to study child bilingualism. To date, most theories of language development are based on what happens in mono-lingual children. Studies of the simultaneous acquisition of two languages can provide facts against which current theories of child language acquisition should be tested. Genesee goes on to point out that studies of these bilingual children allows us to "explore the limits of the language faculty of the human mind" in a way not available elsewhere. He adds that neither the nature nor the nurture view of the development of language (mentioned above) "deals seriously with the case of bi- or multilingual acquisition and, thus, leaves unexplored both the capacity of the mind to acquire different linguistic sys-tems at the same time and the way in which this is accomplished" (p. 154). As we'll see below in section 11.7, current brain-imaging studies already have provided some important results about how language is organized and accessed in language processing.

11.2.5 Problems in studying early child bilingualism

Methodological problems plagued early studies of young bilinguals, although many of them are the same problems that are found in studies of monolingual children as they acquire their L1s. An early problem that still persists to some extent today is that it is hard to compare results across studies because of the **different methodologies** that are used. Then there is the problem of representativeness: Many studies are **case studies** (i.e. they deal only with one or two children).

Problems start at the beginning of data collection: A given study is not very clear on either when the child was exposed to both languages or when he or she began using both languages, or when data collection began systematically, or how consistent it was. For example, consider the best-known early study that includes the most detail on the first two years of life. This is the study by W. Leopold, a German linguist living in the United States who studied his German-English bilingual daughter, publishing four volumes of diaries from 1939 to 1949. A methodological problem in this study, and in many other earlier studies, is that there was only one observer and that observer was the parent (Leopold himself). Also, many early studies did not explicitly describe the circumstances of the child's exposure to both the languages.

Today, child bilingualism studies are more consistent in their methodologies, but many still study only one child or a handful of children. It is most common to study a child who is being raised with one parent speaking one language to the child and the other parent speaking the other language to the child. What parents speak to each other in the child's presence varies. But a continuing problem with many descriptions is that the researcher may use the term **language mixing** as a cover term for a number of quite different types of utterances the child produces. Below, we give examples of *one* type of "mixing" (what is referred to as codeswitching in chapter 9) in the speech of a Norwegian-English bilingual.

Another general problem with studies even today is that the range of languages covered is not very large. Most studies have considered acquisition of European languages, and often these are relatively closely related languages. Also, De Houwer noted that out of 13 combinations she counted, nine of them included English as one of the two languages being acquired.

Finally, yet another general problem is that there is no consensus on how to determine the child's **dominant language**. It is almost a given that even simultaneous bilinguals will not use both languages equally or appear to have equal fluency in both languages. There are a number of explanations for this. First, the child **rarely can be equally exposed to both languages**; usually the child spends more time with one caregiver than others. Second, even very young children rarely hear only their own parents speak; that is, they soon become aware that one language is more used in their community than the other and this can influence the child's own use patterns.

Yet, even though a child's dominance in one of his or her languages seems clear to observers, dominance is extremely hard to measure in any objective way. And in writings on bilingual children the term dominance has been used in different ways. Some researchers use it to refer to more frequent use of one language over the other. Others say it is the language in which the child is most "proficient", but how is that to be measured? One possible measure is to note which language is the source of the morphosyntactic frame when the child produces utterances with words from both languages (cf. chapter 9 on the MLF model of codeswitching). But to our knowledge, no one has used this measure. Problems with assessing dominance also plague studies of adult bilinguals; often the researcher just asks the participants what they think their dominant language is.

11.3 Successes in child bilingualism studies

As noted above, we already know that although young bilinguals must work out the grammatical systems of two languages, they do so within the **same general time frame** as do monolinguals with one language. In addition, today most researchers agree that two other major issues about early child language bilingualism are largely settled. One is an answer to the question, does the child form **two separate language systems** at a young age? The other answers the question, is switching between languages constraint-governed in a grammatical sense? As explained below, the answer to both questions is "yes".

First, consider the issue of separate systems. Not all child language researchers agree, but there is strong evidence that young bilinguals have two systems for their two languages, divisions that are evident once they begin producing words. Earlier researchers assumed that very young bilinguals had a single abstract system joining their two languages. But an in-depth study in 1990 of a Dutch-English bilingual child provided evidence that such children develop two systems, not one, for how to form words and put together larger units into sentences. This study by De Houwer showed that children regularly exposed to two languages from birth according to the "one person, one language" principle (mentioned above) develop two morphosyntactic systems. Also, her study showed that the grammatical development of one language does not have any fundamental effect on the development of the other. That is, once children are at the one-word stage and beyond, research shows they have two systems, not one.

Up until this time, opinions followed Volterra and Taeschner (1978) and other claims that the child had a three-stage model of acquisition, moving from one lexical system, to two such systems but one set of syntactic rules, to finally two separate languages. Researchers spoke of "fusion" of the child's two grammatical systems. But as De Houwer (2005) points out, the "fusion" or "hybrid" view did not offer an explanation of how children eventually manage to differentiate their languages. Those researchers who argue that the child's two language systems are fused have to come up with an explanation for how they eventually become divided.

As the 1990s began, a number of studies had just appeared or were appearing with extensive data supporting De Houwer's research (e.g. Deuchar and Quay, 2001; Genesee et al., 1995; Lanza, 1997; Meisel, 1989). Her **Separate Development Hypothesis** basically states that very young bilinguals employ two separate grammatical systems, one for each language, when they speak their two languages.

11.3.1 Separate languages

Clear evidence supporting this hypothesis is the child's use of a particular structure that varies across his or her two languages, but uses the structure for language A with lexical elements from language A. For example, in English a "yes–no" question involves the presence of a form of the supporting verb *do* at the beginning of the sentence *Do you want some tea?* In Dutch, there is no *do* (e.g. *Wil je thee?* 'Want you tea?'). All such competing structures must be studied in this way in order to conclude that the child has two separate systems. Further, De Houwer (2005) points out that the hypothesis predicts that child bilinguals should show the same structures in their languages at the same developmental stage as monolingual speakers of the languages do. She reports that such comparisons have been undertaken to date for Basque, Dutch, English, French, German, and Spanish. Still, some researchers claim there is cross-linguistic influence in early bilinguals (Döpke, 2000), although some types of influence may be more superficial (e.g. some instances of word order) and may be of little permanent consequence to the grammatical frame.

11.3.2 Is child codeswitching systematic?

Now consider the second issue: Is there a controlling structure when words or phrases in the same clause come from two different languages? The answer is "yes". Systematically, either one language or the other is in control of word order and any other evidence of grammatical structure.

Use of words from two languages in the same utterance was cited as evidence of a fused system by some earlier researchers. They also assumed that a mixed utterance is the sign of linguistic confusion and a stage to be overcome. Unfortunately, many parents and other child caretakers still believe this. But there is growing evidence that a child's use of two languages together (codeswitching) is systematic. In this case, to say it is systematic means that within the same "child clause" (a single utterance), the grammatical patterns of only one language are allowed. (As we've noted before, each language has its own "well-formedness constraints" on how to organize words in a clause.)

11.3.3 The same as adults? Obeying structural constraints in codeswitching

A study in 2000 by J. Paradis, Nicoladis, and Genesee addressed just this issue: Does the codeswitching of young bilingual children obey the same structural constraints as that of adults? Data came from 15 French-English bilinguals who were between about two years old and three years, six months. According to their parents, the children were being raised using the "one language, one parent" model (i.e. one parent spoke only French to a child and the other spoke English). For this study, sessions were conducted in the home with the mother alone or the father alone.

The authors used their own version of the grammatical constraints of the Matrix Language Frame (MLF) model (Myers-Scotton, 1993b) to study the children's grammatical usage. This model claims to explain and predict grammatical usage in adult switching between two languages. The Paradis et al. study tested the MLF model's claim that a Matrix Language (only one of the participating languages) controls the grammatical frame of a mixed constituent (with words from both languages). However, the researchers used their own definition of the Matrix Language as "the language from which the majority of the child's morphemes come in a stretch of discourse" (p. 251). This way of defining the Matrix Language was part of the early version of the MLF model, but was dropped in favor of other ways to identify the Matrix Language.

Establishing the **Matrix Language** on the basis of morpheme count, the researchers then tested children's utterances to see if the word order and the presence of a certain type of grammatical element conformed to the requirements of this Matrix Language. That is, if English was the child's Matrix Language for a mixed utterance, then these structural constraints should come from English and they should come from French if French was the Matrix Language.

In general, the researchers found that these young children did obey the grammatical constraints of the "right language" (which language was deemed the Matrix Language). Thus, when English counted as the Matrix Language, and a child said *rouge bird* 'red bird', this utterance fitted the word order requirement of English. (If French were the Matrix Language, the adjective would generally follow the noun, as in *bird rouge*.) Out of 20 utterances like this, only one seemed to violate the word order of the language in charge.

When French clitics (particles standing for pronouns, used to indicate subjects and objects of the verb) were required for a well-formed French clause, the children generally used them even when the clause had words from both languages. For example, one child said *fish, il mange pas* 'fish, he doesn't eat'. In this example, *fish* can be considered a "topicalizer". As a content word, it can come from either the Matrix Language or the other language (the Embedded Language). But the order of the verb and the negative element (*pas*) follow French rules. (If this utterance were following English order, then the negative element (*pas*) would come before the verb.) There are some examples in which the clitic is not produced as it would be in French, but "violations with respect to pronominals comprise just 13 percent of all mixed utterances with pronominals" (p. 257). Also, the researchers' view of which morphemes violate the MLF model does not always correspond to that of the original model.

Still, the general implication of these findings is very important. The study indicates that, even at a very young age, children follow the **appropriate grammatical constraints** when they engage in codeswitching within the same clause. The data do not support a grammatical deficiency hypothesis indicating that codeswitching was unconstrained before the use of certain grammatical structures, as proposed by Meisel (1994). In addition, the results of this Paradis et al. study also **support the notion of a dominant language as controlling the grammatical frame** of a mixed constituent (according to their definition). Further, this study supports the claim that children possess and can use **language-specific syntactic knowledge**, even at this young age.

The issue of why children engage in codeswitching is still being debated. Genesee (2001) cites support for a proficiency-based hypothesis (e.g. children are filling lexical "gaps" in their knowledge when they insert words from one language in an utterance basically in the other language, or they are filling grammatical gaps when they use a grammatical frame from their more "dominant" language). But this is a controversial claim. Of course, if a child is not exposed to codeswitching (from parents and others), he or she may not use two languages in the same clause. Even then, the child could develop codeswitching spontaneously.

11.3.4 Grammatical constraints on a frame, social constraints on discourse

Studies show many differences in how the young simultaneous bilingual uses his or her two languages. At one extreme, the child may use language A for many multi-clause utterances and use language B only for single words. Other children do a good deal of codeswitching. Studies are mixed in regard to how much parent (or caregiver) input seems to influence children in their preference for one language.

The case study of Siri, a child being raised in Norway as a Norwegian-English bilingual, is an example of studies that support the notion that switching languages is not just a matter of filling lexical gaps. Lanza (1997) argues that not just parental language choices matter, but also that their discourse strategies matter, too. Lanza studied Siri from about age one year, 11 months to two years, seven months. The American mother and the Norwegian father claimed to practice "one language, one parent", although the father had spoken English to the child up to age ten months. Overall, Siri received more outside exposure to Norwegian than English. Her mother was her only regular source of English and she was exposed to her mother's bilingual identity because when they went shopping, the mother spoke Norwegian.

There are two points of special interest in Siri's development of codeswitching, one grammatical and one discourse-related. First, Siri consistently uses Norwegian as the language to frame her utterances that consist of words from English. This is clear because the affixes or other functional elements come from Norwegian (recall the discussion of codeswitching in chapter 9). Given that Norwegian is her dominant language, at least in terms of exposure, this is not surprising. What is interesting is her consistent use of **one language as a frame** because this conforms to predictions of some codeswitching models for adults (the MLF model discussed in chapter 9).

While Siri produces English content words with either English or Norwegian grammatical elements, she only produces Norwegian content words with Norwegian grammatical elements. Lanza states that this indicates the prevalence of a Norwegian grammatical frame. For example, Siri produced English infinitive verbs (e.g. *to walk* in English) with the Norwegian infinitive marker (e.g. *walk-e*, *help-e*, *brush-e*). Of 284 mixed utterances presented in the appendix, 38 percent are of an English verb with a Norwegian verbal inflection. She also produces English nouns with Norwegian determiners or used such utterances with the Norwegian pronoun for first person singular in place of "I" (*jeg back soon* 'I back soon').

A second interesting point is the development of Siri's discourse style, a style that included a good deal of switching while her parents maintained their "one language, one parent" style. Lanza argues that the father's unconscious use of certain **discourse strategies** may have "contributed to negotiating less of a monolingual context with Siri" (p. 302), with the result that Siri consistently engaged in mixing English words in conversations with him despite her dominance in Norwegian. (However, as noted above, any inflections on these English words came from Norwegian.) In contrast, the mother used strategies that Siri seemed to take as not sanctioning using two languages together in the same sentence. The result was a more monolingual conversation (in English only). That is, Siri seemed very aware of what each parent expected or would sanction. Commenting in 2003, Lanza said, "I see this happening over and over again with bilingual families in Norway today" (personal communication).

In addition, Siri also demonstrated an awareness that when all three (parents and child) were together, speaking both languages is appropriate depending on the interaction. Here is an example when Siri is at the age two years and three months and she is eating dinner with her parents with the talk about a skiing trip when both parents had fallen.

(1)

Siri	Parents
jet falt	
I fell	
	F: **Ja, du falt du óg**.
	Yes, you fell, you too.
	M: You went all the way back past our house
	And to the garage. On skis today.
fall	
	M: Mm. You fell sometimes.
nesten/nesten/nesten	
almost/almost/almost	
	F: **Nesten?**
	Almost
ja	
yes	
	M: Almost what?
almost fall	

(Lanza, 1997: 298)

Another study that seems to show the effects of parental input dealt with four Japanese-English pre-school bilingual boys whose production of the minority language (Japanese) increased (Kasuya, 1998). The children were raised with the "one parent, one language" pattern, but they lived in an environment in which they were exposed to English more than Japanese (they were raised in the United States). In fact, generally, they were exposed to Japanese only at home. Still, the parents wanted the children to retain Japanese past their early years so the Japanese-speaking parent always spoke Japanese to the children, even though the parent was bilingual in English.

Three results from this study about the effect of parental language choices are noteworthy. First, there was a relation between what the parent spoke to the child and the language in which the child responded. Second, the children whose overall use of Japanese increased during the course of the study came from the families in which the parents used the most Japanese to the children. Third, "The child who got the least Japanese in both absolute and relative terms was showing the lowest relative use of Japanese compared to the other children" (p. 336).

11.3.5 Summing up on early bilinguals

You can see from the above discussion that language development proceeds without any real hitches in children who are exposed to two languages at a very early age. There are practical and theoretical reasons to study these children. From a practical standpoint, parents are reassured that their child is not "unusual" in any negative way. From a theoretical standpoint, a general theory of acquisition, and indeed a theory of the structure of language, must accommodate research on bilingual children (Genesee, 2001; 2003). Most theories of language acquisition are based on monolingual acquisition. The discussion here has been limited, but studies cited clearly show the following.

- Very young children develop their two or more languages as separate grammatical systems.
- These young bilinguals are able to use their languages appropriately according to their addressee.
- They may develop discourse preferences and strategies based on the input they receive, although not all results support how input matters.
- A child's codeswitching does not reflect an incapacity in the language faculty.
- When children use both of their languages in the same utterance, the evidence points to the child's use of only one as the source of the grammatical frame for that utterance.

11.4 But is bilingualism an advantage or a disadvantage?

Some readers may think that acquiring only one language as an infant is "normal", but Genesee (2003: 207) makes an argument that acquiring two languages is just as normal and reflects the biological capacity that humans have. He goes on to cite a good deal of inferential evidence to support his position.

Of course, young bilinguals are different – because they can speak two languages. But then a number of questions arise as to what this difference *means*. Does this mean bilinguals equal or surpass monolinguals in achievement tests in these languages? Also, does the child develop more or less in those mental abilities thought to be associated with being able to manipulate a language and other abstract systems?

To put the general question negatively, does early bilingualism result in **delayed development**? Some parents used to be told this and they would think this, and some still do. But most of the evidence indicates that, if anything, early bilingualism has advantages, although the **results of studies are mixed**. We offer an overview of research and cite some specific studies on demonstrated abilities in a given language, but also on what is called metalinguistic knowledge (i.e. evidence of abstract thinking transcending ability in any specific language).

11.4.1 Mixed results on demonstrated development in a given language

Early studies that compared monolinguals and bilinguals on language achievement tests seemed to show bilinguals lagged behind on many tests that were intended to demonstrate language abilities. Macnamara (1966) reviewed 77 studies published between 1918 and 1962 that claimed to compare vocabulary, reading, and grammatical complexity in the languages of monolinguals compared with bilinguals. On the basis of his survey, he concluded that "bilinguals have a weaker grasp of language than monoglots" (Macnamara, 1966: 31). But as Bialystok (2001a) points out, it is not surprising that such studies would lead one to this conclusion. If a child learns Spanish at home as the family language and attends school in English, "It is not surprising that the type of competence that the child develops in each of these languages is different." She goes on to say, "The point is that assessing children's linguistic skill requires understanding children's language experiences" (p. 60).

She reports on more recent studies that show other, but mixed, results. Several studies were done involving Spanish-English bilingual children in Miami, Florida. In the first, Pearson, Fernandez, and Oller (1993) compared the receptive and productive vocabulary acquisition of 25 bilingual children with that of 35 monolingual children. They were all between the ages of 8 and 30 months. In a second study, Pearson and Fernandez (1994) evaluated the patterns of productive vocabulary growth in 18 bilingual children in the same age range. They looked at the vocabulary size in each language, the combined total vocabulary for both languages, and the conceptual range given by the number of unique concepts labeled in either language.

In the first study, the total production vocabulary for bilingual children was **not significantly different** from that for monolingual children. Those bilingual children who were dominant in English had about the same productive vocabulary in English as did monolingual English children and the same finding applied regarding Spanish-dominant children. But in the less dominant language, bilinguals fell below the levels for monolingual children.

The second study provided more individual data and it showed **a good deal of individual variability** and goes against findings in the first study. Also, the findings were compared with a study of monolingual vocabulary development by Fenson et al. (1994). The monolinguals knew approximately 75 words at 18 months, 150 words at 20 months, 200 words at 22 months, and 300 words at 24 months. Using these standards, the researchers found that 10 of the 18 bilinguals were within these ranges (demonstrated by monolinguals), and the other eight children were well **below these ranges**. Other studies also report an overall deficit in the vocabulary of bilingual children, but some note that bilinguals displayed better verbal fluency.

Again, studies that compare development on well-formedness conditions on sentence formation (syntax) in their two languages show mixed results. In this test, children were asked if various strings of words could be well-formed sentences in language X or language Y. Gathercole and Montes (1997) compared Spanish-English bilinguals with English monolinguals; all were seven and nine years old. Different types of educational programs and different social classes were represented, but apparently children and their test scores were not grouped in terms of these variables.

For all the structures studied, the **bilingual children lagged behind**. But the older bilinguals were doing better. The **older and stronger bilinguals resembled monolinguals** in their syntactic sensitivity. Across both older monolingual and bilingual children, the progression in mastering structures was the same and the structures were learned in the same order. The difference was that **children learning two languages took longer to learn the subtleties of syntax** than did children concentrating on only one language. How much exposure the bilinguals had to English or Spanish seemed to matter; at least the children with more exposure did better in recognizing acceptable structures in the language being tested.

11.4.2 Metalinguistic knowledge: Is there a bilingual advantage here?

More recently, researchers have been interested in what is called **metalinguistic knowledge** and many conclude that bilingual children may excel in having the **mental flexibility** associated with this type of knowledge. This term has been used in a number of ways, but it basically means knowledge about the abstract character of language – knowledge beyond how to produce certain utterances.

Bialystok refers to metalinguistic knowledge as **linguistic knowledge beyond the details of specific linguistic structures** but knowledge that becomes accessible through knowledge of a particular language. She gives these examples: Children with this knowledge would understand that changes in word order can change meaning, or changes in a verb form change the time at which an event occurred. Why this type of knowledge (or ability) is important is that children would know how "language in general" works. Thus, as Bialystok (2001a: 127) puts it, "To the extent that a learner has metalinguistic knowledge, second-language acquisition is facilitated because a language template is available."

Here are three examples of the type of research that has shown that bilingual children have an advantage over monolingual children in demonstrating **mental agility**. Ben-Zeev (1977) developed a substitution task to test children's awareness that **words are symbols**, typically arbitrary symbols, and their awareness that in a game one symbol can be substituted for another. For example, in the game, children were told that the word *spaghetti* was to be substituted for the word *we*. Children were told this new meaning of *spaghetti* and then were asked to use this word in a sentence to indicate *we are good children*. The response called for would be *spaghetti are good children*. Bilinguals did significantly better in making such substitutions than monolinguals.

Galambos and Hakuta (1988) compared bilinguals and monolinguals in making grammaticality judgments (i.e. answering such questions as "can you say this sentence in English?") and in detecting ambiguities in sentences. (Ambiguous sentences can have two meanings; e.g. *visiting relatives can be a nuisance*, can mean either 'the act of visiting relatives is a nuisance' or 'relatives who visit are a nuisance'.) They found that bilinguals had a consistent advantage over monolinguals in the syntax task, but only older children were better than the monolinguals on the ambiguity task.

Finally, a study in Stockholm seemed to indicate bilinguals have advantages in similar tests (Cromdal, 1999). Schoolchildren whose stronger language was English and who had at least a basic knowledge of Swedish were compared with monolingual English speakers to test a number of metalinguistic benefits between monolinguals and bilinguals. A total of 40 bilinguals and 16 monolinguals were selected between the ages of 6.4 and 7.3, plus two 8-year-olds. Among other results, the bilinguals did better in recognizing ungrammatical sentences in either English or Swedish and in correcting them. They also were more accepting than English monolinguals of marked, but acceptable, ways of constructing a well-formed sentence.

Probably the most influential study of the cognitive effects of bilingualism was the early study of Peal and Lambert (1962). The researchers gave monolinguals and bilinguals a battery of tests to assess difference in the *structure* of intelligence. They found that **bilinguals were especially superior in the area of symbolic reorganization**, leading the researchers to say that bilinguals showed more mental flexibility. There were problems with this research, as there often are with any study. For one thing, the subjects came from a select group of francophone families in Montreal, the type of residents who were also very proficient bilinguals in English. Children from these families were compared with monolingual francophones who probably had less exposure to education and other advantages. Still, this was an important study because it awakened educators and other researchers to the notion that in the important area of ways of processing information bilingualism might be an advantage, not a disadvantage.

11.5 Does early acquisition affect some systems the most?

One of the problems with early ideas about a critical period in child language acquisition is that researchers referred to language as if it were a single system.

In fact, of course, **any language is a set of at least three systems** (phonology, morphology–syntax, and vocabulary). There is no reason to assume that all three are acquired by the same age; most obviously, vocabulary increases through-out the lifetime of most people. But acquisition in general begins very early; this is why those who study early bilingual children insist that to qualify as "early" they must be exposed to both languages within a week of each other.

11.5.1 Pronunciation comes early

One reason for stressing early exposure to both languages is that recent research shows that **infants can distinguish many pronunciation features** of what will be their L1 from other sounds at a very early age. For example, by the age of two months, infants can tell the difference between languages that have different prosodies (think of these as the melodies over stretches of speech longer than a word), if one of the languages is the infant's L1 (Bosch and Sebastián-Gallés, 2001). If the languages are prosodically very similar, telling the difference takes longer. Sebastián-Gallés and Bosch (2001) also demonstrated that very young children can perceive differences between two languages to which they have been exposed. These researchers studied children raised with both Spanish and Catalan in the environment. They demon-strated that as early as $4^{1}/_{2}$ months of age, before they speak their first words, such children can perceive differences in phonological sequences as to whether they are possible parts of one language vs. the other. A number of other studies involving children speaking different languages support these findings. Presumably, the ability to do this would be needed if a child is to establish different mental representations of the two languages.

Also, many studies point to production of **the phonological system** (native-like pronunciation) as having a **different time frame** from other systems of language. Evidence is that pronunciation is set very early. For example, a study by J. Paradis (2001) of two-year-old French-English bilinguals compared with French and English monolinguals of like ages in Canada indicated that bilinguals have separate phonological systems for syllable structure. There was some overlap, however, with apparent influence involving stress patterns from French on the pronunciation of certain types of English words.

Also, studies of immigrants who learn an L2 upon arrival in the host country show that only the youngest children (up to about age 7 at the age of arrival) achieve native-like or near-native-like pronunciations in their new L2. Immigrants arriving as adults rarely achieve such pronunciation. Flege et al. (2002) studied four groups of Italian-English bilinguals living in Canada, with 18 participants in each group. Their dominant language was assessed by means of self-reports and a test of fluency. One of their findings was that all the early bilinguals who were dominant in their second language (English) spoke it with no detectable foreign pronunciation features. Other participants did have foreign features; these included participants who claimed to be balanced bilinguals and both groups of late bilinguals (low or high proficiency in Italian) as well as early bilinguals who were dominant in Italian (cf. an overview in Harley and Wang, 1997).

11.5.2 Later acquisition of morphology and syntax?

The acquisition of patterns of word-formation and sentence structure (morphology and syntax) seem to come later, but still are largely complete by age three or four. This is only one example, but consider a boy who just turned four years old and who is being raised with a father who speaks only English to him and a mother who speaks only Russian to him. His Russian-speaking parent (the mother), who is a linguist, reports that he has acquired the case system of Russian (six different cases) as well the other features to make his Russian well-formed. He only makes a few errors, such as selecting a verb that is a near-synonym instead of the verb that is called for in certain constructions. His English is grammatically well-formed as well, although he doesn't always produce the correct past tense or participial forms for little-used irregular verbs (E. Schmitt, personal communication).

Children acquiring only one language all over the world, no matter what their language, show similar developmental steps in their acquisition of the various systems (that is, they acquire the same sort of structures in roughly the same order). Studies on whether such similarities extend to bilingual children and their two languages give mixed results. This is called **the "lead-lag" issue**, meaning does a bilingual child lead in acquiring certain grammatical structures in one language first?

A case study of a single English-Italian bilingual child showed more similarities than differences in the child's acquisition of the verbal systems of both Italian and English (Serratrice, 2001). Up until the end of the study at about age three, acquisition was largely a matter of gradual verb-specific learning, not a learning of many inflections. But another study of a German-English bilingual child and a Latvian-English child in the same age range produced other results. Sinka and Schelletter (1998) reported that both children produced correct verb endings, one child in German and the other in Latvian, before they did this in English. But both children used word order and grammatical patterns on the same level as monolingual children who were acquiring the languages involved. So whether progress in one language is usually faster remains an issue.

11.5.3 Learning second-language vocabulary

This section offers a brief overview of what's involved in learning words. In contrast to the above two sections, it deals more with the vocabulary learning of late L2 learners than early bilinguals. Clearly, vocabulary learning for child bilinguals differs a great deal because the acquisition of word form and the word meaning **proceed in parallel**, just as they do for monolingual children. In later L2 learning, a word has to be learned for a meaning that is already in place (with some adjustment).

Vocabulary has a critical role in L2 learning; after all, if they need to use their L2, speakers can't get these needs met unless they can talk about them in the L2. Furthermore, it's been claimed that native speakers can better understand ungrammatical utterances if they contain appropriate words than if the utterances have flawless grammar but the wrong words.

But learning words in an L2 can be a daunting task. First, the majority of words in any language have multiple meanings. Further, these meanings aren't stable, but can change over time. Second, to learn each word, a number of types of information have to be learned, all in addition to its possible meanings. These include how the word is pronounced, how it is spelled, how it can fit into a syntactic unit, how it can combine with other words or morphemes to make a larger unit, and what its connotations are when used in that unit.

Vocabulary items are **almost always learned as explicit learning** (i.e. declarative memory is involved). That is, even the young children who acquire their grammar and pronunciation effortlessly have to at least pay overt attention to learn new words. Several studies indicate that knowing a relatively small number of words is sufficient for speaking an L2 (see Hazenberg and Hulstijn, 1996, for an overview). If "only" a few thousand words are needed, then explicit vocabulary learning is a reasonable goal.

When the L2 vocabulary is taught in a formal setting, various methods are in use. We'll only look at one of the most successful methods. It's called the **keyword method**. The two-step process is this. The learners associate a new word with a keyword in their L1 that it "sounds like" or "looks like" Then the learner creates a mental image that somehow includes both the new word and the keyword. So, for example, if the English-speaking learners are studying Chinese and the new word is *gāoxìng* 'happy', the learner can associate it with *glad* and then create an image with the learners feeling "glad" because something happened to make them "gaoxing" or "happy".

This may sound like a lot of effort, but the method seems to work. A number of studies show that learners using the keyword method outperform learners using any other strategy. For example, one study with striking results looked at a 47-year-old university lecturer who learned Italian via this method (Beaton et al., 1995, cited by De Groot and Van Hell, 2005). After ten years, he was tested on his retention of a vocabulary of 350 words even though he had used no Italian in the meantime. The lecturer remembered 35 per cent of the words (about 122 words) he had learned and after ten minutes of relearning, he added an additional 93 words.

Theoretically, the keyword method is of interest because it shows **the role of imaging**. The idea is that the keyword method promotes learning because it uses both the language system and the image system in human memory (Paivio and Desrochers, 1981). However, the few studies that have compared how long it takes a subject to retrieve a word learned via the keyword method with learning via just simple rote learning show that it takes the keyword learner longer to access a word (Van Hell and Candia Mahn, 1997). So, if fluency is a goal the keyword method may not be the best to follow.

The goal of vocabulary learning, obviously, is to retain the words learned. De Groot and Van Hell (2005) report that studies show that **more forgetting** occurs for the types of words that are more difficult to learn in the first place. Evidence shows that concrete words are easier to learn than abstract words and also are easier to "anchor" (tie to other words). Word forms that have familiar pronunciation patterns are easier to learn than words that sound more foreign. This is important because it means that cognate words (words that have similar forms and meanings in another language the speaker knows) are easier to learn. After they are learned, concrete words and cognates are also **easier to retain** than non-cognates and abstract words. Unfortunately, this also means that learning words in a language that is totally unrelated to your L1 are much harder to learn. When your author studied Swahili, learning that *mti* was the word for 'tree' and that *nyumba* was the word for 'house' was harder than learning that *jardin* in French meant 'garden' or that *stuhl* in German meant 'chair'. Whether the actual learning conditions themselves have any effect is another issue and presents something of a puzzle. De Groot and Keijzer (2000) showed that words **learned under difficult learning procedures** actually may be **better retained** than those same words when learned under easy learning conditions.

De Groot and Van Hell present evidence that suggests that for low-proficiency L2 learners, accessing the meaning of a word is **via a route through the word's L1 counterpart**. More proficient learners don't have to do this, but make direct connections between a word and its meaning.

11.6 Learning a second language later

What about becoming bilingual once you are past your early years? The answer is clear: Later second-language learning isn't the same as early childhood bilingualism in many, many ways; it's **more conscious and involves more efforts that don't pay off in great success**. This is the conclusion of both various types of comprehension tests given to L2 speakers who learned the language being tested after childhood and of diverse laboratory experiments. From now on, we'll refer to later second language learning as SLA.

The results of the study by Johnson and Newport (1989) are often cited about differences in learning success. They studied 49 Koreans and Chinese who moved to the United States where they became bilingual in English. Half had moved by age 15 (**early arrivals**) and half after the age of 17 (late arrivals). In a test of acceptability judgments (i.e. "Is this a possible sentence in English?"), not one of the late arrivals performed within the same range of scores that native English speakers showed on the test. Further, anyone who arrived after a very young age did not score well. Even though there wasn't a sudden decline, there was a **clear linear decline** among the L2 speakers starting with an age at arrival of 8 to 10 years old. Then, after an age at arrival of 15, the scores didn't show any real pattern of decline; some subjects with different ages at arrival did much better than others. This finding could be interpreted to mean that external, not innate factors, made the difference. For example, how much exposure they had to the L2 or their attitudes toward the L2 could make the difference. Coming at the study from another perspective, some second-language acquisition researchers raise arguments against this study which are based on its syntactic analysis of the test sentences. These are those researchers who claim that later L2 learners have access to the principles of Universal Grammar that are available to child language learners (e.g. White, 2003b).

11.6.1 A critical period for native-like acquisition or not?

Note that the Johnson and Newport study not only shows that later bilinguals don't perform as well as child bilinguals; it also shows that there **may not be a sharp cut-off point**, even though the ability to acquire a language diminishes beyond an early age. Even without a cut-off point, most researchers still agree that there is indeed a period in early childhood when language acquisition seems more effortless and definitely is more complete (by native speaker standards) than later in life. By the age of 9 to 12, the ability to acquire a second language with native-like ability has fallen off considerably.

Such findings gave rise to what has been called the **Critical Age Hypothesis**. This hypothesis is often attributed to Lenneberg (1967). Certainly, he was the most specific about suggesting the time around the onset of puberty (or age 13) as the end of the period for language acquisition. But far from all researchers agree on a *single* critical age and some don't agree with the idea of a critical age at all.

One of the reasons for lack of agreement is that there is little evidence about any neurological component in the brain that controls when the window of language acquisition is open. So, in some ways, it is no surprise that studies against a clear critical period do continue to appear.

Birdsong and his associates are prominent among those who question the critical period hypothesis. For example, a recent study by Birdsong and Molis (2001) provides empirical evidence from a sample of 61 native speakers of Spanish who immigrated to the United States. In many ways, the study replicated the Johnson and Newport study. The participants were similar, in the sense that they were either students, faculty, or staff members at US

universities. Birdsong and Molis also found a significant decline in performance on test sentences as age of arrival to the US increased.

But the difference is that some of their **late arrivals scored high**. Four
participants who arrived at or after age 17 scored high on the same type
of acceptability judgment test used in the Johnson and Newport study. These
speakers were accurate on 94.8% of the test sentences; on these same sentences, the mean accuracy of native speakers was 95.2%. Interestingly, Birdsong
and Molis also point out that among all their subjects the amount of *current*
English use was a strong predictor of performance. Obviously, one can claim
that the four late arrivals showed native-like results even though they seem to
have had no or little exposure to English before any so-called critical age.

However, Birdsong (2005) makes the point that his argument with claims
about a cut-off age is mainly with the strong version of a Critical Period
Hypothesis. The strong version is that there is a period when acquisition
always happens and after which similar proficiency in the L2 can't be reached.
But if there were an actual cut-off point, then late learners ought not to show
the variation that they do in how well they perform in an L2.

11.6.2 Many studies, many different conclusions

There are many variations on the conclusions regarding the critical period
that researchers reach about comparisons between bilinguals who differ along
various parameters. For example, in another study that used the same type of
grammaticality judgments of L2 sentences as those used in the studies just
mentioned, McDonald (2000), found different results for different groups of
subjects. First she studied two groups of Vietnamese-English bilinguals who
both acquired English quite early, but not equally early. The "early acquirers"
(who learned English before age five) had trouble with the test regarding
those aspects of English that differ markedly from Vietnamese. The "child
acquirers" (who learned English between ages six and ten) had generalized
problems with the English test sentences.

In the second test group, Spanish L1 speakers who only moved to the United
States after the age of 14 also had generalized problems with English test
sentences. But in contrast with that group and both of the Vietnamese groups,
L1 Spanish speakers who were "early acquirers" of English performed in ways
no different from native speakers of English.

McDonald concluded that exposure during the critical period does not always
mean native-like results. She suggested that how different the L2 is from the
L1 may make some difference. Bialystok (2001b) cites two more studies that
argue that first-language similarities and differences (in relation to the L2) are
more important in achieving native-like ability than the age of initial exposure
to the L2. Another possible key to variation in a speaker's performance on
grammaticality items is whether the items are presented in oral or written form.

Another study looked at quite a different aspect of age effects and bilingualism. Izura and A. Ellis (2002) considered the relation of age of acquisition of an L2 and performance on **word recognition experiments**. Many earlier studies show that, all other things being equal, words learned early in life can be recognized and produced faster than later-learned words. This effect is found in a number of different types of tasks (e.g. object picture naming) and seems to be independent of other factors such as frequency of use of words in adult language. Most previous studies with this format have dealt with monolingual subjects.

Izura and Ellis devised studies to see if a second language acquired in late childhood or adulthood showed the same effects. Their study included Spanish participants who acquired Spanish as their L1 in Spain and who then learned English later. These participants were introduced to English at the age of 8 to 10 in school and then they studied English after that throughout their schooling. They were living in England as university students when tested. In one experiment, the subjects named objects in pictures whose names were learned early or late in both Spanish and English. The words were matched for frequency, object familiarity, and word length.

This study showed two main results. First, **response times were faster** for words acquired in their first language (Spanish) than in English (their L2). Second, response times also were faster for earlier acquired words than later acquired ones, but overall were faster for Spanish words. In a second experiment the participants had to carry out a lexical decision task in which they were asked to distinguish words in both English and Spanish from stimuli that were non-words in both languages. Again, results showed that **the order of acquisition was important** for both Spanish and English words, but responses were faster for Spanish.

11.6.3 Generally, late acquisition = less proficiency

But whatever the underlying explanation, the large majority of studies do demonstrate clear differences in L2 proficiency in both grammar and pronunciation seemingly related to age of acquisition. DeKeyser and Larson-Hall (2005) cite studies showing that very few, if any, adults learn an L2 with native-like performance in adulthood.

While DeKeyser and Larson-Hall are careful in their conclusions, they do summarize findings that support the idea of a critical period, if not a cut-off point. They write, "There appears to be **a qualitative change in language learning capacities** somewhere between ages 4 and 18." But what this qualitative change is remains up for debate. DeKeyser and Larson-Hall indicate that they themselves see the difference "in terms of children being largely limited to **implicit learning** and adults being largely limited to **explicit learning**". But they then say that this still doesn't answer the question of *why* there are these differences. True, we have documentation, as you'll see in 11.7, on how some aspects of language seem to be represented in the brain differently in individuals, depending on age of acquisition of an L2.

Even though we now have imaging studies, DeKeyser and Larson-Hall point out that there is no evidence to date to link the learning problems of late L2 speakers to *actual changes* in neurophysiological mechanisms in the brain. This doesn't mean a link can't be found, just that it hasn't been found.

11.6.4 Does utilizing different types of memory figure in late L2 learning?

The suggestion of DeKeyser and Larson-Hall that the difference in L1 and later L2 learning is related to the difference between implicit learning (early) and explicit learning (later) finds support from other quarters. As we noted in chapter 10 when memory was discussed, researchers suggest that there is a fundamental distinction between a memory containing memorized material (called **declarative memory**) and another memory system. This second system contains knowledge that is acquired or learned through repeated execution of a task and it is called **procedural memory**.

We have evidence that these two different types of memory are involved in tasks that humans perform every day. What is in declarative memory was overtly learned and we can call it up when we want to do so. For example, our knowledge of words is in our declarative memory and we can tell someone what a word means. Procedural memory is different: We use what it contains, but we cannot "report" on it in the same way that we can report on declarative memory. For example, researchers suggest that the basis for how to pronounce words or how to construct clauses in our L1 seems to reside in our procedural memory. Procedural memory does not necessarily involve any awareness of learning of the knowledge that is contained there.

How is the existence of two different memory systems relevant to our discussion of second language learning? Ullman (2001) argues that the differences found in L1 and L2 proficiency have to do with which memory system is used, declarative or procedural. His general claim is this: In late learners of an L2, "The processing of linguistic forms that are computed grammatically by procedural memory in L1 is expected to be dependent to a greater extent upon declarative memory in L2" (p. 109). That is, Ullman's hypothesis is that, somehow, procedural memory is **no longer as available** as it is for acquiring an L1 in very young children. Thus, his suggestion is that late exposure to a language means that the learner will have to learn grammatical aspects of that language overtly (to "memorize" them). Why? Because for some reason, the learner has to rely on declarative memory, not procedural memory. In L1 acquisition, declarative memory is only substantially involved in the learning of words (as well as other encyclopedic knowledge, e.g. "What is the name of the big river in Brazil?").

Ullman's hypothesis is based on extensive evidence from imaging techniques and other sources that the two types of memory are located in different areas of the brain. For example, one recent study of language impairment cited by Ullman supports this claim (Ku, Lachmann, and Nagler, 1996). The person studied was a right-handed 16-year-old Chinese-English bilingual who developed a type of encephalitis that involved his left temporal lobe. His L1 was Chinese but he had been living in the United States since age 10. He lost his ability to speak and comprehend English, but retained his ability in Chinese, although he produced only relatively short sentences.

Imaging techniques produce accurate images of the brain region involved in this disease (the region just mentioned above – the left temporal lobe). Other imaging evidence indicates that procedural memory is located in the **left frontal lobes and the basil ganglia areas**, but declarative memory is located in the **left temporal-parietal/medial-temporal lobes**. So it was the site of declarative memory that appeared to be most affected in this patient. The implication is that his problems with English, while retaining Chinese, meant that English (his L2) was situated in declarative memory. After all, it was the left temporal lobe that seemed affected by his disease. In contrast, the fact that he could still produce Chinese is implicational evidence that the grammatical aspects of Chinese were situated in procedural memory (since the supposed sites of procedural memory were not affected by the disease).

The relevance to the issue of L2 acquisition of this discussion about areas of the brain, selective brain damage, and types of memory is that possibly **procedural memory is no longer "available"** for language learning past early childhood. Why it's no longer available is another issue.

In normal L2 learners (with intact brains), the areas of the brain that seem to support procedural memory are still "there", but it's possible that these areas have undergone various changes or that certain relevant neural procedures are no longer available. But if Ullman (and others) are correct in assuming that the problem with achieving a measure of success with an L2 is a problem regarding the type of memory (declarative memory) that is still available to the L2 learner, this finding would be very important to instructors of L2 in designing their curriculum. Obviously, it would be important for instructors to emphasize explicit learning of structures that are assembled implicitly by the L1 learner. The need for SLA practitioners and theorists to consider possible differences in language processing is raised again in 11.8.

11.6.5 Additional evidence tying in with different types of memory

Other implicational evidence supports the idea that sites of memory in the brain are utilized differently for an L1 and an L2 learned later. To recap, in a speaker's L1, different types of memory support different types of language (vocabulary in declarative memory vs. grammar in procedural memory). But most or all of a speaker's L2 (both vocabulary and grammar) is situated in declarative memory.

First, consider implicational evidence from studies of bilingual patients who have aphasia. Fabbro (1999), who has studied such patients extensively, states that when patients have **damage to the left frontal lobes** of their brains, they show **more grammatical impairments in their L1** than in their L2.

Second, a number of brain-imaging studies show **differences between areas that are activated** for the L2 of late bilinguals than those activated for their L1. For example, Perani et al. (1998), also discussed in 11.7, found that late bilinguals show a greater number of activated regions in the temporal regions of *both* the left and right hemispheres in their L2s than in their L1s.

11.6.6 Summary on a critical age of native-like acquisition

In sum, even if there is disagreement over whether there is an end-state for effortless acquisition or over why late L2 learners perform as they do, researchers do agree that late learners are much less successful in language learning than young children. And it is clear to most late L2 learners that their learning is not effortless! Some researchers point to other factors to consider outside of age, such as the type and amount of input (exposure), the amount of practice, the level of motivation, and other variables such as inhibition beyond childhood learning. But age of acquisition keeps showing up in studies with traditional types of empirical evidence. However, newly developed brain imaging studies surveyed in 11.7 give us another type of evidence. These studies present evidence on how a bilingual's languages are represented in the brain.

11.7 Age-related issues and the brain

Studies of brain imaging offer another way to get at the issue of importance of age of acquisition of an L2. Noninvasive neuroimaging techniques are now being used to study the apparent organization of language in the brains of healthy individuals. These techniques include positron emission tomography (PET), functional magnetic resonance imaging (fMRI), event-related brain potentials (ERPs), and magnetoencephalography (MEG). As indicated in chapter 10, most researchers agree that language in general is located in the left hemisphere of the brain, whether it is the L1 or an L2. But what about *where* different languages are in that hemisphere? And what about *how* they are organized? When there are differences, researchers consider the potential role of a number of variables, including age of acquisition. But they are also looking at degree of proficiency and level of exposure.

An overview of brain-imaging studies relevant to bilingualism by Abutalebi, Cappa, and Perani (2001) provides us with some new perspectives on the different results in L2 learning found across studies. We will only report their six general conclusions. First, they make it very clear that such studies indicate that the bilingual brain is definitely **not the sum of two monolingual language systems**. Second, there are **individual differences** across bilinguals in the organization of the neural system. For example, imaging studies do show **some activation in the right hemisphere** for some individuals for some tasks. Third, of the variables that seem to affect the bilingual system, these researchers, at least, conclude that "on the basis of the available evidence, **[degree of] proficiency** seems to be the most important one" (p. 188). Note that this is a different conclusion from that of DeKeyser and Larson-Hall (2005) who place most importance on age of acquisition. Further, other researchers give more credit to other factors. Fourth, it seems that comprehension and production involve different levels of cerebral activation in the bilingual's less proficient language; there is **more activation associated with production**. Bear in mind that the majority of the neuroimaging experiments on language production in bilinguals are based on single word processing (producing a word according to a cue). Their survey also shows that **language comprehension** in bilinguals (as studied via neuroimaging) appears to give **more consistent results** than production studies.

Fifth, the researchers consider the **role of age of acquisition** and conclude that it is less important than other factors. But they qualify this statement by saying that this applies to bilinguals who show the same proficiency. Here is what they say: "What functional imaging has shown is that, when proficiency is kept constant, age of acquisition per se does not seem to have a major impact on brain representations of L2, at least at the macroscopic (brain area) level" (p. 188).

It seems as if Abutalebi et al. partly base this conclusion on the fact that a study by Chee et al. (1999) of early and late bilinguals found little difference when the subjects were producing words. The participants came from Singapore. Abutalebi et al. reasoned that this was a society in which bilingual speakers are often highly proficient in both their languages. Thus, the participants' background suggests that proficiency, not age of acquisition, is important. But these results contrasted with those in a study by Kim et al. (1997) of 12 proficient bilinguals, some early and some late (with their language pairs including diverse languages). The task the participants performed was to tell what they had done on the previous day. Kim and his associates found that in late learners, the L1 and the L2 were represented in different parts of the left inferior frontal cortex (Broca's area). In contrast, overlapping parts of Broca's area were activated for both languages in early learners.

Finally Abutalebi et al. concluded that any evidence of the role of degree of exposure to a language is too limited to draw any conclusions. They recognize that there are important questions that such research does not answer, such as how people learn and acquire a second language.

11.7.1 Two PET imaging studies

We summarize two of the individual studies discussed in the Abutalebi et al. overview above (Perani et al., 1996; 1998). These researchers use Positron Emission Tomography (PET) imaging to study differences between early and late bilinguals. PET imaging shows the chemical function of organs and tissues and can be used to study different levels of activation in different parts of the brain.

Perani and her associates compared patterns of brain activation while the participants listened to stories in their L1 and L2. In the 1996 study, the participants were L1 speakers of Italian with a moderate command of English. In the 1998 study, two groups of bilinguals with high proficiency in their L2 were studied, but speakers who had acquired their L2 at different ages (and presumably in different ways). One group included nine right-handed male native speakers of Italian, who had lived in Italy all of their lives. They had studied English in school from age 10 onwards and all had spent at least a year in an English-speaking country. Spanish-Catalan bilinguals who had acquired their L2 before the age of four made up the other group.

Because of their implications, the two Perani et al. studies had some important results. First, when listening to stories in their L1 (Italian) and their L2 (English), the low-proficiency bilinguals showed **"very different patterns of cortical activity"** (1998: 1845). But no such major difference (in imaging results) was found in either the Italian-English *high-proficiency* bilinguals or the Spanish-Catalan ones.

11.7.2 Implications from imaging studies regarding degree of proficiency

These studies have a number of implications. But first a caveat: Any anatomical similarities or differences regarding L1 and L2 and levels of proficiency in L2 that have been detected are just that, anatomical differences. We can't directly assume that anatomical differences mean that there are cognitive differences (or similarities) in the processes involved in acquiring an L1 vs. an L2. We also can't assume that the cognitive representation of the two languages, if speakers are very proficient bilinguals, is the same as or different from that of less proficient ones or monolinguals. So take the following implications as just implications and not facts.

The first implication is that **differences in neural activity** in the brain reflect **differences in the degree of proficiency in the L2**. A second implication is that if the bilinguals begin L2 learning by age 10 and become very proficient through study, the areas of the brain involved in at least "auditory comprehension" (remember, the participants listened to stories) rely on **similar neural networks of areas for both L1 and L2**.

A final implication is that structural similarities or differences across languages make little difference in influencing brain activity. This seems to be true, at least for the languages studied. The structural differences between Italian and English are much greater than those between Spanish and Catalan, and the differences don't seem to matter regarding brain activity. (However, it is true that the differences between Italian and English aren't so great that they offer as good a test as really different languages, such as Vietnamese or Yoruba, compared with Italian.) Still, Perani et al. can point to "strikingly similar pattern of activation observed for L1 and L2 in Italian-English and in Catalan-Spanish high proficiency bilinguals" (p. 1845). Overall, Perani et al. (1998) seem to conclude that the degree of mastery of the L2 is what makes the difference between the low- and high-proficiency bilinguals in regard to their brain scanning.

Other studies have similar results with similar implications. In light of such evidence and other neuroimaging studies, Green (2005) suggests a **convergence hypothesis**. The hypothesis states that as L2 proficiency increases, its representation (in the brain) and its imaging profile converge with that of native speakers of the relevant language. For an imaging profile, Green refers to PET and fMRI and ERPs (Event Related Potentials that are recordings of cerebral electrical activity during cognitive tasks). Green makes it clear that this is not a claim that an L2 speaker ends up with native-like speech, but rather that neural processing can change. That is, he suggests that **some reorganization may take place** – if, for whatever external reasons, the speaker moves toward more fluency in the L2.

11.7.3 The right hemisphere and language

Finally, there is the issue of the role of the right hemisphere in language. A number of brain-imaging studies have found that tasks related to non-verbal meanings or judgments show activation of the **prefrontal cortex in the right hemisphere in late bilinguals**. In response to these findings, Hahne and Friederici (2002: 13) comment, "This suggests that the right prefrontal cortex supports the processing of conceptual-semantic information whereas the left prefrontal cortex subserves the processing of lexical semantic information." These authors note that these results are in agreement with the distinction various linguists and psycholinguists make between the abstract levels of conceptual-semantic structure (presumably, pre-linguistic) and lexical-semantic structures (presumably, language-specific). (Refer back to 10.5.3 where we discuss this distinction.)

11.7.4 Summing up findings on brain-related differences and later bilingualism

Here are some conclusions about a critical age for acquisition and brain-related differences between L1 and L2. For conclusions about L2 learning and age of acquisition, we rely especially on Harley and Wang (1997).

- Most researchers agree that no matter at what age they are learned, L2s are largely, if not entirely, **in the left hemisphere of the brain**, as is the case with L1s, although an L2 that is learned late may be in slightly different areas of that hemisphere.
- **If exposure to any language is late** (possibly even past the age of four), acquisition is likely to be incomplete. But what "incomplete" means is not easy to pin down. Further, studies on the effect of age of acquisition show mixed results.
- **No single version of the Critical Age Hypothesis** can account for the range of findings.
- Further, some neuroimaging studies indicate that **the degree of L2 proficiency**, not necessarily a very early age of acquisition, matters in predicting how an L2 is represented in the brain in comparison with an L1.
- Although some adult learners are capable of native-like or near-native-like performance in an L2, as the age of initial acquisition goes up (past nine), the attainment of **pronunciation and grammar declines across age groups**. In adults, this is especially the case regarding their speaking and aural comprehension abilities.
- Various studies show that success in grammaticality judgments ("Can this be a sentence in language X?") **declines in a linear fashion** up until about age 12 to 15. Later, there is **no a clear pattern of age related to success**; some late learners do achieve a (surprisingly) high degree of success.
- Why some late second-language learners are much more successful than others is not clear.
- Brain-imaging studies show that **different areas of the brain are activated** when late learners of an L2 perform a task in that language (speaking) than when they perform the task in their L1.
- Thus, mature L2 learners make faster initial progress in learning word-formation and sentence structure than in pronunciation. Recall that pronunciation seems to be set very early in a child's life.
- Finally, and most important, monolingual-like ability in both of a bilingual's languages is probably a myth (at any age). (The explanation doesn't have to do with innate factors, but rather with degree of exposure and use. That is, even very young bilinguals don't use both languages equally and so develop more proficiency in one language.)

11.8 Second language acquisition (SLA) as formal instruction

Why, even after years of study, do speakers of a second language often "make mistakes" (not achieve results resembling native speakers)? And why do some late learners perform better than others? Why haven't instructors come up with methods that work better than they do? These are the questions that are foremost in the minds of students of second languages. You can imagine having no good answers frustrates language classroom teachers, too. In this section, we'll consider current attempts to come up with some answers. That is, we'll look specifically at theories to explain why SLA is as successful (or not) as it is. Certainly, there is a tremendous amount of research going on today, but we warn you that more questions than answers remain.

Recall that we included under second language acquisition any learning of a second language at a later age than when the first language was acquired. But here we will focus on studies of SLA as formal language learning, generally in the classroom and generally past a very young age.

11.8.1 Second language learning around the world

Second language learning in a classroom setting is a necessary fact of life in much of the world. How is this so? Almost every nation state in the world includes populations that are diverse in the sense that each one speaks a different L1. If one of these L1s is the language of the majority, then often minority groups end up having to study that majority language (and many times, schooling is only available in that language). For example, in France, native speakers of French dominate and French is studied by all groups and is the medium of instruction. In nations where no one language group dominates in numbers or politically, then either one regional language or an outside language may be selected as a lingua franca. (Remember that a **lingua franca** is any language used between speakers who do not share the same L1.) In this case, everyone who goes to school may study that lingua franca and it is likely to be the medium of instruction for at least the upper primary grades, too. For example, in Indonesia, Bahasa Indonesian is such a lingua franca as well as the L1 of increasing numbers of Indonesians. In Uganda, English is studied in school and is the main medium of instruction beyond the primary grades, so it becomes a lingua franca in many inter-ethnic group conversations.

In many nations, in addition to studying whatever language is the medium of instruction, upper-level students study one or more international language, such as English. At least 300 to 400 million people speak English as their L1, but at least one billion people study English as a foreign language or as an official second language (Crystal, 1987).

Also, many children in various parts of the world must learn a second dialect of their language when they go to school; that is a standard dialect is expected or required in school settings, whether it is standard German in Germany or Standard American English in the United States. Of course, as we've pointed out in earlier chapters, not only children but also adults learn a second language informally or in classrooms in various places for various reasons; however, this is studied in a less systematic way.

11.8.2 Divisions among SLA researchers

Researchers in Second Language Acquisition (SLA) ask the same questions as learners, but they frame their questions (and answers) in terms of the premises that they hold about the nature of language acquisition in the first place. In a nutshell, they question what cognitive components or mechanisms are available to second language (L2) learners. According to their stand on this matter, we divide researchers into two main and two secondary groups. First, we boil down the differences between the groups; later, we give more details about the groups and their studies.

One group can be called the **Universal Grammar (UG) proponents**; sometimes they are called nativists. This group argues that second language acquisition has distinct similarities to first language acquisition. UG proponents reason that learners have some access to the same **innate language faculty (UG)** that many linguists argue makes first language acquisition so rapid and seemingly effortless. (UG will be explained more fully below.) This group focuses on finding evidence in the performance of L2 learners that UG, and not instruction, must be involved in any successes. This group is most closely allied with generative syntacticians who also refer to UG in their work.

Another group of SLA researchers (probably a larger group) is more **instruction-centered**. This group's premise is that second language learning is very different from first language acquisition. These researchers argue that even if L1 acquisition is based on an innate language faculty, that faculty is no longer active for late L2 learners, or at least not to the extent that it is for L1 acquisition. Therefore, this group focuses on finding evidence for the type of learning that is possible for L2 learners. As you'll see below, there is an important current division in this group. Some argue that learners do best with instruction designed to promote **explicit learning**. Others claim learners achieve the most results through teaching methods that promote **implicit learning** (recall the discussion in sections 11.6.3 and 11.6.4 on declarative and procedural memory and their role in L2 learning).

There is a third group of researchers with theoretical premises more similar to the second than to the first of the main groups just discussed. Researchers in this third group pay more attention to the here and now of classroom instruction; that is, they emphasize the **role of the context** in which learning takes place or **learners' motivations and expectations** related to level of success attained.

Finally, there are those researchers who explain SLA learning within a theory with some important adherents within cognitive science in general, the theory of **connectionism**. One issue is exactly which researchers to include here. In his overview chapter, N. Ellis (2003) includes followers of **construction grammar**, an important group of researchers from linguistics (e.g. Langacker, 1987), and acquisition studies (e.g. Slobin, 1997), among many others. We don't have space to consider construction grammar except to say that it shares with more "pure" connectionism the view that general learning mechanisms enable humans to acquire language, given the necessary environment and motivations based on the functions language can serve. Connectionism per se is a processing model. It emphasizes that structural regularities emerge from the language learner's analysis of linguistic input, driven by the frequency and complexity of the form–function relationships that emerge in the input. Thus, as N. Ellis puts it, "the knowledge of the speaker/hearer cannot be understood as an innate grammar, but rather as a **statistical ensemble of language experiences** that changes slightly every time a new utterance is processed" (p. 64).

Basically, connectionists claim that, with computer-based models of language learning, they can model the process that a language learner goes through to learn to distinguish such forms as past tense version of English irregular and regular verbs. Rumelhart and McClelland (1986) presented the first connectionist model of this construction. The idea of connectionists is that there is no "rule" but on-line "generalizations". Most work to date has concerned L1 acquisition. Gregg (2003) points out that a problem with connectionism is that it has no theory of what it is the learner has acquired, partly because no final state is posited.

In the following sections, we'll only have more to say about the two main groups of SLA researchers. Further, we'll limit discussion to morphology and syntax even though there are many studies on phonology, too. For more on the entire field of SLA research see these edited volumes: Archibald (2000), Doughty and Long (2003), Eubank, Selinker, and Sharwood Smith (1995), Gass and Schachter (1989), and Mitchell and Myles (1998), as well as the textbook by R. Ellis (1994). In addition, there are many new texts every day on related issues, such as an edited volume by Cook (2003) titled *Effects of the Second Language on the First*. Obviously, SLA research is a robust, fast-moving field of study.

11.8.2.1 SLA as the study of learner interlanguages

It's important to recognize that all SLA research (in any of these groups) is concerned with changes of state within the learner, so in this sense it is a **study of internal competence**. Almost all SLA researchers would agree with this statement, but, as you can imagine from the descriptions of the groups above, the disagreement comes over how much innateness specific to language acquisition is involved. And any researcher's stand on this issue indirectly influences the type of study he or she undertakes.

There are many puzzles about L2 learning. This is one reason there are not only the two groups of researchers just mentioned, but many minor divisions within each group, each with its own hypotheses to explain what happens in L2 learning. Although not all researchers agree, there are many similarities between the steps that a speaker goes through in acquiring an L1 and an L2. For example, Klein and Perdue (1997), who report on informal SLA of five European languages among groups of immigrants from very different language backgrounds, indicate that the progression from single content words to more complex clause structures and the use of inflections largely mirrors that of L1 acquisition. The first verb form the immigrants used in their L2 was the present progressive form (the -ing verb, as in *boy singing*). This is also the first grammatical morpheme that Roger Brown (1973) found was acquired by three children from different backgrounds who were acquiring English as their first language. Also, as Nick Ellis (2005) points out, "The fact that L2 learning is influenced by transfer [of structures] from L1 means that a model of SLA must take into account the acquisition and structure of L1." But, again, if there are resemblances between acquiring an L1 and an L2, why are the results so different?

Thus, the subject under study here is the **interlanguage** that develops in L2 learners. Selinker (1972) coined this term. Interlanguage refers to the linguistic systems (note the plural) that an L2 learner constructs as he or she progresses toward the target variety. At any stage, speakers have a system of systematic rules, but they are not the same thing as those of the learner's target, which is presumably a standard dialect of the L2 and which most L2 learners never reach completely. As L2 learners progress toward their target, their interlanguages change and become more like the target.

11.8.2.2 L2 learners and fossilization

Quite often, some features of an interlanguage remain as part of the learner's production of the target, even though they are not well-formed in the target language. This is why we often observe that "so and so speaks language X almost, but not quite, as a native speaker does." Yes, the late L2 learner has learned language X, but it remains an interlanguage variety. For example, a Korean-English bilingual whom we know, who speaks and writes English very fluently, still sporadically uses *he* to refer to a woman. SLA specialists say the learner's grammar has **fossilized** to include such a feature, a feature that he or she may never lose.

11.8.3 The second language learner and innate linguistic competence

Those SLA researchers who are **Universal Grammar (UG) proponents** emphasize the L2 learner as a language processor, with access to language-specific innate components. These researchers are not so interested in the learner's success in acquiring an L2 as they are in uncovering evidence that mental components underlie any success at all. Almost all researchers agree that language is best viewed as a mental grammar that includes **a computational system** that indicates how sentences are formed. The issue is how much of this computational system is specific to language (as opposed to other activities of the mind) and how specific in details is the system.

Researchers who are UG proponents claim that Universal Grammar (UG) is a prominent part of this computational system. Because of how they view an innate component specific to language acquisition (a domain-specific component), and the availability of this component (i.e. UG) in SLA, these researchers clearly stand at one end of the continuum in acquisition studies.

The notion of UG comes from Chomsky (1965; 1981) and others who argue that UG is part of an innate language faculty that makes any type of language acquisition possible. A simple way to describe UG is to say that **the operative word is "constraints"**. That is, the role of UG is to **provide limits** on which structures are possible in human languages and which are not.

According to the theory of UG, speakers do not have to arrive at these limits through overt learning; instead, humans are endowed with the faculty that provides the limits. The main evidence cited for the existence of any innate component like UG is the fact that children acquire their L1s very quickly and seemingly effortlessly with rather limited exposure to their L1s. Many child language researchers explain this fact by saying that UG supplies limits on what is possible in a human language. That is, they say UG explains the mismatch between the rather limited input children receive (speech to which they are exposed) and the unconscious knowledge of their L1 that children display in their speech.

Many other child language researchers argue otherwise, relating success in acquisition to general learning mechanisms that may be innate and various environmental factors. In fact, relatively little of the literature in child language acquisition refers to UG. Many SLA researchers also favor the notion that general universally present learning mechanisms, not a component specific to language, are involved in SLA.

11.8.3.1 SLA studies and UG

Typically, the methodology of these studies is to offer participants strings of words and ask them whether these strings can be considered well-formed sentences in the language in question. That is, they employ grammaticality judgments. However, more recently, other methodologies (testing demonstrated proficiency) are used to supplement such judgments.

And, indeed, some studies do seem to show that L2 learners are able to distinguish between the grammaticality of one form of a sentence and another, even though they never were explicitly taught the grammatically acceptable form. White (2003a) cites such a study by Kanno (1997) of English-speaking learners of Japanese. She sees the results as support for the claim that UG constrains their grammaticality judgments. This study concerned the acceptability of having an overt pronoun or not in certain Japanese sentences (with the pronoun referring back to a certain type of antecedent). White reports that the "L2 learners showed a remarkably similar pattern of results and [that] their responses did not differ significantly from the controls [native speakers of

Japanese]" (p. 24). White herself has conducted a number of studies, especially on French-speaking learners of English and their abilities to correctly recognize the impossibility of certain structures in English.

11.8.3.2 Full or partial access to UG?

One issue that divides UG proponents is how much access L2 learners are seen as having to UG and how much involvement the L1 has. There are at least three positions.

(1) The strongest form of the UG hypothesis is **full access to UG, no transfer**. This position is also called **direct access**. The claim is that the L1 is not involved at all in any first version of the learner's interlanguage and researchers argue that the initial interlanguage must just be based on UG (for support of this hypothesis, see Flynn, 1996).

(2) A second position is for **full access for L2, but also transfer from L1**. Under this hypothesis, learners start with an interlanguage based on their L1 and then reset parameters when they get positive evidence from their exposure to/study of the L2. Parameters supplement universal principles; they are built-in settings that allow for crosslinguistic variation (Schwartz and Sprouse, 2000 *inter alia* offer support for this hypothesis). Earlier, White (e.g. 2000) seemed to support this position but her position is less clear. But she does conclude her book-length study with this comment: "Only Full Transfer Full Access, which allows a role for both the L1 and UG, has the potential to account for native-like ultimate attainment or lack thereof" (2003b: 269). This position allows her to say that the endstate L2 grammar need not be identical in all respects to the L1 grammar that is the putative target language. At the same time, she writes that "non-attainment of native-like competence is fully compatible with the claim that interlanguage grammars are UG-constrained. An interlanguage grammar which diverges from the native grammar can nevertheless fall within the bounds laid down by UG" (2003b: 243).

(3) A third position is only **partial access to UG**, either via L1 or not (see Schachter below). There are many other hypotheses that posit different levels of L1 involvement or of the manner in which UG alone is involved (e.g. Eubank and Grace, 1998; Lardiere, 2000). Evidence of only partial access to UG would be better performance in an L2 that has constraints which are similar to those in the speaker's L1 and therefore are part of the speaker's implicit knowledge.

We illustrate one study testing partial access. Schachter (1989) studied L2 learners' knowledge of a proposed UG universal regarding certain movement rules that go under the term Subjacency (i.e. restrictions on movements of certain elements in a clause from their "initial" place to somewhere else in the clause). We won't go into details about Subjacency, but will just give you the outlines of the experiment Schachter conducted. She tested participants that she referred to as "proficient speakers of English; some were native speakers of Korean, some of Chinese and some of Indonesian".

Results did not support the notion of full access to UG in adult L2 learners; the data from the Korean participants indirectly supported the notion of access only if the learners' language had the feature being tested. Here were the results. First, native speakers of English also were tested as a control group and their performance indicated they knew the construction being tested and which test sentences violated constraints on it. Second, only about one-third of the non-native English speakers showed knowledge of the construction being tested and its violation. Korean does not have this type of movement restriction and the Korean participants performed the least well. Thus, the Korean data support the notion of **partial access to UG** at best. The Chinese and Indonesian subjects performed better on the test sentences and both of their languages have some movement rules that can be considered constraints on Subjacency. Still, neither group performed well enough to give strong support to the position that UG is available to adult learners.

11.8.3.3 *Arguments for and against UG positions on SLA*

An argument for the UG proponents is that they are generally the SLA researchers who have demonstrated the clearest hypotheses and the clearest results in their studies. Further, it is to their credit that they concentrate on the systematicity in language, not on the linear order of words. Among linguists, the assumption of **systematicity** is the assumption that knowledge is organized in a system of abstract representation and that production of language reveals this order. (Recall the Uniform Structure Principle introduced in chapter 9 in reference to language contact phenomena, but with universal application.) Another point in favor of the UG proponents is that their work exploits the premise that late L2 learners are cognitively mature.

There are two main arguments against the notion that UG is available to late L2 learners. First, even if UG is present in young children, the fact that learning an L2 becomes difficult after about the age of 9 to 12 is reason to argue UG is no longer available to older learners. Second, how can UG proponents explain the many studies of the type cited earlier in this chapter that seem to show that late L2 learners do not attain the same level of ability in a language as L1 speakers of that language?

However, proponents of the role of UG in SLA have a good deal of company from the ranks of linguists specializing in the study of syntax. Much current work in generative syntax assumes the existence of UG as an explanation (for a particular language) of why the architecture of a certain linguistic structure takes the form it does (e.g. the syntactic theories of Chomksy (1995) *inter alia*).

11.8.3.4 *A modified view of UG in SLA*

Some researchers, well represented by O'Grady (2003), accept the idea of some innate basis for success in language acquisition, but a basis that is short of the specific claims of the proponents of UG. O'Grady calls the approach he favors **"general nativism"** (also see Croft, 2003; Langacker, 1987). Such an approach includes some sort of innate acquisition system that guides the learner and interacts with experience. But the important feature of this approach is that it **rejects the specific, detailed constraints** as part of UG that proponents of the role of UG in SLA seem to see. That is, theories of this type hold the view that the mind is geared toward processing information, but linguistic information is just one type.

Disagreements with theories based on UG seem to center on the question of whether specific grammatical structures and categories are innate. A short-coming of general nativism, according to O'Grady himself, is that it doesn't include any theory of learnability and development. (The claim of access to UG is, after all, such a theory.) Note that some connectionists claim that proponents of cognitive linguistics, such as Langacker – mentioned above – belong in their camp, not with proponents of any form of UG at all.

11.8.4 Instruction-centered SLA researchers

A large number of SLA researchers can be classified as what we will call **instruction-centered researchers**. But then there are a number of sub-groupings, as you will see. In the following subsections, we'll survey various approaches that have been in vogue. Bear in mind that even though we refer to some of them as prominent in the past, most of them are still very much a part of any current instruction-centered approaches. Old approaches are recycled and refurbished, not lost entirely. Throughout this section, keep in mind the division between approaches that emphasize the possibility of L2 learning through implicit instruction in contrast with those that emphasize explicit learning.

In general, instruction-centered approaches emphasize results in observa-tions or experiments that involve quantification. That is, researchers count the numbers of occurrences of whatever they are studying (usually instances of accurate production of certain features of an L2 that learners are studying) and associate these numbers with some independent variables, such as type of instruction, number of hours of classroom study, etc. Earlier UG approaches relied heavily on grammaticality judgments, as we noted above, but, increas-ingly, they also involve quantification of accurate production of the target features.

11.8.4.1 Emphasis on learning new habits and identifying errors

If we look at the history of SLA research, we see that in the 1950s and 1960s, instructors were much more interested in the practical business of teaching the target language than in explaining successes or their lack thereof. Further, instructors were firmly in the embrace of the prevailing view in psychology,

behaviorism. This all changed by the 1960s, initiated by Chomsky's emphasis on the essential part of language as abstract systematicity – that is, production governed by abstract "rules" that speakers hold in their minds. But for the moment, instructors, along with any researchers there were, believed that success in language learning, like in any other kind of learning, came largely from **forming habits** and the related notion that **practice makes perfect**.

In this vein, two main approaches were advocated to explain successful L2 learning. The first was **contrastive analysis**. The idea was that by analyzing the structure of the learner's first language and comparing it with the target second language, instructors could work out the problem areas for the learner. But you can imagine that the task of comparing the structures of any two languages was a huge task. Further, because of the prevailing view that the structure of language lay only in its surface, linear orders, a real comparison of two languages simply wasn't made (because the abstract nature of language was not considered).

The second approach that took over in the 1970s was called **error analysis**. Now, at least, the interest had shifted to the language produced by the learners themselves. But working out why learners make the errors they do is not easy. The underlying assumption was still that errors occurred because learners were using structures from their L1. The notion of **interference** or **transfer** from the L1 was part of this approach. As R. Ellis (1994: 48) points out, "EA [Error Analysis] provided a methodology for investigating learner language." That is, instructors could identify errors (and use them to see what areas needed to be emphasized in teaching) and researchers could use them to attempt to explain them and the L2 learning process as a whole. However, both of these approaches still emphasized "changing habits". Further, error analysis doesn't necessarily mean that *the source* of errors is identified. As for the L1 as a source of errors through transfer, various studies claimed that anywhere from 3 to 51 per cent of errors could be attributed to the L1; but Mitchell and Myles (1998: 30) cite a survey by Ellis of studies of errors that shows that only about a third of all errors are traceable to the L1.

11.8.4.2 *The role of internal mechanisms*

By the 1980s SLA researchers were more interested in the overall character of SLA and many shifted their interest to the internal mechanisms of language learning. This led some researchers to concentrate on studying the sequence of learning various structures; these resulted in the so-called **morpheme studies**. As part of this interest in sequencing, Krashen (e.g. 1985) produced his **Monitor Model**, which was based on the idea that learning and acquisition are two different processes. Learning is only useful as a "monitor" or "editor" that makes changes in a learner's grammar after he or she has acquired a structure. Krashen's ideas were very influential, but they also were vague. Note that Krashen is mentioned again in section 11.8.4.3.

Many other researchers emphasized the role of psychological variables, such as motivation, language aptitude and personality. The idea that language learning is a matter of **information processing** led not only to connectionism (mentioned above in 11.8.2) but to more function-based explanations of results. Slobin (e.g. 1985) is most associated with the **perceptual saliency approach** to explaining L1 acquisition. The idea is that children organize their language by applying **operating principles** to input. For example, one operating principle is "pay attention to the ends of the words". This idea was taken over by many researchers in SLA studies, too.

Others emphasized sociolinguistic variables, such an environmental factors. The Acculturation Model of Schumann in the late 1970s is an example of this approach in that Schumann linked language learning success to integration into a community. The emphasis on the social context remains evident in many SLA studies today.

At the same time, given the new emphasis on the role of cognitive structures in language that was evident in research by linguists (following Chomsky and therefore especially on syntax), it should come as no surprise that studies of first and second language acquisition took up the cognitive mantle, too. This led to the rise of UG-based studies of SLA discussed above.

Still, as UG-based SLA research proceeds, other researchers have been arguing against the idea that SLA resembles first language acquisition. **The Fundamental Difference Hypothesis** (Bley-Vroman, 1990) contrasts the two types of acquisition. L1 acquisition is a matter of automatic acquisition based on an innate language acquisition component. In contrast, L2 learning is more the result of problem-solving strategies. Note that DeKeyser and Larson-Hall (2005) also view successful L2 learning as the product of explicit learning in contrast to the implicit learning that is possible in L1 acquisition. Their conclusions on the critical age hypothesis were discussed above in section 11.7.

11.8.4.3 Processing competence: an innate capacity that differs from UG

Process-centered researchers share with UG-based proponents an interest in cognitive abilities. But the cognitive component that they posit performs language processing. Further, these researchers do not suggest an innateness of any actual features of language that many of the more strict UG proponents argue exist. For these process-centered researchers, the emphasis is on **learnability** and the idea that what is "learnable" depends on what has already been acquired. The impetus for these studies is the fact that L2 learners do follow a fairly rigid route in their acquisition of certain grammatical structures.

The **processability theory** of Pienemann (2003) is one of these theories. The basic idea of this model is that "at any stage, the learner can produce and comprehend only those L2 forms which the current stage of the language processor can manage" (p. 686). Thus, this model enables the researcher to predict the course of development in acquiring L2 forms. The idea is that after the learner learns one form, grammatical information can be held in a grammatical memory storage, which is highly task-specific. Basically, then, what the learner (L1 or L2) has to do is come up with a new conceptualization that puts together routines in that memory storage.

For example, in order to handle subject–verb agreement (putting the -s on third person singular present tense verbs), the English learner has to have acquired the notion of **feature unification**. This is done in noun phrases where the learner recognizes the feature of "singular or plural" in relation to nouns. But then for subject–verb agreement, the learner has to match features across constituents (from the NP to the VP). This interphrasal matching is not predicted before matching within the phrase (e.g. within the NP). (Note some similarities between the divisions of the 4-M model discussed in chapter 9 in relation to language contact and the divisions between affixes depending on intra-phrase information (early system morphemes) and those outsider late system morphemes that always depend on cross-phrasal information.)

There are similarities between Pienemann's model and several other approaches. Still, be sure to note that neither Pienemann's nor the others is the same thing as connectionism, which does not see the learning of rules as underlying the construction of linguistic knowledge. For example, Pienemann's approach echoes Krashen's Input Hypothesis. Krashen (1985) argued that the learner can only acquire "**comprehensible input**" that came about through inferential learning when the learner achieved a certain stage. While Krashen's model was very popular in the 1980s, it was also criticized; because of its vagueness, it was not clear how it could be tested (and therefore supported or rejected). Another complementary theory is the Autonomous Induction Theory of Carroll (2000). Briefly, her idea is that what a learner can take in is limited by the grammar (interlanguage) the speaker has already constructed of the target language. Van Patten (1996) also distinguishes input and intake, arguing that a set of strategies (under the rubric "attention") is necessary to turn input into intake. Recall both Krashen's views (more or less favoring implicit learning) and Van Patten's views (more or less favoring both explicit instruction and implicit learning) when we discuss these two types of learning in section 11.8.5. Pienemann's proposals seem especially open to testing. In fact, Pienemann (2003: 695) reports on a number of studies of L2 learners of English whose progress in learning English structures follows the implicational table that he predicts for English.

11.8.5 Where is SLA research today?

Doughty (2003) offers an extensive overview of SLA research today. Near the beginning of this survey, she makes it clear that, while UG approaches continue to attract attention, many other researchers are pursuing more learner-based or classroom-based theoretical approaches. She writes, "Even if a UG explanation of SLA were to prevail, the elements of language that are governed solely by UG are limited. Much more of the L2 remains which is potentially acquired more efficiently provided instruction appropriately engages learners' cognitive processing ability" (p. 258).

As she points out, a major division today in SLA revolves around the question of whether **implicit or explicit learning** is possible through formal L2 instruction. Doughty (2003: 268) reproduces details from a study of 250 programs by Norris and Ortega (2000) that shows that 70 percent assume that learning occurs through explicit instruction and only 30 percent assume that implicit learning is possible. (Remember that implicit learning is associated with what can be stored as procedural memory while explicit learning is associated with declarative memory.)

Even though such a study shows that many researchers seem to favor what appears to be explicit instruction, almost as many shy away from referring to explicit instruction when they discuss their approaches. For example, Long (1996) developed an **Interaction Hypothesis** that emphasizes drawing learners' attention to target structures, yes, but doing this specifically in contexts where the attention is meaningful.

Other researchers refer to "noticing" (e.g. Sharwood Smith, 1994) or "conscious-raising" (e.g. Pica, 1994). Overall, such attention is called **focus on form**, but this is not the same as "focus on form-s", which is said to stress more explicit instruction of specific forms. R. Ellis, Basturkmen, and Loewen (2001: 407) define focus on form as "the incidental attention that teachers and L2 learners pay to form in the context of meaning-focused instruction". This focus can be either reactive (focus on corrective feedback) or preemptive (when either the instructor or the student makes form a topic to discuss). No matter what it is called, the assumption seems to be that learning occurs through some attention to form.

Some approaches pay less direct attention to form, such as meaning-based approaches and task-based approaches or interactive approaches (cf. Gass, 2003). The assumption underlying these approaches is that students can learn the structure of the target L2 implicitly through various **tasks that focus on meaning**. Of course, it's unlikely that any instructional program follows any approach exclusively, but more researchers currently seem to argue that successful later L2 learning is more likely to be explicit than implicit learning.

11.9 Summing up

In an overview statement, Nick Ellis (2005) points out three themes that have been present in research on language acquisition. These themes remind us what we know about acquisition and what still needs more study.

- The first theme is **the age factor**. Even though all researchers don't agree on a critical age after which native-like acquisition is near impossible, all do agree that SLA is less successful in older learners. So the question is "why?" In addition, we have to deal with the fact that the success of different L2 learners varies.

- A second theme is **second language processing**. If we accept the notion that SLA is different from child language acquisition, we need a detailed theory of processing, that includes both comprehension and production, that takes account of these two different types of acquisition. We have only some glimmerings of what is involved in SLA processing. For example, recall the views of Pienemann and others in section 11.8.4.3; the views of connectionists mentioned in section 11.8.2; and Ullman on the different roles of procedural memory and declarative memory discussed in section 11.6.4. Also, other researchers not discussed here argue that not all elements are processed in the same way and possibly not in the same area of the brain (e.g. Clahsen, 1999 argues that certain irregular verb forms are processed differently from regularly inflected ones). But, as Doughty (2003) points out, even now the proportion of studies that investigate SLA processes is very small.

- Finally, Ellis's third theme is very specific to SLA. It is **transfer itself** (cf. Odlin, 2003 for an overview). Research seems to show that there is little transfer between the languages in child bilingualism. This is yet another reason to distinguish child and late L2 acquisition because there clearly is almost always some transfer in SLA. Transfer is a hard nut to crack. One intriguing question is this: What **type of transfer** is even *possible* in SLA? Are there innate constraints on which morphemes or structures are open to transfer?

- In addition, a key theme throughout the chapter is the notion that language shows **systematicity**. That is, linguistic knowledge is organized in a system of representations. We see this in child bilingualism where different systems are acquired and the differentiation of the two systems is accomplished implicitly, without conscious effort. We assume that this should be possible in second language learners and we do see at least some systematicity in indications of their underlying competence and in their production.

- **The issue remains** of why young children acquire languages so easily and why adults seem to be unable to reach the same final state as these children do.

11.10 Words and phrases to remember

child bilingualism
bilingualism as an advantage

success in late bilingualism
early and late bilingualism and brain-imaging studies
procedural memory and implicit learning
declarative memory and explicit learning
UG and SLA
instruction-centered SLA

12

Language Policies and Globalization

Multiple voices: The word from an American in Norway

Elizabeth Bellenger is an American living in Norway where she is a university professor. She gives her lectures in Norwegian and occasionally in English, especially if international visitors are present. She is married to a Norwegian and they speak English to each other. But her husband speaks only Norwegian to their children while she speaks mostly English to them, codeswitching between English and Norwegian at times. In addition to these two languages, Elizabeth acquired French as a small child from her French mother while her family was living in North Africa. When the family returned to the United States (Elizabeth was five then), she quickly forgot her French, only to relearn it as a university student. Today, she speaks French on family vacations in southern France and when she meets French friends. Believe it or not, she wants to learn Tagalog in Oslo. She attends a Catholic church where she sings in the choir and so do many of the parishioners who are from the Philippines. The choir often sings Tagalog hymns and Elizabeth is interested in understanding them and her fellow choir members better.

12.1 Introduction

This chapter will present an overview of what **language planning** is as well as a discussion of language policies in representative nation states. The backdrop for this discussion will be **the global language system**, and this will mean we will pay special attention to the role of international languages in the world, even as we discuss policies in individual nation states.

Not a day passes that we don't receive emails that contain news of language policies that affect the more public lives of bilinguals. For example, recently we heard about two new legal measures adopted in Turkey that affect Turkey's numerous minority languages. Under these measures, radio broadcasts in non-official languages are to include translations into Turkish, and TV broadcasts in these languages are to include Turkish subtitles. The measures also restrict the total time for such broadcasting.

And in multilingual India, each week brings news of new policies and counter policies. For example, a 2004 news story tells about the canceling of a Karnataka State government order calling for notifications, orders, and rules to be issued in minority languages in certain cases. This order provoked a lot of controversy in Karnataka State where the order would have affected a number of minority groups. Some locals argued that the **needs of the linguistic minorities** are met by publishing orders in English. But the newspaper *Star of Mysore* commented that publishing notifications in English "only reaches **the creamy layer**" (referring to the cream which is at the top of glass bottles of whole milk, still available in some parts of the world). Whatever the different views, the order ended up being canceled.

Meanwhile, in other nations, minority groups are protesting in various ways the lack of official recognition that their languages receive. For example, in April 2004 representatives of **the Polish minority** in the Czech Republic were collecting signatures in support of local bilingual signposts. In the town with the greatest proportion of Polish speakers (Hrádek), Poles make up 43 percent of the population and in some cities the Polish-speaking minority is 16 or 17 percent.

Protests in Wales were also in the news in mid-2004. Students at the University of Wales in Aberystwyth were protesting what they perceived as a **lack of Welsh language teaching**. They would like to see the establishment of a Welsh-language college.

But there is also news showing how bilingualism affects bilinguals in their private lives. We read news from Romania telling about a **marriage that was not legally recognized** because it wasn't conducted in Romanian. The bridegroom uttered his consent in Hungarian, but he did repeat it in Romanian. A court reversed the ruling, declaring the couple had been caused "moral damages".

The news from the South Tyrol autonomous province in Italy where there is a German minority is about **bilingual labeling**. We find out that starting in 2004, fifteen years after a presidential decree on the use of German in dealings with citizens (the decree was in 1988), pharmaceutical products sold there are going to be labeled in German as well as Italian.

And here's a final example: In 2003, the news from Russia's upper house of parliament (the Federation Council), was that a move to ban the use of

foreign words and vulgarities was rejected. According to the *New York Times*, several senators criticized the legislation as hasty and impractical, saying in particular that foreign words, not to mention obscenities, regularly pepper Russian discourse.

12.1.1 Language in a global system

In his interpretive study of the rationale for existing (and possibly future) language policies, De Swaan (2001) anchors his analysis with the idea of language groups in competition in a global context. From world system theory, he derives the notion that languages should be thought of as competing on one of **three hierarchical levels**: core, intermediate, and peripheral levels. The languages that he calls **supercentral** are at the core level, others can be called **central** languages, and still others are at the **peripheral** level. Placing languages on these levels reflects the idea that languages are not just in competition, they are in unequal competition. This is evident, De Swaan suggests, because "**language learning occurs mostly upward** . . . people usually prefer to learn a language that is at a higher level in the hierarchy" (p. 5).

Using the **metaphor of a galaxy** that includes planets and the moons that circle them, De Swaan says that peripheral languages can be thought of as grouped around a central language. He identifies central languages only in his discussion of individual nation states, but we imagine he would call Kannada in India a central language. It is the Dravidian language with the most speakers in Karnataka State. Also, Wolof in Senegal would be a central language, partly because is the L1 of the majority of the population, but also because many other Senegalese languages are related to it and many people speak it as an L2.

However, De Swaan pays the most attention to a dozen languages that he identifies as supercentral languages today: Arabic, Chinese, English, French, German, Hindi, Japanese, Malay, Portuguese, Russian, Spanish and Swahili. Each has its **constellation of peripheral languages**. Except for Swahili (in East and Central Africa), all these languages have more than a hundred million speakers. But what may be more important, speakers of the peripheral languages often learn the central languages as second languages, but definitely choose to learn the supercentral language in their galaxy if that is a path open to them. (Note the discussion below of languages in general as "collective goods"; supercentral languages achieve this status more than other languages, and central languages achieve it more than peripheral languages. Status, of course, refers to a position relative to that of others, generally used alone to mean a higher position. A group can have high political status or socio-economic status; the two often go together.)

In addition, De Swaan sees English, as the language of global communication, at the center of this galaxy of planets and their moons. English hasn't always had this position and it may lose it, but because of the power of centripetal forces, De Swaan suggests that "in the next decades it [English] is only likely to reinforce its position even further" (p. 6).

Throughout his discussion De Swaan stresses the notion that languages should be thought of as **collective goods**. What this means is that for a language to have value, it must be valued and used by more than one person, a collection of persons. Languages are goods in the economic sense, but they are different from most economic goods in two ways: First, they are not scarce goods; there are languages all over. Second, they do not get "used up"; in fact, an important insight is that **the more a language is used the more valuable it becomes**.

But speaking a language involves **an investment**. As we've indicated in chapter 11, small children have the potential to acquire a number of languages effortlessly. But becoming proficient in a language as an adult is definitely not easy and often not very successful. Experience tells people that learning a second language at all well is an investment of time and effort. Because they recognize this, speakers will choose to learn the language or languages that they think will bring them **more rewards** than other languages. De Swaan refers to a **political economy of languages** and, in the words of **rational choice theory**, says that whatever a nation state's overt policy is, people will try to maximize their opportunities for upward mobility.

12.1.2 The rise of the nation state and national policies

Since before history was recorded, nations have had policies about the use of one language over others in national roles, sometimes put into law, sometimes just implicit, but obvious, in the selection of languages in which official life is conducted. In European **medieval times** there was little need for any language policies on the national level because there was not much of an established national level. Further, few people were necessarily bilingual. This was because the average person had few contacts outside of the local community. They lived under **a feudal system** of loyalty to a noble, not to any larger political entity. Thus, the only type of bilingualism that prevailed was the **horizontal bilingualism** discussed in chapter 4. That is, only if you took into account a large area could you speak about bilingualism and then only in the sense that the area consisted of a number of largely monolingual communities. If any persons were bilingual, they were generally **members of religious orders** who, in addition to their local language, knew a religious language that was also a language for longer-distance communication and in any supra-local administration. In Western Europe clerics knew Latin and in Eastern Europe they knew either Greek or Church Slavonic, for example. In South Asia, religious men learned Sanskrit and in China they knew a version of ancient Chinese spoken by the Han people.

It was only in the eighteenth and especially the nineteenth centuries that nation states became a reality. For this to happen, borders had to be fixed. But establishing nation states and **fixing borders** was a long process, even in Europe, and continued into the mid-twentieth century in parts of Africa and Asia. Even today, new states, such as East Timor, as separate from Indonesia, are being recognized.

12.1.3 The role of borders: an introduction to the problems nation states face

But there is nothing entirely natural about how boundaries have been fixed. Borders cause three general results.

(1) Many times different indigenous groups (or "founding peoples") speaking different languages have found themselves placed next to each other inside the same set of borders by outside powers. This is what happened in Africa when the European powers divided up the continent and established colonies in the nineteenth and early twentieth centuries. When Cameroon's language policies are discussion in section 12.3, you will see how some of its problems are due to its colonial history and where borders were drawn. The fate of the French-speaking population in eastern Canada is another example of an ethnic group that found itself part of a nation state where another language (English) was by far the dominant language. Following a series of wars over the North American territory, France ceded what was called New France to Great Britain in 1763. What was to become Canada was under the British until it was initially established as an independent confederation of provinces in 1867. In section 12.3.1, we discuss recent reactions by the French in Québec Province to their inclusion in Canada.

We could refer to the indigenous peoples in the Americas, as well as peoples who have found themselves inside the boundaries of new nation states, next to other people who do not share their languages.

(2) In many parts of the world, political boundaries cut across linguistic boundaries. That is, the language varieties spoken on either side of borders are related to each other, sometimes so related that they are mutually intelligible. For example, there is a Slavic continuum of languages across Russia and into the Balkans, but there is not one nation state of Slavic speakers, but many. (See Paulston and Peckham, 1998 for more about language policies in Eastern and Central Europe.)

When political boundaries are not linguistic boundaries, then with a change in political relations in a given area, new nation states may be set up. This happened in the 1990s in the Balkans area. New language varieties were cut out of the fabric of the former language variety called Serbo-Croatian. In chapter 2, we discussed the new language varieties that were cut out of the fabric of the former language variety called Serbo-Croatian. We suggest "**planned distinctiveness**" as a cover term for the process involved in creating new language varieties. When something like this creation of new nation states and new language varieties happens, language planners generally work hard on corpus planning (discussed more fully in section 12.4). They try to make the varieties on either side of borders as different from each other as possible. The new Balkan states don't all use the same alphabet; some use a Cyrillic script and some a Roman (Latin) script. Planners in one Balkan state are still creating new forms of words to separate themselves from a neighboring state. Also, something like this happened when India became independent. When we discuss language policy in India in section 12.3, we'll comment on how what was one political entity under colonial rule became three nation states and how this affected the supercentral language of India, Hindi.

(3) In many cases in the world, speakers of the same language, against their will, find themselves on two different sides of a national border. The causes are changes in national borders or changes in the political status of a territory due to wars or political settlements following wars. On one side is the nation state where their language variety is the official language. But the speakers in question end up as a minority group in another national state.

This presents a problem for the nation states on both sides of the border, but especially for the nation state that finds itself with the "stranded" minority of sizeable numbers. In characterizing a specific type of **stranded minority**, Paulston (1998) prefers the term "extrinsic minority". For her, this is a group whose status in the nation where it is located changes from majority status (of whatever kind) to minority status due to circumstances beyond its control.

Some stranded minorities are bigger problems for the majority group than others. This is the situation today in the Baltic states (Lithuania, Latvia, and Estonia) which have sizeable Russian minorities. They either were immigrants there in the past or moved into these countries when the countries were taken over under the USSR. In section 12.5 we discuss Latvia's situation in relation to language education.

Such minorities are also problems in central Eastern Europe, even if the ethnic home state of the stranded minority is not a supercentral power of the same order as Russia. There are several nation states that are homes to minority groups, thanks to the way borders were drawn after various settlements. **Hungarians in particular** find themselves as minorities in several countries. Of course the main home of Hungarians is the nation state of Hungary, and Hungary itself and these Hungarian minorities outside Hungary find continual need to agitate about the language rights of these "stranded" Hungarians. The Hungarian minority in Slovakia and its efforts to have schooling in Hungarian were discussed in chapter 3. Also, the government of Hungary tries to look after the welfare of these Hungarians in various ways. For example, in early 2004 it set up Hungarian TV in the Transylvanian area of Romania.

The situation of the ethnic **Chinese in Taiwan** is a little different, but also is a case of an ethnic group outside its home country. Many Chinese (of the Han ethnic group) found themselves on the island of Taiwan, permanently it seems, having fled there when mainland China fell to Communist rule in the 1950s. However, because of their socio-economic status relative to that of native Taiwanese, these mainland Chinese were able to establish their own language variety as the official language of Taiwan although it is now being threatened by local groups favoring Taiwanese as an official language.

In other parts of South East Asia, there are long-standing groups of ethnic Chinese (not typically L1 speakers of the Putonghua dialect) in places that are now such nation states as Indonesia, Malaysia, and Thailand. When Australia is discussed in section 12.3, we will see there are also many Chinese there today. But they were all voluntary immigrants. In Singapore, the Chinese constitute the largest ethnic group, and it is only in Singapore that Chinese has any official standing (the standard variety, Putonghua, which is called Mandarin in Singapore and sometimes elsewhere). Recall that Singapore's language policy is discussed in chapter 4.

12.1.4 Who plans language policies?

Before we describe the parts of language planning and discuss case studies in sections 12.3 through 12.5, we want to make you aware of a **number of ironies** that arise in any discussion of language policy. One of the ironies is that language policies are **not necessarily really planned** – in the sense of being based on the available objective evidence (e.g. numbers of speakers of language X versus language Y; feasibility of making language X a medium in the schools, etc.). This may be one of the reasons why Bernard Spolsky (2004a; 2004b) prefers the term **language management** over language planning or engineering. That is, language policies are typically the work of politicians who may have agendas quite unrelated to the best interests of all groups in the population. (We have immediately to add, of course, that one of the problems is that it is difficult to identify and then satisfy the interests of all groups in any nation state.)

A **second irony** is that even when governments set language policies, they are not necessarily followed. Here are three examples showing how the public sometimes treats language policies:

(1) In Japan, Japanese teenagers and others who use words such as *hippu hangu* 'hip-hugging jeans' and other foreign-based words are not listening to the government. In 2002, the Prime Minister of Japan (Junichiro Koizumi) was talking about appointing a panel to propose measures to stem "**the foreign word corruption**" of Japanese. He had in mind the influx of foreign words that in Japanese are written in katakana, a syllabic script largely reserved for writing words imported from Western languages. When Prime Minister Koizumi voiced his complaint, he was not referring specifically to the speech

of teenagers, but to various technical words that are not generally understandable, such as *inkyubeetaa* 'incubator'. At the same time, the Council on the Japanese Language said it was going to advise the government and the media to avoid terms it regards as confusing. The problem is that there are lots of **new words that many Japanese don't understand**, not just from English (especially words having to do with fashion, but also technology), but also from German (many medical terms) and French (the stereotypical language of romance in Japan). But a news story in the *New York Times* (October 23, 2002) reported that "the casual use of katakana [foreign words] seems almost uncontrollable, and most Japanese people, especially those under 50, seem unconcerned about the debate."

(2) Not all French academics follow the French government's various laws to limit the role of English. In June 2002, the oldest French journal, the *Comptes Rendus* (Proceedings of the French Academy of Sciences) announced that English would be **the preferred language** for articles that it publishes.

(3) For a final example of how policy makers aren't followed, consider that in Ireland, government-financed efforts and many plans to **revive Irish** have not led to a measurable increase in the number of speakers of Irish after a century of trying.

Yet **a third irony** is that language policy and planning is a subject widely discussed and debated in numerous publications by academics from a wide variety of disciplines, such as sociology, anthropology, and linguistics, as well as language pedagogy. This flurry of interest in language policy was especially strong in the 1960s and 1970s following the independence of a number of new nations in Africa and Asia, **amid idealism** about the possibility of language planning along democratic lines (e.g. an edited volume by Fishman, Ferguson, and Das Gupta, 1968, and several other such volumes edited by Fishman). Once again, language policy drew academic interest in the late twentieth century and receives even more today. Now, however, the reason seems to be more a set of problems than a set of opportunities. The irony of all this academic interest in language policies and planning is that the theories and analyses of academics do not seem to count much when policies are decided by governmental bodies – at least they **haven't had much impact** in the past. Still, there are always possibilities and academics themselves are an eager audience for their own products.

12.1.5 What is facing language planners today

Today, there are at least **four major socio-political developments** (with related problems) that are being discussed today in academic analyses about language policy. They are what language planners ought to consider. These are (1) **the waves of immigration** that nation states all over the world must deal with, (2) the problem of choice of language for **providing education** for these immigrants as well as for indigenous minority groups, (3) the increasing role of **English as a lingua franca** in the world and its potential effect on the use of other languages, (4) the establishment of the **European Union (EU)** and its problems in allowing the languages of its members some part in proceedings (as of May 2004, there are 25 members).

The major part of this chapter consists of studies of language policy outcomes in individual nation states. These case studies indicate how these developments are affecting policy discussions and decisions. They also make clear how policies in individual nation states take account of the world order of languages as discussed in section 12.1.1. (Language policy is the main topic of several journals (*Language Problems and Language Planning*, and two relatively new journals, *Language Policy* and *Language and Politics*), and language policy is a frequent topic in the *International Journal of the Sociology of Language* and the *Journal of Multilingual and Multicultural Development*, as well as elsewhere.)

12.1.6 Language rights and endangered languages

Two issues that are involved in all four of these developments are those of **language rights** and that of **endangered languages**. Language rights are an issue specifically in regard to immigrants and indigenous minorities, but it is also an issue that the EU must wrestle with as it takes in new states that are not the superpowers that formed the original core of the organization. Similar international unions elsewhere, as well as economically based organizations (e.g. the World Bank), are being called upon to consider language rights, too. Behind this issue is the question, Are language rights **part of human rights**? That is, is the right to speak one's own language in public settings a right of the same order as various freedoms and the pursuit of happiness? Some academics, especially those involved with language education for minority groups, argue that language rights are just as important as any other "basic" rights (e.g. Skutnapp-Kangas, 2000).

A special concern for other academics and language planners is the fate of **endangered languages**. These are languages with diminishing numbers of speakers, especially numbers who speak the language as their mother tongue. For example, consider the Australian indigenous languages. At the time of the first European settlement in 1788, Australia had approximately 250 distinct languages spoken by its native peoples. Many languages were lost, especially in the urban and more settled southern areas. As many as 150 were maintained until the mid-twentieth century, but shift to English and creoles has claimed many of these. Today there are only about 15 "strong" languages in the sense they are still being learned and used by children (McConvell and Thieberger, 2003). In various publications, including Fishman (2001), there are arguments about practical steps that can be taken to attempt to save some languages that are being lost.

12.2 What are the parts of language planning?

As Anderson (1983) points out, **communities are largely "imagined"**. That is, communities – or the nation states relevant to this chapter – are "real" only in the minds of members of the community or nation. Few people have ever been able to know the members of their wider community (their nation), or speak to them. Yet, no matter how imagined the nation is, the language that all members of a nation state must speak, at least in certain out-group interactions, is based on policies that are laid down, and these policies are very real.

Discussion of the nuts and bolts of language policies in the modern era goes back to the name Einar Haugen; Cooper (1989: 29) credits him with introducing the term language planning to the community of linguists and sociologists in a 1959 publication. In a 1969 publication, here is what Haugen says: "As I define it, the term LP [language planning] includes the normative work of language academies and committees, all forms of what is commonly known as language cultivation . . . and all proposals for language reform or standardization" (1969a: 701, cited in Cooper, p. 30). But including Haugen's definition, Cooper could list 12 slightly different definitions from the language planning literature (Cooper 1989: 30–1). Haugen (1969b) was especially interested in language planning as it applied to modern Norway (where today there are two standard dialects – yes, two).

12.2.1 Three areas of language planning

Today, language planning is largely considered under three sub-categories: status planning, corpus planning, and acquisition planning.

- **Status planning** largely refers to identifying a language to be the official language; but, as Cooper (1989: 32) notes, the term has been extended to refer to how languages are allocated to a variety of functions, such as medium of instruction and medium of mass communication (e.g. radio and TV).
- **Corpus planning** is a matter of working out what the official language will look like, in terms of its alphabet, its words, and other matters of standardization. Plans to reform spelling and adopt or coin new words fall into this category.
- **Acquisition planning**. This is really an extension of status planning. Most prominently, this type of planning involves ensuring that there are ways – education – for people to acquire whatever languages the planners want them to acquire. Presumably, this includes at least the official language. Thus, plans for language teaching are examples of acquisition planning.

12.2.2 Planning doesn't just solve problems; it also promotes ideologies

In this introduction to planning, we pay special attention to a point that Lo Bianco (2003a) makes in his overview of studies of language policy and language planning. His view is that, although much language planning scholarship has identified the nature of problems in planning, this scholarship has paid insufficient attention to the **ideological character** of these problems. He quotes Calvet (1998: 203) to the effect that "**language policy is a civil war of languages**". Lo Bianco himself stresses the need to recognize that language planning is also politics. Politics is about the **allocation of a nation's scarce resources**. Above, we indicated that languages are not scarce, but the roles of any societal importance that are open to languages are scarce. We think it is in this sense that in 1989 Cooper referred to language planning as the allocation of scarce resources, and concluded, "Thus, in language planning, as in politics, it is **useful to ask who benefits** from any given arrangement" (p. 80).

12.3 Status planning

Status planning is not a very transparent term, but it means deciding on the language varieties that will become the official language of the nation state (or of regions or states within the nation). All other language planning follows from this decision because the official language of a nation state is normally used in all public situations that involve what we have called potential status-raising in earlier chapters. These are all the situations involving governmental actions; normally, to hold a government job above the lowest levels, one must speak the official language. Knowing the official language is especially important in the developing world because many salaried jobs there are government jobs. The official language usually is used in important meetings in the private business sector, too. It is for these reasons that there is so much competition about which language is to be the official language.

Although issues about education do arise over and over in a nation state's history, for the most part decisions about the official language have not really been "made". (The exceptions are the African and some Asian nations that became independent in the middle of the twentieth century or more recently.)

Thus, France only declared French to be its official language in 1992, and in some Western nations, such as the United Kingdom and Sweden, as well as in the United States, there is no official language specified in a constitution or by special law. But in many nations there may be laws making specific languages official for certain purposes. In most nations, even those that do name an official language in their constitutions, official languages have emerged only as part of a political process over time. What happens is that one group becomes politically and economically dominant and its language prevails in official interactions and many ordinary inter-ethnic contacts. Wright (2004: 44) refers to this process by saying that "[S]tatus planning here is the legal acceptance or **recognition of the status quo**." (In the same vein, it is interesting that today many international bodies employ English as their medium of discussion without ever having "ruled" on this decision.) To make things easier, we'll refer to the official language, even though there may be several or many official languages.

Getting the population to accept the central government's ideas about official languages is obviously important. And, as Wright (2004: 43) notes, referring to past attempts at planning, "Accepting of developing standard national languages depended to some extent on the **permeability of elites** and their willingness to adopt a very broad definition of what it means to be a member of the nation." She argues that the elite must do more than accept new policies; it must reinvent itself *and* others as members of a new political entity. So, ideally, the elite must think of everyone as "citizens" and not think of themselves as members of a special ethnic group or social class. Wright also points out that if "peripheral groups" (i.e. groups outside the elite) are excluded from power, this only encourages dissent and separation.

The following subsections give sketches of case studies of a variety of outcomes from status planning. Some of the outcomes reported here are largely ambiguous. This doesn't mean status planning is never successful; it just means the factors promoting success or failure are complex and that unambiguous success is hard to come by! For examples of apparently very successful outcomes, recall the discussion in chapter 4 of language policy in Singapore where a three-language policy (English, Chinese, and Malay) has been very successful, with English as the main language of government and where a largely trilingual population coexists in apparent harmony. Also recall the discussion in chapter 5 of Indonesia's successful policy of uniting the nation around what was an urban "bazaar language", Bahasa Indonesian, now called simply Indonesian. Finally, in section 12.4.3, you'll read about a very successful language policy in Turkey.

12.3.1 Separatism in Canada with language as a symbol

Canada presents perhaps the best current example of the problems that can plague a nation when it includes a large ethnic group that is not satisfied with the status of its language where it finds itself (recall section 12.1.3). **Separation of Québec Province** from the rest of Canada came close to happening in 1976 when the Parti Québécois came into power in the province and passed language laws designed to increase the status of French relative to English. In the late 1960s and the 1970s, language policy was a big issue; it was certainly the major symbol of the Parti Québécois advocating that Québec become its own nation state, separate from the rest of Canada.

The separatist threat has been something Canada has lived with (and re-acted to) for 40 years. Only in 2003 was the Parti Québécois soundly defeated. As we've indicated in earlier chapters, a linguistic reason for the separatist movement was the low status the rest of Canada accorded to French, at least in Canada. Even in Québec itself, English had more prestige and was more widely used (and required) for higher-status jobs.

Three factors militate in Canada's favor against separatists today. First, about 10 percent of the voters in Québec are now immigrants from Eastern Europe, Africa, the Caribbean, and Asia with whom the conquest of Québec by British forces in the mid-eighteenth century does not resonate at all. Québec Bill 101 obligated these immigrants to send their children to French-medium schools, but many of them (called allophones) became trilingual, adding English as well as French. Second, both francophones and anglophones in Québec have increasingly become bilingual. Other anglophones who were unhappy with Parti Québécois policies (or had other reasons to leave) left the province in the 1970s and 1980s. Third, the growing internationalization of the Québec economy (and greater trade with the United States right across the border) has in-creased the need to know English for trade. Still, every time people in Québec have said separatism is dead, the movement has come back again, as it did in 1994. There still are battles there over laws on the books that dictate when and how French or English may be used.

But partly because of Québec's assertion of French rights and the spread of bilingualism, the national government passed an Official Languages Act in 1969. This law increased the number of French-speaking employees in the government so that francophones were represented in proportion to their numbers in the Canadian population. It also provided for schooling and dual government services in the preferred language of individuals whose mother tongue was either French or English where the concentration of these lan-guages was greater than 8 percent.

But such official measures don't necessarily mean that bilingualism is important to Canadians; hockey may be more important! A 1994 poll asked respondents in Québec and in the rest of Canada if they agreed that four factors counted as "things that most tie Canadians together as a nation". More respondents agreed that "health care system" and "hockey" were important than agreed that "national culture" and "bilingualism" were important. Only 40% of Québec respondents and 28% from the rest of Canada said "bilingual-ism" tied Canada together. In contrast, from 62% to 75% of respondents agreed that "the health care system" and "hockey" were unifying factors (cf. Schmid, 2001: 120). The majority of the Canadian population consists of L1 speakers of English. (According to the 2001 census, 60% of the population are L1 speakers of English, 23% speak French, and 17% speak other languages.)

12.3.2 The ups and downs of language policy in Australia

The linguistic makeup of Australia and language policies there have gone through several makeovers since the period after World War II.

Until the 1950s, Australia was **predominantly Anglo-Irish** with a **restrictive immigration policy**. The reason was that the majority of people calling themselves Australians were the descendants of the Anglo-Irish immigrants who settled in Australia in the late nineteenth century and the early twentieth century. (Also, there was a small indigenous population, whose languages are mentioned in section 12.1.6.)

Then, in the 1960s and 1970s, Australia saw a **huge influx of European immigrants**, many of them displaced persons from Eastern Europe. The largest languages represented were Italian, Greek, German, Maltese, Polish, Dutch, and Serbo-Croatian. The term "community languages" came into use in 1975 for the languages of these people and the 1976 census, the first to ask about languages used, found that 12.5 percent of Australians over the age of 5 reported regularly using a community language.

With its history of monolingualism in English, Australia's initial reaction to the new immigrants was that **"they should be like us"** (Clyne, 2004). That is, the official policy was one of assimilation. Thus, the policy was to teach English to immigrants as quickly and as efficiently as possible: on the ships that brought them, in workplaces, and on the radio. Up until the late 1960s, English classes were monolingual, starting from scratch with English, as if the immigrants had no language. Maintenance of the original languages was discouraged and had to take place privately, and by the second generation there was a substantial shift to English, Clyne tells us.

For a good twenty years up until 1987, the general policy was to promote equality among any languages Australians spoke as their L1s and, in effect, to embrace bilingualism between English and other languages. Today, bilingualism is still favored, but bilingualism that includes a few favored languages that the government calculates will bring economic benefit to the nation.

12.3.2.1 Multiculturalism and bilingualism: Everyone is almost equal

All this changed in 1972 when a Labor Government came into power with a policy of **multiculturalism**. This policy was a response to a wide coalition including immigrants that had been lobbying for Australia to recognize its cultural diversity. The new policy to recognize multiculturalism was implemented in such ways as the following: A telephone interpreter service was established for 190 languages; restrictions on broadcasting in languages other than English were lifted; a state-run multilingual radio network was established in the large cities of Sydney and Melbourne; and government subsidies were given to communities to run after-hours ethnic schools. Also, the number of languages available in schools was extended, as well the languages accredited for public examinations. Later (1980) a government multicultural TV network was introduced.

Especially important was the fact this government **terminated racially based immigrant restrictions**. Not only did this change the makeup of the immigrant population, it also changed the position of many immigrants in the class structure. Clyne (2004) points out that most of the recent migrants from Hong Kong, Taiwan, Korea, and India had professional qualifications and/or were wealthy.

Of special interest to readers of this book, **bilingualism became valued**. As Clyne (2004) interprets the situation, "The presence of a significant community [speakers of a given language] became a reason for the teaching of that language as an 'Australian language'." This sent the signal that bilingualism and bilinguals were worth maintaining. In Clyne's view, it meant that children from both English and non-English speaking backgrounds got the message from the outset that school was not a monolingual domain.

It's important to note that at this time the economic or political importance of a language outside of Australia (in the home country or in the world) was not the issue. For example, in the 1980s, about 20 languages were taught in the schools in the state of Victoria. Within the state Education Department in Victoria, the Victorian School of Languages was established. Now it prepares students for final examinations in 43 languages and this organization has been replicated in other states. Clyne stresses the point that this system **treated all languages equally**, whether they were French, German, Japanese, or Farsi (Persian).

12.3.2.2 Priorities count: Economic rationalization

But from 1987 onwards, policies changed and something that can be called "economic rationalization" became the watchword. This was a time of world recession and, Clyne (2004) remarks, "When it comes to the crunch, at most times in history, those in power will not share it" (p. 13). True, the National Policy on Languages (Lo Bianco, 1987) establishes the complementarity of English and other languages used in Australia, but the emphasis on multiculturalism changed. There was more emphasis on raising the level of **literacy in English** and the Australian Language and Literacy Policy of 1991 required states to **prioritize eight languages** from a list of 14 for extra funding, with the implication that there was no longer enough money to fund all languages. In a general comment (not directed at Australia), Fishman (1999: 154) reminds us that "It is difficult to oppose languages without opposing their speakers and their community interests."

The Australian Prime Minister had a policy of "productive diversity". This meant differentiating the community languages as more or less important on the basis of Australia's world economic interests. The idea was that Australia should make use of its linguistic diversity in trade and tourism, but that required

prioritizing languages. Clyne points out that the Rudd Report of 1994 recommended that 60 percent of Australian schoolchildren and 15 percent of those
in years 11 and 12 should study one of the four "super prioritized languages".
These were Japanese, Korean, Indonesian, and the standard dialect of Chinese
(Mandarin/Putonghua). Japanese has led as the main foreign language studied,
but other languages are gaining students.

12.3.2.3 Opening the twentieth century

So where is Australia today and where has it come from? From the time
English-speaking settlers arrived in 1788, it has moved through a long period
of monolingualism, to valuing multiculturalism and bilingualism, and now to
putting a premium on English once again – along with bilingualism, yes, as
long as it's in designated languages. During the 50th anniversary of the Adult
Migrant English Program in the late 1990s, the program was described as
a "passport" to the future. More than 40,000 new arrivals from nearly 90
language backgrounds were learning English under the program in 2001
(Lo Bianco, 2003c). We can assume that today Australia's policy is to say that
English and studying a restricted set of languages are the passport. A complicated scaling system that takes account of students' language backgrounds
gives students all over Australia a score at the end of secondary school. This
score counts toward entry into institutions of higher education and competition is stiff. Everyone can study English and those languages, although, of
course, not everyone begins the race at the same entry point.

12.3.3 Cameroon: Two official languages but little policy

Both the linguistic landscape and the language policy of Cameroon are unique
in Africa. Many other African countries can claim many indigenous languages
(keeping in mind how you count a language versus a dialect). But Cameroon
has an **especially large number of languages** considering the size of the
population (perhaps 260 languages in a population of 16 million, compared
with more than 400 languages in neighboring Nigeria, but in a population of
130 million). Many African nations have a former colonial language as their
official language, but Cameroon has **two official languages**, English and French.
During the colonial period, Cameroon was a German colony. But in 1919,
under the Treaty of Versailles after World War I, Germany lost her colonies
and so part of Cameroon was administered by England (as part of Nigeria)
and about four-fifths became a separate French colony.

Simo Bobda (2004) suggests that the typical anglophone Cameroonian
in Yaoundé, the capital, speaks the following languages daily: one or more
home languages, Cameroonian Pidgin English, English, and French. Even
the notion of identifying your mother tongue (L1) depends on the criteria that
are followed.

The national policies on language, as well as their implementation, are just plain vague. The only mention of language policy in the constitution (the latest is from 1996) is the two following clauses: The first is, "The Republic of Cameroon shall adopt English and French as the official languages with equal status." This clause contrasts with that in a previous constitution, which stated that between French and English versions of a document, the French one should be binding. Second, there is a stipulation that the state "shall guarantee the promotion of bilingualism all over the territory". The previous constitution specified the "protection and promotion of national languages" (national = indigenous languages). There is no mention of Cameroonian Pidgin English in either constitution. From time to time, the prime minister or other ministers issue memos reminding civil servants about their duty to be bilingual, but "should" is used, not anything more binding.

12.3.3.1 *Fluid policies, informal solutions*

Even in the most formal settings, what language will be used varies. At universities, the language used varies between French and English (except for the University of Buea, where English is the only medium). In all seriousness, Simo Bobda states, "Cameroonian universities are probably the only ones in the world where a student never knows in what language a course is going to be taught before the instructor begins to lecture" (p. 5). In study groups outside of class, students may discuss a topic in any of the following: English, French, Cameroonian Pidgin English, or an indigenous language. The same applies to what goes on in a government office.

Simo Bobda argues that on a day-to-day basis, language policy is only a matter of the "survival of the fittest". Indigenous languages are sometimes favored for public discourse, but it depends on the numerical dominance and political dominance of a group associated with a particular language. Also, any prestige attached to the language figures in decisions. For example, **Beti** currently has political dominance; it is the L1 of the current president, who has been in power since 1982. For quite different reasons, **Duala** is a language with high prestige even though it is spoken as an L1 by a minority ethnic group and has never been particularly influential in politics. But Duala is the language of the people who met the first Europeans to come to Cameroon. Further, Duala speakers have traveled to Europe in large numbers. Finally, Duala has prestige because the majority of Cameroonian musicians are Duala and they sing in Duala.

Any promotion of bilingualism or bilingual education involving the local languages is largely done by local organizations, religious institutions, or outside non-governmental agencies. In a few areas, indigenous languages have been introduced into the schools, even though they are not on the official syllabus. The 2001–2002 report of a committee of the National Association of Cameroon Languages reported that indigenous languages are taught, either formally or informally, in more than 300 schools, Simo Bobda indicates.

The government's stance toward language policy seems to be to allow non-governmental groups to act, but not to act itself. And so if any indigenous language is promoted, this is a function of non-governmental agencies or outside groups.

The solution of dividing up Cameroon into francophone and anglophone sections won't work because the languages don't split today in a territorial fashion. Today, especially in urban areas, such as Yaoundé and Douala, there are large communities of both francophones and anglophones.

12.3.3.2 *Attitudes toward Cameroonian Pidgin English and "the anglophone problem"*

Interestingly, the most actively followed "policy" in Cameroon may be the crusade **against speaking Cameroonian Pidgin English** at some schools and in some homes. Cameroonian Pidgin English is not so much a pidgin as it is a creole in the sense that it has the extensive set of grammatical rules that separates creoles from pidgins. Its lexicon is based on English, but its morphosyntactic frame is largely based on local indigenous languages. Simo Bobda reports that one sees banners on the campus of the University of Buea stating "No Pidgin on campus" or more telling banners such as "English is the password, not Pidgin" and "[the] Commonwealth speaks English, not Pidgin". ("Commonwealth" refers to the Commonwealth of largely English-speaking nations in the British realm.) But, as in neighboring Nigeria (where Nigerian Pidgin English is spoken), Cameroonian Pidgin English seems to be an irreplaceable tool in many situations, although it is not an official language there, either. In Cameroon, at least, it is even moving into new domains traditionally reserved for English; members of both the anglophone and francophone elites speak it as well as the majority of the population, who are ordinary people who do not speak either English or French.

Of the two official languages, **English has been the loser**. French-speaking Cameroonians hold the majority of public offices and English is marginalized in official roles. But many **francophones are motivated to learn English**. Simo Bobda states that in 2003 francophones who were studying English represented 95 percent of the students in government bilingual training programs. This, of course, is in line with the spread of English as a world lingua franca; also, English is the main official language in Cameroon's powerful neighbor, Nigeria.

What has been called "the anglophone problem" is a response to the grievances that anglophones have. There is a secessionist movement called the Southern Cameroonian National Council (SCNC). One of the grievances heard from anglophones is that their children do not get admitted to certain prestige schools or do not do well there because of the language barrier. Still, a sense of unity has emerged among the anglophones because they speak the same second language that separates them from other Cameroonians. English, not their ethnic group languages, is their symbol of in-group solidarity (cf. Wolf, 1997).

12.3.4 India: Where official language planning is still waiting for success

India can be considered a case of status planning that did not work out as intended, but many citizens are satisfied with the results. India is an extremely multilingual nation, with perhaps up to 500 different languages. However, in the North most people speak language varieties related to Hindi (many are even mutually intelligible with Hindi), and Hindi supporters always tout Hindi as spoken by a very large percentage of the entire population. In the original Indian constitution written in 1949, Hindi was named the national language as the apparent heir to English, the language of the colonial rulers. But the handover to Hindi as the central-level national language (equivalent to official language status), scheduled to happen in 1965, has never occurred. That is, English remains in place more than fifty years later in many official roles, such as court judgments and the writing of bureaucratic files. (A number of other Indian languages were also declared to be official in the 8th schedule of the constitution, and that number rose to 22 in 2004.)

12.3.4.1 The use of borders and corpus planning

When colonial India was partitioned into the independent states of Pakistan and India, what were two mutually intelligible varieties were turned into two separate languages, Urdu for Pakistan and Hindi for India. They were discussed in chapter 2 when the question of what's a dialect and what's a language was raised. Both are **descendants of Sanskrit**, but speakers of Urdu are largely Moslems and speakers of Hindi are Hindus or members of other religions. Around seven centuries ago, Urdu had developed around Delhi, now the capital of India, under the influence of Persian-speaking sultans and their military administration. It adopted the Persian writing system (the Arabic writing system) and took in **many Persian words**. By the eighteenth century, Urdu had changed enough to differentiate it from related dialects (including Hindi dialects) so that when Pakistan was set up as a separate state, Urdu became its official language.

Meanwhile, back in India, Hindi scholars rose to the task of helping the border with Pakistan remain firm. They brought in a **Sanskrit-derived vocabulary** to add to Hindi and preserved the ancient Sanskrit writing system, too. In fact, one of the complaints of non-Hindi speakers against having Hindi as the main central language was the difficulty in learning it created by all these Sanskrit-based words.

Some time later, East Pakistan became Bangladesh and West Pakistan became simply Pakistan. About 80 percent of the population there is Moslem and up to 98 percent of citizens speak Bengali, also an Indo-Aryan language related to Hindi and Urdu. But of interest in this discussion of corpus planning is the use of names. In Bangladesh, Bengali is **now called Bangla** and is the official language.

12.3.4.2 English and its spread in the states

The individual Indian states have a lot of authority over what languages are to be used for official business and as media of instruction or subjects in the schools. In many states the main state language has millions of speakers and this language is the medium of instruction for local literatures or music, even in universities. This is the case with Tamil, which is a language in the Dravidian family, making it very different from Hindi, an Indo-Aryan language. In addition to having many L1 speakers, Tamil has a literary variety that in mid-2004 was declared a "classical language", meaning that, in terms of prestige, it is on the same level as Sanskrit, the ancient religious language that is evident in loan words in many Indian languages, notably Hindi. But a few years ago, when an international Tamil congress was held in the Tamilnadu State, English was the medium. English is the main medium of higher education and attempts to introduce state languages as media of instruction in other subjects have been soundly rejected because this would put graduates at a disadvantage in competing for jobs requiring English. In some states, English, which was ousted as a medium in the lower grades when India became independent, has been invited back. The reason? English apparently has lost its taint as the language of colonialism and instead is considered the language of international business and is used within India in many businesses, such as banking. However, while an English-speaking elite has developed a wider base across ethnic groups, in the villages English is relatively unknown.

12.3.4.3 The future of Hindi and English

What will the future bring? Adding up the pluses and minuses, political scientist De Swaan concludes that English is the best choice as an L2 for Hindi speakers. But unless you consider global motivations for learning English, he argues that learning Hindi is the best choice as an L2 for non-Hindi speakers in India. Not all India-watchers would agree; they think English is the best choice even for non-Hindus. Certainly, Hindi is robust: There has been a proliferation of Hindi news channels on television and films in Hindi from Bollywood are very successful. Further, Hindi is a language with a rich literature and more than 300 million speakers in the 1991 census. But this number is accurate only if you lump together many "dialects" that would also like to claim "language" status (Schiffman, personal communication).

De Swaan points out general gains for English as an L2. He refers to a 1997 poll that reported 71% of respondents said they "understood" Hindi and 31% said the same for English. But about 40% of all Indians are Hindi L1 speakers, so this means another 31% must have learned Hindi later. De Swaan concludes that "[C]learly, as second languages, Hindi and English are now on a par"

(2001: 78). De Swaan also points out that the fact that so many Hindi-speaking students learn English makes the language more attractive also for students from non-Hindi-speaking areas. So today English may be surging ahead as a favored L2..

India has a policy to promote multilingualism through what is called the "three-language formula". Everyone is supposed to learn Hindi, their own language, and English. For Hindi speakers, this means Hindi, another Indian language, and English. But, not everyone cooperates; Hindi speakers tend not to learn a third language at all (except possibly Sanskrit, which is not a spoken language) and non-Hindi L1 speakers from the larger Dravidian groups tend to learn no Hindi. There is a lot of mutual passive bilingualism. For example, Schiffman reports that Hindi speakers come to South India and speak Hindi and they're answered in English; Tamils learn enough Hindi to understand Bollywood movies (personal communication).

Thus, India remains a nation where state-supported language planning was resisted by the people, and the people seem to be the victors. There is a Department of Official Language in the Ministry of Home Affairs. Its purpose was to help Hindi replace English and bureaucrats there insist that Hindi is the language of "the real India". But the overall official stance on language is ambiguous at best. De Swaan sees the non-Hindi states as successfully following the option of their state language with English as an L2. Still, one can't argue that the future of Hindi is unhealthy – just not as the main official language.

12.3.5 South Africa: A nation that might try "something innovative" – or might not

Emerging from the yoke of *apartheid*, the Republic of South Africa became a democratic nation in 1994 and had a new language policy in its constitution that declared 11 languages as official languages. These include both English and Afrikaans, which had been official under the Afrikaner-dominated government, and nine indigenous African languages. In principle, all the official languages were to be **on equal footing**. Not surprisingly, such a policy was unworkable; English became the *de facto* language of ordinary government business and it replaced Afrikaans in many parts of the private sector.

Even though the majority of South Africans use an African language as their home language (almost 80% according to the 2001 census), the use of English continues to grow. English is the home language of just over 8% of the population (2001 census). At the same time, Afrikaans is still widely used. It is the first language of over 13% of the population (2001 census) and is heard daily, either as a first or second language, from shopkeepers and government employees to rugby players on teams representing South Africa.

What is different about the South African situation, distinguishing it from other sub-Saharan African nations where a European language is the sole official language (or a co-official language), is not just that nine African languages were included in the list of official languages. What is different is that government-sanctioned agencies or advisory boards are vigorously advocating changes to give African languages a role in the government and in society in general that more closely matches the numbers of speakers of these languages. And now, finally, ten years after the move to democracy and following years of protracted discussions, a bill has been sent to parliament that could result in much more use of all the official languages, at least in governmental structures.

One of the earliest bodies working on language policy, that still is very active, is the Pan South African Language Board (PanSALB). From the beginning, at least some members of this board have been pushing for "pluralistic alternatives" to English (and Afrikaans). One suggestion was to develop two new African-based language varieties as the main official languages. One might be called Nguni, to be based on the four Nguni group languages that are official now (isiZulu, isiXhosa, siSwati also called Swazi, and isiNdebele), and the other called Sotho, to be based on the three Sotho languages that are official now (South Sotho/Sesotho, Setswana, and North Sotho/Sepedi). The Nguni group now represents about 46% of the total population and the Sotho group represents more than 25%. These two groupings would represent all the African languages in South Africa that have populations of more than 5% of the total population.

This plan is linguistically feasible in the sense that the varieties in each group are almost mutually intelligible. In the 1920s, when Zimbabwe was the British colony Southern Rhodesia, a standard dialect for the Shona language was created in a similar move. That is, a composite dialect based largely on the Sezuru dialect, but taking account of all the Shona dialects, was put in place as the standard dialect and this variety is one of the official languages of Zimbabwe today (with Ndebele and English). But remember that this was done when the nation was under colonial rule; people weren't free to accept or reject the plan.

However, a different, and in many ways more radical, plan now has passed several official hurdles and therefore may prevail. This plan preserves the African languages, just as they are, but gives them different roles. It is called the National Language Policy Framework (NLPF) and came out of a Language Plan Task Group (LANGTAG) appointed by the Minister of Arts, Culture, Science and Technology. This framework (NLPF) was designed as a package including a policy statement, an implementation plan, and the South African Languages Act. After much consultation with various groups, the NLPF was approved by the government's cabinet (i.e. ministers) in February 2003. Then, in April 2003 the implementation plan was approved by the cabinet and a "revised final draft" of the South African Languages Bill was submitted to the cabinet. As of late 2004, this bill still awaited approval by the National Parliament; of course, it may be changed.

As it stands, the main goal of the South African Languages Bill is to make government documents available simultaneously in 11 languages when feasible and – when not feasible – in six. If this bill is passed by the parliament, the main effect will be a huge increase in demand for translation and editing and interpreting services.

When documents are published in only six languages, then a principle of rotation would apply within the Nguni and Sotho groups. For example, an annual report for 2004 might use isiXhosa from the Nguni group and then in 2005 isiZulu might be used, with siSwati in 2006, etc. The same would apply for the Sotho group languages.

What about the other four languages? In a bold move, the NLPF recommends that the two languages with the fewest native speakers should be included in the six, but not undergo rotation. These are Tshivenda and Xitsonga. Tshivenda is a commonly spoken home language of about 3% of the total population and Xitsonga of under 5%. Not surprisingly, English and Afrikaans will always be included in the six languages. English is to be the language normally used for any communications at the international level.

There are obvious sticking points that could delay passage of the bill or make its implementation difficult. First, the individual languages in the more populous Nguni and Sotho groups would be less represented in government publications and interpreting services than the smallest groups. Second, as the bill now stands, the various departmental ministers have the prerogative to "classify" documents; this means they can state which documents must be in all 11 languages and which may be in the designated six only.

So far, the record of implementing any earlier recommendations of such bodies as PanSALB or LANGTAG has been poor. For example, a trial telephone interpreting service (40 police stations across the country) to have services in all of the official languages was abandoned after eight months (Beukes, 2004). In a 2004 paper, Neville Alexander cites two "dangers" facing policy planners in South Africa. First, he says, there is **"the danger of stagnation"**. He notes that the state authorities and their decision makers do not appear to see changes in existing language policies and the status quo as a matter of urgency. Second, he refers to **"the slippery slope of ethnic politics"** while he recognizes the problem with trying to propagate "an anti-ethnicist language policy" (p. 13). Alexander was an original member of PanSALB, and is a well-known spokesperson for the need to foster linguistic diversity and multilingualism in order to achieve social transformation and promote economic growth in South Africa (cf. Alexander, 1989).

Meanwhile, the use of English in South Africa as a lingua franca across the country expands. For example, those English newspapers and magazines with **a Black readership** are growing. Even so, Alexander (2004) referred to a PanSALB survey claiming that half of Africans surveyed either often or seldom understand speeches made by government officials in English. Still, following a survey among parents conducted in the Xhosa-speaking area that includes Grahamstown, De Klerk (2000b: 212) concludes, "a certain linguistic momentum . . . seems to be involved here, which is driven not so much by the numbers of speakers of the languages but rather by the unequal social, political and economic power of their speakers." Parents voiced widespread preference for education in English in the survey.

12.4 Corpus planning

Corpus planning refers to planning the form of the official language. First, corpus planning means **standardizing** the language. Standardizing is the process of deciding what pronunciations and grammatical structures are to be considered well-formed as part of the dialect that will "represent" the language, the standard dialect. Standardization has an important purpose: It counteracts tendencies for groups within the society to "go their own way". They still will do this (i.e. speak their own regional or social group dialects), but they won't go as far. And, especially when they are in formal situations or when they are writing something to outsiders, they will make an effort to use a variety that approximates the standard dialect. Nation states want to **check too much diversity** because it could encourage groups to separate and form their own state.

Language planners must tread a fine line between being inclusive when they develop a standard dialect and being different enough to separate their language from that of neighboring nation states. The standard dialect has to resemble regional and social dialects in the country enough so that it is comprehensible to them, but it should have features that distinguish it from related languages.

Second, there are other ways in which corpus planning is carried out. Some nation states have language academies that **issue pronouncements**; these statements often select one of two forms that are competing in the public arena (e.g. if English had an academy, it could decide whether to say *I dived* or *I dove*). Dictionaries also are an influential source of corpus planning because they indicate which words and pronunciations the dictionary makers consider acceptable parts of a language and which they do not. Sometimes state legislatures pass laws about the "proper" form of a language. None of these **prescriptive attempts** at corpus planning necessarily works, though. That is, the public may ignore them, although if the educated elite follow such dictums, then they may catch on with the general public.

12.4.1 Corpus planning as against diversity – or for it

Corpus planning often takes the form of a move against diversity. For example, in 2002, a committee of the Russian Duma (parliament) recommended a bill requiring all peoples living in Russia to **use the Cyrillic script**, the script in which Russian and some nearby languages are written. This was a response to five years of efforts by the autonomous region of Tatarstan to reintroduce a Latin-based script. For Tatarstan itself the selection of a script represented a choice to stay closer to Russia (i.e. employ a Cyrillic script) or a choice to move closer to both Turkey and the West (**use a Latin-based (Roman) script**), or have closer relations with Arabic-speaking Moslem nations (use an Arabic script). The transition to a Latin-based script is moving forward to be completed in 2011. It is interesting to note that there are reports that Turkey has been active in the former Soviet republics with efforts to convince various minority groups that speak languages related to Turkish (i.e. they are Turkic languages) to bring their languages closer to Turkish (as spoken in Turkey). Of course, as we indicate below, Turkey now has a Latin-based script. (For more details, see Landau and Kellner-Heinkele (2001) on the ex-Soviet Moslem states.)

Earlier, in reference to the Balkan area and in reference to the Indian subcontinent, we cited cases of corpus planning for diversity. Planners sometimes work to shore up political borders by making their languages more different than those of the languages of their neighbors.

In 12.4.3, we'll see how planners in Turkey worked for diversity on a grand scale.

12.4.2 Script reforms in Asia

In Asia, concerns about script and writing are an even larger part of language planning than they are in Europe. Standardization is a central concern in China and also in Korea and Japan. For example, Lo Bianco (2003c) notes that **policy in Korea** regarding a standard dialect is an oscillation between divergence and convergence of South to North Korea. In South Korea, the Seoul dialect is the basis of a standard dialect, but in the 1950s North Korea designated the dialect of Pyongyang as the basis of its standard dialect. This move of linguistic separation, of course, **symbolized political separation**. As far as script goes, in the South, the government has wavered on permitting Chinese characters alongside the Hankul system (which uses the Roman alphabet) developed in the fifteenth century. In contrast, at first North Korea stressed a policy favoring Hankul to promote mass literacy by abolishing characters, as was done in Viet Nam. But in 1966 it moderated this stance and now permits the teaching of characters in schools, but bans their use in the media. Viet Nam romanized Vietnamese as a symbol of a break from its colonial past. This move to a Roman alphabet for an indigenous language is unique in Asia, but then, Viet Nam is unique, isn't it? (See the edited volume by Lindsay, J. and T. Ying Ying (2003) for more on Asia today.)

12.4.3 The Turkish language reform

Probably the most famous case of corpus planning in modern times involving how the official language is to be written is the case of Turkey. When the

Turkish Republic was established in 1923, one of its goals was to create a distinctively Turkish state and an egalitarian society. One of the reforms was to replace the Arabo-Persian alphabet with a Roman alphabet in 1928. The idea was to separate the new republic from its neighbors with their Arabic or Persian scripts. A little later, a campaign to purge Turkish of its foreign words was launched. Again, the target was to get rid of things that were Arabic or Persian.

Here's a sketch of the history of Turkey. Most of the ancestors of modern Turks in Turkey converted to Islam in the eleventh century and started using the Arabo-Persian alphabet. They borrowed words and grammatical features from Arabic and Persian. **A divide developed** between the common people and the elite (recall the discussion of diglossia in chapter 4). The common people spoke a variety with mostly Turkish words, but the language of literature and administration included many Arabic and Persian elements. There were various attempts in the nineteenth century to simplify literary language, but they weren't very successful.

Enter Atatürk, the founder of the new republic. He wanted to abolish differences in ways of speaking as one way to **make the republic more egalitarian**. He established a Turkish Language Society for the Purification of the Language, which held Turkish Language Congresses in the following years. An example of corpus planning under this new enthusiasm for things Turkish was a campaign to collect Turkish words from regional dialects and from old Turkish texts.

12.4.3.1 *"Authentic Turkish"*

Part of this flurry of interest in "authentic Turkish" produced the **Sun Language theory**. In many ways, this is the example *par excellence* of language engineering to increase the prestige of a language. This theory allowed language planners to claim that Turkish was one of the main ancient languages and the source of words in other languages, including Arabic and Persian. The theory was this: When primitive persons looked at the sun, they said "Aa!" And this expression, it was claimed, was inherently a word in the Turkish language, making Turkey the center/source of all languages. As you might imagine, later this theory was abandoned.

In a book-length study of Turkish language reform, Lewis (2002) details the history of Turkish during this period and up until today. He is critical of the planners involved in the early reforms, arguing that they were not language experts. Note that this comment supports our claim above that language planners don't necessarily pay any attention to language experts. The claim is that many of the replacement words were invented.

12.4.3.2 *A "catastrophic success"?*

What is the situation today? Lewis tells us that the Turkish Language Society was revised in 1983, making it a government agency. It continues to recommend

Turkish alternatives for some new words, but focuses more on scholarly studies. But, as Lewis points out, there has been a great influx of English words into Turkish; that is, in some ways, English, as an external influence, has taken the place of Arabic and Persian from earlier centuries.

Even though most language planners cite Turkish language as a success story, Lewis calls it a **"catastrophic success"**. What does he mean? He says that Ottoman Turkish was discarded, resulting in an impoverished Turkish lexicon (because, remember, the effort was to eliminate Arabic and Persian words). Again, Lewis criticizes the way new words were created.

But in an electronic review of Lewis (Linguist List July 30, 2003), Gokdayi (2003) points out virtues in the reform. For example, he emphasizes that one of the problems that Turkey faced in the 1920s and 1930s was a very low literacy rate. He argues that Ottoman Turkish (with its many Arabic and Persian influences) was really used by only 9% of the population. In contrast, today the literacy rate is around 92%, he states.

In effect, Gokdayi also says **"let the people be the judge"**. In his own words, he says, "we can criticize the way some words are invented or derived in the reform process but since [the] target people, i.e. Turkish speakers, accept the end product, we also have to appreciate the reformers' effort." He chastises Lewis for introducing his book by saying that the story of Turkish language reform is "often bizarre, sometimes tragicomic, but never dull". In response, Gokdayi says in his review, "If TLR [Turkish Language Reform] is bizarre and tragicomic, then all language planning activities and reforms all over the world should be the same. It is part of creating a nation and nation-state started around [the] 1930's" (p. 5).

12.4.3.3 Turkey today and the Kurdish minority

Today, Turkey's main linguistic problem isn't making the Turkish language distinctive, but keeping its large Kurdish minority from asserting itself in various ways, including in its use (and any promotion) of the Kurdish language. Where Turkish officials see ominous signs of separatism, Kurds claim they intend only expressions of ethnic identity. (Kurdish is an Indo-Aryan language and is more closely related to Persian (Farsi) than to Turkish, which is in a different language family.) There are smaller minority groups in Turkey, too; they all are asking for more and more use of their languages in education and the media. A new legal measure adopted in early 2004 allows minority groups to receive teaching in languages other than Turkish, but only so long as students attend schools where they learn Turkish as well.

12.5 Acquisition planning

The third major area of language planning consists of deciding on the medium of instruction in schools and implementing the policies laid down. **Acquisition**

planning is the term that describes policies regarding media instructions in schools and languages required or permitted as school subjects.

Acquisition planners have to recognize two considerations that could lead them in opposite directions. First, policy makers know that statistics show that national economic development seems to be associated with national literacy rates. This is an argument in favor of mother tongue education; at least most educators believe that developing literacy in a child is easier in the child's L1, and there is some evidence supporting this claim. But second, policy makers also believe that education in the official language helps minority children see themselves as more than minority group members and orient towards national goals (Paulston, 1998).

In the poorer nation states, education is not available to children beyond a few years, or teachers and teaching materials are not available enough for educators to try both schemes. However, some countries are introducing bilingual programs to develop biliteracy (i.e. generally meaning being able to read and write in both the child's L1 and the official language) and what is called biculturalism (cf. Hornberger, 1998; 2002a, and 2002b and 12.5.3 on Bolivian bilingual education).

All nations have some minority groups, and if they feel marginalized in various ways by the central government, education is often the area where they will express their discontent. This is because they recognize that education can have both **sentimental and instrumental value** (or either one alone) for their children. Just the fact of including a group's L1 in the education system as a medium, or at least as a school subject, enhances the group's prestige. Such inclusion also can teach children about the group's "great traditions" and its values. Such an education has sentimental value. In contrast, some parents may be more concerned with having an education for their children that will give them a better economic life; they want an education that has instrumental value. If this goal is paramount in their minds, they prefer education in the official language or an international language as providing at least access to socio-economic mobility, if not mobility itself.

If a group is powerful – or desperate – enough, parents or students themselves mount public demonstrations, demanding education in the language of their choice. But implementing the educational demands of its various minority groups is a complicated and costly task for any nation state. The result is that acquisition planning is rarely as easy as it sounds. Here are three incidents that show the type of demands that citizens make regarding language and education:

(1) Perhaps the best-known case of a demonstration against a school language policy occurred in June, 1976 in **the Soweto township** outside Johannesburg in South Africa. South African police fired into a crowd of secondary school students. The official death toll was 23; others put it as high as 200. The students were demonstrating against the plan to have Afrikaans as the medium

of instruction in their schools; they preferred English. Recall from the discussion of South African 12.3.5 that both Afrikaans and English were official languages under the Afrikaner regime, which was in power at the time of the Soweto riots. In South Africa, Afrikaans is the Dutch-based variety that is the L1 of descendants of Dutch settlers and English was the language of a minority of British settlers at this time. This incident only strengthened the resistance to the regime so that, eventually, in 1993 the non-white people of South Africa became free of white minority rule.

(2) In early 2004, the language policy news from Latvia was that from 8,000 to 23,000 **Russian-speaking schoolchildren** (the number varying with the sources) had been demonstrating near the residence of a Latvian official. The reason? They were against announced plans to limit the use of Russian in the schools. The demonstrations were organized by a Latvian-based organization called the Headquarters for the Support of Russian-Language Schools. The language situation in Latvia is discussed further in section 12.5.2 below.

(3) On the other side of the world Cambodian university students protested against the wide use of French in higher education in the mid-1990s. In one instance (May 1995), students at the Institute of Technology disrupted classes for three weeks and burned tires in the university courtyard. They were **demanding English-medium instruction**. We discuss the competition between French and English in Cambodia further in 12.6.3 when the global role of English is discussed.

12.5.1 Types of bilingual education programs

Much acquisition planning in a bilingual state includes providing for some type of bilingual education. If a nation state installs a program in **bilingual education**, this usually means that children begin schooling in one language (often their L1) and then switch to the official language in a later year. In some nation states, the children's L1 is continued as a school subject in later years, or they are taught in more than one language. For information about multilingual programs, see Cenoz and Genesee (1998). When children study another language as a school subject (e.g. study of English in many parts of the world), this is not usually called bilingual education.

Bilingual education programs in many nation states leave something to be desired; they are often not actively supported through legislation nor do they always have teachers with sufficient training. But if, for example, we consider the numbers of children who speak a language other than the official language in many Western European countries, we can see that education systems are dealing with almost unsurmountable problems. For example, in three major cities in Sweden, Stockholm, Gothenburg and Malmo, consider the report that in many schools, fewer than 10 percent of the students are L1 speakers of Swedish (cf. Boyd and Huss, 2001).

When you try to understand different language policies, you cannot be sure exactly what it means to say that "children are in a bilingual education program". To give you an idea of what different programs may look like, we include below a list of five different models of bilingual education, some or all of which have been in place in the United States; programs elsewhere use these models, too, or variations on them. Here are some general facts about bilingual programs: (1) All the children may not speak the same L1 and then the program must be modified. (2) The assumption is that **the main goal** is to learn the official language. In most US programs this is typically the only goal at the time of this writing. (3) In some nation states (e.g. Bolivia, as discussed below) the goal is also to instill the idea of **multiculturalism** or to build the children's pride in their L1. (4) **Mainstream classrooms** are classes of children who are L1 speakers of the target (official) language or otherwise judged to be proficient in that language. Here are the main types of programs:

- **Early exit programs**: Children begin schooling in grades one and sometimes two in their L1, but after that, they go into mainstream classrooms.
- **Late exit programs**: Children continue to receive L1 instruction through primary school, even after they have been classified as proficient in the official language.
- **Structured immersion programs**: Classes consist entirely of children who are not proficient in the official language. Teachers are trained in bilingual education (or especially ESL or English as a Second Language in the United States). Ideally, teachers have some knowledge of the children's language, but use of this language is limited. The goal is to move the children to mainstream classes in two or three years, sometimes in one year. This is the type of program that becomes popular in some US states, such as Arizona.
- **Two-way programs**: Ideally, programs include half L1 speakers of the official language and half non-official language speakers. The idea is for the groups to acquire each other's languages. These programs seem to be rare.
- **Sheltered or content-based programs**: Children who are learning the official language are grouped together in a mainstream classroom. Teachers communicate with them via visual aids initially and other special instructional strategies designed to provide comprehensible input. A popular term for this now in the US is SDAIE (Specially Designed Academic Instruction in English). Focus is on transmitting content but children are expected to acquire the official language, too. These programs also seem to be rare.

12.5.2 Latvia and its Russian minority group

The nation of Latvia is one of the three Baltic nations that border on Russia and are on the Baltic Sea across from Sweden. Each has a relatively small land mass, but each also has a long history of forced occupation and voluntary in-migrations from outside groups. The most important foreign presence in any discussion of Latvian language policy today was the forced occupation of the Baltic states by the Soviet Union (USSR) in 1940. The Russians relinquished control of the Baltic states with the breakup of the Soviet Union in the 1980s. In 1991, Latvia was proclaimed a sovereign (independent) state. But the years of Russian occupation left the new nation state with a **large minority group of Russians**.

Of course other nations have minority groups, but it's hard to find another nation state that has to deal with such a large minority. According to Druviete (1998) the Latvian majority is only 56.4% of the total population of Latvia and the Russian-speaking minority is 37.4% (33% are ethnic Russians, almost 3% are Ukrainians, and 4% are Belorussians); there are a number of other minorities, too, but much smaller groups.

The Russians in Latvia represent two groups. Some came as immigrants in the 1920s and 1930s, fearing religious repression in Russia. Many of these learned Latvian and were integrated into Latvian society. But most of the Russians came after the 1940 incorporation of Latvia into the Soviet Union.

A problem for Latvia is that these newcomers formed a special social group that cannot be defined as immigrants because, after all, they were only moving within the Soviet Union when they arrived in Latvia, and they did not change their Russian citizenship. "Psychologically, [these] Russians **do not feel themselves a minority** nor do Latvians have the feeling of a majority," Druviete notes (p. 169). So Latvia is left with a large minority group, speaking a supercentral language that is the official language of Latvia's powerful neighbor, right across the border. And the Latvians are not blind to where their country is and what has happened to them in the past (e.g. the Republic of Latvia was first established in 1918, before the Soviet takeover).

Given **Russian's credentials** as a major language and the group's size, not surprisingly, the Russian minority has been demanding language rights in Latvia. As Druviete writes, "the symbolic functions of a certain language cannot be undervalued in language policy. The Russian language has always been a symbol of Soviet power, and that power still permeates the attitudes toward Russian in Latvia" (p. 171).

12.5.2.1 Education in Latvia

What to do about education? Usually, nations are called upon to protect minority languages in educational settings; Latvia is in the ironic position of having to try to protect its own official language, Latvian. Writing in 1998, Druviete reported problems along this line. Today a large number of non-Latvian parents, even Russian monolinguals, want to send their children to kindergartens and schools with Latvian as the medium of instruction. But when children arrive without knowing any Latvian and outside of school they don't speak Latvian, progress is slow. Even worse, teachers have to switch to

Russian quite often and "usually Latvian children learn Russian before non-Latvians learn Latvian. The communication among children takes place in Russian even if there are only two or three Russian children among 20 Latvians" (p. 178).

12.5.2.2 *An uncertain future*

Today, new policies, such as **strengthening Latvian teaching in minority schools** (e.g. a new requirement about how much Latvian must be used), may tip the balance toward Latvian. Future developments were unclear at the time of this writing. As noted above, in early 2004 Russian-speaking students protested against any move that would limit the use of Russian in Latvian schools. However, the Latvian parliament went ahead and voted overwhelmingly to require that 60 percent of classes in public schools be taught in Latvian. Obviously, the road ahead in Latvian acquisition planning will be bumpy with its **assertive Russian minority**.

12.5.3 Acquisition planning in the Andes

In recent decades, both Peru and Bolivia have undertaken major education reform initiatives that aim to strengthen the indigenous languages and cultures through bilingual education. When South America is mentioned, most people think of Spanish as the language everyone speaks. In fact, the continent has many indigenous (Amerindian) languages (as well as Portuguese as the official language in Brazil). With 63% of its population speaking an L1 other than Spanish, Bolivia has the highest percentage of Amerindian language speakers as a proportion of its entire population. But with 6 million Amerindian language speakers, Peru has the highest absolute number of L1 speakers of indigenous languages (cf. Hornberger, 1998). Quechua and Aymara are the largest Amerindian languages in both countries. There also are numerous smaller languages.

We will focus on Bolivia, where there are about 2.5 million speakers of Quechua, about 1.6 million speakers of Aymara, and also smaller groups of other Amerindian languages, such as Guarani. Recall that in Ecuador, the variety close to Quechua is called Quichua there. Between Bolivia, Peru, and Chile, there are about 2 million Aymara speakers. There are only about 60,000 Guarani speakers in Bolivia, but there are another 3 million in the neighboring states of Paraguay, Argentina, and Brazil. Guarani is the dominant indigenous language in Paraguay where it is an official language alongside Spanish.

Up until near the end of the twentieth century, the use of indigenous languages was sometimes officially prohibited and often socially denigrated in Bolivia. There is no stated official language, but Spanish is the *de facto* official language. Then, a 1984 government decree established an official Quechua alphabet and also one for Aymara. In the same year, an Education Reform Act stated that the education system was **obliged to offer bilingual education** nationwide for a minimum of the primary school years (eight years). Quechua, Aymara, and Guarani are now official in certain domains and particularly in education. As in most nations, formal education, especially beyond primary school, is perceived as the access route to social mobility. The Reform Act envisions using thirty of Bolivia's Amerindian languages alongside Spanish as subjects and media of instruction. Thus, to introduce the use of Amerindian languages into formal education produces a paradox of sorts. Hornberger (2000b: 183) notes that in Bolivia educational reform seems possible because it "stands on the shoulders of a vigorous indigenous political presence" dating back to the 1952 revolution and a time of reform.

Hornberger visited Bolivia in 2000 and reports the Vice-Minister of Education's welcoming remarks at a workshop on teaching to indicate that changes in the schools may not be to everyone's liking. Hornberger states that the Vice-Minister emphasized that "the key to the Bolivian Education Reform is Bilingual Intercultural Education, and the key to *that* is Spanish as a Second Language". In addition, the Vice-Minister referred to questions that had been raised about the attention to indigenous languages. Specifically, the Vice-Minister said, **parents have begun to demand** that their children be taught Spanish. She seemed to imply that indigenous languages had been stressed to such a degree that the public thinks children are getting monolingual indigenous education (Hornberger, 2000a: 28). But Hornberger herself said that what such scenes as this also show is that "the one language-one nation ideology of language policy and national identity is no longer the only available one worldwide (if it ever was)" (p. 29).

12.5.4 Acquisition planning to reverse language shift: the Cree in Canada

Cree, an Amerindian language spoken in Canada, is making something of a recovery in Cree communities through its use as a medium of instruction in local schools. Cree has been introduced into the schools in at least two locations. Cree definitely is an endangered language with a diminishing number of L1 speakers.

First, in 1993, in Cree communities on the east coast of James Bay and inland (in northern Québec Province) Cree was introduced as a language of instruction in two communities. Burnaby and Mackenzie (2001: 191) report that this project has been expanded so that Cree is now the main language of instruction up to grade four in many of nine targeted communities. While Cree parents could see the point of using oral Cree in school to explain concepts and manage class activities, they were not sure literacy in Cree was necessary; they wanted literacy in English or French first. Cree is written with a syllabary (instead of symbols standing for sounds, symbols stand for syllables). Gradually, parents changed their perspective and accepted that Cree could be used as a first language of literacy. The program, though, is still in its infancy.

Second, teaching Cree is part of a language revival initiative in the community called Cumberland House in the province of Saskatchewan (Bilash, 2004). Residents are either Cree or Metis (persons with a mixed racial background). The community of 1200 people is located 165 kilometers from the nearest town at the end of a 100-kilometer gravel road in an area known to few outsiders except hunters and fishermen. Beginning in 1998, a Cree Bilingual Program opened, with early literacy in Cree as a main goal. In the first class, 22 children were exposed only to Cree in kindergarten and then to 50% Cree and 50% English in grades one through three. By grade three the majority of children were developing literacy skills in both Cree and English. The program was still in effect in early 2004, but with very limited financing.

Commenting at that time on the future, Bilash had this to say: "Only when parents can receive a set of Cree books as a part of their birthing celebration and know that the public library contains hundreds of children's books in Cree that can be and are read by children before they begin school will literacy be a viable key to RLS [reversing language shift]" (p. 13).

12.5.5 Bilingual education in the United States?

Even though this chapter only tries to exemplify a few cases of acquisition planning in the world, even the sketchiest review would have to mention what is happening in the United States. In the United States itself reams of paper have been used to write academic articles about educating the burgeoning immigrant population. Almost every week there are newspaper stories about the problems of providing for immigrants. They often deal with education but also are about other problems, such as getting courtroom and other translators for immigrants. This is also a topic in many book-length studies. Baker (2001) is a well-known general study of bilingual education in the world; it includes a section on the United States. Bilingual education, or the lack of it in the United States, is discussed in many places. Crawford (2000) is a recognized source; see also Crawford (2004). Also, there are many relevant articles in such journals as *The TESOL Quarterly* and the Language Policy Research Unit at Arizona State University issues a number of papers on language policy and bilingual education that are available on the web. (In the following subsections, with apologies to the rest of South and North America, "America" may be used as a cover term for the United States.)

12.5.5.1 *The irony of US fears about bilingual education*

Somewhere we read the apt phrase that "America is the graveyard of languages". Laponce (1987: 189) put it this way about an earlier America, but the words still apply today: "'Give us your immigrants,' the United States said in effect in nineteenth century Europe, 'and we will impose English on them'." Dicker (1996) provides an overview on the history of languages in America.

True, the 2000 census indicated that one in five people aged five and older (47 million US residents) spoke a language other than English at home in 2000. Since 1990, this statistic represents an increase of 15 million people who don't use English at home. But the census also showed that 55% of these people said they spoke English "very well". Just over half of the persons who said they spoke Spanish at home said they spoke English "very well" even though there was a 62% increase in the number of Spanish speakers from 1990 to 2000. Combined with those respondents who spoke only English at home, 92% of the US population aged five and over had no difficulty speaking English. (Nationally, about one in six households were included in the total census sample.)

These data make two facts clear: America is taking in a huge number of immigrants, but even immigrants are following the long-standing American ideology that "**normal people speak English**". Another part of this American ideology is to change immigrants into Americans as quickly as possible; this means asking them to turn in their own languages in exchange for English. Of course, the census data do not reveal this part of the American ethos in regard to language, but it's obvious in American attitudes toward bilingual education (they are against it).

A number of writers have noted the irony in America's near-fear that having other languages used as media in the schools, even at beginning levels, will weaken English. (An "English only" movement began in the mid-1980s and still exists even if it is less strong; it is strong enough that several states passed laws making English their official language.) The irony, of course, is that the role of English in America must only have been strengthened in recent years – because the rest of the world has raised the value of English by installing it as the global lingua franca.

Are we being too cynical to suggest that Anglo-America is so self-absorbed that it's not even aware of what the rest of the world is speaking? To be fair to Americans, we must remember that the United States is a physically huge country with mainly monolingual English communities outside the big urban centers. The result – through no fault of their own – is that many Americans don't meet anyone except other English-speaking Americans. Even though the reality may look different to Europeans who think that half of Kansas City is congregated as tourists in the Louvre in Paris or in St. Mark's Square in Venice, average Americans, even average middle-class Americans, do not travel abroad. They have not been to Europe and heard English spoken there, let alone to Hong Kong and certainly not to India to hear more English. Americans have little cause to think English needs to be protected, but many do. An indication is that they vote against bilingual education; they want everyone to speak English, but they think bilingual education *may even prevent* children from learning English (because there's too much L1 in the classroom). But they don't want a program that puts children with limited English in classrooms *with their children*, either (this was part of a negative campaign against bilingual education in Colorado in 2002).

12.5.5.2 *"Structured immersion" as a version of bilingual education*

The fears of some Americans about languages other than English on US soil have resulted in what Crawford (2000: 84) calls "the political paradox of bilingual education". We can only mention a few of the highlights of what has happened in America. The points to remember are these:

- The Bilingual Education Act is passed by the US Congress in 1968 without a single vote of dissent. This was in the heyday of "the Great Society" and the push for civil rights. The problem was that the Act's purpose was never clear. Its main purpose seemed to be to make it possible for limited-English-proficient children (called LEPs in the schools) to learn English as rapidly as possible. But others thought it might be to encourage bilingualism and biliteracy, or to promote social equality, among other possible goals.
- The US Supreme Court's decision in *Lau v. Nichols* in 1974 has an impact on the way Americans think about bilingual education. The decision, in effect, stated that not making special educational provisions for non-English speakers meant not providing equal access to education. The court's ruling made schools, not parents, responsible for coping with limited English proficiency. The Equal Educational Opportunities Act of 1974 made the *Lau* decision a part of federal law; the result was more attention to bilingual education.
- The 1994 version of the Bilingual Education Act includes among its goals "developing the English skills . . . and to the extent possible the native-language skills" of LEP students.
- Voters in California pass Proposition 227 in 1988. This was a ballot initiative titled "English for Children". It eliminated most L1 instruction, even though California has a huge population of LEP students. Even a large group of Latinos voted for the initiative. What happened? One view is that the ballot passed as an expression of racism that was especially directed at Spanish-speaking immigrants. An opposing hypothesis is that voters didn't understand the initiative; they thought they were voting for English. Crawford (2003) reports on a 1988 *Los Angeles Times* poll in which 73 percent of respondents agreed with the statement "If you live in America, you need to speak English." Crawford says, "Respondents seemed to view bilingual education as a diversion from, rather than a means toward, that end" (p. 4).
- Voters in Arizona pass Proposition 203 in 2000. It requires most English learners to be taught through structured English immersion unless their parents receive a bilingual education waiver.
- More recently, in November 2003, voters in Colorado turn down an initiative that would have installed structured English immersion and would have

effectively banned bilingual education including the students' L1. On the same election day, voters in Massachusetts passed an initiative for structured English immersion.

- In January 2004, the Bilingual Education Act is eliminated as part of a "reform" measure known as No Child Left Behind that was proposed by the Bush administration and passed with broad support from both Democratic and Republican law makers. An English Language Acquisition Act replaces the Bilingual Education Act. Funds will continue to support education for English Limited Students, but rapid teaching of English will take precedence and annual English assessments will be mandated.

- Other states and localities continue with their own versions of bilingual education; these could be structured immersion or mainstreaming (see 12.5.1 again for definitions).

12.5.5.3 *What can we conclude about Americans and bilingual education?*

Here are two more ironies in the recent developments about bilingual education, or the lack of it, as outlined above. First, language-minority communities are **gaining political clout**. For example, in preparation for the 2004 presidential and congressional elections, both Republican and Democratic politicians were concerned about wooing Latinos in key states. Second, more American communities are getting accustomed to having ethnic diversity on their doorstep; there are not Latinos and Asians just in California, but in unexpected places. For example, the percentage of residents in the southeastern state of Georgia who spoke a language other than English at home in the 2000 census increased over 160% from 1990 statistics (there are especially many migrant workers from Central and South America).

Still, the American ideology seems to remain largely unchanged. It is possible that not many Anglo-Americans understand bilingual education; and, as we've indicated above, there is a lot to understand (i.e. what is a specific program designed to accomplish?). But, in general, it seems that the only type of bilingual education that most Anglo-Americans are likely to support are programs that they understand as **a transition to English**. Certainly, they are unlikely to vote to support (financially or otherwise) the multiculturalist programs that may be popular with educators and some ethnic groups. (For more on this, see a special issue of the *International Journal of the Sociology of Language* devoted to "Bilingualism and schooling in the United States", Fishman, ed. 2002 with a focus article by Eugene E. Garcia.)

12.6 English in the world

Throughout this volume, the use of English has been mentioned so often and in so many international contexts that we wonder, does more need to be said?

Thus, this section includes a very limited discussion of English as a world lingua franca.

A headline for a *New York Times* article recently read, "Berlin has a word for its ambitions: English". But not everyone agrees that English should be the one and only main vehicle through which to realize socio-economic mobility. Thus, the headline from another *New York Times* story, this time reporting on Rio de Janeiro in Brazil, is "English is spoken here . . . too much, some say". Books and articles about English in the world abound in the language policy community. (For example, see these book-length studies in recent years: Eggington and Wren, 2002; Maurais and Morris, 2003; Phillipson, 2003; Ricento, 2001; as well as Cenoz and Jessner, 2000 on English in Europe.)

Most who write about English's role in the world do so with superlatives or absolutes, whether they are happy with the situation or not. In the introduction to this chapter, we quoted De Swaan (2001) on placing English as the super-supercentral language in the world. He likes the prefix "hyper-" and goes so far as to say that "English is the hypercentral language that holds the entire world language system together" (p. 17). About the spontaneous aspects of the spread of English as the main second language of the world, Wright (2004: 136) makes this succinct prediction: "One thing is quite clear, however; language planners at the national level can only respond to this phenomenon and not direct it."

12.6.1 Forces behind the spread of English

Since World War II, English has moved with surprising speed into almost all nations and almost all settings, too. Language planners increasingly include English, at least implicitly, in their decisions because they recognize that their own decisions are not isolated from the international context. For example, national planning for education has to take account of this spread of English. The result is that **English is becoming part of school curricula all over** because nation states and private businesses believe that in order to retain their influence in international communication, their citizens and representatives have to be able to use English.

English only achieved its world stature recently. Further, when it spread, its pull may have been more a matter of perceptions about its scope than its actual place in the world. In the nineteenth century, it is true that the language of British colonial rule was English. But although colonialism spread British influence, it did not spread the learning of English. The majority of peoples colonized in Africa and Asia were not given opportunities to acquire English, Wright states. What the British Empire did spread though, we suggest, is **the prestige of English**.

A large part of this prestige was due to its association with scientific advances and technological inventions by Britain and the United States. Wright notes that during the industrial revolution of the nineteenth century, the British went through a period of intense scientific creativity. Throughout the late nineteenth and twentieth centuries, Americans were inventing new devices and developing the mode of mass production for all assembled products. In addition, one might say that after World War II, the American role in that war spread the prestige of all things American. The United States was also a mass producer of cultural inventions in English (e.g. films, pop music), although the UK can claim the Beatles.

But the United States not only became recognized as the world force in science and technology, it also spread the notion of a capitalist system. Wright (2004) argues that the financial networks of global capitalism are not exclusively American; instead, she argues, the network of capitalism is worldwide. She states that of the top 100 transnational corporations, ranked by their foreign assets, 50 percent are actually based in the European Union countries (p. 145). But American-led **thinking about capitalism** is what does dominate, she argues, and this, in turn, has led to the spread of the language of the United States along with the spread of capitalism. Other writers tend to claim that the United States has unchallenged dominance in industry, commerce, and finance.

Whoever is correct, the older members of the elite in many nations do not like the spread of either the use of English or its prestige. Some refer to the spread of English as linguistic imperialism (cf. Phillipson, 2003). On the other side one can argue, as does a 2001 article in the *Wall Street Journal*, that the spread of English takes place voluntarily and with secondary benefits. "It allows members of smaller cultures, such as Hungarians or Finns, to jump into the global mainstream without having to make what would once have been a fateful choice among French, German or Russian." In making an argument that the spread of English does not spell the end of local languages, many writers, including House (2003), distinguish between "languages for communication" and "languages for identification". House argues that in the world outside the L1 English-speaking communities, the speakers' L1s can continue to serve as the speaker's **"language for identification"** and can coexist with English in its role as a **"language for communication"**.

12.6.2 English: A hostile invader or the new Latin?

Whatever viewpoint is expressed, the march of English continues. Many European businesses (and those elsewhere) have already made English their medium. For example, at management meetings at big banks like Deutsche Bank in Germany and Crédit Suisse in Switzerland, the language is English. It's been argued that, in some ways, this march of English is symbolic, born of a wish to have **the image of a global player**. Does this mean people will drop their L1s? Not at all, some argue; it may even accentuate individual ethnicity, they say. At least in 1991 the *Eurobarometer* reported that more than 97 percent of young

Europeans mentioned their national language when asked which language they speak at home (cited in De Swaan, 2001: 218). Perhaps it is only a symbol, but English is now the main foreign language of European secondary school-children, for example. And the reaction of many users of English (especially younger users) is far from negative; in Europe, they consider English simply the new lingua franca, the new Latin.

12.6.3 Languages in competition: French and English in Cambodia

In its spread, English has displaced other languages as the preferred lingua franca. French remains the lingua franca in nations in the French sphere of economic influence (e.g. former French West Africa and former French North Africa). However, in some places where French had been used, a competition still is in process. For example, consider the situation in Cambodia.

There, francophone organizations have spent a good deal of money setting up French-medium universities. But now aid organizations favoring English (and not all are from nations where English is the L1) are competing. Note that this competition between organizations offering financial aid does show that the spread of English in the developing nations is by no means entirely spontaneous.

In Cambodia, 90 percent of the population are L1 speakers of Khmer, now the official language. But Cambodia was a French colony from 1863 to 1953. Then the nation was the site of wars and destruction and communist rule. English and other Western languages were banned to discourage relations with the West. Some Cambodians studied Russian or Vietnamese (just as in China, Russian was the main foreign language studied when China was closely allied with the USSR). In 1989, the Vietnamese withdrew and Cambodia opened relations with the West. France arrived with significant amounts of assistance. But it also came with the requirement that the French-funded Institute of Technology and other higher institutions of education must teach in French. The students who demonstrated in the early 1990s for English instruction were mollified with an offer of four and a half hours per week of English instruction.

But the demand for English accelerates. In 1999 Cambodia was admitted to the Association of Southeast Asian Nations. This organization of 10 nations (dedicated to promoting economic and cultural interactions) uses English as its official language. A Cambodian economist, explaining that 70 percent of his own work requires English, said, "Language choice is market driven, and the market favors English" (Clayton, 2002: 6). At the time of Clayton's writing, French was continuing as a medium of at least some instruction at all universities that receive aid directly from France or through the Francophonie, a French-government-sponsored consortium of French-speaking nations. But in junior high schools, where language choices are generally up to students, students chose English two to one over French in 2000 as their required foreign language, Clayton reports.

12.7 The European Union and Europe's new industry: Translating

Pity the European Union: How can it resolve the problem of satisfying all its member states regarding the medium of discussion? As it stands now, most communiqués are in a few languages (English, French, or German). But the problem is that every time the EU takes in a new member, it has to add to its translation staff to deal with yet another language. When the EU took in 10 new countries in May 2004, they brought with them nine extra languages to add to the EU's existing 11 languages.

The charter states that every official language of members must be provided by the EU's translation service. According to the *BBC News Service* (in May 2004), the European Commission already had 1300 translators who processed 1.5 million pages a year in the EU's then 11 languages. Juhani Lonroth, the Finn who runs the translation service, claims that this translation service costs less than two euros per citizen. He was quoted by the *BBC News Service* as saying, "so that is less than a cup of coffee or a ticket to the cinema. I think it's worth it because it is part of democracy."

There are a number of levels in the EU. There is the European Parliament and the European Council of Ministers in their official sessions and the European Commission in its external contacts. In the Commission the rule that all of the members' languages must be available is in force. At another level, there is the Commission's internal bureaucracy. Here, there are informally a few "working languages" for daily talk and in-house correspondence.

The forerunner of the EU, the European Economic Community (EEC), became the EU in 1993. The EEC had six member states when it was founded in 1957 (Belgium, France, Germany, Italy, Luxembourg, and the Netherlands). Previously a favored language for inter-governmental contacts in Europe, French lost any claim to be the sole lingua franca in the Community. The reason was that the decisions of the Community were to be binding on member states and therefore had to be stated in the languages of its members. Four languages could be used without making deliberations too unwieldy (German, French, Italian, and Dutch). But in 1973, when the UK along with Ireland and Denmark joined, the problems really began. In the EU, English has become the predominant medium of international communication.

One of the problems with the rise of English is that the major European languages are very robust; one can't see the major member states with the most L1 speakers (e.g. France and Germany, but then also Italy and Spain) being willing to see their languages set aside for a Europe-wide medium for the EU that is not even spoken as an L1 on the continent – that is, English. But it is likely that this will happen. That is, it is likely that **the diglossic situation** that already exists will just intensify. That is, members today speak their own language (their L language) and then another language (often English, but sometimes French or German) as a second language (their H language). But whether the EU can settle on only English as its main working language remains to be seen.

National languages do occupy a place in a variety of contexts at the EU, but in second place after English – if we can take the responses of the Swedish delegation as an indication of how other members would respond. Melander (2001) reports on how 16 of the 22 Swedish members of the European Parliament responded to a questionnaire. They estimated that they spoke Swedish 79% of the time in some types of committee meetings vs. 20% for English, but in other committee meetings they spoke English 80% and Swedish only 10.5% of the time. In informal situations they said they spoke Swedish 31.5% and English 52% of the time. Only in plenary sessions did Swedish really dominate for these Swedes; this is not surprising because plenary sessions are the type of session where it's important to "show the national flag". Here they said they spoke Swedish more than 98 percent and English only 1.8 percent of the time. Presumably, they could have spoken Swedish more than they did by making use of translators. Keep in mind, though, that English has been an important L2 in Sweden for a long time and that most Swedes are very good English speakers.

No matter what happens, members will continue to speak their own language, but, as De Swaan implies, every time a new state joined the EU, it increased the extent to which English is more widely used over other choices. Perhaps French will remain privileged. After all, the main seat of the EU is in a francophone location (Brussels, even though it is officially bilingual in French and Brussels Dutch (Flemish)). But in the past, when France has asserted itself to have official status as the second working language, Germany has put forth its call for German as a third working language. Then, other nations jump in with their languages. Thus, the matter is not officially settled.

12.8 Summing up

In this chapter, we discussed what is meant by the terms **language policy and language planning**. We also looked at a number of case studies of the results of language policies. In addition, we've tried to position our overall discussion within the theme of language in a globalizing community and the hierarchies in that community.

- Overall theme of **language groups in competition** for scarce resources that governments can allocate.

- **Three types of planning** (also called management) exist under the rubric language policy. They are:
  - **Status planning:** decisions about which language(s) will fill various official roles. From the standpoint of its speakers, the most important role is as the working language(s) of government because this role means more opportunities of many types for its speakers.
  - **Corpus planning:** decisions about ways to enhance the language(s) selected for official roles. This type of planning refers to preparing dictionaries and developing vocabularies to meet the government's needs. It also can mean making decisions about other features of languages, such as ruling on what will count as the standard dialect of the official language and selecting an official orthography as well as a spelling system.
  - **Acquisition planning:** decisions about how language varieties are to be learned. Especially, deciding on media for instruction in the schools as well as which language(s) will be taught counts as acquisition planning.
- **Problems that language planners** face in today's world:
  - **Borders** and the diverse groups they contain, creating minority groups within a nation state.
  - **The issue of language rights** for speakers of minority languages.
  - **The issue of endangered languages**.
  - **Bilingual education,** practices and attitudes towards it.
- **The reality of English as a global lingua franca**.
- **The European Union** and how it must deal with the many languages of its members.

12.9 Words and phrases to remember

languages of the world as a galaxy
central and peripheral languages
languages as collective goods
language planning to make a nation distinctive
responses of populations to school languages
types of bilingual education
English in the United States
attitudes toward English elsewhere

13

Conclusions

Multiple voices: The word from Haitians in New York

Emile LeBlanc is a taxi driver in New York City. He's a native of Haiti, but lives in New Jersey now where housing costs less. His first language is Haitian Creole and he also speaks the official language of Haiti, French, fairly well. As a taxi driver meeting the public in New York, of course he also speaks English. Emile holds a university degree and is studying for a master's degree. When he finishes that degree, he hopes to become a high-school teacher. His children speak English as their first language and Emile speaks to them only in English because it is the language of their schooling and he's anxious to have them do well in school. They've picked up only limited French and Haitian Creole when Haitian visitors come to the home. But his oldest child, a daughter, graduated from medical school and is now an intern at a New Jersey hospital where she sometimes puts to use the little French she knows with patients from French-speaking backgrounds (some patients are Haitians or African immigrants from francophone countries).

13.1 Some themes to remember

In this brief overview of the entire volume, we want to remind you of the main themes we have stressed in the earlier chapters.

- Being bilingual, or even multilingual, is as normal as being monolingual. There's nothing *wrong* with being monolingual, but it's likely that there are more bilinguals/multilinguals in the world than monolinguals. (We use bilingual as a cover term for both bilinguals and multilinguals here, as elsewhere in the volume.)

- Asymmetries characterize both social and grammatical relations between two languages. That is, things are rarely equal in either type of relation. As we indicated in chapters 3 and 4, not all languages that are spoken in a community are targets to learn as a second language (L2). The socio-economic prestige of the potential target matters as does its official status in the nation state where the potential learner lives. Thus, not all languages are acquired equally or equally maintained.

- But the same set of socio-economic factors figures in whether people acquire any particular language or maintain it, even though the weighting of these factors differs according to the circumstances in the community in question.

- As we indicated in chapters 5, 6, and 7, there also is asymmetry in how speakers value and use languages. Speakers have certain "mind views" (ideologies) about the value of different languages; the culture in which they live partly influences this and how they use their languages. They do not view all languages as serving the same socio-psychological functions. Speakers use and value languages as indices of how they view themselves and as a tool for the negotiation of interpersonal relations.

- In the chapters on structural (grammatical) aspects of language (chapters 8 on borrowing and 9 on the grammars of languages when they are in contact), we see asymmetries. When languages borrow words from another language, it is almost never a reciprocal matter; rather, the language with more social prestige tends to be the donor language. When languages are used together in the same clause, as in codeswitching, they don't participate equally. Also, the implicational evidence is that both languages are "on", but just to different degrees.

- In the chapters especially concerned with the cognitive aspects of language, we also see asymmetries. In chapter 10 we see that psycholinguistic experiments indicate that both of a bilingual's languages are activated in both comprehension and production tasks, but they are not equally activated. There is also asymmetry in the language in which past events are remembered and in recovery of languages when a speaker has suffered brain injuries.

- In chapter 11 we see asymmetry between acquiring a second language as a young child and in learning it later in life. We recognize that late second-language learners almost never have native-like success, and we survey theories about what makes second-language learning as successful as it can be.

- In chapter 12, we see how language policies, almost inevitably, create asymmetries. Not all languages in a nation state are treated equally. The factors to consider in formulating language policies are also generally the same everywhere. The difference between a successful policy and other outcomes depends on how strong a government is and how willing critical groups in the population are to follow the government's ideas. Governments must have the elite and powerful minorities on its side, but these groups do not accept changes readily because their status usually depends on maintaining the status quo.

13.2 Guidelines for understanding speakers in relation to their languages

Probably the most important points to take away from this book are these:

- **First**, do not underestimate the symbolic value that speakers place on the languages they know, most especially their first language.
- **Second**, languages are rarely equally valued; formally assigning them equal status does not make it so.
- **Third**, people should have the right to use whatever language they choose; they just can't always expect to use it for all the situations they meet. They also should have the right to learn and use languages of wider communication.
- **Fourth**, of all the areas to study in relation to bilingualism, we especially have a lot more to learn about the cognitive aspects of language. This means much more study is needed of how languages are organized in the brain and what this organization means for second-language teaching and treating patients with brain injuries or maladies that affect language. More study is also needed of the grammatical effects on the languages involved when people are bilingual because what happens in such circumstances is an empirical window on language in the mind.
- **Finally**, we need to explore more ways to give respect to all languages and their speakers and to provide them access to whatever rewards will make their lives better.

References

Abutalebi, Jubin, Stefano F. Cappa, and Daniela Perani (2001) The bilingual brain as revealed by functional neuroimaging. *Bilingualism: Language and Cognition* 4:179–90.

Acholonu, Catherine, and Joyce Ann Penfield (1980) Linguistic processes of lexical innovation in Igbo. *Anthropological Linguistics* 22:118–30.

Adendorff, Ralph D. (1993) Ethnographic evidence of the social meaning of Fanakalo in South Africa. *Journal of Pidgin and Creole Languages* 8:1–27.

Aikhenvald, Alexandra (2002) *Language Contact in Amazonia*. Oxford: Oxford University Press.

—— (2003) Multilingualism and ethnic stereotypes: The Tariana of northwest Amazonia. *Language in Society* 32:1–22.

Al Batal, Mahmoud (2002) Identity and language tension in Lebanon: The Arabic of local news at LBCI. In Aleya Rouchdy (ed.), *Language Contact and Language Conflict in Arabic*. London: Curzon, 91–115.

Alexander, Neville (1989) *Language Policy and National Unity in South Africa/Azania*. Capetown: Buchu Books.

—— (2004) Socio-political factors in the evolution of language policy in post-apartheid South Africa. Paper presented at 30th International LAUD Symposium, "Empowerment through Language", University of Koblenz-Landau, Campus Landau, Germany, April 19–22.

Al-Khatib, Mahmoud A. (2001) Language shift among the Armenians of Jordan. *International Journal of the Sociology of Language* 152:153–77.

Allard, Réal, and Rodrigue Landry (1992) Ethnolinguistic vitality beliefs and language maintenance and loss. In Willem Fase, Koen Jaspaert and Sjaak Kroon (eds.), *Maintenance and Loss of Minority Languages*. Amsterdam: Benjamins, 171–95.

Alleyne, Mervyn (1980) *Comparative Afro-American*. Ann Arbor, MI: Karoma.

Amuzu, Evershed (1998) Aspects of grammatical structure in Ewe-English codeswitching. M.A. thesis, University of Oslo.

Anderson, Benedict (1983) *Imagined Communities*. London: Verso.

Ansre, Gilbert (1971) The influence of English on West African languages. In John Spencer (ed.), *The English Language in West Africa*. London: Longman, 145–64.

Archibald, John (ed.) (2000) *Second Language Acquisition and Linguistic Theory*. Malden, MA: Blackwell.

Arends, Jacques, Pieter Muysken, and Norval Smith (eds.) (1995) *Pidgins and Creoles: An Introduction*. Amsterdam: Benjamins.

Arutiunov, Sergei (1998) Linguistic minorities in the Caucasus. In Christina Bratt Paulston and Donald Peckham (eds.), *Linguistic Minorities in Central and Eastern Europe*. Clevedon: Multilingual Matters, 98–115.

Atkinson, David (2000) Minoritisation, identity and ethnolinguistic vitality in Catalonia. *Journal of Multilingual and Multicultural Development* 21:185–97.

Auer, Peter (1995) The pragmatics of code-switching: a sequential approach. In Leslie Milroy and Pieter Muysken (eds.), *One Speaker, Two Languages: Cross-disciplinary Perspectives on Code-switching*. Cambridge: Cambridge University Press, 115–35.

—— (1998) Introduction. In Peter Auer (ed.), *Code-switching in Conversation*. London: Routledge, 1–24.

Backus, Ad (1992) *Patterns of Language Mixing: A Study of Turkish-Dutch Bilingualism*. Wiesbaden: Harrassowitz.

—— (1996) *Two in One: Bilingual Speech of Turkish Immigrants in the Netherlands*. Tilburg, The Netherlands: Tilburg University Press.

—— (2003) Units in code-switching: Evidence for multimorphemic elements in the lexicon. *Linguistics*, 14:83–132.

Bailey, Benjamin (1997) Communication of respect in interethnic service encounters. *Language in Society* 26:327–56.

Baker, Colin (2001) *Foundations of Bilingual Education and Bilingualism*. Clevedon: Multilingual Matters.

Barth, Frederick (ed.) (1969) *Ethnic Groups and Boundaries: The Social Organization of Cultural Difference*. Boston: Little Brown.

Béal, Christine (1998) Keeping the peace: A cross-cultural comparison of questions and requests in Australian English and French. In Peter Trudgill and Jenny Cheshire (eds.), *The Sociolinguistics Reader. Vol. 1: Multilingualism and Variation*. London: Arnold, 5–24.

Beaton, Alan, Michael Gruneberg, and Nick Ellis (1995) Retention of foreign vocabulary learned using the keyword method: A ten-year follow-up. *Second Language Research* 11:112–20.

Belazi, Hedi M., Edward Rubin, and Jacqueline Toribio (1994) Code-switching and X-bar theory: The functional head constraint. *Linguistic Inquiry* 25:221–37.

Bell, Allan (1984) Style as audience design. *Language in Society* 13:145–204.

—— (2001) Back in style: Reworking audience design. In Penelope Eckert and John R. Rickford (eds.), *Style and Sociolinguistic Variation*. Cambridge: Cambridge University Press, 139–69.

Bentahila, Abdelali, and Eirlys E. Davies (1983) The syntax of Arabic-French code-switching. *Lingua* 59:301–30.

Ben-Zeev, Sandra (1977) The influence of bilingualism on cognitive strategy and cognitive development. *Child Development* 48:1009–18.

Bernsten, Janice Graham (1990) The integration of English loans in Shona: Social correlates and linguistic consequences. Unpublished Ph.D. dissertation, Michigan State University.

—— (1998) Runyakitara: Uganda's "new" language. *Journal of Multilingual and Multi-cultural Development* 19:93–107.

Bernsten, Janice Graham (1990), and Carol Myers-Scotton (1993) English loans in Shona: Consequences for linguistic systems. *International Journal of the Sociology of Language* 100/101:125–48.

Beukes, Anne-Marie (2004) The First Ten Years of Democracy: Language Policy in South Africa. Paper read at 10th Linguapax Congress on Linguistic Diversity, Sustainability and Peace, 20–3 May, Barcelona.

Bhatia, Tej K., and William C. Ritchie (1996) Bilingual language mixing, universal grammar, and second language acquisition. In William C. Ritchie and Tej K. Bhatia (eds.), *Handbook of Second Language Acquisition*. San Diego: Academic Press, 627–88.

Bialystok, Ellen (2001a) *Bilingualism in Development: Language, Literacy, and Cognition*. Cambridge: Cambridge University Press.

—— (2001b) Metalinguistic aspects of bilingual processing. *The Annual Review of Applied Linguistics* 21:169–81.

Bickerton, Derek (1981) *Roots of Language*. Ann Arbor, MI: Karoma.

Bijeljac-Babic, Ranka, Agnes Biardeau, and Jonathan Grainger (1997) Masked orthographic priming in bilingual word recognition. *Memory and Cognition* 25:447–57.

Bilaniuk, Laada (2003) Gender, language attitudes, and language status in Ukraine. *Language in Society* 32:47–78.

Bilash, Olenka (2004) The rocky road to RLS in a Cree community in Canada. Paper presented at 30th International LAUD Symposium, "Empowerment through Language", University of Koblenz-Landau, Campus Landau, Germany, April 19–22.

Billig, Michael (1995) Discourse, opinions and ideologies: A comment. *Current Issues in Language and Society* 2:162–7.

Birdsong, David (2005) Interpreting age effects in second language acquisition. In Judith Kroll and Annette De Groot (eds.), *Handbook of Bilingualism: Psycholinguistic Approaches*. New York: Oxford University Press, 109–27.

Birdsong, David, and Michelle Molis (2001) On the evidence for maturational constraints in second-language acquisition. *Journal of Memory and Language* 44:235–49.

Bley-Vroman, Robert (1989) What is the logical problem of foreign language learning? In Susan Gass and J. Schachter (eds.) *Linguistic Perspectives on Second Language Acquisition*. Cambridge: Cambridge University Press, 41–68.

—— (1990) The logical problem of foreign language learning. *Linguistic Analysis* 201:3–49.

Blommaert, Jan (ed.) (1999a) *Language Ideological Debates*. Berlin: Mouton de Gruyter.

—— (1999b) The debate is open. In Jan Blommaert (ed.), *Language Ideological Debates*. Berlin: Mouton de Gruyter, 1–38.

—— (1999c) The debate is closed. In Jan Blommaert (ed.), *Language Ideological Debates*. Berlin: Mouton de Gruyter, 425–38.

Blum-Kulka, Shoshana and Juliane House (1989) Cross-cultural and situational variation in requesting behavior. In Shoshana Blum-Kulka, Juliane House and Gabrielle Kasper (eds.), *Cross-cultural Pragmatics, Requests and Apologies*. Norwood, NJ: Ablex, 123–54.

Bolonyai, Agnes (1998) In-between languages: Language shift/maintenance in childhood bilingualism. *The International Journal of Bilingualism* 2:21–43.

—— (1999) The hidden dimensions of language contact: the case of Hungarian-English bilingual children. Ph.D. dissertation, University of South Carolina.

—— (2002) Case systems in contact: Syntactic and lexical case in bilingual child language. *Southwest Journal of Linguistics* 21:1–34.

Boneva, Bonka (1998) Ethnicity and nation: The Bulgarian dilemma. In Christina Bratt Paulston and Donald Peckham (eds.), *Linguistic Minorities in Central and Eastern Europe*. Clevedon, UK: Multilingual Matters, 80–97.

Bosch, Laura, and Nuría Sebastián-Gallés (2001) Evidence of early language discrimination abilities in infants from bilingual environments. *Infancy* 2:29–49.

Bouchereau Bauer, Eurydice, Joan Kelly Hall, and Kirsten Kruth (2002) The pragmatic role of codeswitching in play contexts. *International Journal of Bilingualism* 6:53–74.

Boumans, Louis (1998) *The Syntax of Codeswitching, Analysing Moroccan Arabic/Dutch Conversation*. Tilburg, The Netherlands: Tilburg University Press.

Bourdieu, Pierre (1982) *Ce que parler veut dire: L'Économie des échanges linguistiques*. Paris: Librairie Arthème Fayard.

—— (1991) *Language and Symbolic Power*. Cambridge, MA: Harvard University Press.

Bourhis, Richard Y., and Howard Giles (1977) The language of intergroup distinctiveness. In Howard Giles (ed.), *Language, Ethnicity and Intergroup Relations*. London: Academic Press, 119–35.

Bourhis, Richard Y., and Itesh Sachdev (1984) Vitality perceptions and language attitudes: Some Canadian data. *Journal of Language and Social Psychology* 3:97–126.

Boyd, Sally, and Leena Huss (eds.) (2001) *Managing Multilingualism in a European Nation-State: Challenges for Sweden*. Clevedon, UK: Multilingual Matters.

Braunmüller, Kurt (2000) On types of multilingualism in Northern Europe in the late Middle Ages. In Gudrún Thórhallsdóttir (ed.), *Proceedings of the Tenth International Conference of Nordic and General Linguistics*. Reykjavik, 61–70.

—— (2001) Semi-communication and accommodation: Observations from the linguistic situation in Scandinavia. *International Journal of Applied Linguistics* 12:1–23.

Brown, Gordon D. A., and Charles Hulme (1992) Cognitive psychology and second language processing: The role of short-term memory. In R. J. Harris (ed.), *Cognitive Processing in Bilinguals*. Amsterdam: North Holland, 105–21.

Brown, Penelope, and Stephen C. Levinson (1987) *Politeness: Some Universals in Language Usage*. Cambridge and New York: Cambridge University Press.

Brown, Roger (1973) *A First Language: The Early Stages*. Cambridge, MA: Harvard University Press.

Brown, Roger, and Albert Gilman (1960) The pronouns of power and solidarity. In Thomas A. Sebeok (ed.), *Style in Language*. Cambridge, MA: MIT Press, 253–76.

Budzhak-Jones, Svitlana (1998) Against word-internal codeswitching: Evidence from Ukrainian-English bilingualism. *International Journal of Bilingualism* 2:161–82.

Burnaby, Barbara and Marguerite Mackenzie (2001) Cree decision making concerning language: A case study. *Journal of Multilingual and Multicultural Development* 22:191–209.

Burt, Susan Meredith (1994) Code choice in intercultural conversation: Speech accommodation theory and pragmatics. *Pragmatics* 4:535–59.

Calvet, Louis-Jean (1998) *Language Wars and Linguistic Politics*. Oxford: Oxford University Press.

Canagarajah, A. Suresh (1995) The political economy of code choice in a "revolutionary society": Tamil-English bilingualism in Jaffna, Sri Lanka. *Language in Society* 24:187–212.

Canut, Cécil, and Dominique Caubet (2001) *Comment les languages se mélangent*. Paris: L'Harmattan.

Carroll, Susanne E. (2000) *Input and Evidence: The Raw Material of Second Language Acquisition*. Amsterdam: John Benjamins.

Cenoz, Jasone, and Fred Genesee (eds.) (1998) *Beyond Bilingualism: Multilingualism and Multilingual Education*. Clevedon, UK: Multilingual Matters.

—— (2001) *Psycholinguistics: Trends in Bilingual Acquisition*. Amsterdam: John Benjamins.

Cenoz, Jasone, and Charlotte Hoffman (eds.) (2003) special issue, The effect of bilingualism on third language acquisition. *International Journal of Bilingualism* 7:1.

Cenoz, Jasone, and Ulrike Jessner (eds.) (2000) *English in Europe: the Acquisition of a Third Language*. Clevedon, UK: Multilingual Matters.

Chaudenson, Robert (2001) *Creolization of Language and Culture*. London and New York: Routledge.

Chee, M. W. L., Tan, E. W. L., and Thiel, T. (1999) Mandarin and English single word processing studied with functional Magnetic Resonance Imagining. *Journal of Neuroscience* 19:3050–6.

Cheshire, Jenny, and Lise-Marie Moser (1994) English as a cultural symbol: The case of advertisements in French-speaking Switzerland. *Journal of Multilingual and Multicultural Development* 15: 451–69.

Chomsky, Noam (1965) *Aspects of the Theory of Syntax*. Cambridge, MA: MIT Press.

—— (1981) *Lectures on Government and Binding*. Dordrecht, The Netherlands: Foris.

—— (1995) *The Minimalist Program*. Cambridge, MA: MIT Press.

Clahsen, Harald (1999) Lexical entries and rules of language: A multidisciplinary study of German inflection. *Behavioral and Brain Sciences* 22: 991–1060.

Clayton, Thomas (2002) Language choice in a nation under transition: The struggle between English and French in Cambodia. *Language Policy* 1:3–35.

Clyne, Michael (1994) *Inter-cultural Communication at Work: Cultural Values in Discourse*. Cambridge: Cambridge University Press.

—— (2003) *Dynamics of Language Contact*. Cambridge: Cambridge University Press.

—— (2004) Empowerment through the community language – Does it work? Paper presented at 30th International LAUD Symposium, "Empowerment through Language", University of Koblenz-Landau, Campus Landau, Germany, April 19–22.

Cook, Vivian (ed.) (2003) *Effects of the Second Language on the First*. Clevedon, UK: Multilingual Matters.

Cooper, Robert L. (1989) *Language Planning and Social Change*. Cambridge: Cambridge University Press.

Cortés-Conde, Florencia (1996) Is stable bilingualism possible in an immigrant setting? The Anglo-Argentine case. In Ana Roca and John B. Jensen (eds.), *Spanish in Contact: Issues in Bilingualism*. Somerville, MA: Cascadilla Press, 113–22.

Coulmas, Florian (1981) Poison to your soul: Thanks and apologies contrastively reviewed. In Florian Coulmas (ed.), *Conversational Routine*. The Hague: Mouton, 69–91.

—— (1997) A matter of choice. In Martin Pütz (ed.), *Language Choices: Conditions, Constraints, Consequences*. Amsterdam: Benjamins.

Coupland, Nikolas (2001) Language, situation, and the relational self: Theorizing dialect-style in sociolinguistics. In Penelope Eckert and John R. Rickford (eds.), *Style and Sociolinguistic Variation*. Cambridge: Cambridge University Press, 185–210.

Crawford, James (2000) *At War with Diversity: US Language Policy in an Age of Anxiety*. Clevedon, UK: Multilingual Matters.

—— (2003) Hard sell: Why is bilingual education so unpopular with the American public? *Arizona State University Language Policy Research Unit*, Article No. 8.

—— (2004) *Educating English Learners: Language Diversity in the Classroom*. Los Angeles: Bilingual Educational Services.

Croft, William (2003) *Typology and Universals*, 2nd ed., Cambridge: Cambridge University Press.

Cromdal, Jakob (1999) Childhood bilingualism and metalinguistic skills: Analysis and control in young Swedish-English bilinguals. *Applied Psycholinguistics* 20:1–20.

Crystal, David (1987) *The Cambridge Encyclopedia of Language*. Cambridge: Cambridge University Press.

Daniel, Jack L., and Geneva Smitherman (1990) How I got over: Call-response in communication dynamics in the Black community. In Donal Carbaug (ed.), *Cultural Communication and Inter-cultural Contact*. Hillsdale, NJ: Erlbaum, 27–44.

Daun, Åke (1991) Individualism and collectivity among Swedes. *Ethnos* 56:165–72.

De Graff, Michel (ed.) (1999) *Language Creation and Language Change: Creolization Diachrony and Development*. Cambridge, MA: MIT Press.

De Groot, Annette (1992) Determinants of word translation. *Journal of Experimental Psychology: Learning, Memory, and Cognition* 18:1001–18.

De Groot, Annette, and Rineke Keijzer (2000) What is hard to learn is easy to forget: The roles of word concreteness, cognate status, and word frequency in foreign-language vocabulary learning and forgetting. *Language Learning* 50:1–56.

De Groot, Annette, and Janet G. Van Hell (2005) The learning of foreign language vocabulary. In Judith Kroll and Annette De Groot (eds.), *Handbook of Bilingualism: Psycholinguistic Approaches*. New York: Oxford University Press, 9–29.

De Houwer, Annick (1990) *The Acquisition of Two Languages from Birth: A Case Study*. Cambridge: Cambridge University Press.

—— (2005) Early bilingual acquisition: Focus on morphosyntax and the separate development hypothesis. In Judith Kroll and Annette De Groot (eds.), *Handbook of Bilingualism: Psycholinguistic Aspects*. New York: Oxford University Press, 30–48.

Dejean, Yves (1993) An overview of the language situation in Haiti. *International Journal of the Sociology of Language* 102:73–83.

DeKeyser, Robert (2000) The robustness of critical period effects in second language acquisition. *Studies in Second Language Acquisition* 22:499–533.

DeKeyser, Robert, and Jenifer Larson-Hall (2005) What does the critical period really mean? In Judith Kroll and Annette De Groot (eds.), *Handbook of Bilingualism: Psycholinguistic Aspects*. New York: Oxford University Press, 88–108.

De Klerk, Vivian (2000a) Language shift in Grahamstown: A case study of selected Xhosa-speakers. *International Journal of the Sociology of Language* 146:87–110.

—— (2000b) To be Xhosa or not to be Xhosa . . . That is the question. *Journal of Multilingual and Multicultural Development* 21:198–215.

Dell, Gary S., Lisa K. Burger, and William R. Svec (1997) Language production and serial order: A functional analysis and a model. *Psychological Review* 104:123–47.

De Mejía, Anne-Marie (2002) *Power, Prestige and Bilingualism: International Perspectives on Elite Bilingual Education*. Clevedon, UK: Multilingual Matters.

De Swaan, Abram (2001) *Words of the World*. Cambridge: Polity.

Deuchar, Margaret and Suzanne Quay (2001) *Bilingual Acquisition: Theoretical Implications of a Case Study*. Oxford: Oxford University Press.

Dicker, Susan J. (1996) *Languages in America: A Pluralistic View*. Clevedon, UK: Multilingual Matters.

Dijkstra, Ton and Walter J. B. van Heuven (2002) The architecture of the bilingual word recognition system: From identification to decision. *Bilingualism: Language and Cognition* 5:175–98.

DiSciullo, Anne-Marie, Pieter Muysken, and Rajendra Singh (1986) Government and code-mixing. *Journal of Linguistics* 22:1–24.

Döpke, Susanne (2000) Generation of and retraction from cross-linguistically motivated structures in bilingual first language acquisition. *Bilingualism: Language and Cognition* 3: 209–26.

—— (ed.) (2001) *Crosslinguistic Structures in Simultaneous Bilingualism*. Amsterdam: John Benjamins.

Doughty, Catherine J. (2003) Instructed SLA: Constraints, compensation, and enhancement. In Catherine J. Doughty and Michael H. Long (eds.), *The Handbook of Second Language Acquisition*. Oxford: Blackwell, 256–310.

Doughty, Catherine J., and Michael H. Long (2003) *Handbook of Second Language Acquisition*. Oxford: Blackwell.

Druviete, Ina (1998) Republic of Latvia. In Christina Bratt Paulston and Donald Peckham (eds.) *Linguistic Minorities in Eastern and Central Europe*. Clevedon, UK: Multilingual Matters.

Dua, Hans R. (1992) Hindi language planning: A case study of status change. In Ulrich Ammon and Marlis Hellinger (eds.), *Status Change of Languages*. Berlin: Mouton de Gruyter, 178–99.

Dussias, Paola E. (2001) Psycholinguistic complexity in codeswitching. *International Journal of Bilingualism* 5:87–100.

Dweik, Bader (2000) Linguistic and cultural maintenance among Chechens of Jordan. *Language, Culture and Curriculum* 13:184–95.

Eastman, Carol M. (1983) *Language Planning*. San Francisco: Chandler and Sharp.

Edwards, John (1994) *Language, Society and Identity*. Oxford: Blackwell.

Edwards, John (1999) Refining our understanding of language attitudes. *Journal of Language and Social Psychology* 18:101–10.

Eggington, William, and Helen Wren (eds.) (1997) *Language Policy: Dominant English, Pluralist Challenges*. Amsterdam: John Benjamins.

Ellis, Nick C. (2003) Constructions, chunking, and connectionism: The emergence of second language structure. In Catherine J. Doughty and Michael H. Long (eds.), *The Handbook of Second Language Acquisition*. Oxford: Blackwell, 63–103.

—— (2005) Introduction to section on acquisition. In Judith Kroll and Annette De Groot (eds.), *Handbook of Bilingualism: Psycholinguistic Approaches*. New York: Oxford University Press, 3–8.

Ellis, Rod (1994) *The Study of Second Language Acquisition*. Oxford: Oxford University Press.

—— (1997) *Second Language Acquisition*. Oxford University Press.

Ellis, Rod, Helen Basturkmen, and Shawn Loewen (2001) Preemptive focus on form in the ESL classroom. *TESOL Quarterly* 35: 407–32.

Elster, Jon (1989) *The Cement of Society*. Cambridge: Cambridge University Press.

Ennaji, Moha (2002) Comment. *International Journal of the Sociology of Language* 157:71–83.

Erickson, Frederick, and William Rittenberg (1977) A case of cross-cultural misunderstanding concerning deference in an American hospital situation. Unpublished paper.

Errington, J. Joseph (1998a) Indonesian('s) development: On the state of a language of state. In Bambi Schieffelin, Kathryn Woolard, and Paul Kroskrity (eds.), *Language Ideologies: Practice and Theory*. New York: Oxford University Press, 271–84.

—— (1998b) *Shifting Languages, Interaction and Identity in Javanese Indonesia*. Cambridge: Cambridge University Press.

Errington, Ross (1988) The magic of the Cotabato Manobos. *Studies in Philippine Linguistics* 7:53–64.

Ervin-Tripp, Susan (1976) Is Sybil there? The structure of some American English directives. *Language in Society* 5:25–66.

Essien, Okon (1995) The English language and code-mixing: A case study of the phenomenon in Ibibio. In Ayo Bambose, A. Banjo and A. Thomas (eds.), *New Englishes, a Western African Perspective*. Ibadan, Nigeria: Mosuro, 269–83.

Eubank, Lynn, Larry Selinker, and Michael Sharwood Smith (eds.) (1995) *The Current State of Interlanguage*. Amsterdam: John Benjamins.

Eubank, Lynn, and Sabine Thepaut Grace (1998) V-to-I and inflection in non-native grammars. In Maria-Luise Beck (ed.), *Morphology and Its Interfaces in Second Language Knowledge*. Amsterdam: John Benjamins, 69–88.

Fabbro, Franco (1999) *The Neurolinguistics of Bilingualism: An Introduction*. Hove, UK: Taylor and Francis.

—— (2001) The bilingual brain: Cerebral representation of languages. *Brain and Language* 79: 211–22.

Fasold, Ralph (1984) *The Sociolinguistics of Language*. Oxford: Blackwell.

Fehlen, Fernand (2002) Luxembourg, a multilingual society at the Romance/Germanic language border. *Journal of Multilingual and Multicultural Development* 23:80–97.

Fenson, Larry, P. Dale, J. S. Reznick, E. Bates, D. Thal, and S. Pethick (1994) Variability in early communicative development. *Monographs of the Society for Research in Child Development* 59:1–173.

Fenyvesi, Anna (1998a) Linguistic minorities in Hungary. In Christina Bratt Paulston and Donald Peckham (eds.), *Linguistic Minorities in Central and Eastern Europe*. Clevedon, UK: Multilingual Matters, 135–59.

—— (1998b) Republic of Latvia. In Christina Bratt Paulston and Donald Peckham (eds.), *Linguistic Minorities in East and Central Europe*. Clevedon, UK: Multilingual Matters, 160–83.

Ferguson, Charles A. (1959) Diglossia. *Word* 15:325–40.

—— (1991) South Asia as a sociolinguistic area. Reprinted 1996 in Thom Huebner (ed.), *Sociolinguistic Perspectives: Papers of Charles A. Ferguson*. New York: Oxford University Press, 84–102.

Finlayson, Rosalie, Karen Calteaux, and Carol Myers-Scotton (1998) Orderly mixing and accommodation in South African codeswitching. *Journal of Sociolinguistics* 2:395–420.

Fishman, Joshua A. (1965) Who speaks what language, to whom and when? *La Linguistique* 2:67–88.

—— (1967) Bilingualism with and without diglossia; diglossia with and without bilingualism. *Journal of Social Issues* 23:29–38.

—— (1970) *Sociolinguistics: A Brief Introduction*. Rowley, MA: Newbury House.

—— (1972) *The Sociology of Language*. Rowley, MA: Newbury House.

—— (1991) *Reversing Language Shift: The Theoretical and Practical Foundations of Assistance to Threatened Languages*. Clevedon, UK: Multilingual Matters.

—— (1994) Critiques of language planning: A minority languages perspective. *Journal of Multilingual and Multicultural Development* 15:91–9.

—— (1999) (ed.) *Language and Ethnic Identity*. Oxford: Oxford University Press.

—— (2001) *Can Threatened Languages be Saved?* Clevedon, UK: Multilingual Matters.

—— (2002) (ed.) Bilingualism and Schooling in the United States. (special issue) *International Journal of the Sociology of Language* 155/156.

Fishman, Joshua A., Robert L. Cooper, and Roxana Ma (1971) *Bilingualism in the Barrio*. Bloomington: Indiana University Language Sciences Series.

Fishman, Joshua A., Charles A. Ferguson, and Jyotirindra Das Gupta (1968) (eds.), *Language Problems of Developing Nations*. New York: John Wiley and Sons.

Flege, James E., Ian R. MacKay, and Thorsten Piske (2002) Assessing bilingual dominance. *Applied Psycholinguistics* 23:567–98.

Flynn, Suzanne (1996) A parameter-setting approach to second language acquisition. In W. C. Ritchie and T. K. Bhatia (eds.), *Handbook of Second Language Acquisition*. San Diego, CA: Academic Press, 121–58.

Forson, Barnabas (1979) Code-switching in Akan-English bilingualism. Ph.D. dissertation, University of California at Los Angeles.

Fredsted, Elin (2005) Denmark: Getting to the point. In Leo Hickey and Miranda Stewart (eds.), *Politeness in Europe*. Clevedon, UK: Multilingual Matters, 159–73.

Friday, Robert A. (1991 6th ed.) Contrasts in discussion behaviors of German and American managers. In L. A. Samovar and R. E. Porter (eds.), *Intercultural Communication: A Reader*. Belmont, CA: Wadsworth, 178–84.

Gal, Susan (1979) *Language Shift: Social Determinants of Linguistic Change in Bilingual Austria*. New York: Academic Press.

Gal, Susan, and Judith Irvine (2000) Language ideology and the linguistic imagination. In P. V. Kroskrity (ed.), *Regimes of Language: Ideologies, Politics, and Identities*. Santa Fe, NM: School of American Research Press, 35–84.

Galambos, Sylvia J., and Kenji Hakuta (1988) Subject-specific and task-specific characteristics of metalinguistic awareness in bilingual children. *Applied Psycholinguistics* 9:141–62.

Galván, Roberto and Richard V. Teschner (1977) *El Diccionario Del Espanol Chicano / The Dictionary of Chicano Spanish*. Silver Spring, MD: Institute of Modern Languages.

Garcia, Eugene E. (2002) Bilingualism and schooling in the United States. (special issue) *International Journal of the Sociology of Language* 155/156:1–92.

Gardner-Chloros, Penelope (1991) *Language Selection and Switching in Strasbourg*. Oxford: Clarendon.

Gass, Susan M. (2003) Input and interaction. In Catherine J. Doughty and Michael H. Long (eds.), *The Handbook of Second Language Acquisition*. Oxford: Blackwell, 224–55.

Gass, Susan M., and Jacquelyn Schachter (eds.) (1989) *Linguistic Perspectives on Second Language Acquisition*. Cambridge: Cambridge University Press.

Gathercole, Virginia C., and Cecilia Montes (1997) That-trace effects in Spanish- and English-speaking monolinguals and bilinguals. In Ana Teresa Pérez-Leroux and William R. Glass (eds.), *Contemporary Perspectives on the Acquisition of Spanish*. Somerville, MA: Cascadilla Press, 75–95.

Genesee, Fred (2001) Bilingual first language acquisition: Exploring the limits of the language faculty. *Annual Review of Applied Linguistics* 21:153–68.

—— (2003) Rethinking Bilingual acquisition. In Jean- Marc Dewaele, Alex Housen and Li Wei (eds.), *Bilingualism: Beyond Basic Principles*. Clevedon, UK: Multilingual Matters, 204–28.

Genesee, Fred, Nicoladis, E., and Paradis, J. (1995) Language differentiation in early bilingual development. *Journal of Child Language* 22:611–31.

Gentner, Dedre, and Susan Goldin-Meadow (eds.) (2003) *Language in Mind: Advances in the Study of Language and Thought*. Cambridge: MIT Press.

Giles, Howard (2001) Couplandia and beyond. In Penelope Eckert and John R. Rickford (eds.), *Style and Sociolinguistic Variation*. Cambridge: Cambridge University Press, 211–19.

Giles, Howard, Richard Bourhis, and Donald Taylor (1977) Towards a theory of language in ethnic group relations. In Howard Giles (ed.), *Language, Ethnicity, and Intergroup Relations*. New York: Academic Press, 307–48.

Giles, Howard, Justine Coupland, and Nikolas Coupland (eds.) (1991) *Contexts of Accommodation: Developments in Applied Sociolinguistics*. Cambridge: Cambridge University Press.

Giles, Howard, and Nikolas Coupland (1991) *Language: Contexts and Consequences*. Pacific Grove, CA: Brooks/Cole.

Gokdayi, Hurriyet (2003) Review of Lewis, Geoffrey (1999) *The Turkish Language Reform: A Catastrophic Success*. Linguist List, July 30.

Gollan, Tamar, and Judith F. Kroll (2001) Bilingual lexical access. In B. Rapp (ed.), *The Handbook of Cognitive Neuropsychology: What Deficits Reveal about the Human Mind*. Philadelphia, PA: Psychology Press, 321–45.

Goodwin, Marjorie Harness (1990) *He-said-she-said: Talk as Social Organization among Black Children*. Bloomington: Indiana University Press.

Goody, Esther (ed.) (1978) *Questions and Politeness*. Cambridge: Cambridge University Press.

Grandguillaume, Gilbert (1983) *Arabisation et politique linguistique au Maghreb*. Paris: Maisonneuve and Larose.

Granovetter, Mark (1973) The strength of weak ties. *American Journal of Sociology* 78:1360–80.

Green, David W. (1986) Control, activation, and resource: A framework and a model for the control of speech in bilinguals. *Brain and Language* 27: 210–23.

—— (1998) Mental control of the bilingual lexico-semantic system. *Bilingualism: Language and Cognition* 1:67–81.

—— (2005) The neurocognition of recovery patterns in bilingual aphasics. In Judith Kroll and Annette De Groot (eds.), *Handbook of Bilingualism: Psycholinguistic Perspectives*. New York: Oxford University Press, 516–30.

Greenberg, Joseph H. (1960) Linguistic evidence for the influence of the Kanuri on the Hausa. *Journal of African History* 1:205–12.

Gregg, Kevin R. (2003) SLA theory: Construction and assessment. In Catherine J. Doughty and Michael H. Long (eds.), *The Handbook of Second Language Acquisition*. Oxford: Blackwell, 831–65.

Grice, H. Paul (1975) Logic and conversation. In Peter Cole and Jerry L. Morgan (eds.), *Syntax and Semantics 3: Speech Acts*. New York: Academic Press, 41–58.

Grillo, Ralph D. (1989) *Dominant Language: Language and Hierarchy in Britain and France*. Cambridge: Cambridge University Press.

Grosjean, François (1998a) Transfer and language mode. *Bilingualism: Language and Cognition* 1:175–6.

—— (1998b) Studying bilinguals: Methodological and conceptual issues. *Bilingualism: Language and Cognition* 1:131–149.

—— (2001) The bilingual's language modes. In J. Nicol (ed.), *One Mind, Two Languages: Bilingual Language Processing*. Oxford: Blackwell, 1–25.

Gudykunst, William B. (1994) *Bridging Differences: Effective Intergroup Communication*. Thousand Oaks, CA: Sage.

Gudykunst, William B., and Young Yun Kim (1997) *Communicating with Strangers*. New York: McGraw Hill.

Gumperz, John (1982) *Discourse Strategies*. Cambridge: Cambridge University Press.

Gumperz, John, and Stephen C. Levinson (eds.) (1996) *Rethinking Linguistic Relativity*. New York: Cambridge University Press.

Gupta, Anthea Fraser, and Siew Pui Yeok (1995) Language shift in a Singapore family. *Journal of Multilingual and Multicultural Development* 14: 301–14.

Gynan, Shawn N. (1998) Migration patterns and language maintenance in Paraguay. *Journal of Sociolinguistics* 2:259–70.

Hahne, Anja, and Angela D. Friederici (2001) Processing a second language: Late learners' comprehension mechanisms as revealed by event-related brain potentials. *Bilingualism: Language and Cognition* 4:123–41.

—— (2002) Differential task effects on semantic and syntactic processes as revealed by ERPs. *Cognitive Brain Research* 13:339–56.

Hall, Edward (1959) (reprinted in 1976) *The Silent Language*. New York: Anchor Books.

Hall, Robert A., Jr. (1964) *Introductory Linguistics*. Philadelphia: Chilton.

Halmari, Helena (1997) *Government and Codeswitching: Explaining American Finnish*. Amsterdam: Benjamins.

Harley, Birgit, and Wenxia Wang (1997) The critical period hypothesis: Where are we now? In Annette De Groot and Judith Kroll (eds.), *Tutorials in Bilingualism: Psycholinguistic Perspectives*. London: Erlbaum.

Hartley, Laura C., and Dennis R. Preston (1999) The names of us English: Valley girl, cowboy, Yankee, normal, nasal and ignorant. In Tony Bex and Richard J. Watt (eds.), *Standard English: the Widening Debate*. London: Routledge, 207–38.

Haugen, Einar (1959) Planning for a standard language in modern Norway. *Anthropological Linguistics* 1:8–21.

—— (1966) *Language Conflict and Language Planning: The Case of Modern Norwegian*. Cambridge, MA: Harvard University Press.

—— (1969a) Language planning, theory and practice. In A. Graur (ed.), *Actes du Xe Congrès International des Linguistiques: Bucarest 28 Août–2 September 1967*, vol. I. Bucharest: Éditions de L'Académie de la République Socialiste de Roumanie, 701–11.

—— (1969b) *The Norwegian Language in America: a Study in Bilingual Behavior Vols. I–II. Bloomington*, 2nd ed. Bloomington: Indiana University Press.

—— (1973) Bilingualism, language contact, and immigrant languages in the United States. In Thomas A. Sebeok (ed.), *Current Trends in Linguistics*, Vol. 10. The Hague: Mouton, 505–91.

Hazenberg, Suzane, and Jan H. Hulstijn (1996) Defining a minimal receptive second-language vocabulary for non-native university students: An empirical investigation. *Applied Linguistics*, 17: 145–63.

Heath, Jeffrey (1981) A case of intensive lexical diffusion: Arnhem Land, Australia. *Language* 57:335–67.

Heller, Monica (1994) *Crosswords, Language, Education and Ethnicity in French Ontario.* Berlin: Mouton de Gruyter.

— (1995) Language choice, social institutions, and symbolic domination. *Language in Society* 24:373–405.

Hill, Jane (1980) Culture shock, positive face, and negative face: Being polite in Tlaxcala. *Current Issues in Anthropology* 2:1–14.

Hill, Jane, and Kenneth Hill (1986) *Speaking Mexicano.* Tucson: University of Arizona Press.

Hlavac, Jim (2000) Croatian in Melbourne: Lexicon, switching and morphosyntactic features in the speech of second-generation bilinguals. Ph.D. dissertation, Monash University, Melbourne.

— (2003) *Second-generation Speech: Lexicon, Code-switching and Morpho-syntax of Croatian-English Bilinguals.* Bern/New York: Peter Lang.

Hock, Hans Henrich, and Brian Joseph (1996) *Language History, Language Change, and Language Relationship.* Berlin: Mouton de Gruyter.

Hofstede, Geert (1991) *Cultures and Organizations: Software of the Mind.* London: McGraw Hill.

Hogg, Michael, and Dominic Abrams (eds.) (1993) *Group Motivation: Social Psychological Perspectives.* London: Harvester Wheatsheaf.

Hogg, Michael, and Ninetta Rigoli (1996) Effects of ethnolinguistic vitality, ethnic identification, and linguistic contacts on minority language use. *Journal of Language and Social Psychology* 15:76–89.

Holm, John (2000) *An Introduction To Pidgins and Creoles.* Cambridge: Cambridge University Press.

Hornberger, Nancy (1998) Policy, possibility and paradox: Indigenous multilingualism and education in Peru and Bolivia. In Jasone Cenoz and Fred Genesee (eds.) *Beyond Bilingualism: Multilingualism and Multilingual Education.* Clevedon, UK: Multilingual Matters, 206–42.

— (2002a) Multilingual language policies and the continua of biliteracy: An ecological approach. *Language Policy* 1:27–51.

— (2000b) Bilingual education policy and practice in the Andes: Ideological paradox and intercultural possibility. *Anthropology and Education Quarterly* 31:173–201.

House, Juliane (1996) Developing pragmatic fluency in English as a foreign language: Routines and metapragmatic awareness. *Studies in Second Language Acquisition* 18:225–52.

— (2003) English as a lingua franca: A threat to multilingualism? *Journal of Sociolinguistics* 7:556–78.

Hudson, Alan (1991) Toward a systematic study of diglossia. *Southwest Journal of Linguistics* 10:1–22.

— (2002) Outline of a theory of diglossia. *International Journal of the Sociology of Language* 157:1–48.

Irvine, Judith T. (1974) Strategies of status manipulation in the Wolof greeting. In R. Bauman and J. Sherzer (eds.), *Explorations in the Ethnography of Speaking.* Cambridge: Cambridge University Press, 167–91.

Iwasaki, Shoichi, and Preeya Ingkaphirom Horie (2000) Creating speech register in Thai conversation. *Language in Society* 29:519–54.

Izura, Cristina, and Andy W. Ellis (2002) Age of acquisition effects in word recognition and production in first and second languages. *Psicologia* 23:245–81.

Jacobson, Rodolfo (1992) In search of status: Bahasa Malaysia for national unification. In Ulrich Ammon and Marlis Hellinger (eds.), *Status Change of Languages*. Berlin: Mouton de Gruyter, 200–26.

Jahr, Ernst Håkon (1996) On the pidgin status of Russenorsk. In E. H. Jahr and I. Broch (eds.), *Language Contact in the Arctic: Northern Pidgins and Contact Languages*. Berlin: Mouton de Gruyter, 107–22.

Jake, Janice L. (1994) Intrasentential codeswitching and pronouns: On the categorical status of functional elements. *Linguistics* 32:271–98.

Jake, Janice L., and Carol Myers-Scotton (1997) Codeswitching and compromise strategies: Implications for lexical structure. *International Journal of Bilingualism* 1:25–39.

Jake, Janice L., Carol Myers-Scotton, and Steven Gross (2002) Making a minimalist approach to codeswitching work: Adding the matrix language. *Bilingualism: Language and Cognition* 5:69–91.

James, William (1890) *The Principles of Psychology*. New York: H. Holt.

Jared, Debra, and Judith F. Kroll (2001) Do bilinguals activate phonological representations in one or both of their languages when naming words? *Journal of Memory and Language* 44:2–31.

Jenkins, Rebecca Sue (2000) Language contact phenomena in New Ireland. Ph.D. dissertation, University of South Carolina, Columbia.

Johnson, Jacqueline S., and Elissa L. Newport (1989) Critical period effects in second language learning: The influence of maturational state on the acquisition of English as a second language. *Cognitive Psychology* 21:60–99.

Johnson, Paige, A. Elizabeth Lindsey, and Walter Zakahi (2001) Anglo American, Hispanic American, Chilean, Mexican, and Spanish perceptions of competent communication in initial interactions. *Communication Research Reports* 18:36–43.

Joshi, Aravind (1985) Processing of sentences with intrasentential code switching. In D. J. Dowty, L. Karttunen and A. Zwicky (eds.), *Natural Language Parsing*. Cambridge: Cambridge University Press, 190–205.

Kanno, Kazue (1997) The acquisition of null and overt pronominals in Japanese by English speakers. *Second Language Research* 13:265–87.

Karttunen, Frances (1977) Finnish in America: A case study in monogenerational language change. In Ben Blount and Mary Sanches (eds.), *Sociocultural Dimensions of Language Change*. New York: Academic Press, 173–84.

Kashoki, Mubanga (1978) Between-language communication in Zambia. In Sirarpi Ohannessian and Mubanga Kashoki (eds.), *Language in Zambia*. London: International African Institute.

Kasuya, Hiroko (1998) Determinants of language choice in bilingual children: The role of input. *International Journal of Bilingualism* 2:327–46.

Katriel, Tamar (1986) *Talking Straight: Dugri Speech in Israeli Sabra Culture*. Cambridge: Cambridge University Press.

Kaye, Alan S. (2001) Diglossia: The state of the art. *International Journal of Sociology* 152:117–30.

Keenan, Elinor (1974) Norm-maker, norm-breaker: Uses of speech by men and women in a Malagasy community. In R. Bauman and J. Scherzer (eds.), *Explorations in the Ethnography of Speaking*. Cambridge: Cambridge University Press, 125–43.

Keesing, Roger M. (1974) Transformational linguistics and structural anthropology. *Cultural Hermeneutics* 2:243–66.

—— (1988) *Melanesian Pidgin and the Oceanic Substrate*. Stanford, CA: Stanford University Press.

Kim, Karl H. S., Norman R. Relkin, Kyoung-Min Lee, and Joy Hirsch (1997) Distinct cortical areas associated with native and second languages. *Nature* 388:171–4.

Kim, Young Yun (2001) *Becoming Intercultural*. Thousand Oaks, CA: Sage.

King, Ruth (2000) *The Lexical Basis of Grammatical Borrowing: A Prince Edward Island French Case Study*. Amsterdam: Benjamins.

Klavans, Judith L. (1983) The syntax of code-switching: Spanish and English. In L. D. King and C. A. Matey (eds.), *Selected Papers from the 13th Linguistic Symposium on Romance Languages*. Chapel Hill, NC: 213–31.

Klein, Wolfgang, and Clive Perdue (1997) The basic variety: Couldn't languages be much simpler? *Second Language Research* 13:301–47.

Köpke, Barbara (1999) *L'Attrition de la première langue chez le bilingue tardif: Implications pour l'étude psycholinguistique du bilinguisme*. Ph.D. dissertation, Université de Toulouse–Le Mirail.

Kovács, Magdolna (2001) *Code-switching and language shift in Australian Finnish in comparison with Australian Hungarian*. Åbo, Finland: Åbo Akademi University Press.

Krashen, Stephen D. (1985) *The Input Hypothesis: Issues and Implications*. Harlow: Longman.

Kroll, Judith. F., and Annette De Groot (1997) Lexical and conceptual memory in the bilingual: Mapping form to meaning in two languages. In Annette De Groot and Judith Kroll (eds.), *Tutorials in Bilingualism: Psycholinguistic Perspectives*. Mahwah, NJ: Erlbaum, 169–200.

Kroll, Judith. F., and Annette De Groot (eds.) (2005) *Handbook of Bilingualism: Psycholinguistic Approaches*. New York: Oxford University Press.

Kroll, Judith. F., and A. F. J. Dijkstra (2002) The bilingual lexicon. In R. Kaplan (ed.), *Handbook of Applied Linguistics*. Oxford: Oxford University Press, 301–21.

Kroll, Judith. F., and Erika Stewart (1994) Category interference in translation and picture naming: Evidence for asymmetric connections between bilingual memory representations. *Journal of Memory and Language* 33:149–74.

Kroll, Judith. F., and Gretchen Sunderman (2003) Cognitive processes in second language acquisition: The development of lexical and conceptual representations. In Catherine Doughty and Michael Long (eds.), *Handbook of Second Language Acquisition*. Oxford: Blackwell.

Kroll, Judith. F., and Natasha Tokowicz (2005) Models of bilingual representation and processing: looking back and to the future. In Judith F. Kroll and Annette De Groot (eds.), *Handbook of Bilingualism: Psycholinguistic Approaches*. New York: Oxford University Press, 531–53.

Kroskrity, Paul V. (2000) Language ideologies in the expression and representation of Arizona Tewa identity. In Paul Kroskrity (ed.), *Regimes of Language, Ideologies, Polities, and Identities*. Santa Fe, NM: School of American Research, 329–59.

Ku, A., E. A. Lachmann, and W. Nagler (1996) Selective language aphasia from herpes simplex encephalitis. *Pediatric Neurology* 15:169–71.

Kulick, Don (1992) *Language Shift and Cultural Reproduction*. Cambridge: Cambridge University Press.

Kwan-Terry, Anna (2000) Language shift, mother tongue, and identity in Singapore. *International Journal of the Sociology of Language* 143:85–106.

Labov, William (1972) *Sociolinguistic Patterns*. Philadelphia: University of Pennsylvania Press.

Laitin, David D. (1993) Migration and language shift in India. *International Journal of the Sociology of Language* 103:57–72.

Landau, Jacob M., and Barbara Kellner-Heinkele (2001) *Politics of Language in the ex-Soviet Muslim States*. Ann Arbor: University of Michigan Press.

Landry, Rodrigue and Réal Allard (eds.) (1994) special issue, Ethnolinguistic vitality. *International Journal of the Sociology of Language* 108.

Langacker, Ronald W. (1987) *Foundations of Cognitive Grammar: Theoretical Prerequisites*. Stanford, CA: Stanford University Press.

Langman, Juliet (2002) Mother-tongue education versus bilingual education: Shifting ideologies and policies in the Republic of Slovakia. *International Journal of the Sociology of Language* 154:47–64.

Lanstyák, István, and Gizella Szabómihály (1995) Contact varieties of Hungarian in Slovakia. *International Journal of the Sociology of Language* 112:111–30.

Lanza, Elizabeth (1997) *Language Mixing in Infant Bilingualism*. Oxford: Clarendon Press.

Laponce, Jean A. (1987) *Languages and Their Territories*. Toronto: University of Toronto Press.

—— (1993) Do languages behave like animals? *International Journal of the Sociology of Language* 103:19–30.

Lardière, Donna (2000) Mapping features to forms in second language acquisition. In J. Archibald (ed.), *Second Language Acquisition and Linguistic Theory*. Oxford: Blackwell, 102–29.

LeFebvre, Claire (1998) *Creole Genesis and the Acquisition of Grammar*. Cambridge: Cambridge University Press.

Lenneberg, Eric H. (1967) *Biological Foundations of Language*. New York: John Wiley.

Levelt, Willem J. M. (1989) *Speaking: From Intention to Articulation*. Cambridge, MA: MIT Press.

Levelt, Willem J. M., Ardi Roelofs, and Antje S. Meyer (1999) A theory of lexical access in speech production. *Behavioral and Brain Sciences* 22:1–75.

Levinson, Stephen C. (2000) *Presumptive Meanings: The Theory of Generalized Conversational Implicatures*. Cambridge, MA: MIT Press.

Lewis, Geoffrey (2002) *The Turkish Language Reform: A Catastrophic Success*. Oxford: Oxford University Press. (Hardback edition 1999.)

Li, Wei (1994) *Three Generations, Two Languages, One Family*. Clevedon, UK: Multilingual Matters.

—— (2002) "What do you want me to say?" On the conversational analysis approach to bilingual interaction. *Language in Society* 31:159–80.

Lim, Tae-Seop (2002) Language and verbal communication across cultures. In William B. Gudykunst and Bella Mody (eds.) *Handbook of International and Intercultural Communication*. 2nd ed. Thousand Oaks, CA: Sage.

Lindsay, Jennifer, and Tan Ying Ying (eds.) (2003) *Babel or Behemoth: Language Trends in Asia*. Singapore: National University of Singapore.

Lo Bianco, Joe (1987) *National Policy on Languages*. Canberra: Australian Government Publishing Service.

—— (2003a) Language planning as applied linguistics. In Alan Davies and Catherine Elder (eds.), *The Handbook of Applied Linguistics*. Malden, MA: Blackwell, 738–63.

—— (2003b) The big picture: Language trends in Asia. In J. Lindsay and Tan Ying Ting (eds.) *Babel or Behemoth: Language Trends in Asia*. Singapore: National University of Singapore, 21–43.

—— (2003c) Policy activity for heritage languages: Connections with representation and citizenship. (Manuscript.)

Lo Bianco, Joe, and W. Rhydwen (2001) Is the extinction of Australia's indigenous languages inevitable? In Joshua A. Fishman (ed.), *Can Threatened Languages be Saved? Reversing Language Shift Revisited*. Clevedon, UK: Multilingual Matters, 391–423.

Long, Michael (1996) The role of the linguistic environment in second language acquisition. In W. C. Ritchie, and T. K. Bhatia (eds.), *Handbook of Second Language Acquisition*. San Diego, CA: Academic Press, 413–68.

Luke, Kang-Kwong (1998) Why two languages might be better than one: Motivations of language mixing in Hong Kong. In M. C. Pennington (ed.), *Language in Hong Kong at Century's End*. Hong Kong: Hong Kong University Press, 145–59.

Lumsden, John (1999) The role of relexification in creole genesis. *Journal of Pidgin and Creole Languages* 14:225–58.

Luria, Aleksandr Romanovich (1976) *Cognitive Development: Its Cultural and Social Foundations*. Cambridge, MA: Harvard University Press.

Macnamara, John (1966) *Bilingualism and Primary Education*. Edinburgh: Edinburgh University Press.

MacSwan, Jeff (1999) *A Minimalist Approach to Intrasentential Code Switching: Spanish-Nahuatl Bilingualism in Central Mexico*. New York: Garland.

—— (2000) The architecture of the bilingual language faculty: Evidence from intrasentential code switching. *Bilingualism: Language and Cognition* 3:37–54.

Mansour, Gerda (1993) *Multilingualism and Nation Building*. Clevedon, UK: Multilingual Matters.

Marian, Viorica, and Ulric Neisser (2000) Language-dependent recall of autobiographical memories. *Journal of Experimental Psychology* 129:361–8.

Mar-Molinero, Clare (2000) *The Politics of Language in the Spanish-Speaking World*. London: Routledge.

Martin, Elizabeth (2002a) Mixing English in French advertising. *World Englishes* 21:375–402.

—— (2002b) Cultural images and different varieties of English in French television commercials. *English Today* 18:8–20.

Matras, Yaron and Peter Bakker (eds.) (2003) *The Mixed Language Debate*. Berlin: Mouton de Gruyter.

Maurais, Jacques, and Michael A. Morris (eds.) (2003) *Languages in a Globalising World*. Cambridge: Cambridge University Press.

McConvell, Patrick (2001) Mix-Im-Up speech and emergent mixed languages in indigenous Australia. In Kate Henning, Nicole Netherton and Leighton Peterson (eds.), *Salsa 2001, Texas Linguistic Forum* 44:328–49.

McConvell, Patrick and Nicholas Thieberger (2003) Language data assessment at the national level: Learning from the State of the Environment process in Australia.

In Joe Blythe and R. McKenna Brown (eds.), *Maintaining the Links: Language, Identity and the Land*. Bath, UK: Foundation of Endangered Languages, 51–7.

McDaniel, Edwin R. and Larry A. Samovar (1997 8th ed.) Cultural influences on communication in multinational organizations: The Maquiladora. In L. A. Samovar and R. E. Porter (eds.), *Intercultural Communication: A Reader*. Belmont, CA: Wadsworth, 289–96.

McDonald, Janet L. (2000) Grammaticality judgments in a second language: Influences of age of acquisition and native language. *Applied Psycholinguistics* 21:395–423.

McWhorter, John H. (ed.) (2000) *Language Change and Language Contact in Pidgins and Creoles*. Amsterdam: John Benjamins.

Meisel, Jürgen M. (1989) Early differentiation of languages in bilingual children. In Kenneth Hyltenstam and Loraine K. Obler (eds.), *Bilingualism across the Lifespan: Aspects of Acquisition, Maturity and Loss*. Cambridge: Cambridge University Press, 13–40.

—— (1994) Code-switching in young bilingual children: The acquisition of grammatical constraints. *Studies in Second Language Acquisition* 16:413–41.

Melander, Bjorn (2001) Swedish, English and the European Union. In Sally Boyd and Leena Huss (eds.), *Managing Multilingualism in a European Nation-State: Challenges for Sweden*. Clevedon, UK: Multilingual Matters, 13–31.

Meuter, Renata F., and Alan Allport (1999) Bilingual language switching in naming: Asymmetrical costs of language selection. *Journal of Memory and Language* 40:25–40.

Miao, Ruiqin (2001) Motivational factors for urban immigrant multilingualism in Guangzhou, China. Paper presented at Conference on Language, Migration, and the City. Universität Bayreuth.

Milroy, James, and Leslie Milroy (1985) Linguistic change, social network and speaker innovation. *Journal of Linguistics* 21:339–84.

Milroy, Lesley (1980) *Language and Social Networks*. Baltimore: University Park Press.

Mitchell, Rosamund, and Florence Myles (1998) *Second Language Learning Theories*. London: Arnold.

Moreno, Eva M., Kara D. Federmeier, and Marta Kutas (2002) Switching languages, switching *palabras* (words): An electrophysiological study of code switching. *Brain and Language* 80:188–207.

Morrison, Keith (2000) Ideology, linguistic capital and the medium of instruction in Hong Kong. *Journal of Multilingual and Multicultural Development* 21:471–86.

Mougeon, Raymond, and Édouard Beniak (1989) Language contraction and linguistic change: Welland French. In Nancy Dorian (ed.), *Investigating Obsolescence: Studies in Language Contraction and Death*. Cambridge: Cambridge University Press, 287–312.

—— (1991) *Linguistic consequences of language contact and restriction: The case of French in Ontario, Canada*. Oxford: Clarendon.

Mufwene, Salikoko (2001) *The Ecology of Language Evolution*. Cambridge: Cambridge University Press.

Muysken, Pieter (2000) *Bilingual Speech, A Typology of Code-Mixing*. Cambridge: Cambridge University Press.

Muysken, Pieter, and Norval Smith (eds.) (1986) *Substrata Versus Universals in Creole Genesis*. Amsterdam: John Benjamins.

Myers-Scotton, Carol (1976) Strategies of neutrality: Language choice in uncertain situations. *Language* 52:919–41.

—— (1983) The negotiation of identities in conversation: A theory of markedness and code choice. *International Journal of the Sociology of Language* 44:115–36.

—— (1986) Diglossia and codeswitching. In Joshua A. Fishman et al. (eds.), *The Fergusonian Impact*, vol. 2. Berlin: Mouton de Gruyter, 403–15.

—— (1988) Codeswitching and types of multilingual communities. In Peter Lowenberg (ed.), *Georgetown Round Table 87*. Washington, DC: Georgetown University Press, 61–82.

—— (1990) Elite closure as boundary maintenance: The evidence from Africa. In Brian Weinstein (ed.), *Language Policy and Political Development*. Norwood, NJ: Ablex, 25–41.

—— (1993a) *Social Motivation for Codeswitching: Evidence from Africa*. Oxford: Clarendon Press.

—— (1993b) *Duelling Languages: Grammatical Structure in Codeswitching*. Oxford: Clarendon Press. (Paperback ed. 1997 with new Afterword.)

—— (1993c) Elite closure as a powerful language strategy: The African case. *International Journal of the Sociology of Language* 103:149–63.

—— (2001) Implications of abstract grammatical structure: Two targets in creole formation. *Journal of Pidgin and Creole Languages* 16:217–73.

—— (2002) *Contact Linguistics: Bilingual Encounters and Grammatical Outcomes*. Oxford: Oxford University Press.

—— (2003) What lies beneath: Split (mixed) languages as contact phenomena. In Yaron Matras and Peter Bakker (eds.), *The Mixed Language Debate*. Berlin: Mouton de Gruyter, 73–106.

—— (2005) Supporting a differential access hypothesis: Codeswitching and other contact phenomena. In Judith Kroll and Annette De Groot (eds.), *Handbook of Bilingualism: Psycholinguistic Approaches*. New York: Oxford University Press.

Myers-Scotton, Carol, and Agnes Bolonyai (2001) Calculating speakers: Codeswitching in a rational choice model. *Language in Society* 30:1–28.

Myers-Scotton, Carol, and Janice L. Jake (1995) Matching lemmas in a bilingual language competence and production model: Evidence from intrasentential code switching. *Linguistics* 33:981–1024.

—— (1996) Arabic and constraints on codeswitching. In M. Eid and D. Parkinson (eds.), *Perspectives on Arabic Linguistics IX*. Amsterdam: John Benjamins, 9–43.

—— (2000) Four types of morpheme: Evidence from aphasia, codeswitching and second language acquisition. *Linguistics* 38:1053–100.

—— (2001) Explaining aspects of codeswitching and their implications. In Janet Nicol (ed.), *One Mind, Two Languages: Bilingual Language Processing*. Oxford: Blackwell, 84–116.

Myers-Scotton, Carol, and John Okeju (1973) Neighbors and lexical borrowings. *Language* 49:871–89.

Myhill, John (1999) Identity, territoriality and minority language survival. *Journal of Multilingual and Multicultural Development* 20:34–50.

Nair-Venugopal, Shanta (2001) The sociolinguistics of choice in Malaysian business settings. *International Journal of the Sociology of Language* 152:21–52.

Neville, Helen, and Daphne Bavelier (1996) The extension of visual areas in the deaf: Visual and auditive cortexes are not as distinct as previously believed. *La Recherche* 289:90–3.

Neville, Helen J., Sharon A. Coffey, Donald S. Lawson, Andrew Fischer, Karen Emmorey, and Ursula Bellugi (1997) Neural systems mediating American sign language: Effects of sensory experience and age of acquisition. *Brain and Language* 57:285–308.

Neville, Helen J., Debra L. Mills, and Donald S. Lawson (1992) Fractionating language: Different neural subsystems with different sensitive periods. *Cerebral Cortex* 2:244–58.

Nicol, Janet (ed.) (2001) *One Mind, Two Languages: Bilingual Language Processing*. Malden, MA, and Oxford: Blackwell.

Norris, John M. and Lourdes Ortega (2000) Effectiveness of L2 instruction: A research synthesis and quantitative meta-analysis. *Language Learning* 50:417–528.

Nortier, Jacomine (1990) *Dutch-Moroccan Arabic Code Switching*. Dordrecht, The Netherlands: Foris.

Nwoye, Onuigbo G. (1992) Linguistic politeness and socio-cultural variations of the notion of face. *Journal of Pragmatics* 18:309–28.

Oakes, Leigh (2001) *Language and National Identity: Comparing France and Sweden*. Amsterdam: John Benjamins.

Odlin, Terence (2003) Cross-linguistic influence. In Catherine J. Doughty and Michael H. Long (eds.), *The Handbook of Second Language Acquisition*. Oxford: Blackwell, 436–86.

O'Grady, William (2003) The radical middle: Nativism without universal grammar. In Catherine J. Doughty and Michael H. Long (eds.), *The Handbook of Second Language Acquisition*. Oxford: Blackwell, 43–62.

Omonyi, Tope (1999) Afro-Asian rural border areas in Joshua A. Fishman (ed.), *Handbook of Language and Ethnic Identity*, 369–81.

Owens, Jonathan (2001) Arabic sociolinguistics. *Arabica* 48:421–69.

Oyetade, Solomon Oluwole (1995) A sociolinguistic analysis of address forms in Yoruba. *Language in Society* 24:515–35.

Ozolina, Uldis (1993) *The Politics of Language in Australia*. Cambridge: Cambridge University Press.

Paivio, Allan, and A. Desrochers (1981) Mnemonic techniques in second-language proficiency. *Journal of Educational Psychology* 73:780–95.

Pan, Yuling (2000) Code-switching and social change in Guangzhou and Hong Kong. *International Journal of the Sociology of Language* 146:21–41.

Paradis, Johanne (2001) Do bilingual two-year-olds have separate phonological systems? *International Journal of Bilingualism* 5:19–38.

Paradis, Johanne, Elena Nicoladis, and Fred Genesee (2000) Early emergence of structural constraints on code-mixing: Evidence from French-English bilingual children. *Bilingualism: Language and Cognition* 3:245–62.

Paradis, Michel (1994) Neurolinguistic aspects of implicit and explicit memory: Implications for bilingualism and SLA. In Ellis, N. (ed.), *Implicit and Explicit Learning of Languages*. London: Academic Press, 173–86.

—— (1997) The cognitive neuropsychology of bilingualism. In Annette De Groot and Judith Kroll (eds.), *Tutorials in Bilingualism*. Mahwah, NJ: Erlbaum, 331–54.

—— (2001) Bilingual and polyglot aphasia. In Brenda Rapp (ed.), *The Handbook of Cognitive Neuropsychology: What Deficits Reveal about the Human Mind*. Philadelphia: Psychology Press.

Park, Hyeon-Sook (2000) *Korean-Swedish Code-switching*. Uppsala: Institutionen för Nordiska Språk.

Parkin, Alan J. (2001) The structure and mechanisms of memory. In Brenda Rapp (ed.), *The Handbook of Cognitive Neuropsychology: What Deficits Reveal about the Human Mind*. Philadelphia: Psychology Press, 399–422.

Paulston, Christina Bratt (1998) Linguistic minorities in Central and Eastern Europe: An introduction. In Christina Bratt Paulston and Donald Peckham (eds.), *Linguistic Minorities in Central and Eastern Europe*. Clevedon, UK: Multilingual Matters, 1–17.

Paulston, Christina Bratt, and Donald Peckham (eds.) (1998) *Linguistic Minorities in Central and Eastern Europe*. Clevedon, UK: Multilingual Matters.

Pavlenko, Aneta (2000) New approaches to concepts in bilingual memory. *Bilingualism: Language and Cognition* 3:1–4.

Pavlenko, Aneta, Robert Schrauf, and Jean-Marc Dewaele (eds.) (2003) special issue, Bilingual episodic memory. *International Journal of Bilingualism* 7:3.

Peal, Elizabeth and Wallace E. Lambert (1962) The relation of bilingualism to intelligence. *Psychological Monographs* 76:1–23.

Pearson, Barbara Z., M. C. Fernandez, and D. K. Oller (1993) Lexical development in bilingual infants and toddlers: Comparison to monolingual norms. *Language Learning* 43:93–120.

Pearson, Barbara Z., and Sylvia C. Fernandez (1994). Patterns of interaction in the lexical growth in two languages of bilingual infants and toddlers. *Language Learning* 44:617–53.

Perani, Daniela, Eraldo Paulesu, Nuría Sebastián Gallés, Emmanual Dupoux, Stanislas Dehaene, Valentino Bettinardi, Stefano F. Cappa, Ferruccio Fazio, and Jacques Mehler (1998) The bilingual brain: Proficiency and age of acquisition of the second language. *Brain* 121:1841–52.

Perani, Daniela, S. Dehaene, F. Grassi, L. Cohen, S. F. Cappa, E. Dupoux, F. Fazio, and J. Mehler (1996) Brain processing of native and foreign languages. *NeuroReport* 7:2439–44.

Perdue, Clive (1993) *Adult Language Acquisition: Cross-linguistic Perspectives*, vols. 1 and 2. Cambridge: Cambridge University Press.

Phillipson, Robert (2003) *English-only in Europe: Challenging Language Policy*. London: Routledge.

Pica, Theresa (1994) Research on negotiation: What does it reveal about second-language learning conditions, processes and outcomes? *Language Learning* 44:493–527.

Pienemann, Manfred (2003) Language processing capacity. In Catherine J. Doughty and Michael H. Long (eds.), *The Handbook of Second Language Acquisition*. Oxford: Blackwell, 679–714.

Piller, Ingrid (2001) Identity constructions in multilingual advertising. *Language in Society* 2:61–80.

Pitres, Albert (1895) Étude sur l'aphasie chez les polyglotes. *Revue de Médicine* 15:873–99.

Poplack, Shana (1980) Sometimes I'll start a sentence in Spanish Y TERMINO EN ESPAÑOL: Toward a typology of code-switching. *Linguistics* 18:581–618.

—— (1988) Contrasting patterns of code-switching in two communities. In M. Heller (ed.), *Codeswitching, Anthropological and Sociolinguistic Approaches*. Berlin: Mouton de Gruyter, 217–44.

PuruShotam, Nirmala Srirekam (1998) *Negotiating Language, Constructing Race, Disciplining Difference in Singapore*. Berlin: Mouton de Gruyter.

Rakusan, Jaromira (1985) The function of English loanwords in Canadian Czech. *Revue Canadienne des Slavistes/Canadian Slavonic Papers* 27:178–87.

Rampton, Ben (1995) *Crossing, Language and Ethnicity among Adolescents*. London: Longman.

Raschka, Christine, Wei Li, and Sherman Lee (2002) Bilingual development and social networks of British-born Chinese children. *International Journal of the Sociology of Language* 153:9–25.

Reischauer, Edwin O. (1977) *The Japanese*. Cambridge, MA: Belknap Press.

Reisman, Karl (1974) Contrapuntal conversations in an Antiguan village. In Richard Bauman and Joel Sherzer (eds.), *Explorations in the Ethnography of Speaking*. Cambridge, Cambridge University Press, 110–24.

Ricento, Thomas (ed.) (2001) *Ideology, Politics and Language Policies: Focus on English*. Amsterdam: John Benjamins.

Romaine, Suzanne (ed.) (1991) *Language in Australia*. New York: Cambridge University Press.

Rosaldo, Michelle Z. (1982) The things we do with words: Ilongot speech acts and speech act theory in philosophy. *Language in Society* 11:203–38.

Rumelhart, David E., and James L. McClelland (1986) On learning the past tense of English verbs. In James L. McClelland and David E Rumelhart (eds.), *Parallel Distributed Processing: Explorations in the Microstructure of Cognition. Vol. 2: Psychological and Biological Models*. Cambridge, MA: MIT Press, 216–71.

Safran, William (1999) Politics and language in contemporary France: Facing supranational and infranational challenges. *International Journal of the Sociology of Language* 137:39–66.

Samovar, Larry A., and Richard E. Porter (1991) (eds.) *Intercultural Communication: A Reader*. Belmont, CA: Wadsworth.

Sasanuma, Sumiko and H. Park (1995) Patterns of language deficits in two Korean-Japanese bilingual aphasic patients – a clinical report. In M. Paradis (ed.), *Aspects of Bilingual Aphasia*. Oxford: Oxford University Press.

Schachter, Jacquelyn (1989) Testing a proposed universal. In Susan M. Gass and Jacquelyn Schachter (eds.), *Linguistic Perspectives on Second Language Acquisition*. New York: Cambridge University Press, 73–88.

Schiffman, Harold F. (1993) The balance of power in multiglossic languages: implications for language shift. *International Journal of the Sociology of Language* 103:115–49.

Schmid, Carol L. (2001) *The Politics of Language*. New York: Oxford University Press.

Schmid, Monika S. (2002) *First Language Attrition, Use and Maintenance, The Case of German Jews in Anglophone Countries*. Amsterdam and Philadelphia: John Benjamins.

Schmid, Monika S., Barbara Köpke, Merel Keijzer, and Lina Weilemar (2004) (eds.) *First Language Attrition: Interdisciplinary Perspectives on Methodological Issues*. Amsterdam and Philadelphia: John Benjamins.

Schmitt, Elena (2000) Overt and covert codeswitching in immigrant children from Russia. *International Journal of Bilingualism* 4:9–28.

Schrauf, Robert W., and David C. Rubin (1998) Bilingual autobiographical memory in older adult immigrants: A test of cognitive explanations of the reminiscence bump and the linguistic encoding of memories. *Journal of Memory and Language* 39:437–57.

Schwartz, Bonnie D., and Rex A. Sprouse (2000) When syntactic theories evolve: Consequences for second language acquisition research. In John Archibald (ed.), *Second Language Acquisition and Linguistic Theory*. Malden, MA: Blackwell, 156–86.

Scollon, Ronald, and Suzanne Wong-Scollon (1990) Athabaskan-English interethnic communication. In Donal Carbaugh (ed.), *Cultural Communication and Intercultural Contact*. Hillsdale, NJ: Lawrence Erlbaum, 259–86.

Sebastián-Gallés, Nuría, and Laura Bosch (2001) Building phonotactic knowledge in bilinguals: Role of early exposure. *Journal of Experimental Psychology* 28:974–89.

Seliger, Herbert W., and Robert M. Vago (eds.) (1991) *First Language Attrition*. Cambridge: Cambridge University Press.

Selinker, Larry (1972) Interlanguage. *International Review of Applied Linguistics* 10:209–31.

Serratrice, Ludova (2001) The emergence of verbal morphology and the lead-lag pattern issue in bilingual acquisition. In Jasone Cenoz and Fred Genesee (eds.), *Trends in Bilingualism Acquisition*. Amsterdam: John Benjamins.

Sharwood Smith, Michael (1994) *Second Language Learning: Theoretical Foundations*. Harlow: Longman.

—— (1999) British shibboleths. In Eddie Ronowicz and Colin Yallop (eds.), *English: One Language, Different Cultures*. London: Cassell, 46–82.

Shin, Sarah J. (2002) Differentiating language contact phenomena: Evidence from Korean-English bilingual children. *Applied Psycholinguistics* 23:337–60.

Siachitema, Alice K. (1991) The social significance of language use and choice in a Zambia urban setting. In Jenny Cheshire (ed.), *English Around the World*. Cambridge: Cambridge University Press, 474–90.

Siegel, Jeffrey (1999) Transfer constraints and substrate influence in Melanesian Pidgin. *Journal of Pidgin and Creole Languages* 14:1–44.

—— (2000) Substrate influence in Hawai'i creole English. *Language in Society* 29:197–236.

Simango, Silvester Ron (2000) "My madam is fine": The adaptation of English loans in Chicheŵa. *Journal of Multilingual and Multicultural Development* 21:487–507.

Simo Bobda, Augustin (2004) Life in a tower of Babel without a language policy. Paper presented at 30th International LAUD Symposium, "Empowerment through Language", University of Koblenz-Landau, Campus Landau, Germany, April 19–22.

Sinka, Indra, and Christina Schelletter (1998) Morphosyntactic development in bilingual children. *International Journal of Bilingualism* 2:301–26.

Skutnabb-Kangas, Tove (2000) *Linguistic Genocide in Education or Worldwide Diversity and Human Rights?* Mahwah, NJ: Erlbaum.

Skutnabb-Kangas, Tove, and Robert Phillipson (2001) The world came to Sweden – but did language rights? In Sally Boyd and Leena Huss (eds.), *Managing Multilingualism in a European Nation-state*. Clevedon, UK: Multilingual Matters, 70–86.

Slobin, Dan I. (1985) The child as a linguistic icon-maker. In John Haiman (ed.), *Iconicity in Syntax*. Amsterdam: Benjamins, 221–48.

—— (1997) Operating principles for the construction of language. In Dan I. Slobin (ed.), *The Crosslinguistic Study of Language Acquisition. Vol. 5: Theoretical Issues*. Mahwah, NJ: Lawrence Erlbaum Associates, 1251–6.

Smead, Robert N. (1998) English loanwords in Chicano Spanish: Characterization and rationale. *The Bilingual Review/La Revista Bilingue* 23:113–23.

Smith, Daniel (2003) Personal communication.

Sperber, Dan, and Deirdre Wilson (1986/1995) *Relevance: Communication and Cognition*, 2nd ed. Oxford: Blackwell.

Spolsky, Bernard (2004a) *Language Policy*. Cambridge: Cambridge University Press.

—— (2004b) Language policy failures – why won't they listen? Paper presented at 30th International LAUD Symposium, "Empowerment through Language", University of Koblenz-Landau, Campus Landau, Germany, April 19–22.

Squire, Larry R. (1987) *Memory and Brain*. New York: Oxford University Press.

Stroud, Christopher (1999) Portuguese as ideology and politics in Mozambique: Semiotic (re)constructions of a postcolony. In Jan Blommert (ed.), *Language Ideological Debates*. Berlin: Walter de Gruyter, 342–80.

Swain, Merrill, and S. Lapkin (2000) Task-based second language learning: the uses of the first language. *Language Teaching Research* 4:251–74.

Talmy, Leonard (2000) *Toward a Cognitive Semantics. Vol. I: Concept Structuring Systems*. Cambridge, MA: MIT Press.

Thomason, Sarah G. (2001) *Language Contact: An Introduction*. Edinburgh: Edinburgh University Press and Washington, DC: Georgetown University Press.

Thomason, Sarah G., and Terrence Kaufman (1988) *Language Contact, Creolization, and Genetic Linguistics*. Berkeley: University of California Press.

Ting-Toomey, Stella (1994 7th ed.) Managing intercultural conflicts effectively. In L. Samovar and R. Porter (eds.), *Intercultural Communication: A Reader*. Belmont, CA: Wadsworth, 360–72.

Ting-Toomey, Stella and Leeva Chung (1996) Cross-cultural interpersonal communication: Theoretical trends and research directions. In William B. Gudykunst, Stella Ting-Toomey and Tsukasa Nishida (eds.), *Communication in Personal Relationship across Cultures*. Thousand Oaks, CA: Sage, 237–61.

Toribio, Almedia J., and Edward J. Rubin (1996) Code-switching in generative grammar. In A. Roca and J. B. Jensen (eds.), *Spanish in Contact: Issues in Bilingualism*. Somerville, MA: Cascadilla Press, 203–26.

Torres, Lourdes (2002) Bilingual discourse markers in Puerto Rican Spanish. *Language in Society* 31:65–83.

Treffers-Daller, Jeanine (1994) *Mixing Two Languages: French-Dutch Contact in Comparative Perspective*. Berlin: Mouton de Gruyter.

—— (1999) Borrowing and shift-induced interference: Contrasting patterns in French-Germanic contact in Brussels and Strasbourg. *Bilingualism: Language and Cognition* 2:77–9.

—— (2002) Language use and language contact in Brussels. *Journal of Multilingual and Multicultural Development* 23:50–64.

Triandis, Harry C. (1995) *Individualism and Collectivism*. Boulder, CO: Westview.

Tulviste, Tiia, Luule Mizera, Boel de Geer, and Marja-Terttu Tryggvason (2002) Regulatory comments as tools of family socialization: A comparison of Estonian, Swedish and Finnish mealtime interaction. *Language in Society* 31:655–78.

Tuominen, Anne (1999) Who decides the home language? A look at multilingual families. *International Journal of the Sociology of Language* 140:59–76.

Türker, Emel (2000) Turkish-Norwegian codeswitching: Evidence for intermediate and second generation Turkish immigrants in Norway. Ph.D. dissertation, University of Oslo.

Ullman, Michael T. (2001) The neural basis of lexicon and grammar in first and second language: The declarative/procedural model. *Bilingualism: Language and Cognition* 4:105–22.

Valdés Guadalupe (1981) Codeswitching as deliberate verbal strategy. In Richard P. Duran (ed.), *Latino Language and Communicative Behavior*. Norwood, NJ: Ablex, 95–105.

Van Hell, Janet G., and Andrea Candia Mahn (1997) Keyword mnemonics versus rote rehearsal: Learning concrete and abstract foreign words by experienced and inexperienced learners. *Language Learning* 47:507–46.

Van Heuven, Walter J. B., Ton Dijkstra, and Jonathan Grainger (1998) Orthographic neighborhood effects in bilingual word recognition. *Journal of Memory and Language* 39:458–83.

Van Patten, Bill (1996) *Input Processing and Grammar Instruction*. Norwood, NJ: Ablex.

Victor, David (1992) *International Business Communication*. New York: HarperCollins.

Virtaranta, Pertti (1971) Iiskan i Amerika. *Språk I Norden*. Solna, Sweden: Läromedelsfölagen Svenska Bokförlaget, 79–109.

Volterra, Virginia, and Traute Taeschner (1978) The acquisition and development of language by bilingual children. *Journal of Child Language* 5:311–26.

Von Gleich, Utta (1992) Changes in the status and function of Quechua. In Ulrich Ammon and Marlis Hellinger (eds.), *Status Change of Languages*. Berlin: Mouton de Gruyter, 43–64.

Von Studnitz, Roswitha E., and David W. Green (1997) Lexical decision and language switching. *International Journal of Bilingualism* 1:2–24.

—— (2002a) Interlingual homograph interference in German-English bilinguals: Its modulation and locus of control. *Bilingualism: Language and Cognition* 5:1–23.

—— (2002b) The cost of switching language in a semantic categorization task. *Bilingualism: Language and Cognition* 5:241–51.

Walters, Keith (1996) Gender, identity, and the political economy of language: Anglophone wives in Tunisia. *Language in Society* 25:515–55.

Wasserman, Stanley, and Katherine Faust (1994) *Social Network Analysis*. Cambridge: Cambridge University Press.

Watts, Richard J. (1999) The ideology of dialect in Switzerland. In Jan Blommaert (ed.), *Language Ideological Debates*. Berlin: Mouton de Gruyter, 67–103.

Wei, Longxing (2000) Unequal election of morphemes in adult second language acquisition. *Applied Linguistics* 21:106–40.

—— (2002) The bilingual mental lexicon and speech production process. *Brain and Language* 81:691–707.

Weinstein, Brian (ed.) (1990) *Language Policy and Political Development*. Norwood, NJ: Ablex.

—— (1990) Language policy and political development: An overview. In B. Weinstein (ed.), *Language Policy and Political Development*. Norwood, NJ: Ablex, 1–21.

White, Lydia (1996) Universal grammar and second language acquisition: Current trends and new directions. In W. C. Ritchie and T. K. Bhatia (eds.), *Handbook of Second Language Acquisition*. San Diego, CA: Academic Press, 85–120.

—— (2000) Second language acquisition: From initial to final state. In J. Archibald (ed.), *Second Language Acquisition and Linguistic Theory*. Malden, MA: Blackwell.

—— (2003a) On the nature of interlanguage representation. In Catherine Doughty and Michael H. Long (eds.), *Handbook of Second Language Acquisition*. Oxford: Blackwell, 3–42.

—— (2003b) *Second Language Acquisition and Universal Grammar*. Cambridge: Cambridge University Press.

Wieder, D. Lawrence, and Steven Pratt (1990) On being a recognizable Indian among Indians. In Donal Carbaugh (ed.), *Cultural Communication and Intercultural Contact*. Hillsdale, NJ: Erlbaum, 47–64.

Wierzbicka, Anna (1991a) Japanese key words and core cultural values. *Language in Society* 20:333–86.

—— (1991b) *Cross-cultural Pragmatics*. Berlin: Mouton de Gruyter.

Williams, Glyn (1999) Sociology. In Joshua A. Fishman (ed.), *Handbook of Language and Ethnic Identity*. Oxford: Oxford University Press, 164–80.

Winford, Donald (2003a) *An Introduction to Contact Linguistics*. Malden, MA: Blackwell.

—— (2003b) Ideologies of language and socially-realistic linguistics. In S. Makoni, G. Smitherman, A. Ball and A. Spears (eds.), *Black Linguistics: Language, Society, and Politics in Africa and the Americas*. London and New York: Routledge, 21–39.

Wolf, Hans-Georg (1997) Transcendence of ethnic boundaries: The case of the Anglophones in Cameroon. *Journal of Sociolinguistics* 1:419–26.

Wolfram, Walt, and Natalie Schilling-Estes (1998) *American English*. Oxford: Blackwell.

Woolard, Kathryn A. (1989) *Double Talk, Bilingualism and the Politics of Ethnicity in Catalonia*. Stanford, CA: Stanford University Press.

Woolard, Kathryn A., and Tae-Joong Gahng (1990) Changing language policies and attitudes in autonomous Catalonia. *Language in Society* 19:311–30.

Wright, Sue (2004) *Language Policy and Language Planning*. Edinburgh: Palgrave.

Young, Russell, and Myluong Tran (1999) Language maintenance and shift among Vietnamese in America. *International Journal of the Sociology of Language* 140:77–82.

Yum, June Ock (1991 6th ed.) The impact of Confucianism on interpersonal relationships and communication patterns in East Asia. In L. A. Samovar and R. E. Porter (eds.), *Intercultural Communication: A Reader*. Belmont, CA: Wadsworth, 66–78.

Zentella, Ana Celia (1997) *Growing Up Bilingual: Puerto Rican Children in New York*. Malden, MA: Blackwell.

Zvelebil, Kamil Vaclav (1983) Word-borrowing and word-making in modern South Asian languages: Tamil. In Istvan Fodor (ed.), *Language Reform: History and Future*. Hamburg: Buske, 431–40. (Reprinted from *South Asian Digest of Regional Writing* (1975) 4:86–97.)

Index of Authors

Index of Languages

Note: This index lists the languages mentioned in text; however, minor occurrences of the major languages are not referenced.

Index of Subjects